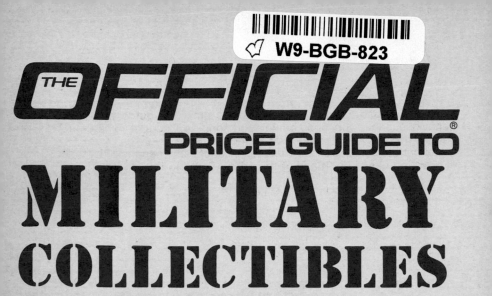

THE OFFICIAL® PRICE GUIDE TO MILITARY COLLECTIBLES

BY
COLONEL ROBERT H. RANKIN

EDITOR
THOMAS E. HUDGEONS III

SECOND EDITION

THE HOUSE OF COLLECTIBLES, INC., ORLANDO, FLORIDA 32809

NOTE

Prices listed in this guide are for items in very good or excellent condition. Prices are those actually realized at the time this guide was written. For items in less than very good but in good condition, deduct 15 percent. This, of course, does not apply to one of a kind items.

Neither the author nor the publisher accepts any responsibility for any loss of any kind based upon any of the prices listed in this guide.

PHOTOGRAPHIC RECOGNITION

Cover Photograph: Photographer — Bernie Markell, Orlando, FL 32806
Color Section Photographs: Photographer — Bernie Markell, Orlando, FL 32806;
Collection — courtesy of Pete Carlson, Boca Raton, FL 33432
Color Separations: World Color, Ormond Beach, FL 32074

Published by: The House of Collectibles, Inc.
                Orlando Central Park
                1900 Premier Row
                Orlando, FL 32809
                Phone: (305) 857-9095

Printed in the United States of America

Library of Congress Catalog Card Number: 81-81806

ISBN: 0-87637-191-8 / Paperback

TABLE OF CONTENTS

ACKNOWLEDGEMENTS

In any presentation such as this price guide, as is true of any work of nonfiction, the major share of credit must go to those cooperative individuals who have so willingly contributed of their time and knowledge to assist the author. Right at this point, the author wants to emphasize that any errors are his own and not in any way those of any of the individuals who assisted him. An attempt has been made to include all those who were of assistance. Any omissions are those of oversight and not of design.

Tom Nelson, President of Collector's Armoury, Inc., was most helpful in providing photographs and other materials. Roderick Jones, Vice President, Collector's Armoury, Inc., was generous in making many references available. Homer Stevens, Advertising Manager, Collector's Armoury, Inc., was always ready to supply needed illustrations.

Norm Flayderman, dean of militaria dealers, antiques authority, author and historian, generously contributed photos and other materials. Roy Butler, Co-Partner in Wallis & Wallis, the world-famous auction house, made many valuable illustrations available. P. A. Cole-King, also of Wallis & Wallis, was of assistance. Major John Harrell, USA-Ret., author and recognized authority on Imperial German Regimental Steins, and Gary Kersner, another recognized authority on the subject and a greatly respected dealer, were generous in providing photos and information in their field of expertise.

Michael Reese, II, author, columnist, dealer, and a worldwide recognized expert on Luger pistols, supplied hard to get Luger photos and contributed from his extensive knowledge.

Ron Manion, author, military expert and owner of the world's largest military antiques auction house, gave expert advice and supplied many materials. Dr. Eric J. Johansson, Editor of *Kaiserzeit*, the Journal of the Imperial German Military Collectors Association, and a widely respected authority on Imperial Germany, contributed photos and valuable information. Joe Walters, well-known dealer in swords and militaria, made photos and information available.

N. R. Belmont-Maitland, publisher of *Tradition* magazine, London, England, and an expert in militaria, also made scarce photos available. Donald E. Closter, Assistant Curator, Division of Military History, The Smithsonian Institution, was of great assistance in the author's search for information. Lieutenant General Alfred Rosenbaum, Belgium Army retired, J. R. Leconte, Le Conservateur in Chef and J. Lorette, Le Conservateur-Adjoint, Musee Royal de l'Armes, Brussels, Belgium; Inga Fl. Rasmussen, Museuminspektor, Tojhusmuset, Copenhagen, Denmark; Olle Cederloff, Director, Karin Oscarsson, Librarian, Svante Ison Warfvinge and Jorgen Lindvist, all of the Royal Army Museum, Stockhom, Sweden, made valuable contributions.

Marvin E. Hoffman, well-known historical arms dealer was always ready to be of assistance with photos and advice. Appreciation must be extended to Robert A. Carlisle, Head Still Photo Branch, Department of the Navy; L. K. Goodstal, Curator, Remington Arms Museum, and Judy Burnham, of Colt Industries. Charles Yust, collector and an outstanding authority on steel combat helmets, furnished valuable information, as well as illustrations not obtainable elsewhere. Thanks are also due Steve McFarland.

Lionel Leventhal, Arms and Armour Press, London, England, very graciously gave permission to use certain illustrations which appeared in my book *Military Headdress* which was published by his press. Margaretta Colt, of The Military Bookman, furnished interesting photos and materials on recruiting posters. The U.S. Marines are always to be depended upon. Colonel F. B. Nihart, Deputy Director for Museums, History and Museum Division, and Lieutenant Colonel F. W. Martino, USMC, Head Support Branch, History and Museum Division, of Headquarters United States Marine Corps, supplied photos and information concerning Marine activities. Personnel of the West Point Museum were also most helpful. Peter Hlinka, dealer in antique military Americana and an expert in his field, has always given assistance to the author in his projects.

Very special thanks must go to Thomas E. Hudgeons, Jr., Executive Vice President, House of Collectibles, for his understanding and for his infinite patience.

Special thanks must also go to Rudolfo A. D'Angelo, military historian and a leading expert in the field of Italian uniforms, particularly headdress.

Appreciation is also extended to William Keys, an expert on Imperial German helmets for his advice and assistance. S. Michael Schnessel, free-lance writer and a member of the staff of The Exhumation, a firm dealing in artwork, posters, prints and illustrated books is thanked for his advice and cooperation.

The cooperation of the Union Cultery Company and the Cole Consumer Products, Inc., in making material available on the KA-BAR Marine Corps fighting/utility knife is greatly appreciated.

David W. Uhrig for contributing information concerning military vehicles.

A special thank you to Mark McNeil of Orlando, Florida for his contribution (Civil War handcuffs) to the cover photograph.

W. T. McCutcheon, Jr., Vice President, Cairns & Brother, Inc., Clifton, N. J.; A. E. Jasper, Ipswich, Suffolk, England; J. C. Fields, Mardon, Tonbridge, Kent, England; E. H. Hounslow, Divosnal Officer, Hampshire Fire Brigade Headquarters, Eastleigh, Hampshire, England; Andre Baegens, Director, Press Information Services, Embassy of France, Washington, D. C., were a great assistance in furnishing information and photographs of firemen's helmets.

Dennis Rydyznski, MIL Distributing, Cincinnati, Ohio, furnished information and photographs on reproduction machine guns.

Washington House Photography, Inc., Arlington, Virginia and Bailey's Photographic Center, Bailey's Cross Roads, Virginia, were most helpful in assisting in certain photographic work.

INTRODUCTION TO THE SECOND EDITION

It is of considerable interest to find that in spite of the prevailing economic conditions, militaria prices are continuing to increase. A survey of the market reveals that there has been some forced selling by a few collectors of limited means who because of job loss or other reasons have been required to sell at least some portion of their collection. When it became necessary to realize a rapid financial return items had to be sold at less than market value. This condition is most apparent at gun shows. It certainly behooves the collector to use judgement and common sense in buying. It is indeed sad to see an individual over spend his budget to acquire a cherished artifact then be required to dispose of his treasure quickly and at a reduced price because of financial pressure.

There is certainly no diminished activity insofar as quality military artifacts are concerned. Prime items are being offered by the better auction houses and retail dealers. However as prices of more sought after items such as Imperial German, Nazi and other militaria have increased there has been a movement on the part of many collectors to explore new fields. For this reason we have included fire helmets and flag pole finials in this edition. As collector interest in these and other new areas develop supplies will quickly diminished and prices increase.

A word as to reproductions. Last year a genuine suit of armor, once belonging to the Duke of Brunswick, was auctioned off in London for a mere $794,200.00 to a dealer. Even suits of lesser historic value are well beyond the means of other than wealthy collectors and museums. The same is true of authentic Japanese feudal armor. These suits are worth a fortune. Prices of other desirable items of militaria have increased so drastically that more and more, attention is turning to *well made* reproductions. In fact a rather large community of collectors of reproductions is developing. It is fortunate that these collectors insist that the reproduction be true to the original in design, detail, and other aspects. In this edition, in addition to the reproductions contained in the First Edition, we have included information on reproduction machine guns which are now attracting much collector attention. In a future edition we plan to include a detailed section on a variety of worthwhile reproductions. As to originals, we plan to go into greater detail and scope on orders, decorations and medals, among other items.

HISTORY OF MILITARY COLLECTIBLES

The collecting of military items has developed into a multimillion dollar business. Action in this field is probably more active than in any other field of collecting. Of course, practically since time immemorial men have collected military gear. In the remote past victorious warriors returned from battle with arms and armor captured from the enemy. These were proudly displayed on the walls of palace, castle and hut. In some cultures these captured items would be displayed together in an artistic arrangement known as a trophy. Hence the origin of the word now meaning an award for victory.

Fighting men have always been inveterate collectors of souvenirs. In many instances, as the veteran grew older, he gradually lost interest in his early military adventures. His trophies were hidden away in an attic, given to children to play with, destroyed and lost, sold for a small sum to a pawn shop, or simply thrown away. This is a condition which prevailed in good part until after World War II. This writer well remembers that after World War I it was possible to buy an Imperial German officer's helmet for $5.00 for an excellent specimen. Other ranks dress helmets sold for even less. German trench helmets could be had for a dollar, while American helmets and gas masks could be bought for less than a dollar each at the small local five-and-ten-cents store. Of some interest is the fact that World Wars I and II British and American helmets are not in great demand. World War I helmets of either nation may be had for around $12.00, post World War helmets for around $8.00 and World War II helmets for $15.00 or less. Such, however, is not at all the case with helmets from other nations today. There was only a moderate increase in prices until a year or two after World War II, then prices began to rapidly escalate and are still rising.

This increase in prices is due to the fact that a regard for military artifacts is continually growing and has spread until it is international in scope. With the number of collectors increasing and with only a limited number of items available, it is easy to understand the present situation. With activities becoming thus restricted in certain areas, new collectors are now turning to other and lesser known artifacts and the whole cycle begins over again. These new fields are noted later in connection with such items as tropical helmets and certain American collectibles.

Perhaps the most popular collectibles today in the military field are those of Imperial Germany and Nazi Germany. German military items have always had a worldwide fascination, more so than those of any other country. There are several reasons for this. Among others is the fact that, particularly since the beginning of the reign of Kaiser Wilhelm II and continuing on through the Third Reich of Hitler, there has been a profusion of colorful uniforms unequaled elsewhere. In addition, the German Army, *except for the Nazi thug units,* has always enjoyed a most high regard among fighting men of all lands. The Germans are professionals among professionals. The proud manner in which they wear their uniforms reflects this.

Kaiser Wilhelm II was not at all normal, as is well-known. A withered left arm gave him an inferiority complex which he attempted to overcome by assuming a belligerent attitude and becoming a self-styled "All Highest" and "War Lord." His army was his first love and nothing was too good for it. He fancied himself an expert in all departments and he dearly loved uniforms. It is well-known that he had complete uniform outfits for all regiments which he wore when he visited with them. To the great delight of military tailors of the time and to modern collectors, he was constantly designing new uniforms. The variety seems almost endless. In no other army, even that of Austria, was there such a colorful selection.

Fortunately for the collector, the Germans have documented their uniform development. This has been done in a way which few other nations have attempted, with the possible exception of France and England and even these to a lesser extent. Over a long period of time, the Germans have published detailed studies, most often with beautifully colored illustrations. Many of these studies are collectors' items in their own right. Fortunately, a number of them are now being reproduced. At the present time, there has been a marked resurgence in the field and German researchers are producing a volume of informative and reliable studies. All of this, of course, adds much to collecting interest. Unfortunately this is an area which, in the United States, was largely neglected until recently. Now interest is being awakened by the studies being made by the erudite Company of Military Historians, the staff of the Military Division of the Smithsonian Institution and several serious researchers and writers.

Now as to the word "militaria." It is a newly coined word and, as far as is known, has not been picked up by any dictionary editors. Nonetheless, it has achieved international acceptance. No precise definition of the word has been developed to date. **Generally** the word may be applied to any military collectibles. Some collectors would exclude all weapons except those used by the individual fighting man, such as handguns, rifles, bayonets and swords. Machine guns and all heavier weapons would be excluded. Others would exclude **all** weapons. For the purpose of this book, it has been decided to include only those personal weapons deemed to be of some interest to the general military collector such as Lugers, Mausers, Walthers, Colts, Springfields, and certain personal weapons of some historical significance. In this regard, attention is invited to the section on Lugers which is believed to be the most complete, accurate and up-to-date pricing of these weapons. Another reason for not going into detail on firearms is that such a field is extremely large and merits special and separate treatment. A number of these specialized books are recommended in the Reference section of this guide.

NAZI ITEMS

The interest in the collecting of Nazi militaria is an absolute phenomenon. There is probably more activity in this area of collecting than in any other. This is so despite the terrible record of Hitler and his thugs. The Army of the Third Reich, apart from the Nazi elements, was always given respect by professional fighting men. However the brutal Nazi elements, such as the S S, the dreaded and hated Nazi military arm, have an appeal for some collectors. The writer will not attempt to explain this. In this connection, the majority of dealers and auction houses handling Nazi collectibles publish a disclaimer to the effect that they do not espouse the Nazi cause; that they are handling the material as a matter of satisfying a demand. Another reason for the popularity of Third Reich items, particularly uniforms, is the fact that there is such a great variety of colorful items available and some of them are still comparatively reasonable. Some helmets, decorations, badges and personal equipment are not too expensive now, but are increasing in value.

In contrast to these less costly artifacts are those which can and do reach astronomical heights. Witness, for example, that Herman Goering's personal yacht was put up for auction not too long ago at a reserve bid of half a million dollars! A prisoner of war post card from him to Frau Goering had a reserve bid of around $500.00. A personal letter from Hitler's mistress Eva Braun had a reserve bid of around $1,000.00. Field Marshal Model's marshal's baton was assigned a reserve bid of around $30,000.00, while Goering's wedding sword presented by the Luftwaffe had a reserve bid of $60,000.00.

HISTORICAL NOTE

Other than Nazi items, the most interesting and colorful military items date from prior to World War I. This is particularly true with respect to uniforms, but also applies to weapons generally. Distinctive military garb may have originated as long ago as Caesar's Legionnaires for there are accounts of Roman troops of the time being similarly clothed. Certainly their armor and weapons were alike, including the deadly short spear or **pilum** and the terrible short broad blade sword or **gladius.** Incidentally, these weapons are rarely, if ever, found outside museums. Not much is known about uniforms from this time. The levies of common men called to follow the nobles during the Middle Ages were actually a rabble wearing whatever clothing they had.

Their weapons were most often the tools which they used on their masters' farms or modifications thereof. These included spiked clubs, axes and scythes, among others. Gradually these were developed over the years into more practicable tools of war. More sophisticated weapons, such as swords, halberds, and such, were first used by the nobles before eventually being given to the common folk. Of some note is the fact that the bow and arrow in its various forms and sizes was one of the earliest weapons known and was used by fighting men of all cultures, both Oriental and Occidental, until forced into discard by firearms. The fame of the English long bow is a permanent part of military history. The crossbow in its time was considered a most horrible weapon. The often very painful and fatal wounds which it caused and its ability to penetrate armor made it quite fearsome. For a time it was considered much too cruel to use against Christians and several Papal decrees forbade its use except against infidels! These decrees were ignored for the most part. The weapon was far too effective and it was used until made obsolete by firearms. Crossbows are available to the collector but they are very expensive.

The armor of the medieval knights was not too uniform in appearance. It was very costly and was designed to fit the individual wearer. The design and the quality depended much upon the size of the purse of the knight. In order to be identified when fully armored, knights took to wearing a surcoat or loose jacket over the armor, bearing an identifying device such as some form of a cross or a heraldic design. Knights were also identified by a crest worn on the helmet.

The discovery of invention of gunpowder spelled an end to armor in the usual sense. As firearms became more accurate, far-ranged and powerful, the thickness of body armor had to be increased to the point where it became far too heavy to wear. Breast and back plate (cuirass) and metal helmet would continue to survive for the use of heavy cavalry up until the early days of World War I when the machine gun, rapid firing field guns and trench warfare brought about the demise of cavalry units. Cuirass and metal helmet survive today for use by certain ceremonial units. The development of firearms also brought about the end of edged weapons except for swords and bayonets. Today the sword too is merely a ceremonial thing with the bayonet alone surviving as a weapon. Of course, metal helmets are still being worn in combat and body armor first introduced into modern warfare by Germany during World War I is now an accepted part of the equipment of combat troops. The development of ballistic materials, such as fiberglass, plastics, and others is allowing the design of lightweight but effective protection. It is suggested that those collectors who are able to secure these new examples of armor hold on to them for they are certain to increase in value.

Admittedly, the uniforms of the Papal Guard, designed by none other than Michelangelo himself, and the uniforms of Yeoman of the Guard, the so-called "Beef Eaters," first raised in Tudor times in England, were probably the first uniforms as we know them today. These units wear almost the same uniforms today. Nonetheless, they were uniforms for small units. Thus it may be said that the French Army of Louis XIV (1636 to 1715) was the first army to be completely uniformed. Military historians do consider this to be the actual beginning of military uniforms. Soon other nations adopted the idea. The idea was most appealing in that buying great quantities of the same kind of material and equipment lowered the cost. Above all, perhaps, is the fact that uniforms have a tremendous morale factor. This is a factor given most serious consideration even today in uniform design.

After the beginning of the uniform in France, the idea rapidly proliferated all over the world but particularly in the British and European services. The era immediately preceding World War I saw all this at its highest and it is in this era that collectors find great delight. Then World War I put an end to the most fancy and colorful era. Trench warfare with men burrowing in the ground like moles ruled out anything but the most practicable garb. Certain ceremonial troops did retain some items of their dress uniform. Somewhat recently in addition to the development of sensible battle dress, there has been a return to dress uniforms. As colorful as these may be, they can in no way compare with the peacock uniforms of earlier times.

SOURCES OF ARTIFACTS

The most obvious source of military collectibles is the militaria dealer. General antique dealers at times have items of interest. There was a time when excellent items might be secured from antique shops, particularly in smaller towns for a very low price. This is not very often true anymore, for even the small dealers have learned more and more about values. Although the majority of dealers in militaria and other antiques are conscious of their good reputation, there are some rascally individuals and companies which must be guarded against. **Never do business with anyone who will not guarantee the authenticity of what you buy.** All reputable dealers are ready to stand behind their merchandise. Junk yards and shops and yard sales are also sources. Here the buyer must be on the alert lest he be "taken to the cleaners."

Reputable mail auction houses are an excellent source of supply. The names and addresses of those which the writer can recommend appear in a section at the end of this book. These auction houses issue regular illustrated catalogs at a modest fee. Information furnished covers a description of the article and the reserve or minimum bid acceptable. The buyer pays an auctioneer's fee over and above the bid price and pays for transportation. Bid forms and complete information about submitting bids are found in each catalog. After the auction has been completed, some houses will sell the article at the reserve bid price in the event no person submitted a bid. The firms noted are reliable and will stand behind all sales. Auction houses are located in many of our larger cities and these, from time to time, have military items. These houses usually issue catalogs for sale and biddings can be done in person. All auction catalogs are a valuable reference tool, as are dealers' catalogs.

Gun shows and flea markets are also likely sources of militaria. Here again, the collector must be sure that the seller is reputable. The better shows carefully screen all exhibitors and will not allow. individuals of questionable ethics to participate. In the writer's own experience, a greater proportion of "sharp shooting," unscrupulous characters are found at unregulated gun shows than at any other place.

Of course, personal dealings with a fellow collector is another source of artifacts. Here again, one must be sure of the integrity of the individual concerned.

WHERE TO BUY

AUCTION HOUSES

AAGI Militaria Mail Auction, 75 East Main Street, Nanticoke, Pennsylvania, 18634. Illustrated catalogs. Write for subscription price.

The Centurion, 219 North Jackson, El Dorado, Arkansas, 71730. Illustrated catalogs. Write for subscription price.

The Fox Hole, Mr. Ron Manion, Post Office Box 12214, Kansas City, Kansas, 66112. This is the largest auction house in the world handling only military antiques. There are approximately 10 auctions each year and an illustrated catalog listing reserve bid prices is published well in advance of each. The subscription price is $15.00 a year for the United States and Canada, $20.00 a year for Europe and Asia. Approximately 1700 to 2000 items are listed for each auction. Each item is described. No reproductions, current issue material, "Army and Navy Store" used uniforms of no collector value, reprinted photographs or books of no collector value are handled. Service is prompt and all items are well-packed for insured shipment. This establishment is given the highest recommendation.

Graf Klenau oHG, 8000 Munchen 1, Postfach 122, West Germany. Well established auction house handling all kinds of military antiques of very high quality. Worldwide militaria is auctioned but the selection of both Imperial German and Third Reich items is extremely good. Frequent auctions held and an illustrated catalog is issued well in advance of each auction. Each item is well-described and a reserve bid is given. Catalog is in German. Mail bids accepted. For information regarding current catalog subscription prices, a request should be addressed to this firm. Highly recommended.

Jan K. Kube, Herzostrasse 34, 8 Muchen 40, West Germany. Another well-known German auction house handling military antiques of extra high quality. A good source of better quality Imperial German items. Also highly recommended.

Wallis & Wallis, Regency House, 1 Albion Street, Lewes, Sussex, England, BN7 2NJ. This is an old and well respected auction house offering antique military items from all over the world. The selection is wide and the offerings are of extremely high quality. Mail bids accepted. Illustrated catalog issued well in advance of each auction. Items are well described. This is a particularly good source of British and German militaria. For information regarding current catalog subscription prices, a letter should be addressed to this firm. Highly recommended.

J. Curtis Earl, 5512 North Sixth Street, Phoenix, Arizona 85012. Mr. Earl is a most knowledgeable and reliable dealer in machine guns. His inventory, which is constantly changing, is the largest in this country and perhaps in the world as far as private dealers are concerned. He issues an illustrated brochure which lists all weapons currently available and includes valuable information for the collector, including laws governing the collecting and possession of machine guns. This brochure is priced at $4.00 and is of especial interest to the beginning collector.

BOOKS

Arco Publishing, Inc., 219 Park Avenue South, New York, New York., 10003. Publishers of a list of outstanding books of interest to militaria collectors, with particular attention to books on the Third Reich. Highly recommended.

Arms and Armour Press, 2-6 Hampstead High Street, London NW3 1 QQ England. One of the world's largest publishers of authoritative military books. Subjects cover the whole range of military history, including many in the specific area of militaria collector interest. Catalogs issued.

Fairfield Book Company, Box 289, Brookfield Center, Connecticut, 06805. This concern stocks a complete inventory of books on all military areas. It is very often possible to obtain books here which are unavailable elsewhere. Emphasis is largely on current titles. Very swift and courteous service. The president of the firm, Mr. Harold C. Kurfehs, is a militaria collector and historian and is very knowledgeable in the field. The firm is the successor to N. Flayderman & Company, Booksellers. Annual catalog is $2.00. Most highly recommended.

Hippocrene Books, Inc., 171 Madison Avenue, New York, New York, 10016. Publishers of a list of excellent books on military books. Many of these titles are valuable references for militaria collectors and historians. Catalog issued. Highly recommended.

Peter Hlinka, Post Office Box 310, New York, New York, 10028. An excellent source for rare books on military subjects and for military manuals. Inventory changes rapidly. Fast reliable service. Highly recommended.

Mr. A. A. Johnston, Military Books and Prints, Pitney, Langport, Somerset, England. Constantly changing inventory of rare and out-of-print books, as well as recent releases, of interest to collectors. Service is excellent, lists are published regularly. Recommended.

Lyle Publications, Glenmayne, Galashiels, Selkirkshire, Scotland. Publishers of authoritative reference books on antiques. "The Lyle Official Arms and Armour Review," published annually, is an essential reference work for all dealers, collectors and investors. Emphasis is on British, Continental and Oriental artifacts. The best reference work in the field, catalog issued.

The Military Bookman, 29 East 93rd Street, New York, New York, 10028. This organization carries an extremely wide selection of books on every aspect of military history and military science. Limited editions and out-of-print titles are a specialty. This is also an excellent source of recruiting posters and other posters of military aspect. Comprehensive catalogs are published and illustrations of posters are used. Fast service, most highly recommended.

The Soldier Shop, 1013 Madison Avenue, New York, New York, 10021. Carries an extremely wide inventory of military titles, the majority of which are of especial interest to militaria collectors. Catalog issued, recommended.

Ken Trotman, 2-6 Hampstead High Street, London NW3 1QQ, England. A most complete inventory of books on all military subjects worldwide. Carries books of all publishers. Catalogs issued, one of the best.

RETAIL DEALERS

The Exhumation, P. O. Box 2057, Princeton, New Jersey, 08540. Has a complete inventory of World War I and II posters. Periodic catalogs issued, $3.00 each.

William Fagan, 126 Belleview, Mt. Clemens, Michigan, 48043. Illustrated catalogs. Write for subscription price. Good source of ancient militaria.

Jacques Noel Jacobsen, Jr., 60 Manor Road, Staten Island, NY 10310. Antique militaria. Very good source of supply for firemen's helmets. Illustrated catalogs. Write for subscription price.

MIL Distributing, P. O. Box 33129, Cincinnati, Ohio. Excellent machine gun reproductions. Write for information.

Fairfax Military Antiques and Equipment, P. O. Box 461, Sayville, New York, 11782. Small military items including firearms parts, insignia, cross belt plates and a very good selection of bayonets from all over the world. Lists issued. Very good.

Norm Flayderman & Co., Inc., R. D. 2, New Milford, Connecticut, 06776. This is the largest retail dealer of military and nautical antiques in the world. Only better quality items are handled. Is one of the largest sources of truly rare and museum quality antiques to be found. Stock ranges through the entire range of militaria, including weapons, paintings, nautical gear, rare military books, helmets and headdress, and recruiting posters. Internationally known with reputation for integrity. Mail order only, catalog with illustration issued annually, subscription price $4.00 for two years.

Glentiques, Ltd. (Mr. Gary Kirsner), P. O. Box 337, Glenford, New York, 12433. Specializes in Mettlach, Musterchutz, Character and German Regimental steins. Periodical lists issued. Excellent.

Peter Hlinka, Post Office Box 310, New York, New York, 10028. Offers a variety of smaller military items including insignia and medals. Catalog issued. Very good.

The House of Swords and Militaria, 2804 Hawthorne, Independence, Missouri, 64052. Offers a most complete catalog of military antiques. The sword, dagger and other edged weapon offerings are most complete. All offerings are illustrated. Also a great variety of other militaria, including Imperial German helmets, shoulder straps, medals and uniforms. Catalogs are $5.00. Excellent.

Seven Seas Corporation, Post Office Box 920, Williamsburg, Virginia, 23185. Excellent offering of decorations and medals of all nations. Stock changes constantly, lists issued. Excellent.

Roger S. Steffen, 14 Murnan Road, Cold Spring, Kentucky, 41076. General militaria. Illustrated catalogs. Write for subscription price.

Army Jeep Parts Inc., David W. Uhrig, President, P.O. Box 726-A, Chillicothe, Ohio, 45601. A list of currently available military vehicles and parts is issued. Write for price of list.

The Soldier Shop, Inc., 1013 Madison Avenue, New York, New York, 10021. Has extremely high quality militaria, including headdress, medals and decorations, swords, prints, paintings and model soldiers. Catalog issued.

Collector's Armoury, Inc., Post Office Box 388, 800 Slaters Lane, Alexandria, Virginia, 22313. Has a wide and changing stock of both original and reproduction military items. Strong in Third Reich collectibles. All reproductions are plainly marked. Largely a mail order business but has a retail store of many one-of-a-kind collectibles. Excellent.

Gun shows are usually a good source of military collectibles. At the larger and well-organized shows, the collector usually has the assurance that the vendors have been screened for reliability and that if any reproductions are sold, all are plainly identified as such. At many smaller shows, the collector should be most careful in his selections. General antique shows and antique shops will occasionally have very worthwhile items. The author has at times bought excellent Imperial German helmets at dusty little country crossroads shops for a mere fraction of what they would have cost at an antique military shop in the city. Such instances are now becoming fewer as dealers and collectors have begun to range abroad. However, rewarding finds are still possible if the collector has patience. Thrift shops, yard sales and secondhand stores are also sources. Advertising in the "WANT" sections of newspapers will sometimes bring rewarding results. A close reading of the classified as well as the display ads in such publications as "Shotgun News," Box 669, Hastings, Nebraska, 68901, may also be rewarding.

THE MATTER OF APPRAISALS

As collections grow larger and more valuable, the matter of having their worth appraised may arise. By careful study of price trends, the individual collector can, of course, fairly accurately assign values to his collection. It is important to note that while such appraisal may be satisfactory for insurance purposes, a professional appraiser's estimate is required for such matters as taxes and many insurance purposes. Militaria appraisers are not nearly as available as appraisers in other fields. By all means have nothing to do with less than a professional if your collection in of great value. Most larger dealers and auction houses can make recommendations.

Professional appraisers do not come at a cheap price. They have spent many years in training to spot fakes and reproductions and in learning the value of artifacts. Charges will vary. For items or collections of $1,000.00 or less, the fee is usually anywhere from five to 10 percent. This is in addition to any travel or lodging. For collections of considerable value, charges of between $100.00 to $250.00 per day, plus travel and lodging may be expected. Some appraisers will also quote a flat fee. The appraiser will furnish his appraisal in writing, including a description of each item, the value of the object and the date of the appraisal. A statement of the appraiser's qualifications will be included. The entire appraisal will be signed and notarized.

REPLACEMENT PARTS, REPRODUCTIONS AND FAKES

The subject of replacement parts and reproductions is one of greatly divided opinion among serious collectors, with one school of thought not willing to make concessions to the other.

Some purists maintain that to be of worth, the artifact must be 100 percent original. They would rather have a less than complete original than the same item with replacement parts. It is not unusual for incomplete Imperial German helmets to be completed with reproduction chin straps, chin scales, cockades and such. These are the parts most often lost over the years. At times front plates may be recovered from badly damaged helmets and together with other parts used to complete another. Some less than honest persons, in an attempt to upgrade a helmet, will substitute a rare helmet plate from a famous regiment and/or alter the spike and spike base. In many instances, these changes and additions may be identified by extra holes under the spike base or behind the front plate. This is not always an accurate guide, however, for during the closing days of World War I, when materials were in short supply in Germany, helmets were turned back to the arsenals and reworked. Here again be sure of your source. Insist upon the truth and, if possible, call in an expert.

A few reproduction Imperial German helmets and other items of headdress have appeared on the American market. These have been made in Germany and at times have been passed off as the genuine article. The specimens which the writer has examined are of lighter materials, both leather and metal work, and are of inferior workmanship. The front plates in particular lack a fineness in detail. Here again, if you are undecided, consult an expert.

The constantly increasing scarcity of Nazi items has led to mass reproduction of everything from badges to decorations to caps and daggers. Daggers in particular may be fabricated from parts left over from World War I and combined with reproduced parts or they may be made more recently from parts struck from original or reproduced dies. Caps, insigna and decorations, among other things, are fairly easy to reproduce. The reputable manufacturer will honestly describe these pieces and will not attempt to pass them off as originals.

It may be observed that in some instances military items are so rare and unobtainable, consequently so costly, that it takes little less than a millionaire to acquire them. Medieval armor, for instance, is much desired but when available costs a fortune. The same is true of authentic Japanese feudal armor and weapons. In a less costly bracket certain martial weapons such as Lugers, Mausers, Walthers and Colts, are too costly for a collector of modest means. As for submachine guns, they may be had only after compliance with Federal regulations and a high tax fee. Fortunately, excellent reproductions of these items and others are available.

This writer can see no harm in having these reproductions to fill a gap in a collection or to be had as an interesting item in themselves. After all, not many people can afford an original painting by Van Gogh, Manet, Michelangelo, Gainsborough, Turner or Copley, yet no harm is attached to displaying a good reproduction in one's home. **The important factor involved is that the reproduction must be plainly tagged as a reproduction. A reproduction becomes a fake when it is passed off as an original.** It is indeed regrettable that the militaria field has far too many characters who are out for "a fast buck." Be constantly on guard against such people and see to it that they are blacklisted.

LEARNING ABOUT YOUR COLLECTION

A great part of the enjoyment of any collection of artifacts is becoming thoroughly acquainted with background. This is interesting as well as informative. In collecting helmets, for instance, it is well to know the dates of original introduction and withdrawal from service, as well as facts about the army and regiment using it. Methods of manufacture are also interesting. More and more references are becoming available. A section later in this guide gives more detailed information on this subject.

A WORD AS TO LISTINGS AND PRICES

Price has not been a factor in the selection of items to be included in this guide. **Interest** and **availability** have dictated the choice. Obviously, there is little purpose in a book of this nature to include artifacts in which collectors have demonstrated little or no interest. Nor is there purpose in listing items which exist only in museums or which may be acquired only by millionaires. A few very rare pieces have been included because of their general interest and because they **are** available even if only infrequently. Items listed are those observed for sale by dealers at their own shops and at shows, by individuals at shows, and those offered at auction, both in this country and abroad. It is always possible that a reader may not find his favorite among the listings. In such a case, he probably has a rare item which is not often available.

As an example of all the above, I have not listed the very beautiful and extremely rare eagle crested helmet of the Prussian Lige Guard Gendarmerie, a small elite unit whose personnel were transferred from various Prussian cavalry regiments. Their duty was to act as personal escorts to the Kaiser and the Kaiserin. This unit was commanded by one of the Kaiser's Aides-de-Camp. On a few occasions, I have heard that one of these helments is in the hands of a private collector. Yet I have never been able to locate the private owner. The only specimen I have seen is in a German museum. Obviously it is impossible to assign a value in dollars and cents to such an item. The same thing is true of many Imperial German general officers' helmets.

Prices of militaria in this guide are based upon the average prevailing at the time of preparation. In some instances an allowance has been made for some anticipated increases. Prices are constantly escalating and nothing short of a major depression will halt the rise. The prices indicated herein can be regarded as the lowest or base price for artifacts of good to excellent condition. At all times it is well to remember that a rare item in only fair condition may be expected to bring more than an excellent condition item which is in fairly abundant supply.

Another factor is the desire for a certain object. The writer has on occasion seen a wealthy collector pay much more than the normal price for an item simply because it struck his fancy. Above all, remember that you cannot expect to sell to a dealer for the going market price. He plans to sell at the competitive retail price but from that price he must in payment to you deduct such expenses as insurance on his store and stock, rent, taxes, light, heat, salaries of employees, advertising and so on. As a rule of thumb, you cannot expect him to pay you much more than the retail price.

ORGANIZATION OF THIS GUIDE

And now a word as to the organization of the remainder of this guide. It opens with a price guide to armor, followed by price guides to other items of militaria. Information sections complete the book. There is a good reason for giving considerable attention to headdress. The collecting of military headdress is extremely popular no doubt due to the fact that it has a most fascinating history, is easy to display and does not require a great amount of care.

Each price guide section is introduced by a brief historical account of the particular items. All Nazi items are treated in a separate section except for steel combat helmets which are included in the combat helmet section pricing the helmet of all nations.

As one militaria collector to another, the very best of luck and enjoyment in your collecting.

Robert H. Rankin
Colonel
U.S. Marine Corps (Ret.)

Falls Church, Virginia
August 31, 1979

REFERENCE BOOK LIST

In order to properly understand and appreciate one's collection of military collectibles, a good reference library is a "must." Knowing the background of the items in the collection adds much to their interest and assists in assigning values.

There is, of course, a host of books on militaria. Unfortunately, some of these are of little use to the serious collector. The following items are recommended because of their reliability and their completeness. With very few exceptions, these may be obtained from the book dealers listed in this guide.

ARMOR (and Arms)

Arms and Armor, Frederick Wilkinson. Good general discussion of the development of arms and armor from prehistoric times to the present. Includes Oriental and Japanese armor, many illustrations, including color, $10.95.

Arms-Armor From the Atelier of Ernst Schmidt, Munich, E. Andrew Mowbray. A fully illustrated review of the reproduction armor made by this famous German armorer during the late 1800's and early 1900's. Also includes reproduction arms, a most valuable aid in detecting fake arms and armor, $12.00.

British and Continental Arms and Armour, Charles Henry Ashdown. A definitive coverage of the subject. Reprint of an old classic, includes several hundred illustrations, $4.00.

European Armour in the Tower of London, A. R. Duffy. Comprehensive and beautifully illustrated description of many outstanding examples of armor in the Tower of London collections, $15.00.

Fine Arms and Armor, Johannes Schobel. Descriptive catalog of the arms and armor in the Historisches Museum, Dresden, Germany. Many examples of priceless items, excellent illustrations including many in full color, $20.00.

A Glossary of the Construction, Decoration and Use of Arms and Armor in all Countries and in all Times, George Cameron Stone. The title fully describes all that this volume covers. It is necessary to **any** study of arms and armor. If the collector in this area were restricted to just one book, this would be the volume to buy. EXCELLENT! $10.98.

Japanese Armour, L. T. Anderson. Short but interesting monograph on Japanese armor in general, black and white photos, $4.95.

Japanese Arms and Armor, H. Russel Robinson. Extremely well-done volume on armor and weapons of the Edo Period (1614-1867). Many excellent photos including many in color, $15.00.

The John Woodman Higgins Armory, Stephen V. Grancsay. Well-done catalog describing the medieval armor in one of the most famous collections in the United States. Fully illustrated with scholarly text, $8.95.

The Samurai, A Military History, S. R. Turnbull. Principally a military history of feudal Japan, this book has some very good information on arms and armor. The illustrations of arms and armor are especially good, $25.00.

Secrets of the Samurai, Oscar Ratti and Adele Westbrook. Subtitled "A Survey of the Martial Arts of Feudal Japan," this comprehensive volume describes in detail the arms and armor of old Japan and explains just how they were used. Fully illustrated with excellent line drawings which lend details not possible in photos, $30.00.

Warriors and Worthies, Helmut Nickel. Description with illustrations of some of the outstanding examples of arms and armor in the Metropolitan Museum of Art. Of especial interest to the beginning collector, $10.00.

BAYONETS

The American Bayonet, Albert N. Hardin, Jr. The most complete study available on American bayonets and by an acknowledged expert. A detailed illustrated account, $24.50.

Bayonets of the World, Paul Kiesling. A four volume study of hundreds of bayonets from all over the world. Identification made easy inasmuch as the weapons are classified by overall length. Excellent line drawings with full details of each bayonet. Volumes One, Two and Three, $19.95 each. Volume Four, $23.95.

The Collector's Pictorial Book of Bayonets, Frederick J. Stephens. A well-defined pictorial treatment of some 250 weapons from 20 countries. Excellent reference, $3.95.

The German Bayonet, John Walter. Covers bayonets of the Imperial German Army from the late 1800's on through World War I to the Third Reich. This well-illustrated study is a "must" for German bayonet collectors, $12.50.

EDGED WEAPONS (Daggers and Swords)

The American Sword, Harold L. Peterson. The Blue Book of American swords. Includes photos and description of all swords worn by the U.S. Army, Navy, Marine Corps and Coast Guard (and its predecessors) from the Revolutionary War to the Present. One of the very best, $18.50.

The Arts of the Japanese Sword, B. W. Robinson. An important history of Japanese sword making, given details of forging and an excellent account of the noted swordsmiths, $17.50.

Bluebook of Identification of Reproduction Nazi Edged Weapons, R. McFarlane. Valuable assistance in spotting fake Nazi swords and daggers, $4.50.

Collecting the Edged Weapons of the Third Reich, LTC Thomas M. Johnson. Three volumes. An essential reference work for Nazi edged weapons collectors. Complete and comprehensive, fully illustrated. The author is a widely recognized authority in his field, excellent. Volume One, $18.50; Volume Two, $18.50. Volume Three, $20.00.

Japanese Sword Fittings, Henri L. Joly. Reprint of an earlier work by a well-known authority on Japanese weapons. The collecting of Japanese sword guards or tsubas ia a very special field and this volume is an invaluable guide. Fully illustrated, $50.00.

The Samurai Sword, Gary D. Murtha. An interesting account covering the origin and development of the Samurai sword. Deals with the weapon both as a tool of war and as an art form. Many drawings, black and white and color photographs. A valuable reference source.

The Samurai Sword, John M. Yumoto. Treats of the origin, development and identification of this unique weapon. Interesting and informative text by an expert, $9.50.

Shinto Bengi Oshigata, W. M. Hawley. Extremely valuable guide to the identification of swordblade smiths. Contains detailed drawings of the smith's or armorer's marks on the sword tang. Important to the serious Japanese sword collector, $12.50.

Small Arms of the Sea Services, Colonel Robert H. Rankin. Chapters on all edged weapons, including battle axes and pikes, used by all of the U.S. Armed Forces from the Revolutionary War through Vietnam. Fully illustrated with sharp photos, $14.50.

Swords of the British Army, Brian Robson. Includes a well-illustrated study of British Army swords, including the Scots basket hilt, from 1788 to 1914. Interesting, $22.50.

The Tsuba, Gary D. Murtha. An excellent reference work on the tsuba. Contains history and evolution of the tsuba, schools, groups and stylesm artists, care and cleaning and clubs, books and booksellers. Well illustrated with black and white photos.

The World of the Javanese Keris, Garrett and Bronwen Solyom. An in-depth examination of this fascinating Oriental weapon. Facts not available elsewhere, fully illustrated, $7.50.

FLAGS AND BANNERS

British Cavalry Standards, Dino Lemonofides. This and the following volume are essential to the collector of British Army flags and standards. Both color and black and white illustrations, $7.95.

British Infantry Colors. Illustrations in color, $7.95.

Flags and Standards of the Third Reich-Army, Navy and Air Force, Brian Davis. Complete coverage of the military and naval flags of the Nazi armed forces. Party and civilian examples not included. Fully illustrated with both color and black and white illustrations. This is a necessary reference book on the subject, $15.00.

Flags - Through the Ages and Across the World, Dr. Whitney Smith. An interesting encyclopedic general study of the origin and development of flags in all countries. Thousands of flags in full color, a scholarly and reliable presentation, $39.95.

The Standards, Guidons and Colors of the Household Division, 1660-1973, Major Nicolas Payan Dawnay. Important to the advanced collector. Complete history, illustrated in full color, of flags of the Household Division during the period indicated. Also contains numerous black and white illustrations, excellent, $29.95.

HELMETS AND HEADDRESS

Die Geschichte Des Deutschen Stahlhelmes, Ludwig Baer. Largely German text with some explanatory text in English. A most complete account of the development of the German steel combat helmet from 1915 through 1945. Contains several hundred color and black and white photographs of individual helmets as well as views of troops wearing the helmet. Much valuable information on the use of steel helmets by Free Corps units. This is the only book to picture the rare experimental German steel and leather head protection used during 1915-1916 just prior to the introduction of the first steel combat helmet. A required book for any serious collector of German steel helmets, $39.95.

Dress and Field Service Hats of the Third Reich, Tom Shutt. Definitive discussion of the hats and caps of the Nazi era, both military and political. Goes into great detail and is the most complete reference of its kind available. Very well illustrated with photos and charts. All headdress is shown in color. Black and white photos show the headdress being worn by individuals and by groups. Highly recommended.

Europaische Helme, Heinrich Muller and Fritz Kunter. This large and extremely lavish volume is of a type that could only be produced where cost was of little consequence. It is a **most** complete coverage of both dress and steel helmets from the fifteenth century to the present time. Has a total of 449 large detailed photos, prints and other illustrations, including a great number in color. Many rare and little known artifacts are pictured here for the first time. Contains the only available complete discussion of the development of Russian helmets from World War I to the present. All illustrations supplemented by detailed data. Text in German. This volume is not easy to find but is available from English military book dealers from time to time. The advanced collector will consider his library incomplete without it, $100.00.

Helme und Mutzen der Armee, Gerd M. Schulz. Price guide and a description of German dress helmets, combat helmets, caps and other military headdress of both the armies of Imperial German and the Third Reich. Excellent photos of each. German text and prices in German currency but is fairly easy to follow. Is valuable for the identification photos alone, recommended highly, $18.95.

The Helmet Plates and Cyphers of the German Army. An exact reprint of the four extra large black and white prints which was originally published by the famous German military publisher, Ruhl of Leipzig, Germany, in 1914. Clearly pictures and identifies all of the helmet and headdress plates used in the Imperial German Army at the beginning of World War I. In addition has identifying examples of the insignia worn on shoulder boards. An absolute necessity for proper identification, $10.00.

Helmets and Body Armor in Modern Warfare (with supplement to World War II). This is a reprint of the original study by Bashford Dean describing and picturing the development of steel helmets, face masks and body armor of World War I, including the many experimentals. The supplement, with foreword by the late Harold L. Peterson, armor expert, is a reprint of the U.S. Army Ordnance Department's summation of the development of helmets and body armor in World War II. Excellent for the combat helmet collector, $25.00.

Helmets and Headdress of the Imperial German Army, Colonel Robert H. Rankin. A basic manual for collectors of Imperial German Army headdress. Fully illustrated with black and white photos. Lists principal German regiments with their honorary titles, $9.50.

Military Headdress, Colonel Robert H. Rankin. This is a basic reference book containing 230 large photos of military headdress from 1660 to 1914, the classic years insofar as collectors are concerned. Full description of each item included, valuable for identification purposes, $14.95.

Stahlhelm, Floyd R. Tubbs. Interesting discussion of the development of the German steel helmet from its inception in World War I through the Third Reich. English text, fully illustrated with black and white photos. Gives interesting information on linings, chin straps and other details, a good reference work, $7.50.

Stahlhelm, Franz Thaler. Probably the most complete coverage of the steel combat helmets of **all** nations from 1915 to the present. Good photos of around 400 examples including many oddball and experimental types. Includes a set of two photos of the rare French steel skull cap of 1914-1915. Also the great variety of French and Italian helmets is covered. Text in both German and English with prices given in German currency. This book is a necessity for any steel helmet collector, $18.95.

2,500 Years of European Helmets 800 B.C.-1700 A.D., Howard M. Curtis. Until the publication of this work, the collector of the very old and genuine antique helmets had little in the way of definitive literature. This most interesting and instructive volume is very well illustrated with both color and black and white photos, supplemented by a scholarly text. Is of positive value to both beginning and advanced collector alike, $20.00.

INSIGNIA (and Badges)

American Badges and Insignia, Evans E. Kerrigan. An original interesting study of the subject. Covers the wide range of insignia of rank, qualification badges, shooting badges, corps badges and shoulder insignia. Hundreds of black and white line drawings of each, very good reference for the American collector, $6.95.

Aviation Badges and Insignia of the United States Army, 1913-1946, J. Duncan Campbell. A reliable in-depth study of American aviation badges and insignia by an acknowledged expert. Contains important information relative to the identification of fakes, restrikes and reproductions. A valuable tool for the serious collector, $12.00.

Fur Fuhrer and Fatherland (Awards of the Third Reich), LTC John R. Angolia. This volume covers medals and decorations but also examines in depth and illustrates the many badges and insignia of the Third Reich army. The author is well recognized for his research. Volume One concerns military awards, $18.95. Volume Two covers political and civil awards, $18.95.

German Army Uniforms and Insignia 1933-1945, Brian Davis. Although this very important reference book deals also with uniforms, it contains a great abundance of authentic information on Third Reich military insignia not available elsewhere. The author is an expert, highly recommended, $16.95.

Insignia, Decorations and Badges of the Third Reich and Occupied Coun-

tries. Rather complete coverage with illustrations of orders and decorations, Nazi party insignia, propaganda badges. Very good, $17.50.

Regimental Badges, Major T. J. Edwards. Detailed black and white line drawings of all the British army regimental badges prior to the amalgamation of some of the regiments following World War II. Contains complete description of badges and information as to their use, $9.75.

Tinnies of the Third Reich, Ron Manion. Two volumes picturing and describing hundreds of the plastic and cheap metal propaganda badges of Nazi Germany. The only such study in the field. List of manufacturers, and rarity and price guide included. Other volumes to follow will completely cover the field. The author, Ron Manion, is an acknowledged expert in the field. Volume One, $8.95. Volume Two, $8.95.

MEDALS AND DECORATIONS

Fur Fuhrer and Fatherland. See description under Insignia above.

Orders and Decorations of All Nations, Robert Werlich. This is an outstanding reference work. With it at hand the collector in reality has no particular need for other references on the subject. All items are fully described and the text is supplemented by over 1000 black and white photos plus color plates. Probably the best book on the subject, $36.00.

Orders, Decorations, Medals and Badges of the Third Reich, David Littlejohn and Colonel C. M. Dodkins. Both black and white and color illustrations, a two volume definitive study of the subject. Of particular interest and value to the advanced collector, includes a fascinating amount of details and documentation, highly recommended. Volume One, $12.95. Volume Two, $12.95.

Uniforms of the Sea Services, Colonel Robert H. Rankin. Although devoted principally to the historical development of uniforms of the U.S. sea services, this volume contains an excellent section on all awards of the U.S. Navy, Marine Corps and Coast Guard. Both color and black and white illustrations, $50.00.

MILITARIA (General)

Collecting Militaria, R. J. Wilkinson-Lathan. Good treatment of all aspects of military relic collecting. Illustrated with both color and black and white photographs, very instructive, $15.00.

The Lyle Official Arms and Armour Review 1980. An excellent annual review of arms, armor and other military antiques auctioned by Wallis & Wallis of Lewes, Sussex, England, one of the world's largest and most respected antique military auction houses. Each item is pictured and the selling price given, an excellent guide, $16.95.

Military Antiques, Frederick Wilkinson. An excellent general coverage of all fields of antique military gear. Many color and black and white illustrations. Both this and *Collecting Militaria* are extremely worthwhile as general reference books, $14.95.

PISTOLS AND REVOLVERS

Colt Automatic Pistols, Donald B. Bady. Illustrated account of the development of all the Colt automatic pistols. This book, together with *A History of the Colt Revolver,* will give a rather complete account of Colt hand guns, $15.00.

The Complete Illustrated Encyclopedia of the World's Firearms, Ian V. Hogg. As the title infers this is an encyclopedia covering the development of all types of pistols, revolvers and rifles. Photos and line drawings of exceptional quality. Describes weapons and gives brief biographical data on gun designers. A one volume library, $24.95.

Famous Pistols and Hand Guns, excellent general coverage of Luger, Mauser, Walther, Colt, Browning, Webley and Scott, Beretta and Astra automatic pistols. Informative and authentic text completely illustrated with excellent color and black and white photos, $8.75.

Flayderman's Guide to Antique American Firearms and Their Values, Norm Flayderman. This is without a doubt the most important book on the subject to yet appear. Illustrates and describes all antique American firearms and gives their current value. Includes all variations, chapters on development and the state of the art of collecting. Well-organized for easy reference, includes muskets and rifles as well as pistols and revolvers. A required book in any gun collector's library, $12.95.

German Pistols and Holsters 1934/1945 Military-Police-NSDAP, Major Robert D. Whittington III. Concerns the handguns and holsters of the Third Reich with attention to those for the Nazi party members and the police, as well as the armed forces. Also treats of handguns acquired from other countries. Much information pertaining to identification, illustrated, $15.00.

The Gun Collector's Handbook of Values, Charles Edward Chapel. First published in 1940, this important volume has been revised regularly to reflect the constant change in prices. Covers both small arms and long arms, fully illustrated. Although principally concerned with U.S. weapons, it also includes significant foreign examples, an important book, $16.95.

A History of the Colt Revolver, Charles T. Haven and Frank A. Belden. New edition of a classic covering all aspects of the origin and development of Colonel Colt's revolver. Hundreds of excellent illustrations, $10.98.

The Luger Pistol, Fred Datig. Interesting and most informative study of the history of the Luger from the original Borchardt on through to the final Luger models. Much information not found in other Luger books. Based on original research, illustrated, $9.50.

Lugers at Random, Charles Kenyon, Jr. Full scale photos of hundreds of Luger models and variations with accompanying detailed text. Accessories fully covered. This is a true Luger classic and is required reading for the Luger collector, $17.50.

Luger Tips, Michael Reese II. Little known facts on each and every major model. Also much on holsters and accessories, many original photos, required Luger reading, $6.95.

Luger Variations, Harry E. Jones. Splendid reference on the subject. Three-view presentation of each weapon discussed with complete description. The 160 full page photos are supplemented with four color plates of extremely rare examples, $22.50.

Mauser Pocket Pistols 1910-1946, Roy G. Pender. A comprehensive study of all Mauser pistols produced during the period indicated, each is illustrated, $12.95.

Mauser Self-Loading Pistols, James N. Belford and H. J. Dunlap. Presents little known and complete information on the development of the famous "broom handle" Mauser. All models, including experimentals, covered. A valuable tool for the Mauser collector, $12.50.

1900 Luger - U.S. Test Trials, Michael Reese II. The only comprehensive report on these trials. Complete with original photos and reproductions of official correspondence. By one of the world's outstanding Luger experts, $4.95.

Small Arms of the Sea Services, Colonel Robert H. Rankin. Well-illustrated chapters on the development and use of pistols and revolvers of the U.S. sea services from the Revolutionary War to the present. The only study of its kind, $14.95.

Small Arms of the World, W. H. B. Smith, revised by Edward Ezell. Universally recognized classic on small arms of 42 countries. Beautiful volume with some 2000 photos and drawings. Covers the entire universe of small arms. Probably the most important single book on all small arms and ammunition in print today. Originally published around 1950, it has been revised and updated, $20.00.

United States Single Shot Martial Pistols, C. W. Sawyer. This is an excellent reprint of the original 1911 edition of this classic discussion of these historically important pistols. Contains both photos and line drawings, $6.00.

Walther P-38 Pistol, George Nonte. Devoted to this single famous Walther, this work, although not too long, is an excellent and detailed treatment of the subject. All features covered including operation and identification, of much interest to all Walther collectors, $3.95.

RIFLES AND MUSKETS

British Military Longarms, D. W. Bailey. Two volumes. An excellent coverage of these British weapons. Much detail, including much on variations, proof marks and other subjects. An important addition to the gun collector's library. Volume One, 1715-1815, $4.50. Volume Two, 1850-1865, $4.50. Both volumes well illustrated.

Civil War Guns. William B. Edwards. Excellent coverage of its subject. Although it treats with all firearms, including the crude machine guns of the era, the chapters on rifles are of especial interest to the collector. Much interesting material on gun designers and smiths, $7.98.

The Complete Illustrated Encyclopedia of the World's Firearms. Ian V. Hogg. As the title infers this is an encyclopedia covering the development of all types of pistols, revolvers and rifles. Photos and line drawings of exceptional quality. Describes weapons and gives brief biographical data on gun designers. A one volume library, $24.95.

Flayderman's Guide to Antique American Firearms and Their Values, Norm Flayderman. This is without a doubt the most important book on the subject to yet appear. Illustrates and describes all antique American firearms and gives their current value. Includes all variations, chapters on development and the state of the art of collecting. Well-organized for easy reference, includes muskets and rifles as well as pistols and revolvers. A required book in any gun collector's library, $12.95.

The Gun Collector's Handbook of Values, Charles Edward Chapel. First published in 1940, this important volume has been revised regularly to reflect the constant change in prices. Covers both small arms and long arms, fully illustrated. Although principally concerned with U.S. weapons, it also includes significant foreign examples, an important book, $16.95.

Small Arms of the Sea Services, Colonel Robert H. Rankin. Well-illustrated chapters on the development and use of pistols and revolvers of the U.S. sea services from the Revolutionary War to the present. Contains much information on muskets and rifles as well as one of the few accurate accounts of military shotguns or trench guns. The only study of its kind, $14.95.

UNIFORMS

Army Uniforms of World War I, Andrew Mollo and Pierre Turner. Interesting and informative guide to the army uniforms of all nations engaged in World War I. Illustrated in color, recommended, $6.95.

Cavalry Uniforms, Robert and Christopher Wilkinson-Latham. British, Commonwealth and other mounted units. A companion volume to *Infantry Uniforms,* 96 full color plates plus detailed descriptive text, an excellent account of value to uniform collectors, $6.95.

A Dictionary of Military Uniform, W. Y. Carman. The author is a well-known authority on military history and uniforms. Before his retirement, he was Deputy Director of the National Army Museum, London. He has drawn upon his vast knowledge and resources to definition and background information of all the various parts of uniforms of the world and their accessories. Illustrated with both color and black and white plates. This is an indispensable book for a military collector, $12.50.

Dress Regulations for the Army 1900. Excellent reprint of the British Army dress regulations. The detailed regulations are supplemented by a host of black and white photos picturing the articles described. The collector of British militaria will need this volume, $10.00.

German Army Uniforms, Brian L. Davis. Listed previously under Insignia, this extremely important book gives an excellent description of all the various uniforms worn by the armies of the Third Reich. Nearly 400 large clear photos and detailed line drawings. The author of this book is an expert in his field, $16.95.

Infantry Uniforms, Robert and Christopher Wilkinson-Latham. Also includes material on artillery and other supporting units of the British Army. Two volumes, each with nearly 100 color plates plus text. Volume One, 1742-1855, $6.95. Volume Two, 1855-1939, $6.95.

Militaria, Jan K. Kube. This valuable reference could very well have been listed under helmets as well as uniforms. The text is in German but the 200 or so clear photos dramatically illustrate the details of Imperial German helmets and uniforms. The descriptive text under each illustration is easy to follow. In addition to the black and white photos and detailed drawings, there are seven color plates of rare headdress and shoulder straps, all of the Imperial German Army. Highly recommended, $19.95.

Militaria, Von Wolfgang Hermann. Descriptive catalog and price guide of over 300 pieces, including helmets, other headdress, uniforms, accessories, steins, accoutrements, weapons, and other military gear of the Imperial German Army, together with a few examples from Great Britain, France, Russia and Belgium. The catalog itself is prefaced by a historical essay on uniforms and weapons with a short dictionary of terms. Of particular interest is the series of color plates of some of the uniforms of the army of Freidrich the Great. This is a real bonus. Text in German but an important reference for the serious uniform collector, $19.95.

Military Fashion, John Mollo. Lavishly illustrated volume in color giving an excellent general history of world uniforms. Includes many uniform details not available elsewhere, an excellent reference, $20.00.

Military Uniforms in America, the Company of Military Historians. Two volumes, large format. Pictures in full color, accompanied by excellent descriptive text, the various American uniforms and uniforms worn by foreign armies campaigning in the United States. An interesting and thoroughly reliable source of information. Volume One covers the era of the

American Revolution — 1755-1795, $25.00. Volume Two covers the so-called "years of growth" — 1796-1851, $25.00. Other volumes are in preparation.

Naval, Marine and Air Force Uniforms of World War II, Mollo and McGregor. General description of the uniforms of all nations engaged in World War II. A helpful resource book, illustrated in color, $6.95.

Uniforms of the Army, Colonel Robert H. Rankin. A survey of U.S. Army uniforms from the Revolutionary War to modern times. General in its scope, well-illustrated with both color and black and white plates, $6.95.

Uniforms of the Civil War, P. Haythornthwaite. Good study, with color plates of the Union and Confederate armies, worthwhile, $6.95.

Uniforms of the Imperial Russian Army, Boris Mollo. This is the first book in English to give an insight into the many colorful uniforms worn by Imperial Russian troops. It is excellent, interesting text supported by color plates. Necessary to the Imperial Russian collector and of great interest to anyone interested in uniforms, $12.95.

Uniforms of the Marines, Colonel Robert H. Rankin. Same format and coverage as **Uniforms of the Army** but of the U.S. Marines, $6.95.

United States Army Headgear 1855-1902, Edgar M. Howell. Complete treatment of the development and use of headgear for the period indicated. Much valuable information on the spiked and plumed helmets worn by the U.S. Army, fully illustrated, $7.95.

MISCELLANEOUS

American Polearms 1526-1865, Rodney Hilton Brown. This is the only book available on this particular area of military collecting. Covers in-depth the development of lances, halberds, spontoons, pikes and other naval boarding weapons in the U.S. service. This is an important study in a little known field which is now beginning to attract the notice of more and more collectors. Fully illustrated with photos and diagrams, $14.50.

Civil War Collector's Encyclopedia, Dr. Frank A. Lord. Three volumes. Remarkably complete coverage of Civil War artifacts by an acknowledged expert in the field. Large format, illustrated with photos and drawings. Each succeeding volume supplements the other with no duplication but with facts about artifacts acquired after the publication of the previous volume. Civil War collectors should have these. Volume One, $7.98. Volume Two, $19.50. Volume Three, $19.50.

Collector's Illustrated Encyclopedia of the American Revolution, George C. Neuman and Frank J. Kravic. Pictorial study of American Revolution military artifacts, minimum of text, all items illustrated, $17.95.

Gorgets of the Third Reich, Richard Deeter and Warren Odegard. The interest in collecting gorgets is steadily increasing, particularly gorgets of the Third Reich. This is the only book presently available on the subject and it is of great value to the specialized collector in the field. Well-illustrated with representative gorgets, $9.95.

Regimental Steins, Major J. L. Harrell. Although regimental steins have been of collector interest since World War I, this is the first and only book on the subject. It pictures and describes 376 steins of all types and sizes. The steins are covered in great detail. Additionally, there is an abundance of information not readily available elsewhere of name and honorary name, date of formation and garrison of all military units. Similar applicable information is furnished for naval units. There is also valuable information on the

history of the Imperial German Army. The author is an acknowledged expert in the field. Of interest to anyone interested in the Imperial German Army, it is required reading for the regimental stein collector, $19.75.
Note: The above list includes but a few of the rapidly increasing number of books on militaria which are available. Military collecting is one of the fastest growing, if not the fastest, of any area of the antiques field. However, each of the books listed above are or have been in the personal library of the author and each bears his personal recommendation.

MUSEUMS

For the serious collector, museums and their reference libraries can be of important reference sources. In many instances the public exhibitions include just a portion of the artifact holdings. The remainder are held in so-called study collections not generally open to the public except by special arrangement. The museum reference libraries often contain valuable materials which may be of considerable value to the collector. Many museums will, upon application, make their study collections and libraries available to serious researchers and will answer inquiries. In this respect it is well to remember that museum personnel are very very busy with their own responsibilities and should not be burdened with trivia. Requests for permission to use study collections and libraries should be made well in advance of an anticipated visit. Both black and white and color prints, as well as color transparencies, are usually available upon order. The price of these will vary from museum to museum.

Do not expect museum personnel to appraise an article for you. Almost, without exception, museum policy forbids this.

There are many museums in this country featuring militaria. The majority of these are listed here. Listed first are major museums with some indication as to their holdings. These are followed by a list of smaller institutions. More complete information, including hours of opening, a brief account of holdings and more complete addresses may be found in "The Directory of Museums," by Kenneth Hudson and Ann Nicholls, New York, 1975. This volume is available in many public libraries. Additionally, many of these museums have descriptive brochures which they will furnish upon request. These contain complete information on their collections.

Aberdeen Ordnance Museum, Aberdeen, Maryland.
A most complete collection of weapons of all nations in all catagories from a giant Nazi railway gun to bayonets. Interior exhibits cover small arms, helmets, and automatic weapons, among others. Outdoor exhibits include large tank and artillery parks of weapons of all nations.
Engineer Museum, Fort Belvoir, Virginia.
Very good exhibits relating to the development of military engineering.
Metropolitan Museum of Art, New York, New York.
Most complete collection of high quality European and Oriental arms and armor. Beautifully displayed.
Museum of the Confederacy, Richmond, Virginia.
Very good collection of uniforms of famous officers as well as other interesting and important artifacts of the Confederacy.

National Rifle Association Firearms Museum, Washington, D.C.
Most complete collections illustrating the development of firearms.
Patton Museum, Fort Knox, Kentucky.
Interior exhibits trace history of U.S. Cavalry, with attention to a special collection of the memorabilia of the famous American tank general George Patton. Outdoor exhibits include an extensive park of armored vehicles.
Remington Arms Museum, Ilion, New York.
An interesting and important museum featuring the many arms made by the famous Remington organization.
Smithsonian Institution, Washington, D.C.
National Air and Space Museum.
Comprehensive exhibit of the development of aviation from the very beginning through space travel. Special attention to military and naval aviation.
National Museum of History and Technology.
Excellent exhibits of military and naval subjects from early times to the present.
Springfield Armory Museum, Springfield, Massachusetts.
One of the most extensive collections of small arms in this country. An excellent reference collection.
The John Woodman Higgins Armory, Worcester, Massachusetts.
Excellent collection of medieval arms and armor, both European and Oriental. Well displayed.
U.S. Air Force Museum, Wright Field, Dayton, Ohio.
Excellent collection of aircraft and artifacts pertaining to the history of military aviation.
U.S. Army Infantry Museum, Fort Benning, Georgia.
Important collection of items pertaining to infantry and to military small arms.
U.S. Army Quartermaster Corps Museum, Fort Lee, Virginia.
Exhibits pertaining to military quartermaster activities. Some excellent uniform exhibits.
U.S. Army Signal Corps Museum, Fort Monmouth, New Jersey.
Located at an interesting old military post. History of the development of signal equipment and similar material.
U.S. Army Transportation Musuem, Fort Eustis, Virginia.
History of military transportation depicted in exhibits. Good.
U.S. Artillery Museum, Fort Sill, Oklahoma.
This museum located at a famous old Army artillery post gives a most interesting insight into the development of artillery.
U.S. Cavalry Museum, Fort Riley, Kansas.
Housed at a famous old cavalry post. Interesting history of cavalry, particularly horse mounted units.
U.S. Marine Corps Aviation Museum, Quantico, Virginia.
Collections include Marine aircraft from before World War I on through to the present.
U.S. Marine Corps Museum, Washington, D.C.
Colorful exhibits covering the history of the U.S. Marine Corps, including uniforms and weapons. Exhibit of machine guns is one of the very best.
U.S. Military Academy Museum, West Point, New York.
Important and rather complete collection of arms, uniforms and other memorabilia of all U.S. wars.

U.S. Naval Academy Museum, Annapolis, Maryland.
A small but most excellent collection of artifacts related to naval history, including very many excellent models.
U.S. Naval Aviation Museum, Pensacola, Florida.
Important exhibits of the history of naval aviation.
U.S. Navy Memorial Museum, Washington, D.C.
Well designed exhibits depict the entire span of naval history of the United States. Indoor exhibits include many ship models and much ordnance. Outdoor exhibits include tanks, heavy guns, guided missiles, midget submarines and others.
War Memorial Museum of Virginia, Newport News, Virginia.
Good collection of military artifacts, particularly of World Wars I and II and later wars.
Winchester Museum, Buffalo Bill Historical Center, Cody, Wyoming.
Collections trace the history of firearms from their inception with particular attention to Winchester made arms. These collections are from the Winchester Gun Museum formerly located in New Haven, Connecticut.

OTHER MUSEUMS

Several military posts and Navy and Marine Corps installations have small museums, as do National Parks, states and cities and even a few private organizations. These vary greatly in size and quality. In many instances they are highly specialized as to interest. In this connection the following listing should be of some assistance.
Appomatox Court House National Historic Park Museum, Appomatox, Virginia.
Browning Gun Museum, Ogden, Utah.
Confederate Naval Museum, Columbus, Georgia.
First U.S. Army Museum, Fort George G. Meade, Maryland.
Fort Leavenworth Museum, Fort Leavenworth, Kansas.
Fort Lewis Military Museum, Fort Lewis, Washington.
Fort Ward Museum, Alexandria, Virginia.
Gettysburg National Museum, Gettysburg, Pennsylvania.
Guilford Courthouse National Military Park, Greensboro, North Carolina.
Kings Mountain National Military Park, Kings Mountain, North Carolina.
Manassas National Battlefield Park Museum, Manassas, Virginia.
Museum of the Ancient and Honourable Artillery Company of Massachusetts, Boston, Massachusetts.
Soldiers Memorial, St. Louis, Missouri.
Texas Confederate Museum, Austin, Texas.

COLLECTOR TERMINOLOGY

ACCOUTREMENT. Articles or equipment worn with the uniform. May include such items as belts, straps, ammunition pouches, first aid kits, canteen, and similar articles.
AIGUILLETTES. For service dress, one or more loops worn about the left shoulder. For full dress plaited cord worn about the left shoulder and draped across the left chest. The ends are fitted with tapering metal points. In the U.S. Service, worn by aides-de camp.

AIR COOLED. Various methods used to cool the gun barrel, particularly of machine guns.

ARTILLERY. Combat arm embracing a variety of weapons from light field guns to missiles. In the U.S. Service at one time there was coast artillery, using large howitzers and guns to protect harbors; field artillery using horse drawn and later motorized mobile cannon. Other nations have a variety of special artillery units, including fortress artillery, light artillery, heavy artillery and foot artillery. A speciality of modern warfare is antitank artillery especially designed to stop enemy tanks.

AUTOMATIC PISTOL. A weapon designed to be fully automatic. When the trigger is depressed the gun will continue to fire until the ammunition is exhausted. However the term is now loosely applied to weapons which are self-loading, that is the weapon reloads itself after each firing.

BADGE. Any of a variety of devices, usually metal or plastic used to identify the wearer's organization or speciality. Commonly worn on caps, shoulder straps and lapels.

BATTLE HONORS. Names of battles, campaigns and other engagements in which the unit has participated with honor. May appear as part of the unit's cap badge or headdress plate, on drums, belt plates, cuff bands, flags and banners, and elsewhere. Probably more common with the British Army and with the Imperial German Army.

BEARSKIN. A type of military headdress usually of fairly high cylindrical form. May be a development of the grenadier cap. Most generally worn by elite units.

BELL CROWN CAP. A military or naval cap with a top larger than the band, the two joined by concave sides.

BELT PLATE. May be applied to waist belts or shoulder belts. Bears the regimental or unit identifying device.

BICORNE. Military headdress with two sides of the broad brim turned back up against the crown. Sometimes called a cocked hat.

BUGLEHORN. Sometimes called a light infantry horn. Originally made from an animal horn. Later a horn with a fairly large loop in the instrument.

BOLT ACTION. Method of closing the breech of a gun by a bolt which moves along the axis of the gun barrel. A turn bolt is one which when pushed forward is turned to lock the action. A straight pull bolt is one in which the bolt is locked by cam action.

BOX MAGAZINE. A metal box for holding and feeding ammunition into the chamber of the weapon. This is accomplished by a metal plate which by spring action causes each round to ascent as the spent round is ejected. May be within the weapon itself or attached to the outside.

BUSBY. Usually a medium high cylindrical headdress of fur. Worn by hussars. Never worn in the U.S. Service except by drum majors.

BUSBY BAG. A decorative bag hanging down over the right side of the busby. Usually of different colors to identify the wearer's unit.

CALIBER. Sometimes spelled calibre. The interior diameter of a gun barrel. Is the measurement from the top of the rifling grooves. The American and British Services usually measure this in thousandths of an inch, as .30; .303; .45, etc. Continental services use millimeters in expressing this measure, as 7.65-mm, 9-mm and so on.

CARTRIDGE BOX. Simply a box to conveniently carry pistol or rifle ammunition. At times decorated with the unit badge or other identifying device.

CENTER FIRE. Method of cartridge ignition where the percussion cap is mounted in the center of the base of the cartridge.

CHAMBER. That portion of the rear of the gun barrel shaped to closely accommodate and align the cartridge.

CHAPEAU de BRAS. From the French. A cocked hat flexible enough to be folded back upon itself to permit easy carrying under the arm.

CHEVRON. A "V" shape device worn on the arm to denote grade of enlisted men or other ranks. At one time also worn to denote rank of officers. To denote grade these are usually worn point up on one or both upper sleeves. Small chevrons were worn by the American military during and following World War I to denote wounds or overseas service. These were worn on the lower arm and were of different material for wounds than those for overseas service.

COCKADE. An identifying device worn on the headdress. Usually of the national or state color. May be of metal, leather, cloth or similar other material.

CUIRASS. Breastplate and backplate. Formerly worn for protection, usually by pikemen and mounted troops. One of the last uses to which armor was put. Now used for ceremonial occasions by certain elite units.

CYPHER. The monogram of a soverign. Initials may be reversed and intertwined. Most often seen on flags, banners, drums, and forming cap devices.

CZAPSKA. Also known as a lancer cap. Originated in the four sided cap worn by Polish peasants and adopted by the Polish lancers. Worn by British and Continental lancers, light cavalry, uhlans, and similar troops.

DIRK. A small dagger-like weapon usually worn by naval midshipmen and still worn by officers and other ranks of the Scots regiments.

DRAGOON. Basically a mounted infantryman. Originally armed with carbine or rifle and on occasion with bayonet and sword. Tactics called for the infantryman to ride to the scene of battle, then dismount and go into action.

EJECTOR. Mechanism which in cooperation with the extractor throws the spent cartridge out of the weapon.

EPAULETTE. Originally metal shoulder defenses of armor. When armor became impractical it became a decorative shoulder device around about the early 1700's. Consists basically of a strap running along the shoulder seam to the top of the sleeve where it terminates in an oval pad. The strap is usually decorated with heavy flat embroidery. The pad often has a metal crescent about the outer edge and may be further decorated with hanging fringe.

EXTRACTOR. That part of the weapon mechanism which withdraws the spent cartridge out of the chamber and presents it to the ejector.

FELDMUTZE. German Army undress cap.

FIELD ARTILLERY. Artillery mobile enough to provide close support to troops in the field.

FLUGELMUTZE. A tall cylindrical headpiece with a long "wing" or piece of fabric which may be wound about the piece or allowed to flow free. The German word translates as "winged cap."

FULL DRESS. The uniform worn for ceremonial and/or formal occasions. Is much more elaborate than that worn for general duty.

FUSILIER. A flintlock musket was formerly known as a fusil. It replaced the matchlock but for a time was so expensive that it was used only by certain select troops. These troops were known as fusiliers. Later the term was given to crack infantry units.

GORGET. Last vestige of armor to be worn. A miniature representation of the throat protection. Most often half-moon in shape. Usually worn at one time by officers and enlisted men or other ranks assigned to special duties. Worn in the German Service long after it had been abandoned by other armies. Was used during the Third Reich to identify color guards, police and certain other special personnel. The device is decorated with cyphers, coats of arms, or other decorations.

GRENADE. A small container containing a bursting charge and designed to fragment upon detonation. Earlier grenades were ignited by a fuse. Later grenades are detonated by a mechanical igniter.

GRENADIER. Especially selected tall strong soldiers whose duty it was to hurl the then heavy grenades into the enemy ranks. Later the term was applied to elite infantry units.

GRENADIER CAP. Medium to tall military headpiece without brim. Originated according to legend far back in the days when broad brim hats were worn by the military personnel. The wide brim hindered the efficient use of the grenadier's throwing arm and the straight sided cap was devised to eliminate the difficulty. Of fur or cloth in the shape of a bishop's mitre. Variously decorated with a full metal or cloth front plate or national or regimental insignia and often with cords and tassels.

GUARDS. Elite units whose duty it is to closely guard the sovereign. Noteable examples are the British Foot Guards, the Prussian Garde du Corps, the Prussian Palace Guard Company, the Bavarian Archers of the Guard, the Wurttemberg Place Guard Company, and others. These units wore a very elaborate dress uniform befitting their high station.

HELMET. A military headdress consisting basically of a semi-spherical skull with a front and sometimes a back visor. Of cloth or metal. Usually has a decorative crest or other type of top adornment including a spike or a ball fixture. Trimmed with an identifying plate or insignia on the front and equipped with chin strap or chin scales. May be very elaborate. Helmets for modern combat, however, are strictly utilitarian, being designed for protection of the head but may have some identifying device on the front or side.

HAT. A military hat is somewhat similar to a civilian hat with a brim around a crown. May have one or more sides turned up and is usually decorated with colored cord and various insignia.

HUSSAR. Light cavalryman. Usually armed with a lance and carbine or a pistol. Fought mounted. Were regarded as among the elite of an army and wore a special and fancy uniform, including the busby.

IMPERIAL CROWN (or Royal Crown). Representation of the crown worn by the ruling sovereign as contrasted to those worn by nobility. Worn as a part of the insignia on headdress, drums, flags, banners and such.

INFANTRY. The so-called "Queen of Battles." Units organized and trained to fight on foot armed with light weapons. The backbone of military combat forces. Early infantry regiments were known as Foot regiments.

JACK BOOTS. Originally high top leather cavalry boots which had been treated or jacked with tar and wax to give them a hard surface which was quite protective against the weapons of that day. In more recent times the term has been applied to the medium high boots worn in the German Army.

KEPI. Originally a cloth cap with visor. Was without anything to stiffen the cloth, thus causing it to fall forward toward the visor. Later had a stiffened band and top arranged to make the top slant forward. Often decorated with braid and identifying devices.

KHAKI. Name derives from the Indian "dust." The white and/or red coats worn by British troops in India caused them to be easy targets for native sharpshooters. The troops soon learned to dye their uniforms in coffee or mud and other substances to cause them to blend in with the background. Was later adopted by many armies as a color for field uniforms.

KOKARDE. Plural is kockarden. From the German. A cockade. A device, usually circular in shape, of metal, cloth, plastic or other material in the national colors of the wearer. May also be in the regimental colors.

LANCER CAP. Sometimes known as a tschapka. Cap with a rounded skull with front visor. Has a four sided mortor board on top. Most often highly decorated with unit identifying devices, badges and cords. Lancers were rated as medium cavalry. In the German Army lancers were called uhlans.

LANYARD. A stout cord or leather strap attached to a ring in the butt of a pistol, revolver or carbine and attached to the body of the wearer to prevent loss in combat. In earlier times it was also the cord or strap used to fire an artillery piece.

MACHINE GUN. Light to fairly heavy weapon, usually of rifle caliber or slightly larger designed to fire automatically. Fired in short bursts to preserve the rifling of the barrel.

MAMELUKE. Originally Turkish or Circassian captives who were incorporated into a very elite combat unit. They were known for their terrible fighting ability and devotion. At first slaves, they eventually became so strong that they became virtual rulers of Egypt. They wore a saber with a characteristic pistol shape hilt.

MEDALS. Along with decorations these are defined in the section on decorations and medals.

MILITIA. Generally, civilians who have been enrolled and trained in a military unit for call to active duty in event of an emergency.

MIRLETON. From the French. See **Fugel Mutze.**

MUSKET. A smoothbore shoulder arm, commonly muzzleloading. Used the matchlock and flintlock means of ignition. These methods are described in the section on small arms.

NUMBER. It has long been military custom to number regiments and other units consecutively, i.e., 1st Infantry Regiment. 7th Cavalry Regiment, etc.

ORNAMENT. The various ornamentation on uniforms may be said to have begun for a very practical reason. Among other examples, the decorative slits on the cuffs of the uniforms of some regiments are a reminder of when the large cuff was turned back and up and secured.

OTHER RANKS. Name or term applied to private soldiers in British and other armies. In the U.S. Service, the term enlisted men is used.

OVERSEAS CAP. A soft cloth cap which could be easily and quickly folded. Originally designed to replace the heavy steel combat helmet when the wearer did not need that protection. First used by the U.S. Army in overseas areas, hence the name. At one time its wear was restricted to those serving or who had served overseas during Wiorld War I. Its use was then extended for wear with service dress.

PEAK. Known as a visor in the U.S. Services.

PELZMUTZE. The German name for the fur busby worn by hussars.

PERCUSSION CAP. Small copper cap filled with detonating powder which, when struck by the weapon's trigger, caused a flash into the power charge of the cartridge.

PICKELHAUBE. German name for the spiked helmet.

PIONEERS. Used by the British and Continental armies to designate the troops known as engineers in the U.S. Army.

PLATE. The plate on the front of the military headdress, usually of metal, cloth or plastic, bearing the unit identification of the wearer or the national arms. May be known as shako plate, helmet plate, etc., or simply as a front plate.

POMPOM. Cloth tuft worn for identification purposes on military headdress. Usually appears on the front or either side of the headdress. May be a ball or elongated. May be in the national colors, the colors of the arm or service or of the unit.

POUCH. Originally a large pouch to hold grenades and, in the case of mounted men, pistol ammunition. Those for enlisted men or other ranks were fairly plain and bore a simple identification. Those for officers were elaborately decorated.

PRUSSIAN EAGLE. The traditional heraldic eagle of Prussia.

QUEEN'S CROWN. A distinctive form of royal crown worn during the reign of Queen Victoria of England.

RAUPENHELME. Helmet with a worsted crest. Particularly popular in the Bavarian Army at one time.

RIFLE. A shoulder arm with a spirally groved bore. This causes the bullet to spiral vertically along its axis, Importing range and accuracy.

ROMAN HELMET. A helmet of more recent times, generally patterned after the high crested helmet of the Roman legionaire.

ROSETTE. Circular metal, cloth or plastic ornament worn on military headdress. If of cloth, it's usually pleated. In the national or unit colors.

ROUND HAT. Very similar to the civilian hat of the same name. Most often decorated in the military service. A hat with a small round top crown and a fairly narrow rim all around.

ROYAL ARMS. The personal coat of arms of the reigning monarch. Often used as an identifying device on various parts of the uniform.

SABRETACHE. Ornamented pouch carried with the sword. Hussar breeches were so light that they could not be fitted with pockets and the pouch was worn on the waist belt to hold the hussar's personal belongings. Was sometimes worn by other mounted troops including horse artillery.

SCALES. May be chin scales or shoulder scales. Chin scales are overlapping pieces of metal attached to leather straps which pass under the chin of the wearer of a military headdress. Shoulder scales are overlapping metal pieces attached to a cloth shoulder strap.

SCHABRACKLE. Ornamental cloth which was worn under the saddle. Might be highly ornamented with royal devices and regimental insignia.

SCHAKO. Alternate spelling for tschako or shako.

SCHAPSKA. The distinctive cap worn by lancers. See lancer cap.

SPONTOON. A type of pole arm carried by officers until around the early 1800's. Sometimes called espontoon.

TANK. Armored mobile vehicle for use in infantry support or used in much the same manner as cavalry. Classified into light, medium and heavy catagories. Tanks are now referred to as armor. This is logical inasmuch as they are an extension of the old suits of armor except that, in the modern usage, the armor protects several men instead of just one.

TIN HAT. Nickname for the combat helmet.

UHLAN. A German lancer. The name comes, it is believed, from an ancient

Tartar word meaning "belonging to the horse." It was introduced into the German Army about 1808.

VOLUNTEER. An individual who enters the military or naval service of his own free will. In some armies there were certain differences in uniform to distinguish volunteer units from those of the regular establishment. For instance, in the British service helmets had silver or white metal helmet plates and trim instead of gilt or brass.

WAR SERVICE STRIPES. May be chevrons of small size or bars worn on a lower sleeve to indicate the amount of time the wearer had served outside his own country. Usually authorized only in war time. A single stripe might indicate either six months or a year of overseas service according to the army. Color of these also varied from army to army.

WOUND STRIPES. Similar in form to War Service Stripes but of a different color and material to distinguish them. Might also be worn on a different lower sleeve. Ordinarily a stripe was awarded for each wound sustained in combat.

YEOMANRY. In the British service, volunteer cavalry.

ZOUAVE DRESS. A type of uniform adopted from that worn by Algerian troops. Oriental in pattern with very baggy trousers, gaiters, short jacket and fez-like cap. Worn by some troops (volunteers and militia) of both the Union and the Confederacy during the American Civil War.

ARMOR

Armor presents one of the most exotic areas of military collecting. Armor, whether it be of Oriental or Occidental origin, possesses a fascination for nearly everyone whether or not they are military minded. Well executed suits of armor and helmets are true objects of art as well as being essential items of military gear. Many art museums which would in fact refuse to display other impedimenta of war will proudly display armor as an expression of the art form. Indeed the rare suits of armor which are highly engraved, etched or embossed do represent the highest artistic skill.

Some forms of protective devices have existed since earliest times. These have varied throughout the years to conform with the changing concepts of war and of the weapons employed. Specimens of the earliest types of armor are very few and far between. These, for the most part, were made of leather or quilted cloth and the few artifacts which have survived the ages, along with the few bronze helmets, are to be found only in museums.

Greek and Roman armor reached a high degree of development and although it consisted for the most part of helmet, breastplate and backplate, and greaves or protection for the legs, it was particularly well suited to the type of warfare in which it was used. Greek and Roman helmets are particularly beautiful art examples. Unfortunately, very few specimens of this armor have survived and these too are in the hands of museums and a few wealthy collectors.

The type of warfare which later developed in Europe and England, including the introduction of new weapons, brought about a different kind of armor. Heavily quilted clothing, sometimes reinforced with metal plates and chain mail (composed of thousands of closely linked metal rings) was largely used until around the beginning of the 13th-century. Armor composed almost entirely of this chain mail was also employed. This type of armor was supplanted sometime during the following century by plate armor, which is the type of armor with which we are most familiar today. Complete suits of plate armor, encasing the wearer from head to toe continued in use until well into the 1600's. Then the development of firearms put an end to its use, although it was discarded gradually, piece by piece. In order to make the armor proof against gunfire, it would have been necessary to make it so thick that it would have been far too heavy to wear. First, parts were discarded which had protected the feet and legs and the armor would be known as "three-quarter" armor. Then the upper leg defenses disappeared and we had "half" armor. This continued until only the cuirass (breast and backplates) and the helmet were left. This armor would be worn almost exclusively by heavy cavalry (cuirassiers) and foot troops known as pikemen. Armor was worn by heavy cavalrymen into World War I, particularly by French and Belgium. Soon high powered rifle fire put an end to its use completely. It has since been worn only by a few elite guard troops.

It is extremely doubtful if any **complete** suits of armor of the 1500's and earlier still exist. The numerous pieces of this armor were held together with leather straps. In time, these frayed or rotted away and parts were lost and had to be replaced. Additionally, through the years, as weapons and tactics were improved, changes in armor design were called for and many of the older suits were reworked and modified. Today, even in the best museums and collections, it is impossible to find a completely original suit of the old armor. Luckily, this is not true of the later periods. Three-quarter armor, half armor, cuirassier and pikeman's armor and helmets of the mid-1600's on are available. Although not cheap, it is within the means of many collectors. Helmets of the 1500's, unlike the armor itself, are also available both at auctions and from dealers. These helmets are of a number of types, including close helmets, burgonets, morions, funerary helmets, and others. Helmets of the 1600's and later are more plentiful, particularly cabassets, burgonets and lobster tail helmets, both with nasal bar and hinged bar visor.

Oriental armor, including Turkish and Indian variations, is very different from that of Europe. Japanese armor differs drastically from that of any other nation. Turkish and Indian armor consists mainly of a helmet and chain mail. This chain mail may be only a shirt-like affair or may cover the entire body. In some specimens metal plates protect the vital areas of the body, legs and arms. These plates are linked together by chain mail. The helmets are of odd but interesting and artistic design. Generally these consist of a medium shallow metal skull, often decorated all around with chiseled, etched or engraved floral designs or with quotations from the **Koran.** A spike, plume holder or crescent usually decorates the top of the helmet. A sliding nasal bar is attached to the front. So-called "devil's head" helmets will have large curved metal horns attached to the sides. The front of these helmets are embossed with a devil's face. A spike adorns the top of the skull. On all these helmets a chain mail "camail" hangs down to protect the back and sides of the head and the brow. An especially interesting and desirable helmet is the Turkish "turban" helmet which is of extra large size so that it can be worn over the turban.

One really enters a complicated field in Japanese armor. It is very beautiful with its varicolored silk lancing and is a distinct art form which reflects the artistic as well as the military aspect of the Japanese culture. This is a field in which the collector, unless he is a past-master himself, would do well to consult an expert. Generally speaking, Japanese armor is very loose fitting, not conforming to the shape of the body of the wearer as is the case with European armor. The skull of the helmet is large and may be fabricated of several sections. A family **mon** or crest or other device decorates the front. The sides of the face and the neck are protected by large metal lames laced to each other with silk cords. The helmet is held secure on the head by an intricate arrangement of silk cords. Protection for the face was provided by a metal mask which could cover the whole face or just a portion. This too was held in place by silk cords. Some breast and backplates might be of single piece construction or might be composed of a number of metal lames, again held together with silk cords. Shoulders and upper legs were protected by apron-like arrangements of silk laced lames. Arms and lower legs were usually protected by metal plates connected with chain mail. All metal parts were highly lacquered.

The rank of the wearer was indicated by the color of the silk cord lacing and by the manner in which this lacing was used. Certain colors were reserved for particularly important and noble families or clans. The backplate was often provided with a holder into which a shaft, bearing a small standard or other identifying device, could be inserted. As odd as Japanese armor may seem to many Occidentals, it was particularly well adapted to the warfare for which it was intended. Japanese armor, including helmets, offer a complex variety. Details may be had from Stone's *"A Glossary of the Construction,*

Decoration and Use of Arms and Armor in All Countries in All Times," and from the references listed elsewhere in this guide.

The most valuable and historic Japanese armor dates from those periods of intense strife and civil wars among the noble families. The value of a single suit of this classic armor was often measured in terms of an entire province and was later designated a "National Treasure." Very, very few suits of this armor ever left Japan. Those in the hands of a very few museums and private collectors are worth a considerable fortune.

During the latter part of the Tokugawa Era (1600-1867), the government achieved stability and peace was established. Armor was now worn largely for court appearances, ceremonies and parade. Protective qualities were sacrificed for art form. Most of these suits are extremely beautiful and it is these that are most likely to be found at auctions and for sale by dealers. With the end of the feudal period in Japan in 1868 and the entry of Japan into the modern world, and with increased communication and commerce with the western world, a great interest in Japanese culture developed in Europe, England and America. To supply the demand on the part of westerners for armor for decorative purposes, the armorers began fabricating copies to satisfy the mass of new customers. The identification of these requires an expert.

Collecting miniature armor, both Eurpoean and Japanese, is an interesting field of collecting, especially for those with limited funds and space. The older examples were made by experienced armorers and are truly gems. Consequently, they are rather expensive. Modern made miniatures of reasonable quality are not expensive.

Reproduction European and Japanese armor is also available. This armor varies in quality from the downright awful to the elegant. A little study will enable one to be able to identify fine reproductions which closely approximate the original.

ORIGINAL ITEMS

Price Range

☐ **Burgonet,** *German, c. 1500's. One-piece skull with well-defined comb with roped decoration, medium width umbril or brim projecting over the brow, with roped edge, hinged defense or flaps over the ears. These too have roped edges and are decorated with an etched circle with a rayed design within. One each side of the skull is another and larger etched circle enclosing the scene of a contemporary soldier and a masonry wall.* 800.00   875.00

☐ **As above,** *but of plain pattern without decoration. These may be from several countries.* 600.00   650.00

☐ **Cabassets,** *16th century. The cabasset is an open helmet with a narrow brim. Some have a small point projecting from the top. The name itself is from the Italian, meaning "pear." These helmets are usually decorated about the base of the skull and just above the brim with brass rosettes. Specimens may vary slightly in pattern and in decoration.* 300.00   350.00

☐ **Cabassets,** *17th century. Same as above but of later date.* 225.00   300.00

☐ **Complete Suit of Japanese armor,** *c. early 1800's. Conventional style helmet or kabuto with wide flaring neck protector of curved lames. The lacquered breast and backplates are covered with small metal scales laced together with colored silk binding. Large lacqured menpo or face mask covering three-fourths of the face, shoulder defenses of metal lames laced together with colored silk, tassets of similar construction, arm and leg defenses of metal plates and chain mail.* 3200.00   3800.00

☐ **Complete Suit of Japanese armor,** *c. mid-1800's. Deep skull or hashi made up of formed steel sections firmly riveted together, raised gilted rib marks sections, small brim in front, circular opening in top of skull surrounded by a stylized chrysanthemum design. Neck guard made of four curved strips of lacquered metal attached to the rim of the skull with colored silk cords, lacquered half face mask with gorget attached, solid breast and backplates with laced scale covering, no shoulder defenses. Chain mail and metal plate arm defenses attached to richly brocaded cloth, thigh and upper leg defenses of metal scales laced together, lower leg defenses of metal strips joined by chain mail.* 3200.00   3800.00

Complete suite of Japanese armor, c. mid-1800's.

Cromwellian armor, c. 17 century.

Price Range

☐ **Cromwellian armor,** *17th century. This interesting suit of what may be defined as half armor has an interesting helmet with lobster tail neck guard and an adjustable nasal bar. The breastplate and backplate have a large gorget and shoulder and upper arm defenses attached. Tassets are attached to the breastplate. This is a type of armor not to be confused with the usual suits of pikeman's armor.* 2000.00   2500.00

☐ **English Close Helmet,** *c. 1500's. An extra fine specimen with one-piece skull with well-defined roped crest. The visor has long vision slits with roped decorative treatment on the lower part. Right front side of visor pierced with five breathing holes in form of a cross. Attached gorget is in two pieces decorated with rivets and roped edge.* 2250.00   2600.00

☐ **English Pikeman's armor,** *c. early 1600's. Consists of breast and backplates, with two tassets, decorative hinges attach tassets to front or breastplate, two-piece "pot" helmet with plume holder.* 1000.00   1200.00

☐ **English Pikeman's armor,** *c. 1600. Consists of the usual pot-type helmet, together with breast and backplates and tassets attached to the breastplate with ornamental hinges. In addition, this suit has a gorget or protective neck armor, the front fastenings of the scaled shoulder straps are very ornamental, and the bottom of the tassets are decorated with a diamond and heart design.* 1100.00   1300.00

English pikeman's armor, c. 1600's.

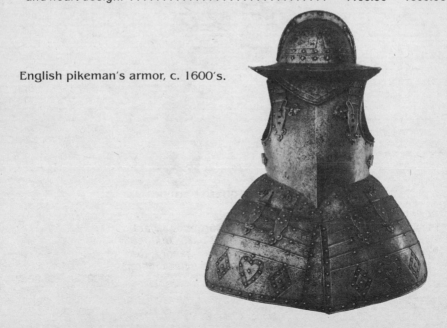

Note: Pikeman's armor of the 1600's is relatively plentiful insofar as authentic armor is concerned. Although that for officers is not as plentiful, that of the common pikeman was made in some quantity and is well preserved. It may be noted that this type of armor was worn by the early American colonists. All of the armor is very similar in pattern, differing largely in decoration. On the current market these are available without much searching, all within the $1000.00 range.

Price Range

☐ **English Lobster Tail Helmet,** c. 1600's. Moveable
visor and triple bars in front protecting the face. 350.00 400.00
☐ **As above,** but with sliding nasal. 350.00 400.00

German three quarter armor
with burgonet.

☐ **German Three-quarter armor with Burgonet.** Black
and white breastplate, all original, all parts marked
with the City of Vienna Arsenal mark, except the
breast and backplates which bear the Nuremberg
city mark, dated 1546. . . . . 8400.00 9500.00

Price Range

☐ **Indian Helmet,** *c. 1600's. Of the so-called "Devil Head" pattern. Well-rounded steel skull topped with a long spike, large metal horn projects from the top front, moveable nasal bar, one plume socket on each side of skull below the horns, front of skull embossed with stylized devil face. Helmet is highly decorated with scrolls, arabesques and Arabic writing. Chain mail camail is incomplete.* 300.00 350.00

Indo-Persian helmet, c. 1600's.

☐ **Indo-Persian Helmet,** *c. 1600's. Extremely fine example of this type of helmet (Kula-Khud). Semi-conical steel skull is topped by an ornate plume holder. Plume holders, attached by screws on each side of the front area, sliding nasal with flat ornament at top and bottom, skull is segmented by embossed lines radiating from the top, each segment and lower rim decorated with inlay designs, chain mail camail is complete.* 400.00 450.00

☐ **Italian Close Helmet,** *c. 1600's. One-piece skull, undecorated pointed brim, riveted removeable visor with eye slits and with four pierced breathing holes on the lower front.* 600.00 650.00

☐ **Italian Close Helmet,** *c. early 1600's. One-piece skull with medium wide brim at bottom rear, visor attached to each side of skull with decorative rivets. Visor is of the barred pattern.* 850.00 950.00

Price Range

☐ **Japanese armor,** c. mid-1800's. Complete suit, lacquered, all lancing intact, conventional type helmet or kubuto with neck guard or shikoro of five lames with top lame turned back to form a wing like piece on each side called the fuki-gayeshi, each bears the owner's mon, half face mask or mempo with four lame throat protector attached, breastplate and backplate are lacquered iron segments laced together with silk tape, six laced tassets attached, chain mail arm and leg protectors. This is a better than average suit but is unmounted. 1500.00   1750.00

☐ **Japanese armor,** c. mid-1800's. Complete suit, mounted, most interesting and rather unusual helmet or kabuto in the form of a snail shell. Neck protector or kozane is composed of four lames, crest or mayedate in the form small stylized antlers, full face iron face protector or mempo, chest armor and back armor have all appendages, chain mail sleeve and leg protectors. In excellent condition. 1400.00   1500.00

☐ **Persian Chain Mail Coat,** c. 1500's. High collar. The bottom third of the coat has opening which permits it to be wrapped about each leg and secured with leather thongs, some missing links. 700.00   775.00

☐ **Persian "Devil Head" Pattern Helmet.** Similar to Indian helmet in general pattern, long spike decoration on top of skull of flat blade-like design, very large curved horns project from the sides of the skull, flat sliding nasal bar with high ornamented ends, skull decorated in detail with geometric patterns, chain mail camail is not complete. 375.00   425.00

☐ **Persian Helmet,** c. 1600's. Steel skull of slightly conical pattern etched with floral designs, plume holder on top of skull and on each side at front, sliding nasal bar with flat decorative arrowhead design at bottom, several links missing from the camail. 400.00   450.00

☐ **Persian Helmet,** c. 1600's. Well-rounded steel skull with small ball device topped by long spike on top of skull, plume holder at each side, center front, sliding nasal bar with flat decorative devices at each end, entire skull decorated in floral designs in gold inlay, chain mail camail is complete. 600.00   650.00

☐ **Small Full Suit of Plate Armor for a Boy,** c. mid-1600's. Such armor was made for the sons of nobles and was complete in every way. 11000.00   12500.00

☐ **Mid-Eastern Three-quarter Armor,** c. 1500's. Chain mail of two-piece pattern with shirt covering the upper part of the body and trousers of chain mail extending to cover the knees, metal scale additional protection at abdominal area, skull of helmet is of fluted design with hinged ear pieces and sliding nasal bar. 3000.00   3500.00

Small full suit
of plate armor for a boy.

Price Range

☐ **Italian Three-quarter Suit of Horseman's Armor,** *c.
1600's. Black finish overall, interesting and unusual
close helmet of the Savoyard pattern. This pattern is
sometimes referred to as the "Death Head" type
because of its fancied resemblance to a human skull.
Breast and backplates with large gorget and complete defenses for the arms, completely articulated
metal scaled gauntlets, leg defenses of metal lames
extending to cover the knees.* 3900.00   4500.00
☐ **Polish Three-quarter Suit of Horseman's Armor,** *c.
1600's. Burgonet type helmet, breast and backplate
with shoulder and upper arms defenses attached,
overlapping lames in the thigh and upper leg
defenses which extended to protect the knees, some
replaced lames. This is an interesting functional
armor to be used in actual combat.* 3900.00   4500.00

Price Range

☐ **Turkish Horseman's Helmet,** c. 1600's. Tall semi-conial skull with top ornament in the form of a crescent, skull is without decoration, banded design about the lower edge of skull, large disk boss on each side of bottom of skull bearing an embossed five-point star, sliding nasal bar in the form of an arrow with the pointed head at the bottom and embossed feathers at the top end, chain mail camail is incomplete. 390.00   425.00

JAPANESE HELMETS OR KABUTO

The Japanese helmet or kabuto is in itself a most desirable collectible. The kabuto is usually easier to find than complete armor but many of them are by no means reasonable. Those made by famous armorers are very expensive indeed. The following helmets which have appeared for sale offer an interesting variety of the several different types.

☐ **Kabuto.** In the definitive classification of Japanese helmets this offering is identified as a kawagasa helmet. It is of the type worn by the lower class of armed retainers of a samurai. Consists of all leather construction heavily lacquered both on the inside and outside to produce a tough helmet. Heavily ribbed skull with large visor. The mon of the family to which the retainer belonged appears on the front in gold paint. Rather rare. Of some age but in excellent condition. 725.00   790.00

☐ **Kabuto.** Of kamurai or ceremonial hat pattern. Five curved shikoro or neck protectors. Short visor. Crest or maidate in the form of two stylized dolphins forming a "U." Curved wing piece or fuki-gayeshi on each side of helmet bears the owner's mon. Of considerable age. In excellent condition. 1150.00   1800.00

☐ **Kabuto.** Of momo-nari or peach shape pattern, unique one piece skull heavily embossed with floral designs. Short embossed visor. Skull has low ridge from front to back. Four lame curved shikoro with fuki-gayeshi on each side. Maidate is missing. 850.00   950.00

☐ **Kabuto.** This offering is patterned after a Portugese cabasset. It is of modified design having a flat steel brim a fourth of the way up the skull. The skull itself is decorated with stylized chrysanthemum shape studs. Shikoro of five curved lames. No maidate. This kabuto is of all Japanese manufacture. With the advent of the first Europeans in Japan the Japanese armorers at times would attach the typical tassets of lames to the European breastplate and modify the European helmet, usually a babasset or morian, by adding a neckguard or shikoro of laced lames. Sometimes a crest was added. Converted European armor was known as "southern barbarian armor" since the

Price Range

Europeans first were restricted to a few settlements in the south of Japan. This unusual offering is rare and is a good collectible. 950.00   1050.00

JINGASA

The jingasa is an interesting and most often a beautiful helmet which is not often offered for sale. It is characterized by a shallow basin like skull tapering off into a wide brim. Size and shape vary greatly. This helmet was worn by the higher order of armed retainers. Those used for combat were most often of steel while those used for parade purposes were usually of wood. Some are plain but the majority are lacquered in various colors and elaborately decorated with various designs. The inside of the skull is padded and a padded loop hangs down on each side. A folded cloth is passed under the chin and through these loops to hold the jingasa firmly on the head. The jingasa makes an excellent wall decorator.

☐ **Jingasa.** *Iron made of eight plates riveted together to form an octagonal brim, deeper than usual skull giving the helmet somewhat the appearance of a fully open morning glory, opening or hachimanza at the top, lacquered red. Old.* 675.00   750.00

☐ **Jingasa.** *One piece iron with extremely shallow skull with wide circular brim, embossed all over with demon and sea monsters, lacquered brown. Old.* 675.00   750.00

☐ **Jingasa.** *Shallow wood skull tapering off into narrow brim, high quality black lacquer finish with a gold mon on three sides with flecked gold design all over, ceremonial. Excellent.* 680.00   645.00

☐ **Jingasa.** *Unusual pattern with low cylindrical flat top skull tapering off into a sloping brim, all of iron. Front of brim heavily embossed with a dragon, skull is also heavily embossed. On the outside rear of the brim is a kasajircuhi-no-kuwan or ornamental ring to which is attached a kasajiruchi or elaborate stylized knot of silk cord with two hanging tassels. This was a combat helmet probably belonging to a highly placed retainer. Not usually seen.* 700.00   790.00

☐ **Jingasa,** *c. mid-1800's. Parade type with large shallow skull with narrow brim, lacquered black with large gold dragon encircling the base of the skull, wood construction.* 550.00   600.00

☐ **Jingasa,** *c. mid-1800's. Parade type of wood lacquered black, large shallow skull ornamented with gold lacquered Ho Birds, narrow brim, has hachimanza at top of skull. Very good condition.* 550.00   600.00

☐ **Jingasa,** *c. mid-1800's. Parade type of wood lacquered black, deeper skull with narrow brim, two dragons in gold lacquer encircle the bowl, in front is a Tokagawa mon in gold lacquer. In excellent condition and interesting.* 550.00   600.00

REPRODUCTION ARMOR   Price Range

☐ **English Made Reproduction,** c. 1500's. Full suit of
armor, made in Victorian England, well-proportioned,
with reproduction two-handed sword. 1600.00   1800.00

☐ **Modern Made Italian Three-quarter Suit.** Horseman's
armor, fully articulated and well-proportioned,
closely approximates the original in appearance,
barred visor to helmet. 1500.00   1700.00

☐ **Newly Made Copy of an English Close Helmet,** c.
1500's. An especially well made helmet closely
approximating the original in appearance, roped
edges to crest and gorget. 450.00   500.00

☐ **Spanish Made Reproduction Armor,** 15th century.
Well-proportioned with close helmet and reproduc-
tion two-handed sword, modern made. 1800.00   2100.00

AUTHENTIC CUIRASSIER ARMOR AND
OTHER BREAST AND BACKPLATES

These artifacts present what amounts to a separate field of armor collecting. Since, in general, they are less costly they attract a wider group of collectors. Complete breastplate and backplate, plus the associated helmet
makes a most interesting collector's item. Separate breastplates and
backplates are especially attractive as decorators.

☐ **European Armor Backplate,** c. 1500's. From an exceptionally fine suit. The metal is blackened and is
decorated overall with gold inlaid designs, edges of
the backplate are roped. 2500.00   2800.00

☐ **German Armor Breastplate,** c. 1500's. Of the peascot
form, so-called because the lower part projects outward and downward in the pattern of the peascot or
civilian doublet of the day, well defined median ridge,
top and bottom of the breastplate are heavily roped. .   1500.00   1700.00

☐ **Bavarian Complete Cuirassier Armor,** c. mid-1800's.
Burnished breast and backplates connected at shoulders by metal scale covered leather straps, sides and
bottom of breastplate decorated with large brass
rivets, steel helmet with deep front visor and long
rear neck piece with brass edging, high classical
Roman pattern crest with black hair on top, front of
helmet bears a device within which is the cypher "L"
for the soverign Ludwig. 1550.00   1675.00

☐ **French Cuirassier Breastplate and Backplate,** c. late
1800's. Polished steel, leather straps at shoulders
covered with brass chains. 450.00   600.00

☐ **As above,** but c. early 1800's. Frontplate decorated
with brass studs. 650.00   700.00

☐ **French Cuirass Front Plate,** c. mid-1800's. Apparently
from a guard unit. Made of polished steel with bright
brass trim about edges, studded with large brass
rivets. In very good condition. Attractive decorator. . .   250.00   300.00

French Cuirass Front Plate.

Price Range

☐ **French Cuirassier Backplate,** *c. 1830.Complete with chain covered straps.* **100.00   125.00**

MINIATURE ARMOR

Extremely well detailed
miniature armor
for horse and man.

Price Range

☐ **Armor for Horse and Man.** *Extremely well-detailed, fully articulated, figure holds jousting lance in right hand, jousting armor with barred helmet and complete beautifully decorated armor for horse. Rider is fitted with proper type spurs.* 500.00   550.00

Well detailed miniature suite of typical plate armor, fully articulated.

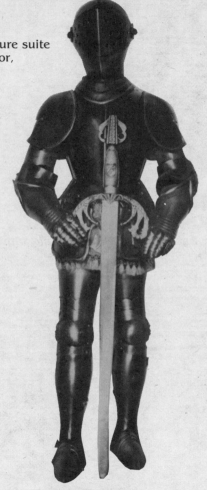

☐ **Modern Made Suit of Typical Plate Armor.** *Well-detailed, fully articulated, well-proportioned.* 225.00   250.00

AUTOMATIC PISTOLS

The term "automatic" as applied to pistols is really a misnomer. An automatic pistol is one which continues firing until the magazine is empty, once the trigger has been activated. Only a few of these have been manufactured and even fewer actually used. They are far too difficult to control once the firing has started. What we are talking about here is the **self-loading** pistol which reloads itself after each round is discharged and is ready for the new round to be fired. However, inasmuch as the term "automatic" has over the years been used to denote the self-loading pistol, it is used here.

COLT

Of American automatic military pistols, the Colt .45 caliber model 1911 and the improved model 1911A1 are the most popular with collectors. However, many pistol collectors rank it behind the Luger, Mauser and Walther insofar as military firearms are concerned. This weapon was designed by that versatile and prolific arms designer John Browning whose credits include a variety of automatic pistols, shotguns, automatic rifles and machine guns. His gun designs were manufactured by Colt, Remington, Winchester and by Fabrique National d'Armes de Guerre of Herstal, Liege, Belgium. They were selected by the U.S. Army after several trials which included Luger, Savage and others. More of these Colts were produced for the U.S. Army than any other hand gun. The demand for them was so great, that Colt was unable to supply enough and the automatics were made under license by several other manufacturers. These are noted in the price list. All prices are for weapons in **very good** condition. For specimens in excellent condition, the prices are twice as much or even more. The model 1911 was also made for civilian sales and is known as the Civilian Series. These are identical with the military model but along with other markings bear the legend "GOVERNMENT MODEL" on the left side of the slide. Military models are easily identified by government markings. Among other markings the words "UNITED STATES PROPERTY" on the frame and on the right slide appears the model number followed by "U.S. ARMY," "U.S. NAVY," and in very rare instances "U.S.M.C." Guns manufactured by other contractors under license are identified on the slide.

MILITARY COLT	Price Range	
☐ **Model 1911 Colt,** *.45 A.C.P. U.S. Army*	160.00	180.00
☐ **Model 1911 Colt,** *.45 A.C.P. U.S. Navy*	225.00	250.00
☐ **Model 1911 North American Arms Company,** *.45 A.C.P.*	1500.00	1700.00
☐ **Model 1911 Springfield Armory,** *.45 A.C.P.*	300.00	250.00
☐ **Model 1911 Remington-UMC,** *.45 A.C.P.*	200.00	225.00
☐ **Model 1911A1 Colt,** *.45 A.C.P.*	200.00	225.00
☐ **Model 1911A1 Singer Manufacturing Company,** *.45 A.C.P.*	450.00	500.00
☐ **Model 1911A1 Union Switch & Signal Company,** *.45 A.C.P.*	180.00	200.00
☐ **Model 1911A1 Remington Rand, Inc.,** *.45 A.C.P.*	180.00	200.00
☐ **Model 1911A1 Ithaca Gun Company, Inc.,** *.45 A.C.P.*	180.00	200.00

Note: Manufacture of the Model 1911A1 began in 1924 by Colt.

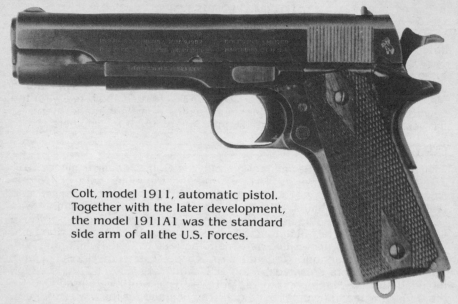

Colt, model 1911, automatic pistol.
Together with the later development,
the model 1911A1 was the standard
side arm of all the U.S. Forces.

THE LUGER

Of all military automatic pistols, the Luger is by far the most popular. It is extremely reliable and easy to handle. It has good weight and balance; it is easy to maintain and beautiful in appearance. If a weapon may be said to have glamour, the Luger most certainly has it. Over the years, legend and romance have been built up about this weapon. Few writers of mystery or spy stories would dare not to mention it.

The Luger itself is a development of an earlier automatic, the Brochardt. Hugo Brochardt, an outstanding American arms designer, after working for the American gun makers Sharps and Winchester, moved to Hungary where, for a time, he was director of the state arsenal at Budapest. He then moved on to the important German arms firm of Ludwig Loewe at Berlin. It was there that he developed the pistol bearing his name. It was the first successful toggle action pistol. It was a fairly large weapon, weighing in the neighborhood of two and a half pounds. It was an accurate weapon but was awkward in appearance and, from a strictly military point of view, was not practical.

The Brochardt was manufactured by Ludwig Loewe for about two years until that firm merged with another arms maker to form the famous Deutsche Waffen und Munitions Fabriken, more familiarly known as DWM.

In 1897 an attempt was made to sell the Brochardt to the U.S. Army. DWM sent over one of their assistant engineers, Georg Luger, to demonstrate the weapon. Typical military conservatism precluded the testing of the pistol. It is reported that a total of some 3000 Brochardt pistols were made, 1100 by Loewe and 1900 by DWM. Some 1100 were sold commercially in this country. Today the Brochardt is a prized collector's item.

Greatly concerned by the lack of acceptance of the Brochardt by military authorities, DWM assigned Luger, upon his return from the United States, to redesign the weapon. An outstanding gun designer in his own right, Luger, taking advantage of the suggestions as well as the criticisms of military people, set about to design the pistol which was to make his name a legend.

The new pistol was offered to the German Government but was refused. However, it was accepted by the Swiss Government, after trials in 1898 which clearly demonstrated its superiority over a number of other automatics. This resulted in an order for 3000 for the Swiss military and 2000 for the Swiss civilian market. This weapon was in 7.65-mm caliber. The military version is identified by a Swiss cross superimposed upon a heraldic sunburst on top of the receiver.

A small number of Lugers was purchased by the Bulgarian Government in 1900. These bear the Bulgarian Coat of Arms on the receiver. They are extremely rare collector's items today. Only a mere "handful" are known to exist.

For American collectors, one of the most interesting Lugers is the 1900 Army Test Model. By the beginning of the early 1900's, military people all over the world were finally accepting the possibility that the automatic pistol had come to stay. At this time the U.S. Army decided to find such a weapon. As a result of preliminary trials of two Lugers, the Army purchased 1000 Model 1900 Lugers, together with extra magazines, tools and 200,000 rounds of ammunition, all for the purpose of testing the weapon under actual field conditions. In the meantime, the Rock Island Arsenal was ordered to manufacture 1000 special holsters for the Lugers. The pistols and holsters were sent to various Army installations and organizations for shakedown trials. These trials lasted for approximately two years. Less than a hundred of these trial Lugers are known to exist today and only a very few holsters are to be found. It is little wonder that they are rare items.

These trial Lugers have the Great Seal of the United States over the chamber. The cypher "DWM" (Deutsche Waffen und Munitions) appears on top of the toggle. These trial Lugers have a serial number range of 6099 to 7099 only. Commercial Lugers made for sale in this country may also have the Great Seal of the United States on the chamber but they are **not** within this range of numbers.

One of the most consistent criticisms of these Lugers during the field trials was that they were of insufficient caliber; and that they lacked stopping power. Heavy caliber pistols were and still are favored by our military people. Luger now redesigned his automatic to fire a 9-mm cartridge. A total of 50 of these was made for the U.S. Army Trials to select a heavier caliber pistol. These incorporated a so-called "cartridge counter" developed by G. H. Powell, a device which indicated the number of rounds remaining in the magazine. This consists of a long narrow slot cut in the left front of the butt, with a numbered metal strip along the back of the slot. On the metal strip there appear the numbers "1" through "7," the number "1" being at the very top. As each round is fed into the chamber, an indicator moves up one number. This is a fancy but unnecessary arrangement. Once again the Luger was rejected. Of the 50 which DWM furnished to the Army, only 11 or 12 are known to exist today. They also have the Great Seal of the United States on top of the chamber and the DWM cypher on the toggle. The serial number range is from 22401 to 22450. They are readily identified by the cartridge counter.

By far the most valuable of all Lugers is the model 1907 .45 caliber pistol made for the last of the Army trials to select an automatic pistol. This is a big weapon. It weighs two and a half pounds and has a five-inch barrel. These pistols were furnished as a result of the Army's decision to use a .45 caliber weapon. As a result of extremely grueling tests, the Colt and Savage .45's were selected for further competition, with the Luger as a third choice. Both Colt and Savage were requested to submit 200 additional .45's for a final shakedown test, these to be delivered within 10 months. Colt accepted but Savage did not. Thereupon DWM was asked to supply 200 pistols for competition against the Colt. DWM rejected the order. It seems probable that the success of the Luger in Europe and elsewhere and the "off again, on again" maneuvers of the U.S. Army may have influenced the decision. In any event the Colt .45 caliber was accepted, going into production as the model 1911. Some arms experts are of the opinion that the Luger would have won out in the final trials.

Apparently there is no way of determining exactly how many .45 caliber Lugers were brought to this country for the final trials. It appears that there were at least five. Serial numbers "2" and "5" are known to exist. Number 2 is in the possession of a private collector and is valued at $200,000.00! Number 1 is supposed to have been fired to destruction during trials. There is some doubt about this and it may turn up one day. From time to time, one hears that numbers 3 and 4 have been located. If so, they haven't been seen.

All military Mausers are in 9-mm caliber. The Imperial German Army versions are especially popular with collectors, including the Army model with four-inch barrel. In 1914 a Luger with an eight-inch barrel and adjustable rear sight was produced. This weapon was provided with a detachable shoulder stock which could be rapidly and easily attached to the weapon to convert it into a carbine. This so-called Artillery model was developed for cavalry and artillery units, these not usually being provided with the Mauser 98 rifle or carbine. This model was also popular with the Imperial German Navy, it being deemed more practical for boat crews and shore landing parties than a rifle or a carbine. These World War I Lugers were manufactured by both DWM and the Royal Arsenal at Erfurt.

In addition to the Lugers furnished to Bulgaria, Germany, Switzerland and the United States, these weapons were supplied to a number of other countries including France, Russia, Portugal and a small number to England. The majority of these were marked on the top of the receiver with the arms or other distinguishing mark of the particular country. Over a period of years, in addition to DWM and the Royal Arsenal, Lugers were made in Germany by the arsenal at Spandau, Simson & Co., Suhl; Mauser, Oberndorf A/Neckar and Krieghoff, Suhl. They were also made in England by the famous munitions makers Vickers, Ltd. (for the Netherlands Government) and in Switzerland by Waffenfabrik, Bern. Commercial Lugers were very popular in this country. Many were marketed by such top flight firms as Abercrombie & Fitch and A. F. Stoeger.

The Army of Germany's Weimar Republic used the Luger as its official sidearm. These were manufactured by Simson & Company from parts left over from World War I. Later Mauser and Krieghoff began manufacturing the pistols, using surplus parts. Mauser continued the Luger production until 1942.

Mr. Michael Reese II, one of the world's foremost Luger experts, estimates that at least 8,000,000 Lugers were produced and that there are in excess of 300 variations. Obviously it is not possible to catalog all of these here.

As might be expected, anything connected with Luger pistols is highly collectible, including conversion units, magazines, loaders, stocks, tools, and holsters. For a detailed study of Lugers, it is recommended that use be made of the recommended reading list given elsewhere in this book.

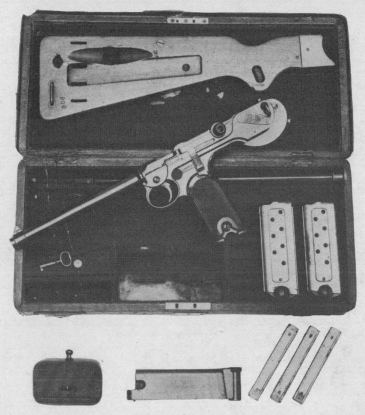

Brochardt, model 1893, automatic pistol complete with leather covered wood case with red velvet lining. The case contains tools and accessories. A complete cased Brochardt pistol is a much sought after collector's item.

Left side view of the Brochardt automatic pistol. This is the forerunner of the famous Lugers.

Price Range

☐ **Borchardt, 1893 pistol,** *7.63-mm. Complete with leather covered wood case with red felt lining. Compartment contains shoulder stock, spare magazine, dummy wood magazine, oil bottle, demountable three-piece ramrod, cleaning rod, three cartridge clips and key to case. This rare pistol is listed here because it is the forerunner of the Luger*............ 6000.00   6750.00

☐ **Model 1900 prototype,** *marked "GL," 7" barrel, special rear sight*.................................. 18200.00   22000.00

☐ **Model 1900 Commercial** 2000.00   2200.00

☐ **Model 1900 Swiss prototype,** *without "GL," two digit serial number.*................................ 2000.00   2200.00

☐ **Model 1900 Swiss.** 1100.00   1250.00

☐ **Model 1900 American Eagle Commercial.**.......... 1100.00   1250.00

Left side view of the
model 1900 Luger
used in the U.S. Army Trials.

Top view of the model 1900 Luger used in the U.S. Army Trials. The American Eagle and DWM markings may be clearly identified.

	Price Range	
☐ Model 1900 American Eagle, *Army Trials.*	2100.00	2300.00
☐ Model 1900 Carbine prototype.	11900.00	13200.00
☐ Model 1902 Carbine.	4150.00	4600.00
☐ Model 1902 Carbine, *marked to A. F. Stoeger.*	4050.00	5600.00
☐ Model 1902 prototype, *without "GL" marking.*	3200.00	3560.00
☐ Model 1902 Commercial.	3200.00	3560.00
☐ Model 1902 American Eagle crest commercial.	2800.00	3100.00

Left side view of the
model 1902 American Eagle crest
9-mm. cartridge counter Luger
made for the U.S. Army Trials.
This view clearly shows
cartridge counter in the grip.

☐ Model 1902 American Eagle crest, *9 mm, cartridge counter, Army Trials.*	6500.00	7200.00
☐ Model 1904 Naval Model, *(first accepted by the Imperial German Army.)*	5950.00	6600.00
☐ Model 1906 Commercial.	900.00	1000.00
☐ Model 1906 Swiss Military.	900.00	1000.00
☐ Model 1906 Swiss Police.	900.00	1000.00
☐ Model 1906 Swiss Commercial.	2350.00	2800.00
☐ Model 1906 American Eagle crest, *7.65-mm.*	900.00	1000.00
☐ Model 1906 American Eagle crest, *9-mm.*	1125.00	1500.00
☐ Model 1906 Commercial, *(safety marked)*	1130.00	1300.00
☐ Model 1906 French Contract Commercial.	3800.00	4200.00
☐ Model 1906 U.S. Army Test, *.45 A.C.P.*	190000.00	210000.00
☐ Model 1906 Dutch.	810.00	900.00
☐ Model 1906 Portuguese Army, *7.65-mm.*	475.00	550.00
☐ Model 1906 Portuguese Navy, *9-mm.*	5500.00	6100.00
☐ Model 1906 Brazilian, *7.65-mm.*	700.00	800.00
☐ Model 1906 Bulgarian Military, *7.65-mm.*	3675.00	4075.00
☐ Model 1906 Russian Contract.	1000.00	1100.00
☐ Model 1906 Vickers, *(British) made for Netherlands Government.*	8200.00	9100.00

	Price Range	
☐ **Model 1906 Naval,** *1st issue.*	1900.00	2100.00
☐ **Model 1906 Naval,** *2nd issue.*	1900.00	2100.00
☐ **Model 1908 Military.**	700.00	775.00
☐ **Model 1908 Commercial.**	650.00	725.00

Left side view of the
model 1908 Luger made by the Erfurt Arsenal.

Top view of the model 1908 Luger made at the Erfurt Arsenal. This view clearly
shows the erfurst marking.

☐ **Model 1908 Erfurt Arsenal.**	400.00	450.00
☐ **Model 1908 Naval/Commercial.**	2500.00	2750.00
☐ **Model 1913 Commercial,** *(with grip safety).*	750.00	850.00
☐ **Model 1914 Commercial.**	660.00	750.00
☐ **Model 1914 Naval.**	950.00	1050.00
☐ **Model 1914 Military,** *made by DWM.*	375.00	425.00
☐ **Model 1914 Military,** *made by Erfurt Arsenal.*	375.00	425.00

Top view of Luger 1914 artillery model made by DWM. Note the long barrel.

	Price Range	
☐ **Model 1914 Artillery,** *made by DWM.*	750.00	825.00
☐ **Model 1914 Artillery,** *made by Erfurt Arsenal.*	850.00	950.00
☐ **Model 1920, Police Marked,** *made by DWM.*	385.00	425.00
☐ **Model 1920 Commercial,** *made by DWM.*	425.00	475.00
☐ **Model 1920 Naval/Commercial.**	825.00	930.00
☐ **Model 1920 Artillery/Commercial.**	1200.00	1300.00
☐ **Model 1920 Naval Carbine.**	4650.00	5150.00
☐ **Model 1920 Carbine.**	3350.00	3750.00
☐ **Baby Model Luger.** *During the 1920's four scaled down Lugers were manufactured. Two were in 9-mm.(Browning Short) and the other two were in .32-mm. ACP. To date, only one of these Baby Lugers is known to exist. It has an overall length of 6-1/4." The barrel measures just 2-15/16." The magazine holds five rounds.*	18000.00	20000.00

Note: DWM (Deutsche Waffen und Munitions Fabriken) the original makers of Lugers was merged with BerlinKartsruhn Industrie Werk (BKIW), then this firm was taken over by Mauser in 1930. Originally intended as a devious means of circumventing arms controls imposed by the Treaty of Versailles, following World War I, a number of codes were developed by the government and by munitions makers to conceal both the makers of the weapons and the number of weapons being produced. This subterfuge lasted into and throughout the Third Reich. Mauser arms were identified by the symbols "S/42," "42" and "byf." Luger production was terminated in 1942-1943. It is of considerable interest to know that during 1945 the French Army seized the Mauser plant, finding an abundance of parts. These were assembled into weapons and were issued to the French Army.

The attractiveness of the Luger, or parabellum, as it is sometimes known, is still so great that after World War II the world famous firm of Interarms, of Alexandria, Virginia, arranged with Mauser for the production of the German Army P. 08 Model and the Swiss 1929 version. These were rapidly bought up and are now collector's items themselves, selling for in the neighborhood of $700.00 to $800.00. Mauser also produced 250 sets each of two matched weapons, each numbered. These were known as "Commemorative sets." 250 matched pairs or sets were made of the Russian Model, the Bulgarian Model and the Naval Model. These originally sold for $3600.00 for each matched set. They are now being offered for around $6000.00 a set on the collectors' market. At this time Mauser plans to issue commemorative sets of the 1914 Artillery Model.

☐ **"byf"/Code KU.**	750.00	850.00
☐ **"byf" code Mauser.**	525.00	575.00
☐ **Death's Head,** *(DWM).*	750.00	825.00

	Price Range	
☐ 42/Code KU............................	750.00	800.00
☐ 42 with code date......................	380.00	425.00
☐ Model 1906/24, *Waffenfabrik, Bern.*	900.00	1000.00
☐ Model 1922 Abercrombie & Fitch Commercial, *originally DWM made for Swiss*......................	2475.00	2775.00
☐ Model 1923 American Eagle, *marked A. F. Stoeger*....	3175.00	3575.00
☐ Model 1923 Commercial........................	550.00	625.00
☐ Model 1923 Dutch............................	925.00	1025.00
☐ Model 1923, *marked "safe" and "Loaded" in English.*	750.00	825.00
☐ Model 1929 Swiss.	875.00	975.00
☐ Model 1930, *(DWM), marked A. F. Stoeger, 9-mm.*	1850.00	2075.00
☐ Model 1930, *as above but in 7.65-mm.*	2750.00	3075.00
☐ Model 1930 Mauser, *(DWM) 8" Artillery, marked A. F. Stoeger.*	3700.00	4075.00
☐ Model 1934, *dated, (grip safety).*	1300.00	1450.00
☐ Model 1934 Mauser Banner Contract.	1475.00	1650.00
☐ Model 1934 Mauser Commercial.	1100.00	1225.00
☐ Model 1934 Mauser Commercial, *(grip safety).*	1300.00	1425.00
☐ Model 1934 Mauser, Dutch......................	1100.00	1235.00
☐ Model 1934 Swedish Commercial Mauser.	825.00	935.00
☐ Model 1934 Swiss Commercial Mauser, *(grip safety).*	1475.00	1635.00
☐ Model 1935 GNR Portuguese.	800.00	875.00
☐ Model 1942 Mauser Banner, *with 2 digit date.*	835.00	950.00
☐ Persian Mauser.	4550.00	5500.00
☐ S/42 with dated chamber.......................	375.00	435.00
☐ S/42 with G-date.............................	425.00	475.00
☐ S/42 with K-date.............................	950.00	1050.00
☐ Simson & Co. Military Model.	750.00	835.00
☐ Simson & Co. Model, *(grip safety).*	800.00	875.00
☐ Simson & Co. Model, *(Suhl)*.....................	750.00	825.00
☐ Simson "S" Code.............................	1100.00	1225.00

The following Lugers were made by H. Krieghoff Waffenfabrik, Suhl, Germany:

☐ Model 1923 DWM/Krieghoff, Commercial...........	650.00	725.00
☐ Krieghoff, Commercial, *with side frame inscription.*	3650.00	4050.00
☐ Krieghoff, early S Code........................	1100.00	1230.00
☐ Krieghoff, late S Code.........................	1175.00	1300.00
☐ Model 1936 Krieghoff, *dated*....................	1560.00	1750.00
☐ Post War 1945 Krieghoff.	1850.00	2050.00

A limited number of Lugers were manufactured with certain sections cut away so that the action of the weapon could be easily observed. These were used by salesmen in demonstrating the weapon to prospective buyers.

☐ Model 1906 DWM cutaway.	1850.00	2050.00
☐ Model 1914 DWM cutaway.	1850.00	2050.00
☐ Model 1914 Simson cutaway.	1850.00	2050.00
☐ Model 1930 Mauser cutaway.	1850.00	2050.00

Right side view of a cutway Luger
used by salesmen for demonstration purposes.

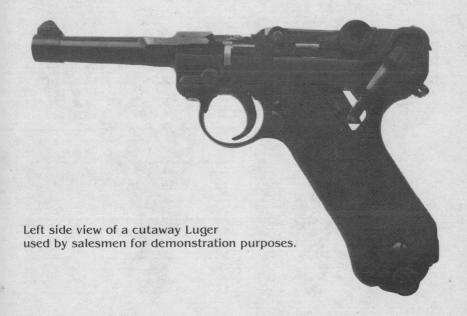

Left side view of a cutaway Luger
used by salesmen for demonstration purposes.

ACCESSORIES   Price Range

As might be expected, just about any item associated with the Luger is a collector's item in itself. The following prices are typical.

☐ **Artillery holster,** *complete with tools*.............	100.00	115.00
☐ **Artillery stock,** *proofed, with leather.*	200.00	225.00
☐ **Conversion unit,** *Swiss, .22 l.r. In wood box.*	350.00	375.00
☐ **Drum magazine,** *32 round, 9-mm. First issue.*	225.00	250.00
☐ **Drum magazine,** *32 round, 9-mm. Second issue.*	265.00	285.00
☐ **Leather carbine case.**...........................	650.00	750.00
☐ **Leather carrier for drum magazine.**................	475.00	525.00
☐ **Loader for 32 round drum magazine.**	340.00	375.00
☐ **Luger manuals,** *in either German or English.*........	150.00	175.00
☐ **Luger wall chart.**...............................	475.00	525.00
☐ **M-2 holster,** *with tool.*..........................	40.00	45.00
☐ **Naval holsters.**................................	150.00	175.00
☐ **Naval stock,** *proofed, with leather.*	250.00	275.00
☐ **Ordinary military model holsters.**..................	40.00	45.00
☐ **Prewar conversion unit,** *.22 l.r. Complete.*	300.00	325.00
☐ **Stock/holster,** *artillery, wood.*	575.00	650.00
☐ **Stock/holster,** *telescoping.*	335.00	375.00
☐ **Swiss holster for 06 Luger.**.......................	65.00	80.00
☐ **Swiss holster for 24 Luger.**.......................	40.00	45.00
☐ **U.S. Test holster.**...............................	875.00	975.00

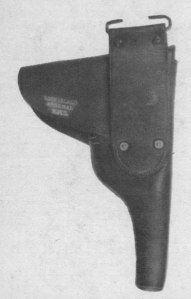
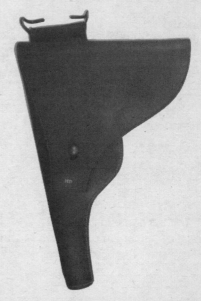

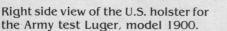

Right side view of the U.S. holster for the Army test Luger, model 1900.

Left side view of the U.S. holsters for the Army test Luger, model 1900.

THE MAUSER

The name of Mauser has a unique importance in the weapons field. The brothers Paul and Peter Mauser founded what was to become one of the most famous weapons plants in the world. The father of the brothers was what was known as a Master Gunsmith at the Government Firearms Factory, at Oberndorf, in the Kingdom of Wurttemberg, Germany. During their early teens, the brothers had been apprenticed as gunsmiths at the arms factory. When the plant was closed down due to lack of business, the brothers took their severance pay and used it to develop their own weapons designs.

The story of Mauser success began with their development of their famous breech-loading rifle which is discussed in some detail later in this book. It is sufficient to say here that their rifle was so successful that it was adopted by the Prussian Government, followed soon thereafter by a multitude of other nations. The brothers established a small arms manufacturing plant at Oberndorf. In the meantime the Government of Wurttemberg became interested in assuring a supply of arms in the event of an emergency and sold the Government Firearms Factory to the Mausers, arranging easy financial terms. There Mauser Brothers & Company was founded in 1874. A few years later, William Mauser died and the concern was then organized as Waffenfabrick Mauser. In 1887 Paul Mauser sold his controlling interest in the firm to Ludwig Loewe & Company. This firm has been mentioned before in connection with the development of the Luger pistol. Later the Mauser firm came under the control of Deutsche Waffen und Munitions Fabriken (DWM) but the Mauser name was retained.

Perhaps the most desirable Mauser pistol as far as collectors are concerned is the model 1896 and its variations. This is the so-called "broomhandle" Mauser because its grip resembles that homely household item. This weapon is something of a paradox. It is ugly looking, lacks the balance and refinement of the Luger, is complicated in design and is expensive to manufacture. On the other hand, it is accurate and efficient. It is so well designed that only a few and minor changes were made in it during the nearly 50 years during which it was manufactured. All parts are interlocking and there are no screws except for those holding the sides of the grip.

An interesting fact about this pistol is that although it was never officially adopted by any major power, it was extremely popular with military people. More than a million of these pistols were made and great numbers of copies were made in Spain and China. Thousands were used during World War I by the Imperial German and Austrian armies.

The model 1896 was manufactured over the years in a number of variations. First made in the then popular 7.63-mm., the demands of the German military for a heavier caliber resulted in it being manufactured in a 9-mm. version. These 9-mm.'s are readily identifiable by the large figure "9" burned into the grip on each side of the handle, filled with red paint. All broomhandle Mausers have the magazine in front of the trigger guard. This, with the broomhandle grip, gives the weapon an odd look.

Although Mauser produced several other pistols, the most popular from the collector's point of view, other than the broomhandle, are the several versions of the model 1910 7.65-mm. pocket pistol of conventional appearance, used by some German officers in World War I, and the model H Sc, 32 caliber, a straight blow-back double action pistol used as a substitute weapon by Nazi police and army officers.

BROOMHANDLE MAUSERS   Price Range

☐ **Chinese manufacture,** *(handmade).* 575.00   650.00
☐ **Chinese manufacture,** *(Shanshei Arsenal) .45 A.C.P.* .   1850.00   2050.00
☐ **Italian Navy contract.** 1035.00   1150.00
☐ **Model 1930,** *7.63-mm.* 560.00   625.00
☐ **Model 1930,** *8.15-mm.* 750.00   825.00
☐ **Ordinary model,** *with conehammer.* 790.00   875.00
☐ **Persian contract.** 3650.00   4050.00
☐ **Post World War I "Bolo."** *(Used extensively by the*
  Bolsheviks). 650.00   735.00
☐ **Spanish manufacture,** *by Astra, Azul, Royal and*
  other factories. 560.00   625.00
☐ **Standard Pre-World War I Commercial model.** 560.00   625.00
☐ **Turkish contract,** *with conehammer.* 3650.00   4050.00
☐ **World War I Commercial.** 575.00   625.00
☐ **World War I Military,** *.30-mm.* 565.00   625.00

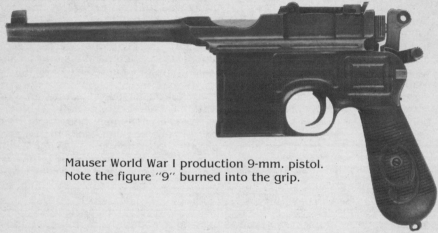

Mauser World War I production 9-mm. pistol.
Note the figure "9" burned into the grip.

☐ **World War I Military,** *9-mm.* 650.00   725.00

OTHER MAUSERS

☐ **Model 1910.** 250.00   275.00
☐ **Model H Sc.** 300.00   350.00

ACCESSORIES

☐ **Leather holster,** *standard type.* 75.00   90.00
☐ **Leather holster,** *for Bolo model.* 110.00   135.00
☐ **Leather holster,** *for Chinese .45 A.C.P.* 250.00   280.00
☐ **Various manuals,** *each.* 55.00   65.00

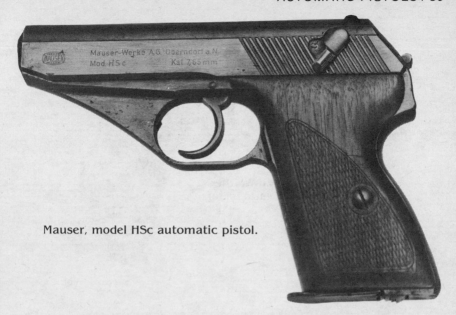

Mauser, model HSc automatic pistol.

WALTHER

Of the several models of Walther pistols, those of the Nazi era, particularly the justly famed P.38, are most sought after by militaria collectors.

Karl Walther, the founder of the arms firm bearing his name, began manufacturing automatic pistols in 1908. His first weapon was a small 6.35-mm. blow-back model aptly designated Model 1. In 1929 the Model PP (Polizei Pistole or Police Pistol) was introduced. It was made in several calibers, including 7.65-mm., 9-mm. and a very few in 5.6-mm. Originally designed for police use, it quickly became something of a favorite and it was used by some Nazi police and army officers during World War II. In 1931 the Model PPK (Polizei Pistole Krimminal or Criminal Police Pistol) was introduced. Manufactured in .22 long rifle caliber, 6.35-mm., 7.65-mm. and 9-mm. it soon became a favorite with police officers all over the world with the exception of police in the United States and Canada. In Nazi Germany it was one of the favorite weapons of the dreaded Gestapo. In 7.65-mm. it was also a substitute standard weapon for both the SS and the Wehrmacht combat forces.

The collectors' delight, the P.38, is an efficient, rugged, trouble free weapon of excellent balance which is a delight to look at as well as to shoot. The P.38 is a refinement of the Model HP (Heeres Pistole or Army Pistol) introduced in the late 1930's and made available on the commercial market. The standard caliber was 9-mm but a few were made in .30 and .45 caliber for the American commercial market. The HP was offered to the German Government in 1937 and a quantity was delivered. With a few minor modifications, the pistol was officially adopted in 1938 as the standard service pistol, being designated the P.38.

The HP's are extremely well made and are beautifully finished as are the

Rare Nazi marked Walther,
model PP automatic pistol.

A rare Nazi marked Walther, model PPK.

early P.38's. Inasmuch as the war demanded rapid production of weapons, the P.38's of these war years are not as well finished but the workmanship is still excellent. Because of their Nazi association the wartime P.38's are much sought after, particularly the few engraved presentation pieces made for Nazi leaders of higher rank.

With the defeat of Nazi Germany, the Walther plant was seized by the Russians inasmuch as it was located in the newly created East Germany. Fortunately, Walther went to West Germany where he reestablished his business with a new and modern plant. A variety of Walther weapons is now being produced, including target rifles, target pistols, air rifles and pistols. Most popular, however, are the updated versions of the PP, PPK and the P.38. These are available in this country through Interarms of Alexandria, Virginia (22313). Interarms is also making the PPK in its own plant in Virginia as the PPK/S.

For the vast army of collectors unable to afford the price of the genuine weapons, Unique Imports of Alexandria, Virginia (22313) has available a series of replicas which may be disassembled and have the same appearance, weight and feel of the originals. However, they cannot under any circumstances be made to fire live ammunition. The prices of these are listed, together with the prices of the modern Walthers.

MODEL HP

	Price Range	
☐ **Early manufacture,** *with rectangular firing pin*	550.00	625.00
☐ **Later manufacture,** *with round firing pin*	550.00	625.00
☐ **Swedish Army.**	750.00	825.00
☐ **7.65-mm,** *with plastic grips*	2175.00	2450.00
☐ **7.65-mm,** *single action with wood grips.*	2915.00	3250.00
☐ **Late production,** *commercial finish, army markings.*	650.00	725.00

MODEL P.38

☐ **Early production.**	400.00	450.00
☐ **Walther made,** *zero series, first model.*	750.00	825.00
☐ **Walther made,** *zero series, second model.*	650.00	725.00
☐ **Walther made,** *zero series, third model.*	625.00	700.00
☐ **Walther made,** *bearing code 480.*	825.00	925.00
☐ **Walther made,** *bearing code "ac" but not dated.*	825.00	925.00
☐ **Walther made,** *bearing code "ac" with "40" added.*	650.00	725.00
☐ **Walther made,** *1940, marked "ac."*	550.00	625.00
☐ **Walther made,** *1941, marked "ac" on frame.*	475.00	525.00
☐ **Walther made,** *1941, no code mark on frame.*	295.00	325.00
☐ **Walther made,** *1941, military finish, marked "ac."*	295.00	325.00
☐ **Walther made,** *1942, marked "ac."*	295.00	325.00
☐ **Walther made,** *1943, marked "ac" double line slide markings.*	225.00	250.00
☐ **Walther made,** *1943, marked "ac" single line slide markings.*	225.00	250.00
☐ **Walther made,** *1943, marked "ac," with police acceptance marks.*	600.00	675.00
☐ **Walther made,** *1944, marked "ac."*	200.00	225.00
☐ **Walther made,** *1944, marked "ac," with police acceptance marks.*	575.00	625.00
☐ **Walther made,** *1945, marked "ac" with all factory matching numbers.*	200.00	225.00
☐ **Walther made,** *1945, marked "ac" with factory mismatched numbers.*	200.00	225.00
☐ **Mauser made,** *1942, marked "byf."*	475.00	550.00
☐ **Mauser made,** *1943, marked "byf."*	200.00	225.00
☐ **Mauser made,** *1943, marked "byf" police acceptance marks.*	575.00	650.00

	Price Range	
☐ **Mauser made**, *1944, marked "byf" with "military blue" finish.*	250.00	275.00
☐ **Mauser made**, *1944, marked "byf" with dual tone finish.*	250.00	275.00
☐ **Mauser made**, *1944, marked "byf" with light blue police finish.*	575.00	640.00
☐ **Mauser made**, *1945, marked "SVW."*	295.00	325.00
☐ **Mauser made**, *1945, marked "SVW" with police markings.*	825.00	925.00
☐ **Mauser made**, *1945, marked "SVW" French production after end of war.*	385.00	425.00
☐ **Mauser made**, *1946, marked "SVW" all marking variations.*	575.00	650.00
☐ **Speerwerke made**, *1943-44, marked "cyq."*	225.00	250.00
☐ **Speerwerke made**, *1945, letter "a" prefix to serial number, "cyq."*	300.00	340.00
☐ **Speerwerke made**, *"zero series" marked "cyq."*	2725.00	3025.00

MODERN MADE WALTHERS

☐ **Model PP**, *.22 A.C.P. Long rifle.*	400.00	475.00
☐ **Model PP**, *.32 A.C.P. ACP.*	375.00	450.00
☐ **PPK/S**, *American made, .22 l.r. Long rifle.*	475.00	525.00
☐ **PPK/S**, *American made, .32 A.C.P.*	425.00	525.00
☐ **P-38**, *.22 l.r. Long rifle.*	650.00	725.00
☐ **P-38**, *9-mm. Luger.*	575.00	625.00

REPRODUCTIONS

The following nonshooting reproductions are advertised and sold as reproductions by Unique Imports of Alexandria, Virginia. They are of the same size, weight and appearance as the originals. They may be taken apart and reassembled. All parts work and move. **Dummy** cartridges are available. Under no circumstances can they be made to fire live ammunition. These reproduction weapons are steadily advancing in price and are themselves becoming collectors' items.

☐ **Colt U.S. Government**, *.45 cal.*	45.00	50.00
☐ **Dummy ammunition**, *Luger, Mauser or Walther.*	7.00	8.00
☐ **Dummy ammunition**, *for Colt .45 cal.*	8.95	10.00
☐ **Luger**, *long barrel artillery model.*	75.00	80.00
☐ **Luger**, *naval model.*	70.00	80.00
☐ **Luger**, *parabellum model, (P-08) standard infantry model.*	55.00	60.00
☐ **Mauser HSc.**	45.00	50.00
☐ **Mauser**, *model 1896, broomhandle, 7.63-mm.*	85.00	90.00
☐ **Mauser**, *model 1896, broomhandle, 9-mm. Marked grips.*	85.00	90.00
☐ **Walther PPK.**	40.00	50.00
☐ **Walther P.38.**	50.00	60.00

Replica Walther PPK automatic pistol. One of a series of non firing models similar in appearance, weight and action to the original weapons. All models have moving parts and may be disassembled.

AVIATION COLLECTIBLES

Aviation artifacts, although not in any great abundance on the market at the present time, are interesting a growing group of specialized collectors. More and more aviation items are being unearthed from long forgotten places and are being made available as interest increases. The following is a sample of recent offerings.

PROPELLORS

All complete and intact. Prices are basic for offerings with age cracked varnish finish. Examples in excellent condition with all markings, including manufacturers trade mark, will be priced at least $100.00 more.

	Price Range	
☐ **British,** *wood two blade, World War I*	400.00	450.00
☐ **British,** *as above, but four blade.*	600.00	675.00
☐ **German,** *wood two blade, World War I*	600.00	675.00
☐ **French,** *wood, two blade, World War I.*	400.00	450.00
☐ **U.S.,** *wood, two blade, World War I*	200.00	250.00
☐ **U.S.,** *as above, but four blade, World War I.*	335.00	375.00
☐ **U.S.,** *wood, two blade, 1920's to 1930's*	175.00	200.00
☐ **U.S.,** *metal, two blade, non adjustable, 1930's.*	175.00	200.00

FABRIC

All specimens should be documented.

	Price	Range
☐ **British,** *wing or fuselage, no markings.*	50.00	65.00
☐ **British,** *fuselage, with red, white and blue insignia. . .*	200.00	250.00
☐ **German,** *portion of fuselage showing all of black Maltese cross with white border, World War I........*	300.00	325.00
☐ **German,** *fuselage, with black straight sided cross with white border, World War I. ....*	275.00	300.00

Portion of fabric wing covering of a Nazi Heinkel He 51 fighter bomber in the service of the Spanish Nationalist Army during the Spanish Civil War.

☐ **German,** *wing covering portion from a Heinkel He 51 fighter/close support aircraft in the service of the Spanish Nationalist Army during the Spanish civil war, yellow and red circles on grey fabric ....*	75.00	95.00
☐ **Japan,** *portion of fuselage showing "meat ball" insignia, World War II. ....*	150.00	175.00
☐ **United States,** *portion of fuselage showing star in circle insignia, World War I. ....*	240.00	275.00

INSTRUMENTS

☐ **British compass,** *World War I. ....*	100.00	125.00
☐ **British tachometer,** *World War I. ....*	100.00	125.00
☐ **German compass,** *World War I. ....*	125.00	150.00
☐ **German tachometer,** *World War I. ....*	125.00	150.00
☐ **Identification plate** *from the engine of a Royal Air Force aircraft. Marked "ROLLS ROYCE LTD," with the address of Derby and London. Bears the legend "MERLIN AERO ENGINE." Contains information relative to the engine model and number, as well as the notation that it is for the right hand tractor engine. A unique RAF collectible. ....*	18.00	25.00
☐ **Japanese Bomber Compass.** *Black metal housing. Fluid mounted compass on spring loaded base permitting adjustment. Japanese manufacturers plates, fully functional. An interesting Japanese aviation item ....*	50.00	75.00

Identification plate from the engine of a Royal Air Force aircraft.

Japanese bomber compass.

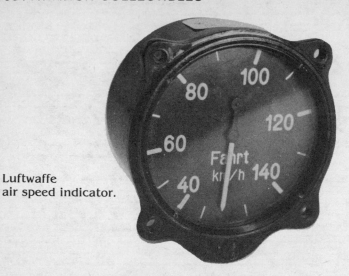

Luftwaffe
air speed indicator.

	Price Range	

☐ **Japanese Turn and Bank Indicator.** *Documented that it was taken from the cockpit of a Zero fighter plane. Japanese characters on dial. Has oil bubble indicator and maker's name plate. Fully operable.* 40.00   50.00

☐ **Luftwaffe Air Speed Indicator.** *Black blakelite body. Black dial with white fluorescent numerals recording speed range from 40 to 140 kph. In excellent condition. Removed from a Fulke-Wulf advanced trainer/ fighter* 50.00   75.00

☐ **Luftwaffe Clock.** *From the cockpit of a Nazi fighter plane. Is operating and in excellent condition. Fine memento.* 150.00   165.00

☐ **Luftwaffe Celestial Navagation Compass.** *In very well made Luftwaffe gray/blue wood chest, in excellent condition, complete with spare lenses and tools. Interesting.* 80.00   90.00

☐ **U.S. Army Air Flare Discharger.** *Model M5. c. World War II. This is a six barrel remote control device and is complete with all attachments. This one dated 1942. Is an interesting relic of the old Army Air Force.* 30.00   35.00

☐ **U.S. Army Air Force Sextant.** *Early World War I era. Comes in original Government fitted case. Is complete and operable. Specimen of the type used early in World War II by bomber navigators. Excellent condition.* 65.00   75.00

☐ **U.S. Compass,** *World War I.* 80.00   90.00

☐ **U.S. Navy Bomb and Rocket Console Instrument.** *Mark 5 type. Has various switches and controls allowing single or multiple release, on-off switch, safety*

	Price Range	

switch, choice of other operations, etc. Korean War era. **40.00**   **45.00**

☐ **U.S. Navy Dive Bomber Sight.** *Complete with all lenses and adjustment knobs. This is an early World War II type which attached to the fuselage ahead of the cockpit. Excellent.* **70.00**   **80.00**

☐ **U.S. Tachometer,** *World War I.* **80.00**   **90.00**

METAL

☐ **Metal Wing Covering.** *Portion of covering of a famed Junkers JU 87 Stuka dive bomber. Black swastika with white outline on blue/gray background. Authenticated* **325.00**   **400.00**

MISCELLANEOUS

U.S. aerial bombs, all inert.

☐   *25 pound, World War I.* **15.00**   **20.00**
☐   *50 pound, World War I.* **20.00**   **25.00**
☐   *100 pound, World War I.* **25.00**   **30.00**
☐   *100 pound practice bomb, World War II.* **25.00**   **30.00**

☐ **Portion of engine cowling** *from German Messerschmidt heavy fighter shot down in English Channel. Documented.* **85.00**   **95.00**

☐ **Portion of Engine Cowling,** *coral encrusted, of Japanese Zero shot down in the South Pacific. Documented.* **120.00**   **150.00**

BADGES AND OTHER INSIGNIA

The use of military badges and other identifying devices is very old. The obvious purpose of these is to make known the affiliation or special qualifications of the wearer. Heraldic devices are an early expression of the identity aspect of the subject. These often took the form of an animal or a familiar object. For instance, we know from Old Testament history that the Tribe of Benjamin has a ravening wolf as a symbol, Zebulen had a ship, and so on. The relatively simple armorial bearings which appeared in the 1200's became increasingly elaborate and complicated as time went on until an entire art and craft had been built up about them. Moving rapidly on down to modern times, we instantly recognize the badge of the Geneva Red Cross as a universal device worn by the medical personnel of all armies of Christian nations, while the Red Crescent is similarly worn by medical personnel of many Moslem armies.

Today there is a tremendous profusion of military badges and insignia, ranging all the way from cap devices to sleeve insignia denoting rank and military specialties.

At the present time, it would appear that the greatest interest among collectors is in Nazi items. For that reason, they are listed first in the following price guide. There is also much interest in British Army insignia. Interest in badges and insignia of the United States Armed Forces is not nearly as great except for a limited number of specialists. Although the variety is wide ranging all the way from elaborately enameled metal regimental and corps coats of arms, proficiency awards and rank chevrons, the quality available is still quite large. It is still possible to pick up highly desirable specimens at military surplus goods stores and small shops catering to military personnel. Many militaria dealers just don't want to take the time and trouble to stock items which are so readily available elsewhere. One exception to this is in a few rarer items such as aviator's and air crew wings and some early branch and arm insignia. Interest in wings tapers off in post World War II items.

BADGES

GERMANY (Imperial)

☐ Army Zeppelin badge.	325.00	400.00
☐ Bavarian Pilot's badge, *Hall marked.*	550.00	800.00
☐ Navy Zeppelin badge.	325.00	400.00
☐ Observer's badge, *2 piece construction.*	275.00	300.00
☐ Observer's badge. *3 piece construction.*	335.00	425.00
☐ Pilot's badge, *hollow back.*	325.00	400.00

Note: The above six items are among the most sought after of Imperial German artifacts.

GERMANY (Third Reich)

A word of caution. There are probably more outright fake Third Reich badges, medals, decorations and insignia being made than any other fake items of militaria. This is also true to a lesser extent of Imperial German artifacts. Be on guard! Be sure you **know** the person or organization with whom you are dealing.

☐ Anti-Partisan badge, *bronze.*	225.00	250.00
☐ Anti-Partisan badge, *silver.*	362.00	400.00
☐ Army Parachutist's badge, *breast badge.*	220.00	350.00
☐ Auxiliary Cruiser War badge, *marked.*	125.00	150.00
☐ Battle Shields. Metal badge attached to cloth, worn on upper left sleeve of coat. All shields listed below have this cloth backing.		
☐ Cholm shield.	91.00	100.00
☐ Demjansk shield.	80.00	90.00
☐ Krim (Crimea) shield.	35.00	40.00
☐ Kuban shield.	36.00	37.00
☐ Navrik shield.	55.00	75.00
☐ Blockade Runner badge, *marked.*	120.00	140.00
☐ Blockade Runner badge, *with stick pin, marked, cased.*	140.00	155.00
☐ Close Combat badge, *bronze, 10 days close combat.*	75.00	85.00
☐ Close Combat badge, *gold, 50 days close combat....*	190.00	200.00
☐ Close Combat badge, *silver, 30 days close combat...*	100.00	110.00
☐ Coast Artillery War badge, *marked.*	90.00	100.00
☐ Destroyer badge, *marked.*	90.00	100.00
☐ General Assault badge, *25 assaults, breast badge.*	500.00	550.00
☐ General Assault badge, *50 assaults, breast badge.*	565.00	625.00
☐ High Seas Fleet War badge.	125.00	150.00

Navy High Seas Fleet War Badge.

	Price Range	
☐ **Infantry Assault badge**, *bronze*.	28.00	30.00
☐ **Infantry Assault badge**, *silver*.	28.00	52.00
☐ **Infantry Assault badge**, *bronze, breast badge*.	40.00	45.00
☐ **Infantry Assault badge**, *silver, breast badge*.	32.00	35.00
☐ **Luftwaffe Air Gunner and Flight Engineer badge,** *marked*.	275.00	300.00
☐ **Luftwaffe Air Gunner and Flight Engineer badge,** *marked and cased*.	400.00	440.00
☐ **Luftwaffe Antiaircraft (Flack) badge,** *marked*.	70.00	80.00
☐ **Luftwaffe Bomber Clasp,** *silver, marked*.	225.00	250.00
☐ **Luftwaffe Day Fighter Operational Clasp,** *gold with "300" pendant, indicating 300 operational flights*. . . .	270.00	300.00
☐ **Luftwaffe Ground Combat badge,** *marked*.	60.00	75.00
☐ **Luftwaffe Ground Combat badge,** *unmarked*.	40.00	45.00
☐ **Luftwaffe Ground Combat badge** *with "25" number shield, indicating that number of engagements*.	300.00	370.00
☐ **Luftwaffe Observer's badge,** *marked*.	500.00	550.00
☐ **Luftwaffe Parachutists (Paratrooper) badge,** *marked*.	225.00	250.00
☐ **Luftwaffe Pilot's and Observer's badge,** *embroidered in gold, silver and aluminum on cloth*.	325.00	365.00
☐ **Luftwaffe Pilot's and Observer's badge,** *marked*.	405.00	450.00
☐ **Luftwaffe Pilot's badge,** *late war, unmarked*.	90.00	100.00
☐ **Luftwaffe Pilot's badge,** *marked*.	225.00	250.00
☐ **Luftwaffe Pilot's badge,** *marked and cased*.	300.00	325.00

Luftwaffe Anti-Aircraft Badge.

Luftwaffe Observer's Operational Flying clasp.

Luftwaffe Operational Bomber clasp.

Luftwaffe Ground Combat Badge.

	Price Range	
☐ **Luftwaffe Radio Operator/Air Gunner badge,** *cased.*	275.00	300.00
☐ **Luftwaffe Radio Operator/Air Gunner badge,** *marked.*	200.00	240.00
☐ **Luftwaffe Reconnaissance Clasp.**	253.00	280.00
☐ **Mine Sweepers, Sub-Chasers and Escort Vessels War badge,** *marked.*	80.00	90.00

Luftwaffe Radio Operational / Air Gunner's Badge.

Navy Mine Sweepers, Sub-Chasers and Escoert Vessels War Badge.

Price Range

☐ **Patrol-Torpedo Boat (E Boat) War badge,** *1st type,* *marked.*	400.00	440.00
☐ **Patrol-Torpedo Boat (E Boat) War badge,** *2nd type,* *marked.*	225.00	230.00
☐ **Submarine War badge,** *marked.*	170.00	190.00
☐ **Submarine War badge,** *unmarked.*	70.00	80.00
☐ **Tank Destruction badge,** *silver, sleeve badge.*	135.00	150.00
☐ **Wound badge** *for German Volunteers in the Spanish Civil War.*	95.00	120.00
☐ **Wound badge,** *World War II, black, one or two wounds.*	12.00	14.00
☐ **Above badge,** *cased.*	30.00	32.00
☐ **Wound badge,** *World War II, gold, five or more wounds.*	30.00	32.00
☐ **Above badge,** *cased.*	55.00	60.00
☐ **Wound badge,** *World War II, silver, three or four wounds.*	18.00	20.00
☐ **Above badge,** *cased.*	35.00	40.00

UNITED STATES

Perhaps the most sought after of the badges of the United States Armed Forces are the aviation pilot and air crew wings. There is a great variety of these but unfortunately the older items are in extremely short supply and are not at all easy to obtain. The first pilot's badge, known officially as the Military Aviator Badge was authorized in 1913. Made in gold, it consists of a small bar bearing the words "MILITARY AVIATOR." Suspended from the bar is an American eagle in full flight with signal flags grasped in its talons. The air arm was a part of the Signal Corps at that time and all pilots were officers of the Signal Corps. Since only 14 of these badges were ever made, it can readily be seen that they are extremely rare and will not be found in the market place.

The next wings were authorized in 1917 and in addition to pilot's insignia included a number of distinctions and specialties. The wings authorized in 1917 were embroidered in bullion on cloth or were of silk embroidery on cloth. Many of these have not withstood the ravages of time and so are difficult to find. The first medal badges, in oxidized silver, were authorized in 1918. The greatest variety of aviation badges was authorized by both the Army and the Navy during World War II. The following list of World War I and II Army wings is typical.

☐ **Aerial Gunner badge,** *World War II.*	35.00	40.00
☐ **Airship Pilot badge,** *c. 1921. Authorized in 1921, a dirigible took the place of the balloon in this badge.* . .	160.00	180.00
☐ **Bombardier badge,** *World War II.*	35.00	40.00
☐ **Combat (Aircraft) Observer badge,** *World War II.*	45.00	50.00
☐ **Command Pilot badge,** *World War II.*	50.00	55.00
☐ **Flight Surgeon's badge,** *c. 1943.*	55.00	60.00
☐ **Glider Pilot badge,** *World War II.*	50.00	55.00
☐ **Liaison Pilot badge,** *World War II.*	35.00	40.00

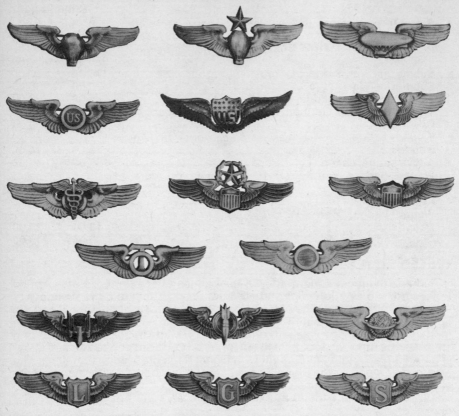

Aviation Badges of the United States.

Top Row: Military Aeronaut and Junior and Reserve Military Aeronaut, c. 1919; Senior Balloon Pilot, c. 1941; Airship Pilot, c. 1921.

Second Row: Pilot Observer Badge, c. 1920; Military Aviator (fourth style) and Junior and Reserve Military Aviator, c. 1918; Women's Army Service Pilot, World War II.

Third Row: Flight Surgeon's Badge, c. 1943; Command Pilot's Badge, World War II; Pilot's Badge, World War II.

Fourth Row: Technical Observer Badge, World War II; Combat (Aircraft) Observer Badge, World War II.

Fifth Row: Aerial Gunner Badge, World War II; Bombardier Badge, World War II; Navigator Badge, World War II.

Sixth Row: Liaison Pilot Badge, World War II; Glider Pilot Badge, World War II; Service Pilot Badge, World War II.

Price Range

☐ **Military Aeronaut and Junior and Reserve Military Aeronaut.** *At the time this badge was authorized in 1919, "aeronaut" referred to a pilot of a free balloon. A free balloon is the central design of the badge.* 115.00 130.00
☐ **Military Aviator (Fourth Style) and Junior and Reserve Military Aviator,** *c. 1918. One of the first oxidized silver aviation badges authorized.* 380.00 425.00
☐ **Navigator badge,** *World War II.* 35.00 40.00
☐ **Navy, Marine Corps and Coast Guard Aviation badges.** *The Naval Aviator Badge design is the same as that first authorized for Naval aviation. This badge is readily obtainable at commercial outlets dealing in uniforms and are rarely handled by militaria dealers. Generally the same holds true for the many and various naval specialized aviation badges.*
☐ **Pilot badge,** *World War II.* 35.00 40.00
☐ **Pilot-Observer badge,** *c. 1920. For military observers also qualified as pilots.* 115.00 125.00
☐ **Senior Balloon Pilot badge,** *c. 1941. By the time this badge was authorized in 1941, the aeronaut was called a balloon pilot. Similar to the Military Aeronaut badge but with a star above the balloon.* 115.00 125.00
☐ **Senior Pilot badge,** *World War II.* 50.00 55.00
☐ **Service Pilot badge,** *World War II.* 45.00 50.00
☐ **Technical Observer badge,** *World War II.* 60.00 65.00
☐ **Women's Army Service Pilot's badge,** *c. World War II.* 95.00 110.00

BELT PLATES

GREAT BRITAIN

☐ **Officer's Shoulder Belt Plate,** *38th Regiment (1st Straffordshire), in gilt and silver.* 180.00 200.00
☐ **Officer's Shoulder Belt Plate,** *4th Regiment (King's Own).* 195.00 225.00
☐ **Officer's Shoulder Belt Plate,** *Royal Berkshire Militia, gilt and silver.* 245.00 270.00
☐ **Officer's Shoulder Belt Plate,** *c. 1850. 59th Regiment of Food (2nd Nottinghamshire), gilt on copper.* 580.00 650.00
☐ **Officer's Shoulder Belt Plate,** *c. 1850. The Royal Marine Light Infantry, gilt on copper.* 130.00 150.00
☐ **Volunteer Officer's Shoulder Belt Plate.** *1st Renfrew Brigade, the Argyll and Sutherland Highlanders, gilt on copper.* 130.00 140.00
☐ **Volunteer Officer's Shoulder Belt Plate.** *The Royal Scots Fusiliers, silvered.* 100.00 115.00

CAP BADGES

GREAT BRITAIN

☐ **Officer's Cap badge,** *c. 1890. The Royal Welsh Fusiliers.* 76.00 85.00

	Price Range	
☐ **Officer's Cap badge,** *c. 1895. 15th King's Own Hussars.*	45.00	49.00
☐ **Officer's Cap badge.** *The Carabiners.*	30.00	35.00
☐ **Other Ranks Cap badge.** *14th Canadian Hussars.*	12.00	15.00
☐ **Other Ranks Cap badge.** *Le Regiment de Joliette, Canada.*	10.00	12.00
☐ **Other Ranks Cap badge.** *Royal Army Medical Corps.*	15.00	17.00
☐ **Other Ranks Cap badge.** *Royal Berkshire Regiment.*	20.00	23.00
☐ **Other Ranks Cap badge.** *Royal Tank Corps, interesting.*	30.00	33.00
☐ **Other Ranks Cap badge.** *The Governor General's Guards, Canada.*	15.00	17.50
☐ **Other Ranks Cap badge.** *The Grenadier Guards.*	12.00	14.00
☐ **Other Ranks Cap badge.** *The Royal Artillery.*	15.00	17.00
☐ **Other Ranks Cap badge.** *The Royal Flying Corps.*	15.00	17.00
☐ **Other Ranks Cap badge.** *The West Nova Scotia Regiment, Canada.*	10.00	11.00
☐ **Other Ranks Cap badge.** *The York and Lancaster Regiment.*	12.00	13.00

ITALY

☐ **Other Ranks Bersaglieri Cap badge.** *Brass light infantry bugle-horn with a flaming grenade in the center and with a black enameled cross on the grenade, all superimposed upon crossed rifles. This device is backed by a pleated red, white and green cockade.*	50.00	55.00

CUFF TITLES (Sleeve Bands)

Cuff Titles were another means of identification in the Nazi forces. These were used to identify members of certain elite groups or formations, personnel assigned to certain duties or participation in certain campaigns. Early on, these were worn on the right sleeve but later regulations changed the wear to the left sleeve. They were very highly thought of.

Cuff Title: Africa.

GERMANY (Third Reich)

☐ **Adolph Hitler** *cuff title.*	175.00	190.00
☐ **Afrika** *(Africa) cuff title.*	100.00	115.00
☐ **Der Fuhrer SS Officer's** *cuff title.*	200.00	220.00
☐ **Deutscher Volksstrum Wermacht** *cuff title.*	32.00	35.00
☐ **Deutschland SS Officer's** *cuff title.*	195.00	220.00
☐ **Feld Polizei** *arm band.*	50.00	55.00
☐ **Fuhrehuptquartier** *cuff title.*	125.00	135.00
☐ **Hitler Youth** *arm band.*	20.00	25.00

Cuff Titles: Fallschrim-Division, Grossdeutschland, Adolph Hitler, Jagdeschwader Richthofen, Deutscher Volkssturm Weracht.

	Price Range	
☐ **Im Dienste der Sicherheitspolizei** *(In the service of the Security Police.) arm band.*	35.00	40.00
☐ **Jagdeschwader Richthofen** *cuff title.*	85.00	95.00
☐ **Kreta** *(Crete) cuff title.*	125.00	138.00
☐ **Kyffhauserbund, Other Ranks,** *arm band.*	30.00	35.00
☐ **Motorisierte Gendarmerie** *(Motorized Police) cuff title.*	85.00	95.00
☐ **Ostturkischer Waffen Verba s der SS** *SS Turkish cuff title.*	120.00	130.00
☐ **Propagandakompanie** *cuff title.*	85.00	95.00
☐ **Red Cross Workers'** *arm band.*	25.00	28.00
☐ **Wesland SS Other Ranks** *cuff title.*	165.00	180.00

HELMET AND SHAKO PLATES

GERMANY (Imperial)

Bavaria

☐ **Chevaulegers Regiments, Schweres Regiment No. 2 and War Ministry officials.**		
☐ **Officer's,** *gilt.*	65.00	75.00
☐ **Other Ranks,** *brass.*	40.00	45.00
☐ **Crown and initial "L" for model 1868 rauprmhelm.**		
☐ **Officer's** *in gilt/gold.*	75.00	80.00
☐ **Other Ranks** *in brass.*	50.00	60.00
☐ **Crowned "L" superimposed upon heraldic star,** *c. 1880's. Gilt, for Landwehr officer.*	80.00	90.00

Price Range

☐ **General officer's.** *Enameled Bavarian arms in full color with gilt/gold supporters. For model 1886 leather helmet.* 125.00   150.00

☐ **Infantry regiments.** *Bavarian arms with supporters.*

☐   **Officer's,** *gilt.* 50.00   55.00

☐   **Other Ranks,** *brass.* 32.00   50.00

Brunswick

☐ **First and Second Battalions, Infantry Regiment No. 92.** *Prussian heraldic eagle with scroll across breast with words "MIT GOTT FUR FURST UND VATERLAND." Superimposed over this is a cross, circle, tower and horse. Under this is a scroll bearing the word "PENINSULA." Rarely offered for sale.*

☐   **Officer's,** *gilt and enamel.* 130.00   150.00

☐   **Other Ranks,** *brass and white metal.* 65.00   75.00

☐ **Third Battalion, Infantry Regiment No. 92.** *As above but with skull and cross bones in lieu of the cross, circle, tower and horse and with a scroll bearing the words "PENINSULA" below.*

☐   **Officer's,** *gilt.* 140.00   165.00

☐   **Other Ranks,** *brass.* 65.00   70.00

Hesse

☐ **General Officer.** *Gilt Hessian lion facing left within a gilt wreath of oak and laurel leaves. Superimposed upon the lion is the sliver and enamel star of the Order of Louis.* 600.00   675.00

☐ **Infantry Regiment No. 115.** *Similar to the above but with a large scroll above bearing the date "1621." Less elaborate than the general officer's plate.*

☐   **Officer's,** *gilt with enameled Order of Louis.* 260.00   285.00

☐   **Other Ranks,** *brass with silver metal Order of Louis.* 80.00   87.50

☐ **Infantry Regiment No. 117, 9th Company.** *Hessian lion within wreath with scroll bearing date "1697" on the left and scroll bearing the date "1897" on the right. Superimposed upon the legs of the lion are an upright anchor and crossed pickax and an ax.*

☐   **Officer's,** *gilt.* 150.00   170.00

☐   **Other Ranks,** *brass.* 72.00   80.00

Imperial German Marine-Infantry

☐ **Imperial German Eagle** *superimposed upon an upright fouled anchor with the Imperial Crown above.*

☐   **Officer's,** *gilt.* 90.00   125.00

☐   **Other Ranks,** *brass.* 55.00   60.00

Mecklenburg-Schwerin

☐ **The Arms of Mecklenburg-Schwerin** *superimposed upon a heraldic star.*

☐   **Officer's,** *silver arms on gilt star.* 95.00   110.00

☐   **Other Ranks,** *silver color arms on brass star.* 74.00   80.00

Officer's Shako Plate,
Imperial German Marine-Infantry.

	Price Range	

Mecklenburg-Strelitz
☐ **Arms of Mecklenburg-Strelitz** *superimposed upon a heraldic star.*

☐ **Officer's,** *silver arms on gilt star.*	95.00	110.00
☐ **Other Ranks,** *silver color metal arms on brass star.*	70.00	79.00

Oldenburg
☐ **Dragoon Regiment No. 19.** *Prussian dragoon eagle with the arms of Oldenburg superimposed upon the breast.*

☐ **Officer's** *silver eagle, gilt heraldic star with gilt arms*	80.00	89.00
☐ **Other Ranks** *silver color eagle, brass heraldic star with silver color arms*	50.00	55.00

☐ **Infantry Regiment No. 91.** *Prussian heraldic eagle with the arms of Oldenburg superimposed upon the breast.*

☐ **Officers,** *gilt with silver arms*	70.00	80.00
☐ **Other Ranks,** *brass eagle with silver color arms* ..	40.00	45.00

Prussia
☐ **Cuirassier Regiment No. 2.** Large Prussian heraldic line eagle with scroll across the bottom reading "HOHENFRIEDBERG 4. JUNI. 1745."

☐ **Officer's,** *gilt with black enameled letters*	185.00	215.00
☐ **Other Ranks,** *brass with black letters*	95.00	110.00
☐ **General Officer's, eagle plate for the model 1842 helmet.** *This is an extremely rare offering. Very large gilt guard eagle with the star of the Order of the Black Eagle superimposed upon the breast. Star in silver with remainder of the order in enamel*	910.00	1175.00
☐ **General Officer's eagle plate,** *c. 1900's. As above but of smaller size. Star is more pronounced*	280.00	325.00
☐ **Line regiments.** *Heraldic eagle.*		
☐ **Officer's** *gilt*	55.00	60.00
☐ **Other Ranks,** *brass*	35.00	40.00

Price Range

☐ **Grenadier Regiment No. 1.** *Grenadier eagle with scroll above eagle's head bearing the date "1655."*

☐ Officer's, *gilt*	120.00	135.00
☐ Other Ranks, *brass*	65.00	75.00

☐ **Grenadier Regiment No. 4.** *As above but with date "1626."*

☐ Officer's, *gilt*	115.00	130.00
☐ Other Ranks, *brass*	65.00	73.00

☐ **Hussar Regiments No. 3, 5, 8, 11 to 15.** *Scroll bearing the legend "MIT GOTT FUR KOENIG UND VATER-LAND."*

☐ Officer's, *gilt*	95.00	105.00
☐ Other Ranks, *brass*	60.00	65.00

☐ **Hussar Regiments No. 4, 6, 9 and 10.** *As above but silver.*

☐ Officer's, *silver*	95.00	105.00
☐ Other Ranks, *silver color metal*	60.00	65.00

☐ **Hussar Regiment No. 7.** *Cypher "WR" with "I" below and with crown above. Scroll under all with legend reading "MIT GOTT FUR KOENIG UND VATERLAND."*

☐ Officer's, *gilt*	160.00	175.00
☐ Other Ranks, *brass*	85.00	95.00

☐ **Hussar Regiment No. 15.** *Large Scroll bearing the legend "MIT GOTT FUR KOENIG UND VATERLAND" with four smaller scrolls under reading "PENINSULA" "WATERLOO" "EL BODON" "BAROSSA."*

☐ Officer's, *silver with black enameled lettering*	185.00	210.00
☐ Other Ranks, *silver color metal with black lettering*	95.00	105.00

☐ **Infantry Regiment No. 33, 5th and 6th Companies.** *Line heraldic eagle with scroll across the bottom reading "FUR AUSZEICHNUNG D. VORMALIGEN KONIGL. SCHWEDISCHEN LINREGT. KONIGIN."*

☐ Officer's, *gilt with black enameled letters*	120.00	135.00
☐ Other Ranks, *brass with black letters*	60.00	65.00

☐ **Infantry Regiment No. 74, 77 and 78.** *Line heraldic eagle with scroll across the neck of the eagle reading "WATERLOO."*

☐ Officer's, *gilt with black enamel letters*	95.00	105.00
☐ Other Ranks, *brass with black letters*	40.00	45.00

☐ **Infantry Regiment No. 87.** *Line heraldic eagle with scroll across the wings and behind the neck with the words "LA BELLE" on one side and "ALLIANCE" on the other.*

☐ Officer's, *gilt with black enameled letters*	116.00	130.00
☐ Other Ranks, *brass with black letters*	58.00	65.00

☐ **Life Cuirassier Regiment No. 1.** *Eagle of Frederick The Great with a scroll above bearing the legend "PRO GLORIA ET PATRIA." Plate is of large size.*

☐ Officer's *gilt*	280.00	325.00

	Price Range	

☐   **Other Ranks,** *brass* 117.00   130.00

☐ **Life Hussar Regiments No. 1 and 2.** *Skull and crossbones with scroll above bearing the legend "MIT GOTT FUR KOING UND VATERLAND."*

☐   **Officer's,** *silver* 190.00   215.00

☐   **Other Ranks,** *silver color metal* 85.00   100.00

☐ **Line Grenadier Regiments.** *Grenadier eagle.*

☐   **Officer's,** *gilt* 67.00   75.00

☐   **Other Ranks** 42.00   45.00

☐ **Shako eagle plate for line Jager and Train units.** *Line heraldic eagle but of smaller size than the helmet eagle.*

☐   **Officer's,** *gilt* 70.00   78.00

☐   **Other Ranks,** *brass* 40.00   45.00

☐ **Shako Plate, Jager Battalion No. 10.** *As above but with scroll forming a circle behind the wings and in front of the neck and legs. Above appears "WATERLOO." Below appears "PENINSULA" "VENTA POZO."*

☐   **Officer's,** *gilt with black enameled lettering* 100.00   115.00

☐   **Other Ranks,** *brass with black lettering* 49.00   55.00

☐ **Shako Plate, Guard Jager and Schutzen Battalions.** *Star of the Order of the Black Eagle.*

☐   **Officer's,** *silver and enamel* 116.00   130.00

☐   **Other Ranks,** *silver color metal* 45.00   50.00

Saxony

☐ **Line Regiments.** *Saxon Arms superimposed upon a heraldic star. Some regiments will have silver arms upon a gilt star while others will have gilt arms upon a silver star. Prices are the same for both varieties.*

☐   **Officer's,** 92.50   105.00

☐   **Other Ranks,** 45.00   50.00

Wurttemberg

☐ **Dragoon Regiment No. 26.** *Wurttemberg Arms upon which is superimposed the Star of the Order of the Crown of Wuttemberg.*

☐   **Officer's,** *silver star with enameled center* 95.00   105.00

☐   **Other Ranks,** *silver color metal star and center* ...   45.00   50.00

☐ **Line Regiments.** *Large size Arms of Wurttemberg. May be either silver or gilt according to regiment or unit.*

☐   **Officer's,** *silver or gilt* 65.00   75.00

☐   **Other Ranks,** *silver color metal or brass* 40.00   45.00

GREAT BRITAIN

☐ **Noncommissioned Officer's Helmet Plate.** *1879-1902 pattern. The Royal Marine Light Infantry Band, gilt* ..   240.00   265.00

☐ **Officer's Helmet Plate.** *Victorian. The Royal Marine Light Infantry, silver, gilt and enamel* 215.00   240.00

☐ **Officer's Shako Plate,** *c. 1810. The Royal Marines Artillery, gilt, a beautiful and unique plate* 590.00   660.00

Price Range

☐ **Officer's Shako Plate,** *c. 1855. 2nd Royal Tower Hamlets Militia of The Queen's Own Light Infantry, silver and gilt* 65.00   75.00

☐ **Officer's Shako Plate,** *1845-1855 pattern. The Royal Marines, gilt and silver* 175.00   195.00

☐ **Other Ranks Helmet Plate,** *1878 pattern. 97th Regiment of Foot, brass* 45.00   50.00

Ranks Lancer Cap front plate, 17th Lancers, Duke of Cambridge's own.

☐ **Other Ranks Lancer Cap Front Plate,** *c. 1902. All brass plate with the Royal Arms, trophy of arms, battle honors, title of regiment and skull and cross bones under which is a scroll bearing the legend "OR GLORY." This carries out the motto of the regiment "Death or Glory." This famous British regiment was one of those involved in the famous "Charge of the Light Brigad." Of great historic interest* 100.00   125.00

☐ **Other Ranks Shako Plate,** *c. 1844. The 89th Foot* 220.00   246.00

☐ **Other Ranks Shako Plate,** *1869 pattern. 1st Regiment of Foot, brass* 75.00   85.00

☐ **Other Ranks Shako Plate,** *1869 pattern. 13th Regiment of Foot, brass* 48.00   55.00

☐ **Volunteer Officer's Artillery Shako Plate,** *c. 1830. Silvered* 95.00   107.00

POLAND   Price Range
☐ **Other Ranks Lancer Cap Eagle Front Plate.** *Brass*
   Polish Eagle 30.00   35.00
RUSSIA (Imperial)

Russian Officer's Helmet plate, Guard Cuirassier Regiment.

☐ **Officer's Helmet Plate,** *Guard Cuirassier Regiment.*
Silver heraldic star upon which is superimposed a
silver outlined blue enameled band bearing the gilt
letters in Russian which translate "FOR FAITH AND
LOYALTY." Within the band upon a gilt background is
a black enameled Russian Imperal Eagle with a small
gilt St. Andrew's cross upon its breast. All of the
above constitutes the Star of the Order of St. Andrew
First Called, the highest decoration awarded in Impe-
rial Russia. This is a very, very rare offering but is
occasionally offered for sale 1200.00   1350.00
☐ **Other Ranks Infantry Helmet Front Plate,** *c.*
mid-1800's. All brass. Imperial Russian Eagle with

Price Range

crown. Upon the breast is an embossed shield showing St. George slaying a dragon. Under the eagle is a
cartouche of plain brass but ornamented with highly
decorative border. In the center of the cartouche
appears the pierced numeral of the regiment. Not too
common 140.00   155.00

SWEDEN

☐ **Officer's Helmet Plate,** *Life Foot Guard. Blue enameled Arms of Sweden with gilt border and crowns, all
superimposed upon silver flags and lions. The collar
of the Order of the Seraphim is about the arms* 100.00   115.00
☐ **Other Ranks Infantry Helmet Front Plate,** *c. early
1900's. As above but the Arms of Sweden and the collar of the Order of the Seraphim are in yellow metal
and the flags and lions are in white metal* 50.00   55.00

UNITED STATES

☐ **Eagle Front Plate** *for the model 1872 Light Artillery-
Cavalry Helmet. Large American eagle with the
Shield of the United States on its breast. In a semicircle above the eagle's head is a scroll bearing the
words "E PLURBUS UNUM." Scroll joins the olive
branch and war arrows held in the rght and left talon
respectively.*
☐   **Officer's,** *gilt* 60.00   67.50
☐   **Enlisted Man's,** *brass* 35.00   38.00
☐ **Eagle Front Plate** *for the model 1881 helmet. American eagle as above but with scroll held in the eagle's
beak. Officers' helmet plates will be found with gilt
crossed cannon, rifles or sabers behind the U.S.
Shield and the regimental number in silver may
appear on the front. Enlisted helmet plates may be
found with crossed cannon, crossed sabers or crossed
rifles behind the shield all in brass. On the bottom of
the shield may be found the regimental number in
German silver. For staff troops in lieu of the above
the staff device in German silver will be found, i.e.,
hospital stewards, a caduceus; commissary stewards, a crescent; engineers, a castle; ordinance sergeants, a flaming grenada and signal service, crossed
signal flags, all placed on the face of the shield.*
☐   **Officer's,** *gilt* 40.00   45.00
☐   **Enlisted Man's,** *brass* 15.00   20.00
☐ **Officer's Shako Eagle Front Plate,** *early 1800's. Silver
eagle with the Arms of the United States on its
breast. The right talon holds an olive branch while
the right grasps war arrows. Rare* 100.00   110.00
☐ **Enlisted Man's Dragoon Shako Plate,** *c. 1834. Brass
heraldic star upon which is superimposed an eagle in
silver color metal. Rare* 100.00   110.00

WINGS

Price Range

GREAT BRITAIN

☐ **Pilot's Wings,** *Royal Flying Corps, c. World War I. An infrequent offering of these wings, bullion embroidery on cloth. A wreath enclosing the initials "RFC" with a wing on each side and Royal Crown above* ...   75.00   85.00

JAPAN

☐ **Pilot's Wings,** *c. World War II. Silver embroidered wings with gold wreath and star in center on green cloth* 60.00   70.00

BAYONETS

Bayonets have always had a fascination for militaria collectors. They are interesting looking, fairly easy to display, have considerable legend connected with them and do not require as great an outlay of funds as do other military collectibles. But prices are shifting upwards as is true for all militaria. Not too many years ago it was possible to acquire, except for a few extremely rare specimens, a wide variety of interesting specimens for a dollar or two. This was especially true in the years immediately following World War II when thousands of surplus arms were being imported especially for sale to collectors.

Insofar as the practical value of the bayonet is concerned, it has always been grossly overrated. A detailed study of military surgical reports reveals that the numbers killed and seriously wounded by the bayonet have always been very small compared to other causes. Yet the myth of the bayonet has been aided and abetted by fiction writers, who glory in writing about bloody bayonet charges. The late Colonel Melvin M. Johnson, Marine officer and world known ordnance expert and small arms designer, took a dim view of the worth of the bayonet. This inventor of a light machine gun and semiautomatic rifle noted in one of his authoritative studies that the modern military rifle has a velocity of some 2000 feet per second, whereas the rifle and bayonet in the hands of even a combat experienced soldier is less than 30 feet per second. The lesson here is obvious.

The bayonet enjoyed whatever success it may have had during the days of short range, difficult to reload, inaccurate firearms and massed tactics. It could be used with some effect when troops clashed hand to hand. Certainly it went into decline with the advent of the high power accurate rifle and most positive decline with the advent of the self-loading magazine rifle. Interesting enough, doubt as to the value of the bayonet was expressed as early as the 1770's. A respected French military analyst of the period regarded the weapon as being of limited value. Some 60 years later, in 1831, a British Army officer, one Lieutenant Colonel John Mitchell, remarked that the bayonet was "the grand mystifier of modern tactics." Other military students called it "a grand military illusion."

The imaginative and efficient employment of the rifle in the American Civil War, the Franco-Prussian War, the Russo-Japanese War and in many conflicts, including both World Wars I and II and Korea demonstrated that the enemy can be kept as a distance where the bayonet is useless. Rapid fire weapons of the more recent wars has underscored this point time and again. Nonetheless the bayonet still remains a great favorite with the troops. Its appeal is largely a matter of morale. Somehow the knife-like blade stuck on the muzzle of the gun gives the soldier added assurance regardless of the facts in the case.

The bayonet, regardless of its value as a weapon, has an interesting history. Several stories are told as to its origin. There is no reliable historic fact to support any of them. Among one of the more interesting is that the name stems from the French town of Bayonne, once famous for the excellence of its dagger craftsmanship. Another tale has it that the word derives from **baionier,** the crossbowman of the Middle Ages who carried a large dagger as an auxiliary weapon.

In the absence of anything more positive, it might be supposed that the bayonet originated as a defense weapon. Early firearms were extremely inaccurate and were time consuming to reload. A determined enemy could charge among the musketeers while they were reloading, giving them a merciless drubbing. To prevent this very thing from happening, tactics were developed whereby the musketeers immediately upon firing their pieces would retire behind a line of pikemen who attempted to hold off the enemy until reloading could be completed. This was inefficient at best.

Perhaps a more convincing episode relating to the origin of the bayonet is revealed in the famous French military leader De Puysegur's memoirs. He related that his musketeers at the battles of Bergues, Ypres and Dixmude, during the early 1500's, carried **bayonettes,** which were long dagger-like weapons with a tapering handle which the men forced into the muzzles of their muskets to turn them into a sort of lance.

It is known for a fact that British troops in Tangier were issued a similar weapon, now known as a **blug bayonet** in 1663. The tapering handle allowed the bayonet to be more firmly seated in the musket barrel.

The plug bayonet was used for more than half a century by practically all armies. Despite its wide use, the plug bayonet was far from satisfactory. If not firmly seated in the gun barrel, it could shake loose or stick in the body of the enemy. If too firmly seated it could be more difficult to remove. This could be embarrassing to the point of disaster as happened at the Battle of Killiecrankie in 1689. The English troops fired volley after volley at the fiercely charging Scots clansmen, then plugged in their bayonets to receive the enemy. The Scots were not as close as the English commander General Hugh Mackay had estimated. Believing he had enough time to fire another volley at the onrushing clansmen, he ordered bayonets unplugged and another round fired. Unhappily, difficulty in removing the bayonets allowed the Scots to be among the hapless English and a bloody slaughter ensued.

In the meantime the French had devised what was known as the **ring bayonet.** This had two rings through the handle which allowed the bayonet to slide down the barrel to hold it fast. This was something of an improvement for it allowed the gun to be fired with the bayonet in place. It wasn't too practical, however, for there was such a wide difference in the diameter of the barrels of the time (standardization being unknown) that it was not at all possible to achieve a snug fit. Additionally, the rings had a tendency to stretch out of shape after continued used and the bayonet became all but useless.

The next development was the **socket bayonet** around 1724. The socket

Early socket bayonet and scabbard.

bayonet was simply a socket or sleeve to which a blade was attached. It was an improvement but here again lack of standardization of gun barrels precluded a tight fit. The search for a more practical weapon went on. Next was the **split socket bayonet** which was like the original socket bayonet except that the socket was split open to allow it to be open or closed, usually by hammering, to insure a tight fit. Continued search led to several arrangements of clips and springs to enable the bayonet to be locked in position. The vast majority of these early socket type bayonets had a long blade with a triangular cross section. The problem of a firm fit was not solved unitl the advent of standardized barrels. Then the split socket bayonet gave way to a modified split socket type with a locking ring. At long last the bayonet became a practical adjunct of the musket or rifle.

The sword and the knife blade bayonets with which we are more familiar today came into use around the middle of the 1800's with such blades being fitted with the ring locking socket.

The modern method of attaching the bayonet by means of a muzzle ring and a slot and spring arrangement or attaching by means of a long spring locking device was developed also around the mid-1800's.

In all fields of endeavor (and it seems particularly in the weapons field), there has always been a wealth of hair-brained designs supposed to make a given device do double duty by attempting to combine it with another. Even so with the bayonet. Only a few can be noted here. In each instance, they were failures insofar as their value as weapons is concerned but they usually bring premium prices on today's collectors' market. One of the most absurd of these was the so-called **rod bayonet** designed to be used as both a cleaning rod and a bayonet. This item was threaded at one end so that a sharply pointed end could be screwed on and the rod locked in place. Closely related to this number was a rod with a pointed end which replaced the cleaning rod in the channel under the rifle barrel. When not in use, it was shoved back under the barrel and was pulled forward and locked in place when needed. Of some interest is the fact that this latter type was the type of bayonet furnished originally with the Springfield 1903 rifle. All these rod types were so fragile as to be utterly useless and were soon abandoned.

Yet another item was a bayonet hinged so as to fold back against the rifle barrel when not in use and was arranged to spring forward and lock in place when a spring motivated latch was released. Some of these weird ideas die a lingering death and some Italian rifles during World War II were equipped with a manually operated folding bayonet.

One of the most absurd of these odd-ball contraptions was the **trowel** or **spade-blade bayonets.** These were designed to assist in digging trenches but were most thoroughly impractical. Still another was a bayonet with a barong-type blade to assist in slashing through brush. The use of any of these would have certainly subjected the rifle to considerable damage for the rifle would have been the long handle to use the tool. Interesting enough, many of these Rube Goldberg designs originated in the United States and the trowel, spade and barong types were actually issued to troops!

From time to time bayonets with a sawtooth edge or back have been tried, at least one as late as World War II. Just when and where the idea of this type weapon originated is unknown. We do know that there was an official issue of sawtooth bayonets to some British troops during the 1800's. They were also being issued to other armies about the same time. Basically, they were intended to provide engineer or pioneer troops with a weapon which could double as a saw to cut through wire and posts. An absurdity of Allied World War I propaganda was the charge that the brutal Germans originated and used this bayonet as a terror weapon. The sawtooth bayonet was used, principally by pioneers, by the Germans early on in the war just as it was by many Allied troops.

Because of their uniqueness and because of the difficulty in some instances of determining the country of origin, plug bayonets have been listed separately in the following guide.

PLUG BAYONETS

	Price Range	
☐ **Dutch,** c. mid-1600's. Double edge long tapered blade, brass crossguard with reversed quillons, turned and tapering wood handle with brass pommel, some pitting to blade	165.00	180.00
☐ **English,** c. 1670. Long bulbous shape wood grip with brass pommel, brass crossguard with short quillons, long single edge blade, pitting and aging consistent with age, a good military type	380.00	425.00
☐ **Oriental Origin,** c. mid-1600's. Long tapering single edge blade which is fairly wide at handle. Tapering, well turned wood handle with brass pommel and crossguard. Some decoration to blade and crossguard as is common in Oriental weapons. An extra long weapon overall, in good condition with some pitting	210.00	232.00
☐ **Probably French,** c. 1680. Turned wood handle with iron pommel and crossguard, some pitting to blade but a very good specimen.	165.00	180.00
☐ **Probably German,** c. early 1700's. Medium length blade which is fairly wide at handle, steel crossguard, blade double edged, tapering horn handle, fairly rare type	320.00	360.00
☐ **Probably Spanish,** c. late 1600's. Long single edge blade, tapering wood handle with brass pommel, iron crossguard, shows use and age with some pitting to blade, all is consistent with age of weapon.	355.00	390.00
☐ **Spanish,** c. early 1800's. Fairly short blade of a flattened diamond cross-section, crossguard of steel with reversed quillons, turn wood handled without pommel, interesting.	100.00	110.00

ARGENTINA

Price Range

☐ **Model 1891 bayonet.** *For the Argentine Mauser rifle. White metal hilt, complete with national coat of arms, hooked crossguard.* 45.00   50.00

☐ **Model 1891 bayonet.** *As above but with brass hilt.* . . .   50.00   55.00

☐ **Model 1891 bayonet.** *As above but with wood grips.* . .   40.00   45.00

☐ **Rolling Block bayonet.** *Brass hilt with hooked crossguard.* 66.00   75.00

AUSTRIA

☐ **Sword Blade bayonet.** *Made for the Model 1886 Austrian rifle made for the Portuguese Government, with scabbard.* 40.00   45.00

☐ **Sword Blade Socket bayonet,** *c. 1809. Single edge fullered blade, diagonal locking slot and ring. Bayonet could do double duty as a sword. Leather covered wood scabbard, important early type.* 120.00   135.00

BELGIUM

☐ **Brunswick Rifle bayonet.** *Broad sword-type blade, single edge. Stamped "P. J. Mahlerbe A Liege." Brass hilt and crossguard with down turned quillons, complete with brass mounted leather scabbard.* 185.00   210.00

BRAZIL

☐ **Bayonet.** *For the model 1908 Mauser rifle. Long single edge blade with fuller, wood and steel hilt, steel crossguard with turned down blade breaker quillon, muzzle ring.* 20.00   25.00

BRITISH COMMONWEALTH

British Enfield, model 1907. Used by all Commonwealth troops.

☐ **Enfield bayonet.** *Model 1907. This bayonet was used by all British Commonwealth troops in both World Wars and after. Long fullered single edge blade, wood grips, steel pommel and short steel crossguard with muzzle ring arrangement to accommodate studs under barrel. Shortly after World War II, these could be had for a dollar or two each.* 20.00   22.00

BRITISH INDIA

☐ **Brown Bess Type bayonet.** *For the India pattern*

Price Range

musket, long blade with fairly long socket, steel is of
low grade, manufactured for colonial troops. 36.00   40.00
☐ **Enfield bayonet.** 1907 pattern. (So-called "India Pat-
tern.") Plain single edge unfullered blade, various
Indian arsenal markings, with scabbard, unissued. . .   57.50   65.00
☐ **As above,** with scabbard, but used condition. 27.00   30.00

CZECHOSLOVAKIA
☐ **Bayonet.** For the M98 Czech Mauser. With muzzle
ring, complete with scabbard.   26.00   30.00
☐ **As above** but without muzzle ring, complete with
scabbard. 35.00   38.00

FRANCE
☐ **Bayonet.** For the model 1874 Gras rifle, with scab-
bard. 50.00   55.00
☐ **Bayonet.** 1892, knife-type blade. 50.00   55.00
☐ **Bayonet.** Model 1936 for the M.A.S. rifle. Cruciform
blade. 38.00   45.00
☐ **Fusil Socket bayonet,** c. early 1700's. Fairly short
double edge spear point blade, wide at the hilt, some
decoration to blade, silver socket without locking
ring, extremely high quality black leather scabbard
with white metal mountings, fancy and interesting.   325.00   360.00
☐ **Socket bayonet.** For the model 1866 Chassepot "needle gun." Very long blade with unique locking
arrangement. 125.00   135.00

GERMANY (Imperial and Pre-Imperial)
☐ **Imperial German bayonet.** Model 1898. Long straight
narrow sword blade with quill back. This specimen
dated "1912." Has initials of the maker "WK&C" on
ricasso, complete with metal mounted black leather
scabbard, not as common as other model 1898
bayonets. 60.00   65.00
☐ **Imperial German bayonet.** Model 98/05 so-called
"Butcher Knife" bayonet. Knife-type blade swells
somewhat as it nears the point causing it to resemble an old-fashioned butcher knife. This specimen is
complete with stamped metal scabbard and leather
frog carrier, full flash guard, short crossguard. 40.00   45.00
☐ **Imperial German Ersatz bayonet,** c. 1917. As World
War I progressed far beyond the time the General
Staff had planned, the demands for war material
became so great that the nation was forced to make
all sorts of improvisions. Among other things obsolete and captured enemy bayonets were modified to
fit German rifles. At times this resulted in a rather
weird looking, but nevertheless fairly efficient
weapon. This specimen has the fairly long triangular
cross section blade of an old socket bayonet welded

Price Range

to a steel hilt with slot, locking spring and muzzle
ring. It is rather crudely made. With metal scabbard.   60.00   65.00

☐ **Imperial German Ersatz bayonet,** *c. 1917. Identified*
as model 83/98/15. Bavarian proof marks, serrated
two piece metal grips fastened with domed rivets,
medium length fullered blade, steel crossguard with
muzzle ring, opposite end of guard is turned slightly
backward, no scabbard. 27.00   29.00

☐ **Imperial German Ersatz bayonet,** *c. 1917. This varia-*
tion has a fairly short knife-type blade attached to a
steel hilt. There is no crossguard and the muzzle ring
is open, no scabbard. 30.00   35.00

Imperial German Ersatz Bayonet, World War I.

☐ **Imperial German Ersatz bayonet,** *c. World War I.*
Fullered blade similar to that of model 98/05 bayonet,
medium length and medium width, somewhat unique
in that it has a one piece cast metal grip, grips are
serrated, stamped metal scabbard. 30.00   35.00

☐ **Imperial German Ersatz bayonet,** *c. World War I.*
Medium length, medium width plain unfullered
sharply pointed blade, flat metal grips, short cross-
guard with muzzle ring, stamped metal scabbard. . . .   30.00   35.00

☐ **Imperial German Pioneer bayonet.** *Model 98/05. Saw-*
tooth back. Maker's name "R. Stock & Co., Mari-
enthal-Berlin" on ricasso. It was this type bayonet
which created all of the absurd propaganda in the
Allied press. Complete with leather scabbard.   45.00   50.00

☐ **Prussian bayonet.** *Model 1842. This interesting*
specimen is one of the type imported with Prussian
made muskets used during the American Civil War.   36.00   40.00

☐ **Prussian bayonet.** *Model 1871. As below but a full*
dress or parade version, more finely finished, blade
decorated with etched trophies and floral designs,
brass hilt, white metal crossguard, good quality
polished black leather scabbard with brass mounts,
intended for parade and not for combat. 110.00   125.00

☐ **Prussian bayonet.** *Model 1871. Long plain sword type*
blade, one piece ribbed brass hilt with eagle shape

Price Range

pommel, fairly long quillons with reversed ends, slotted hilt, complete with its brass mounted black leather scabbard, muzzle ring. 85.00   95.00

☐ **Schleswig-Holstein bayonet.** *Model 1848. Straight single edge blade is fairly long and plain, sword type, flattened brass hilt with very short crossguard, brass mounted black leather scabbard, arsenal marks.* 210.00   230.00

Note: Third Reich (Nazi) bayonets are listed in the section of this guide entitled NAZI DAGGERS, SWORDS AND BAYONETS.

GREAT BRITAIN

☐ **Baker bayonet.** *Extremely long blade sword bayonet with detachable sword hilt with "D" type hand guard and turned down quillon. This weapon was for use with the Cambridge University Volunteers Baker rifle, interesting and rare.* 210.00   230.00

☐ **Brown Bess Socket bayonet.** *Early model. This item is unique in that it has a "U.S." surcharge. May be a captured British bayonet taken into government inventory and so marked, interesting.* 105.00   116.00

☐ **Brown Bess Socket bayonet.** *Long socket and long blade, blade is marked with a crowned "5," clean and in very good condition.* 60.00   65.00

☐ **Brown Bess Socket bayonet.** *Model 1839. Marked "G Salter & Co." Bayonet has extra large collar and the blade has been modified to accommodate the model 1839 scabbard, excellent.* 95.00   110.00

☐ **Brown Bess Socket bayonet.** *Shorter socket, also somewhat shorter blade, marked with crown over "B 16" and also marked "John Roe," an outstanding example.* 95.00   110.00

☐ **Enfield Socket bayonet.** *1853/71 pattern. This is the 1853 pattern but with the socket bushed to accommodate the Martini-Henry rifle.* 40.00   45.00

☐ **Enfield Socket bayonet.** *Type supplied with the quantities of Enfield rifle-muskets imported by both the Union and the Confederacy.* 50.00   55.00

☐ **Jacobs bayonet.** *Extremely long double edge fullered sword blade with semibasket hand guard and turned down quillon, steel pommel, checked black leather grips. This bayonet was for the double barrel Jacobs percussion rifle, rare and interesting.* 155.00   170.00

☐ **No. 4, Mark I bayonet.** *Cruciform blade, with scabbard.* 36.00   40.00

☐ **No. 4, Mark II Spike bayonet.** *Common, blade and socket, made separately then welded together.* 7.00   8.00

☐ **No. 4, Mark II Spike bayonet.** *Common, straight side metal scabbard.* 10.00   11.00

☐ **No. 4, Mark II Spike bayonet.** *Easily found, with scabbard.* 5.00   5.50

Price Range

☐ **No. 5, So-called "Jungle Bayonet."** *For the Lee-Enfield Jungle carbine, short Bowie-type blade, large muzzle ring, no scabbard.* 55.00   60.00

☐ **Martini-Henry bayonet.** *1875 pattern with sawtooth back. Long sword-type fullered blade, checked leather grips to hilt, steel pommel and crossguard with muzzle ring, no scabbard, not too common.* 80.00   92.00

☐ **Martini-Henry bayonet.** *1876 pattern. Long fullered sword-type blade. Steel crossguard with muzzle ring, checked grips, steel pommel. These bayonets are offered quite frequently with various British markings, complete with scabbard.* 50.00   55.00

ITALY

☐ **Bayonet.** *For the model 1871 Vetterli Vitale, long blade.* 35.00   38.00

☐ **Bayonet.** *Model 1891 for the Carcano rifle. These are offered with several scabbard variations as below:*

☐   **Leather Scabbard** *with metal tip.* 20.00   23.00
☐   **Leather Scabbard** *with brass tip.* 25.00   27.00
☐   **All Metal Scabbard.** 25.00   27.50

☐ **Folding bayonet.** *For the Mannlicher Carcano model 1891 carbine. An interesting weapon but impractical.* 15.00   16.50

JAPAN

☐ **Arisaka bayonet,** *c. late World War II. Generally the same as above except that it is of rough finish and shows the general state of manufacturing in Japan as the emergency continued and materials and men were in shorter supply. As with the above specimen, these will be found with markings of different arsenals. This offering does not have the turned down blade breaker quillon. This particular characteristic had been borrowed from older swords. In practice it was practically useless and dropped from bayonet design, no scabbard.* 40.00   45.00

Japanese Arisaka, model 30, bayonet.

Price Range

☐ **Arisaka bayonet.** *Model 30. Long fullered knife-type blade, steel crossguard with muzzle ring on one side and sharply curved blade breaker on the other, wood grips and steel pommel. This type bayonet was used by Japanese troops in the Russo-Japanese War and on through the end of World War II. Complete with metal scabbard.* 26.00   28.00

MEXICO

☐ **Remington Rolling Block 7-mm Single Shot Rifle bayonet.** *This particular rifle was made for the armies of many nations and it was a great favorite in Central and South America. The export rifles and the bayonets were marked with the name of the maker "Remington Arms Co., Ilion, N.Y. U.S.A." These will be found in all kinds of condition. The specimens quoted here are for bayonets in very good condition with metal mounted scabbard. This specimen is the long blade or so-called "long tooth" model. Fullered blade, steel crossguard and pommel, wood grips, crossguard had muzzle ring and blade breaker quillon, blade is maker marked.* 59.00   65.00
☐ **As above** *but short blade ("short tooth") model.* 50.00   55.00

RUSSIA (Imperial)

☐ **Berdan II Socket bayonet.** *For the Berdan II rifle developed by Colonel Hiram S. Berdan of the United States. The original rifle modified from percussion to a bolt action metalic cartridge rifle in the 1870's in Russian's Tula Arsenal. Bayonet has a medium length cruciform blade ending in a so-called screw driver tip. Slotted socket equipped with locking ring.*   59.00   65.00
☐ **Mosin Nagant bayonet.** *Model 1891 1st and 2nd models. Fairly long cruciform blade attached to socket by extremely short elbow, screw driver tip. Some difference in socket slot and dimensions between two patterns. There is no scabbard for these bayonets since it was the practice in the Imperial Russian Army for the bayonet to be fixed at all times when used by the infantry. However, cavalry troopers carried it in a scabbard incorporated in the saber scabbard.* 40.00   45.00
☐ **Mosin Nagant Socket bayonet.** *Model 1891/30. Very similar to the above bayonet, the principal difference being that the locking ring was replaced by a knurled stud in elbow to release bayonet. This model came with and without a foresight guard attached to the socket. Price for both is the same.* 40.00   45.00

SIAM

☐ **Mannlicher bayonet.** *Model 1888. Fairly short single edge fullered knife blade, wood grips with steel*

Price Range

crossguard with muzzle ring and no counterguard, blued steel scabbard, Siamese and German markings, old stock sold to the Siamese or may be obsolete Bulgarian bayonets. 36.00 40.00

☐ **Mauser bayonet.** *In general follows Mauser bayonet pattern of the period. Blackened metal parts, single edge fullered knife blade, short crossguard with muzzle ring and pommel, all of steel, blackened steel scabbard. These weapons were made in Japanese arsenals and bear Siamese and Japanese marks.* . . . 31.00 35.00

☐ **Royal Police Bayonet** *(so-called). Siamese markings, together with the "Grinning Tiger" or Royal Tiger Head marking. Patterned on the British Enfield model 1907 bayonet, well made fairly long fullered blade of English steel, complete with metal scabbard.* 31.00 35.00

SPAIN

☐ **Mauser bayonet.** *Model 93. Bright steel blade, crossguard and pommel, knife blade is single edge and fullered, crossguard has muzzle ring. Earlier bayonets have straight back to grips, those of later manufacture have shaped back to grips. "TOLEDO" marked, leather scabbard, metal mounts.* 31.00 35.00

☐ **Remington Rolling Blocket bayonet.** *Socket bayonet with long triangular cross section blade. Slotted socket with locking ring. Socket, shank and small section of rear blade blackened, rest of blade bright.* 40.00 45.00

SPANISH

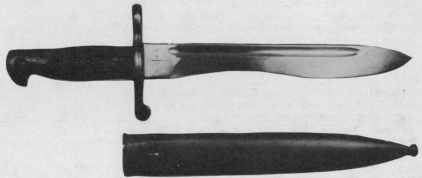

Spanish, model 1941, bayonet.

☐ **Spanish bayonet.** *Model 1941. For the Spanish '98 Mauser. Heavy steel blade is fullered and is of modified bolo type, bright steel finish to blade, blued steel crossguard with muzzle ring and counterguard, blue steel bird type pommel, blued steel scabbard.* 22.00 25.00

SWITZERLAND

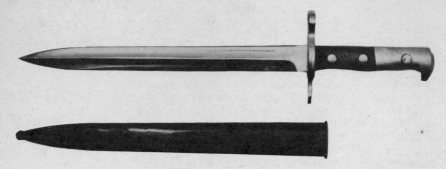

Schmidt-Rubin, model 1931, bayonet.

	Price Range	

Schmidt-Rubin bayonet. *Model 1931. Medium large double edge blade, steel crossguard with muzzle ring and steel pommel, all metal parts chrome plated, wood grips.* 31.00 35.00

Schmidt-Rubin Pioneer bayonet. *Model 1914. Fairly long fullered single edge blade is brightly polished as are the crossguard with muzzle ring and pommel, wood grips, back of blade has saw teeth. May be found with blued steel scabbard or brown leather scabbard with bright steel mounts.* 40.00 45.00

UNITED STATES

Bannerman Cadet bayonet. *In the early 1900's there was an interest in elementary military drill in some boy's schools and local organizations usually known as "Boy's Brigades." These units usually drilled with dummy muskets or rifles. This bayonet was designed for these guns. Socket bayonet with long slender blade, roughly made of cast iron, an interesting oddity.* 60.00 65.00

Bayonet. *Model 55. Long bright fullered modified yataghan-type blade. Brass one piece hilt and crossguard with muzzle ring.* 76.00 85.00

Bayonet. *Model 1860. For the Sharps rifle. Long recurved fullered blade of bright finish steel, brass hilt and crossguard with large muzzle ring, without scabbard.* 110.00 120.00

Bayonet. *Model 1942. War time expediency production. The model 1905 bayonet with ribbed plastic grips and parkerized finished, scabbard of olive drab plasticized webbing with parkerized throat. Not nearly as well finished as previous model 1905 bayonets.* 58.00 65.00

British-made bayonet. *Identical to the U.S. bayonet but marked "U.S." on the wood grips.* 36.00 40.00

Top: Dahlgren saber type bayonet for the Plymouth/Whitneyville Navy Rifle.
Bottom: Bowie knife bayonet for the Plymouth/Whitneyville rifle.

Price Range

☐ **Dahlgren Bowie Knife bayonet.** *For the Plymouth/ Whitneyville .69-mm. muzzle loading Navy rifle. Bowie profile knife blade with hilt and crossguard fashion from a single brass casting. Wood grips inset into the hilt, muzzle ring on crossguard with reverse guillons, black leather scabbard with bright brass mounts. This bayonet will not fit the rifle for which it was intended without some alteration of the muzzle ring and slot in hilt. There is considerable conjecture as to the reason for this. Apparently this bayonet was* **primarily** *intended for use as a hand weapon. It is one of the rarest of U.S. bayonets.* 475.00   530.00

☐ **Dahlgren Saber Pattern bayonet.** *For the Plymouth/ Whitneyville .69-mm. Navy rifle. Yataghan blade, closely resembles the model 1855 bayonet. It appears that these bayonets were each made for a specific rifle for in most instances they will only fit a rifle bearing the same serial number. Long bright blade with brass crossguard and large muzzle ring.*   110.00   120.00

☐ **E-1 or Simply E-1.** *Model 1905. Shortened version of the model 1905. Manufactured at the request of the U.S. Cavalry command for a short version which would be more handy for use of motorized troops. Interestingly enough, the short blade was just as effective as the long blade for all that is necessary is for the blade to penetrate the vital organs and not run all the way through the body. Consequently, bayonets are shorter now. For use with both the Springfield '03 and the Garand M-1.* 40.00   45.00

☐ **Experimental Ramrod bayonet.** *Model 1880. For the U.S. model 1880 rifle, conical point with triangular cross section. This was the first U.S. ramrod bayonet with such a point. Rear end of rod threaded to accommodate extension with cleaning cloth slot.* 40.00   45.00

Price Range

☐ **Fencing bayonet.** *Model 1912. This is a rather oddball item. It has a flat steel blade with considerable spring with a half twist to the blade and a ball end. Blade and ball leather covered, two steel crossguard arrangements, rear one is short with muzzle ring, front has both muzzle ring and small counterguard. Unthreaded small holes in sides through which a small screw passes to engage threads in holes in fencing musket barrel.* 60.00   65.00

☐ **Johnson bayonet.** *For the Johnson semiautomatic rifle, short parkerized triangular blade, parkerized hilt is merely a flat tang with a special attachment to secure it to the rifle barrel. Very lightweight fullered blade, necessarily lightweight so as not to impede recoil of the Johnson gas operated rifle. A very limited number was used by the U.S. Marines but was issued in some quantity to Royal Netherlands Marines who during World War II were armed, uniformed, equipped and trained by the U.S. Marines. Colonel Johnson, the designer, was no believer in the bayonet but he devised it to satisfy the demand for the weapon. It is interesting, unique and fairly rare.*

☐   *Mint condition with scabbard.* 120.00   130.00
☐   *Used but very good to excellent condition.* 40.00   45.00

☐ **Krag bayonet.** *For the 1892-98 U.S. Krag-Jorgensen rifle. Fullered knife blade with single edge, steel crossguard and pommel with wood grips, muzzle ring in crossguard with short counterguard. The blades were first blued but later production bayonets have bright blades, blued steel scabbard. This bayonet is said to have been patterned on the Swiss Schmidt-Rubin.* 50.00   55.00

☐ **Krag Bolo Blade bayonet.** *For the U.S. model 1892-98 Krag-Jorgensen rifle. Same hilt as above but fitted with a medium weight and fairly short bolo blade, blued pommel with bright crossguard and blade. Too small and too light to be of real use in cutting away jungle growth except for small brush. Blued steel scabbard, bayonet useless except as a prized collector's item.* 77.00   85.00

☐ **Krag Bowie Knife bayonet.** *For the U.S. model 1892-98 Krag-Jorgensen rifle. Same hilt as above but fitted with steel Bowie knife pattern blade. Extremely well-made wicked looking weapon but thoroughly impractical, valuable only as a rare collector's item.* .. 475.00   525.00

☐ **M-1 bayonet.** *Generally same as E-1 but with different fullered blade, for use with the U.S. Garand M-1 and the Italian Baretta assault rifle.* 40.00   45.00

☐ **M-6 bayonet.** *Knife blade bayonet for the M-1 rifle. Used by both Army and Marine Corps, short blade*

Price Range

with straight crossguard with muzzle ring and short counterguard, flat steel pommel, black plastic grips, parkerized, complete with scabbard. 27.00   35.00

☐ **Mark I Navy Training bayonet.** *Model 1942. Model 1905 blade made of black* **plastic,** *steel hilt with ribbed black plastic grips, black plastic counterguard with muzzle ring and short guard, for use with the dummy model 1903 training rifle.* 50.00   60.00

☐ **Ramrod bayonet.** *Model 1884. For the U.S. model 1884 rifle, has round blade and threaded rear to accommodate extension with cleaning cloth slot.* 65.00   70.00

M-6 Bayonet.

☐ **Ramrod bayonet.** *Model 1903. Round blade, all over blue finish. There is no provision for a cleaning cloth slotted extension. This is the bayonet originally furnished with the Springfield '03.* 20.00   22.00

☐ **Ross bayonet.** *Model 1905. During World War I the U.S. Government purchased several thousand Canadian-made Ross Mark II rifles for use in training U.S. Army troops. These were accompanied by the Ross model 1905 bayonet. Knife blade, steel crossguard and pommel, crossguard with muzzle ring with short counterguard with disk finial, bright steel parts. Identical with the Canadian weapon except stamped with U.S. Ordnance bom and initials "US."* 67.00   75.00

☐ **Socket bayonet.** *Model 1855-70. Long blued triangular cross section blade with ring lock, a basic Civil War pattern.* 40.00   45.00

☐ **Socket bayonet.** *Model 1873. For the U.S. model 1873 rifle, fairly long triangular blade and ring locked slotted socket, medium elbow, entire bayonet blued.* 40.00   45.00

☐ **Springfield bayonet.** *Model 1905. For the famous Springfield model 1903 rifle. Like the rifle, in use*

Parkerized World War II version of the model 1905, Springfield bayonet.

Price Range

longer than any other weapon in the U.S. Services. Replaced the absurd ramrod bayonet, the rifles being recalled by the Springfield arsenal to be altered to accommodate the new bayonet. Long fullered blade with steel crossguard and pommel, crossguard has muzzle ring and short counterguard, first production numbers have blued hilt and bright blade. Following this the entire weapon was blued, then later the weapon was parkerized. Walnut grips. Those of earlier production are corrugated, others are smooth. This was a good weapon as far as bayonets go, used in both World Wars I and II. 60.00   65.00

☐ **Springfield bayonet.** *Model 1905. U.S. Navy issue. Identical with the above but with U.S. Navy markings.* 68.00   75.00

Stoner M-16 wire cutting bayonet.

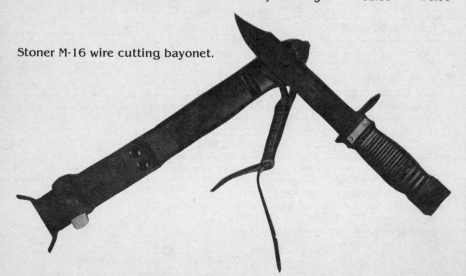

Price Range

☐ **Stoner M-16 Wire Cutting bayonet.** *Interesting saw-tooth back Bowie-type steel blade, steel counter-guard with muzzle ring, on one side only, flat steel pommel, grips of black plastic, for use in cutting through barbed wire, high impact plastic scabbard.*   55.00   60.00

☐ **Trowel bayonet.** *Model 1873. Bright steel blade with wedge shape reinforcing ridge under the slightly up-curved blade. Blued socket and elbow, unique lock-ing arrangement within the socket. Came with walnut wood insert for rear of socket to keep dirt from socket when bayonet used for digging. May be offered with a substantial brown leather scabbard with brass tip and leather belt loop with brass hook or with brown leather scabbard with the then stand-ard belt loop with brass swivel stamped "US." It would appear that this item was intended as a tool first and as a weapon second, extremely interesting.*   130.00   145.00

☐ **United States bayonet,** *model 1917. For use with the U.S. model 1917 rifle (.30 cal. version of the British Enfield Pattern 14 rifle.) Identical to the British bayonet. Long fullered blade, steel crossguard with muzzle ring and short counterguard, steel pommel. Bayonet issued in several finishes, bright, blued, parkerized or browned. This bayonet was also used with the Remington and Winchester trench guns issued to Marines in World War I.* 50.00   55.00

☐ **Winchester Socket bayonet,** *model 1873. For the model 1873 Winchester repeating rifle, fairly long tri-angular blade with slotted ring locked socket, all bright finish, has bridge on right side of socket.* 50.00   55.00

CANNONS, MORTARS AND ANTI-TANK RIFLES

Cannon and mortar collectors form a rather exclusive fraternity. The cost of these artifacts is high. Considerable space is required for their display. A long range is needed for those members of the fraternity who are "cannon cockers," who like to shoot their pieces. Ammunition too is rather expensive. Nonetheless there is considerable activity in this field of collecting. Some examples grace the lawns of collectors (the author once proudly displayed three field pieces on his lawn), others use their pieces regularly on ranges. As is the case with machine guns, **cannons and mortars must be registered with the Federal Government and in some jurisdictions with either or both state and local authorities.** A $200.00 Federal tax must be paid each time the col-lectible changes hands and is paid by the purchaser. This tax is in addition to the selling price. Those desiring to enter this field of collecting are strongly urged to consult with the local Office of the Bureau of Alcohol, Tobacco and Firearms Control, Internal Revenue Service, U.S. Treasury Department and local law enforcement authorities.

Cannons and mortars are in extremely short supply. The price trend is always upward. These collectibles were imported in considerable numbers shortly after World War II and sold rapidly. Importation was closed off a few years later and no more will be coming in. This means that the demand far exceeds the supply.

The following list includes only original weapons in firing order. Reproductions, particularly of Civil War artillery, are being offered to collectors. These are not collectibles within the meaning of this particular guide and therefore are not included. Their interest is restricted to those uniformed units of Civil War buffs who enjoy re-enacting battles.

CANNONS

ARGENTINA
Price Range

☐ **Hotchkiss Rapid Firing Gun.** *six-pounder, mounted on naval type pedestal mount. Made by the British firm of Hotchkiss-Armstrong. Marked both to the maker and to the Argentine Navy.* 2000.00   1230.00

FRANCE

☐ **Canon de 75,** *modele 1897. This is the famous "French 75" with the box trail. Used so effectively by American Field Artillery in World War I as well as by French artillery units. After that was exported by France in large quantities to a number of foreign governments. The United States 75-mm M1897 A2 and A4 guns were patterned on the original. This offering is French made and is in firing order. Complete with gunners' shield.* 7000.00   7700.00

☐ **Canon Leger de 25 Antichar SAL,** *modele 1934 L/72. Mounted on carriage with split trail. Semi-solid tires. Sliding breech. Gunners' shield. Compact anti-tank gun used early in World War II by French and a few by British Expedionary Force. Proved to be too light to be effective against heavy tanks. Is both a good decorator and shooter. Complete in firing order.* 1500.00   1650.00

☐ **Canon leger de 25 Antichar SAL,** *modele 1937 L/77. An improved model of the above gun. Better and more rugged looking gun with graceful lines. Much too light for use against heavy tanks. Another excellent decorator and shooter. With gunners' shield. Complete in firing order. Semi-solid tires.* 1600.00   1775.00

GERMANY

☐ **Gebirgskanone 15,** *7.5-cm. First German Army World War II mountain gun. Skoda design. Wood wheels with steel rims. Gunners' shield. Box trail. Breaks down into pack loads. Well designed and well made. In firing order.* 1500.00   1650.00

☐ **Krupp Mountain Gun,** *c. late 1800's. Beautiful example of famed Krupp workmanship. Sliding breech-block. Elevated front sight. Wood spoke wheels with iron tires. Elevating screw, no traverse mechanism. Designed to be broken down into several pack loads.*

Price Range

No gunners' shield in this design. Made for export. In
firing order. Interesting piece. Box trail. 1100.00   1225.00

☐ **Leichtes Infanterie Geschutz 18,** 7.5-cm. A most interesting item. First new German field piece since
World War I. Introduced in 1927 and used to some
extent in World War II. Made by the famed Rheinmetall works. Designed as an infantry support
weapon. Short barrel pivots near the muzzle. Unusual
loading operation which consists in pulling back a
lever which tips the breech up for loading. Reversing
the movement drops the breech in front of the
breechblock, ready for firing. Made in three versions.
The infantry type has a box trail and either solid rubber tired wheels or steel rim wood wheels. The model
for mountain troops has tubular steel trail and is
lighter. Both the infantry and mountain types are
priced the same. The mountain type is identified as
the Gebrig IG 18. A third type, the 18F was made for
paratroopers. It was similar to the mountain model
but had smaller and lighter wheels. This type has not
been offered to collectors. The infantry and mountain
types are available and are offered in firing order with
gunners' shield. All complete.   1100.00   1225.00

☐ **Nebelwerfer 41,** 15-cm. Rocket launcher holding
seven rockets which were fired electrically at two-
second intervals. Rocket tubes are fixed in a cluster
and mounted on a steel split trail carriage mounted
on steel disk wheels with solid rubber tires. Weapon
aimed in the same manner as the regular artillery
cannon. Known to German troops as the "smoke
thrower" and by the Allies as "moaning Minnie."
Most used on Russian front employing both smoke
and high explosive rockets with great effect. No
rockets available but weapon makes a most inter-
esting and attractive decorator. 600.00   650.00

GREAT BRITAIN

☐ **Howitzer Quick Firing Field Gun,** 4.5-inch. Built in
parallel with the 18-pounder Mark I field gun at
Coventry Ordnance Works. Wood wheels with steel
rims. Gunners' shield. Box trail. Used in quantity by
the British in World War I and to some extent by the
Imperial Russian Army. Operable. Interesting display
piece. 1000.00   1100.00

☐ **Mark I Field Gun,** 18-pounder. Field Gun. Built by the
Coventry Ordnance Works. Introduced in 1909 and
used until World War II. Gunners' shield. Wood
wheels with steel tires. Steel tublar trail. Very
interesting World War I gun. Operable. 1000.00   1100.00

GUATEMALA

Price Range

☐ **Hotchkiss Mountain Gun,** *2-pounder. Imported, with Hotchkiss and Guatemalan Army marks. This is a little beauty with wood wheels with steel tires. Steel trail with elevating screw. No traversing mechanism. In working condition but no ammunition available. Is a graceful design and is light enough to be displayed even in a large apartment or a small house.........* 1400.00 1550.00

☐ **As above** *but with identification marks of the Costa Rica Government.................................* 1300.00 1400.00

ITALY

☐ **47/32 Anti-tank Gun,** *Model 1935. A most interesting light weight and highly mobile piece. Split trail. Steel wheels with solid rubber tires. No gunners' shield. Could be maneuvered and serviced by a small crew. Designed by the Austrian armament firm of Bohler and built under license by the Italian firm of Terni-OTO. Some appeared on heavy duty motorcycle type wheels with tires. This weapon was a failure as an antitank gun but was a success as a close-support infantry weapon. Imported in considerable quantity into this country following World War II. No ammunition available but this weapon makes a most excellent display piece and is an interesting artifact of the Italian effort in North Africa.....................* 850.00 950.00

JAPAN

☐ **Infantry Support Howitzer,** *type 92, 70-mm. This weapon was so small that it looked like a toy artillery piece. It weighs only 467 pounds, has a gunners' shield and is mounted on split trail carriage with all steel wheels. A unique feature is the mounting of the wheels on crank like axles which allow the weapon to be raised to allow for recoil in high angle firing or lowered to permit concealment. This gun was particularly adaptable to jungle warfare and was much thought of. These interesting little weapons are also excellent decorators.............................* 775.00 860.00

☐ **Mountain Gun,** *model 41, 75-mm. Design based on the export Krupp Model 08 mountain gun. First produced in 1908 and used throughout World War II. An efficient light weight weapon. Easily broken down into pack units for mule transport. It is reported that a few of these where used by Chinese forces well into the 1970's. No gunners' shield. Wood wheels with steel tires. An extremely limited number of Japanese field pieces have ever reached this country. Good display piece. ....* 875.00 975.00

MORTARS

FINLAND

☐ **Chemical Mortar,** *81-mm. In original wood ordnance chest. Complete with bipod, baseplate, sight and other accessories.* 200.00   225.00

☐ **Portable Spike Mortar,** *.47-mm. Specimen offered with sights, range tables, bipod mount and muzzle cover.* 200.00   225.00

GERMANY (Third Reich)

☐ **Mortar,** *50-mm. This model may be dropped fired or fired by trigger. An interesting Nazi collectible.* 200.00   225.00

RUSSIA

☐ **Mortar,** *50-mm. Highly portable weapon. Complete with tube, bipod, elevating and traversing mechanisms and baseplate. Small enough for indoor display. The author has one of these by the fireplace in his study.* 165.00   180.00

☐ **Mortar,** *81-mm. At the time of manufacture was the lightest weight mortar of its caliber in any army. Complete with carrying handle, tube, bipod, baseplate and elevating and traversing mechanism. Beautifully made weapon of pleasing design which makes it ideal for indoor display.* 245.00   275.00

☐ **Mortar,** *120-mm. A larger model. Also complete with tube, bipod, baseplate and elevating and traversing mechanism. Offered complete in a sturdy custom fitted carrying case with all accessories. Another ideal display piece for outdoors.* 200.00   225.00

ANTI-TANK RIFLES

These interesting weapons fall into a special category. Although they are called rifles they are much to large too ever be considered in the same category as the regular weapons. They are excellent collectibles and are much sought after by "big gun" fanceriers. Anti-tank rifles are offered in operating condition and are often used for competitative shooting. The following weapons are those most often offered for sale.

FINLAND

☐ **Lahti anti-tank rifle,** *20-mm. Redesigned from the Lhati anti-craft gun, not too successful. Used by the Finnish Army against Soviet armor in 1939. Later used by Nazi Army utilizing captured supplies. Top feed. Offered in original heavy duty wood case with replacement parts and accessories. May be used for display or firing.* 600.00   750.00

☐   *Live ammunition for the above is available, per round.* 7.00   8.00

GERMANY (Imperial)

☐ **Mauser T-Gewehr,** *13-mm. Single shot, bolt action. An over-size version of the famous Mauser 98 rifle. Its*

Price Range

steel core bullet could pierce one inch of armor plate
at 200 yards. Was a successful weapon for its time
but had a tremendous recoil. German soldiers for this
reason were reluctant to be assigned to fire it.
Offered as relic only. Is rare. 350.00   400.00

GERMANY (Third Reich)

☐ **Rheinmetall anti-tank gun,** *20-mm. Single shot,
recoil operated, not too successful. Good decorator.* 330.00   370.00

GREAT BRITAIN

☐ **Boys Mark I anti-tank rifle,** *55-mm. Monopod
mounted. Had a very heavy recoil, bolt action, feeding from a magazine on top of the weapon. Barrel and
breech recoiled to help dampen shock. A muzzle
brake further reduced the recoil. Although this
weapon saw some active service in Egypt, France,
Libya, Malaya and Burma, it was not considered
much of a success. It is historically important as the
sole British anti-tank weapon to enter service. Inter-
esting decorator.* 250.00   275.00

CIVIL WAR HANDGUNS AND LONGARMS

As mentioned elsewhere in this guide, interest in all collectibles having to
do with the American Civil War continues unabated. It has, in fact, developed
into a rather highly specialized field of collecting. For this reason it is
believed that a separate listing of the small arms of that period is justified.
Now during that conflict a vast array of firearms was used by both the North
and the South. Just about everything from an ancient family fowling piece to
government issue weapons were pressed into service. In a guide such as this
it is not feasible to enter into all the weapons used. Such specialized volume
as "Flayderman's Guide to Antique American Firearms" is highly recommended for that area. That work is listed elsewhere in this volume. This present work treats only of those weapons thought to be more interesting
historically and which are available on the collector's market. The choice is,
of course largely a matter of opinion. The guide first deals with the weapons
of the Union Army, then of the Confederacy. It should be noted that a few
guns of the Civil War era have been included in the WEAPONS section of this
guide, which is designed as a chronological approach to the general subject
of weapons.

UNION

HANDGUNS

☐ **Colt Army Revolver,** *model 1860, .44 cal. Most used of
all revolvers during the Civil War, with fluted cylinder.* 600.00   1450.00
☐ **Colt Army Revolver,** *model 1860. As above but with
plain round cylinder.* 360.00   835.00
☐ **Colt Navy Revolver,** *4th model 1851, .36 cal. Govern-
ment inspection marks, brass or iron straps.* 450.00   1050.00

Price Range

☐ **Colt Navy Revolver,** *model 1861, .36 cal. Limited number furnished only to Navy, Navy markings* 735.00   1785.00

☐ **Remington Army Revolver,** *model 1861, .44 cal. Government marked* 275.00   575.00

☐ **Remington-Beals Revolver,** *Army model, .44 cal. Government marked.* 725.00   1435.00

Remington-Beals Navy model revolver.

☐ **Remington-Beals Revolver,** *Navy model, .36 cal. Similar to the above but smaller, government marked.*   325.00   675.00

☐ **Remington Navy Revolver,** *model 1861, .36 cal. Government marked.* 325.00   600.00

☐ **Remington Navy Revolver,** *new model, .36 cal. Reported to have been popular with Navy personnel, government marked.* 600.00   1125.00

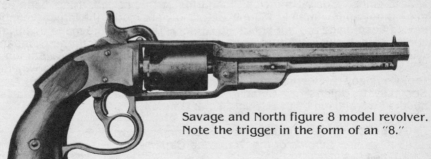

Savage and North figure 8 model revolver. Note the trigger in the form of an "8."

☐ **Savage & North Revolver,** *figure 8 model, .36 cal. So-called because trigger is in the form of an "8," limited production for the U.S. Government, martially marked. This specimen is the second variation of the first production model, very limited production.* 1450.00   2250.00

☐ **Savage & North Revolver,** *third figure 8 model. Extremely limited production for Navy.* 1550.00   2450.00

	Price Range	

☐ **Savage Revolving Firearms Company,** *Navy model, .36 cal. Produced in some numbers for Navy, government marked.* **335.00** **525.00**

☐ **Whitney Navy Revolver,** *.36 cal. Extremely popular with both the U.S. Army and Navy, as well as with many state militia units. Along with the Colt model 1851 revolver it often served as the pattern for Confederate made revolvers. For some unexplained reason the legend "EAGLE CO" appear on some of the 1st models instead of the Whitney markings.*

☐ **First model.**

☐   **Type I,** *very limited number made.* **375.00** **925.00**

☐   **Type II,** *very limited number made.* **275.00** **650.00**

☐   **Type III.** **275.00** **675.00**

☐   **Type IV.** **300.00** **725.00**

☐ **Second model,** *made in considerable numbers.*

☐   **Type I,** *heavy frame, Whitney markings.* **225.00** **575.00**

☐   **Type II,** *made in greater numbers than any of the others.* **195.00** **435.00**

☐   **Type III.** **195.00** **435.00**

☐   **Type IV.** **195.00** **435.00**

☐   **Type V.** **195.00** **435.00**

☐   **Type VI,** *changed rifling.* **195.00** **435.00**

LONGARMS

The tremendous demand for longarms during the Civil War required that arms manufacturers were taxed to the limit. The caliber .58 Rifled Musket was the most widely used of all longarms of this period. It has been estimated that approximately 150 million or so were made, the largest number having been made at the Springfield Armory. The rest were made by private contractors, including Alfred Jenks & Son, Eagle Manufacturing Company, William Mason, James D. Mowry, William Muir and Company, Sarson & Roberts, Welch, Brown & Company, Parker's Snow & Company, Providence Tool Company, E. Remington & Sons, E. Robinson, Savage Revolving Arms Company, C. Union Arms Company and others. Interestingly enough a few hundred were made by C. H. Funk, Suhl, Germany.

☐ **Gwyn & Campbell Carbine,** *.52 cal. Sometimes known as the Union Carbine or the Grapevine Carbine.*

☐   **Type I.** **350.00** **575.00**

☐   **Type II.** **325.00** **525.00**

☐ **Jenks "Mule Ear" Carbine,** *.54 cal. So-called because of the side hammer action, percussion, made by N. P. Ames, marked to the U.S. Navy.* **375.00** **675.00**

☐ **Jenks "Mule Ear" Carbine.** *As above but marked to the U.S. Revenue Cutter Service.* **625.00** **1125.00**

☐ **Jenks "Mule Ear" Carbine.** *As above but with tape primer instead of percussion, made by E. Remington & Son.* **450.00** **830.00**

☐ **Jenks "Mule Ear" Navy Rifle,** *.54 cal. A few were made in .52 cal. made by N. P. Ames.* **450.00** **950.00**

Jenks "Mule Ear" carbine with tape primer.
Made by E. Remington & Son.

	Price Range	

☐ **Joslyn Carbines,** *model 1862 and 1864, .52 cal. Rimfire, much used by Union cavalry, government marked.* 350.00 575.00

☐ **Remington 1863 Percussion Contract Rifle,** *.58 cal. So-called Zouave rifle, for saber type bayonet, extremely well made, because so many are found in excellent condition it is believed that they were never issued, government marked.* 525.00 830.00

☐ **Rifled Musket,** *.58 cal. Made by any of the above contractors or by the Springfield Armory.* 325.00 725.00

☐ **Rifled Musket,** *.58 cal. As above but made by either C. H. Funk or Union Arms Company.* 475.00 875.00

☐ **Sharps Carbines and Rifles.** *Of all the firearms used by Federal troops during the Civil War without a doubt those made by the firm headed by Christian Sharps were among the most popular. Thousands of them were delivered and they were all well designed and serviceable weapons. Only a sampling are listed here.*

☐ **Sharps Carbines and Rifles,** *new model 1859, 1863, and 1865, .52 cal. Well over 100,000 of these delivered to the Army and the Navy.*

☐   **1859 Carbine,** *brass furniture with patchbox.* 480.00 725.00
☐   **1859 Carbine,** *iron furniture with patchbox.* 325.00 525.00
☐   **1863 Carbine,** *iron furniture with patchbox.* 325.00 525.00
☐   **1863 Carbine,** *iron furniture without patchbox.* 325.00 525.00
☐   **1865 Carbine,** *iron furniture without patchbox.* 400.00 750.00
☐   **1859 Rifle,** *lug for saber type bayonet.* 425.00 750.00
☐   **1859 Rifle,** *as above but longer barrel.* 535.00 875.00
☐   **1863 Rifle,** *no bayonet lug.* 450.00 750.00
☐   **1865 Rifle,** *no bayonet lug.* 575.00 1150.00

☐ **Sharps "Coffee Mill" Carbine.** *In the days before instant or ready ground coffee it was necessary for the user to grind coffee beans before he could prepare his brew. This could be a major problem in campaigning in the field. Experiments were made to build a coffee mill or grinder into the buttstock of a longarm. Condemned Sharps new model 1859 and 1863 carbines were used for these experiments. The special coffee mill was designed, built and installed by a private firm by the name of McMurphy. The mill was*

Price Range

turned by a removable handle. Trials determined the
idea to be impracticable and the idea was never put
to use. The few trial weapons bring a premium price.
Collectors are warned that fake coffee mill carbines
are being offered for sale.

☐ **Sharps "Coffee Mill" Carbine.** Authentic. 3350.00 6350.00
☐ **Sharps & Hankins Carbine,** model 1862, .52 cal.
☐   **Army Model.** Similar to Navy model but never fitted
   with leather cover although screw holes for retain-
   ing cover are present. 325.00 550.00
☐   **Cavalry Model.** Similar to Navy model but barrel is
   shorter and coated with tin. Of the limited number
   made, some went to the 11th New York Volunteer
   Cavalry and some went to the Navy. It was believed
   that the tinned barrel would prevent corrosion. 400.00 700.00
☐   **Navy Model.** Leather covered barrel. Leather
   resisted corrosive effect of salt air at sea. It also
   prevented heated barrel from burning hand of user
   after continual firing. An interesting offering. 300.00 570.00
☐   **Navy Model.** As above but with leather missing. . . . 175.00 250.00
☐ **Spencer Carbine,** model 1863-1865, .52 cal. Rimfire.
Spencer weapons were also used in considerable
quantity by Federal troops during the Civil War. The
Spencer Repeating Rifle Company did not have ade-
quate facilities to fill its government orders, con-
sequently some were made under contract from
Spencer to the Burnside Rifle Company.
☐   **Model 1863-1865,** carbine. 350.00 650.00
☐   **Model 1865,** carbine. 300.00 575.00
☐   **Model 1865,** carbine made by Burnside. 300.00 575.00
☐ **Spencer Rifle,** Army model, .52 cal. Provision for the
socket type bayonet. 425.00 850.00
☐ **Spencer Rifle,** Navy model, .52 cal. Lug for saber type
bayonet, limited production. 500.00 975.00
☐ **Spencer Rifle,** model 1865, .52 cal. Socket bayonet. . . 375.00 700.00
☐ **U.S. Rifle Musket,** model 1863, .58 cal. Made by
Springfield Armory, type I or II. 325.00 575.00

CONFEDERATE

HANDGUNS

All Confederate made weapons are in a rare category. Production, except
for arms made in the Richmond, Virginia, Government Armory, was never very
large, varying from less than a hundred to a few thousand. Although the total
number of arms made at the Richmond Armory is unknown reliable authorities estimate that it was greater than the total made by all the other manufacturers in the Confederacy. Compared to the arms made in the North, those
made in the South are usually poorer in workmanship. Much machinery had
to be improvised, arms were needed in a hurry and there was a shortage of
skilled workers. Most specimens which have been found have seen service.

Production was so small and the demand was so great that all were pressed into use, unlike in the North where some arms never left the Government warehouses. It is of some interest to observe that the vast majority of Confederate handguns were patterned after the Colt model 1851 Navy and the Whitney Navy. The following list concerns only a few of the many specimens which have been offered for sale. However it does give an insight into what is available as well as an index to prices.

Price Range

☐ **Augusta Machine Works Revolver,** *.36 cal. Patterned on the Colt, Navy model 1851, very well made for a Confederate piece. Very few made, very rare.* 1250.00   3650.00

☐ **Columbus Fire Arms Manufacturing Company Revolver,** *.36 cal. Patterned on the Colt, Navy model 1851. Only a very few manufactured and fewer offered for sale.* 2800.00   9050.00

☐ **Leech and Ridgon Revolver,** *.36 cal. Patterned on the Colt, Navy model 1851. Made upon contract from the Confederate Government, rather highly regarded.*   1300.00   2850.00

☐ **Spiller and Burr Revolver,** *.36 cal. Less than a thousand made on a government contract for 15,000. The company was purchased by the government and some 700 were made at the government's Macon armory.* . . .   1500.00   3050.00

☐ **T. F. Cofer Revolver,** *.36 cal. Patterned on the Whitney, Navy model. Total production not known but only a very few have ever been offered. The rarest of all Confederate firearms and priced accordingly, unique spur type trigger. Three types have been offered for sale at various times.*

  ☐ **Type I,** *with so-called split cylinder which could use the percussion type cartridges of the period or the metallic cartridge with nipple.* 8100.00 25600.00

  ☐ **Type II,** *for percussion cartridges only.* 5350.00 17850.00

  ☐ **Type III,** *a shoulder where the barrel breech joins the cylinder precludes rifling being seen.* 5275.00 17825.00

LONGARMS

☐ **Fayetteville Armory Rifles,** *.58 cal. Production believed limited to no more than a few thousand. Interesting piece inasmuch as many were fabricated from parts from the captured Harper's Ferry Armory. Usually have lug for saber type bayonet.*

  ☐ **Early production examples,** *Harpers Ferry parts.* . .   950.00   2300.00

  ☐ **Second production type,** *also Harpers Ferry parts.*   675.00   1825.00

  ☐ **Standard type,** *most common although still rare.*   525.00   2100.00

☐ **H. C. Lamb Muzzle-Loading Rifle,** *.58 cal. Lug for saber type bayonet, probably patterned on the U.S. model 1841 rifle, sometimes known as the Mississippi rifle.* 1075.00   3650.00

☐ **Morse Carbine,** *.50 cal. Designed by George Morse and manufactured on captured machinery from the Harpers Ferry Armory at the factory of H. Marshall &*

	Price Range	

Company. *Some delivered to the Confederate Army but the majority to the South Carolina State Militia. Production later moved from Atlanta, Georgia to Greenville, S.C.*

☐ **Atlanta production specimens,** *limited*.	1625.00	3625.00
☐ **Greenville production.**		
☐ **Type I**.	1375.00	3225.00
☐ **Type II**.	925.00	2025.00
☐ **Type III**.	925.00	2025.00

☐ **Morse Inside Lock Musket,** *.71 cal. Manufactured by George Morse in his shop in Greenville, S.C., reputed to be the simplest made of all Confederate longarms. Rare.* 1425.00   4300.00

☐ **Richmond Armory Carbines,** *.58 cal. Also made on machinery captured at Harpers Ferry. Musketoons and rifle-muskets were produced in greater quantity than all other Confederate manufactured firearms combined. Several fakes, made from parts picked up following the Civil War, are being offered for sale. These are cleverly made and the collector should be wary!*

☐ **Carbine**.	675.00	1850.00
☐ **Musketoon,** *for both naval and artillery use*.	875.00	2400.00
☐ **Rifled Musket,** *for socket bayonet*.	500.00	1350.00

☐ **Tallassee Enfield Pattern Carbine,** *.58 cal.This rather interesting offering was made at the Confederate Armory at Tallassee, Alabama, and followed the design of the British Army's carbine. Enfield designed firearms have always been of the best and this design is no exception. As far as can be learned this was the only cavalry carbine* **officially** *adopted by the Confederacy. Production began too late for these weapons to see service. Only a few hundred were ever made. A most rare collector's piece.* 1450.00   4250.00

EPAULETS

Among the more ornate and interesting military collectibles are epaulets. In the beginning these were shoulder defenses of a suit of armor. At that time they had a variety of names, including pauldrons, shoulder guards, shoulder cops, epaulieres and epauletts. Around about the mid-1700's, long after armor had been discarded, epaulets reappeared in greatly modified form as decorative devices, usually indicative of rank. As such their form changed but slightly over the years. Except for a very few exceptions these modified epaulets fell into disuse in the early 1900's. They now comprise a specialized area of collecting.

Basically the epaulet consists of a strap extending from the shoulder seam to the top of the sleeve, terminating in an oval pad. This strap is usually of plain cloth or of heavy flat embroidery. The pad may have an embroidered edge and may be wholly or partially enclosed within a metal crescent. In many instances cloth cord or bullion fringe hangs from the crescent. Enlisted men or other ranks wear epaulets with cloth straps and pads with a brass or white metal crescents with cord fringe. Officers have straps of gold or silver embroidery, silk pads and gilt/gold or silver crescents with bullion fringe. A corps or branch of service device may appear on the pad of the epaulet of enlisted men or other ranks. Officers may wear both corps and rank devices on theirs.

BRITISH

Price Range

☐ **Officer of the Coldstream Guards,** *full dress, c. early 1800's. Wide yellow cloth straps covered with silver embroidery, bearing the cypher of George IV, the Garter Star, and the Royal Crown, appear along the strap. Silver crescents are plain, with silver bullion fringe attached. Leather and velvet backing. This is an ornate and most beautiful pair of epaulets from a most distinguished British regiment.* 320.00   375.00

☐ **Officer of the Cheshire Militia,** *dress, c. early 1800's. An interesting pair of epaulets of early design, of silver bullion lace. Large reversed crescents with silver fringe are flexible to fit the shoulders. Wide straps, each bearing a flaming grenade. Unusual, rare.* 475.00   525.00

☐ **Volunteer General Officer,** *c. mid 1800's. Beautiful pair of full dress epaulets of silver bullion. Wide straps with raised edges, silver crescents enclosing crossed baton and sword surmounted with Royal Crown, silver bullion fringe.* 125.00   137.00

FRENCH

☐ **Officer's,** *pair, c. early 1900's. Army, gilt/gold straps with heavy embroidered chevron design on straps. Highly ornamented gilt/gold crescents enclosing surgeon's device. Gilt/gold bullion fringe, beautiful and unusual, in wooden storage case.* 300.00   335.00

GERMANY

☐ **Army Artillery Officer's,** *pair, red wide strap with gold lace edges. Red pad nearly completely enclosed within a gilt/gold crescent. The numeral "30" appears in the center of each pad in gilt/gold with a flaming grenade above and an oberleutnant's rank device below. From the 2nd Baden Field Artillery Regiment, No. 30. Excellent condition and colorful.* 150.00   165.00

☐ **Other Ranks,** *pair, 3rd Saxon Uhlan Regiment (Emperor William II, King of Prussia's Uhlans) No. 21. Strap composed of overlapping silver colored metal disks terminating in an oval metal pad with raised edges. In the center of each of these is the Prussian*

	Price Range	

crown in high relief. There is a blue cloth lining under all, unique and colorful. **140.00   155.00**

☐ **Other Ranks,** *pair, Hennings v. Treffenfeld's Uhlans (Altmark) No. 16. Blue straps with scaled gold color metal edges. Gold color metal crescents enclosing a blue pad upon which appears the cypher "G.R." with crown above.* **140.00   155.00**

☐ **Bavarian Army Ministerial Official,** *pair, heavy wide straps covered with bullions embroidery in floral designs with heavily embroidered and raised edges. Silver pad enclosed within a gold metal crescent which in turn is enclosed within a heavy gold embroidered crescent. In the center of the pad is the monogram "M." (Maximilian II). Heavy gold bullion fringe descending from the crescent. Enclosed in extra high quality silk lined, leather carrying/storage case, beautiful and rare.* **285.00   320.00**

SPAIN

☐ **Officer of the Life Guards,** *c. 1910, unusual pair, large scaled straps in gold/gilt. In lieu of the usual pads there are long gilt/gold oval caps with raised edges designed to fit loosely about the shoulder. Each of these in the center bears the cypher "A XIII" (Alphonso XIII), not often seen.* **120.00   225.00**

UNITED STATES

☐ **Captain of Engoneers,** *c. 1861, gold bullion lace strap with raised edges. Gold bullion lace pad with crescent, bullion fringe desends from the crescent. Two embroidered bars in silver appear on each strap. A silver metal turreted castle appears in the center of each pad, pair.* **117.00   130.00**

☐ **Englisted Man's,** *c. 1861, brass shoulder scales terminating in a brass oval with raised edges to form a crescent, pair.* **50.00   55.00**

☐ **Navy Commander's,** *c. 1852, heavy gold lace strap with raised edges. Bullion crescent of elaborate design with dependent bullion fringe, crossed metal fouled anchors on the pad. It should be noted that at this particular time the rank of commander was held by those having command of ships from twenty four to forty guns. Epaulets of this period are extremely rare, pair.* **300.00   335.00**

☐ **Navy Commander,** *medical officer with the rank of commander, c. 1930's. Heavy gold lace ornamental strap with raised edges, bullion crescent of elaborate design with dependent bullion fringe. The medical corps device in gold appears on the strap and a silver*

Price Range

oak leaf rank device appears on the pad. Pair in silk lined, leather carrying/storage case. **185.00**   **200.00**

☐ **Marine Officer's,** *c. 1912, gold lace strap and crescent. On the pad appears the Marine Corps emblem in silver and gold, on the strap appears the twin silver bars of a captain. Pair, not often offered.* **250.00**   **275.00**

☐ **Marine Enlisted Man's,** *c. 1860, scaled brass straps and brass crescent with dependent yellow worsted fringe, pair.* **85.00**   **90.00**

☐ **Marine Enlisted Man's,** *c. 1895, scarlet cord shoulder knot terminating in a cloth scarlet pad and brass crescent. A brass Marine Corps emblem appears in the center of the pad, pair.* **50.00**   **55.00**

FIGHTING KNIVES

The knife is primarily designed for cutting or slashing whereas the dagger is meant for stabbing or thrusting. However there are times when the words are used interchangeably. Some references to military collecting do not include knives. This may be due to the idea that they are primarily a civilian weapon. Interestingly enough, in spite of the publicity given it at times, the knife, like the bayonet, has not been much of a major factor in combat. Some fighting knives have been items of military use. These were usually issued to special troops such as commandos. Again, like the bayonet, the knife's principal value is as a morale booster and that, perhaps, is not to be mitigated. It is well known that, in instances, men in the armed forces have privately purchased knives.

Among the vast array of knives, perhaps the most popular is the Bowie, then the military issue trench knives. The Bowie knife is named for "Colonel" James Bowie, American frontier hero and one of the defenders of the famed Alamo. The true account of the origin and exact pattern of the Bowie knife has been sadly distorted by legend. As far as may be **accurately** determined, it appears that Bowie preferred a fairly broad heavy blade with a sharply turned up saber like sharp point, with the false edge sharpened for about three inches and with the cutting edge of the blade extra sharp. This could be a most deadly weapon in close combat. It could be used equally well for slashing or thrusting and would require little effort to disembowel an opponent. It is recounted that Bowie took the design for his knife to James Black, an Arkansas blacksmith who was widely known for his ability to harden the temper steel knife blades. Bowie's successful fights with his new knife led to its adoption by a majority of frontier knife fighters. Subsequent "Bowie" knives have varied in size and weight but generally retain the general pattern of the original.

The Bowie knife was a much used weapon on the frontier and during the Civil War. Many were made locally by blacksmiths and were modified to suit the desires of the particular user. Quality varied according to the skill of the local smith. Great numbers of high quality Bowies were manufactured in England and imported into this country. The Bowie is perhaps the most prized among American collectors and fairly expensive. They are listed separately in the following price list.

With the development of trench warfare in World War I, involving trench raids and small unit actions, close combat ensued and the U.S. Army developed a so-called trench knife. This type was also developed separately by other armies at the time. The U.S. Army originally issued the model 1917. This has a medium length, narrow, sharply pointed triangular blade which easily penetrates leather and cloth. The grips are of wood and have four shallow scallops cut out to accommodate the fingers. The knuckle bow is a sheet iron stamping with a row of pyramidal projections about the outside. This allowed the weapon to also be used as a "knuckle duster." A modification, the model 1918 was similar except that in lieu of the pyramidal projections on the knuckle bow it had projecting triangular projections on the outside on each side. Late in 1918 the Mark I appeared. It has a flat stabbing blade with a median ridge. The cast bronze hilt has four finger loops with pointed projections on the outside to also permit this weapon to be used as a "knuckle duster." These weapons were used by both the Army and the Marine Corps.

During World War II the Marine Corps issued a combined fighting/utility knife named the KA-BAR, KA-BAR being the trade mark of the Union Cutlery Company, makers of the knife. It is identical with the Navy Mark 2 fighting/utility knife except for Marine markings in lieu of Navy. It has a clipped point blade. The blade is parkasized. The top of the point is sharpened for a length of two and seven sixteenths inches and the bottom of the blade is sharpened and honed. The guard is of steel and the grips are grooved compacted leather. The pommel is of steel.

Some U.S. troops in World War II were issued with a stiletto. This was patterned after the Sykes-Fairborn design used by British commandos. Various other types of close combat knives are included in the following price guide.

BOWIE KNIVES · AMERICAN MADE

	Price Range	
☐ Bowie knife, *c. late 1800's. 9" blade, blade marked "Bridgeport, G.I. Co." together with serial number, German silver crossguard, two piece stag handle.* . . .	**125.00**	**140.00**
☐ **Bowie knife,** *c. late 1800's. 10½" blade, clipped back. The blade etched with stylized U.S. shield and the initials "N.Y." brass crossguard, horn grips.*	**85.00**	**94.00**
☐ **Bowie knife,** *c. 1860's. Type used by some Union soldiers in the Civil War. Classic Bowie type blade 9" long, single edged, iron crossguard, ribbed wood grips with brass ferrule at lower end, brass pommel in form of eagle's head. Shows use and wear but overall condition is very good, unusual. Believed to have been made by Roby of West Chelmsford, Massachusetts, manufacturer of U.S. cavalry sabers.*	**925.00**	**1030.00**
☐ **Bowie knife,** *c. mid-1800's. Massive Bowie type blade 12½" long marked "Rose/New York" in two lines, German silver crossguard, one piece ivory grips carved in spiral design, German silver pommel. A large and beautifully made knife in excellent condition, considering age.*	**1285.00**	**1430.00**

	Price Range	

☐ **Bowie knife,** c. Civil War era. This massive knife shows the rough workmanship of a local blacksmith. The modified Bowie pattern blade is rather well curved, is single edged and is 2" wide. The blade has been attached to the hilt of a typical artillery sword of the War of 1812 era. The hilt is in excellent condition with leather cover and wire binding intact. Some pitting, was used by a Confederate soldier.......... **250.00 275.00**

BOWIE KNIVES · BRITISH MADE

Interestingly enough some of the very best Bowie knives were made in England. They found a ready market in the United States and were imported in very great numbers. The following are English made Bowies imported into this country.

☐ **Bowie knife.** c. mid-1800's. A rather heavy, well made Bowie blade 6½" long, marked to Ellin & Co., Sheffield, thick German silver crossguard, two piece stag grips, flat German silver pommel. Blade shows wear but is rated very good. **235.00 265.00**

☐ **Bowie knife.** Clipped blade 11½" long, marked to "G. Wostemholm & Son, Washington Works, Sheffield." This is a famous old English cutlery works. Has German silver oval crossguard and wood grips with a long narrow German silver plaque on each side...... **160.00 175.00**

☐ **Bowie knife.** c. Civil War era. Extremely fine quality 8" Bowie blade, marked "CAST STEEL," together with serial number, German silver crossguard and handle. This handle is decorated in well defined relief on both sides with stylized American Eagle and Shield, scroll, a floral design and cluster of stars. ... **315.00 350.00**

☐ **Bowie knife.** Excellent Bowie pattern blade with typical sharp cut back point. Blade is 9¾" long, marked "Joseph Rodgers & Sons, 6 Norfolk Street, Sheffield." Also marked with "V.R." under a crown. Heavy brass crossguard, two piece horn grips with inset oval brass plaque on each side. Excellent example by another famous old English blade maker...... **165.00 180.00**

☐ **Bowie knife.** This is an interesting specimen having a large 13" blade with long clipped point. The most of the back edge of the blade is sheathed with soft brass. Brass reverse counterguard, wood handles. Not marked to maker.. .... **150.00 175.00**

☐ **Bowie knife. A reproduction.** This is one of the very few reproductions listed in all of this guide. When the Wostenholm firm merged with the Rodgers firm, both long time English makers of Bowie knives, one hundred copies of their last pattern Bowie knives were made to mark the event. These are all handmade and have a massive 10" blade. This blade is of unaltered

Price Range

Bowie pattern and the back is marked "G. Wostenholm & Son/Washington Works, Sheffield, England, together with the company's mark of "I*XK." A large etched panel bears the following inscription "ONE OF ONE HUNDRED OF THE LAST BOWIE KNIVES MADE BY GEORGE WOSTENHOLM & SON PRIOR TO OUR MERGER WITH JOSEPH RODGERS & SONS, SHEFFIELD, 1971," together with the serial number of the knife. German silver crossguard and horn grips. This weapon is attractively boxed in a velvet and silk lined red leatherette hinged case with "I*XL" imprinted in gold on the cover. Blade wrapped in thin paper on which the original warranty is printed. The price listed here is that for which this offering sold at the time this guide was being written. An item such as this will steadily increase in value. 150.00   175.00

FIGHTING KNIVES AND STILETTOS
BRITISH

☐ **Commando fighting knife.** c. World War II. Single edge stabbing blade with fuller, flat plain brass "knuckle duster" hilt. Identified as a Middle East Commando Knife. 125.00   140.00

☐ **Commando stiletto.** c. World War II. Sykes-Fairborn pattern made by Wilkinson Sword. Blade is 6½" long, white metal oval crossguard and crosshatch pattern aluminum grips, complete with metal tipped leather sheath. 75.00   85.00

☐ **Trench knife.** Curved 8½" saber-like blade, has sword pattern hilt with handguard, greatly resembles a naval dirk, complete with scabbard, odd and interesting. Marked to Robbins Dudley. 215.00   240.00

☐ **Trench knife.** c. World War I. Hollow ground 8" blade, oval steel counterguard, aluminum hilt with bulbous disk pommel, complete with leather sheath, odd. Made by Robbins Dudley. 165.00   185.00

☐ **Trench knife.** c. World War I. Short double edge stabbing blade with median line on each side, brass hilt in form of "knuckle duster" rivetted to blade. Similar in general appearance to the Mark I U.S. Army trench knife, complete with leather scabbard. Made by Robert Kelley & Sons, Liverpool and so marked. 170.00   190.00

FRANCE

☐ **World War I trench knife.** Double edge stabbing 8" blade with median line, has etched inscription "Le Nettoyeur de Tranchees Campagne 1914-15-16" (The Trench Cleaner Campaigns of 1914-15-16.) Metal bulb pattern hilt with rugged metal crossguard, has its original leather scabbard, unusual. 75.00   85.00

GERMANY

Price Range

☐ **Luftwaffe fighting/utility knife.** *c. Third Reich. 8½"
modified Bowie pattern blade which folds back into
staghorn handle, locking lugs, complete with brown
leather sheath.* 75.00   85.00

☐ **Trench knife.** *c. World War I. 8" broad, sharply
pointed blade attached to off-set leather covered hilt
with brass pommel and reverse brass quillion on one
side opposite the off-set. Has two inscriptions, one in
German reads "I was forged in the Iron Age from
France's ravaged fields," this on the obverse side.
On the reverse side in Flemish an inscription reads "I
come from the fires of the sun, 1916." Complete with
brass-mounted leather scabbard. It has been suggested that this knife originally belonged to a German soldier who was captured and the second
inscription added. Most interesting, one of a kind.* . . . 80.00   90.00

☐ **Trench knife.** *c. World War I. Straight 9" blade with
sawtooth back, odd sharp pointed beak, small steel
crossguard, horn grips with steel pommel. Marked
"Kriegshead."* 80.00   90.00

ITALY

☐ **Fascist dagger/knife.** *This particular weapon is
usually listed with daggers but from the shape of its
blade, it might well be listed as a knife. Plated 8"
blade bearing a facsimile of Mussolini's signature,
plated steel crossguard, black wood grips with
shallow scallops to accommodate fingers, plated
metal scabbard.* 825.00   925.00

☐ **Trench knife.** *c. World War II. Broad, flat, sharp
pointed stabbing blade, roughly finished wood handle secured to tang with two steel rivets, thin steel
crossguard, handle die-marked with number "677,"
complete with leather scabbard, wartime workman-
ship.* 40.00   45.00

SPAIN

☐ **Combat knife.** *c. Spanish Civil War era. Double edged
wide blade with spear point, fuller down center of
blade, reverse steel quillions, plain wood grips
secured by three small steel rivets, leather scabbard.
This knife is reputed to have been carried by a
member of the famous "Battalion of Death." Inter-
esting.* 140.00   150.00

UNITED STATES

☐ **Confederate fighting knife.** *Generally resembles a
scaled down version of the Model 1833 U.S. Foot
Artillery Sword. However it is not a **cut-down** version.
12" medium width spear point blade with median
ridge, brass hilt with overlapping scales design cast*

Price Range

in one piece with crossguard and pommel, unusual, very good condition with some minor pitting. 300.00   340.00

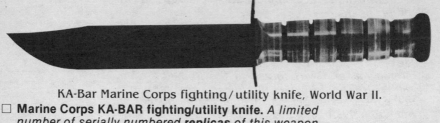

KA-Bar Marine Corps fighting / utility knife, World War II.

- ☐ **Marine Corps KA-BAR fighting/utility knife.** *A limited number of serially numbered **replicas** of this weapon have been released by the original manufacturer. The price of these will no doubt increase in the future.* 25.00   30.00
- ☐ **Marine Corps KAR-BAR fighting/utility knife.** *See introduction to this section for description.* 50.00   55.00
- ☐ **Trench knife,** *Model 1917. See introduction to this section for description.* 55.00   60.00
- ☐ **Trench knife,** *Model 1918. See introduction to this section for description.* 65.00   70.00
- ☐ **Trench knife,** *Mark I. See introduction of this section for description.* 75.00   90.00
- ☐ **Stiletto,** *c. World War II. Sykes-Fairborn design.* 55.00   60.00

FIREMEN'S HELMETS

Of increasing interest to militaria collectors are firemen's helmets. This is not at all unusual inasmuch as the majority of foreign fire fighting organizations are either paramilitary or quasi-military in organization and responsibility. In fact some firefighting organizations began years ago as an intergral part of the regular military establishment and wore slightly modified military uniforms. However, it has not been until comparatively recent that firemen's helmets have achieved prominence in the militaria field. With strictly military headdress becoming more and more difficult to obtain, prices have esculated to the level where only more affulent collectors can afford them. Whereas only a very few years ago excellent specimens of firemen's helmets could be had for a few dollars, ordinary items may now sell for a hundred dollars or more. German fire officer's helmets, patterned on the artillery officer's helmet, are selling for several hundreds of dollars. Brass English firemen's helmets command similar prices. It would appear that this is a very good investment field. Because of their distinctly military appearance, French items are also much in demand.

It appears from a review of history that the famous French brass firemen's helmets had their origin when Napoleon Bonapart, following a disasterous fire in Paris in the early 1800's, replaced the ill equipped and thoroughly inefficient civilian fire brigades with two companies of regular dragoons. These troops continued to wear their military helmets. French firemen wore military type helmets from that time on. The helmet front plates were rather elaborate and usually reflected the firefighting duties of the unit with a display of fire fighting equipment. Throughout the 1800's the helmets were of a modified Roman pattern with a high brass skull and high comb bearing a large wool roach. There was a socket on the left side of the helmet for a plume which was worn for dress. The large front visor was moveable and was often decorated with crossed fire axes within a floral design.

In the 1820's only officers were wearing the very ornate helmet noted above. Other members of the organization wore a helmet of similar design but with a lower skull and crest and without the roach. Around the beginning of the 1900's the helmet assumed the shape which, with minor modifications, has been worn since. This helmet has a low profile skull and low crest. It is of nickled brass and the earlier model served as a pattern for the French military helmets of World Wars I and II. All French firemen's helmets have an ornate front plate, often incorporating the crest of the city, town or other unit. All French firemen's helmets command a very good price.

Ancient English records reveal that a very early form of firemen's head-dress was a thick leather "fire hat" with a medium height cylindrical crown with flat top and wide brim. Probably the next development, early in the 1700's, was a so-called "fire cap" or helmet. This consisted principally of a reinforced, heavy leather skull which was rounded on top and was of medium height. The skull was formed of four segments with the joining sides stitched together to form a ridge or comb. Later this cap or helmet was developed into a military type leather helmet with well rounded skull. There was a short visor in front, a narrow side brim and a long rear visor. Visors and skull were bound in brass and there was usually a brass front plate with a design identifying the unit to which the wearer belonged. The comb or crest was of leather or brass and varied considerably in ornamentation. Modifications of these leather helmets have continued to be worn until fairly modern times.

Some historians on the subject of helmets affirm that the brass fireman's helmet was introduced into England in 1850 by an official of the London Fire Brigade who recommended that the English helmet be patterned on that worn by the French. Others maintain that the first English brass firemen's helmets were influenced by those worn by the British Army. In any event these helmets are much sought after. The high metal skull is provided with a medium length pointed or round front visor and a long rounded rear visor. The comb or crest is high in front and tapers down to the rear. Leather lined metal chin chains or scales are provided. The comb or crest is highly ornamented, often with a dragon design. The front of the helmet is decorated usually with a device of fire fighting axes and other tools or with large size initials of the name of the fire fighting organization. Firemen's helmets are of brass. Officer's are silver plated or of white metal.

Latest English firemen's helmets are of reinforced plastic and are of semi-military design. These have not attracted much collector interest to date. However there will come a time in the future when these helmets will be of interest.

German firemen's helmets, particularly those of the Imperial era, are of great interest. For the most part these are patterned on the army helmets of the period. Many use the same leather skull but with a metal comb or crest instead of the spike or ball top. In some instances the front and rear visors are larger than the military versions. Both visors are usually trimmed with brass. Officer's helmets may be of this design but with much more ornate decoration and trim and with chin scales instead of a leather chin strap. Other officer's helmets are of conventional Imperial Army design with an artillery pattern ball top or with a modified spike. Helmet plates vary considerably. Many incorporate provincial or national arms encircled with a floral wreath. Firemen's helmets of the Nazi era are also in good demand. The steel helmet, similar in pattern to the M35 combat helmet, is of lighter weight. It may have seven small ventilation holes arranged in a circular cluster, with one or two clusters to each side of the skull. Others may have a larger single hole on each side fitted with a fine wire mesh screen. A chrome or aluminum crest fits the top of the skull. The helmets are painted black with the Nazi police insignia on the left side and the party swastika shield in red, white and black on the right. Other examples may be found with a tilted white swastika on the right side and a tilted national red, white and black shield on the left. During the later years of the war all forms of war material became extremely scarce in Germany and a variety of substitute measures had to be taken. Among other things, captured enemy helmets were repainted and given Nazi decals. A few of these odd firemen's helmets are being offered for sale. Since it is extremely easy to fake these, the collector should be positive about the authenticity of the helmet he contemplates buying.

Other European countries and several South American nations had firemen's helmets similar to those of Imperial Germany and were made there. These are easily identified by the front plate. These helmets bring a good price. It should be noted that some South and Central American helmets were made in the United States. These were of the so-called Roman pattern with a high comb and large front plate. This particular helmet was also used as a presentation item for some American fire department officials. All of these are very desireable.

Japanese firemen's helmets are of the same pattern as the samurai helmets but are much lighter in weight. They were known as "fire watcher's" helmets. All samurai were expected to "turn to" in the event of a fire.

Firemen's helmets in the United States developed entirely independently of those in other countries. Fire fighting organizations were first of a private nature, then were part of the civic government. The first headgear probably dates from around 1740 and is of the so-called stove-pipe pattern worn by civilians of the era. The tall cylindrical flat top crown and wide brim are of heavy black leather. Identifying insignia is painted in bright colors on the front. A few years later a design change resulted in the crown having a rounded instead of a flat top. A heavy wire was sewn into the outer edge of the brim to prevent it from warping in heat and moisture.

The traditional fireman's helmet as we know it today was introduced about the mid-1800's. It roughly resembles a jockey cap turned backwards. The high skull, fitted with a large front piece, carrying the identification of the fire fighting organization, the fairly narrow front brim and side brims and the long turned down brim in back, are characteristic. The skull has raised rims extending from the top of the skull down the sides. These ribs varied in number according to the desire of the individual or organization. Modern helmets follow the same general design but with a smaller front piece, somewhat lower skull and narrower brim. Although the earlier helmets were made of hardened leather, modern helmets may also be made of aluminum or special plastic compounds. Some modern helmets, of plastic, generally resemble the safety helmets worn by construction workers. Helmets are designed to withstand falling objects and protect the back of the neck. Large clear plastic face shields are another improvement in addition to much improved suspension of the helmet. Carin and Brother, one of the very early pioneers in the design and manufacture of fire helmets, is still in business and is the largest manufacturer of such headgear. The company was founded over 123 years ago when it took over the business of the original designer of fire helmets.

ENGLAND

Price Range

☐ **Ashford Kent Volunteer Fire Brigade Dress helmet.** *Stiff black felt skull with crest of same material. Black leather band about base of skull. Fairly wide felt brim all around. No front plate.* 250.00   300.00

☐ **Fire Chief's helmet.** *Silver plated skull, visors and crest. Crest heavily embossed. Silver chin chain secured to each side of skull with embossed rose fasteners. Large front plate embossed with fire fighting trophies.* 350.00   400.00

☐ **Fireman's helmet.** *Highly polished black leather helmet with squared plain brass comb with lion mask on the front. Brass trim about base of skull and visors. Fairly large rounded front visors. Extremely long rear visors. Embossed decorative brass strip down front of helmet joining crest to the brass band around skull of helmet. This in lieu of an identifying front plate. Leather chin strap attached to each side of skull by embossed rose attachments.* 125.00   175.00

☐ **Fireman's helmet.** *Polished black leather skull and visors. Square leather crest trimmed along top and front in brass. Lion mask embossed on front. Brass strip about base of skull. Fairly wide pointed front visor and long square cut rear visor. Front visor only has brass trim to edge. The leather chin strap attached to each side of skull by embossed rose fixtures. Large embossed brass front plate in form of fire fighting trophies.* 125.00   175.00

☐ **Fireman's helmet.** *Same as above, but with high brass comb embossed with floral designs. Leather back brass chin scales.* 140.00   190.00

☐ **Fireman's helmet.** *Polished brass skull and front and rear visors. High brass comb decorated on each side with a dragon design. Metal rope affect trim about base of skull. Brass chin chains backed with leather and attached with fixtures of a rose design. Large front plate in the form of embossed fire fighting trophies.* 225.00   350.00

☐ **Fireman's helmet.** *So-called "salave" pattern. Black leather skull and visors. Front and rear visors of equal size with narrow side brims. Square cut leather crest without decoration. Leather chin strap attached*

Price Range

to each side of skull with embossed brass rose fixtures. A medium width brass band without decoration about the front base of the skull joins these fixtures. No front plate. This probably is the plainest of all English fire helmets. 100.00   150.00

☐ **Norwich Union Fire Chief's Dress or Parade helmet.** *Stiff red felt skull with gilt crest and gilt laurel band about base of skull. Brim trimmed with silver edging. Brass rosette side buttons. No front plate. These felt dress helmets are not often offered.* 550.00   650.00

☐ **Oxford Fire Brigade helmet.** *Bright brass skull and visors. Highly embossed comb. Brass chin chain backed with leather. Front plate in the form of a large cartouche with decorated border and with "O F B" in center.* 350.00   400.00

FRANCE

French Sapeurs-Pompies
Officer's helmet, c. 1822.

☐ **Early Officer's Fire Fighting helmet.** *Classical style highly polished brass "Roman" type helmet. Brass crest decorated with embossed volutes and surmounted by a black hair roach. A flaming grenade on the front of the crest. Socket on left side of skull holding a red feather plume. Front plate is an embossed brass cartouche with decorative border with a shield in the center bearing three embossed*

Price Range

fleur-de-lis. Crossed fire axes below. A royal crown surmounts the cartouche. Moveable deep front visor with embossed crossed fire axes. Leather lined brass chin strap simulates scales. Large side bosses. Royalist. 450.00   600.00

☐ **Early Fireman's helmet.** *Same as above, except the front plate consists of a large embossed cartouche with a rooster with out-spread wings at the top within a laurel wreath. A trophy of flags in the background. A large circular wreath at the bottom encloses crossed fire axes and other fire fighting tools. This surrounded by a ribbon bearing the legend "SAPEURS POMPIERS DE BOURGES." . . . .*   450.00   600.00

☐ **Early Fireman's helmet.** *Same as above, but with no plume socket on left side. Front plate is large cartouche with a ribbon about the sides bearing the legend "SAPEURS DE POMPIERS DE LA VILLE DE PARIS." Eagle at top of trophy of flags. In center of cartouche a shield bearing an early one mast ship, all within a wreath with crossed fire axes below. . . . . . .*   450.00   600.00

☐ **Fireman's helmet,** *c. 1805. One of the earliest examples. Brass casque without front or rear visors. Brass "Roman" pattern crest decorated with embossed volutes. Bear skin band surrounds base of skull, extending approximately half way up the skull. Large embossed front plate bearing the image of a three mast warship. Socket on right side of skull for plume. Rare. . . . .*   550.00   600.00

☐ **Fireman's helmet.** *Nickel plated helmet with well rounded and fairly low crown. Fairly narrow front and rear visors and side brims. Ornate gilt/brass front plate bearing the arms of the city of Paris and the legend SAPEURS - POMPIERS DE PARIS." Black leather chin strap. The French Army steel helmets of World Wars I and II were patterned on this helmet. Not rare but interesting. . . . .*   75.00   125.00

☐ **Fireman's helmet.** *This particular helmet very closely follows the English pattern. Polished brass skull and visors. The visors are fairly narrow. No moveable visor in this design. High brass "Roman" type crest decorated with embossed volutes. Leather back brass chin scales. Plume socket on left side of skull. Large brass front piece larger in the front than on the sides. Extends about front half of base of skull and is attached to bosses on each side. Sides embossed with floral designs with embossed shield in front bearing a three mast ship. Above the shield is a large crown. A ribbon about the crown and shield bears the inscription "SAPEURS POMPIERS DE PARIS." An unusual example. . . . .*   375.00   450.00

GERMANY

☐ **Bavarian Fire Official's Ball Top helmet.** *Except for the front plate this is quite similar to the typical Imperial German artillery officer's helmet. Black patent leather skull and visors. Gilt trim to front visor. Gilt ball top fixture with cross piece base. Brass chin scales. Leather and silk lining. Large gilt wreath encloses enameled arms of Bavaria with crown above. Crossed fire axes behind shield. Unusual piece.* 250.00   375.00

Bavarian
Fireman's helmet.

☐ **Bavarian Fireman's helmet.** *Glossy black metal skull. Bottom of skull trimmed with broad brass band with simulated rivets. Brass "Roman" type crest with large ventilation holes on each side. Leather chin strap attached to each side of skull by lion mask bosses. Front plate consists of embossed brass cypher "L" (Ludwing) with crown above. Leather lining. An unusual specimen.* 100.00   135.00

☐ **NASSAUISCHER Fireman's helmet.** *Like the above, except for the front plate which consists of an embossed silver metal shield encircled with laurel wreath. At the top of the shield, in two lines, appears the legend "NASSAUISCHER/FEUERWEHR VER-BAND." Under this the shield is divided in two by a vertical line. On the left appears the heraldic Lion of Nassau. On the right appears a stylized fireman's helmet upon crossed fire axes. Under the shield is a*

Price Range

scroll bearing the legend "GOTT ZUR EHR-DEM NACHSTEN ZUR WEHR." Unusual front plate. 80.00   100.00

Ersatz Nazi Fireman's helmet converted from a French fireman's helmet.

☐ **Nazi Fireman's helmet.** *As World War II dragged on, all kinds of material and materiel became in short supply in the Third Reich. An example is this ersatz fireman's helmet converted from a French fireman's helmet of the period. Original nickeled skull painted black but comb left bright. Nazi fireman's decals applied to sides of skull. Original French liner and chin strap.* 75.00   90.00

☐ **Nazi Fireman's helmet.** *Early issue. Army pattern skull but with square instead of rounded dip at sides. Painted black. Bright aluminum crest or comb. Light weight liner. A tilted swastika on right side. Tilted national red, white and black shield on left. A cluster of seven ventilation holes on each side of skull. Some with leather neck protector.* 100.00   125.00

☐ **Nazi Fireman's helmet.** *Later issue. Same as above, but with a double cluster of seven ventilation holes on each side of skull. Nazi party shield on right side of skull. Silver and black police shield on left.* 90.00   100.00

☐ **Obeplottbach Village Fireman's helmet.** *Black metal helmet with visors joined at side to form small brim. All trimmed in brass. Usual brass crest. Front plate consists of a brass ring with a bar across the center*

Nazi
Fireman's helmet.

Obeplottbach Village
Fireman's helmet.

Price Range

reading "OBEPOLTTBACH." On the upper part of the
ring appears "FREIWLLIGE." On the lower half
appears "FEUERWEHR." All this superimposed upon
a vertical ladder, crossed fire axes and a fireman's
helmet. Leather chin strap attached by lion mask and
ring. 80.00   100.00

☐ **Prussian Fireman's helmet.** Same as NASSAUI-
SCHER, except that the white metal front plate is the
embossed heraldic star of the ORDER OF THE BLACK
EAGLE. 80.00   100.00

Raschala Village
Officer's Fire helmet.

Price Range

☐ **Raschala Village Officer's Fire helmet.** *Black metal helmet, high ornate brass crest embossed on sides with floral design. Front plate similar to the Obeplott-bach Village Fireman's helmet, except that "RAS-CHALA" appears on center bar and the whole is enclosed within a large brass wreath. Ornate brass leather lined chin scales attached to each side of skull by ornate round bosses. Leather chin strap attached to each side of helmet interior. Very fancy.* . 100.00   125.00

☐ **SAARLOUIS Fireman's helmet.** *Polished black leather skull and front and rear visors. Visors trimmed in white metal. Leather chin strap attached on each side of skull with embossed circular bosses. White metal crest on top. Front plate consists of the arms of Saarlouis with crown above and scroll below bearing the word "SAARLOUIS," all in white metal and enamel. This is the typical Imperial German fireman's helmet with skull and visors like those of the army helmet.* 80.00   100.00

☐ **Unidentified Fireman's helmet.** *All leather black helmet with modified "Roman" pattern leather crest. Front and back visors connected at sides with narrow brim. Black leather visor attached to inside of skull. Device of crossed arrows and lightening bolts profes-sionally hand painted in gilt on front of skull. Leather in excellent condition. An attractive and unusual item.* 80.00   100.00

Unidentified German Fireman's helmet.

Price Range

☐ **Unidentified Fireman's helmet.** *Similar to Prussian helmet, except for narrow brim along sides. All metal is brass. Brass crest extends all the way from base of skull in front to base of skull in back. Attached by brass studs. A very plain helmet.* 55.00   65.00

☐ **Unidentified Fireman's helmet.** *Well rounded polished black leather skull with polished black leather visors. The front visor trimmed with brass edge. Front plate is in brass and consists of crossed fire axes with a fireman's helmet above. Usual brass crest on top of skull. Black leather chinstrap attached to each side of helmet by a brass disk.* 80.00   100.00

☐ **Wurttemberg Fire Officials Spiked helmet.** *Another fireman's helmet similar to that of an Imperial Army helmet. Patent leather (black) skull and visors with gilt trim to front visor. Large silver spike with small ball on the top as is seen in some custom officer's helmets. Silver cross piece spike base. Silver chin scales. Leather and silk lining. Arms of Wurttemberg within a laurel wreath superimposed upon crossed fire axes. Conventional German fireman's helmet on top of all. This front plate in silver and gilt. These specimens in demand.* 225.00   350.00

ITALY

Italian Fireman's
Dress helmet,
model 1926.

Price Range

☐ **Fireman's Dress helmet,** *model 1926. Well rounded heavy leather polished skull with heavy black leather visors. Heavy leather bead about base of skull. Polished brass comb and polished brass trim to both visors. Circular brass boss with lion mask on each side of skull at the bottom. Leather chin strap attached to inside of helmet. Front plate consists of embossed large brass flaming grenade superimposed upon crossed fire axes. Center of grenade is enameled red with the figure "22" superimposed upon it. These helmets will be found with different numbers on the front signifying different fire brigades. Helmets worn during World War may have a cross instead of a number. These were worn by firemen still in training school or not yet assigned to a brigade. The price is the same for all such helmets.* 85.00   125.00

☐ **Fireman's helmet,** *Fascist period. Same as World War II style, except that the front plate consists of a stamped brass device consisting of a flaming grenade with fasces in the center of the grenade.* 85.00   125.00

☐ **Fireman's helmet,** *present day. One piece black fiberglass skull with comb. Suspension liner. Leather chin strap. Specimens will be found with the front plate of various cities and towns. This example has the front plate of the arms of the city of Torino, and a flaming* *grenade superimposed upon crossed fire axes with the numerial "1" on the body of the grenade. Modern but traditional.* 75.00   100.00

Italian Fireman's helmet,
World War II era.

☐ **Fireman's helmet,** *World War II era. Skull roughly resembles the Italian military helmet of the period. Skull of grey/green fiber with green painted metal comb. Green leather chin strap. Front plate in brass consists of crossed fire axes and flaming grenade upon which is superimposed a shield bearing the arms of the particular city/province to whose brigade the wearer belonged. The price is the same for all helmets of this type.* 85.00   125.00

JAPAN

☐ **Antique Fireman's or Fire Watchers helmet.** *Characteristic samurai helmet of light weight, complete ;with provision for attaching protective fire cloak. Such helmets are extremely rare.* 3500.00   4000.00

UNITED STATES

☐ **Fire Boat Lieutenant's helmet.** *Black leather Carin made helmet with large white leather front plate bearing a large "9" in green in the center with a cartouche with the legend "LIEUTENANT" below. This helmet belonged to an officer aboard the fire boat*

Price Range

"FIREFIGHTER" of Marine 9 of the New York Fire
Department. 140.00   165.00

☐ **Enginme Company Lieutenant's helmet.** *Carin black
leather helmet with large front plate of white leather
bearing a large black sewn "51." Above is a black car-
touche bearing the word "LIEUTENANT" in white.
Below is a similar cartouche bearing the word
"ENGINE." This helmet belonged to a lieutenant of
Engine Company No. 51 of the Philadelphia Fire
Department.* 120.00   150.00

☐ **Old Aluminum Fireman's helmet.** *Black aluminum
helmet of classic style, made by Cairns. Tall leather
front plate bearing large painted "18" with the legend
"LADDER P. F. D. This is an interesting example of an
aluminum helmet.* 160.00   180.00

☐ **So-called Roman or South American Style Fireman's
helmet.** *White leather Roman helmet with crest.
Large brass front plate with brass scroll front plate
holder. Large "1" in brass applied in center of front
plate. Brass unit identifying scroll above numeral is
missing. Under the numerial is a cartouche bearing
"E & H."* 300.00   350.00

☐ **So-called Roman or South American Style Fireman's
helmet.** *As above, but of black leather. Front, side
and rear brim and visors somewhat wider however.
Large white leather front plate embossed in elaborate pattern. Legend "VICE PRESIDENT" in curved
cartouche across the top. Applied cypher "H & L 1" in
center of front plate.* 250.00   300.00

FLAGS, STANDARDS AND BANNERS

A **flag** is generally meant to mean a piece of cloth of different colors and
with different devices on it to identify the state, nation or organization which
it represents. It is usually attached to a staff or halyard. A **standard** may
mean a flag of a high ranking official or organization. Flags and **banners**
usually mean the same thing although some purists may use the term to indicate a modified type of flag used for decorative purposes. Although the terminology may differ in foreign usage and among specialists, the terms are
most often used interchangeably in the English language.

Military flags date back to very early times. We know that distinguishing
symbols carried at the top of a staff or pole were used by many ancient
peoples. However, it remained for the Romans of the Caesars to systematize
their use. By the Middle Ages military flags as we recognize them today were
being used by all armies in Europe and England and in some Eastern armies.
At first these were extremely large and became increasingly so. At length
they became too impractical for carrying into battle, as was the custom of
the times. Gradually they became smaller and more manageable. National

flags, monarch's standards and regimental colors were expensively made of colored silk and gold and silver embroidery. They were highly revered as high and holy things. They were carried by especially selected men, in many instances an officer, usually of a junior rank. In fact, the rank of ensign was given to the honored young officer who carried the flag or ensign as it was sometimes called.

On occasions the national flag alone was carried into battle, then the colors of the regiment and at times both. In any event, it was regarded as a great disgrace to lose the colors to the enemy. Many interesting accounts exist of the bravery displayed to protect the flag. Sometimes it was wrapped about the body of a soldier under his uniform so that he could escape with it. At times it might be burned or otherwise destroyed to prevent its capture. Such importance was placed on the flag that its capture signaled defeat and the troops to which it belonged gave up in despair.

The flag or colors in most armies were indeed high and holy and when worn out they were hung in the regimental church or kept in the regimental museum. Replacements were presented by royalty, high ranking government officials or military officers. Both the presentation and the "lay up" of the flags involved elaborate religious ceremonies.

In some armies the newly joined recruit took his oath to support, defend and give his life for his leaders and his country while placing one hand on the colors. This was considered a most serious action.

The very nature of modern warfare is such that it is highly impractical to carry flags into battle. Now they are kept at the unit's headquarters or church at home and are carried only on parade and other ceremonial occasions. It is rather interesting to note that following the defeat of Germany and the occupation of Berlin, Russian troops removed the German colors, many of the famous old Imperial regiments, and carried them in a victory parade in Moscow. Following the parade, they were placed on display in the Red Army Museum in Moscow. Other captured German flags are displayed in the Hall of Victory in the Army Museum in Warsaw, Poland. Still others are in military museums in England, West Germany and the United States. A few are in private hands and appear for sale or auction occasionally.

Small flags, guidons and banners of smaller military units of the Third Reich are much sought after collectors' items. Nazi leaders, fully realizing the morale value of such things, provided for a profusion and variety of flags of all sizes and kinds, ranging all the way from the personal standards of high ranking officials to smaller unit flags. By far the greatest interest today is in these flags of the Third Reich. They predominate in the following list because more of them are available. It is much easier to find a Nazi flag than it is to find those of other countries.

GERMANY (Third Reich)   Price Range

☐ **Afrika Korps Flag.** *Good quality bunting, black bordered flag with a silver color square forming the upper left quarter and the lower right quarter. Black squares form the lower left quarter and the upper right quarter. On the upper left silver quarter appears the Afrika Korps insignia of palm tree and swastika. On the lower right silver quarter appears the unit designation of "II/21."* 55.00   60.00

Price Range

☐ **Command Flag.** *For the Reich Minister for Air Travel. This flag also appeared in several sizes and materials according to the use to which it was to be put. This offering is a flag of bright red bunting. In the center is a white wreath surrounding a white center upon which appears a black eagle facing toward the staff. Details of the eagle are in yellow. Suspended from the bottom of the wreath is the blue and gold cross of the Pour le Merite. Gray color wings extend out from each side of the wreath. Extending from the wreath to the four corners of the flag are four white wedges trimmed in black. At the extreme outer end of each wedge is a black swastika. The reverse of this flag is the same as for the obverse except that the eagle within the wreath is replaced by a canted black swastika. The black swastikas at each corner of the flag are replaced by black eagles with yellow details.*   475.00   530.00

☐ **Command and Rank Flag.** *For a Grand Admiral of the German Navy. It was made in several sizes and materials depending upon the use to which it was to be put. This example which was offered for sale is two sided of white bunting material. Both sides of the flag are identical, consisting of a printed black Iron Cross outlined in black and white. Upon the cross appear two crossed admiral's batons printed in gold with white and black details. Superimposed upon the batons is a Wehrmacht eagle printed in gold, with details in black, grasping a gold color swastika. This specimen complete with lanyards. ....*   380.00   425.00

☐ **DAF Pennon.** *Intended for mounting on an automobile. Red cloth pennon shape flag with white outlined black cogwheel in the center. White disk occupies the center of the cogwheel upon which appears a canted black swastika, white district triangle on upper staff side, no protective case.* 65.00   90.00

☐ **Engineer Standarte.** *Basically the same as Infantry Standarte except that the flag itself is of high quality black silk.* 4600.00   5500.00

☐ **German Labor Front Flag** *(DAF). Red cloth flag with DAF insignia of black cogwheel, outlined in white with a white center upon which appears a canted black swastika, all sewed on. In the upper left hand corner of the flag appears a small brown rectangle upon which the DAF district name and number "Munster 7" are embroidered in white. The rectangle is enclosed in a blue border, silver fringe to three sides of the flag.* 360.00   400.00

☐ **Hitler Youth Banner.** *To be mounted on an automobile. Square yellow cloth flag bearing the eagle, diamond and swastika insignia of Hitler Youth in color.*

DAF Pennon for automobile mounting.

Hitler Youth Banner for automobile mounting.

Price Range

Flag bound in narrow leather, interesting and fairly rare, bears the embroidered inscription "Reichsjugenfuhrung." 340.00   375.00

Price Range

☐ **Infantry Standarte.** *Flag of high quality white silk, upon this is a black silk Iron Cross extending out to all edges of the flag. The sides of the cross are outlined in aluminum thread. Superimposed upon the center of the cross is a white silk disk outlined in appliqued oak leaves. Occupying the center of the disk is a black Wehrmacht eagle grasping a canted black swastika. In each of the corners of the flag is a black silk swastika outlined in aluminum thread. Three sides of the flag bear aluminum fringe.* 4600.00 5500.00

☐ **Kreigsmarine Standarte.** *Light blue flag of excellent quality silk. In the center is a white silk disk surrounded by appliqued garland of oak leaves in gold. Upon the disk is a black swastika outlined in white and black and in a canted position. Radiating from the disk to each of the four corners of the flag are the white silk arms of a cross outlined in gold. The top end of the cross on the staff side bears a gold anchor. The bottom one bears a black Iron Cross. The position of these is reversed on the outer end of the flag. The anchors are embroidered in gold thread and gold fringe appears on three sides of the flag. The other side of this flag is basically the same except that a black Iron Cross edged in silver replaces the swastika and a gold embroidered Wehrmacht eagle replaces the Iron Crosses. This is a beautiful example of a rare flag.* 3700.00 4100.00

☐ **Luftwaffe Squadron Flag.** *Will be found in several sizes, top and bottom bars of black with a gold bar between, in the center of the flag, a silver Luftwaffe eagle and swastika, printed on good quality bunting.* 50.00 55.00

☐ **Luftwaffe Standarte.** *Flag of high quality dark yellowish silk, in the center is a white silk disk outlined in silver oak leaves. Upon the disk is a black silk Iron Cross outlined in aluminum. Radiating from the disk to the four corners of the flag are the arms of a cross in white silk. At the end of each arm of the cross is a black silk swastika outlined in silver thread. Aluminum thread decorates three sides of the flag, the other side of the flag is the same except that the leaves encircling the central white disk are laurel instead of oak. In lieu of the Iron Cross on the disk, there appears a Luftwaffe eagle with the outstretched wings extending beyond the wreath. The eagle faces toward the staff side of the flag and grasps a silver swastika. A black silk swastika outlined in silver decorates the extreme ends of the cross.* 4600.00 5100.00

☐ **National War Flag of the Third Reich.** *This flag appeared in several sizes according to use. This offer is of very good quality bunting printed in highest*

Price Range

quality dye. The red flag has a white disk in the center outlined in white, black, white. Upon the disk appears a canted swastika outlined in white and black. The arms of a black cross extends to each side of the flag. This cross is outlined in white, black, white. In the upper left corner of the flag appears a black Iron Cross outlined in white, black, white. Frequently offered for sale. 100.00   110.00

☐ **Nazi Naval Flag.** Red cloth field with printed black anchor upon which is superimposed a white disk and black swastika. 15 x 22." 50.00   55.00

☐ **Nazi Panzer Standarte.** Flag of pink color high quality silk. Finely embroidered brown Reich's eagle within silver embroidered wreath, all superimposed upon a black Iron Cross outlined in black and white. A black swastika outlined in white in each corner, silver fringe. 3800.00   4200.00

☐ **NSDAP Reichsleiter Pennon.** Black and white cloth pennon shape flag with stylized NSDAP eagle in silver with black details. Eagle grasps a swastika within a wreath. On the left side of this device appears the German Gothic initial "R," on the other "L." Complete with clear plastic and red leather foul weather protective case and metal mounting brackets, unusual offering. 835.00   930.00

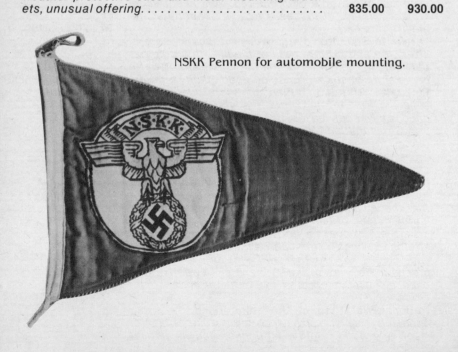

NSKK Pennon for automobile mounting.

Price Range

☐ **NSKK Pennon.** *For automobile mounting, red cloth pennon shape flag bound with black and white cord. Silver color NSKK insignia in cloth of spread wing eagle grasping a black swastika within a wreath and with a silver ribbon above the eagle's head, bearing the initials "NSKK" in black, appears in the center of the flag, upon a white disk outlined in black, white, black. An interesting offering but not at all rare.* **45.00** **50.00**

NSKK Pennon for wall hanging.

☐ **NSKK War Pennon.** *Intended for hanging with the point down. Red cloth pennon shape flag with NSKK insignia embroidered on a white disk.* **100.00** **115.00**

☐ **Personal Standard.** *For Adolph Hitler as Leader and Supreme Commander of the Armed Forces. An interesting and most prized offering. Again as was the case with many other flags, this standard was made in several materials. For parade and ceremonial purposes, the flag was of highest quality silk with silver*

Price Range

and gold embroidery, size varied. For other occasions, the flag as of bunting with bright colorfast designs and symbols. It is this type which is sometimes (but not very often) offered for sale or at auctions. The present offering is of good quality bunting, the square flag being a bright red outlined with a narrow black band, a wider white band and a still wider black band on the outside. In the center of the flag is a large white disk upon which is printed a wreath of gold color oak leaves, bound top and bottom and sides with a gold ribbon. Within this, the arms touching the wreath, is a large upright swastika outlined in white and black. In the upper left and lower right corners of the flag, within the border, appears the Nazi Party eagle printed in gold. In the other corners appear gold printed Wehrmacht eagles, thus signifying that Hitler was head of both party and armed forces. **475.00   525.00**

☐ **Personal Standard.** For Adolph Hitler as Leader and Supreme Commander of the Armed Forces. This is a once in a life time offering of Hitler's ceremonial and parade standard. Heavy superior quality red silk with a white silk disk upon which is a heavy gold bullion wreath. Within the wreath is a black swastika with narrow black and white border. On the upper left corner and the lower right corner are the Nazi party emblems of eagle wreath and swastika embroidered in gold bullion. In the upper right hand corner and the lower left hand corner are the Wermach emblems of an eagle grasping a swastika, all embroidered in gold bullion. The standard has a wide black outer border with a narrow silver border and a still narrower black border within. The standard is the same on both sides. This standard is fully documented as authentic. 38 x 38". **13200.00   14575.00**

☐ **Personal Standard.** For Herman Goering as Reichmarschall of the Greater German Reich (2nd Pattern). This was an extremely rare item which aroused great interest when it was offered at auction. Pale blue flag of extremely fine silk. In the center of the flag appears a large Wehrmacht eagle embroidered in gold thread facing toward the staff. The eagle grasps a wreath of gold laurel leaves upon which are superimposed crossed Reichmarschall's batons in white with details worked in gold and gray. Superimposed upon the batons is a gold swastika with small black Iron Crosses within the inner angle of each arm. The wreath is bound top and bottom with gold edged crimson ribbon. About the flag is a blue border formed by a narrow yellow/gold line on

Top Row: American Flag; British Flag; World War I Imperial German Battle Flag; Weimer Republic Naval Ensign; Third Reich (Nazi) Battle Flag.
Middle Row: Reichsmarshall Goering's Personal Standard (1st pattern); Hitler's Personal Standard; Command Flag for the Reich Minister of Air Travel; Japanese Rising Sun Battle Flag.
Botton Row: Luftwaffe Squadron Flag; SS Headquarters Flag; Afrika Korps Flag.

	Price Range	

the inside and a wider line on the outside. Within this border is a pattern of laurel leaves and berries. The wreath is tied at each corner by a gold bordered crimson ribbon upon which is superimposed a Balken Cross in black and white and black edges. A historically important offering. **7800.00   8650.00**

☐ **Reichs Labor Service Flag** *(RAD). Red cloth flag with large black cloth canted swastika in the center. Superimposed upon the center of the swastika is a large circle of leaves with the RAD shovel and grain insignia on the white background in the center. The top left corner bears the name "Peter Muhlenberg" in silver thread, three sides of this flag bear silver fringe.* .   **330.00   375.00**

☐ **SS Headquarters Flag.** *Good quality bunting, printed. A silver color triangle with the base at each end of the rectangular flag meet in the center with their apex. Black triangles form the top and the bottom of the flag with the apex meeting in the center. Superimposed in the center of the flag is the Nazi Party eagle in silver with black details.* **50.00   55.00**

☐ **SS Unit Car Pennon.** *White rectangular flag printed with a wide black outline triangle occupying half of the flag with the base forming the left or staff side*

Price Range

and the apex extending to the upper right corner. Within the triangle appears the Party eagle in silver with black details, on the lower right half of the flag appears the Roman numeral "VIII." This flag was intended for display on an automobile. 300.00   335.00

☐ **Staff Pennon.** *Of the National Master of the Forests. This was an office once occupied by Herman Goering. Pennon shape flag for display on an automobile. This offering came complete with the nickel-steel mounting staff. Green pennon embroidered in silver with a stag's head with a disk between the antlers bearing a black canted swastika. On the flag in two lines appears the inscription in silver "Stab/Reichsjagermeister," all embroidered. Pennon edged in silver, all complete within its clear plastic foul weather case. This was a rare offering.* 600.00   675.00

☐ **Trumpet Banner.** *Silk parade banner of the 34th Infantry Regiment. Fine quality white silk banner with Iron Cross outlined in silver wire. In the center of the cross is a Wermach eagle embroidered in natural colors, all on a white silk background. About the eagle is a silver embroidered wreath with a gold embroidered knot at the bottom. In each corner of the standard is a black silk swastika outlined in silver wire. There is silver fringe about three sides of the banner. On the reverse of the banner on the white field is a silver embroidered wreath enclosing the regimental cypher, "JR" over "34," 18 x 18".* 575.00   650.00

☐ **Trumpet Banner.** *Silk parade trumpet banner of the NSDAP - the Nazi Party. Front side of banner is of high quality red silk upon which is the gold wire embroidered eagle, wreath and swastika of the Nazi Party. The reverse of the banner is white silk with a city coat of arms finely embroidered in full color. Gold fringe appears on three sides of the banner.* . . .   575.00   650.00

GERMANY (Imperial)

☐ **Jager zu Pferde Shellambaum Banner.** *This extremely interesting flag was suspended from the shellambaum or "Jingling Johnny" which was an essential part of every German military band. The extremely high quality silk banner is composed of gold silk wedges forming an Iron Cross within the arms of which appear alternate black and white silk wedges which form a cross of their own. In the center is a black eagle of Frederick the Great grasping a gold sword in one talon and thunderbolts in the other, all embroidered on a white silk disk outlined with a gold wreath of oak and laurel leaves. At the top of the wreath appears a royal crown embroidered in red and gold. On each arm of the Iron Cross is an embroi-*

Jager zu Pferde Shellabaum Banner.

Price Range

dered gold flaming bomb, edges of the banner
trimmed in gold color cord with long fringe at the bottom, banner hangs from a bronze rod with a large
gold thread tassel at each end. An Imperial German
banner of this type and quality is seldom offered. ... 1210.00 2100.00

☐ **War Flag.** These came in several sizes and of different materials depending upon the use for which
intended. The very large ones were used on battleships and for garrison flags. Smaller sizes had a
variety of use. This specimen is of very fine quality
bunting with printed details. It is marked to the
Imperial Navy and is of a size which was probably
used on a medium size war craft. On the white field
appears a black cross with straight arms extending
to each edge of the flag. This cross is outlined in
white and black. In the center of the cross appears a
white disk upon which is a black Imperial Eagle with
gold details. In the upper left side of the flag (staff
side) between the arms of the cross appear three
horizontal bars — black, white, red, from top to bottom. Superimposed upon the center of this is a black
Iron Cross outlined in white and black. 335.00   375.00

GERMANY (Weirmar Republic)

Flag of a Feri Korps Unit.

Price Range

☐ **Flag of a Frei Korps Unit.** *This homemade flag was used by a unit of the infamous Free Corps which literally ruled Germany shortly after World War I. Many of these units formed the basis of the later Nazi outfits. The reverse side of the flag is the same as the obverse. In the center of the black cloth rectangular flag is sewn a fairly crude skull and crossbones, under which appears in red the letter "W." This letter no doubt refers to "Werewolf" since that name was frequently used by some of these units. In the upper left hand corner of the obverse of the flag is a well-executed black Iron Cross outlined in white and black. On the upper arm in white appears the Imperial Crown. On the lower arm appears the date "1813," the date of the institution of the Iron Cross. In the center of the cross, in white, is a "W" for Wilhelm II. The members of the Free Corps were former officers and men of the Imperial Germany army. The use of the Iron Cross indicates their loyalty to the ideals of the old government. Flags of this kind were carried in the Free Corps' many deadly street battles. Free Corps flags are not often seen.* 750.00 825.00

GREAT BRITAIN

Price Range

☐ **1st Life Guards Standard,** *c. 1890. This is a crimson silk damask banner of very high quality. Three sides are trimmed with gold fringe, bullion Union Badge in the center of Thistle, Rose and Shamrock, with gold and red Royal Crown above. The badge bears a ribbon reading "DIEU ET MON DROIT." On one side of the badge is a gold crowned "V" and on the other a gold crowned "R." The lower part of the standard, from side to side, carries the battle honors "DETTINGEN" "PENINSULA" "WATERLOO" "EGYPT 1882" "TEL-EL-KEBIR." Mounted on original fluted staff, finial is a lion standing on a crown, complete with bullion cords and tassels.* **875.00   975.00**

☐ **21st Light Dragoons Standard,** *c. 1780. High quality double thickness crimson banner with heavy silver fringe about all but the staff edge. Flag is of the so-called swallow tail design. In the center appears a hand-painted design of thistles and roses in color. Across the bottom of this design on a ribbon appears the legend "DIEU ET MON DROIT" (God is my Right.). In the upper left and lower right of the flag appears a gold cartouche within which is the Horse of Hannover. In the other corners appears a gold cartouche bearing the Roman numerals "XXI" together with the initials "LD," referring to the 21st Light Dragoons. Over the central design in the center of the flag appears the Royal Crown. Attached to the staff side of the banner is the original gold bullion, silk and worsted cord and tassels. This is a most rare and beautiful flag of a famous British Regiment.* **4700.00   5200.00**

Note: At the present time the major interest in this country appears to be, as far as British flags are concerned, regimental standards. The Union Jack itself attracts little note unless proof exists that the particular artifact has a positive historic connotation. This type of item appears very rarely and therefore is not included here.

AUSTRIA-HUNGARY

☐ **Printed Banner.** *On good quality cotton cloth, black and white background with the arms of the Dual Kingdom in full color in the center. Surrounding the lower half of the black double-headed eagle, which forms the background for the armorial shield, is a wreath in full color tied at the bottom with colored ribbons. The purpose for which this type of banner was made is unknown. However, it is a most beautiful and desirable artifact.* **180.00   200.00**

UNITED STATES OF AMERICA

☐ **18 Regiment, U.S. Infantry.** *This offering consisted of important identifying portions of a regimental color*

Price Range

of a famous Regular Army Infantry Regiment. The blue silk flag itself has disintegrated but all identifying portions remain, including a large American eagle with shield on breast. One talon grasps laurel leaves and berries while the other grasps war arrows, all in proper colors. In its beak it holds a ribbon bearing the legend "E PLURIBUS UNUM." In the collection is the scroll which goes below the eagle with the words "18th REGIMENT U.S. INFANTRY." In themselves these pieces are very valuable artifacts of a famous regiment which distinguished itself, particularly during the Civil War. 1900.00   2100.00

☐ **Naval Jack.** This is the famous rectangular Confederate flag of bright red with a blue St. Andrew's cross superimposed upon it, with 13 white stars evenly spaced on the arms of the cross. Officially, the rectangular flag was for the naval service and the square flag, bearing the same design, was for the army. It is most often referred to as the "battle flag." This particular specimen is made of heavy linen and is entirely handmade. It shows aging and is somewhat tattered on the fly end. It is entirely authentic, genuine flags of the American Civil War are extremely difficult to find. 1650.00   1850.00

☐ **91st AAA AW Battalion Flag.** Rectangular red silk flag with large American eagle in the center with brown body, white head and tail, holding green laurel leaves in the right talon and white war arrows in the left. Gold triangular device on a red and blue shield superimposed upon the breast of the eagle. A winged bomb appears within the triangular device, scroll under the eagle bears the legend "NINETY FIRST AAA AW BATTALION." 650.00   725.00

CONFEDERATE STATES OF AMERICA

☐ **Texas Regimental Flag.** Rectangular shape handmade flag of extremely high quality linen bound with white silk. The entire field in the upper left corner bears a single large white star, the remainder of the flag is occupied with a wide red bar top and bottom with a wide white bar between. Flag reflects normal aging, colors still bright, few age holes. This is an extremely rare find, an authentic artifact, first such flag to be offered at public sale. 1875.00   2075.00

Note: The American Flag, Stars and Stripes, is not sought after by collectors unless documentation exists that it is historically important. There are a few collectors who have an interest in earlier flags whose stars reflect the number of states at a given time, for instance a 48 star flag. The price for this sort of flag varies so greatly that they are not considered here.

JAPAN

The two Japanese flags best known to Americans are the National flag and a variation. The National Flag has a red disk (the sun disk) on an all white field. It is known that this flag was used as early as 1592 and possibly earlier. This flag is sometimes referred to as a battle flag and to Americans fighting in the South Pacific it was known as the "meatball" flag. In various smaller sizes and usually made of silk, it was carried by the individual soldier on his person. These usually had Shinto prayers inscribed upon the white section. Others might have the names and/or comments written upon the white field. These inscriptions did not extend into the red disk. This is the type of Japanese flag sought after by collectors. The variation of the flag is a white field with the red sun disk slightly left of center and with red rays extending out to all sides of the flag. This type is not so popular unless it bears inscriptions or can be documented as an artifact with important historical association.

	Price Range	
☐ **Sun Disk Flag,** *silk, without inscriptions*............	27.00	30.00
☐ **Sun Disk Flag,** *silk, with numerous hand inscribed inscriptions.*	100.00	110.00

FLAG STAFF FINALS

The finials or ornaments decorating the top of a flag staff or pole are attracting increased collector interest. These items are fairly easy to display. They are easily mounted on a block of highly polished wood and require little maintenance except for an occasional dusting. All are extremely attractive. German finials are in most demand at the present time, particularly those of the Third Reich. The Napoleon "Eagle" which adorned the top of the staff of elite French regiments are also in considerable demand.

The origin of the flag staff finial is unknown. It appears that the earliest were in the form of a spear or pike head, the flags or banners simply being attached to a spear or pike shaft. Over the years, however, a variety of finials have been developed, usually of artistic design. The spear head type finial is still in use, particularly in this country.

AUSTRIA

☐ **Finial,** *c. mid-1800's. Large polished brass spear head finial with engraved edge on both sides. Both sides display an engraved cypher "FI," (Francis I) over which is an engraved Austrial royal crown.*	400.00	480.00

FRANCE

☐ **Finial,** *c. 1791. Large polished brass spear head finial with beveled edges. The lower part of the finial is pierced with a large fleur-de-lis. Infabtry use.*	300.00	350.00
☐ **Eagle finial,** *model of 1804. Large extremely well detailed bronze eagle, with wings wide spread and grasping thunder bolts. Extremely rare.*	1000.00	1200.00

GERMANY (Imperial Germany)

☐ **Finial From A Saxon Veterans, Organization Standard Staff.** *Gilt figure of Germania with sword in right hand and holding a large shield hearing the Imperial Eagle in the left. Mounted on an ornate socket. Unusual.* 900.00 1000.00

☐ **Finial From An Old Wurttemberg Infantry Regiment.** *This old finial dates from around 1807. Of gilt over bronze it is a rather solid and plain spear point design with some engraving around the edges. In the lower center is engraved the cypher "FR: (Fredrich Rex) under a crown. The finial is mounted on a rather long plain socket. This specimen shows some age but is historically important.* 850.00 900.00

☐ **Finial Of A Mecklenburg-Schwerin Infantry Regiment.** *An open work bronze spear head shape finial enclosing the crowned arms of Mecklenburg-Schwerin with the cypher "FF" (Friedrich Franz) on each quarter of the arms. This item has a long screw for attaching to the staff instead of being attached by a sleeve.* 450.00 650.00

☐ **Finial Of An Oldenburg Cavalry Standard.** *Open work bronze spear head design as above but attachment for staff is a sleeve or socket. There is a small ball at the point of the finial. Black enameled Iron Cross with silver edges within a floral wreath.* 400.00 450.00

☐ **Finial Of First Bodyguard Hussars, No. 1.** *This particular finial is from the shaft of the standard of a very famous Prussian hussar regiment. It is similar in design to the above except that there is no ball on the point. Also the finial is of silver instead of bronze. Accompanying the finial is a silver shaft collar bearing the inscription "TOBITSCHAU 15. JUIL 1866" and "H.R.No. 1." Also with the finial is a silver plate from the staff showing that the standard was presented to the regiment by the German Crown Prince on November 29, 1914. This is, of course, an extremely historic collection.* 2300.00 2600.00

☐ **Finial Of The Third Battalion,** *first Grand Ducal Hessian (Liebrade) Infantry, No. 115. Decorative open work spear head shape polished bronze finial enclosing a black enameled Iron Cross with silver edges. A crowned initial "L" is superimposed upon the cross. This striking finial belonged to a very famous unit.* . . 1000.00 1200.00

☐ **Reichsbahn Finial.** *This beautiful item once adorned the flag staff of a unit of the Imperial German rail system. The heavy open work spear head shape ornament is of gilt metal and encloses an ancient pattern winged railroad wheel with pierced spokes. All is enclosed within a delicate floral werath design. Extremely attractive. The workmanship is very good.* 125.00 175.00

Imperial German Reichsbahn Finial.

GERMANY (Third Reich)   Price Range

☐ **Deutschland Erwacht Finial.** *A very rare early Nazi finial. Extremely fine gilt, silver and enamel example. The large full figure eagle with much detail, in gilt, faces forward as though just alighting on top of a wreath made of silver oak leaves. A gilt ribbon winds about the wreath. The black enameled swastika with silver edges sets square within the wreath. The wreath is attached to a long silver flag staff socket. This is an excellent work of art which is seldom offered for sale.* 3300.00   3500.00

☐ **Enginner Unit Finial.** *Open work spear head of polished aluminium. Within the spear head is a silver Wehrmachtadler emblem of the Nazi eagle perched on a swastika. This was the standard Army finial.* . . . 175.00   200.00

☐ **HJ (Hitler Youth) Finial.** *Made in gold color plastic. A wreath encircling a swastika upon which is superimposed a Roman pattern sword with the blade extending well above the wreath. An Iron Cross within a circle occupies the lower end of the sword. Unique.* 75.00   100.00

☐ **Hoch-Und Deutschmeister Finial Of Grenadier-Regiment 134.** *This finial consists only of a broad gilt brass spear head without design of any kind. Since it is of such plain design it can be easily duplicated. Should be purchased only with complete authentication. This Austrian unit made up of three famous old regiments was part of the Nazi army. Thus finial is extremely rate.* 500.00   550.00

Luftwaffe Finial.

Price Range

☐ **Luftwaffe (Air Force) finial.** *Fairly well detailed Air Force eagle cast from silver colored metal alloy. This eagle is three dimensional. In its talons it clutches a silver alloy swastika which rests upon two sprigs of oak leaves which form a "V."* 175.00   200.00

☐ **Luftwaffe (Air Force) Finial.** *This example is similar in design but is rare for the excellent detailed execution of all parts. It is of nickeled steel as is the long socket which attaches to the staff. Heavy construction. Much finer than the usual Luftwaffe finial.* 800.00   850.00

☐ **Luftwaffe (Air Force) Schellenbaum Finial.** *This is by far the most beautiful Luftwaffe finial to yet be offered for sale. Similar in pattern to above but larger and in much finer detail. Eagle is of silver, as are the oak leaves. Swastika is high quality gilt. Cylindrical peg in base for attaching to staff.* 3000.00   3400.00

☐ **National Socialist Work Assistance Finial.** *Nickel cog wheel upon which is superimposed a swastika on a workman's hammer. Two sprigs of oak leaves at the base of the handle form a "V." Also at the base of the handle is a black rectangle with nickel border within which are the nickeled letters "NSAO." An acorn appears on each side of a cylindrical piece fitted with a metal spike for attaching to the shaft. One of a great variety of non-military finials.* 50.00   75.00

☐ **National Sports Association Finial.** *Nickel open work spear point finial enclosing the Sports Association*

	Price Range	

eagle with black swastika on breast. Fitted with long screw for attaching to staff. **50.00** **75.00**

☐ **Naval Land Unit Finial.** *Similar to the engineer unit except that the finial is made of gilt brass. This was the standard navy finial.* **175.00** **200.00**

☐ **NSDAP (Nazi Party) Finial.** *First type party eagle with little detail mounted over a flat open work circle enclosing a flat swastika. Very plain.* **70.00** **80.00**

☐ **NSDAP (Nazi Party) Finial.** *Similar to the above except that all is in fine detail and instead of the open work disk there is a well detailed wreath.* **100.00** **125.00**

Three Variations of the NSDAP (Nazi Party) Finial.

☐ **NSDAP (Nazi Party) Finial.** *Nickel plated party emblem of eagle atop wreath with black swastika with nickeled edge within the wreath. Common* **120.00** **150.00**

☐ **RAD (Labor Corps) Finial.** *Large silver finial in the form of a shovel with short handle merging into staff socket. Extending out from each side of the handle is a wheat head forming a "V."* **175.00** **200.00**

☐ **Reich's National Food Estate Finial.** *Large black swastika on long silvered socket. Across the swastika are a silver color Roman pattern sword and a gilt head of barley. A most interesting offering.* **250.00** **275.00**

☐ **Troop Carrier Finial.** *Large silvered open work wreath with fairly wee detailed 2x4 troop carrier at inside bottom. Wreath mounted on thich ornamented disk*

Reich's National Food Estate Finial.

	Price Range	
from the bottom of which projects a screw for attaching to shaft.	**125.00**	**150.00**

☐ **Veteran League Finial.** *Cast and polished bronze device consisting of an open work circle supporting an open work spear head. Within the lower half of the spear head is a balck and white painted shield of the Kyffhauser Memorial. Within the circle is a large swastika in polished bronze upon which is supperimposed an Iron Cross painted black with white edge. Supporting the bottom of the circle is a bronze "V" device upon which appear oak leaves. . . . .*   **80.00**   **90.00**

ITALY

☐ **Savoy Cavalry Finial.** *Tall, graceful open work spear head with the metal embossed in scroll design. Enclosed in the lower half is the cross of Savoy on a crowned shield within a laurel wreath. Bottom of finial has short peg for attaching to staff. All in gilt metal. . . . .*   **250.00**   **300.00**

RUSSIA (Imperial)

☐ **Infantry Finial.** *Open work bronze spear head enclosing the crowned two head Imperial Russian eagle. Very little detail. Long socket attached to staff. Only fairly attractive but historically interesting. . . . .*   **250.00**   **300.00**

Savoy (Italy) Cavalry Finial.

RUSSIA (Soviet)	Price Range	
☐ **Military Finial.** *Plain open work spear head. Five-point star in upper angle. Crossed hammer and sickle in lower half. Heavy staff socket with flange on each side. All of highly polished nickeled steel.*	200.00	250.00

GORGETS

A gorget, in the sense in which it is used here, refers to a small metal shield or crescent shape decorative device worn by officers and certain elite personnel such as standard bearers. It originated in the metal protective piece, sometimes a part of the helmet but more often a separate piece of armor. In the latter instance, it usually had a collar to which the helmet attached. Its purpose was to provide protection for the neck and at times, depending upon the style of the armor, protection for the shoulders as well. The gorget which we are not considering is but a mere vestige of the original. It bears some identifying device and is attached usually to a silk cord or chain links which encircle the neck. It was sometimes attached directly to the front of the uniform. In any instance it hung over the breast. It was quite popular as a means of identifying officers of all armies during the 1700's and the early 1800's. Its use thereafter was largely restricted to the Imperial German armies. Then with the advent of Nazi control, the gorget was given a new lease on life, appearing in several patterns. Most Nazi organizations, military or political, had their own identifying gorget. English gorgets are, of course, particularly popular in England and to a lesser extent in Europe and the

Price Range

United States. Nazi gorgets, however, are almost universally popular as collectors' items.

☐ **Bavarian gorget,** *pre-1886 period. Half-moon pattern, silver plate, center device consisting of the Bavarian lion and a shield bearing the cypher "L" (Ludwig), no neck chain.* 100.00   110.00

☐ **British Officer's gorget.** *Georgian period, 1714-1830. Deep crescent shape, of gilted copper. Engraved with the cypher "GR" with the Royal Crown above and a spray of laurel leaves on each side. The gorgets of this period are those most often offered for sale. They are of beautiful workmanship. Without the lining these gorgets are usually offered in the price range indicated, the price depending upon the size and the quality of workmanship.* 125.00   225.00

☐ **As above,** *but a gorget belonging to an officer of the 2nd Foot Guards. Bears the Royal Arms in relief in lieu of engraved cypher.* 225.00   250.00

☐ **As above,** *engraved with the cypher "GR" with Royal Crown above and with laurel leaves on each side, excellent workmanship, reverse side lined with chamois, blue lace rosette at each end.* 200.00   225.00

☐ **As above,** *but specifically of the reign of George III. Beautifully engraved with the King's Arms and with delicate engraving at each end of gorget.* 200.00   225.00

☐ **As above,** *but a gorget of an Irish volunteer or militia unit. This gorget is engraved with a crowned Irish harp with motto below and decorative treatment about the harp. Lace rosette at each end.* 400.00   435.00

☐ **As above,** *pre-1801. Engraved with the Arms of George III with the initial "G" on one side of the crown and "R" on the other.* 220.00   250.00

☐ **As above,** *but a rare gorget belonging to an officer of the East India Company. Center deeply engraved with the Company Arms, decorative engraving on each arm of the gorget.* 475.00   525.00

☐ **Nazi Labor Corps RAD Standard Bearer's gorget.** *Heart shape silver color gorget, liner, identifying device on the center consisting of a pointed shovel bearing a large relief swastika. Two wheat stalks form a "V" with the shovel handle. The RAD motto "ARBEIT ADELT" or "WORK ENOBLES" appears near the top of the gorget. Link neck chain.* 300.00   340.00

☐ **Nazi NSKK or Nationalsozialistischen Kraftfahr-Korps (National Socialist Motor Corps) Standard Bearer's gorget.** *Metal half-moon shape gorget with raised and rounded edges, gilt-plated. The remainder of the gorget is gray. In the center of the gorget is an applied gilt NSKK insignia of a stylized Nazi eagle with outspread wings grasping the usual wreath*

Officer's Gorget, Georgian Period.

Officer Gorget,
Honorable East India Company.

Price Range

encircling a swastika. Above the eagle appears a curved bandeau bearing the initials "N S K K." Cloth covered reverse side to gorget, neck chain of closely interlocking nickel-plated rings. 385.00   425.00

Price Range

☐ **Nazi Political Leaders gorget.** *The standard bearer's gorget of this organization is of a modified shield pattern in plated bronze. There is an ornamented embossed edge to the gorget. In the center is a styl-ized eagle with slightly upswept wings. The eagle's talons grasp a wreath within which is a swastika. The neck chain is composed of flat sections joined by chain links. The design on these sections is alter-nated, one bearing a swastika within a wreath and the other bearing an eagle grasping a swastika within a wreath. This gorget is lined with green felt...*   325.00   365.00

☐ **Nazi Polizei (Police) Flag Bearer's gorget.** *Half-moon shape gorget of aluminum, matte finish with raised and polished ridge about the edges. The center is occupied by an aluminum Polizei device of an eagle with widespread wings grasping a wreath within which is a swastika in relief. All this is superimposed on a large wreath of oak leaves and acorns. Orna-mental boss at each end of gorget, cloth liner on reverse of gorget, neck chain of aluminum links and wire loops.* 420.00   465.00

Nazi SA Standard Bearer's Gorget.

Price Range

☐ **Nazi SA or Sturmabteilung (Storm Detachment) Standard Bearers gorget.** *This was the first official gorget of the Third Reich. Nickel-plated shield or heart-shape metal gorget. Affixed to the center is a gilt heraldic star in the center of which is a gilt rope edge disk. Within the circle formed by the edge is another rope circle design together with a silver color eagle with outspread wings. The eagle grasps a wreath within which is a mobile swastika. Under this is a half wreath. A large gilt boss appears on each side of the top of the gorget. Nickel-plated rings form the neck chain. Back lined with dark blue cloth.* 560.00   625.00

☐ **Nazi SS or Schutzstaffel (Protective Squad) Guard Duty gorget.** *Half-moon shape nickel-plated gorget with raised edge. At the top center is a metal circle enclosing a black disk. In the center of the disk are two nickel-plated SS runes. Below this disk appears a bandeau bearing the word "STREIFENDIENST" (Guard Duty). At each corner of the gorget is a gilt boss. Neck chain is of wire links.* 560.00   625.00

☐ **Nazi Veterans League (Deutscher Reichskrieger-bund) Standard Bearers gorget.** *Modified half-moon pattern of silver color metal with raised edge. In the center is a white shield upon which appears a profile of the German War Memorial, the Kyffhauser, in black. This rests on a red base upon which is super-imposed a white disk with a black swastika. All of this is in enamel. On either side of the shield is a branch of oak leaves. Behind all this is a trophy of Imperial German battle flags, two on each side of the shield. At each corner of the gorget is a button-like fastener of brass or gilt. The neck chain is composed of flat links joined by oval rings. The design on these links alternates. On one is a swastika, on the other is the Iron Cross.* 300.00   335.00

☐ **NSKK Verkehrs-Erziehungsdienst (Traffic Control) gorget.** *Extremely wide half-moon shape stamped aluminum gorget with raised edges. Stamped into the gorget are the NSKK insignia with the legend "N.S.K.K. VERKEHRS - ERZIEHUNGSDIENST" stamped around the bottom curve of the gorget. The gorget plate is spray painted black while the raised insignia and legend are aluminum. Earlier gorgets have a serial number above the insignia, each numeral being sepa-rate and attached by prongs. Later gorgets had the serial number stamped into the gorget. In either case they are aluminum color. This gorget is backed with green cloth. The neck chain is attached to each end of the gorget by aluminum unornamented bosses and consists of an oval link connected to a smaller double link, all in aluminum.* 385.00   425.00

Nazi Veterans League Standard Bearer's Gorget.

NSKK Traffic Control Man's Gorget.

Prussian Flag Bearer's Gorget, Imperial Germany.

	Price Range	

☐ **Prussian Flag Bearer's gorget,** *Imperial Germany. White metal open crescent or half-moon pattern. Applied gilt Prussian Crown in center with crossed flags behind. Under the crown is the cypher "WR" (Wilhelm Rex). At each corner of the gorget an applied gilt flaming grenade, neck chain of gilt oval and alternate round links.* 250.00   275.00

☐ **Prussian Officer's gorget,** *Prussian Guard Infantry Regiments, c. late 1700's. Extremely wide and deep, polished steel gorget. This more closely approximates a piece of armor but is, of course, smaller. Gilt edges and a gilt boss at each end. Covering almost the entire gorget is an applied gilt design consisting of the Prussian Crown below which is a large inset white disk upon which is a black Prussian Eagle with gilt beak, crown, scepter and other details. Upon the breast of the eagle appears the crowned royal cypher "FWR," all in enamel work. About this disk and the large crown above appears a gilt well detailed trophy of arms, armor and flags. This is a rare and beautiful item much sought after by advanced collectors.* 655.00   725.00

☐ **Prussian Standard Bearer's gorget,** *Prussian Guard Infantry Regiments. Highly polished silver color half-moon shape gorget. The entire center is occupied with a stamped Star of the Order of the Black Eagle with the Prussian Crown above, superimposed upon*

	Price Range	
crossed regimental flags, all in brass. At each end of the gorget is a stamped brass flaming grenade. Neck chain of alternating flat oval and round pieces joined by small rings....................................	315.00	350.00

HALBERDS

Basically the halberd is a weapon with an ax-like head with a point or beak on the opposite end, mounted on a fairly long shaft or pole, with a long spike projecting above the ax head. It first appeared in the 1200's. Introduced in northern Europe its use soon spread to France and other European countries and to England. As originally conceived it was intended for use by unmounted soldiers. The side opposite the ax blade was sometimes curved and forged in the shape of a knife. All in all it was a wicked weapon as an ax like weapon can be. The long spike added to its utility and the beak opposite the ax could be used to unhorse a mounted warrior or at least cut the horse's bridle. The halberd gradually fell into disuse with the development of more efficient weapons, particularly firearms, being retained largely as an insignia of rank and for use by ceremonial guards. The latter day halberds were often issued with a velvet covered shaft and extremely ornate engraved and ornamented head. In this country collector interest is particularly active in the area of native American halberds of the Revolutionary War era.

GREAT BRITAIN

☐ **Artillery halberd,** c. mid-1700's. Long four sided spike, pierced ax blade with broad leaf shaped projection opposite the ax head, which is deeply crescent, stout long oak shaft. This is probably a sergeants' halberd.................................. 940.00 1050.00
☐ **Ceremonial halberd,** head only, c. mid-1800's. Extremely ornate pierced ax head with unusually long four-sided spike........................... 290.00 325.00

GERMANY

☐ **Combat halberd,** c. mid-1500's. Fairly small ax head and beak with pierced design on crescent shaped blade, very long diamond section spike, long shaft protected with straps. 245.00 275.00
☐ **Combat halberd,** probable late 1500's. Fairly large ax head and beak, both with pierced designs. Heavy medium length diamond section spike, deep crescent blade, mounted on long shaft with protective straps. An excellent well preserved example. 350.00 400.00

SWITZERLAND

☐ **Authentic halberds.** Famed Swiss foot troops of earlier times are very few and far between. However

Price Range

this offering is an excellent specimen from the mid-1500's. Mounted on a long octagonal shaft is a large ax head with pierced shallow crescent blade. In lieu of the usual beak to the rear of the blade there is a claw like device in steel. The diamond section spike is only fairly long. Shaft decorated with brass studs. There is a red silk tasseled decoration at the base of the head. This is a very unusual specimen. 695.00 775.00

UNITED STATES

☐ **Colonial halberd,** *American-made. Large fancy pierced shallow crescent blade with pierced beak terminating in a sharp point. Flat long spear point with etched and pierced design. Socket and side straps. Original maple shaft. Museum quality, showing normal aging. Rarely offered on the collector's market.* 2750.00 3050.00

☐ **Colonial halberd,** *American-made. The blade and beak of this offering is generally similar to the above specimens, but has a different pierced design. The narrow leaf spear point is similar in design to the above but is larger and bears pierced "S" shaped designs. Straps to shaft all intact. The oak shaft is original. Condition of halberd is consistent with age. Some pitting, no rust and no worming of wood.* 2650.00 2950.00

☐ **Colonial halberd,** *American-made. This specimen is crudely made and was obviously hammered out by some local blacksmith for a member of the militia. Fairly small curved ax blade with plain simple semi-hooked beak. Medium length narrow leaf shaped spear point. In lieu of a socket and side straps the halberd head has a spike which was forced into the top of the shaft. No shaft. Halberds of this type are hardly ever found with the shaft for it became easily detached. Nonetheless specimens of the local blacksmith's weaponery are much sought after by colonial arms collectors. Normal pitting consistent with age.* 950.00 1060.00

☐ **Colonial halberd,** *American-made. Very similar to the above specimen and by the same maker. Although the design is the same there are some minor differences due to hand crafting. Among other things the narrow leaf type spear point is smaller. Rarely offered. Original shaft. Normal aging.* 2625.00 3000.00

☐ **Revolutionary War Period halberd,** *head only. Large pierced deep crescent blade with large pierced beak to rear. Fairly short diamond section spike, socket and long straps for attachment to shaft. Shaft has rotted away. Good specimen.* 325.00 375.00

HEADDRESS

MILITARY CAPS

The cap, along with the hat, is one of the oldest uniform items. Its origin is unknown. Quite likely it was at first an adaptation of a similar kind of civilian headgear. Very broadly defined, a cap is a type of headdress without an all-around brim. It may or may not have a visor. It appears in a great variety of shapes, colors and materials. Patterns vary from stylish to downright ugly. Caps with a visor and with either a stiff or a soft crown are often worn for both dress and off-duty wear. Soft caps without a visor and with little or no form, sometimes known as forage caps, are often worn for field duty. A fairly small soft cap sometimes used for both field service and off-duty wear is common to most armies. In the American service, this particular type of cap is frequently referred to as an "overseas cap" inasmuch as its wear was first restricted to American troops serving in Europe during World War I. It immediately became so popular with the troops that its design was greatly improved and its use is prescribed in this country where it is still worn on certain occasions.

As might be expected, caps of the Imperial German Army came in a great variety of colors. Generally this headdress was known in its several forms as a field cap (feldmutze), duty cap (dienstmutze) and officer's cap (offiziersmutze). The officer's and noncommissioned officer's cap were provided with a black visor and were rather sharp looking, particularly the caps of officers which were of extremely high quality. The other ranks cap did not have a visor. No chin strap was worn. The band about the bottom of the cap and the braid trim varied according to the branch of service and the regiment. On the front of the cap were two metal cockarden or rosettes, worn one above the other. The upper one was in the national colors — red, white and black. The lower was in the color of the country to which the regiment or unit belonged, i.e., black and white for Prussia; dark green, Anhalt; yellow and red, Baden; light blue and white, Bavaria; light blue and yellow, Brunswick; white and red, Hanse Towns of Bremen, Hamburg and Lubeck; red and white, Hesse; yellow and red, Lippe, red, yellow and blue, Mecklenburg; blue and red, Oldenburg; yellow, red and black, Reuss; green and white, Saxony; green and white, Saxon Dutchies; green, black and yellow, Saxe-Weimar; dark blue and white, Schwarzburg; black, red and yellow, Waldeck and black and red, Wurttemberg.

The cockarden of officers are extremely well detailed and well made and those of noncommissioned officers are also distinctive from those of other ranks which are not as ornate. In the case of reserve units, a small silver or silver color Maltese cross appears on the lower cockarden. The 1st and 2nd Body Guard Hussars and the 17th Hussars have a small silver or silver color metal skull and crossbones between the two cockarden.

The uniforms of the Third Reich, although utilitarian, were extremely well designed and were perhaps the smartest worn by any of the World War II armies. They had a certain "dash" about them that made them neat and distinctive. This is particularly true of the headdress. The visored cap or **schirmmutze** had a certain flair about it unequalled by any other military cap. It was worn with certain modifications by all members of the land and aviation forces. The color and insignia varied from service branch to service branch and according to rank, a feature which delights collectors. Although originally intended as a dress cap, it was so popular that it was often worn in the field. Another interesting item of headdress is the M-38 Other Ranks Field Service Cap. Of gray/green material, this somewhat resembled in pattern the old American overseas caps except that it was of a larger pattern. On the front of this cap was an inverted cloth "V" in the color of the branch of service. These colors, "Waffenfarben," were as follows: infantry, white; mountain troops, bright green; cavalry, yellow; tank troops, pink; artillery, red; signals, lemon yellow; engineers, black; and medical, cornflower blue. A red, white and black rosette appeared in the angle of the "V" and over this was the conventional Nazi emblem of stylized Nazi eagle with outspread wings grasping a wreath with swastika within it.

All members of the Nazi Army mountain troups and ski troops wore a field gray/gray-green cloth soft cap with stiff cloth covered visor. It had a turn down flap arrangement which folded up and back against the body of the cap and was secured by two pebble grain aluminum buttons. Above these appeared the cloth red, white and black cockard and Nazi eagle, wreath and swastika. On the left side of this cap, known as the **Bergmutze** (mountain cap), was a metal pin in the design of the leaves and bloom of the Edelweiss. This cap was patterned after the service cap of the old Imperial Austrian Army and the Edelweiss device was borrowed from the Austrian mountain troops. This cap with its rather long rakish visor had a very smart appearance and such style that the pattern has been copied for recent winter caps in this country for civilian wear. Incidentally, the field gray/gray-green color was the same as that for most headgear of the Nazi troops, except tank units which was black.

The M-43 general issue field cap or **Einheitsfeldmutze** was worn by nearly all ranks of the Nazi army and was perhaps one of the most widely used soft hats of World War II. It appeared in field gray for army units other than Panzer units which had black. It was a comfortable soft round cap with flat top and with the flaps similar to the mountain cap. The same devices appeared on the front. German army personnel in Africa wore a similar pattern cap made of olive/green cotton drill. It also had the long visor which gave it a rakish look. The red, white and black cockade and the eagle wreath and swastika (in light blue thread rather than white thread of the other field caps) was worn on the front. Luftwaffe units had this cap of blue/gray material.

Another type of field service cap also somewhat similar to the old familiar American "overseas cap" differed from the earlier model field cap in that the turnback of the cap was quite wider and formed a sharp curve to the front of the cap until it was half as wide. This came in field gray for troops other than Panzers and had the usual cloth insignia. Panzer units had a black cap and in lieu of the red, white and black cockade wore a skull and crossbones.

Nazi party and organizations, both political, civil and semimilitary wore a variety of headgear similar to those worn by the military. These are usually distinguished by their various unit or other organizational insignia.

Imperial German and German Third Reich headdress is the most sought after by American collectors. British collectors apparently maintain a great interest in their own historic military headdress, perhaps to a somewhat greater degree than Nazi items or those of Imperial Germany. Caps of other armies, although of some limited interest, do not figure very much in sales or auctions. Except for a comparatively few collectors in this country interested in American military history, there has been no great demand for caps

Price Range

of the U.S. forces. A few of these of particular interest are listed in the following guide.

AUSTRIA

☐ **Dragoon Service Other Ranks cap,** *c. late 1800's. Medium height red cloth cylindrical cap with flat top. Cloth ear flaps turn back to fit closely about the cap. At the front are two plain slightly domed brass buttons. At the top front is a pierced brass disk bearing the cypher "FJI."* 100.00   120.00

☐ **Field Artillery Service Officer's cap,** *c. early 1900's. High quality gray/green cloth of the same pattern as below. Two flat gilt buttons each bearing embossed crossed cannons are at the lower front where the flaps meet. At the top front is a gold cord circular cockade with maroon velvet center bearing the cypher "FJI" in gold thread.* 125.00   150.00

☐ **Field Artillery Service Other Ranks cap,** *c. early 1900's. Felt cloth cap of gray, blue, green color, black leather untrimmed visor, turn down flaps which fold back closely about the cap. Fastening these flaps in front are two plain brass semidomed buttons. At the top front of the cap is a shaped brass disk with the initials and number "FJI" cut out. This is the cypher of the then reigning monarch.* 100.00   120.00

BRITAIN/CANADA

☐ **Canadian Militia Officer's Forage cap,** *c. late 1800's. The body of this cap is very similar to that of the pillbox cap described below. However, there is a thick black leather visor attached on the front edge of which appears a wide band of silver embroidery. A wide band of decorative silver lace encircles this cap. On the flat top is a silver net ball surrounded with silver decorative loops. A similar cap was worn by the Regular Service but with gold trimmings.* 100.00   120.00

☐ **Canadian Militia Officer's Forage cap,** *(67th Carleton Light Infantry), c. late 1800's. Here again we have a cap of a militia officer similar in pattern to that of an officer of the regulars. It is interesting to observe that the Canadian militia units, unlike many of their counterparts in the United States, did not go in for circus and comic opera headgear. This cap, similar in pattern to the officer's patrol caps described below, is of medium height, is cylindrical and flared slightly outward at the top. It is of dark blue cloth with black leather visor. The front edge of this is decorated with a band of gold lace. The number of the regiment "67" appears in gold embroidery on the lower front of the cap. The flat top is decorated with a black woven wool button surrounded with black braid decorative*

Canadian Militia Officer's Forage cap.,
c. late 1800's.

	Price Range	

knots. This militia headpiece is somewhat unusual in
that such outfits usually had silver trim. **100.00**   **120.00**

☐ **Royal Welsh Fusiliers Officer's Forage cap.** *This cap*
differs from the forage caps discussed above in that
it is of a modified "overseas" pattern. Of dark blue
cloth it has flaps which turn back against the crown.
Two gilt buttons decorate the front. They bear the
regimental device of the Prince of Wales coronet and
plumes. On the left side of the cap, about a fourth of
the way back, appears a gold thread embroidered
flaming grenade. **100.00**   **120.00**

☐ **Gloucester Regiment Officer's Patrol cap,** *late Vic-*
torian period. Dark blue medium height cylindrical
hat with black leather visor trimmed on the outer
edge with gold lace. Front plate is the badge of the
Gloucester Regiment. Thin gold piping about the top
of the cap. **145.00**   **165.00**

☐ **Monmouthshire Regiment Officer's Patrol cap,** *Vic-*
torian period. Medium high blue cylindrical cap with
slight flare or bell at the top, gold lace trim about the
outer edge of the visor, cap device in the form of a
griffin within a wreath with a Royal Crown above. . . .   **100.00**   **120.00**

☐ **Royal Norfolk Regiment Officer's Patrol cap,** *Volun-*
teer Battalion. Similar pattern to the above but with
silver wire lace about the outer edge of the visor. Sil-
ver cap made in the form of the figure of Britannia,
the badge of the regiment. **175.00**   **200.00**

☐ **North West Mounted Police Officer's Pillbox cap,** *c.*
late 1800's. This cap resembles nothing quite as
much as the cap worn by hotel bell hops. A pattern

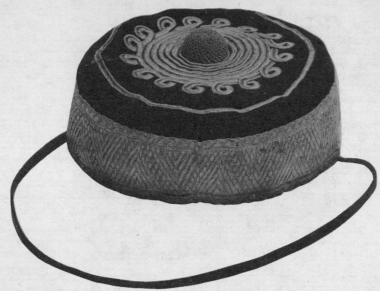

North West Mounted Police Officer's Pillbox cap, c. late 1800's.

Price Range

very similar to this was also worn by British officers and U.S. Marines of the period. It was usually worn tilted or cocked to one side. It was never very popular. The specimen described here is of soft dark blue cloth with a wide band of figured gold braid about it. The top is decorated with a large circle of gold braid encircling the flat top of the cap. The remainder of the top of the cap is elaborately decorated with circles and swirls of gold braid in the center of which is a gold net ball. 100.00   110.00

☐ **Canadian Militia Officer's Undress cap,** *c. mid-1850's. This cap, as was the case with many uniform items of the Canadian service, is very similar in pattern to that worn by officers in the British Army, the principal difference being the cap badges. This cap is of dark blue cloth with an extremely wide crown. Visor and chin strap are of black leather. The cap device consists of the initials "VR" intertwined and made of silver thread. The initials are the cypher meaning Victoria Regina. Above the cypher is the Royal Crown, also in silver thread. About the cap is a wide embroidered black band bearing an oak leaf and acorn design.* . . .   90.00   100.00

FRANCE

☐ **Foreign Legion, Other Ranks Field or Service cap.** *"Overseas" style of medium height, green wool cloth with scarlet wool cloth insert at the top.* 16.50   20.00

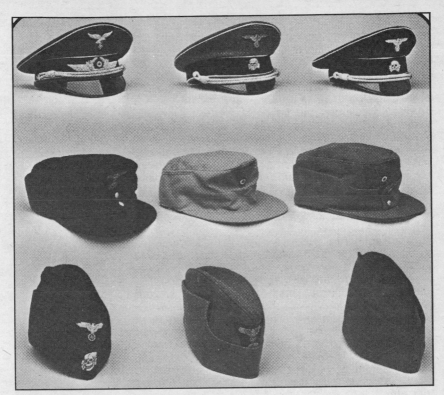

Top Row, left to right: Luftwaffe Officer's cap, Waffen SS Officer's cap, Aligemeine SS Officer's cap.
Middle Row, left to right: Panzer M-43 Other Ranks cap, Africa Corps M-43 Other Ranks cap, Wehrmacht M-43 Other Ranks cap.
Bottom Row, left to right: Panzer Field Service Other Ranks cap, Wehrmacht Field Service Other Ranks cap, French Foreign Legion Service cap.

GERMAN (Imperial)

Price Range

☐ **Bavarian Infantry and the 1st and 2nd Schwere-Reiter (Heavy Cavalry) Regiments Officer's cap.** *Same pattern as Bavarian Jager Battalions 1 and 2, but with light blue crown, scarlet cap band and scarlet piping about the crown, Imperial German and Bavarian cockades at the front.* 165.00 175.00

☐ **Bavarian Jager Battalions 1 and 2 Officer's cap.** *Same pattern as Hussar Regiment 17, but with light blue crown, light blue cap band and light blue piping about crown, Imperial and Bavarian cockades (blue/white/blue).* 180.00 200.00

☐ **Bavarian Leibgarde der Hartschiere or Archers of the Guard.** *Same pattern as Bavarian Infantry, but with light blue crown, black cap band and black piping*

	Price Range	

about the crown, Imperial German and Bavarian cockades. 365.00 400.00

☐ **Dragoon Regiment 2 Officer's cap.** *Same pattern as Field Artillery Regiments, Foot Artillery Regiments, and Pioneers, but with cornflower blue crown, black cap band with black piping about the crown. Between the upper and lower cockades is a small traditional German Dragoon Eagle. This is the only Dragoon regiment to have this distinction.* 275.00 300.00

☐ **Field Artillery Regiments, Foot Artillery Regiments, and Pioneers.** *Same pattern cap as Uhlan Regiments 9 and 13, but with dark blue crown, black cap band and scarlet piping about the crown and about the top and bottom of the cap band. Imperial German upper cockade, lower cockade in the colors of the country to which the unit belonged.* 110.00 125.00

☐ **Hussar Regiment 8 Officer's cap.** *Well designed bell crown cap with medium width band. Crown of cap is dark blue with a cornflower blue band. White piping about the top of the crown and on top and bottom of the band, black leather visor. Lower cockade at front center of the band is of black enameled metal with a silver (white) circular overlay. These are the Prussian colors. At the front center of the crown is a red and black enameled cockade with a circular silver (white) overlay. These are the colors of Imperial Germany.* .. 185.00 200.00

☐ **Hussar Regiment 14 Officer's cap.** *Same pattern as Infantry Regiments, but with dark blue crown, white trim about top, scarlet cap band and white piping above and below cap band, Imperial German and Prussian cockades.* 110.00 125.00

☐ **Hussar Regiment 17 Officer's cap.** *Same pattern as Royal Body Guard Hussars 2, but with black crown, yellow piping about the crown, and above and below the cap band. Imperial German and Brunswick cockades. The Brunswick cockade is blue, gold and blue. Silver skull and crossbones between the two cockades.* 365.00 400.00

☐ **Infantry Regiments Officer's cap.** *This is the typical cap for all Imperial German infantry officers, other than those of the Bavarian infantry regiments. Dark blue crown with scarlet (red) cap band, scarlet trim about the top of the crown, black leather visor, upper cockade (Imperial German colors) the same for all regiments. Lower cockade in the colors of the kingdom, or country, within Imperial Germany from which the regiment came, as follows: Anhalt, dark green; Baden, yellow and red; Bavaria, light blue and white; Brunswick, light blue and yellow; Hanse Towns of Bremen, Hamburg and Lubeck, white and red; Hesse,*

Price Range

red and white; Lippe, yellow and red; Mecklenburg, red, yellow and blue; Oldenburg, blue and red; Prussia, black and white; Reuss, yellow, red, and black; Saxony and the Saxon Duchies, green and white; Saxe-Weimar, green, black and yellow; Schwarzburg, dark blue and white; Waldeck, black, red and yellow; and Wurttemberg, black and white. 110.00   125.00

☐ **92nd Infantry Regiment Officer's cap.** *Same as above, but with the lower cockade for Brunswick, has a small silver skull and crossbones between the upper and the lower cockades.* 155.00   175.00

☐ **Other Ranks caps.** *In addition to those noted above, heavy oilcloth caps were issued to some of the reserve ranks, usually those of Bavaria, Prussia and Saxony. These oilcloth caps appear in both black and gray oilcloth and may or may not have a leather visor. At the center front of the cap band appears either the Imperial German cockade or the cockade of the country to which the unit belongs. Above the cap band and on the front of the cap appears a large Landwehr (Reserve Cross) bearing the inscription "MIT GOTT FUR KONIG UND VATERLAND" and the date "1812." This cross may be attached to the cap either with thread passing through holes in the arms of the cross or by prongs.* 100.00   110.00

☐ **Other Ranks caps.** *These caps were roughly similar to the officer pattern except that there was no visor, the caps were of cheaper cloth and the rosettes were of considerably lesser quality and had two small holes in them where thread passed to secure them to the cap. The officer cockades were highly detailed and of two-piece construction. They were usually fastened to the caps by small prongs. Color combinations were the same as for the officer's cap. In excellent condition these other ranks caps range from $50.00 for more common regiments to $100.00 for the more famous regiments.*

☐ **Royal Body Guard Hussars 1 Officer's cap.** *Same pattern as Dragoon Regiment 2, but with black crown, scarlet cap band, white piping about the crown and with the Imperial German and Prussian cockades. Between the cockades is a silver skull and crossbones.* 365.00   400.00

☐ **Royal Body Guard Hussars 2 Officer's cap.** *Same pattern as Royal Body Guard Hussars 1, but with black crown, black cap band and white piping about the crown and about the top and bottom of the cap band, Imperial German and Prussian cockades with a silver skull and crossbones between.* 365.00   400.00

☐ **Train Battalions Officer's cap.** *Same pattern cap as above, but with dark blue crown and light blue band,*

Price Range

light blue trim about crown, black leather visor, cockades at front as above. 100.00   115.00

☐ **Uhlan Regiments 9 and 13 Officer's cap.** *Same pattern as Hussar Regiment 14, but with dark blue crown with white cap band, white piping about the crown and on each side of the cap band, Imperial and Prussian cockades.* 180.00   200.00

☐ **Uhlan Regiments 12 and 16 Officer's cap.** *Same pattern as above, but with dark blue crown, light blue band, light blue trim about crown, white trim to top and bottom of cap band, black leather visor, cockades as above.* 135.00   150.00

Note: Although all Imperial German regimental caps are not covered above, all of the variations and rare specimens are noted and this list may be used as a reliable guide to the caps not listed.

JAPAN

☐ **Other Ranks Field cap,** *c. World War II. Soft cloth cap (at times semisoft) of extremely full overseas pattern without flaps, semistiff cloth visor. After some use the crown of these caps could become shapeless. They came in a variety of colors from shades of olive drab through dark brown to khaki. They were made of a variety of cloth materials and even in woven straw. The cloth versions appear on the collector's market but this writer has never seen a woven straw cap offered for sale. A yellow cloth star usually appears on the lower front of the cap. Price for all cloth versions.* .   85.00   100.00

RUSSIA

☐ **His Majesty's Life Guard Hussar Regiment Officer's cap,** *c. late 1800's. Crimson/dark reddish cloth cap of excellent material, gold piping about the edge and above the cap band. Highly polished black leather visor, large silver, black enamel and gilt oval rosette on the front of the cap. The crown of this cap is somewhat smaller than that of similar caps of other armies, no chin strap was used.* 135.00   155.00

☐ **Line Infantry Regiment Officer's cap,** *c. early 1900's. Similar pattern to the above but of high quality olive/drab cloth. Black leather visor and chin strap. Cockade similar to the above.* 130.00   140.00

THIRD REICH (German - Nazi)

☐ **Africa Corps Visored Field cap,** *with inverted "V" (soutache).* 150.00   175.00

☐ **Africa Corps Visored Field cap,** *without inverted "V" (soutache)* 100.00   115.00

☐ **Allgemeine SS (General Elite Guard) Officer's Black Visor cap.** *Nazi insignia above on front and with skull and crossbones below, Officer's chin cords.* 800.00   875.00

Price Range

☐ **Allgemeine SS Other Ranks Visored cap.** *As above, but of less costly materials, leather chin strap.* 800.00   875.00

☐ **Army Black Panzer Beret.** *Crash liner within.* 615.00   800.00

☐ **Army Officer's Visored cap.** *High quality silver colored Nazi national insignia and red, white and black rondell, silver color (aluminum) chin cords.* 150.00   175.00

☐ **Army Officer's M-38 cap.** 70.00   80.00

☐ **Army Officer's M-43 Field cap.** 100.00   115.00

☐ **Army Other Ranks M-38 cap.** 50.00   55.00

☐ **Army Other Ranks Visored cap.** *Leather chin strap, silver color Nazi national insignia and red, white and black rondell.* 110.00   110.00

☐ **Army (Wehrmacht) General Officer's Visored cap.** *Black velvet cap band, gold chin cords and Nazi national insignia with high quality red, white and black rondell.* 785.00   875.00

☐ **Kreigsmarine (Navy) Officer's Dark Blue Visored cap.**   165.00   180.00

☐ **Luftwaffe (Air Force) Officer's Visored cap.** *Field gray with black leather visor. Silver color piping about top of cap and above and below black cap band. Aluminum wire woven chin cords. On front of the cap band is red, white and black cockade in center of wreath and outspread wings. At top of cap is flying eagle grasping a swastika. These devices are in silver color.* 125.00   140.00

☐ **As above,** *but with white top. Not often offered for sale.* 215.00   240.00

☐ **Luftwaffe Other Ranks Visored cap.** *Field gray with black leather, same pattern as Officer's cap but of lesser quality and with leather chin strap.* 100.00   110.00

☐ **As above,** *but with white top.* 125.00   135.00

☐ **Navy Officer's cap.** *White top.* 250.00   275.00

☐ **Officer's M-43 Black Panzer cap.** 220.00   250.00

☐ **Other Ranks M-43 Field cap.** 50.00   55.00

☐ **Other Ranks Blue cap,** *so-called "Donald Duck" type without visor and with a large flat soft crown overhanging the cap band. This cap with "KREIGSMARINE" cap band.* 45.00   50.00

☐ **As above,** *but with white top or cover.* 125.00   150.00

☐ **Waffen SS (Army SS - Elite Guard) Officer's cap.** *Gray/green with black velvet band, gold color Nazi emblem at top front and silver skull and crossbones below, white piping about crown, aluminum wire chin cords.* 550.00   600.00

☐ **Waffen SS Other Ranks Visored cap.** *As above, but with less costly materials and trim, black leather chin strap.* 425.00   475.00

☐ **Waffen SS Panzer Field Service cap.** *Black with silver Nazi emblem and skull and crossbones.* 250.00   275.00

Note: As Nazi collectors well know, all organizations within the Third

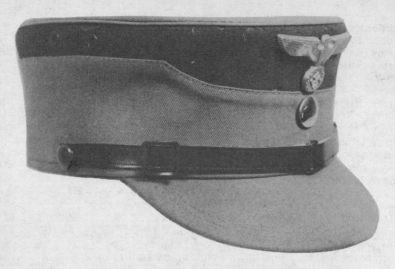

Wermacht (Nazi Army) Other Ranks M-43 Field cap.

Reich were under very strict Nazi party control. There was a host of organizations, both civilian and semimilitary, all uniformed and subject to the strictest discipline. Although the uniforms of these organizations do not fall within a strict definition of militaria, they are related and are of great interest to collectors of Nazi military gear. For this reason, the following list is included.

	Price Range	
☐ **Deutscher Reichskriegerbund (DRB),** *the German Veterans' Association.*		
☐ **Dark Blue Visored cap.** *Cap insignia.*	65.00	75.00
☐ **Hitler Youth (Hitlerjugend)**		
☐ **Leaders cap.** *Not often offered for sale.*	280.00	310.00
☐ **Overseas Type cap.** *For other than leaders.*	45.00	50.00
☐ **National Socialist German Workers Party (NSDAP).** *The Official Nazi Political Organization.*		
☐ **Coffee Can cap.** *Pattern originally used by party members. Brown cloth cylindrical cap with flat top, cloth covered visor and leather chin strap. Later caps may differ slightly in pattern. Nazi party devices on the front. A much desired item and fairly rare.*	300.00	340.00
☐ **Other Ranks Overseas Type cap.** *Blue piping.*	75.00	80.00
☐ **Political Leaders Overseas Type cap.** *Blue piping.* . .	150.00	165.00
☐ **Political Leaders M-43 cap.** *Red piping.*	350.00	385.00
☐ **Political Leaders Visored cap.** *Red piping.*	310.00	350.00
☐ **Political Leaders Visored cap.** *White or blue piping.*	360.00	400.00

Wermacht (Nazi Army)
Other Ranks M-43 Field cap.

	Price Range	
☐ **National Socialist Motor Corps (NSKK),** *National Sozialistischen Kraftfahr-Korps.*		
☐ Coffee Can cap.	250.00	275.00
☐ Officer's Overseas Type cap.	60.00	65.00
☐ Other Ranks Overseas Type cap.	45.00	50.00
☐ **Police (Polizei).**		
☐ Other Ranks Fire Police Visored cap.	75.00	85.00
☐ Other Ranks Visored cap.	75.00	85.00

THIRD REICH REPRODUCTION CAPS (Nazi)

The growing demand by collectors for Nazi caps has led to the production of a multitude of reproductions and outright fakes. This is certainly an area in which the beginner can very well be taken for the proverbial "ride." Some reproductions being passed off as genuine are extremely well made and it requires a rather knowledgeable person to detect them. Reliable dealers, traders and collectors with an honest reputation to maintain will always identify the reproductions. It is of some interest to know that a well made reproduction today sells for more than an original did just a few years ago. Some reliable dealers, including Unique Imports of Alexandria, Virginia 22312, upon request will special order reproduction caps. These are fabricated by the original German manufacturers and may be ordered in a wide variety of branch, rank and size. Prices begin in the neighborhood of $165.00. Other Ranks Kreigsmarine (Navy) caps, reproductions with original insignia, are in stock and are priced at about $75.00. These are sold as reproductions or replicas and no attempt whatsoever is made to sell them as originals. Be aware of any so-called genuine headgear of any kind offered at "Bargain Basement" prices. There is no such thing as a cheap original. Beginners should be especially on guard against some of the merchandise being offered as "bargains" at some of the gun shows.

UNITED STATES

☐ **Enlisted Man's Forage cap,** *c. early 1800's. Flat crown cloth cap with the crown considerably larger than the cap band. Made of dark blue wool with large flat black leather visor. From a plain small brass but-*

U.S. Enlisted Man's Forage cap, c. early 1800's.

Price Range

ton on the top of the cap, dark green cords radiate to the edge and under the crown. At the top and bottom of the wide dark blue cap band is piping of white cord. Although this particular piping varied for the color of the arm or service, few specimens of this cap are to be found but there is not any great demand for them at this time. 115.00 125.00

☐ **Enlisted Man's Forage cap,** c. 1830's. This cap was worn by Regular Army personnel as well as by cadets at the United States Military Academy at West Point. It was completely utilitarian. It is an unattractive piece of headgear. Of heavy black leather about its only recommendations were that it was extremely rugged and could be folded flat for easy storage. May be found with a brass company number on the front. Rarely found but not in demand. 115.00 125.00

☐ **Militia Versions** of the above cap are found occasionally. These vary from cloth covered cardboard caps with leather visors to fairly heavy leather examples. As might be expected, these are all decked out with fancy trimmings, often not in the best of taste. . 115.00 125.00

☐ **Enlisted Man's Fatigue cap,** c. late 1830's. In this cap the design began to take on a more stylish look. Cap of dark blue wool with turn down flap attached to rear half. When turned up it was held in place by the buttons holding the end of the black leather chin strap.

U.S. Enlisted Man's cap,
c. late 1930's.

U. S. Enlisted Man's Fatigue cap,
c. late 1830's.

Price Range

These brass buttons were embossed with the Arms of the U.S. Flap was further secured by cloth tape passing around the front of the cap. Untrimmed black leather visor. This visor extended straight down over the wearer's brow. Regulations provided that a colored cloth band could be worn. This band was white for infantry, red for artillery, yellow for dragoons and light blue for ordnance. Cadets at the United States Military Academy wore a black velvet band with the initials "USMA" embroidered in Old English script within a wreath of olive and laurel leaves. 100.00   125.00

U.S. Enlisted Man's cap, c. early 1900's.

☐ **Enlisted Man's cap,** *c. early 1900's. Blue cloth cap of medium height with slight bell crown, black leather visor and chin strap. Strap is adjustable by means of a small brass buckle on the right side. A small brass button bearing the Arms of the U.S. holds the chin strap to each side of the cap. These caps are found with a colored felt band around the top and bottom of the cap band. This was in the color of the arm or service. The device on the front of the cap varies according to the arm or service. The specimen shown here is an artilleryman's cap. The bands at the top and bottom of the cap band are red. The cap device con-*

Price Range

sists of brass crossed cannons with the figure "I"
above and the initial "A" below. This identified A Bat-
tery of the First Field Artillery. Prices vary only
slightly as to arm or service. A similar specimen was
recently priced as follows **50.00   75.00**

There is little or no interest in more recent U.S. caps except for a few collectors specializing in the area. In many instances, specimens may be had for $10.00 or less. Some dealers find it difficult to dispose of caps of the World War II era. It is possible, of course, that a market for them may develop sometime in the future.

THE GRENADIER CAP

One of the most interesting items of military headdress is the grenadier cap. This is a miter-shape cap somewhat resembling the miter worn by bishops and abbots. In the military service it began as a medium high conical cap with a stiff cloth front, usually with a round or pointed top. An embroidered device on this front piece identified the unit to which the wearer belonged. Later the stiff cloth front was replaced by a large metal front plate. The embellishment of this front plate consisted of the elaborate use of royal arms, cyphers of rulers and the insignia of military orders, all supplemented with trophies of arms and an assortment of other military items. The sides and the back of the cap were also usually highly decorated.

It has been maintained by some military historians that the use of the grenadier cap was necessitated by the fact that the brim of the military hat of the period was a hindrance to the throwing of a grenade. This supposition is laid to rest by the fact that the crude hand grenade was most often thrown underhand! Although the real reason is unknown, it could well be that this distinctive cap was introduced simply because it was unique and colorful; that it constituted a morale factor useful in identifying certain elite troops which the grenadiers most certainly were. Grenadiers first appeared in the early 1700's. They were individuals selected for their physical prowess, capable of accurately throwing a heavy grenade a great distance. They were banded together in special units. When the use of grenades became obsolete, the term "grenadiers" was retained to honor outstanding infantry units.

This particular style of headdress was worn by a number of armies, particularly in England, France, Germany (then composed of many independent states), Austria and Russia. The German states, especially Prussia, were particularly fond of it. In fact, Prussia used a multitude of variations on the theme. Interestingly enough, some units of our American Revolutionary War army used the grenadier cap at one time or another. It appears that to most Americans the use of the grenadier cap during the American Revolution is associated with the Hessian troops employed by the British Government.

Although the use of the grenadier was comparatively short-lived, it was retained for parade wear in the Imperial German Army by certain elite groups, namely The First Guard Regiment of Foot, Emperor Alexander's Guard Grenadiers and the Prussian Palace Guard Company, until World War I. This unique style of headdress was certainly far too colorful for the uniform loving Kaiser Wilhelm II to discard.

To date only a few copies or reproductions of the grenadier cap have appeared. These are most often those made up for dramatic productions and are most easily identified by anyone who has seen a genuine grenadier cap.

Although a great variety of grenadier caps were worn by many armies, only a comparatively few ever appear on the market. Those which do are usually those of the Imperial German Army. The following price list is restricted to those items which actually have appeared for sale. As is the case with all military headdress, items belonging to officers are made of much better materials and details. Front plates and decorations in particular are more finely executed.

AUSTRIA   Price Range

☐ **Army Other Ranks grenadier cap,** *c. 1750. An interesting cap with the medium high front and the sides of black bearskin. The top and back of red cloth trimmed in white tape ending in a flap with a tassel attached. A large brass flaming grenade decorates the front of the cap. This item is typical of the fur grenadier caps worn in the Austrian army.* 7400.00   8250.00

☐ **Army Other Ranks grenadier cap,** *c. 1830. Fairly tall grenadier cap with bearskin front and sides and cloth top and back. A brass front plate reaches up half way to the top. The front plate bears the embossed crowned double-headed Austrian eagle. A flaming grenade appears at each lower end of the front plate.*   3800.00   4200.00

ENGLAND

☐ **43rd Foot Officer's grenadier cap,** *Grenadier Company. High miter front of buff color velvet edged with gold cord. At the top of the front is a royal crown worked out in red, gold and silver. Under the crown is a large cypher "GR" for "George Rex," embroidered in gold cord. On either side are intertwined roses and thistles worked in gold with the roses in crimson and the thistles in silver. The back of the cap is scarlet trimmed in a gold foliate design. A broad band about the bottom of the cap is also embroidered with a gold foliate design with a flaming grenade at the rear with a "4" on one side and a "3" on the other. This is another very rare grenadier cap.* 8400.00   9300.00

☐ **Other Ranks grenadier cap,** *c. 1770. Similar to the fur grenadier caps of the Austrian army of the period. Tall cap of bearskin with a red cloth insert trimmed in white set in the back. A black japanned metal front plate extends approximately one-third of the way up the front. Within an elaborate silver color cartouche appears a large medieval royal helmet (full face) with a large lion crest. On one side appears "G" and on the other appears "R." Around this design appears a ribbon bearing the motto "NEC ASPERA TERRENT."*   7400.00   8250.00

☐ **12th Foot Other Ranks grenadier cap,** *Grenadier Company, c. mid-1700's. Buff cloth miter type front decorated on the upper half by a large embroidered crown and the cypher "GR" for "George Rex." A*

Bearskin Grenadier cap, British Army, c. 1770. Worn during Revolutionary War.

Price Range

foliate design decorates the sides of the front. The lower half of the front has a scarlet turnback featuring the "Horse of Hannover" within an embroidered band bearing the motto "NEC ASPERA TERRENT." The embroidered cloth grenadier cap was used extensively by the British. A wide buff band about the bottom of the cap bears a foliate design with a grenade at the back with "X" on one side and "II" on the other. 4750.00   5250.00

GERMANY

☐ **Hesse Cassel Other Ranks grenadier cap.** *Large miter-type brass front plate on the upper two-thirds occupied by an embossed Hessian crowned lion standing on an elaborately embossed cartouche. Red cloth cap with wide metal band about the bottom elaborately embossed with trophies of arms and a flaming grenade at the center back. . . . .*   7400.00   8250.00

☐ **32nd Prussian Officer's grenadier cap,** *Grenadier Regiment, c. 1760. Tall miter-type metal front piece of gilt with elaborately embossed trophies of arms. Covering almost the upper half of the front plate is the so-called eagle of Frederick the Great above which is a crown*

British Other Ranks Grenadier cap, Grenadier Company, 12th Foot, c. mid-1700's.

Price Range

and the motto "PRO GLORIA ET PATRIA." The cloth cap is green in color and is topped with a gilt half grenade and flame. A wide green band surrounds the bottom of the cap which is decorated on each side and back with a large Prussian heraldic eagle standing on a trophy of arms.................................   7400.00   8250.00

PRUSSIA

☐ **First Guard Officer's grenadier cap,** *Regiment of Foot, but for the Fusilier Battalion. Generally similar to the Officer's grenadier cap, but with red backing to the front plate and with yellow/gold cloth cap. The chin scales are attached by a knob and a medium size Prussian heraldic eagle appears on each side and the back of the white band around the bottom of the cap.* 8250.00   9200.00

☐ **First Guard Officer's grenadier cap,** *Regiment of Foot. Fairly high gilt miter pattern front plate with large star of The Order of the Black Eagle in silver and enamel with a large silver crown overall. These are separate pieces which have been applied to the front plate. Silver chin scales, blue cloth backing to the front plate. Body of the cap in red cloth with white and black tape stripes from the top down each side and the back to the wide*

32nd Prussian Officer's
Grenadier cap,
Grenadier Regiment, c. 1760.

Price Range

*white cloth border at the bottom. A large gilt flaming
grenade attached the end of the chin scales to each
side of the cap. There is a similar grenade decorating
the back. A decorative device with silver cup base and
black and silver bullion was fixed to the top of the front
plate. After May 1890 the 1st Battalion and Regimental
Staff had a metalic ribbon device bearing the motto
"SEMPER TALIS" between the star and the crown. This
was silver for Officers and brass for Other Ranks. The
letters of the motto were worked out in red.* 8250.00   9200.00

☐ **As above,** *but with the addition of the "SEMPER TALIS"
ribbon.* 8875.00   9875.00

☐ **First Guard Other Ranks grenadier cap,** *Regiment of
Foot,* **but for the Fusilier Battalion.** *Generally similar to
the Officer's cap of the fusilier battalion, but with less
costly materials.* 3340.00   3700.00

☐ **First Guard Other Ranks grenadier cap,** *Regiment of
Foot. Similar to the Officer's cap, but of less costly
materials. The front plate is of brass and the star of The
Order of the Black Eagle and the Crown are in relief.
The decoration atop the front plate is of black and
white wool.* 1550.00   1800.00

☐ **As above,** *but with "SEMPER TALIS" ribbon.* 3350.00   3800.00

Price Range

☐ **Prussian Palace Guard Other Ranks grenadier cap.**
*Generally similar to the grenadier cap worn by the First
Guard Regiment of Foot prior to February 1894. There
was no "SEMPTER TALIS" motto on the front plate. The
white metal tall miter type front plate was topped by a
wool decorative device. The Star of The Order of the
Black Eagle with large crown above was embossed on
the front. The cap is of red cloth with a white tape stripe
down each side and the back. A white cloth band surrounds the bottom of the cap. The metal chin scales are
attached at each side with a metal grenade.* 3800.00   4200.00

UNITED STATES

Other Ranks Grenadier cap, Kaiser
Alexander Guard, Grenadier Regiment 1, c. after 1894.

☐ **First Guard Officer's grenadier cap,** *Regiment of
Foot, after February 1894. Tall miter pattern silver
front plate elaborately embossed in fine detail with
trophies of arms and grenades with a crown at the
top and with the cypher "FR" in a cartouche at the
bottom. In the center part of the front plate appears
the so-called eagle of Frederick the Great. For other
than the Fusilier Battalion, a ribbon above this eagle
bears the motto "SEMPER TALIS." The backing of
the front plate is red as is the cloth cap. About the
bottom of the cap is a wide silver band of elaborate
embossed designs with a large grenade at the sides*

Price Range

and back. Chin scales are silver. Atop the front plate
is a silver bullion cup and knob device. White tape
extends from the top of the cap down each side and
the back. 2900.00   3200.00

☐ **First Guard Officer's grenadier cap,** *First Guard Regi-*
ment of Foot, **but of the Fusilier Battalion.** *Similar to*
the above but with a yellow/gold cloth cap and with
the motto "PRO GLORIA ET PATRIA" on the ribbon
above the eagle's head. 3300.00   3650.00

☐ **First Guard Other Ranks grenadier cap,** *Regiment of*
Foot, **but of the Fusilier Battalion.** *Similar to the*
Officer's cap of the Fusilier Battalion but of less
costly materials................................. 1720.00   1900.00

☐ **First Guard Other Ranks grenadier cap,** *First Guard*
Regiment of Foot, other than the Fusilier Battalion.
Similar to the Officer's cap but of less costly
materials, including white metal for silver. 1550.00   1850.00

☐ **George Washington grenadier cap,** *Regiment of*
Grenadiers (of Gloucester, Massachusetts). Con-
structed of homespun red wool, tall pointed front of
cloth stiffened by cardboard. The front plate is red
with a white overlay covering almost the bottom
third. On the upper portion of the front appears the
cypher "GW" in white. On the white overlay appears
the word "REGIMENT" in an embroidered semicircle
above an embroidered flaming bomb. A wide decora-
tive band surrounds the bottom of the cap. This is an
extremely rare item. **14700.00**   **16300.00**

Special Note: *After February 1894 the First Guard Regiment of Foot was*
given a new pattern cap and their former caps were assigned to the Kaiser
Alexander Guard Grenadier Regiment 1. The new caps were patterned
after those worn by Frederick the Great's Regimental Guard. The caps
turned over to the other regiment had the "SEMPER TALIS" ribbon removed.

THE LANCER CAP (Czapka)

One of the more interesting items of military headdress is the lancer cap.
This is often known in the continental armies as the czapka or tschapka. It is
distinguished by a skull or body with a front visor but no rear visor. There is a
mortar board or trencher (board) top. Most often it is elaborately decorated,
lancers being particularly proud of their tradition, heritage and dress. The
lancer cap originated in Poland in the form of a four-sided cap, the
konfederatku, worn by the peasants. It was later adopted and modified by the
Polish lancers, who were rather famous in Europe at one time. It really
received its first international recognition when it was introduced into the
French service by Napoleon in 1807 when he inducted several Polish lancer
units into his army. It was not long after this that the lancer cap began to gain
in popularity among the lancer units of other nations, eventually spreading to
a multitude of other nations.

Although it was used by many armies, it never achieved quite the popularity in other countries as it did in Austria, England, France and Germany,

being used up until World War I. In each of the armies, it was modified considerably to conform with national tastes. The lancer cap was known as the tschapka in the German service where it received considerable publicity worldwide as the headdress of the famed uhlan regiments. The uhlans were medium cavalry, armed with lance, light sabers, carbines and pistols. "Uhlan" is a word which comes from a name used in ancient Tartary to mean "belonging to the hoof." The Prussian lancers adopted it in 1808.

The colorful lancer cap never was adopted by the United States Army. In fact, it was used by only a very few militia outfits. For the most part these American lancer caps are gaudy, flimsy affairs, few of which have survived. The American version is not sought after by many collectors although the lancer caps of other armies are quite popular.

AUSTRIA   Price Range

☐ **Uhlan Officer's czapka**, *Regiment 1, c. 1900. Polished black leather skull or crown, with black leather front visor, gilt front edge, gilt chin scales attached on each side of cap with large gilt bosses. Front plate consists of the double-headed Austrian eagle, with crown overall, in gilt. There is a small polished shield on the breast of the eagle. On the shield is the silver numeral "1." As is typical of Austrian lancer caps, the mortar board top is small. A long black horsehair plume hangs from a fixture above the left side of the mortar board. This plume is formed into a ball shape at the top. On the top of this ball is a gilt disk with a three stepped edge. In the center of the disk appears the pierced cypher "FJI," signifying the Austrian Emperor Francis Joseph 1st. The hanging plume is held to the side of the cap by a gilt chain.* 560.00   625.00

☐ **Uhlan Senior (Field Grade) Officer's Dress czapka**, *Regiment 3, c. 1900. Similar in pattern and profile to the above, but much more elaborately decorated. There is a narrow gilt front edge to the visor. Also around the front of the visor is a medium width band of gold lace. The gilt chin scales are made to resemble leaves and are attached to each side of the cap by large lion mask bosses. About the cap are three rows of medium width figured gold lace with a narrow band of gold cord above and below. The front plate consists of a gilt double-headed eagle with crown above. On the breast of the eagle is a polished shield upon which appears the numeral "3." The mortar board is covered on the top and bottom with maroon velvet cloth. This is trimmed across the top and down the sides with gold cord. The plume is same as the above lancer cap but in lieu of the gilt disk on top of the plume ball, there is a rosette of gold braid with a maroon velvet center. The cypher "FJI" is worked out in gold thread on the velvet center. The plume is held close to the cap by two gilt chains.* 750.00   840.00

BELGIUM

☐ **Officer's (Field Grade) tschapka,** *1st Lancers, c. 1914. Polished black leather cap and visor, gilt chin scales attached to each side of cap by gilt lion mask bosses. The front plate consists of a large half sunburst upon which is superimposed a silver half disk bearing gilt cross lanced with lance flags behind a shield bearing the numeral "1." The top and underside of the mortar board is covered with crimson velvet. A red and black oval rosette surrounded by gilt cord is on the left side of the mortar board. This supports a white aigrette of heron feathers.* **750.00   840.00**

ENGLAND

☐ **Officer's lancer cap,** *9th Lancers, c. 1905. The profile of this cap is somewhat different from those that follow in that the skull continued on up into the mortar board top in a straight line instead of curving in to meet the base of the mortar board, then curving out again. This pattern closely resembles that of some of the early French lancer caps. Cap, as usual, is of black leather with a black leather visor. The front of the visor has a gilt edge. Lion mask side bosses are of gilt. The gilt chin chain is backed with leather. The gilt triangular front plate is of slightly different shape, the points of the rays forming the background being more pronounced. On the plate appears the Royal Arms with a scroll beneath bearing the regimental title, all backed with a floral design. Each corner of the mortar board top is decorated with a gilt ornament. The underside has a cloth cover and a strip of gilt metal extends down from each corner to the top of a wide stripe of highly ornamented gold lace which encircles the base of the mortar board top. A fine cord rosette in the colors of the regiment at the front left side holds a gilt plume holder supporting a falling plume of black and white cocktail feathers.* **1450.00   1600.00**

☐ **Officer's lancer cap,** *17th Lancers, c. 1900. This cap is the same basic design and pattern as other ranks below. The fittings, however, are much more elaborate and are of finer quality. The visor is decorated with one narrow and one wide band of gold lace. The lion mask bosses are of gilt as is the leather backed chin chain. The front plate, triangular in form, bears the Royal Arms with a skull and crossbones below. Under the skull and crossbones appears a scroll bearing the words "or Glory." This signifies the regiment's motto, "Death or Glory." The skull and crossbones motif was also a distinguishing feature of certain elite German Army regiments. The front*

British Officer's Lancer cap,
17th Lancers, c. 1900.

Price Range

plate also contains the regiment's many battle
honors superimposed upon an elaborate floral background. The top and underside of the mortar board
top are covered with white cloth. Across the top and
down each corner of the mortar board is a heavy strip
of gold cord. At the bottom of the mortar board are
two bands of gold lace with a narrow band of blue
silk lace between. Below these are a wide and a narrow band of gold cord. At the left front of the top of
the cap is a large gold and blue cord rosette. In the
center of this is a blue velvet background bearing the
Cypher of Edward VII worked out in gold thread. This
rosette supports a gilt plume holder supporting a
plume of white feathers. 1550.00   1725.00

☐ **Other Ranks lancer cap,** 12th Lancers, c. 1900. This
lancer cap and the officer's pattern above are typical
of the lancer caps used in the British Army. The
prices will generally hold for the same grades and
ranks of the other British lancer regiments. The cap
and visor are of black leather as is the mortar board
top. There is no trim to the front of the visor. The
brass chin chain is backed with leather. The very
elaborate stamped out brass front plate is triangular
in shape. It bears the Royal Arms, the battle honors
of the regiment and the plume, coronet and motto of

British Other Ranks Lancer cap,
12th Lancers, c. 1900.

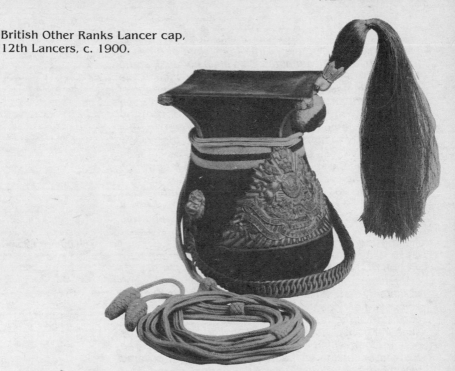

Price Range

the Prince of Wales. This appears over the Royal
Arms. Under the arms appears a Sphinx over the
word "Egypt." There is a brass ornament at each corner of the mortar board. The underside of the mortar
board is covered with red wool cloth with a stripe of
blue between two stripes of white at the bottom. A
stripe of yellow cord runs down from each corner
ornament to the top of the white band. On the left
front of the mortar board appears a yellow and blue
rosette with a brass regimental button in the center.
An ornamental brass plume holder projecting up
from this rosette holds a falling red horsehair plume.   750.00   825.00

FRANCE

☐ **Other Ranks czapka,** *Chevaux-legers-lanciers de la
Vistule, c. 1813.* This is one of the earliest of the French
lancer caps. It is of black leather and the sides of the
cap extend up in almost a straight line into the mortar
board top. The visor is of black leather with a small leaf
design embossed down the center. There is a broad
brass edge to the front of the visor. Chin chains of brass
rings are backed by leather. These are attached to each

Price Range

side of the cap by a large lion mask boss on a large brass base. The extremely large front plate of brass is in the form of a half sunburst. On a plain half disk at the lower part of the plate appears an embossed eagle grasping thunderbolts in its talons. Behind the eagle, and crossed, are lances and lance flags, two on each side. A crown appears above the eagle's head. The mortar board is completely covered with black cloth with a plain brass ornament at each corner of the top. Yellow cord forms a cross on the top and extends down each corner to meet a wide band of yellow cloth lace which surrounds the cap. At the top left center of the top is a yellow cloth rosette upon which is superimposed a black Maltese cross with yellow edges. A small brass button appears in the center of the cross. Behind this rosette is a plume holder which supports a faded elongated wool pompon. 750.00   825.00

☐ **Other Ranks lancer cap**, c. 1850's. This is a much later version of the lancer cap than that described above. Of all black leather, it has an extremely small visor which is scarcely distinguishable as such. Brass chin chain is composed of rings backed with leather and attached to each side of the cap by lion mask bosses. The huge half sunburst front plate has a plain polished half disk at the bottom upon which is embossed the numeral "4." The top and underside of the mortar board top is covered with blue wool cloth. Around the bottom of this is a board band of yellow braid. There is a small brass ornament at each point of the mortar board. The edges of the top are trimmed with yellow cord which extends down each corner to join the wide band. A strand of small brass chain is looped about the four sides of the top. A black horsehair plume droops from the left front corner of the top. 375.00   425.00

GERMANY
Bavaria
☐ **Uhlan Officer's tschapka**, Regiments 1 and 2, model 1873. Black leather cap and visor. Top of cap is semiconical and terminates in a short small neck supporting the mortar board top. Front edge of visor trimmed in silver metal, flat silver metal chin scales attached to each side of cap by lion mask bosses in silver. Two bands of silver lace about the cap above which appears a silver "L" with crown above, silver and blue oval field badge on left side of mortar board. 1010.00   1125.00

☐ **Uhlan Officer's tschapka**, Regiment 1, 1873-1886. Lancer cap similar in pattern to above, but with no lace trim about the body. Gilt edge to visor, gilt chin scales attached to cap by gilt lion mask bosses, front plate is

Price Range

*large and consists of the Arms of Bavaria in gilt, oval
silver and blue field badge on left center of top.* **1010.00   1125.00**

☐ **Uhlan Other Ranks tschapka,** *Regiment 1, 1873-1886.
As above, but of less costly materials, brass metal
parts and cloth field badge.* **560.00   625.00**

☐ **Uhlan Officer's tschapka,** *Regiment 2, 1873-1886.
Same as above Officer's lancer cap, except that all
metal fittings and trim are in silver.* **1015.00   1125.00**

☐ **Uhlan Other Ranks tschapka,** *Regiment 2, 1873-1886.
Same as above Other Ranks lancer helmet, except
that all metal fittings and trim are in white metal.* . . .   **600.00   675.00**

☐ **Uhlan Officer's tschapka,** *Regiment 1, after 1886.
This model has a well rounded skull or crown similar
to a conventional helmet. Of black leather with black
leather visor, base of mortar board top is larger, as is
top, gilt trim to front visor, gilt chin scales, large gilt
front plate consisting of the Bavarian Arms, silver
and blue metal rosette under end of chin scales on
right side, oval field badge of silver cord with blue
velvet center.* **600.00   675.00**

☐ **Uhlan Other Ranks tschapka,** *Regiment 1, after 1886.
Lancer cap of same pattern as above, but with brass
metal fittings and trim, blue and white oval cloth field
badge.* **375.00   425.00**

☐ **Unlan Officer's tschapka,** *Regiment 2, after 1886. As
above, except that metal fittings and trim are of silver
metal.* **600.00   675.00**

☐ **Uhlan Other Ranks tschapka,** *Regiment 2, after 1886.
Lancer cap as above, except that metal fittings and
trim are of white metal, blue and white oval cloth
field badge.* **375.00   425.00**

Prussia

☐ **Guard Uhlan Officer's tschapka,** *Regiments 1, 2 and
3, c. 1910. Conventional pattern German lancer cap
of black leather with fairly low well rounded skull and
gracefully shaped base to the mortar board top.
Black leather visor with gilt trim to front edge, gilt
chin scales with a silver and black rosette under the
end of the chin scales on the right. Front plate is a
silver Guard Eagle with a silver and enamel Star of
the Order of the Black Eagle on its breast. (For Uhlan
Regiment 2, however, the Eagle is gilt with a silver
and enamel star on its breast.) Silver cord oval field
badge with black velvet center on left front of the top.*   **1450.00   1600.00**

☐ **Guard Uhlan Other Ranks tschapka,** *Regiments 1, 2
and 3, c. 1910. (As above, except that brass or white
metal is used and the field badge is of cloth.)* **1000.00   1015.00**

☐ **Uhlan Officer's tschapka,** *Regiments 1, 2, and 3, c.
1910. Basic lancer cap as above. Gilt edge to front of
visor. Gilt front plate is the "Grenadier Eagle," the*

Price Range

heraldic Prussian eagle with the cypher "FR" on the breast of the eagle replaced by an oval bearing the cypher "FWR." Gilt chin scales, field badge as above. 1400.00   1550.00

☐ **Uhaln Other Ranks tschapka,** *Regiments 1, 2 and 3. As above, but all metal parts of brass, field badge of white cord with black cloth center.* 600.00   675.00

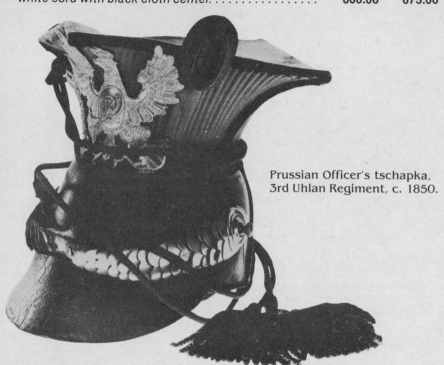

Prussian Officer's tschapka,
3rd Uhlan Regiment, c. 1850.

☐ **Uhlan Officer's tschapka,** *Regiment 3, c. 1850. Cap and visor of black leather, thick base to mortar board top, no trim to front of visor, gilt chin scales, large gilt Prussian heraldic eagle with a polished oval on the breast bearing the cypher "FWR," (Freidrich Wilhelm Rex). Typical of the Prussian lancer caps of this period, this eagle front plate appeared on the front underside of the mortar board top instead of on the front of the skull. The underside of the top is covered with gold color cloth trimmed with black cord. On the left front of the top appears an oval silver cord field badge with black velvet center. The silver cap lines are flecked with black and terminate in tassels.* 1200.00   1350.00

Price Range

☐ **Uhlan Officer's tschapka,** *Regiments 4, 9, 10, 11 and 14. Lancer cap as above, gilt edge to front of visor, gilt chin scales with silver and black rosette under right end, front plate consisting of gilt Prussian heraldic eagle (with cypher "FR" on breast), silver cord oval field badge with black velvet center.* 1460.00   1650.00

☐ **Uhlan Other Ranks tschapka,** *Regiments 4, 9, 10, 11, and 14. As above, except that metal parts are of brass and the field badge is of white cord with a black cloth center.* 600.00   675.00

☐ **Uhlan Officer's tschapka,** *Regiments 5, 6, 8, 15, 16, and 7 (before 1913). Lancer cap as above, but with gilt edge to visor. Silver and black rosette on right side, gilt chin scales, silver Prussian heraldic eagle front plate, silver cord and black velvet field badge.* 1460.00   1650.00

☐ **Uhlan Other Ranks tschapka,** *Regiments 5, 6, 8, 15, 16 and 7 (before 1913). As above, but white metal and brass metal fixtures and trim, white cord and black cloth oval field badge.* 600.00   675.00

☐ **Uhlan Officer's tschapka,** *Regiment 7, after 1913. Officer's pattern lancer cap as above, gilt fittings and trim except for front plate which is silver eagle similar to the Guard Eagle except that there is no Star of the Order of the Black Eagle on the breast.* 1650.00   1850.00

☐ **Uhlan Other Ranks tschapka,** *Regiment 7, after 1913. Other Ranks lancer cap with white metal and brass trim and fittings.* 785.00   875.00

☐ **Uhlan Officer's tschapka,** *Regiment 13, after January 1899. Officer's pattern lancer cap with gilt fittings and trim, except for front plate which is a silver Guard Eagle with the Star of the Order of the Black Eagle in silver and enamel. Appearing on a ribbon which appears on each side and over the star are the black enameled battle honors "PENINSULA -WATERLOO -GARZIA-HERNANDEZ."* 1460.00   1650.00

☐ **Uhlan Other Ranks tschapka,** *Regiment 13, after January 1899. Other Ranks pattern lancer cap with white metal and brass trim and fittings, as above.* 835.00   925.00

☐ **Uhlan Officer Ranks tschapka,** *Regiment 14, after January 1899. Officer's pattern tschapka with gilt trim and fittings. The gilt Prussian line (heraldic eagle has a circular band or ribbon which passes over the eagle's talons, behind the wings and over the neck). The battle honors "WATERLOO - PENINSULA - GARZIA HERNANDEZ" appears in black enamel on this band.* 1650.00   1835.00

☐ **Uhlan Other Ranks tschapka,** *Regiment 14, after January 1899. Other Ranks pattern lancer cap with brass trim and fittings.* 925.00   1025.00

Saxon (Imperial German) Officer's lancer cap,
Uhlan Regiments 17 and 18, c. 1910.

Saxony

	Price Range	
☐ **Uhlan Officer's tschapka,** *Regiments 17 and 18, c. 1910. Officer's pattern lancer cap, gilt trim to front of visor, gilt chin scales with silver and green rosette under boss on right side, gilt heraldic star upon which is superimposed the Arms of Saxony in silver, silver cord oval field badge with green velvet center.*	1300.00	1450.00
☐ **Uhlan Other Ranks tschapka,** *Regiments 17 and 18, c. 1910. Other Ranks pattern lancer cap with brass and white metal trim and fittings and white cord and green cloth field badge.*	650.00	725.00
☐ **Uhlan Officer's tschapka,** *Regiment 21, c. 1910. Officer's pattern lancer cap as above, but with silver trim and fittings. Front plate consists of a silver heraldic star with the Arms of Saxony in gilt.*	1460.00	1625.00
☐ **Uhlan Other Ranks tschapka,** *Regiment 21, c. 1910. Other ranks pattern lancer cap with white metal and brass fittings and trim, white cord and green cloth field badge.*	550.00	625.00

Note: On certain occasions, such as for parade, a colored cloth cover was worn on the underside of the mortar board top. These were known variously as a curvet or as a rabatten. They had a cord binding at the edges and a cord loop through which the cap lines passed. The cap lines were of silver flecked with black for Prussian Officers and of white braid flecked with black for Other Ranks. For Saxon Officers they were of silver flecked with green and green flecked white braid for Saxon Other Ranks. Bavarian

Officers had silver flecked with blue and the Other Ranks had white cord flecked with green. A haarbusch or falling plume was also worn for parade and other special occasions. These were blue and white or white for Bavarian uhlans, black and white or black or white for Prussian uhlans and white for Saxon uhlans. As is the case in all headdress, that of Officer's was of much finer quality than that of Other Ranks.

The following rabatten colors were used: White: 1st Guard uhlans, 5th uhlans, 9th uhlans, 13th uhlans and the 17th uhlans. Dark Red: 18th uhlans. Scarlet: 2nd Guard uhlans, 2nd uhlans, 6th uhlans and 19th uhlans. Crimson: 10th uhlans, 14th uhlans, 1st Bavarian uhlans, 2nd Bavarian uhlans. Yellow: 3rd Guard uhlans, 3rd uhlans, 7th uhlans, 11th uhlans, 15th uhlans and 20th uhlans. Light Blue: 4th uhlans, 8th uhlans, 12th uhlans, 16th uhlans and 21st uhlans.

German lancer caps are infrequently found with plume, rabatten and cap lines. When they are found in this complete condition, $125.00 may be added to their value. Caps with lines and rabatten will be found more often. These may be valued at $75.00 more. Caps with either lines or a rabatten may be valued at $40.00 more.

POLAND   Price Range

☐ **Other Ranks lancer cap,** *c. 1885. Black leather cap and visor of rather conventional pattern with fairly high rounded crown. Front edge of visor bound with black leather. About the bottom of the skull is a medium width band of red wool cloth, trimmed top and bottom with narrow gilt braid. The brass chin scales are attached to each side of the cap by a brass boss bearing an embossed Polish Eagle. The large brass front plate is in the form of the Polish Eagle. The mortar board top is covered with red wool cloth trimmed about the top and down the edges with gilt braid. There is a white horsehair plume at the left front of the cap.* **375.00   425.00**

☐ **Other Ranks lancer cap,** *c. 1914. This is among the last forms of the Polish czapka, as the lancer cap was known in Poland. Again the cap and visor are of black leather. The base of the mortar top is fairly thin. Black leather binding to front of visor, brass chin scales, bosses and front plate as in above lancer cap, mortar board top covered with red wool cloth. Only top edges of mortar board trimmed with yellow braid, hanging black horsehair plume.* **300.00   325.00**

RUSSIA

☐ **Officer's czapka or lancer cap,** *14th Lancer Regiment, c. mid-1850's. Cap and visor of black leather. Cap extends up in a straight line into outward curve to form mortar board top. Silver trim to the front edge of visor, silver chin scales and side bosses. Halfway up the cap is a broad band of figured silver lace. The front plate is a silver cartouche with decorative border, with the numeral "14" in the center. Atop the cartouche is the*

Russian Officer's czapka,
14th Lancer Regiment, c. mid-1850's.

Price Range

Russian double-headed eagle with crown. The mortar board is covered with fine black cloth. There is a small silver ornament at each point of the top. About the edges of the top and across it to form an "X" and down each of the four corners is silver braid. A large plume of black and white feathers appears on the left top front of the cap.. 1100.00   1225.00

☐ **Officer's czapka or lancer cap,** His Majesty's Life Guard Lancer Regiment, c. 1914. This is probably one of the most beautiful of all lancer caps. Like most items of Russia of the Czarsa, it does not appear very frequently on the collector's market. Cap of rather conventional lancer pattern of polished black leather. The front edge of the visor is trimmed in silver. Silver chin scales attached to each side of the cap by small bosses. The beautiful front plate consists of the crowned double-headed Russian eagle and is in silver. On the breast of the eagle is the silver and enamel Star of the Order of St. Andrew First Called. Above the eagle is a scroll bearing battle honors in Russian. The underside of the mortar board top is covered with fine heavily ribbed yellow/gold cloth which joins a cap of silver bullion on

Price Range

top of the crown of the cap. At the center left of the mortar board is an oval field badge of silver upon which appear yellow, black, yellow, black ovals. The underside of the edges of the top are lines with silver cord, flecked with gold. The silver cap lines are also flecked in gold and terminate in two silver bullion tassels. **2300.00   2550.00**

UNITED STATES

As has been mentioned previously, the lancer cap was never very popular in the United States and was worn by only a few militia organizations who were looking for something rather fancy. The American specimens are rather shoddy and ill-proportioned as compared with those of the British and Continental Armies. Few American lancer caps have survived and these are not in any great demand, apparently being of most interest to collectors of Americana. The two examples described below are typical of what may be found.

U.S. Militia Officer's lancer cap
of an unknown lancer regiment, c. 1940.

☐ **Officer's lancer cap.** *Of an unknown militia unit, c. 1840. The cap is of conventional pattern. The skull is of dark red felt on a frame. The black leather visor is trimmed with a brass edge about the front. Encircling the base of the cap is a medium width black leather band. The front plate, which appears much too large for the cap, is a sunburst upon which is superimposed a stylized eagle, all in brass. The mortar board top is of black leather and the underside is covered with light tan* cloth. Gold lace trims the sides of the top and base of the mortar board and extends down each corner. Small brass pieces decorate each corner of the top. **300.00 325.00**

☐ **Officer's lancer cap.** Of a pattern perhaps used by the National Lancers of Boston, conventional pattern skull and top. Skull is covered with blue cloth. The front of the visor is trimmed with brass. Brass chin scales of unique square scales, attached to sides of cap by a large brass boss embossed with a flaming grenade. There is a medium black leather band about the bottom of the cap. The front plate is an extra large brass sunburst without any device or insignia. The mortar board top is covered with red cloth. Brass corners to top and gilt trim to top and bottom of mortar board, two gilt tassels hang from the right side of the mortar board. (From the large size of the front plates on these lancer caps and since they are out of proportion to the cap, it is quite possible that they were left over from an order for shakos.). **300.00 325.00**

ADDENDUM: The following listed three lancer caps do not often appear on the collectors' market. The first two appear most infrequently and the French cap does not often appear outside of museums. However, they are important additions to any lancer cap collection.

French lancer cap
of the 8th Chevau Leger
Lanciers Polomais, c. 1812.

☐ **Lancer cap or czapka.** Of the 8th Chevau Legers Lanciers Polomais, c. 1812. The plume, chin chain scales, cap lines and flounders are missing, which is

Price Range

usual in these specimens. Black leather skull and visor, visor trimmed with brass, embossed brass front plate with the initial "N" in the center, lion mask side bosses to which the chin chain attached, fluted green cloth top, painted leather cockade on the left side. 675.00 750.00

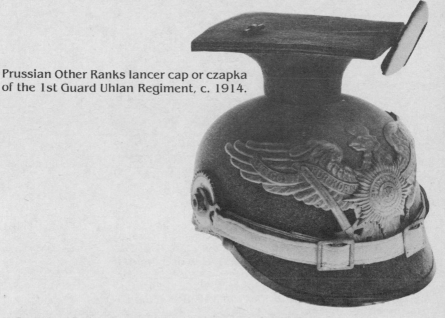

Prussian Other Ranks lancer cap or czapka of the 1st Guard Uhlan Regiment, c. 1914.

☐ **Prussian Other Ranks lancer cap or czapka.** *Of the Guard Uhlan Regiment 1, c. 1914. This cap is a wartime expedient made of gray-green felt in lieu of leather which was needed for more important purposes. Lancer cap of conventional lancer type, gray metal side fittings, visor trim and chin strap fittings. The chin strap is of reinforced khaki cloth, another saving of scarce leather. Gray metal front plate in the form of the Guard Eagle with a scroll bearing the motto "MIT GOTT FUR KONIG UND VATERLAND" across the wings. On the breast appears the Star of the Order of the Black Eagle. Red, white and black painted metal cockarden on the right side under the end of the chin strap. Black and white cockarden on the left side. Black and white cloth field badge on the left front of the top of the cap. . . . .* 375.00 425.00

☐ **Imperial German (Wurttemberg) lancer cap or czapka.** *Of the 2nd Wurttemberg Uhlans. This Other*

Imperial German
(Wurttenburg) czapka of
the 2nd Wurttemburg
Uhlans.

Price Range

*Ranks cap, c. 1900, is of black leather with brass
trim, fittings and front plate. The front plate is in the
form of the Royal Arms of Wurttemberg. Right metal
cockarden painted in red, white and black. Left
cockarden in red and black, the colors of Wurttemberg. Cloth field badge at the front left of the top of
the cap is red and black.* 300.00   325.00

THE MILITARY HAT

The earliest form of military headdress was the hat. It was simply an adaptation of the civilian headpiece, a broad brim item with a round crown. Inasmuch as the wide brim was somewhat awkward and impeded the use of
shoulder weapons, it was usually turned up on one side and secured to the
crown by a pin, a bunch of ribbons, a rosette or some other identifying device.
If the wearer were an officer, various color plumes might be added. The
military types kept experimenting to improve the style and the utility of the
hat. It was turned up on two sides to form a bicorne or was turned up on three
sides to become the tricorne. The tricorne is the pattern most often
associated with the American troops of the Revolutionary War. As a matter of
fact, it was worn by a multitude of armies. All were usually decorated about
the edges with white or colored tape for enlisted men and with gold or silver
lace for officers. They were further decorated by various kinds of plumes,
rosettes, tassels and other trimmings.

Eventually the bicorne was modified into the chapeau, sometimes called a
cocked hat. If constructed in such a manner that the sides could be pressed
in and folded against each other, the hat became a chapeau-de-bras.

The chapeau in its various forms was worn in many ways. At times it was worn with the turned up sides facing forward and back. At other times it might be worn with the ends of the hat facing front and back. Or it might be cocked over one or the other of the eyes. At times the chapeau-de-bras was so absurdly large and each end was so low that it was virtually impossible for the wearer to turn his head. This was really the height of military vanity. Although the chapeau was comparatively short lived for lower ranks, it was retained until well into this present century for wear by generals and for other special officer types.

The military hat has been largely ignored by militaria collectors. However, within the last year or two it has begun to be an item of interest. At the present time, even choice and historically important specimens may be secured for comparatively reasonable prices.

Example of the earliest form of military headdress.
Adaptation of a mid-1600's civilian hat worn by a Swedish soldier.

AUSTRIA   Price Range

☐ **General's Chapeau or Cocked hat,** *c. 1900's. Extra high quality black beaver cocked hat of high pattern, edges bound with very wide figured gold bullion lace. On the right side, from the top middle of the hat, a wide strip of gold bullion lace with pointed end extends down to almost the bottom, with a gilt button at the lower end. At the top of the hat is a plume of blue/white feathers. At the bottom front of the hat is a half-dome device of gold bullion cord with a black velvet center. Traced out in gold thread on this center is the cypher "FJ" (Francis Joseph)*. 385.00   425.00

☐ **General's Chapeau or Cocked hat,** *c. 1815. Of very high quality black beaver with the turn up on the right side higher than that on the left. Edges trimmed with figured gold lace, gold lace strap three-quarters of*

Price Range

the way down to gilt button. At the upper end of the strap is a greenish black plume of feathers, bullion tassels at each end. 300.00   325.00

☐ **Officer's hat,** *Field Jager Battalion No. 18, c. 1890's. Black of modified civilian pattern made of fine quality beaver with edges bound in black leather, bullion cord about the bottom of the crown. At left front of the hat is a light infantry horn with the bell and mouthpiece pointing up, supporting a high quality green/black plume. The figure "18" appears within the circle of the horn.* 330.00   375.00

☐ **Other Ranks Artillery hat,** *c. 1806. Large civilian type hat of the period of black felt or beaver. Medium height crown with straight sides and slightly rounded top, brim bound with black tape. Medium width brim except on left side where it is considerably wider and is turned up against the side of the crown. Front decorated with a vertical strip of cloth lace, with a yellow and black wool pompon at the top.* 250.00   275.00

☐ **Other Ranks hat,** *Jager Battalion No. 5, c. 1860's. Black felt hat of modified civilian pattern, much like an Austrian hunters hat of the period. Medium height crown with flat top and narrow brim turned up on left side but not fastened to the crown, greenish cord band about bottom. On the left side of the hat a brass light infantry horn with the bell to the top and the mouthpiece to the bottom. In the circle of the horn is the figure "5." A plume of black cock feathers is held in place by this device.* 275.00   300.00

FRANCE

☐ **Marines Other Ranks hat,** *c. 1800. Black felt with flat black leather top and upper band, fairly high crown, narrow cloth band about the bottom. Brim is narrow except on the left side where it is extremely wide and is turned back against the crown, extending above the top of the hat. In the center of the turn back is a brass foul anchor. The top of the turn back, which is rounded at the top, is a red, white and blue rosette with two white cloth bands forming a "V" to the bottom rear of the rosette.* 350.00   400.00

☐ **Other Ranks Cavalry Tricorne,** *c. 1760's. Black felt hat with fairly low crown, round on top with the wide brim turned up on three sides. On the turn up on the left side appears a cockade of yellow cloth. Edges of hat are unbound.* 200.00   275.00

☐ **Other Ranks Cocked hat,** *c. 1815. Hat of good quality black felt with medium/low crown. The edges of the brim are untrimmed. The brim is turned back in front and is rounded to follow the curved contour of the*

French Other Ranks Marine's hat, c. 1800.

Price Range

crown. The brim is much larger at the back and is
turned back to form a "fan" which extends well
above the crown. A red, white and blue cloth rosette
is at the top left front of the hat. 200.00   275.00

GREAT BRITAIN

☐ **Staff Officer's Cocked hat,** *c. early 1800's.* Fine quality black beaver hat designed to be worn front to
back with the turn backs on the side. Right front side
decorated with a highly ornamented badge of silver
bullion wire, the central figure being an eight star
with leaf-like rays. Gold bullion wire tassels are at
front and rear. On the top and falling to the back is a
large plume of white and red swan feathers. 300.00   345.00

British Army Surgeon's Cocked hat, c. 1890's.

PRUSSIA
Price Range

☐ **General's Bicorne,** *c. 1830's. Good quality black beaver with broad turn back brims to front and back, edges unbound, turnback to rear is higher than that in front. At top left of the front is a metal rosette enameled silver and black. Extending from the top of the hat down over this rosette almost to the bottom are five strands of silver bullion wire, secured at the bottom by a gilt button. There are gold bullion tassels at each end of the fold backs. At the top left is a large plume of black and white feathers. Although this may be an interesting historical item, the demand is low.* .   200.00   225.00

☐ **Other Ranks Fusilier hat,** *c. 1790's. Bicorne pattern of black felt. Medium high crown with wide brim turned back in front and back, edges bound with white cloth tape. On the front appears a white metal eagle of rather crude design. At the top left of the front turn back is a black and white wool pompon.* 150.00   175.00

☐ **Other Ranks hat,** *c. 1780's. Black felt with narrow sides and broad front and back brims, medium height round top crown. Front and back brims turned back and fastened to crown, edges bound in white cloth tape. The cypher "FWR" (Friedrich Wilhelm) in white tape appears on the front.* 150.00   175.00

UNITED STATES

U.S. Army Enlisted Man's
Artillery hat, c. late 1850's.

Price Range

☐ **Enlisted Man's Artillery hat,** *c. late 1850's. So-called "Hardee" hat. Made of black felt with medium height crown with sunken top. Sides taper inward toward the top giving the crown the appearance of an upside down flower pot. Broad brim trimmed with black cloth and turned up on right side and held by a brass device in the form of the U.S. Arms. A double red cord encircles the bottom of the crown and terminates in front with two tassels. On the front are large brass crossed cannons. A flimsy black feather adorns the left side. With changed front insignia, i.e., crossed sabers for cavalry, flaming bomb for ordnance, a castle for engineers, etc., and with the proper color hat cord, this hat was worn by all enlisted men. The price is the same for all.* 250.00   275.00

☐ **Marine Officer's Chapeau,** *(majors, lieutenant colonels and colonels) c. 1860's. Very dark blue felt cocked hat with the turn back on the right side slightly higher than that on the left. Edges bound with black silk braid, gold bullion tassels at front and rear. At top left is a large black silk rosette. Extending down over this, at a forward angle from top to bottom, are two bands of gold bullion lace terminating in a pointed end and secured by a large gilt button. A large plume of scarlet vulture feathers extends over the top of the hat from front to rear.* 400.00   450.00

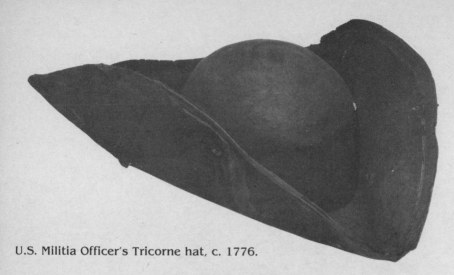

U.S. Militia Officer's Tricorne hat, c. 1776.

U.S. Army Officer's Cocked hat,
c. early 1800's.

Price Range

☐ **Militia Officer's Tricorne hat.** *This is simply a wide brim civilian hat with the brim turned back on three sides. The crown is fairly low and is rounded on top, edges bound with black silk. On the right side there is a black silk rosette.* 400.00   450.00

Price Range

☐ **Officer's Chapeau-de-bras.** *An extremely large, black felt hat designed so that it may be folded and carried under the arm. Silver wire tassels hang from each end. At the top front, slightly to the right, is a large black leather rosette with a small metal American eagle. Extending down from this rosette is a double strand of silver bullion cord which forms a loop about a button at the bottom. At the top left of the hat is a red feather plume.* 400.00   450.00

☐ **Officer's Cocked hat,** *c. early 1800's. Bicorne of black felt designed to be worn with the ends over each side of the head. The turn back to the rear is slightly larger than that in front. Edges bound with wide black silk. From top to bottom on each side of the front is a strip of wide black silk. At the top left front is a black leather rosette bearing a small stylized gilt metal eagle. On either side of the rosette, extending from top to bottom, are two strands of gold wire looping about a small gilt button at the bottom. In this specimen there is provision for a plume but the plume is not present.* 400.00   450.00

MIRLETON, BUSBY AND BEARSKIN

With the possible exception of the Imperial German version of the busby, called the **pelzmutze,** to date there has not been too great an interest in these three types of headdress except by specialized collectors. Except for the Imperial German items, which command a fancy price, many specimens from other armies may be had fairly reasonably. Here again is another field of collecting which the beginning collector or the collector of limited financial means might want to consider.

There is some question as to the origin of the mirleton which was worn at one time by the British, French and German hussars, among others. Some military historians affirm that this type of headdress was introduced by the French hussars and that it was inspired by a similar type of headdress worn in the Orient. The German version was known as a flugelmutze or winged cap. In any event this type of headdress consists of a high cylindrical felt or cloth cap with a very long loose piece of cloth which could be wrapped about the cap as a sort of turban or could be allowed to fly free. There were several variations of the mirleton. Some were conical at the top, others were flat. Some were rather plain around the bottom, others had a wide band about the bottom with a turned-up peak resting against the cap. A death design was popular with the Prussian regiments and was carried over in later times to the pelzmutze. This particular design may have originated from the death's head design in the funeral trappings used during the burial of King Frederick William I.

The busby is typically a fairly low profile cylindrical fur headpiece. The name "busby" is said to derive from the cylindrical fur caps made for the British Army originally by the London military outfitter W. Busby in the early 1800's.

The bearskin, the tall fur cap most often associated with the British Foot Guards, may be the least collected of all the various types of military headdress. Their large size and difficulty of preservation and display may have much to do with this. However, inasmuch as there are a few collectors interested in them, they must be included here. It is of some interest that the bearskin was never worn by any units of the U.S. Army and Marine Corps except in some instances by drum majors. These are one of a kind items which remain U.S. Government property and are never offered for sale but are assigned to military museums when no longer used. Of course, some of the more affluent militia units wore them for a time but these are very few and far between on the collectors' market. The items listed in the following price guide are those which have been offered for sale from time to time.

GERMANY (Imperial)

Brunswick   **Price Range**

☐ **Officer's busby,** *17th Hussar Regiment. Black bearskin busby with scarlet cloth top and bag, gilt chin scales. On the front appears a silver skull and crossbones. Above is a gilt metal band or ribbon bearing the inscription "PENINSULA, SICILIEN, WATERLOO, MARS LA TOUR." At top front is an oval field badge of silver wire with a black velvet center.* 2500.00   2800.00

☐ **Other Ranks busby,** *17th Hussar Regiment. Busby similar in pattern to the above but of black sealskin and with brass fittings. Oval field badge at top front of black and white cloth.* 1125.00   1250.00

Prussia

☐ **Other Ranks mirleton or flugelmutze,** *c. mid-1700's. Black felt high conical cap with a cloth skull and crossbones on the lower front. A long black and white piece of cloth ("wing") hangs down on the right side as does white plaited cord, "waffles" and tassels.* 450.00   525.00

☐ **Other Ranks mirleton or flugelmutze,** *Hussar Regiment von Belling. Black cloth covered conical body of medium height with flat top of black leather, black leather binding about the bottom, white cord about the top and bottom of the headdress, black and white cloth wing. On the front of the flugelmutze is the figure of reclining skeleton holding a scythe with the motto "VINCERE-AUT-MORI" below. Translated this motto reads "Victory or Death."* 430.00   475.00

☐ **Officer's busby,** *Life Guard Hussar Regiment. Otter fur, scarlet cloth top and bag hanging down on the left side, gilt chin scales. Front plate consisting of the Guard Star in silver and enamel with a bandeau bearing the motto "MIT GOTT FUR KONIG UND VATERLAND" intertwined with the rays of the star. Oval field badge at the top front of silver wire with a black velvet center.* 2350.00   2600.00

☐ **Other Ranks busby,** *Life Guard Hussar Regiment. Same pattern as above but of black sealskin and with*

Prussian Other Ranks Mirlton
or Flugelmutze, c. mid-1700's.

	Price Range	

silver color metal front plate and chin scales. Oval
field badge at top front of black and white cloth. **1015.00 1200.00**

☐ **Officer's busby,** *1st and 2nd Royal Body Guard
Hussars. These were the famous "Death's Head
Hussars." Before 1912 this busby was of brown otter
fur. After that it was of gray opossum. The cloth top
and busby of the 1st Body Guard Hussars were scarlet. For the 2nd Life Guard Hussars these were white.
Both regimental busbies had gilt chin scales. The
front plate for both consisted of a large silver skull
and crossbones over which was a silver bandeau
bearing the motto "MIT GOTT FUR KONIG UND
VATERLAND." Oval field badge of silver with black
velvet center. This is a much sought after item.* **2210.00 2550.00**

☐ **Other Ranks busby,** *1st and 2nd Royal Body Guard
Hussars. Busby of the same pattern as above but of
black sealskin. Fittings and trim of brass and silver
color metal. Cloth black and white field badge.* **1265.00 1400.00**

Officer's Busby, 1st Prussian Royal Body Guard Hussars.

Price Range

☐ **Officer's busby,** *3rd, 4th, 5th, 6th, 8th, 9th, 10th, 11th, 12th, 13th and 14th Hussar Regiments. Otter fur busby before 1912, opossum fur thereafter. Officer's pattern busby as above, gilt chin scales. The front plate consisted of a metal bandeau bearing the motto "MIT GOTT FUR KONIG UND VATERLAND." This was of gilt for the 4th, 6th, 9th and 10th Hussars and silver for the 3rd, 5th, 8th, 11th, 12th, 13th and 14th Hussars. Silver wire and black velvet field badge for all regiments. Scarlet cloth top and bag for the 3rd, 6th, 7th, 11th, and 14th Hussars. White cloth top and bag for the 12th Hussars, yellow for the 4th Hussars, crimson for the 5th Hussars, light blue for the 8th and 9th Hussars, purple for the 10th Hussars. Prices are the same for any of these regiments.* 1450.00   1600.00

☐ **Other Ranks busby.** *Same regiments as above. Black sealskin busby similar in pattern to the officer's model, but with brass or white metal fittings and trim, as appropriate. Black and white cloth field badge.* 775.00   860.00

Price Range

☐ **Officer's busby,** *7th Hussar Regiment. Otter fur until 1912, opossum fur thereafter, scarlet cloth top and bag, gilt chin scales. Front plate consisting of the initials "W.R." intertwined with the numeral "1" (William 1st) with a Royal Crown above. Under this device is a bandeau bearing the motto "MIT GOTT FUR KONIG UND VATERLAND," all in gilt. Silver and black velvet field badge at the top front.* 2500.00   2775.00

☐ **Other Ranks busby,** *7th Hussar Regiment. As above except that the busby is of black sealskin and fittings are of brass, cloth black and white field badge.* 1100.00   1225.00

☐ **Officer's busby,** *15th Hussar Regiment. Opossum fur busby with gilt chin scales. Front plate consisting of silver bandeau bearing the motto "MIT GOTT FUR KONIG UND VATERLAND." Under this are four laurel leaves bearing the battle honors "PENINSULA-WATERLOO-EL BONDON-BAROSSA." Silver and black velvet field badge.* 2400.00   3000.00

☐ **Other Ranks busby,** *15th Hussar Regiment. As above except that the busby is of black sealskin and fittings are brass and silver color metal.* 1015.00   1150.00

Saxony
☐ **Officer's busby.** *18th, 19th and 20th Hussar Regiments. Otter fur before 1912, opossum fur thereafter, gilt chin scales, front plate consisting of the Arms of Saxony on a gilt heraldic star. Scarlet cloth top and bag for the 18th Hussars, dark red for the 19th Hussars and light blue for the 20th Hussars. Field badge at top front of silver wire with green velvet center.* 1825.00   2150.00

☐ **Other Ranks busby,** *18th, 19th and 20th Hussar Regiments. Same pattern as above except that the busby was of black sealskin. All fittings in brass and silver color metal, oval field badge of white and green cloth.* 1125.00   1250.00

Note: For parade all hussar regiments wore long ornamental lines which attached the busby to the body of the wearer. This was originally intended to prevent loss of the headpiece in the rapid movement of combat. For the Prussian regiments, this was silver cord flecked with black silk. For other ranks, it was white cord flecked with black. For the Saxon hussar regiments, it was silver cord flecked with green silk and for other ranks, it was white cord flecked with green. An upright plume of white or white and black heron feathers was worn by Prussian hussar officers and a white hair plume by other ranks. The Saxon regiments had a green and white heron feather plume while other ranks had a white hair plume. During World War I a gray cloth cover was worn over the busby to conceal the bright trim and fittings. During this period the later issue busbies were issued with dull gray fittings and a leather chin strap. Busbies with cords and plume increase in value to $25.00 more while for other ranks, the value increases to $15.00 more. Busbies with leather chin strap and gray metal fittings will sell for around half the value of the headdress with gilt, silver, brass and silver color metal fittings. Gray cloth busby covers will sell in the neighborhood of $30.00.

Replica busbies are offered for sale from time to time. The materials used and the method of construction are such that they present no problem to the experienced collector. The beginning collector would do well to consult an expert if in doubt. These replica busbies sell for around $100.00. Certainly no authentic specimen may be had for that price.

GREAT BRITAIN

British Officer's Fur busby, 15th Hussars, c. late 1800's.

Price Range

☐ **Officer's Fur busby,** *15th Hussars, c. late 1800's. Black fur busby of medium height, blue cloth top and bag with gold cord trim. At the top front of the busby is a boss of gold cord. The flaming grenade-type plume holder at top front holds red vulture feathers which in turn support white ostrich feathers. Gilt/gold chin scales with leather backing.* **300.00 350.00**

☐ **Officer's Fur busby,** *Hussars, c. mid-1800's. Brown fur with a scarlet bag with gilt lace trim hanging down over the right side. This bag is a holdover from the days when hussars wore a long bag-like cap which fell over on one side. Leather-lined gilt chin chain. At the top front is an ornamental gilt device*

Price Range

holding a plume of white egret feathers set into
scarlet vulture feathers. 215.00   237.00

☐ **Other Ranks Black Fur busby,** *the Welsh Fusiliers.*
Front plate of the regimental badge in the form of a
flaming grenade on the front and with a small white
hair plume on the right side. 160.00   175.00

☐ **Other Ranks Black Fur busby,** *the Royal Fusiliers.*
Front plate of the regimental badge in the form of a
flaming grenade in brass, a white hair plume on the
left. 125.00   150.00

☐ **Other Ranks busby,** *the Rifle Brigade, c. late 1800's.*
Although the busby was usually worn by hussars,
during the late 1800's certain elite rifle units and certain horse artillery units, because of their ability to
maneuver quickly and easily in the manner of cavalry,
adopted a modified version of the busby. This particular specimen is of the so-called envelope pattern.
It is made of black fur and is trimmed with black
plaited cords. On the lower front of the busby is the
bronze badge of the regiment consisting of a maltese
cross within a wreath with crown above. Above this
badge and separated from it is a Royal Crown. Above
this is a bronze plume holder in the form of a flaming
grenade holding a hair plume. 250.00   275.00

☐ **Other Ranks Fur busby,** *11th Hussars. Black fur busby*
with crimson cloth top and bag hanging down on
right side, bag trimmed with gilt cord, crimson and
white hair plume at top front. 160.00   175.00

☐ **Royal Artillery Officer's Fur busby,** *c. late 1850's. This*
volunteer officer's headdress, so indicated by the
silver color fittings in lieu of the gilt of the Regular
Service, is of brown fur. It has a red cloth top and a
red bag hanging over on the right side. On the left
side is a silver flaming grenade with the Royal Artillery crest on the grenade body. This badge forms a
holder for a white hair plume. The chin chain is of
silver lined with leather. 185.00   200.00

☐ **Royal Fusiliers Officer's Bearskin cap,** *c. early*
1900's. Black bearskin cap with leather-lined gilt chin
chain, gilt regimental badge on the front and white
feather on the left side. 335.00   380.00

☐ **Royal Fusiliers Officer's Raccoon skin cap,** *c. late*
1800's. Leather-lined gilt chin chain. Front plate in
the form of the regimental badge, consisting of a circular grenade design upon which appears the Garter
with gilt motto against a blue enamel background
with a red and white heraldic rose in the center, gilt
flame issuing from the top of the grenade. 435.00   490.00

☐ **Royal Scots Greys Other Ranks Bearskin cap,** *c. early*
1900's. Black fur bearskin with leather-lined brass

British Royal Artillery Officer's Fur busby, c. late 1850's.

	Price Range	

chin chain, brass regimental badge of flaming grenade on the left side. On the ball of the grenade appears the Royal Arms, white plume above the badge. 305.00   350.00

ITALY

☐ **Royal Italian Cavalry busby,** *c. early 1900's. Officer's high quality black fur busby with silver bullion intertwined cord about the bottom, flaming grenade superimposed upon crossed lances with flags. Superimposed upon the body of the grenade is a stylized hunting horn with the ring of the horn encircling the body of the grenade. Upon the body of the grenade is the cross of Savoy. This total device is superimposed upon a rosette of red, silver and green. At the top front of the busby is a feather holder in the form of a red pompon. This holds a large cut and formed eagle feather for parade.* 615.00   690.00

☐ **Royal Italian Cavalry busby,** *c. early 1900's. Other Ranks model. Same pattern as above. Red cloth cord about the bottom of the busby. Brass front plate on red, white and green cloth cockade. Red felt feather*

British Royal Fusiliers
Raccoon Skin cap,
c. late 1800's.

Price Range

*holder with eagle feather smaller than that worn by
officers.* **325.00**   **350.00**
*Note: The front plate noted on the above two busbies was the same as
that worn by all personnel attached to the cavalry school cavalry depot,
remount centers and cavalry squadrons.*

NETHERLANDS

☐ **Officer's Fur busby,** *a horse artillery regiment. As in
the British service the hussar-type busby was worn
by certain other elite units. This specimen is in black
fur with a red cloth top. A red bag hangs down on the
right side and red plaited cords and tassel hang
down from the left. The large front device consists of
large gilt crossed cannons with a large Royal Crown
above. At the top front is a white plume.* **210.00**   **250.00**

Royal Italian Cavalry
Other Ranks busby,
c. early 1900's.

THE SHAKO (Including the Kepi)

Of all the many kinds of military headdress, the shako was perhaps the most popular and the most universally adopted of all. Introduced in the late 1700's, it appeared in a wide variety of patterns throughout the years. For a time it was a most important part of the uniform of the armies of Austria, Great Britain, Germany, the United States, and many others, including the armies of many South American countries.

Military historians are rather well agreed that the shako originally developed from the flat top cylindrical headpiece worn by the Austrian Frontier Force, and modified in the 1790's with the addition of a front visor or peak (as it is known in Europe). The word "shako" itself is thought to derive from the Magyr word for "peaked cap."

At first the body of the shako was rather high, then over the years it gradually became lower. One pattern had a stiff leather front piece extending well above the crown. Another pattern, the bell top shako, had a crown considerably wider at the top than the bottom of the shako. In time these two patterns gave way to other distinctive patterns. One had straight sides and a low flat crown. The other also had a low flat crown but was well rounded in profile at the back. This particular pattern was extremely popular in the German states. All shakos had a front visor and some had a rear visor also.

As may be expected, the decorations on the front of the shakos consisted of national arms, regimental or royal crests or cyphers, or colored rosettes and unit numbers. The top front was most often decorated with a colored tuft, pompon or similar device. A wide variety of chin scales, chin chains and leather chin straps were used. Shakos were usually made of felt or leather or a combination of the two.

In a desire to dress up the shako, some nations went beyond the bounds of good taste to the ridiculous, ending up with headdress which would give credit to the comic opera. The Prussians and the Russians seemed to have a particular flair for this sort of thing. They draped an abundance of cords about the shako and added enormous elongated plumes to the top front of the headdress. Interestingly enough, some of the American militia units in the early 1800's also showed a similar lack of good taste.

During the 1880's the French developed a stiff felt shako with sloping sides and a small flat top. It had a flat leather visor. The new pattern shako was first used by French troops in Africa. After a time this item developed into a small cloth cap with a flat leather visor and a small flat top. The cloth body was soft enough to allow the top to slope down forward. Known to the French as the **kepi**, it was adopted by a number of armies, including those of the Union and the Confederacy during the American Civil War. It was also used by the U.S. Army for several years thereafter, as well as by a number of militia outfits.

AUSTRIA   Price Range

☐ **Hussar Officer's shako,** *c. early 1900's. Medium high stiff black felt body, straight sides and front, with slight outward slope at back. Leather top and visor, leather band about bottom. Visor not decorated. A wide figured bullion band surrounds almost the top half of the shako. Bullion shako cords and "waffles" are draped about the headpiece. At the top front appears a gilt metal rosette bearing the cypher "FJ." Projecting up from this rosette is a stiff black hair aigrette. The front plate is the double-headed Austrian eagle in gilt metal. The regimental number appears on a shield upon the breast of the eagle.....*   **700.00**   **775.00**

☐ **Hussar Officer's shako.** *Similar in general profile to the above but with the top three-quarters of the shako surrounded by rich bullion cloth. Gold bullion decoration covers the outer two-thirds of the visor. Gilt cords in elaborate design are draped about the shako with large "waffles" hanging down on the right side. Top front decorated with gilt rosette bearing the cypher "FJ." A long stiff feather aigrette projects up from this rosette. The front plate consists of a richly gilted Austrian double-head eagle.................*   **1375.00**   **1525.00**

☐ **Infantry Officer's shako,** *c. 1854. Stiff black felt body with flat leather top and black leather band around the bottom. Top front is decorated with gold bullion cockade bearing the cypher "FJ" (Francis Joseph). About the top of the shako are three wide bands of figured bullion tape. These cover almost the top half*

Austrian Officer's shako, c. 1854.

Price Range

of the shako. The front edge of the visor is trimmed with gold bullion. A thin gilt chain extends around the front of the shako from one end of the visor to the other. This shako is fairly high and, while the front and sides are straight, the rear flares out slightly to the bottom. 375.00   425.00

☐ **Infantry Other Ranks shako,** c. 1809. Black leather with the top slightly larger than the bottom. Flat top, large visors front and back. Decorative yellow wool device with black center at top front. Brass sunburst on center front of shako with decorative brass device extending from center of sunburst to top of shako. . .   750.00   850.00

FRANCE

☐ **Artillery Officer's shako,** c. 1860's. Stiff black felt shako, straight in front, with considerable flare out toward the bottom on the sides and back. Black leather top and flat black leather visor. Wide black leather band about the bottom and wide gold braid band around the top. A wide gold braid "V" appears on each side of the shako. The front plate consists of a large gilt eagle standing upon a cannon ball which in turn rests on crossed cannons. Behind the eagle's head is the usual red, white and blue metal cockade. A falling white horsehair plume decorates the top front. 475.00   525.00

Price Range

☐ **Grenadier Officer's shako,** *c. mid-1800's. Stiff black felt shako with flat leather top and black leather band about the bottom. Flat black leather visor, wide fancy silver braid around the top of the shako. Silver chin scales attached at each side with embossed disk of silver, each bearing a flaming grenade. Ornate front plate consisting of a cock atop a globe superimposed on crossed fasces. A banner appears on each side of the globe bearing the legend "LIBERTY, EGALITE, FRATERNITE." Below the globe appears a ribbon bearing "REPUBLIQUE FRANCAISE." Between the front plate and the top of the shako appears a metal red, white and blue rosette. A red ball with red pompon on top of it appears at the top front of the shako.* 475.00   525.00

☐ **Marshal's shako or casquette** *for use in North Africa, c. 1860. Tall stiff red felt shako smaller at the top than at the bottom, flat black leather visor. Six rows of gold braid about the top of the shako, wide black velvet band about the bottom with a row of gold braid above. Gold chin strap backed with leather, flat red cloth top decorated with small gold braid quarterfoil, red and white metal cockade at center front of shako. Six lines of gold braid extend from under a gilt button in the middle of the rosette up to the top of the shako.*   475.00   525.00

French National Guard
Officer's shako, c. 1830's.

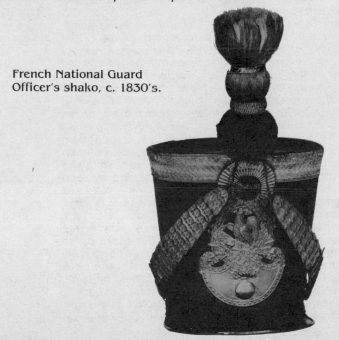

Price Range

☐ **National Guard Officer's shako,** *c. early 1830's. Stiff black felt shako with flat black leather top and black flat leather visor. Medium width black leather band about the bottom. Gold lace surrounds the top of the shako. The extra wide chin scales are gilt. The gilt front plate consists of a cartouche with flaming grenade in the center. The cartouche has a decorative edge. Atop the cartouche is a cock surrounded by a wreath. The cock stands on a trophy of arms. There is a red, white and blue rosette between the front plate and the top of the shako. At top front is a wool ball topped by a standing hair tuft.* 750.00   825.00

☐ **Hussar Officer's shako,** *c. 1825. Black leather shako somewhat wider at the top than at the bottom, flat black leather top, high quality gold bullion band around the top. Gold bullion interwoven cords looped about shako and held on each side by gilt hook at top of shako. "Waffles" and tassels hang down on left side. Gilt front plate is fine detail consisting of oval upon which appear three fleur-de-lis. Royal crown above oval, oval superimposed on stand of flags. Gilt chin scales attached at each side by large embossed disk, bearing a fleur-de-lis. Gold bullion oval shape rosette with red center at top front. Regimental number in bullion thread appears in center. Also at top front is an absurdly tall white feather plume.* 1100.00   1225.00

☐ **Hussar Officer's shako,** *c. 1890. This shako is something of a departure from the foregoing shakos in that the body is of light blue felt instead of black. A number of other French hussar shakos of this period and the shako of the French military academy to this day is blue. The flat leather top is black as is the wide band around the bottom of the headpiece. The slightly arched visor is also of black leather. Around the top of the shako is a wide band of silver lace. A silver chin chain attaches to each side to a lion head boss. At the bottom front of the shako is a silver flaming grenade. Between it and the top of the shako is the usual red, white and blue metal rosette. Three strands of silver braid loop around a silver button in the center of the rosette and extend to the top of the shako. At the top front is a ball ornament made of silver braid* 330.00   395.00

☐ **Officer's shako,** *7e Regiment Infanterie Suisse dea Garde de Roi, c. 1815. This is a colorful shako but is absurdly tall and is of the toy soldier, comic opera type. Extremely tall stiff cylindrical red felt shako with cloth red flat top. Wide gold bullion lace, backed by black leather about the top. Black leather circular turn back at the back, flat black leather visor, gilt chin chains, gilt lion mask and hook on left side of shako. Gilt rosette on*

Price Range

*bottom front third of shako with plain gilt button, joined
to top of headpiece by two ornate bullion bands. Large
yellow (gold) wool pompon at the top front.* 650.00   725.00

☐ **Other Ranks shako,** *c. early 1800's. Stiff black felt
shako, slightly wider at the top than at the bottom. Flat
black leather top, black leather band about top and bottom, black leather visor. Front plate consists of large
brass half sunburst with small plain button at top.
Lower part of sunburst is plain with a light infantry horn
embossed in the center. Red, white and blue rosette
above and half covered by the front plate. Red wool
two-part pompon at top front of shako.* 475.00   525.00

French Other Ranks shako,
c. 1808.

☐ **Other Ranks shako,** *c. 1808. Stiff black felt shako of
medium height with flat leather top. Black leather band
around top and bottom, black leather "V" on each side
of shako joins top and bottom bands. Black leather
visor, large metal front plate in form of ornate cartouche
with eagle at top. Napoleon's profile embossed in
center of cartouche with "N" on one side and "IR" on
other. Regimental number below. Red, white and blue
cockade between eagle's head and top of shako, red
wool pompon, brass chin scales* 1375.00   1530.00

☐ **Other Ranks shako or casquette,** *3rd African
Chausseurs, c. 1840. Tall stiff red felt shako similar in
profile to Marshal's shako. Flat black visor with cut,*

Price Range

unfinished edge. Wide black wool band about the bottom of the shako, narrow black braid down each side and the back. Red flat top has round brass button in the center with two lines of black braid extending to the back. Red, white and blue metal rosette at center front of shako, a brass figure "3" appears below. Four lines of black braid extend from a brass button in center of rosette to top of shako. A yellow wool ball decorates the top front................................... 200.00   225.00

GERMANY (Including the Third Reich)

☐ **Bavaria, Landwehr Artillery Other Ranks shako,** c. 1825. Large black felt shako with an extreme flare at the very top. Flat black leather top with black leather band about the top. Black leather visor, white metal chin scales attached on each side of the shako to a lion head boss. Large white metal front plate consisting of a cartouche within a wreath and with a crown above. An embossed flaming grenade appears in the center of the cartouche. At the top left side of the shako is a white metal hook attached to a lion head. This was for attaching shako lines, which are not present. 520.00   575.00

☐ **Bavaria, Officer's shako,** 1st and 2nd Jager Battalions, after 1895. High quality black felt over leather shako with slightly sunken flat black leather top. Short black front and rear visors. Flat gilt chin scales attached on each side under a gilt boss with a rosette in the national colors (red, white and black) under the right one. Highly detailed gilt front plate consisting of the Bavarian arms. Large oval field badge at top front of silver bullion and blue velvet. Shako straight in front and rounded profile at back. 520.00   575.00

☐ **Bavaria, Other Ranks shako,** 1st and 2nd Jager Battalions, after 1895. As above, but with all leather shako, leather chin strap, brass front plate, cloth field badge. 300.00   325.00

☐ **Bavaria, Officer's shako,** Railway Battalion, after 1911. As above, Jager Officer's helmet, but with silver front plate and flat silver chin scales. 520.00   575.00

☐ **Bavaria, Other Ranks shako,** Railway Battalion, after 1911. As above, Jager Other Ranks Jager shako but with white metal front plate. 400.00   550.00

☐ **Brunswick, Officer's shako,** III Battalion, Infantry Regiment 92, before March 30, 1889. Fairly tall black leather shako with flat top and front and rear visor, flat gilt chin scales. Front plate of silver in the form of a skull and crossbones with a scroll below with the legend "PENINSULA." Gilt oval field badge with blue velvet center. National red, white and black rosette under chin strap................................. 1100.00   1225.00

Price Range

☐ **Brunswick, Other Ranks shako,** *III Battalion, Infantry Regiment 92, before March 30, 1889. Shako of leather but not felt covered, leather chin strap with single buckle in front, white metal front plate, cloth field badge.* 825.00   925.00

☐ **Brunswick, Officer's shako,** *I and II Battalions, Infantry Regiment 92, before March 30, 1889. Similar to above, but with front plate consisting of the Star of the House Order of Henry the Lion in gilt and enamel, round silver chin scales.* 1050.00   1175.00

☐ **Brunswick, Other Ranks shako,** *I and II Battalions, Infantry Regiment 92, before March 30, 1889. Shako as above of leather, black leather chin strap, field badge of cloth.* 700.00   775.00

☐ **Mecklenburg-Schwerin, Officer's shako,** *Jager Battalion 14. Officer's shako as above. Flat gilt chin scales. National red, white and black rosette under right end of chin scales. Silver arms of Mecklenburg-Schwerin superimposed upon a silver heraldic star in the front plate. Field badge at top front consisting of gold cord oval with gold cord cross on center oval of velvet dividing it into red and blue and blue and red portions.* 655.00   745.00

☐ **Mecklenburg-Schwerin Other Ranks shako,** *Jager Battalion 14. All leather shako, the same pattern as above. Leather chin strap, white metal front plate, cloth field badge.* 430.00   475.00

☐ **Prussia, Other Ranks shako,** *Guard Fusilier Battalion, c. 1815. Medium height black felt shako with the top slightly larger than the bottom, white band about the top, leather visor and chin strap. White metal Star of The Order of the Black Eagle for front plate. White and black cloth field badge, black visor, tall clumsy-looking black plume at top front of shako. This absurd plume exceeds the shako itself in height and is as big around as the top of the shako.* 560.00   630.00

☐ **Above shako** *without plume.* 475.00   525.00

☐ **Prussia, Other Ranks shako,** *Landwehr Infantry, c. early 1800's. Black felt bell top shako very similar to the British bell top shako. Black leather top (flat) and band about the top. Black leather band about the bottom and black leather visor. Brass scale chin straps, large front plate of metal, circular in shape with a white border. In the center, on a black background is a white metal Landwehr cross similar to a Maltese cross. On the upper arms of the cross appears "MIT GOTT" (WITH GOD). Across the horizontal arms of the cross appears "FUR KONIG UND VATERLAND" (FOR KING AND FATHERLAND). On the bottom arm of the cross appears the date "1813," when the Landwehr was formed. Heavy plaited white shako lines*

Prussian Landwehr Infantry
Other Ranks shako, c. early 1800's.

Price Range

*drape from the sides of the shako down across the
front. Tassels and cords hang from a ring attached to
the top of the shako on the right side. A black and
white cloth field badge is attached to the top front...* 560.00 675.00

☐ **Prussia, Dragoon Officer's shako,** *c. 1830. Medium
height black felt shako slightly larger at the top than
at the bottom. Flat black top and band about the top,
all of leather, leather band about the bottom. Deep
black leather visors both front and back trimmed on
the edges with a brass binding. Brass chin scales
attached to each side of the shako by a brass Prussian heraldic eagle device. White cord plaited shako
lines drape from the top of each side to drape down
across the front of the shako. Long shako lines with
"waffles" and tassels, all in white, hang from the
right side. White metal star of The Order of the Black
Eagle, with brass center, makes up the front plate.
Oval silver field badge with black velvet center.
Above this is an absurdly tall plume of feathers,
white over black.* 830.00 945.00

☐ **Above shako** *without feather plume.* 650.00 725.00

☐ **Prussia, Officer's shako,** *Jager Battalions 3, 4, 8, 9,
11. Shako is Officer's pattern, flat chin scales in gilt,
gilt front plate in the form of the Prussian heraldic
eagle. National red, white and black rosette under*

Price Range

*end of chin scales on left side. Silver cord oval field
badge with black velvet center.* 430.00   475.00

☐ **Prussia, Other Ranks shako,** *Jager Battalions 3, 4, 8,
9, 11. Other Ranks pattern shako, leather chin strap,
brass front plate, cloth field badge, red, white and
black metal rosette under end of chin strap on right
side.* 275.00   300.00

☐ **Prussia, Officer's shako,** *Jager Battalion 10. Officer's
shako as above, but with gilt Prussian heraldic eagle
with a circular band over the eagle's neck, behind the
wings and over the legs, bearing the inscription
"PENINSULA-WATERLOO-VENTA-DEL POZO."* 725.00   800.00

☐ **Prussia, Other Ranks shako,** *Jager Battalion 10. As
above but Other Ranks pattern shako, with brass
front plate, leather chin strap and cloth field badge.*   475.00   530.00

☐ **Prussia, Officer's shako,** *Machine Gun Units 1 to 7.
Officer's pattern shako as above but body covered
with green felt. Flat gilt chin scales, gilt Prussian
heraldic eagle, brown leather top and front and rear
visors.* 565.00   625.00

☐ **Prussia, Other Ranks shako,** *Machine Gun Units 1 to
7. Other Ranks pattern shako but body covered with
green felt. Brass Prussian heraldic eagle, brown
leather chin strap and front and rear visors.* 430.00   480.00

☐ **Rostock, Officer's shako,** *Burgerwehr, c. 1850. Black
felt shako of medium height with straight sides.
Black leather top with black leather band about the
top, black leather band about the bottom and large
black leather visor. Large gilt front plate in the form
of a griffin, tall white horsehair plume at top front.* 340.00   380.00

☐ **Saxony, Officer's shako,** *Infantry Regiment 108
(Saxon Sharpshooters) and Jager Battalions 12 and
13. Black felt shako with flat sunken black leather
top and black leather bottom band. About top are gilt
or silver bands of lace, the number of bands depending upon the rank of the wearer. Silver arms of
Saxony with light infantry horn below, all upon a gilt
heraldic star compose the front plate. Silver cord
oval field badge with green velvet center at top front,
leather chin strap. Small rosette in red, white and
black under end of chin strap on right side. For
parade a falling horsehair plume (black) secured to
the left side of the shako as it falls from the top front.*   655.00   750.00

☐ **Saxony, Other Ranks shako,** *Infantry Regiment 108
(Saxon Sharpshooters) and Jager Battalions 12 and
13. Black felt shako as above, but without lace bands
about the top. Brass and white metal front plate,
cloth field badge.* 385.00   435.00

*Note: The Saxon shakos differ considerably from those of the other Ger-
man states in that they are not as high, have a shorter arc to the curve at*

Saxon Officer's shako, Infantry Regiment 108 (Saxon Sharpshooters).

back and the top is tilted slightly down in front. The plume worn for dress droops down and is secured to the side, whereas for the shakos of the other German states, the plume stands upright before falling slightly.

Imperial German Navy, Marine Infantry Officer's shako.

Price Range

☐ **Imperial German Navy, Marine Infantry Officer's shako.** *Conventional Officer's Jager pattern shako with the Imperial German Eagle superimposed upon an anchor with the Imperial Crown above, all in gilt.*   775.00   875.00

Imperial German Navy, Other Ranks Marine Infantry shako.

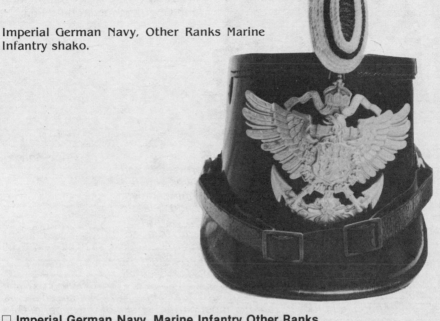

☐ **Imperial German Navy, Marine Infantry Other Ranks shako.** *As above but Other Ranks Jager pattern shako with brass insignia and chin scales.* 400.00   460.00

☐ **Prussia, Guard Jager Battalion and Guard Schutzen Battalion Officer's shako.** *Conventional Officer's Jager pattern shako but with front plate consisting of gilt and enamel Guard Star.* 565.00   625.00

☐ **Prussia, Guard Jager Battalion and Guard Schutzen Battalion, Other Ranks shako.** *Conventional Other Ranks Jager shako but with brass front plate consisting of white metal Guard Star.* 200.00   225.00

GERMANY (Third Reich)

☐ **Nazi Police (Polizei) Officer's shako.** *Jager pattern shako with body covered with green felt. Silver color police insignia (large size) as the front plate (Nazi Eagle with widespread wings standing on a wreath enclosing a canted swastika with a larger wreath,*

Prussian Guard Jager Battalion and Guard Schutzen Battalion.

Price Range

open at the top surrounding the smaller wreath and the body of the eagle). Silver, black, silver and red oval field badge, silver color metal chin scales, slightly sunken plastic top and upper band. Plastic band about the bottom, with plastic front and rear visors. For urban police the plastic and trim are black, for rural police they are brown. 190.00   225.00

☐ **Nazi Police (Polizei) Other Ranks shako.** *Similar to above but with brown leather chin strap with less costly front plate and field badge.* 150.00   175.00

Note: It is of some interest to note that this Nazi Police shako is something of a holdover from the Jager pattern shako of the Imperial German Army. This is the only headdress to be so copied. This pattern shako was also used by the police units of Imperial Germany and is still used by the police units of the Federal Republic of Germany.

    Note: The above prices are for urban police. Rural police shakos will cost around $25.00 more in each case.

GREAT BRITAIN

☐ **Infantry Officer's shako,** *c. early 1800's. Stiff black felt shako of medium height, sunken flat black leather top and top band, black leather visor with untrimmed edge. Black silk "turban" about the bottom of the shako, gilt chin scales. Fancy plaited cords drape down in front and back and are attached to the upper band on the sides. Two tassels hang down on the right side. Front plate consists of a gilt light infantry bugle-horn. At the top front of the shako is a leather cockade and a holder for a plume.* 565.00   625.00

Nazi Police (Polizei) Officer's shako.

British Infantry Officer's shako, c. early 1800's.

☐ **Infantry Officer's shako,** *c. 1835. Similar in profile and construction to Light Dragoon officer's shako but with leather band about the top and narrow leather bands down around the back and sides connecting the top band to the lower black leather band. Gilt chin scales attached to large gilt bosses on each side. Front plate consisting of the regimental badge* *superimposed upon a silver heraldic star with crown above, white over red wool ball shape pompon at top front.* 1435.00   1650.00

☐ **Infantry Officer's shako,** 2nd or Coldstream Regiment of Foot Guards. *Regimental badge in the center of the front plate. This consists of the Garter bearing the inscription "HONI SOIT MAL Y PENSE" all in pierced gilt. Within the Garter is a red enameled cross on a silver background. All of the above is superimposed upon a silver heraldic star.* 1925.00   2125.00

British Infantry Officer's shako, c. 1870.

☐ **Infantry Officer's shako,** *c. 1870. Dark blue cloth covered cork shako with flat top. The back of the shako flares out slightly toward the bottom to accommodate the bottom which is larger than the top. The front of this shako pattern is shorter than the back, thus causing the top of tilt forward. Two bands of gold braid encircle the top and a single band encircles the bottom. A strip of gold braid extends down the sides and back. Flat black leather visor, gilt chin chain attached on each side to a gilt Tudor rose. Front plate consists of a gilt Garter bearing the motto "HONI SOIT OUI MAL Y PENSE," all within a gilt laurel wreath with a crown above. The regimental number usually appears within the Garter but in some instances the regimental badge may appear in lieu of the number. At the top front of the shako is a silver ball and cup supporting a white over red wool ball. The silver ball on the front bears the cypher "VR"(Victoria Regina).* 285.00   325.00

☐ **Light Dragoon Officer's shako,** *c. 1835. Black beaver on felt bell topped shako with the top considerably larger than the bottom. Sunken black leather flat top, fancy gold lace band about the top, gilt chin scales*

British Officer's Light Dragoon shako, c. 1835.

Price Range

attached to each side with gilt bosses. Gold shako lines, front plate in the form of a large Maltese cross, regimental numbers in Roman numerals within a wreath in the center. Gilt crown above the cross, drooping white horsehair plume attached to gilt fixture at the top front. 1475.00 1650.00

☐ **Officer's shako**, c. 1812. This shako is of the so-called Waterloo or Belgic pattern. Of stiff black felt with black felt false front piece extending well above the crown of the shako. This is bound in black braid. The shako tapers slightly from bottom to top. Crimson and gilt plaited cords are draped down across the front. Flat black leather visor. Crimson and gilt tassels hang down from the right side. Large gilt front plate in the form of a cartouche with raised edge and a crown at the top. The cypher "GR" appears in the center of the cartouche. On the left side is a red and white feather plume extending well above the top of the shako. 1650.00 1845.00

☐ **Yeomanry Officer's shako**, c. 1835. Bell top shako, broad silver lace about the top, silver chin scales attached at the sides with large silver bosses, gold shako lines. Large front plate, in this case a silver Maltese cross with slightly domed disk in center bearing a Staffordshire knot insignia. Large gilt crown on black rosette above cross. Socket for plume at top front but plume is missing. 1600.00 1775.00

British Officer's shako, c. 1812.

British Other Ranks shako,
Highland Light Infantry.

Price Range

☐ **Highland Light Infantry Other Ranks shako,** *c. 1900. Dark blue stiff felt shako with flat top of the same material. The top of the shako is smaller than the bottom. The front is shorter than the back, giving the top a downward slant to the front. The front is straight but the back has a pronounced outward flare to the bottom. There is a black metal ventilator on each side near the top middle. About the bottom is a band diced in white, red and green. Flat black leather visor with untrimmed edge. Plaited black cord attached to the top of the shako on each side drapes down across the front. Twin black cords are draped down across the back. Twin black cords held together by a black knot, terminates in cord acorns hanging down on the right side. The front plate consists of the regimental badge. This consists of the Star of the Order of the Thistle. Upon this appears a light infantry bugle-horn with the initials "HLI" within the circle of the horn. A boss of black braid appears above the front plate. Above this is a dark green wool ball-shaped pompon.* 300.00   325.00

☐ **Volunteer Officer's "Albert" Pattern shako,** *Light Company, The Royal Sussex Regiment. Stiff black felt, beaver covered medium high with almost straight sides, black leather flat top and upper band, narrow black leather band around the bottom. Black leather visors in front and back. Silver chin chain attached at sides to silver bosses, each in the form of a Tudor rose. Front plate consists of the gilt, silver and enameled badge of the regiment. At the top front of the shako is a green ball in a silver holder.* 650.00   630.00

RUSSIA

☐ **Life Guard Hussar Regiments Other Ranks shako,** *Medium high red felt shako with black leather flat top and upper band. Black leather band about the bottom, black leather visor. Gold color cloth lace extends between top and bottom bands, two on each side spaced a distance apart, brass chin scales. Gold color shako lines with double lines hanging from the right top side of the shako, terminating in gold and black knots and "waffles." Extremely large shako plate consisting of the double-headed Russian eagle in brass holding torches in the right talon and a wreath in the left. On the breast of the eagle is a shield with the embossed figure of St. George and the dragon, above the eagle is a large crown. A gold color wool ball shape pompon decorates the top front.* 775.00   860.00

☐ **Infantry Regiments Officer's shako,** *c. 1840's. Dark green felt typical bell crown shako of medium height.*

Russian Infantry Officer's shako, c. 1840's.

Price Range

Black leather top and top band, black leather band about the bottom and black leather visor, gilt chin scales. Across the lower front of the shako are two well plaited cords. These are attached to each side at the top. Tassels and "waffles" hang down on the left side. The large shako plate consists of a gilt double-headed Russian eagle with large crown above. On the breast of the eagle is a shield depicting St. George and the dragon. This is another headdress with an absurdly tall plume on the front. This black wool plume is slender and is at least twice the height of the shako itself. **775.00 860.00**

☐ **General Staff Officer's shako or kiwer.** This type of shako was peculiar to the Russian service. It was fairly low in profile. The top was larger than the bottom, causing the sides to flare out sharply. In this particular item, the body is of scarlet felt of high quality. The front of the shako is slightly higher than the back, causing a dip in the black leather top. A bullion cord is around the top of the shako and a broad band of gold bullion lace is about the bottom. The black leather visor has gilt edging. Intricately woven gold bullion cords attached to each side drape down across the front sides and back of the shako. Chin scales are of gilt. The front plate is a gilt double-headed Russian eagle with crown above. On the breast of the eagle appears a shield with St. George

Price Range

and the dragon. A silver metal field badge with yellow and black enameled center is at the top front. Atop this is a gold bullion wire ball and inverted cone like device. This is certainly one of the most elaborate shakos of recent times. 1200.00 1350.00

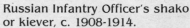

Russian Infantry Officer's shako or kiever, c. 1908-1914.

☐ **Infantry Officer's shako or kiwer,** *c. 1908-1914. This shako is similar in pattern to the above. Black leather top, body of shako is of blue/green felt. About the top is a silver lace band, about the bottom is a black velvet band with red piping on top and bottom edges. Silver chin scales, silver plaited cords desend from a silver color button on each side of the shako and drape down across the front, sides and back. The front plate is the silver double-headed eagle of Imperial Russia with crown above. At the top front is a silver metal field badge with yellow and black enameled center. Above this is a silver wire ball with inverted cone on top.* 1000.00 1100.00

UNITED STATES
☐ **Enlisted Man's Artillery shako,** *c. 1854. This is one of the most ungainly patterns of headdress ever used by the U.S. Army. It is a dark blue felt shako with flat*

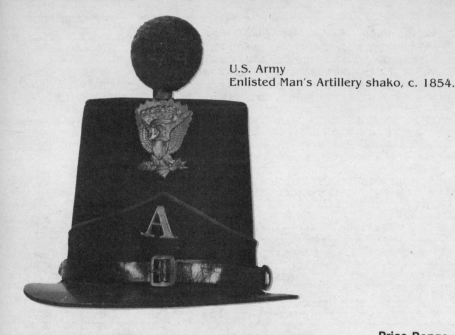

U.S. Army
Enlisted Man's Artillery shako, c. 1854.

Price Range

top and is slightly conical in form, much like an inverted flower pot. It has a large awkward flat leather visor with unfinished edge. Black leather chin strap secured on each side by a brass button. Red braid encircles the shako about a fifth of the way up and forms an inverted "V" in the front. A large initial "A" appears near the point of the "V," and indicates the particular company to which the wearer belonged. At the top front of the shako is an eagle in brass with upstretched wings with a U.S. shield on its breast. A bundle of arrows is clutched in the left talon and olive branches in the right. About the eagle's head are stars and in its beak is a ribbon bearing the motto of the United States. Above the front plate is a red pompon......................   325.00   355.00

☐ **Enlisted Man's Artillery shako,** *Regular Army, c. 1870's. While the infantry and cavalry of this period were issued the rather smart looking kepi described below, the artillery was issued a fancy shako of definite European design which was not nearly as becoming to the American fighting man regardless of how colorful it was. This is a dark blue felt shako, medium in height, and of conventional French design. The front was straight and the back was rounded, the top being smaller than the bottom of the shako. The visor was of flat black leather and has an*

U.S. Army Enlisted Man's Artillery shako, c. 1870's.

Price Range

unfinished edge. The thin black leather chin strap is attached at each end by a medium size brass button bearing the U.S. Arms. The insignia on the front is in two parts. Over crossed brass cannon is a stylized American eagle with U.S. shield and laurel leaves and arrows. In an arch over the eagle's head is a ribbon bearing the motto, "E PLURIBUS UNUM." In the center of the flat top is a black metal ventilator. About the top and bottom of the shako is a single line of red braid. These are joined on each side by a similar line of braid. At the top front is an inverted pear shape pompon of red wool. This shako was also worn by some other arms and services with the change in insignia under the eagle and the color of the braid and pompon. This is a fairly rare item. 325.00   335.00

☐ **Enlisted Man's kepi or forage cap**, *Regular Army, c. late 1850's to early 1870's. An ungainly design which like all kepi patterns is a development of the French Army headgear worn in North Africa. In general appearance it resembles a rather conventional French pattern shako without any support to the sides and back. Thus the limber blue felt has a tendency to fall in upon itself with the top falling over forward. Simple black leather chin strap attached to each side with a small brass button bearing the U.S. Arms. Black leather visor, sometimes flat and sometimes slightly arched. At first a brass initial identifying the wearer's company was worn on the front. During the Civil War brass insignia, i.e., crossed cannon,*

crossed sabers, a light infantry horn and such was
often worn on the top. This item may be found with
slight variations from the above description. WARN-
ING: THIS ITEM IS ONE OF THE MOST OFTEN
REPRODUCED OF ALL MILITARY HEADGEAR. The
price here is for an original specimen. 200.00   225.00

U.S. Army
Enlisted Man's
kepi, c. 1870's.

☐ **Enlisted Man's kepi,** *Regular Army, c. 1870's. This is
a refined and more graceful development of the kepi
described above. It was officially designated as a
forage cap. Body of dark blue cloth with stiffening
material within the body to cause it to retain its
shape. Thick flat black leather visor with unfinished
edge. Thin black leather chin strap attached to each
side with a large brass button bearing the U.S. Arms.
The front of the kepi bears large crossed rifles or
crossed sabers and sometimes had the wearer's
company or troop initial below and the regimental
number above. This is a choice item not too often
found in the original.* 250.00   275.00

☐ **Enlisted Man's Light Artillery shako,** *Regular Army, c.
1860's. Fairly large shako of black felt with straight
front and slightly sloping back toward the top. Black
leather flat top and upper band, black leather bottom
band, flat black leather visor of large size. Black
leather chin strap attached to each side with small
brass button, medium size brass front plate in two
parts. A stylized U.S. eagle with breast shield, laurel*

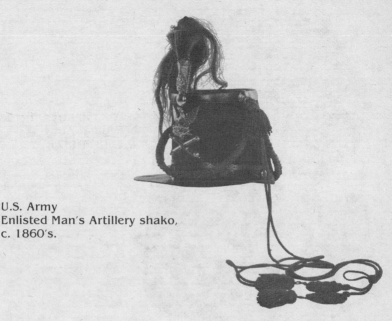

U.S. Army
Enlisted Man's Artillery shako,
c. 1860's.

Price Range

branch and arrows positioned over crossed brass
cannon. At the top front of the shako is a flaming
grenade device helping to support a brass plume
socket of ornate design. This supports a falling red
horsehair plume. At the top side of the shako is a circular brass fixture holding a small brass ring. To this
is attached fancy plaited red cords which drape
down in front and back. A red tassel is attached to
the left ring and from the same ring desends long red
shako cords terminating in "waffles" and tassels....   325.00   360.00

☐ **Enlisted Man's shako,** *Chester County Union Troop,
c. 1850's. Medium tall dark blue felt shako with flat
top smaller than the bottom. Shako straight in front
with sides and back tapering in toward the top. Thin
black leather visor and thin black leather chin strap,
small brass buttons attach each end of the chin
strap. An orange braid encircles the shako about a
fourth of the way up with a very shallow "V" in front.
Between the bottom front of the shako and this "V"
appear the brass letters "U" and "T" with considerable space between them. At the top front of the
shako is a large brass domed device upon which is
an eagle design. This merges into a brass plume
socket which holds an elongated orange wool pompon with a falling white horsehair plume sticking out
from the top.* 275.00   300.00

U.S. Infantry Officer's shako,
Regular Army,
c. 1814-1821.

Price Range

☐ **Infantry Officer's shako,** *Regular Army, c. 1814-1821. To date no* **complete** *specimen has ever appeared and even incomplete specimens are extremely rare. This shako is patterned after the British "Waterloo" shako introduced around 1810. Tall black leather shako with a front piece extending up above the flat crown, black leather visor. The front plate is large and is placed at the top front. Of silver, it has straight sides and scalloped top and bottom. It has embossed edges and a large embossed oval in the center. Within this oval is an American eagle with outstretched wings perched on a trophy of flags, cannon and cannon balls. Above the eagle appears a scroll bearing the motto "E PLURIBUS UNUM." Above the scroll appears an arc of 13 stars. A silver three strand cord extends around the base of the visor and is attached on each side by a silver button. There is a large silver button at the top right of the shako, indicating that shako lines were attached at one time.* 850.00   875.00

☐ **Infantry Officer's shako,** *Regular Army, c. 1825. Black leather bell crown shako with black leather visor, gilt/brass chin scales. Chain plaited gold braid attaches to the top side of the shako and drapes down in front and back. Gold tassels hang down from*

Price Range

*the right side. The front plate is a small silver eagle
with outstretched wings clasping olive leaves in one
talon and arrows in the other. A U.S. shield appears
on the eagle's breast. At the top front of the shako is
a small pressed black leather rosette with a gilt button in the center bearing the arms of the U.S. Above
this is a white wool pompon.* 650.00   725.00

U.S. Militia Officer's shako,
c. 1835.

☐ **Militia shako,** *c. 1835. Another example of the gaudy
headdress favored by some militia units. The particular unit to which this shako belonged is unknown.
Cylindrical black leather shako of medium height
with flat leather top and with a brass band around the
top. Black leather band around the bottom except in
the area of the visor. Large brass visor attached to
the shako by a narrow brass band, narrow black
leather chin strap. Large brass eagle with outstretched wings grasping olive leaves in the right
talon and arrows in the left. U.S. shield on eagle's
breast. At the top front of the shako is a pressed
leather rosette with an eagle button of brass in the
center. Attached to the button is chain plaited gold
cord which drapes slightly down around the right
side and is attached to a similar button at the top
rear of the shako.* 575.00   640.00

☐ **Regular Army Officer's shako,** *3rd Artillery Regiment.
Tall bell crown black leather shako, black leather
visor. Shako is incomplete but has bullion cord chain
suspended from each side at the top and draped*

U.S. Officer's shako,
3rd Artillery Regiment,
Regular Army.

Price Range

down across the front. Medium size gilt eagle grasping olive leaves and arrows in its talons. United
States shield on breast of eagle pierced with the
numeral "3." Black leather rosette at top front with a
gilt button in the center bearing the initial "A"
(Artillery) on a shield on an eagle's breast. To be complete, this shako should have chin scales and a pom-
pon at top front. 575.00   650.00

☐ **Regular Army Other Ranks Dragoon shako,** c. 1840.
Tall black felt shako tapering slightly toward the top.
Black leather top and upper band, black leather band
about the bottom. Large black leather visor with untrimmed edge, black leather chin strap attached at
each side with a brass button. Plaited yellow cords
are attached to the top band of the shako on either
side. These drape down in front and back. From the
left side hang two yellow cords terminating in
tassels and "waffles." The large front plate consists
of a brass heraldic star upon which appears an eagle
in silvered brass. At the top front of the shako is a
flaming grenade device in brass which supports a
white horsehair plume 655.00   725.00

☐ **Militia Other Ranks shako,** c. 1860. There is no mistaking the French influence in the pattern of this
shako. In fact this particular pattern was manufactured in France for a number of U.S. militia units.
Shako may be found with black leather body or with
leather body covered with dark blue cloth. Flat black

U.S. Army Enlisted Man's shako,
Dragoon Regiment, c. 1840.

U.S. Militia Other Ranks shako, c. 1860.

Price Range

leather top and upper band. Top is smaller than the bottom of the shako and so designed that the shako is straight in front and tapers slightly in on sides and back. Black leather band about the bottom. Back of shako may be slightly lower. Flat black leather visor with finished edges. A "V" of black leather bands on both sides of the shako join the top and bottom bands. On each side at the top is a black metal ventilator. The rather elaborate brass front plate consists of an American eagle with outstretched wings and with a U.S. shield on the breast, perched upon a wreath of oak and laurel leaves. Within the wreath is a domed disk bearing a light infantry horn. Above the eagle but partly behind its head is a large stamped red, white and blue rosette. Above this is a brass plume holder with a small red wool ball on top of which is a green pompon. In this particular version the shako is rather graceful and tasteful. However, some militia used a large red, white and blue plume in lieu of the pompon, a feature which added nothing to the appearance. At the present time, these shakos are not hard to find. 155.00   175.00

☐ **Militia Other Ranks shako,** *1st Pennsylvania Artillery, c. 1840.* Rather restrained in design as compared to earlier patterns. Black felt shako with straight front and with sides which incline slightly inward toward the top. Sunken black leather top and top band, black leather band about the bottom, thick heavy black leather visor. Black leather chin strap secured at each side with a brass button bearing crossed cannon. The large front plate consists of the arms of the State of Pennsylvania within a wreath. Across the bottom of the wreath is a scroll bearing the words "FIRST ARTILLERY." At the top front of the shako is a cartouche in brass bearing two crossed cannons superimposed upon a flaming grenade. There is no plume nor pompon although there is provision for one. 115.00   125.00

☐ **Militia Other Ranks shako,** *unidentified militia unit, c. 1835.* Black leather bell crown shako with black leather top and black leather visor. This shako is of rather large size and clumsy looking. Brass chin scales with brass color metalic cords plaited in chain pattern attached at the top on each side of the shako and draping down in front and back. The huge brass front plate is in the form of a shield with raised edges. On the shield is an eagle with outstretched wings holding a large U.S. shield in its talons. Back of the eagle and U.S. shield is a trophy of flags, cannon and cannon balls. There is no plume or pompon in this example although there is provision for one. ... 565.00   625.00

Price Range

☐ **Militia shako,** *unidentified militia unit, c. 1816.*
Although this shako is not nearly as gaudy as some
other militia headdress, it still lacks some of the
dignity of a Regular Army shako. Black leather body
with flat black leather top and black leather visor
with brass edging around the front. The shako is
slightly larger at the top so that the sides flare out
slightly. Flexible black leather neck piece at rear
which may be turned up and secured by a small brass
button on each side. There is a red leather band
about the bottom of the shako. The front plate is of
brass and is similar to that of the above shako. A red
feather plume appears at the top front. 565.00   625.00

ADDENDUM

Prussian Other Ranks shako,
c. late 1800's.

☐ **Early Prussian Landstrum Other Ranks shako.** *This*
interesting shako was a regular issue to Landstrum
units in the mid-1880's to the early 1900's. The Land-
strum was a division of the reserve composed of
older men who had served with the colors. For a time
it was the identifying badge of this reserve. The black
leather body is taller than that of the later shakos
and is of a less graceful design. Both the front and
rear visors are larger than those of later models. The
leather chin strap of black leather had a slit in each

end which fit over a small ball-like fixture. No cockades were worn in the sides of this shako. The large oval front plate had raised rays and a black center with white edge (the Prussian state colors). In the center of the oval is a large Maltese cross of matte silver color metal. This is the so-called Landwehr Cross and bears the inscription "MIT GOTT FUR KONIG UND VATERLAND" and the date "1813" when the Landwehr, of which the Landstrum was a part, was founded. At the top front of the shako is a black and white cloth field badge. **325.00**   **375.00**

Nazi Prussian Police Other Ranks shako.

☐ **Nazi Prussian Police Other Ranks shako.** This interesting Nazi item is not too frequently offered for sale. It may be considered fairly rare. Body is of a hard black plastic-like material covered with greenish material (cloth). Visor and strip about top of shako, as well as chin strap, are black. The front plate is in the form of a silver metal eagle of the so-called Frederick the Great pattern. On the breast of the eagle is a black enameled swastika. At the top front of the shako is a red, white and black metal field badge. This shako is very similar to the later Nazi police shako except for the front plate. This is the shako worn by the Prussian police under Goering and later under Himmler............................. **755.00**   **825.00**

Early Prussian Other Ranks shako.

Price Range

☐ **Prussian Other Ranks shako,** *c. late 1800's. This is an artifact not seen too often on the collector's market. However, it is a "must" for shako collectors. It differs largely from later pattern Imperial German shakos in that it is considerably higher and the chin strap had a single slide or buckle as opposed to the single slide chin strap of later models. All trim and fittings are of brass including the Prussian heraldic eagle front plate. The field badge is of black and white cloth.* ...　400.00　450.00

SPIKED HELMETS (Pickelhauben)

The helmets of Imperial Germany, in particular, the spiked helmets or picklehauben are in very great demand among collectors. In fact, they are probably the most popular of all helmets. This is reflected in an interest which has grown most rapidly over the past 25 years with the result that prices are increasing at a great rate.

Although the spiked helmet did not originate with Imperial Germany, it was popularized by the Imperial armies. The exact origin is lost far back in military history and it was worn by soldiers in the near east for centuries. The Moslem armies of ancient times were particularly partial to it. However, it was not at all common among Western armies.

The use of the spiked helmet in more modern times probably originated with Nicholas I of Russia who in the early 1840's was toying with the design of such a helmet for certain units of his armies. During a visit to his fellow monarch, William IV of Prussia saw a sample spiked helmet on Nicholas' desk. The Prussian ruler liked the design so much that upon his return to his own country, he immediately introduced his own version in 1842. This was some time before the Russians began using the helmet.

Prussian Pickelhaub, model 1842, first of the famous German spiked helmets.

The Model 1842 pickelhaube has a high crown and deep visors, the front visor being square cut. A spike on a cross bar base decorates the top. Metal chin scales are worn. On the front of the helmet appears a metal Prussian heraldic eagle, that of the line infantry differing slightly from that of the elite grenadiers. Guard troops and general officers wore the so-called Guard eagle with widespread wings and the Star of the Order of the Eagle on the breast. Metal parts were gilt for officers and brass for other ranks.

In 1846 a ball-type ornament was introduced for artillery units, the ball suggesting the cannonball of the era. This helmet, as was the spiked version, was soon adopted by the other German states, the majority of which took the lead of Prussia in military matters.

The leather pickelhaube underwent changes in 1857, 1860, 1867, 1888 and 1890, with the crown gradually becoming lower and more rounded. Following 1857 the square front visor was retained only for general officers, reserve (Landwehr) officers and some elite units, including dragoons, the Prussian Palace Guard. Design was somewhat different in the Bavarian Army. In 1887 the metal trim about the front visor was eliminated, along with the metal chin scales for other ranks, a leather chin strap being substituted. The metal trim was readopted in 1891, along with metal chin scales for other ranks of certain elite regiments, including the Prussian Guard.

For parade a drooping plume was worn in lieu of the spike or ball ornament. Certain regiments wore black plumes, except musicians, other than Saxon, who wore red. Prussian generals had white and black plumes, Prussian General Staff, white; Bavarian generals, white and blue; Hessian generals, white and red; Saxon generals, white; Wurttenburg generals, black and red, and so on, the plumes being in the color or colors of the state.

An all metal cuirassier helmet with lobster tail rear was also introduced in 1842 with helmet plates similar to those of the other units. It too underwent a series of design changes during the following years, somewhat similar to those of the leather helmet.

The identifying plates appearing on the front of these helmets are of a great variety and add much interest to helmet collecting. Practically every state (land) had its own distinctive plate, usually consisting of the coat of arms, or some modification thereof. For instance in Prussia, in addition to the Prussian heraldic eagle of line regiments, there were modifications of the eagle for elite regiments. There were even differences within a single regiment. As an example, the first and second battalions of the 92nd Infantry Regiment (Brunswick) wore the Prussian heraldic eagle with the heraldic Star of Henry the Lion superimposed upon the breast with a scroll bearing the word "Peninsula." The third battalion of this same regiment had a death's head (totenkoff) or skull and crossbones superimposed on the breast of the eagle, with the word "Peninsula" on a scroll below. This particular skull and crossbones and the "Peninsula" scroll was a holdover from the headdress plate worn by the troops of Brunswick when that state was independent of Prussia. Helmets of such elite units are extremely rare and command a great price. It is believed that no **complete** collection of all the vast variety of helmet plates exist. Such a collection would certainly be without price!

The helmets of Prussia and Bavaria are perhaps the easiest to find and usually are not as costly as others. Helmets of Wurttemberg and Saxony are perhaps the next most common. The helmets with plates of the smaller states, such as Anhalt, Hesse, Mecklenburg, Reuss and Schwarzburg-Rudolstadt are very rare and are high priced.

The Imperial Russian helmet was similar to the Prussian models, both for mounted and unmounted units. The unmounted units had a cartouche with the regimental number, under a stylized Russian double-headed eagle. Helmets of mounted units and certain elite units bore the heraldic Star of the Order of St. Andrew First Born. Some helmets have an ornament on top in the form of stylized grenade with pointed flame projecting from the top. Other units had a crest in the form of a crowned Imperial double-headed eagle. Of some interest is the fact that the crowned double-headed eagle is really of Byzantine origin. Early Russian Czars contended that they were the lawful heirs of the rulers of the old Byzantine Empire and that it was right and proper that they adopt that ancient symbol. It remained in use until the Communist takeover.

It is an historic fact that nations successful in their military efforts set the uniform styles for other nations. Thus France, Germany, Great Britain, the United States, and others, have at one time or another set military uniform styles. Following the success of Prussian arms in the Franco-Prussian War, nations large and small copied the Prussian uniform including the pickelhaube. These nations ranged all the way from tiny Parma and Hawaii to Mexico, Sweden, Netherlands, Great Britain, and others. Interestingly enough, even the United States jumped on the bandwagon and for a time the U.S. Army, Marines and the Navy band wore a form of the pickelhaube.

The British spiked helmet adopted in 1878 showed a decided Prussian influence. It was made of cloth-covered cork, although some militia units had leather and metal helmets. Some elite regular regiments also had metal helmets. The front visor of officer helmets is trimmed in gilt, other ranks in leather. A spike on top of the helmet is attached to a crosspiece. The rear of the crosspiece at the back of the helmet has a small hook to which the metal chin chain attaches when not in use. A metal heraldic rose boss is on each side of the helmet, the leather backed chin chain attaching under that on the left. Metal was gilt for officers and brass for other ranks, except for militia units in which case the metal was silver or white metal. The helmet plates varied in design according to the regiment or arm or branch of service. The service branches wore a ball device in lieu of the spike, as did the Royal Marines. For regular army officers, the front visor was usually pointed, while that of other ranks was round. An exception of the old Royal Marine Artillery where visors for all personnel were round. The vast majority of these helmets were covered with dark blue cloth. However, some militia units had a gray cloth color while light infantry helmets were covered with dark green cloth and had bronzed fittings. The great variety of different helmet plates allows the collector a large area within which to collect.

The United States adopted a Prussian influenced helmet in 1872. It was worn until 1903. During this time it underwent several modifications. Basically, the helmet was of black felt with gilt metal work for officers and brass for enlisted men. The first model which was introduced had a long (lobster tail) rear visor. The chin strap was leather. An ornate tassel hung down on the left side of the helmet, which was fitted with helmet lines, bullion for officers and worsted for enlisted men. The worsted varied in the color of the arm. A gilt/brass ball and socket device held a plume, the color of which varied according to the arm. The light artillery plume was red; cavalry, yellow; signal service, dark orange. Gilt/brass side buttons bore the insignia of the arm. The front plate, in gilt or brass, was the American eagle of the United States arms with a scroll bearing the motto, "E PLURIBUS UNUM" in a semicircle about the eagle and extending down on each side to the eagle's claws. The unit number appeared in silver/white metal on the U.S. shield on the eagle's breast.

A modified helmet, the Model 1881 had a much shorter rear visor. The cross-type base for the plume was replaced by a circular base of oak leaves. This supported either a spike or a plume. Officers could wear either a black felt helmet or a black cloth covered cork helmet. Majors and above of infantry wore a white plume. Officers of artillery wore a red plume; of cavalry, yellow. Officers of mounted units had a gilt chin chain. The helmet plate was the American eagle with the shield of the United States on the chest. The motto scroll bearing "E PLURIBUS UNUM" was held in the eagle's beak. Regimental or unit numbers appeared in silver/white metal on the face of the shield. Behind the shield appeared crossed rifles (infantry), crossed cannon (artillery) or crossed sabers (cavalry). These were in silver for officers and in white metal for enlisted men. The side buttons bore the same designs of rifles, cannon or sabers.

In lieu of the unit number, enlisted men of the signal service had crossed signal flags in white metal on the face of the shield. Commissary steward had a crescent; hospital steward, a caduceus; engineer troops, a castle; and ordnance sergeants, a flaming bomb. By far the rarest and most interesting helmet plate was that worn by the famed native Indian Scouts. This elite unit had crossed white metal arrows on the shield's face and a red and white plume was worn. In fact an Indian Scout helmet is worth twice as much as a helmet of any other U.S. Army outfit.

Even the U.S. Marines felt the Prussian influence for in 1880 a white cloth covered cork helmet with brass spike, chin chain, and a front plate consisting of the Marine Corps emblem of eagle, anchor and globe, within a wreath, all mounted on a U.S. shield was authorized for enlisted Marines alone. In 1882 a black helmet was authorized. Two years later the helmet, with gilt trim, was authorized for officers. This same year the shield and wreath were deleted and a large eagle, anchor and globe device was substituted. For special full dress, in lieu of the spike, officers of the grade of major and above wore a scarlet plume. All Marine Corps spiked helmets are rather rare and command a premium price.

Perhaps the rarest of all American spiked helmets is that worn by the U.S. Navy Band of the late 1900's. Authorized in 1897 it was worn for only a short time. It was the Army Model 1881 helmet with brass chin chain and spike. The large eagle front plate of the Army helmet was modified by having a large white metal lyre superimposed upon the shield on the eagle's breast.

Neither the spiked nor the plumed helmet became the American fighting man. It never looked quite right and it could be most inconvenient at times, witness the complaint of enlisted Marines that because of the low overhead between decks they were continually knocking the spike against the overhead.

Prussian influenced helmets of other nations often followed the original design even more closely than did those of the United States and Great Britain. This was no doubt due to the fact that they were ordered from and made by the same German firms which made the German helmets. The distinctive feature of these helmets is that they have a front plate in the form of the nation's arms or other identifying device.

CRESTED HELMETS

Associated with the spiked helmets are those having a crest in lieu of the spike. In addition to the Russian eagle crested helmet already mentioned, perhaps the rarest of these is that of the Bavarian Archers of the Guard (Liebgarde der Hartschiere). This is a nickeled helmet with a very high rounded crown and deep visors, with ornate chin scales attached to each side by ornamented bosses bearing the crown of Bavaria in high relief. The front plate consists of the arms of Bavaria within an elaborate floral design. The front visor is trimmed in gilt and gilt studs decorate the edge. On top of the helmet is a large standing lion. A falling white plume replaces the lion for full dress (gala) occasions.

Another rare Imperial German crested helmet is the full dress (gala) helmet of the Saxon Garde-Reiter-Regiment, post 1907. It is rated as one of the most beautiful and is much sought after by advanced collectors. The shell or skull of this helmet is of tombac (an alloy of copper and zinc) with a bright copper finish. The chin scales are also of tombac, although those of officers are of gilt. A large silver (officers) or white metal (other ranks) lion is on top of this helmet. The lion's forepaws rest upon the top of a shield which bears the crowned initials "FAR," (Friedrich Augustus Rex). The front plate consists of the ancient arms of Saxony upon a heraldic star. For other than full dress, a spike replaces the lion. Only a very limited number of these helmets were ever issued.

Another much sought after Imperial German helmet is the full dress (gala) helmet of the famed Prussian Grade du Corps and Garde Kurassier Regiment. This is a lobster tail helmet of tombac with a round front visor for other ranks and a stepped square front visor for officers. An eagle with extended wings (silver for officers with gilt crown and tombac crowned white metal eagle for other ranks) appears on top of the helmet. The front plate consists of the Star of the Order of the Black Eagle, in silver for officers and in white metal for other ranks. That of officers is of high relief and enamel. Gilt/tombac chin scales and silver/white metal edging trims the visors. A gilt/tombac spike replaces the eagle for other than full dress wear.

The rarest of all those German crested helmets is that of the Lieb-Gendarmerie. This unit was never very large and very few helmets of this unit are known to exist. It is so rare that it is seldom available for sale. The lobster tail helmet is nickeled with a gilt crowned eagle as the crest. This eagle, with wings extended wide, is much more defiant in appearance than that atop the Grade du Corps helmet. Gilt chin scales and the Star of the Order of the Black Eagle in silver and enamel further decorate this helmet.

Apart from the crested helmets of Imperial Germany, such helmets have been extremely popular in the armies of other nations. **Metal** helmets, crested in the manner of the classic Greek and Roman manner, with a highly ornamented large crest, and topped with fur or horsehair were quite popular. These were usually decorated with chin chains or scales and had an identifying front plate. Used at first as a protective covering for mounted troops, they later became more decorative and less protective. Such helmets were used extensively by Napoleon's mounted troops and were adopted by a great number of other nations, including Austria, Great Britain, and Brazil. This type helmet was also adopted by a few American militia units but not by the Regular Army. The crested **leather** helmet was also a popular item of military headdress all over the world for many years. These **leather** crested helmets vary from a simple jockey style cap with a strip of bearskin decorating the top from front to back, worn by very early American militia units to the extremely elaborate fur crested helmets of the British and European armies of the 1800's.

Of particular interest among the metal crested helmets is that of the 1st (Royal) Dragoons 1834-1843. This much desired British helmet is of marked Roman design. It was of gilt for officers and brass for other ranks. A high ornate crest with a lion head in front decorates the top of the helmet. The British Hanoverian arms make up the front plate and the sides of the skull are decorated with an elaborate overlay. The chin scales are held in place by large bosses in the form of a heraldic rose. The regimental title was embossed on a decorative metal band just above the pointed front visor. On full dress occasions, the lion head was removed from the front of the crest and a very large bearskin crest was substituted, extending from front to back.

In the field of crested helmets, the Bavarian "Raupenhelm" is also a much desired collector's item and to date are not too expensive, although like all items of militaria, their value is increasing steadily. This helmet consists basically of a polished black leather skull. Some types have the front and rear visors edged with gilt/brass metal, others have plain visors. On the left side appears the blue and white national cockade, sometimes with a plume or pompon holder. The plume or pompon varied according to the service. The front plate was the crowned initial of the reigning ruler, the most common being "L" for King Ludwig.

One of the most rare and certainly one of the most beautiful of crested helmets is that of the British Life Guards, the pattern of 1817. It is of silver and a large gilt front plate consisting of a half sunburst upon which is superimposed the British Royal Arms, together with the battle honors of the regiment. The ornate chin scales are attached to the helmet by gilt lion head bosses. The sides and back of this headdress are decorated with a gilt floral design. The helmet is set off by a huge bearskin crest.

Just as rare and certainly almost as beautiful is the helmet, c. 1840, of the First City Troop of Philadelphia, an elite militia organization. Some experts affirm that the British Life Guards helmet, described above, was the inspiration for this item. Of polished black leather, the skull is topped by a giant black bearskin crest. Side bosses, chin scales and a large half sunburst front plate are in white metal. A yellow metal American eagle with the U.S. shield on the breast appears on the half sunburst front plate. The sides and back of this elaborate helmet are decorated with highly detailed leaves of white metal.

SPIKED AND PLUMED HELMETS

GERMANY (Imperial)

	Price Range	
☐ Bavarian General Officer, *with plume*.	1700.00	1875.00
☐ Bavarian General Officer, *with spike*.	1150.00	1275.00
☐ Bavarian General a la Suite, *spike*.	1150.00	1275.00
Bavarian Infantry Life Regiment, *Cadet Corps, Pioneer Battalions 1-4, Train and Telegraph Battalions, Paymaster and Justice officials, spike.*		
☐ Officer.	500.00	550.00
☐ Other Ranks.	325.00	350.00
Line Infantry Regiments, *1-23, Under Officer's School, spike.*		
☐ Officer.	325.00	350.00
☐ Other Ranks.	200.00	225.00
Bavarian Jager Battalions, *1886 to 1895, spike.*		
☐ Officer.	400.00	450.00
☐ Other Ranks.	300.00	325.00
Bavarian Chevaulger Regiments, *1, 3, 5, 7; Schweres Relter Regiment 2 and War Ministry (gilt/brass front plate).*		
☐ Officer.	400.00	450.00
☐ Other Ranks.	300.00	325.00
Bavarian Chevaulger Regiments, *2, 4, 6, 8; Schweres Reiter Regiment 1 (silver/white metal front plate).*		
☐ Officer.	400.00	450.00
☐ Other Ranks.	300.00	325.00
Bavarian Reiter Regiments, *1 and 2 (old model helmet, 1886). Gilt/brass crowned "L" front plate.*		
☐ Officer.	750.00	825.00
☐ Other Ranks.	475.00	525.00
Bavarian Field Artillery Regiments, *1-12 (spike to 1916).*		
☐ Officer.	400.00	450.00
☐ Other Ranks.	250.00	275.00
Bavarian Field Artillery Regiments, *1-12 (ball ornament after 1916).*		
☐ Officer.	300.00	450.00

	Price Range	
☐ Other Ranks...................................	250.00	275.00
Bavarian Foot Artillery Regiments, *1-3 (spike to 1916).*		
☐ Officer.......................................	350.00	375.00
☐ Other Ranks...................................	250.00	275.00
Bavarian Foot Artillery Regiments, *1-3 (ball ornament after 1916).*		
☐ Officer.......................................	350.00	375.00
☐ Other Ranks...................................	250.00	275.00
Bavarian Train Battalions, *1-3, Jager zu Pfred.*		
☐ Officer.......................................	400.00	450.00
☐ Other Ranks...................................	275.00	300.00

Brunswick Infantry Officer's helmet, Regiment 92, 1st Batallion.

Brunswick Infantry Regiment, *92 I and II Battalions (after 1889) with Star of Henry the Lion and scroll bearing "Peninsula."*		
☐ Officer.......................................	1225.00	1350.00
☐ Other Ranks...................................	370.00	400.00
Brunswick Infantry Regiment, *92 III, 1912, skull and crossbones with scroll bearing "Peninsula."*	1225.00	1350.00
☐ **Hesse General Staff Officer,** *with Star of the Order of Ludwig and Lion within wreath.*	1500.00	1675.00
Hesse Guard Under Officer Company, *Star, Lion, Wreath and "1623."*		
☐ Under Officers.	775.00	850.00

Price Range

Hesse Infantry Regiment, *115, Star, Lion, Wreath and scroll bearing "1623."*

☐ Officer.................................	800.00	875.00
☐ Other Ranks............................	475.00	550.00

Hesse Infantry Regiments, *116, 118 and 168, Wreath and Lion.*

☐ Officer.................................	475.00	525.00
☐ Other Ranks............................	365.00	400.00

Hesse Field Artillery Regiment, *25 to 1915 with spike.*

☐ Officer.................................	420.00	575.00
☐ Other Ranks............................	430.00	475.00

Hesse Field Artillery Regiment, *25 after 1915 with ball ornament and Star of the Order of Ludwig.*

☐ Officer.................................	950.00	1050.00
☐ Other Ranks............................	700.00	775.00

Hesse Train Battalion, *18, Wreath and Lion.*

☐ Officer.................................	520.00	575.00
☐ Other Ranks............................	410.00	450.00

Mecklenburg-Schwerin Infantry Regiment, *89, I and II Battalions, Fusilier Regiment, 90.*

☐ Officer.................................	650.00	725.00
☐ Other Ranks............................	450.00	500.00

Mecklenburg-Schwerin Dragoon Regiment, *17 (gilt/brass chin scales).*

☐ Officer.................................	750.00	825.00
☐ Other Ranks............................	450.00	500.00

Mecklenburg-Schwerin Dragoon Regiment, *18 (silver/white metal chin scales).*

☐ Officer.................................	750.00	825.00
☐ Other Ranks............................	455.00	500.00

Mecklenburg-Schwerin Field Artillery Regiment, *60.*

☐ Officer.................................	750.00	850.00
☐ Other Ranks............................	450.00	500.00

Mecklenburg-Strelitz Infantry Regiment, *89, II Battalion.*

☐ Officer.................................	785.00	875.00
☐ Other Ranks............................	420.00	575.00

Mecklenburg-Strelitz Field Artillery Regiment, *24, III Battalion.*

☐ Officer.................................	785.00	875.00
☐ Other Ranks............................	420.00	575.00

Oldenburg Infantry Regiment, *91.*

☐ Officer.................................	700.00	775.00
☐ Other Ranks............................	455.00	500.00

Oldenburg Dragoon Regiment, *19.*

☐ Officer.................................	750.00	825.00
☐ Other Ranks............................	475.00	525.00

Oldenburg Field Artillery Regiment, *62, II and III Battalions.*

☐ Officer.................................	785.00	875.00

	Price Range	

☐   **Other Ranks.** 520.00   575.00
☐ **Prussia General Officer,** *spike.* 1200.00   1325.00
☐ **Prussia General Officer,** *plume.* 1400.00   1550.00
☐ **Prussia General Staff Officer,** *spike.* 900.00   1000.00
☐ **Prussia General Staff Officer,** *plume.* 1055.00   1175.00

Prussia 1st Guard Regiment of Foot, *to 1889, Guard Eagle with Star of the Order of the Black Eagle.*

☐   **Officer.** 725.00   800.00
☐   **Other Ranks.** 425.00   475.00

Prussian 1st Guard Regiment of Foot, *after 1889, Guard Eagle with Star of the Order of the Black Eagle and scroll bearing "Semper Talis."*

☐   **Officer.** 1025.00   1125.00
☐   **Other Ranks.** 510.00   675.00

Prussia Guard Regiments of Foot, *2, 3 and 4; Guard Grenadier Regiments 1 and 2 until 1889, and Guard Grenadier Regiments 3 and 4.*

☐   **Officer.** 700.00   775.00
☐   **Other Ranks.** 450.00   500.00

Prussia Guard Grenadier Regiments, *1 and 2, after 1889.*

☐   **Officer.** 650.00   725.00
☐   **Other Ranks.** 427.00   475.00

Prussia Guard Fusilier Regiment *and 5th Guard Regiment of Foot.*

☐   **Officer.** 750.00   825.00
☐   **Other Ranks.** 460.00   500.00

☐ **Prussia 1st Guard Dragoon Regiment.**
☐   **Officer.** 730.00   825.00
☐   **Other Ranks.** 525.00   575.00

Prussia 2nd Guard Dragoon Regiment.
☐   **Officer.** 750.00   825.00
☐   **Other Ranks.** 450.00   500.00

Prussia Guard Field Artillery Regiments, *1-4.*
☐   **Officer.** 700.00   775.00
☐   **Other Ranks.** 450.00   500.00

Prussia Guard Foot Artillery Regiment, *spike.*
☐   **Officer.** 700.00   775.00
☐   **Other Ranks.** 455.00   500.00

Prussia Guard Foot Artillery Regiment, *plume.*
☐   **Officer.** 800.00   900.00
☐   **Other Ranks.** 525.00   575.00

Prussia Guard Foot Artillery Regiment, *4th Company, with scroll bearing "Colberg 1807" under Guard Eagle and Star.*

☐   **Officer.** 915.00   1125.00
☐   **Other Ranks.** 655.00   725.00

Prussia Guard Pioneer Battalion, *Guard Railroad Regiments 1-3.*

☐   **Officer.** 700.00   775.00

	Price Range	
☐ Other Ranks..	455.00	500.00
Prussia Guard Train Battalion.		
☐ Officer..	700.00	775.00
☐ Other Ranks..	450.00	500.00
Prussia Grenadier Regiment, *1, before 1888, scroll above Grenadier eagle bearing date "1619."*		
☐ Officer..	900.00	1000.00
☐ Other Ranks..	615.00	675.00
Prussia Guard Regiment, *1, 1888-1900, scroll above the eagle bearing the date "1615."*		
☐ Officer..	835.00	925.00
☐ Other Ranks..	565.00	625.00
Prussia Grenadier Regiment, *1, after 1900, scroll below eagle with widespread wings bearing the date "1655."*		
☐ Officer..	790.00	875.00
☐ Other Ranks..	420.00	575.00
Prussia Grenadier Regiments, *2 (before 1897), 3 (before 1901), 4 (before 1888) and 5, 5, 10, 11 and 12. Grenadier eagle.*		
☐ Officer..	425.00	475.00
☐ Other Ranks..	340.00	375.00
Prussia Grenadier Regiments, *2 (after 1897), 3 (after 1901) and Guard Grenadier Regiments 1 and 2 (before 1889). Grenadier eagle with widespread wings.*		
☐ Officer..	625.00	675.00
☐ Other Ranks..	430.00	475.00
Prussia Grenadier Regiment, *4, 1888-1911, with scroll above eagle bearing date "1626."*		
☐ Officer..	880.00	975.00
☐ Other Ranks..	610.00	675.00
Prussia Grenadier Regiment, *4, 1911 on, with scroll above eagle with widespread wings bearing the date "1626."*		
☐ Officer..	880.00	975.00
☐ Other Ranks..	610.00	675.00
Prussia Grenadier Regiment, *7, 1897 on. Eagle with widespread wings.*		
☐ **Officer.** *(Ornamental disk holding chin scales bearing initials "WRII" with crown above).*	745.00	825.00
☐ Other Ranks..	420.00	575.00
Above helmets have scroll bearing date and legend "22 March 1797" below eagle.		
Prussia Grenadier Regiment, *8, to 1898.*		
☐ **Officer.** *(Ornamental disk holding chin scales bearing initials "FWR")*	745.00	825.00
☐ **Other Ranks.** *(Ornamental disk holding chin scales of 1st and 2nd Battalions bear a star, the 3rd Battalion a horn.)*	520.00	575.00
Prussia Grenadier Regiment, *8, 1898 on (as above but with eagle with widespread wings.)*		

	Price	Range
☐ Officer...	745.00	825.00
☐ Other Ranks...................................	520.00	575.00

Prussia Grenadier Regiment, *9, 1849-1913, Grenadier eagle with scoll across legs of eagle bearing the legend "COLBERG 1807."*

☐ Officer...	745.00	825.00
☐ Other Ranks...................................	520.00	575.00

Prussia Grenadier Regiment, *9, 1913 on, as above but with eagle with widespread wings.*

☐ Officer...	870.00	975.00
☐ Other Ranks...................................	600.00	670.00

Prussia Infantry Regiments, *13-33, 35-72, 75, 76, 79-86, 1st Battalion 96, 97-99, 128-132, 135-138, 140, 141, 143-152, 154-163, 166, 167, 171-176.*

☐ Officer...	345.00	380.00
☐ Other Ranks...................................	275.00	300.00

Prussia Infantry Regiment, *33 (the 5th and 6th Companies, Other Ranks from 1865, Officers from 1891, eagle bearing a scroll across its legs with the legend "Fur Auszeichnung d. vormaligen Konigl. Schwedischen Leibregt. Konigin."*

☐ Officer...	750.00	825.00
☐ Other Ranks...................................	555.00	600.00

Prussia Infantry Regiments, *74, 77, 78, 164, 165, 1899 on. (Eagle with scroll across the neck of the eagle with the legend "WATERLOO").*

☐ Officer...	485.00	550.00
☐ Other Ranks...................................	385.00	425.00

Prussia Infantry Regiment, *87, 1899 on (Eagle with scroll behind the neck of the eagle bearing the legend "PENINSULA-WATERLOO").*

☐ Officer...	575.00	650.00
☐ Other Ranks...................................	450.00	500.00

Prussia Fusilier Regiment, *73, 1899 on (Eagle with scroll behind the neck of the eagle bearing the legend "LA BELLE-ALLIANCE").*

☐ Officer...	575.00	650.00
☐ Other Ranks...................................	450.00	500.00

Prussia Infantry Regiment, *88, 1899 on (Eagle with long scroll behind the neck and wings of the eagle bearing the legend "LA BELLE ALLIANCE-MESA DE IBOR-MEDELLIN."*

Prussia Life Cuirassier Regiment, *1 (Eagle of Frederick the Great with scroll above the eagle bearing the legend "PRO GLORIA ET PATRIA."*

☐ Officer...	2495.00	2750.00
☐ Other Ranks...................................	1487.00	1625.00

Prussia Cuirassier Regiment, *2 (Line eagle with scroll across the lower wings and breast bearing the legend "HOLENFRIEDBERG 4. JUNI 1745") (This is a metal helmet.)*

	Price Range	
☐ **Officer**...............................	2350.00	2600.00
☐ **Other Ranks**............................	1360.00	1500.00

Prussia Other Ranks Metal Cuirasser helmet, Cuirassier Regiments 1, 3, 4, 5 and 7.

Prussia Cuirassier Regiments, *1, 3, 4, 5, 7 and 8.*
Metal helmet with line eagle.

☐ **Officer**..................................	1315.00	1450.00
☐ **Other Ranks**.............................	955.00	1050.00

Prussia Cuirassier Regiment, *6, as above but with line eagle in silver/white metal instead of gilt/brass.*

☐ **Officer**..................................	2350.00	2600.00
☐ **Other Ranks**.............................	1360.00	1500.00

Prussia Jager zu Pfred Regiments, *1-7, black metal helmet with silver eagle for Regiments 1-6 and brass Dragoon eagle for Regiment 7.*

☐ **Other Ranks**.............................	950.00	1000.00

Prussia Jager zu Pfred Regiments, *1-13, silver metal helmet, with silver Dragoon eagle for Regiments. 1-6 and gilt Dragoon eagle for Regiments 7-13.*

☐ **Officer**..................................	2825.00	2575.00

Prussia Jager zu Pfred Regiments, *7-13, leather helmet with brass Dragoon eagle.*

☐ **Other Ranks**.............................	500.00	550.00

Price Range

Prussia Dragoon Regiment, *1, leather helmet with Grenadier eagle with widespread wings.*

☐ Officer. 680.00   750.00
☐ Other Ranks. 450.00   500.00

Prussian Dragoon Officer's helmet, Dragoon Regiment 2.

Prussia Dragoon Regiment, *2, Dragoon eagle with a scepter in the center of an oval, the oval circled by a border. Over the oval is a crown. In the case of Officer's helmets, the oval is blue enamel and the crown has a red enamel background.*

☐ Officer. 925.00   1125.00
☐ Other Ranks. 750.00   850.00

Prussia Dragoon Regiments, *3 (to 1897), 4-6, 10, 11 and 15. Silver/white metal Dragoon eagle.*

☐ Officer. 475.00   525.00
☐ Other Ranks. 380.00   425.00

Prussia Grenadier Regiment zu Pfred, *3, after 1897. Silver/white metal Grenadier eagle with widespread wings. Chin scales attached to helmet with flaming grenade device.*

☐ Officer. 1015.00   1125.00
☐ Other Ranks. 750.00   825.00

Prussia Dragoon Regiments, *2 (to 1913), 9 (to 1899), 7, 8, 11, 13 and 14. Gilt/brass Dragoon eagle.*

☐ Officer. 475.00   525.00
☐ Other Ranks. 380.00   425.00

Price Range

Prussia Dragoon Regiment, *16, (from 1899 on), gilt/brass Dragoon eagle with scroll across the eagle's neck bearing the legend "WATERLOO-PENIN-SULA-GOHRDE."*

☐ Officer....................................	750.00	825.00
☐ Other Ranks................................	610.00	675.00

Prussia Dragoon Regiment, *9, 1899 on. Silver Dragoon eagle with scroll across neck of eagle bearing the legend "WATERLOO."*

☐ Officer....................................	750.00	825.00
☐ Other Ranks................................	610.00	675.00

Prussia Field Artillery Regiments, *1, 2 (less 1st Battery), 3 (less 6th Battery) and 6. Ball top ornament and gilt/brass Grenadier eagle.*

☐ Officer....................................	475.00	525.00
☐ Other Ranks................................	365.00	400.00

Prussia Field Artillery Battery, *2 (1st Battery) and 3 (6th Battery). Ball top ornament with gilt/brass Grenadier eagle with scroll across the legs bearing the legend "COLBERG 1807."*

☐ Officer....................................	790.00	875.00
☐ Other Ranks................................	610.00	675.00

Prussia Field Artillery Regiment, *10, 2nd Horse Battery, and the 1st, 4th, 5th and 6th Batteries of the 46th Field Artillery Regiment, gilt/brass line eagle with a scroll over the wings and behind the head bearing the legend "PENINSULA-WATERLOO-GOHRDE." Ball top ornament.*

☐ Officer....................................	880.00	975.00
☐ Other Ranks................................	610.00	675.00

Prussia Field Artillery Regiments, *4, 5, 7-9, 15-24, 26, 27, 31, 33-45, 46 (2nd and 3rd Battalions), 47, 51-59, 62, 63, 67, 69-75. Gilt/brass line eagle, ball top ornament.*

☐ Officer....................................	430.00	475.00
☐ Other Ranks................................	325.00	360.00

Prussia Field Artillery Regiment, *10 (2nd Battery), 46 (2nd Battery), 35 (2nd and 4th Batteries), gilt/brass line eagle with scroll across the wings and behind the head bearing the legend "PENINSULA-WATERLOO-GOHRDE" and a scroll across the legs bearing the legend "COLBERG 1807," ball top ornament.*

☐ Officer....................................	920.00	975.00
☐ Other Ranks................................	610.00	675.00

Prussia Foot Artillery Regiments, *1, 2, 3 and 6, ball top ornament with gilt/brass Grenadier eagle.*

☐ Officer....................................	455.00	500.00
☐ Other Ranks................................	320.00	350.00

Prussia Foot Artillery Regiments, *4, 5, 7-11, 13, 15, 18, ball top ornament with gilt/brass line eagle.*

☐ Officer....................................	430.00	475.00
☐ Other Ranks................................	325.00	360.00

Price Range

Prussia Foot Artillery Regiment, *2 (3rd Company),* *ball top ornament gilt/brass Grenadier eagle with scroll across the legs bearing the legend "COLBERG 1807."*

☐ Officer..	880.00	975.00
☐ Other Ranks.................................	610.00	675.00

Prussia Pioneer Battalions, *1 and 3, silver/white metal Grenadier eagle.*

☐ Officer..	520.00	575.00
☐ Other Ranks.................................	390.00	430.00

Prussia Pioneer Battalions, *2, 4-9, 11, 15-21, 23 and 24, silver/white metal line eagle.*

☐ Officer..	610.00	675.00
☐ Other Ranks.................................	320.00	350.00

Prussia Pioneer Battalion, *10, silver line eagle with a scroll across each wing and behind the neck bearing the legend "PENINSULA-WATERLOO."*

☐ Officer..	565.00	625.00
☐ Other Ranks.................................	435.00	475.00

Prussia Train Battalions, *1-11 and 15-17, gilt/brass line eagle.*

☐ Officer..	430.00	465.00
☐ Other Ranks.................................	300.00	325.00

Prussia Underofficers' School, *gilt/brass line eagle with Star of the Order of the Black Eagle.*

☐ Officer..	565.00	625.00
☐ Other Ranks.................................	455.00	500.00

Reuss Infantry Regiment, *96 (2nd Battalion), line eagle bearing the arms of Reuss on a heraldic star.*

☐ Officer	880.00	975.00
☐ Other Ranks.................................	615.00	675.00

Sachsen-Thuringen Infantry Regiment, *95 and 153 (1st and 2nd Battalions), line eagle bearing the arms of the Saxon Dutchies on a heraldic star.*

☐ Officer..	750.00	825.00
☐ Other Ranks.................................	420.00	575.00

Sachsen-Weimar Infantry Regiment, *94, line eagle with a heraldic star bearing the arms of Sachsen-Weimar.*

☐ Officer..	860.00	950.00
☐ Other Ranks.................................	565.00	625.00

Schwarzburg-Rudolstadt Infantry Regiment, *96 (3rd Battalion) line eagle with heraldic star bearing the arms of Schwarzburg.*

☐ Officer..	880.00	975.00
☐ Other Ranks.................................	620.00	675.00

Saxony Life-Grenadier Regiment, *100, silver/white metal arms of Saxony on heraldic star.*

☐ Officer..	565.00	625.00
☐ Other Ranks.................................	430.00	475.00

Price Range

Saxony Grenadier Regiment, *101, Infantry Regiments 102-107, 133, 134, 139, 177, 178, 179, 181, 182, gilt/brass arms of Saxony on a heraldic star.*

☐ Officer..	455.00	500.00
☐ Other Ranks..................................	365.00	400.00

Saxony Field Artillery Regiments, *12, 28, 32, 48, 64, 77 and 78. Ball top ornament with gilt/brass arms of Saxony on a heraldic star.*

☐ Officer..	520.00	575.00
☐ Other Ranks..................................	385.00	425.00

Saxony Foot Artillery Regiment, *12, ball top ornament with silver/white metal arms of Saxony on a gilt/brass heraldic star.*

☐ Officer..	520.00	575.00
☐ Other Ranks..................................	385.00	430.00

Saxony Pioneer Battalions, *12 and 22, Railway Company 15, silver/white metal heraldic star with gilt/brass arms of Saxony.*

☐ Officer......................................	550.00	600.00
☐ Other Ranks..................................	430.00	475.00

Saxony Train Battalions, *12 and 19, gilt/brass heraldic star with silver/white metal arms of Saxony.*

☐ Officer..	520.00	575.00
☐ Other Ranks..................................	385.00	425.00

Saxony Telegraph Battalion, *7, silver/white metal heraldic star with gilt/brass arms of Saxony.*

☐ Officer..	745.00	825.00
☐ Other Ranks..................................	520.00	575.00

Wurttemberg General Officer, *arms of Wurttemberg in gilt, bearing a silver and enamel Star of the Order of the Wurttemberg Crown.*

☐ With gilt spike...............................	2395.00	2650.00
☐ With white, black and red plume.............	2710.00	3000.00
☐ **Wurttemberg Palace Guard Company,** *arms of Wurttemberg in silver.*	635.00	700.00

Wurttemberg Grenadier Regiments, *119 and 123, arms of Wurttemberg is silver/white metal.*

☐ Officer..	500.00	550.00
☐ Other Ranks..................................	385.00	425.00

Wurttemberg Infantry Regiments, *120-122, 124-127 and 180, arms of Wurttemberg in gilt/brass.*

☐ Officer..	475.00	525.00
☐ Other Ranks..................................	300.00	335.00

Wurttemberg Dragoon Regiment, *25, silver/white metal arms of Wurttemberg.*

☐ Officer..	635.00	700.00
☐ Other Ranks..................................	475.00	525.00

Wurttemberg Dragoon Regiment, *26, silver/white metal arms of Wurttemberg with the silver and enamel Star of the Order of the Wurttemberg Crown for officers and a white metal Star for other Ranks.*

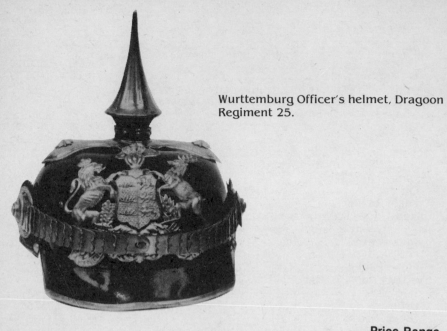

Wurttemburg Officer's helmet, Dragoon Regiment 25.

	Price Range	
☐ Officer..	905.00	1000.00
☐ Other Ranks.................................	565.00	625.00

Wurttemberg Artillery Regiments, *13 and 29, ball top ornament and gilt/brass Arms of Wurttemberg.*

☐ Officer..	475.00	525.00
☐ Other Ranks.................................	320.00	350.00

Wurttemberg Pioneer Battalion, *13, spike and silver/white metal Arms of Wurttemberg.*

☐ Officer..	550.00	600.00
☐ Other Ranks.................................	385.00	425.00

Wurttemberg Train Battalion, *13, gilt/white metal Arms of Wurttemberg.*

☐ Officer..	475.00	525.00
☐ Other Ranks.................................	365.00	405.00

GREAT BRITAIN

☐ **1871 Pattern Officer's helmet,** *British Dragoon Guards Regiments, gilt helmet with gilt trim. The regimental badge with plume, coronet and motto of the Prince of Wales, within the Garter, superimposed upon a heraldic star, all in silver, gilt and enamel, identifies this as a helmet of the 3rd (Prince of Wales) Dragoon Guards. Falling black and red plume.* 925.00 1025.00

☐ **1881-1901 Leicestershire Officer's helmet,** *gilt spike and fittings with the badge of the regiment on a heraldic star with royal crown above.* 145.00 155.00

British Royal Artillery Officer's helmet, c. 1881 to 1901.

	Price Range	
☐ **1881-1901 Period Royal Artillery Officer's helmet,** *blue cloth with gilt ball top ornament and fittings, badge of the Royal artillery.*	185.00	200.00
☐ **Home Service 1878 Model Royal Marines Light Infantry Officer's helmet,** *gilt spike and fittings, Royal Marines badge superimposed on a heraldic star with royal crown above.*	250.00	275.00
☐ **Home Service Helmet Post 1901 Cheshire Regiment Officer's helmet,** *gilt spike and fittings, regimental badge on heraldic star with royal crown above.*	145.00	175.00
☐ **Post 1902 Army Service Corps Officer's helmet,** *blue cloth with gilt spike and trim*	125.00	135.00
☐ **Post 1902 East Kent Regiment Officer's helmet,** *blue cloth with gilt spike and trim.*	125.00	140.00
☐ **Post 1902 Manchester Regiment (6th Volunteer Battalion) Officer's helmet,** *blue cloth with silver spike and trim.*	145 00	175.00
☐ **Post 1902 Officer's helmet,** *Aberdeenshire Artillery Volunteers, blue cloth with silver ball top and fittings, badge of the Royal Artillery with the regimental title on a scroll below.*	185.00	200.00
☐ **Post 1902 Officer's helmet,** *Volunteer Artillery, blue cloth with silver ball top and fittings, badge of the Royal Artillery with regimental title on scroll below.* . .	225.00	250.00
☐ **Post 1902 Officer's helmet,** *Royal Army Medical Corps, blue cloth with gilt ball ornament and trimmings, badge of the Corps.*	150.00	175.00

British Officer's Home Service helmet,
The Cheshire Regiment, Post 1901.

	Price Range	
☐ **Post 1902 Officer's helmet,** *Royal Service Corps, blue cloth with gilt ball top and fittings, badge of the corps.*	205.00	225.00
☐ **Post 1902 Royal Engineers Officer's helmet,** *blue cloth with gilt ball top and gilt fittings.*	140.00	160.00
☐ **Post 1902 Royal Sussex Regiment Officer's helmet,** *blue cloth with gilt spike and trim.*	215.00	235.00
☐ **Victorian Officer's Albert Pattern Metal Gilt helmet,** *Royal Irish Dragoon Guards, with drooping white plume, helmet elaborately decorated with leaf designs, regimental badge within wreath with royal crown above.*	340.00	375.00
☐ **Victorian Officer's Albert Pattern Metal helmet,** *Gentlemen-at-Arms, gilt skull elaborately decorated with floral design, badge composed of crowned badge of the unit surrounded by an oak wreath, Order of the Garter, all superimposed on a heraldic star. This is one of the most desired of all British helmets with its white swan feather plume.*	1375.00	1525.00
☐ **Victorian Officer's Albert Pattern Silver Metal helmet,** *Life Guards, gilt mounts, badge of the organization with enameled center, falling white plume.*	835.00	915.00
☐ **Victorian Officer's Black Leather helmet,** *Queen's Own Royal Yeomanry (Staffordshire), elaborate silver*		

Price Range

trim about base of skull and decorating the edge of the front visor, large silver badge of the regiment in silver with the Stafford knot in gilt, all superimposed upon a heraldic star, encircled by a silver wreath with the royal crown above. 1175.00 1300.00

☐ **Victorian Officer's Black Silk Fur Covered helmet,** *Royal 1st Devon Yeomanry Cavalry, silver trim and fittings, large silver and gilt badge of the regiment, encircled by a wreath with scrolls below bearing the title "ROYAL DEVON YEOMANRY CAVALRY," red and white falling plume.* 1175.00 1300.00

☐ **Victorian Officer's helmet,** *Black Watch, black cloth with gilt spike and furnishings, badge of the regiment on a heraldic star with crown above.* 250.00 275.00

☐ **Victorian Officer's helmet,** *Fermanagh Light Infantry, green cloth helmet with silver spike and fittings, regimental badge on heraldic star with royal crown above.* 185.00 200.00

☐ **Victorian Officer's helmet,** *Royal London Militia, black cloth with silver spike and trim, badge of the regiment on heraldic star with royal crown above.* 133.00 150.00

☐ **Victorian Officer's helmet,** *Royal West Kent Regiment (1st Volunteer Brigade), blue cloth helmet with silver spike and fittings, badge of the regiment on a heraldic star.* 250.00 275.00

☐ **Victorian Officer's helmet,** *Volunteer Medical Staff Corps, blue cloth with white metal ball top and fittings, badge of the corps.* 187.00 200.00

MEXICO

Black leather Officer's German-style helmet. *Gilt fittings, gilt helmet plate in form of the Mexican Eagle perched on a cactus, holding a serpent in its beak, silver "B" on one side of the eagle's legs, silver "Z" on the other.*

☐   *As above, but with gilt spike.* 655.00 725.00

☐   *As above, but with black horsehair plume.* 835.00 925.00

Post 1905 Black Leather Officer's German-style helmet. *Gilt helmet plate and fittings as above, but without the initials "B" and "Z."*

☐   *As above, but with white feather plume (general officers)* 1015.00 1125.00

☐   *As above, but with black feather plume (staff and field grade officers)* 925.00 1025.00

☐   *As above, but with black horsehair plume (company grade officers)* 835.00 925.00

☐   *As above, but with white horsehair plume (cadets).* 835.00 925.00

☐   *As above, but with gilt spike* 655.00 725.00

RUSSIA (Imperial)

Guard Cuirassier helmet, *c. 1914. Yellow metal helmet with round front visor and so-called lobster tail*

Imperial Russian Guard Cuirassier helmet, c. 1914.

Price Range

back, edging in white metal, gilt chin scales. Spike in form of grenade with elongated flame. Front plate in the form of a heraldic star of the Order of St. Andrew First Called. Circular center with silver rimmed blue enamel circle with the double-head Imperial Russian Eagle in black enamel on a gilt background. Small gilt St. Andrew's cross on the breast of the eagle. On the blue enamel circle appears the legend in Russian "FOR FAITH AND LOYALTY." This is a much sought after collector's item.

☐ Officer.	4075.00	4525.00
☐ Other Ranks.	1285.00	1425.00

☐ **Mid-1800's Other Ranks black leather helmet** (artillery). Gray chin scales and badges, badges consist of crossed cannon with flaming bomb above pierced with the regimental number, brass flaming bomb top ornament. 835.00   925.00

☐ **Mid-1800's Other Ranks Infantry Black Leather helmet.** Brass fittings, top ornament in form of flaming bomb with pointed flame. Helmet plate consists of a cartouche with the regimental number pierced in the center. Above the cartouche is the Imperial Russian double-headed eagle with a shield on its breast showing St. George slaying a dragon. 735.00   825.00

SWEDEN

Price Range

☐ **1880's Officer's German-style Leather helmet.** *Gilt spike and trim. Helmet plate consists of blue enameled and gilt Arms of Sweden surrounded by the Collar of the Order of the Seraphim, all superimposed on flags and lions.* 430.00   475.00

Swedish Other Ranks Spiked helmet, c. 1850.

☐ **Mid-1850's Early Style German-type Black Leather helmet.** *Brass spike and fittings, Other Ranks model. Oval badge bearing the Arms of Sweden, surrounded by the Collar of the Order of the Seraphim.* 365.00   400.00

☐ **German-influenced Black Leather helmet, model 1900.** *White metal spike and trim, front plate consisting of the Arms of Sweden and the Collar of the Order of the Seraphim in brass superimposed upon flags and lions of brass.* 385.00   425.00

UNITED STATES

Plumed helmet, model 1872. *Gilt/brass fittings and various colored plumes and helmet lines (see descriptive text on spiked helmets.)*

☐   **Officer.** 300.00   325.00

☐   **Enlisted men.** 250.00   275.00

Swedish Other Ranks Spiked helmet, c. 1900.

U.S. Army Enlisted Man's Dress helmet, model 1872.

U.S. Army Officer's Dress helmet (unmounted), model 1881.

Price Range

Spiked and/or Plumed helmets, model 1881.
*Gilt/brass fittings and various colored plumes
and/or helmet lines (see descriptive text or spiked
helmets.)*

☐ **Officer.** 250.00   275.00
☐ **Enlisted men.** 185.00   225.00

*Special Note: It is of some interest to note that spiked and/or plumed U.S.
helmets are in very short supply even in this country. The relatively few
Army helmets which are available are rapidly increasing in price.
Reproductions are beginning to appear in quantity but **not** in quality. The
collector should be on guard. As for U.S. Marine spiked/plumed helmets,
this writer has seen only three offered for private sale over a long period of
years. These brought an extremely high price. To this writer's knowledge, a
U.S. Navy musician's spiked helmet has never been offered for public sale.*

CRESTED HELMETS

AUSTRIA

☐ **1850's Imperial Officer's Black Leather helmet.** *High
Roman style crest with black and yellow fur comb or
crest, elaborate embossing of metal crest, gilt trim
and fittings. Large gilt front plate bearing the
Austrian eagle with a shield on its breast bearing the
cypher "F.J.I" (Francis Joseph I).* 1220.00   1350.00

☐ **Imperial Trooper's Heavy Black Leather helmet,** *c.
1798. Crest similar to that of an ancient Roman
gladiator's helmet, brass trim and fittings, large plain*

Imperial Austrian Trooper's helmet, c. 1798.

Price Range

brass front plate bearing the cypher "F.II," black and
yellow wool comb. 390.00   430.00

BELGIUM

☐ **Cuirassier Other Ranks helmet,** c. 1842. Helmet of
white metal with brass comb and trim. The Roman-
style helmet has a highly ornate comb with black
horsehair tuft in a brass holder at the front. A black
horsehair tail hangs from the back of the comb. A red
feather plume is inserted in a socket on the right side
of the helmet. The front plate is a highly detailed and
embossed lion's head (the lion is one of the heraldic
beasts in the Arms of Belgium). 850.00   950.00

ENGLAND

☐ **20th Light Dragoons Officer's helmet,** c. 1796. Black
leather helmet silver plated copper crest and trim,
cloth turban about the lower third of the helmet, front
plate bearing an embossed alligator, commemorating the regiments service in Jamaica in 1791, red and
white horsehair plume atop the crest.............   1220.00   1350.00
☐ **Worcestershire Yeomanry Officer's helmet,** c. 1850.
Black leather helmet with silvered crest and trim,
large front plate gilt backed by silver. The plate consists of the royal cypher "VR" within an oval
inscribed "QUEEN'S OWN REGIMENT," with the

Belgium Cuirassier Other Ranks helmet, c. 1842.

British Army Officer's helmet, 20th Light Dragoons, c. 1796.

royal crest and supporters. Under the oval appears a scroll bearing the legend "WORCESTERSHIRE YEOMANRY." A red and white horsehair plume on the crest is ornamented by a gilt heraldic rose. . . . .

Price Range

1400.00   1550.00

British Army
Officer's helmet,
Worcestershire Yeomanry,
c. 1850.

FRANCE

☐ **Chasseur Other Ranks helmet,** *c. 1910. Bright steel skull and visors, brass trim, brass comb of elaborate design bears a black horsehair mane, Medusa head on front of comb which extends down and around helmet. Five-pointed star with radiating rays on front, plume socket on the left side of helmet.* ....

Price Range

400.00   450.00

French Dragoon Officer's helmet, 1852-1870.

Price Range

☐ **Dragoon Officer's helmet,** *1852-1870. Gilt copper skull with a band of leopard skin about the lower half of the skull and extending over the visors. Ornate comb, horsehair tail and tuft, no plume in the plume holder.* 500.00   550.00

☐ **Other Ranks Chasseur a Cheval helmet,** *c. 1910. Similar to Chasseur, Other Ranks helmet except that instead of the star, there is a light infantry bugle horn with radiating rays.* 400.00   450.00

French Cuirassier Other Ranks'
helmet, c. 1830.

☐ **Post 1830 Cuirassier Other Ranks helmet.** *Steel skull and visors with brass trim and fittings, horsehair mane atop ornate comb, brass tuft holder with red tuft at the front of the comb. Socket for plume on the left side of helmet, ornate front plate, extending down from front of crest and around sides of skull, oak leaf embossing with a flaming grenade at the lower front.* 500.00   550.00

☐ **Post 1840 Cuirassier Other Ranks helmet.** *Bright steel helmet with wide black fur band about the bottom and above the visors, brass trim, large brass decorated comb with trailing black horsehair at rear. At the top front is a tuft holder with red tuft. Red plume in a socket on the left side of skull, front of comb bears embossed face of Medusa with a flaming grenade below.* 500.00   550.00

French Cuirassier Officer's helmet, pre-1830.

	Price Range	
☐ **Pre-1830 Cuirassier Officer's helmet.** *Silvered copper skull and visors, gilt comb and fittings, high ornately decorated comb bears a black horsehair crest. Front plate is large and continues in a wide band around the bottom of the skull and is decorated with oak leaves. On an embossed oval with a wreath of laurel leaves appears the Royal fleur-de-lis.*	600.00	650.00

GERMANY (Imperial)

Bavaria Archers of the Guard (Lieb-Garde der Hart-schiere). *Nickeled helmet with high crown and deep visors, ornate chin scales. Front plate consists of the Arms of Bavaria within an elaborate floral design. Falling white plume for dress (gala). A large standing lion replaces the plume on other occasions.*

☐ **As above,** *but with plume.*	3000.00	3300.00
☐ **As above,** *but with lion crest.*	4350.00	4800.00

Bavaria Chevaulegers, Artillery, Train organizations. *Raupemhelm model 1868 black leather helmet with gilt/brass fittings, black fur comb, hair plume falling on left side. Chevaulegers, white; Artillery, red; Train, black. Front plate is gilt/brass crowned cypher "L."*

☐ **Officer.**	475.00	525.00
☐ **Other Ranks.**	475.00	525.00

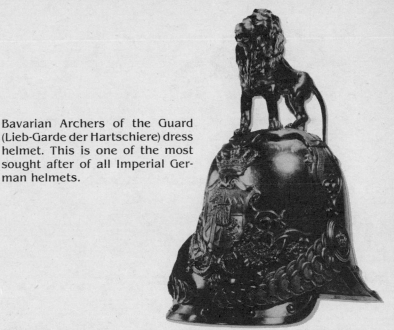

Bavarian Archers of the Guard (Lieb-Garde der Hartschiere) dress helmet. This is one of the most sought after of all Imperial German helmets.

Price Range

Bavaria Cuirassier Regiments, *1 and 2, to 1878. Bright steel helmet with gilt/brass trim and fixtures. Black horsehair roach or comb atop gilt/brass comb. Earlier helmets have crowned "M" (Maximillian) in gilt/brass for a front plate. Later helmets have a crowned "L" (Ludwig).*

☐ **Officer.** 1720.00   1900.00
☐ **Other Ranks.** 955.00   1050.00

Bavaria Jager, Schutzen and Infantry Regiments. *Raupenhelm model 1868 black leather helmet with gilt/brass fittings, black wool comb or crest, front plate is gilt/brass crowned cypher "L."*

☐ **Officer,** *long green pompon on left side.* 525.00   580.00
☐ **Other Ranks,** *long green pompon on left side.* 400.00   450.00

Prussia Garde du Corps Regiment, Garde Kurassier Regiment. *Metal tombac helmet with eagle crest (see descriptive text).*

☐ **Officer.** 2000.00   2325.00
☐ **Other Ranks.** 1540.00   1700.00

Saxony Garde Reiter and Karabinier Regiments, *1875 on. Gilt/tombac metal helmet with silver/white metal trim. Silver/white eagle with gilt/brass crown atop helmet with its forepaws upon the tip of a shield bearing the initials "FAR," (Friedrich Augustus Rex). Front plate is a silver/white metal heraldic star with the gilt/brass Arms of Saxony.*

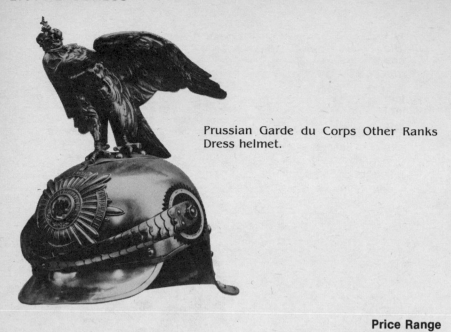

Prussian Garde du Corps Other Ranks Dress helmet.

		Price Range	
☐	**Officer**..	**3500.00**	**3900.00**
☐	**Other Ranks**.................................	**2000.00**	**2200.00**

Saxon Garde Reiter Other Ranks Dress helmet.

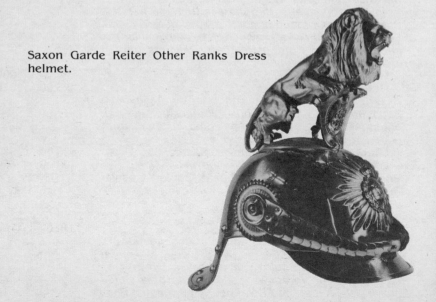

Price Range

Saxony Garde Reiter and Karabinier Regiments, *to 1875. Black leather helmet with gilt/brass trim, black wool comb atop black comb, gilt/brass Arms of Saxony superimposed on silver/white metal heraldic star.*

☐   **Officer** 875.00   965.00

☐   **Other Ranks** 670.00   750.00

GREAT BRITAIN

Imperial Russian Life Horse Guards Regiment, c. 1914.

☐ **1st Oxfordshire Light Horse Volunteers Officer's helmet,** *1864 to 1870. Rare helmet of a disbanded regiment, dark blue felt with leather visors, white metal trim and fittings, metal comb with ventilation openings, red horsehair mane atop the crest. The front plate consists of the regimental cypher reversed and interlaced with the numeral "1" above and a scroll bearing the legend "FORTIS EST RITAS." Over the cypher is the Royal Crown.* 1440.00   1600.00

1st Royal Dragoons Officer's helmet, *1834 to 1843. This is one of the most prized of collectors' helmets. Gilt metal helmet of Roman style with very ornately embossed comb with head, mane and forepaws of a springing lion in front. Scroll designs decorate the sides of the helmet which is encircled about the bot-*

Price Range

tom and above the visors with the title "THE ROYAL DRAGOONS" in front. The helmet plate consists of the Royal Hanoverian Arms with scrolls bearing the words "PENINSULA" and "WATERLOO" below, all on a half sunburst. This helmet is also found with a very large bearskin crest atop the metal crest.

☐   **As above,** but without bearskin crest. 1800.00   2000.00
☐   **As above,** but with bearskin crest. 2070.00   2300.00

Officer's helmet of the 1st Kings Dragoon Guards, c. 1800. Similar to foregoing helmet but with rounded instead of pointed front visor, with a scroll under the Royal Arms bearing the word "WATERLOO," and with the title "1st THE KING'S DRAGOON GUARDS" on the front of the band encircling the bottom of the helmet. This helmet, too, may be found with a very large bearskin crest.

☐   **As above,** but with bearskin crest. 2070.00   2300.00
☐   **As above,** but without bearskin crest. 1800.00   2000.00

ITALY

☐ **Royal Piedmont Cavalry Officer's helmet.** Polished steel skull and visors, lower half of skull and visors covered with black fur, gilt trim and fixtures, extremely high gilt comb, silver cross with equal length arms appears as front plate at lower front of helmet. 400.00   450.00

RUMANIA

☐ **Early 1920's Officer's helmet.** Highly polished green leather with black leather visors, back visor twice as long as the front, silvered comb with eagle with widespread wings at front, silvered trim and fixtures. Front plate consists of interwoven cyphers "C" (Carl) with crown above. 525.00   580.00

RUSSIA

Imperial Life Horse Guard Regiment. Tombac helmet with gilt/yellow metal double-headed Imperial eagle with crown. On the breast of the eagle is a shield showing St. George slaying a dragon. Trim and fittings in silver/white metal. Helmet plate in the form of a silver/white metal heraldic upon which appears the Star of the Order of St. Andrew, First Called, in yellow metal for other ranks and in gilt and yellow and blue enamel for Officers.

☐   **Officer.** 5100.00   5650.00
☐   **Other Ranks.** 1340.00   1475.00

Helmets. As above, but with gilt/yellow metal flaming grenade with elongated flame, in lieu of the double-headed eagle are less costly.

☐   **Officer.** 4150.00   4600.00

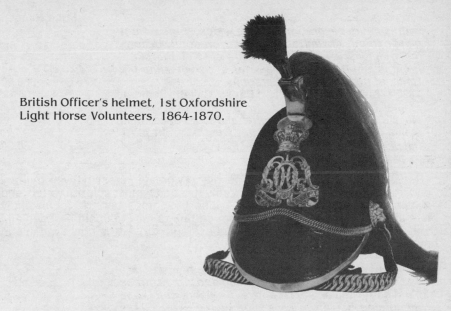

British Officer's helmet, 1st Oxfordshire
Light Horse Volunteers, 1864-1870.

	Price Range	
☐ **Other Ranks.**	1000.00	1100.00

SPAIN

To date there has not been a very great interest in Spanish helmets. In the event such interest does develop, dealers and others will search them out. Interestingly enough several Spanish concerns are, along with fabricating reproduction medieval arms and armor and Japanese weapons of the feudal period, are also reproducing some dress helmets of the monarchy. This is an area in which the collector must be careful. Generally speaking, an authentic Spanish dress helmet will sell in a range from $300.00 to $450.00. The helmet described below is an exception and is an example of what may be expected to be available if the demand increases.

☐ **Dress helmet of the Life Guard of Alphonso XIII** *(reigned 1902-1931). Large silvered skull and visors with gilt trim and fittings, gilt front plate consisting of detailed laurel wreath about a five-pointed star, with the Royal Crown above, large drooping feather plume.* 1270.00 1400.00

SWEDEN

As is the case with Spanish helmets, there has not to date been a very great demand on the part of collectors for Swedish items. Here again as interest increases, dealers will search them out in numbers. The following examples are typical of what is now available.

☐ **Life Guard Dragoons Other Ranks Leather helmet.** *Brass trim and fixtures, moderately high brass comb*

Price Range

with simple decoration on the sides. Brass front plate extends down from the comb, gradually becoming wider as it passes along the side of the skull. Front is embossed with the Arms of Sweden and the Collar of the Order of the Seraphin. 270.00 300.00

☐ **1850's Black Leather Other Ranks Cavalry helmet.** Similar to the above helmet but with higher and more classic shaped skull and higher and more decorative comb. Same crowned Swedish badge on front plate but of larger size. 315.00 350.00

SWITZERLAND

Here again to date there has not been a very great interest in Swiss military headdress. Nonetheless, the Swiss Army has had a most colorful variety and as items of Imperial German and British headdress become increasingly more difficult to secure, collectors are certain to turn to Spain, Sweden and Switzerland. The following is a typical example of what is now available in limited numbers.

☐ **Other Ranks Black Leather Infantry helmet,** late 1800's. Polished black leather skull and visors, brass band about the skull just above the visors and brass reinforcing bar down each side of the skull. Brass chin scales with bosses bearing an embossed light infantry bugle design, large black fur crest atop the skull, front plate in the form of a rimmed oval, in brass, bears a Swiss cross in silver. 205.00 225.00

ADDENDUM

In addition to all of the above crested helmets, there are a few others which, although not of general availability or collectibility, are of interest to some advanced or specialized collectors.

AUSTRIAN

☐ **Dragoon Officer's helmet,** c. early 1900's. High quality black lacquered metal helmet with gilt trim and fittings, high ornate comb with highly detailed embossed lion and serpent, gilt front plate in the form of the Austrian double-headed eagle with the Arms of Austria on its breast. 450.00 500.00

☐ **Dragoon Other Ranks helmet.** Polished black leather with plain black metal comb with yellow metal trim and with skull trimmed in yellow metal and with yellow metal front plate. 185.00 200.00

☐ **Dragoon Warrant Officer Private Purchase helmet.** Black lacquered metal, similar to Dragoon Officer's helmet but with plain black metal comb trimmed in yellow metal and with yellow metal trim and fittings, including the front plate. 225.00 250.00

BAVARIAN

☐ **Early 1800's Other Ranks Raupenhelm.** Tall black leather skull with black wool comb, plain brass trim,

Price Range

scarlet plume on left side of skull, medium size brass front plate of oval shape with embossed cypher "M.K.," with embossed crown over the oval. 600.00   675.00

LUXEMBOURG

☐ **Cavalry Officer's helmet,** *c. 1900. Blue wool covered metal skull and visors, with detailed gilt lion head crest, gilt trim and fittings. Front plate is of gilt and consists of a flaming grenade surrounded by a wreath, with crossed lances behind. Directly above the badge is a red, white and blue cockade. On the left side is a plume socket holding a cloth ball and red feather plume.* 300.00   325.00

SAXONY

Saxon Horse Artillery Officer's helmet, 1848-1864.

☐ **Horse Artillery Officer's helmet,** *c. 1848-1864. Highly polished heavy black leather, with two heavy gilt reinforcing bars on each side of the skull. Wide gilt band decorated with embossed oak leaves about front lower part of skull just above the visor. Front plate is slightly dished rimmed oval bearing the cypher "FR" (Friedrich Rex). Black fur crest, gilt trim and fixtures.*   575.00   635.00

SPAIN

☐ **Cavalry Officer's helmet,** *c. 1900. Highly polished steel skull and visors, gilt trim and fixtures, elaborate*

overlaid floral designs on both visors, extremely high
classic style gilt comb decorated on sides with finely
detailed floral design, silver star on each side of
comb. Front plate consists of the Royal Arms of
Spain in silver on a gilt half sunburst. ....

Price Range

575.00   635.00

UNITED STATES

As of this writing, there has not been a lively interest in American military
headdress, other than that of the American Civil War period. Even during the
Revolutionary War Bicentennial, there was not much interest on the part of
collectors for these items. In addition to the headdress of the Regular
Establishment, the great number and varied designs of the militia units allow
for a wide range of interest. As with other items, this writer believes that
eventually a demand for these items will develop and prices will be such that
the helmets will come out of hiding. Only two examples are shown here.
These are very rare items but they illustrate the possibilities existing for
knowledgeable collectors.

Helmet of the First City Troop
of Philadelphia, c. 1840. This
is perhaps the most ornate of
all U.S. helmets and is one of
the most beautiful in all the
world.

☐ **Helmet of the First City Troop of Philadelphia,** *c.
1840. This headdress dates from the beginning of a
period when militia units in many instances were
made up of men of considerable wealth, a fact which
is reflected in their uniforms. This is certainly one of
the most beautiful helmets in existence. It rivals the
helmets of any of the other armies. It is quite similar*

U.S. Militia Dragoon Cap
with bearskin crest,
post Revolutionary War.

Price Range

to and was probably copied from the large bearskin crested helmets of either the 1st Royal Dragoons or the 1st King's Dragoon Guards. Very highly polished black leather skull and visors, white metal trim and fixtures, including chin scales and bosses. Finely detailed laurel leaves decorate the top and sides of the skull. Extremely large fine quality bearskin crest decorates the top of the helmet. A very rare item.....   4700.00   5200.00

☐ **Militia Dragoon helmet,** *post Revolutionary War. So-called jockey cap type with polished high crown skull and large flat black leather visor. No front plate, wide painted red band about the bottom third of the skull, large red and black painted rosette on left side of skull, secured by plain brass button. Crest consists of a strip of bearskin over the top of the skull from front to back...................................*   500.00   550.00

STEEL COMBAT HELMETS

Since World War II there has been an increasing interest in steel combat helmets of the modern era. Although much of this interest centered about Imperial Germany and Third Reich examples, there is now considerable attention being given to those of other armies. Prices are still comparatively modest in this field but there is every indication that as interest grows, the prices will go up. Collectors with any interest in these helmets would be well advised to begin acquiring specimens. Enough variations exist to make the subject most interesting. But again, a word of caution! Inasmuch as the value of some helmets is dependent upon the insignia or organization identifying device which these carry, usually in the form of a painted insignia or decals, some dishonest operators have attempted to upgrade an otherwise ordinary specimen by adding phony insignia. Know the person with whom you deal! Consult an expert!

The French are credited with the introduction of the steel combat helmet into modern warfare. A French general named Adrian, of an inventive turn of mind, while talking to a wounded soldier observed that he had not been killed although struck in the head by a shell fragment. The soldier explained that at the time he had his metal mess bowl under his cap. This allowed enough deflection of the fragment to prevent his death. General Adrian, much impressed, experimented with various metal skull caps, finally developing one to be worn under the cap with the rim resting within the cap band. Approximately 700,000 of these were manufactured and their use reduced fatalities to a marked degree. Sometime not long after the introduction of the metal cap liner, General Adrian modified the design by addition of a front and rear visor and a decorative crest covering a ventilation slot. **This immediately became known as the model 1915 Adrian helmet.** It was modified in 1926 and 1933 and in that form was worn throughout World War II. Although this helmet did reduce the number of casualties, it was not nearly as effective as it could have been due to the type of steel used. It had a positive artistic appearance, however, and was proudly worn by the troops. In this connection it is interesting to observe that the **appearance** of a helmet has a very great influence upon the fighting man's morale. He wants to wear a helmet as a means of identifying him as a **combat** soldier. The better he likes his helmet, the less likely he is to throw it away when he becomes tired and his helmet grows heavy!

The French did experiment with several other helmets which were better as far as ballistics are concerned but these helmets added nothing to the military appearance of the man and were not accepted.

The French World War I helmets, as well as some of those of World War II bore a metal or painted device on the front identifying the kind of organization to which the wearer belonged. For instance, infantry, cavalry and train units wore a flaming bomb in metal, with "RF" (Republic of France) embossed on the bomb. The majority of these helmets were blue or blue gray, while some were painted khaki or even black. Many of the helmets used in World War II were painted khaki.

The French also developed special helmets for tank crews, and later for air crews. Basically these consisted of an Adrian model with a thick leather pad replacing the front visors. Following World War II a new model helmet was issued to the troops. This, the Model 51, was generally similar in appearance to the American helmet of World War II. It had a separate liner and was olive green in color.

During 1915 the British introduced a basin-shape steel helmet which became a sort of "trademark" of the "Tommy" in two World Wars. Although it was ballistically superior to the French model, it was far too shallow to be of much protection except to the top of the head. Dubbed the "tin hat," it was simple in design and easy and cheap to manufacture. It weighs two pounds, three ounces. During World War II a paratrooper helmet and an improved combat helmet were developed. All these British helmets are easily available at modest prices.

The United States had no helmets when we entered World War I. Upon our entry into that conflict, a committee was appointed to study the subject. This committee soon recommended the adoption of the British helmet as an interim measure. In the meantime, experiments were conducted with several designs, none of which proved to be practicable. Only small test lots of these helmets were ever made; consequently, they command a fairly high price on the collectors' market.

Manufacturing a somewhat modified version of the British helmet was started in this country and high production figures were soon attained. In the meantime, the British made 400,000 helmets immediately available to us. The U.S. model of the British helmet was used in a slightly modified form into the early months of World War II.

In the late 1940's the first positive steps were taken in this country to develop a helmet more suited to modern combat conditions. In this connection it may be well to consider a few of the important factors involved in helmet design. It is important that the helmet cover as much of the head as possible. The helmet should be proof against the majority of small missiles likely to be encountered in combat. It is indeed interesting to note that a helmet has yet to be developed (may never be developed) which will negate high velocity rifle and machine gun fire at close range.

Comfort is another consideration. The helmet should be light enough so that the wearer would rather not be without it. It should be well fitting, well balanced, and at the same time should shield from sun and rain as well as from missiles. Utility requires that the shape of the helmet be such that it will not hamper vision and hearing. As mentioned previously, morale requires that the helmet have a striking military appearance so that the individual will be proud to wear it as a symbol of a **combat** soldier.

Any helmet at best is awkward to wear when not actually needed; therefore, some sort of field cap must be provided for wear at such times. The American designers at length solved this problem by fitting the helmet suspension within a lightweight liner similar in shape to and slightly smaller than the metal skull. Worn by itself this liner is martial looking. In combat zones the helmet fits quickly and closely over the liner. Although a decided improvement over the "wash basin" type of World War I and early World War II, it is still somewhat clumsy and has a tendency to echo the voice of the wearer. Presently progress is being made in developing helmets of ballistic fiberglass and other lightweight materials.

This American helmet, the M-1, was the result of considerable experimentation. It was issued to personnel of all the U.S. services and soon became one of the distinguishing badges of the American fighting man. It was provided with a camouflaged cover as well as with a net cover into which twigs and leaves could be easily inserted. This helmet was modified for paratrooper use by being fitted with a special chin strap which was attached to **both** the helmet and the liner to prevent it from being displaced during the jump. For aircraft crews it was worn without the liner, the head suspension being attached to the helmet itself. Both sides of this helmet were cut away in a small semicircle to accommodate headphones. Hinged shallow metal cups came down over the phones. Other modifications were developed for tanks crews.

The U.S. Navy developed a special helmet for the use of certain exposed shipboard personnel, particularly antiaircraft gun crews. This was a very large one piece steel shell with an extremely thick soft sponge rubber lining. Although these Navy helmets were not produced in nearly as great a number as the M-1, it has not attracted any great collector interest to the present time and it is available for a most modest price. It is quite probable that the price will go up in the future.

Insofar as protection is concerned, the German helmet of both World Wars I and II was by far the superior to that of any other nation. At the advent of World War I, no provision had been made for a protective headdress for German combat soldiers. The great number of head wounds in early combat underscored the fact that something had to be done about the matter. A makeshift device consisting of an adjustable leather headpiece with an attached shaped steel plate covering the front of the head and nose was devised and issued in some numbers. Use was restricted to the Vosges sector on Army Group Gaede's front. It was withdrawn upon the introduction of the combat helmet. It is now extremely rare. The writer has seen only two or three for sale within recent years and these were selling for around $700.00 each.

German army authorities, particularly doctors, were greatly concerned and began intensified research into the problem in 1915. After exhaustive experimentation, the first of what would become standarized helmets were issued to assault troops at bloody Verdum during January 1916. In modified form it would be used throughout both World Wars I and II. Dubbed a "coalscuttle" in supposed ridicule by Allied propagandists, it was far superior to anything the Allies had and was quickly accepted by the German Fighting man as an elite status symbol. It was the central design of the much honored wounds badge (the equivalent of our Purple Heart) and the design was incorporated into flags, banners and other objects.

The original 1916 pattern helmet weighs two and one-fourth pounds. This helmet is most often referred to as the Model 16 helmet even in many German language publications. However, some expert military historians maintain that the term "Model" was not **officially** used until the Model 35 helmet appeared during the early days of the Third Reich. In any event the helmet has a well rounded skull, somewhat flat on top, with a well defined visor extending out low over the brows and a neck guard flared out behind. It is fitted with a comfortable liner which kept the helmet away from the head. It has excellent ballistic characteristics and gives very good protection to the head, brows, neck and ears from missiles and from the elements. This helmet has a chin strap which attaches to the inside of the flared side rim by means of a bayonet-type lug. Helmets with either leather or heavy cloth will be found, cloth straps appearing late in the war when leather became in short supply.

One interesting characteristic of the German World War I helmets is seen in the side lugs or "horns" which were armored ventilators and also served as attachments for an armor frontal plate, which is described below. The 1917 pattern helmet was like the earlier pattern except that the chin strap was attached to a "D-ring" attached directly to the helmet liner.

A yet later pattern helmet appeared in 1918. In this pattern the helmet rim was cut out over the ears to allow better hearing. Some collectors maintain that this model was introduced to provide for the accommodation of headphones. Some maintain that it is a special cavalry model. There is little known to validate these opinions. In the 1916 and 1917 patterns there was a tendency for the voice to reverberate, a characteristic which was largely eliminated by providing the cutouts over the ears.

A so-called Turkish Model, of which less than 6,000 were manufactured, was produced for the Turkish Government. This was the 1917 Pattern helmet without the front visor. It was designed to permit the Moslem soldier to touch his forehead to the ground while praying, a requirement of his religion. None of these helmets was delivered to Turkey. They were used after the war mainly by the Freikorps (Free Corps) about which there will be more later.

Pattern 17 helmets with minor front visor variations appeared late in the war, as did a rather heavy "siege" model. It has a well rounded skull and fairly flat front and rear visors. A protective portion extends down over the ears. This item weighs in the neighborhood of 14 pounds. Even with its heavily quilted liner, it was very tiresome to wear for any length of time. Only a very limited number was ever manufactured. The few in service were used by machine gunners and special troops expected to be under heavy fire.

German helmets were issued in a variety of greenish/gray colors. Camouflage pattern painting was sometimes employed. This painting was done either at the time of manufacturer or by the individual in the field. No insignia or other identifying devices were used on these helmets during World War I. Both white and field gray cloth covers were issued for use with these helmets.

For the use of machine gunners and other troops in exposed positions, there was a heavy metal frontal shield, designed to fit closely over the front of the helmet. A slot on each side fitted over the ventilation lugs of the helmet and the frontal piece was secured by a strap passing around the base of the skull. Few of these were ever made. Interestingly enough, to date these have not attracted much collector interest and may be bought for a fairly reasonable price.

During 1916 the Austrian armies began using the 1916 pattern helmet. In addition they used their own Austrian model 1916 which is almost identical to the German version in appearance and construction. A distinguishing feature is a rivet on each side below and slightly to the rear of the ventilation lugs. This attaches the chin strap to the helmet. Other Austrian M-16 helmets have the chin strap fastened to a "D" ring on the helmet liner. Chin straps of the Austrian made helmets were of stout cloth. These helmets were painted brown and also accommodated the protective frontal plate.

Also used was the Berndorfer helmet, manufactured by Berndorfer Metallwarenfabrik Arthur Krupp, A.G., Berndorfer, Austria. It had a more shallow shell than the German model and was somewhat rounder on top. The front visor is crimped up, forming an eagle. Ventilation is provided through a flat round plug on top of the shell. A small frontal plate was also provided. It may be attached by a brown cloth strap secured under the top ventilator plug, by a metal strap at each end of the frontal plate extending down and passing under the rim of the front visor, and by a brown cloth strap passing around the base of the skull. Both this helmet and the frontal plate are very rare and command a good price.

From the end of World War I to the beginning of the Nazi reign, 1919 to 1933, Germany went through a series of political evolutions. The military forces were drastically reduced in size and armaments. Military meteriel consisted largely of Surplus World War I items. The helmets of the new German states bore on the left side a painted shield in the colors of the state (land) as follows: Bavarian, white and blue; Wurttemberg, black and red; Saxony, white and green; Baden, yellow/red yellow; Hessen Bremen, red and white; Oldenberg, blue and red; Brunswick, blue and yellow; Scahaumberg Lippe, white/red/blue; Anhalt, red/green/white; Lippe Detmold, yellow and red; Twuringen Lubek, white and red; Mecklenburg, blue/yellow/red. The Navy had a white shield within a yellow border with a blue anchor on the white. Some special units wore these painted shields on both sides of the helmet.

Out of the complexities of post World War I Germany came the formation and rapid growth of the Free Corps (Freikorps) units. Economic and political conditions were so calamitous that little or no order prevailed. The small regular army was unable to contain the situation but groups of dedicated exservice men banded together to restore order, if necessary by force of arms. Operating at first for purely patriotic reasons, these Free Corps units after a time degenerated into what amounted to brutal freebooters. Each unit was responsible only to the men who organized and commanded it. Patriotism gave way to the political ambitions of the leaders.

These Free Corps companies were clothed, equipped and armed from surplus stocks. The steel helmets were decorated in various ways to identify the various units. A white swastika painted on the front was popular, as was a large painted white skull and crossbones. Other units used a variation of the state or city colors as a shield on the sides of the helmet.

A rather interesting and rare variation of the German steel helmet is that of the Austrian Guard Battalion, 1935 to 1938. This Austrian made German pattern steel helmet is painted black. There is a large bronze colored Austrian double-headed eagle front plate. On the left side of the helmet is a large cluster of green enameled oak leaves attached in the ventilation lug. These helmets are very rare.

World War I pattern German helmets were used in many armies, including Afghanistan, Bulgaria, Czechoslovakia, Finland, Hungary, Mexico, Poland, Turkey, Latvia, Lithuania, and others. These helmets were distinguished by metal badges or painted devices. Of particular interest is the fact that one front line unit of the Russian Army during the early days of World War II was equipped with 1916 and 1917 pattern German helmets. It is probable that these helmets came from the captured Latvian and Lithuanian army stocks. These unique helmets have the traditional Red Star on the front.

FEDERAL REPUBLIC OF GERMANY

Three patterns of helmets for ground troops and two for paratroopers have been or are being worn by the military forces of West Germany. The old M35 helmet of the Third Reich was retained and worn by the border guards. Modifications of this helmet include a lighter metal shell and a modified liner. A second pattern has the M35 profile with an entirely new liner. The third pattern is based upon the profile of the current American helmet but with less flare in the rim. This rim edge is rolled in whereas the American design has a separate edging. The liner is also different. These helmets are painted various shades of green. No identifying devices are worn on these helmets. One style of paratrooper helmet is most similar to that used by the Nazi Luftwaffe but has a modified liner, chin and neck straps. A later model has a more rounded shell and entirely different liner, chin and neck straps. Both are painted olive green. No identifying devices appear on these paratrooper helmets.

GERMAN DEMOCRATIC REPUBLIC

The army (VOPO) of the German Democratic Republic has a helmet with a profile quite unlike that of any other country. The shell has a well rounded top and is widely flaring on all sides. The front visor and the longer rear visor are a straight continuation of the lines of the skull. This item is well balanced and has a comfortable lining. The shell itself has a cork inner lining. Of the two types of chin straps, one is a two-piece design which buckles by means of a prong and a type with a "V" surrounding each ear. This helmet is painted gray/green. A small shield in black/red/gold appears on the left side. These helmets do not often appear on the collectors' market.

NAZI HELMETS

With the advent of Hitler to power in Germany, World War I helmets with modifications were being used. These are known as "transitional helmets" to most collectors and military historians. They differ from the old helmets in that they have an improved liner and chin strap and various devices appear on one or both sides to identify the organization to which the wearer belonged.

A new helmet appeared in 1935, known as the M35. Although it has the same general silhouette as the older 1916/1917 helmets, it was much improved to accommodate new concepts of warfare. It has a considerably lower profile with smaller rim/visors. There are no ventilator lugs. The much improved liner is very comfortable. Chin strap, with attachments, as well as the suspension are also greatly improved. It was stamped out of one piece of metal and has rolled edges. All in all, this helmet has very good ballistic characteristics. In 1942 the M42 was introduced. Almost identical to the M35, the rim is unrolled and is more prominate. All this made for quicker and easier manufacture.

A modified form of helmet, identified as the police model, has a square cut instead of a rounded dip in the sides of the rim. The vent holes and the liner are also different. For firemen (a quasi-military organization in the Third Reich of Hitler), a model similar to that of the police but with an aluminum or chrome crest was issued. For paratroopers, the standard helmet, much modified by being manufactured without rim or visors was issued. This model also had a special shock absorbing liner and chin strap. The Luftschutz (Air Defense) early model helmet has extended rim/visors with a cutout over the ears. It is known as the "gladiator type." A later model was similar in general profile but was of three-piece construction, has a different liner, and enlarged rim/visors. The Luftschutz is the standard army helmet with a pronounced "bead" around the base of the skull.

Prior to World War II military officers of the Third Reich were permitted to privately purchase what were known as parade helmets. These were the standard pattern helmets with some slight modifications, made of fiber or aluminum.

Helmets were painted differently and bore different insignia for various units. Army, Navy, Waffen-SS and some police units wore shades of gray/green. Other police units, firemen and a few other units wore black. Some Navy helmets were issued in blue/gray. Bahnschultz (Railway Police) had dark green. Luftwaffe and Luftschutz had shades of dark blue or gray/blue. Africa Corps helmets appeared in sand-color and brown. Helmets used on the Russian front were painted white.

Colored decals appeared on the sides of the helmets, except for the Luftschutz and the early R.L.B. (Air Defense) helmets, in which case they appeared on the front. There were cases where a decal appeared on only one side of the helmet. Captured enemy helmets were used quite frequently by Germany as the war moved along to its unsuccessful conclusion. These were reworked when necessary and given German decals. No decals were ever authorized for the Africa Corps. However, some individuals painted a design of a swastika or cross superimposed upon a palm tree on the left side of the helmet. As the war progressed and individuals became more frequently transferred, and with materiel in increasingly short supply, a variation of colors appeared in different units and decals disappeared from use.

ADDENDUM

Model 31 and model 35 Nazi helmets were at times painted with camouflage designs. There were no standard patterns. Cloth covers with camouflage designs were issued as were cloth bands, wire and cloth netting. The bands and netting provided a means of holding twigs and leaves to provide a kind of camouflage.

Model 31 and model 35 helmets were also used at one time or another by other armies, principally those of China, Spain, Norway and Finland. The Spanish helmet was often issued with a metal slot on the front to which a brass and enameled Spanish double-headed eagle and cross could be attached.

Helmets of other designs and profiles were used by nations other than those mentioned above. For the most part, these were of inferior design and profile. Many had low ballistic characteristics.

In the following price list an attempt has been made in the majority of cases to include enough descriptive data to provide for identification of each helmet.

AUSTRIA   Price Range

☐ **Austrian Guard Battalion helmet.** *Bronzed Austrian double-headed eagle front plate and oak leaves on side. See text above for more complete description.*   575.00   635.00

☐ **Berndorfer helmet.** *See text above for more complete description.* 400.00   450.00

Austrian Pattern
1916 helmet.

Price Range

☐ **M16 helmet.** *This helmet has a shell almost identical to that of the German 1916 pattern except that a rivet head is located below and slightly to the rear of the ventilating horns. See text above for more complete description.* 125.00   135.00

BELGIUM

☐ **Army helmet.** *M15 French Adrian pattern with front plate in the form of a lion head from the Belgium Arms, clay colored.* 55.00   60.00

Belgium Steel helmet, with lion head insignia on the front. This helmet is similar in many respects to the French model 1915 helmet, although it is designated the Belgium model 1930.

☐ **Army helmet.** *M33 French Adrian pattern, front plate in the form of a lion head from the Belgium Arms, khaki color.* 32.00   35.00

☐ **Experimental helmet.** *Similar to the French Dunand experimental helmet. Slotted visor pulled down to protect the eyes and upper part of the face. Black/yellow/red rosettes or cockades on each side where the visor attaches to the helmet, khaki color.* 600.00   660.00

DENMARK

☐ **Army helmet M23.** *Shell as below. Dark brown, rough finish to the outside of shell. Brass front plate consisting of the State Arms and crown within a wreath.* 140.00   150.00

☐ **Navy helmet M23.** *Shell as below. Front plate consisting of a brass fouled anchor under a crown, blue color.* 140.00   150.00

Price Range

☐ **Police helmet M23.** *High rounded shell with sides sloping out at bottom to form pronounced rim, painted black. Brass front plate consisting of the State Arms (Three lions on a rimmed oval with a royal crown on top of the oval.)* 90.00   100.00

FRANCE

☐ **1915 Steel Skull Cap.** *Worn under cloth cap.* 150.00   175.00

☐ **Steel Trench helmet** *model 1915. The first true helmet, made in four pieces, usually painted blue/gray. Hereafter this will be referred to as the Adrian helmet. For infantry, cavalry and train, with metal front badge of flaming bomb with "RF."* 46.00   50.00

French Steel Combat helmets, model 1915. From the left: Infantry, Colonial Army, Artillery, side view of this model helmet.

☐ **Artillery.** *Model 15 Adrian. Flaming bomb with "RF" superimposed upon crossed cannon, blue/gray.* 46.00   50.00

☐ **Chasseurs.** *Model 15 Adrian. Blue/gray with metal front plate consisting of a light infantry horn with "RF" within the circle of the horn.* 55.00   60.00

☐ **Colonial Infantry.** *Model 15 Adrian. Blue/gray with metal badge on front consisting of flaming bomb with "RF" superimposed upon an anchor, rifle on each side.* 46.00   50.00

☐ **Constabulary.** *Model 15 Adrian. Black with metal front plate of bright white metal flaming bomb.* 55.00   60.00

☐ **Dunand Experimental helmet.** *Appeared in two models, one with a fairly shallow skull, the other with*

Price Range

a deep shell. Both had a small but well defined rim.
Both had a slotted visor which could be pulled down
to protect the face. Blue/gray in color. Some had a
blue/white/red cockade under the visor ends where
they attached to the helmet. Visor was ballistically
weak. 600.00   650.00

☐ **Engineers.** *Model 15 Adrian. Blue/gray with metal
badge consisting of cuirass with "RF" under a
cuirassier helmet.* 46.00   50.00

☐ **Tank Crew helmet model 19.** *Model 15 Adrian helmet
modified by removable front rim with leather pad
substituted. Blue with front plate consisting of flam-
ing bomb with "RF."* 100.00   110.00

☐ **M23 Infantry helmet.** *Improved Adrian pattern. Khaki
color with front plate is flaming bomb with "RF."* 42.00   45.00

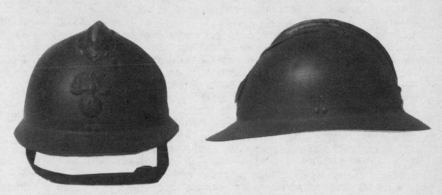

French Steel helmet, model 1923.

☐ **M26 Infantry helmet.** *As above but without front
badge.* 25.00   27.00

☐ **M26 Engineer (pioneer) helmet.** *As above but with a
front badge consisting of cuirassier helmet over
cuirassier armor.* 42.00   45.00

☐ **M26 Chausseurs helmet.** *As above but with front
badge consisting of a light infantry horn with "RF"
with the circle of the horn.* 55.00   60.00

☐ **M26 Artillery helmet.** *As above but with front badge
consisting of flaming bomb with "RF" superimposed
upon crossed cannon.* 42.00   45.00

☐ **M26 Navy helmet.** *As above but with front badge con-
sisting of a vertical fouled anchor.* 55.00   60.00

☐ **M26 Navy helmet.** *As above except that the fouled
anchor is mounted on a small metal disk.* 64.00   70.00

Price Range

☐ **M26 Native North African Troops.** *As above but with front badge consisting of a crescent with the horns pointing upward, with an "RF" between the horns.* ..   55.00   60.00

☐ **M26 Red Cross helmet.** *As above but painted white and with a metal red cross badge in front.* 55.00   60.00

☐ **M26 French Resistance Movement helmet.** *As above but khaki color helmet with painted Cross of Lorraine (Free French) on the front.* 69.00   75.00

☐ **M26 Free French Air Forces helmet.** *As above but with a metal front badge consisting of the Cross of Lorraine with upswept wings on each side. Only a few ever made.* 430.00   475.00

☐ **M35 Tank Crew helmet.** *Deep, well rounded shell with straight sides. No crest (comb). Medium long rear visor, no front visor which is replaced by thick leather pad. Front badge consisting of medieval close helmet superimposed upon crossed cannon with "R" on one side and "F" on the other. All this on a disk with raised rim, khaki color.* 55.00   60.00

☐ **M37 Air Force helmet.** *Similar to above but painted blue/gray and with metal front badge consisting of upswept wings with five-pointed star at bottom.* 78.00   85.00

☐ **Vichy Government helmet.** *Life Guard of Marshal Petain. Similar to above helmet but painted blue and with front plate consisting of colored shield upon which is superimposed a fasces with double blade ax.*   190.00   210.00

☐ **M45 Tank and Air Crews helmet.** *Well rounded deep shell with straight sides. Medium long rear visor and heavy leather pad replacing the front visor. Low metal crest similar to that of the Adrian pattern helmet. Painted blue/gray for air crews and khaki for tank crews. Price is the same for either.* 42.00   55.00

☐ **M51 Combat helmet.** *Deep, well rounded shell with almost straight sides. Somewhat similar in general profile to U.S. helmet but with extremely shallow brim with no dip around circumference. Separate lining within plastic/fiberglass shell. Chin strap is attached to sides of shell, painted olive/green.* 33.00   35.00

☐ **Native North African Troops.** *Model 15 Adrian. Sand color with metal badge on front consisting of a crescent with horns pointing upward, with "RF" between.*   64.00   70.00

☐ **St. Cyr Military School** *(the French West Point). Model 15 Adrian. Blue with bright white metal front plate consisting of the badge of the school, a flaming bomb (without "RF") with scroll below.* 130.00   140.00

GERMANY (To the Third Reich)

☐ **1916 Pattern helmet.** *See above text for description. Gray/green color.* 64.00   70.00

☐ **1916 Pattern helmet.** *Camouflage painted.* 87.00   95.00

☐ **1916 Pattern helmet.** *With frontal plate attached.* 280.00   310.00

Imperial German Army 1916 Steel helmet. Note the rivet on the lower side which held the chin strap fastner.

Imperial German Army Pattern 1916 Steel helmet with cutouts above the ear.

Imperial German Army 1918 Pattern Steel helmet. Note the absence of the rivet on the brim. In this pattern the chin strap attached to the head band.

	Price Range	

☐ **1916 Pattern helmet.** *With cut-outs above the ears. These are sometimes referred to as "double dip" helmets. See above text for description.* . . . . | 375.00 | 450.00

☐ **1918 Pattern helmets.** *Prices same as for 1916 pattern helmets.* . . . . | 96.00 | 105.00

☐ **Reichwehr helmets.** *1916 and 1918 pattern, with painted emblems of various Reichwehr states on side.* . . . . | 175.00 | 190.00

☐ **Reichwehr helmets.** *As above, but "double-dip."* . . . . | 205.00 | 225.00

☐ **Freikorps (Free Corps) helmets.** *1916 and 1918 pattern helmets with painted emblems of various Freikorps units.* . . . . | 205.00 | 225.00

☐ **Freikorps (Free Corps) helmets.** *As above but "double-dip."* . . . . | 250.00 | 275.00

GERMANY (Third Reich-Nazi)

NOTE: Model 35 helmets have a rolled edge and high quality lining. Model 43 helmets have an unrolled edge (sometimes referred to as a "raw" edge). Some Model 43 helmets have a cheaper and inferior lining. Some were issued without decals.

Nazi Germany made abundant use of insignia of all kinds. Colorful decals on helmets identified various organizations. In the following price list, helmets are identified by organizational name as follows: Wehrmacht (Army), Luftwaffe (Air Force), Kreigsmarine (Navy), Allgemeine-SS (general Elite Guard or Schutzstaffel), Waffen-SS (Army Elite Guard or Schutzstaffel), RAD (Reichsarbeitsdienst or Reichs Labor Service), Police and Fire Organizations (Polizei und Feuerwehr), RLB (Reichsluftsschutzbubd or German Air Protection Federations) and Luftschutz (Air Raid Protection, a division of RLB).

☐ **Army paratrooper helmet.** *These helmets were a new development of World War II. Basically the M35 helmet without visor and neckguard and with specially designed heavily padded liner. Early type with Army and National decals.* . . . . | 400.00 | 450.00

☐ **Paratrooper helmet.** *Similar to above but with single Luftwaffe decal (in silver) on the left side.* . . . . | 340.00 | 375.00

☐ **Luftschutz helmet.** *So-called "gladiator" pattern. Upper shell somewhat similar to M35 but has very deep visor and neck guard. Is lighter in weight than the combat helmet and has cheaper liner and different vents. Dark blue color with large Luftschutz in silver and black on the front.* . . . . | 78.00 | 85.00

☐ **Luftschutz helmet.** *So-called "Army" pattern. Similar to M35 helmet but with a ridge or bead around the base of the skull, dark blue color, with large silver and black Luftschutz decal on front.* . . . . | 78.00 | 85.00

☐ **M35 helmet.** *With both Army and National decals, gray/green.* . . . . | 87.00 | 95.00

☐ **M43 helmet.** *As above but with single Army decal.* . . . . | 69.00 | 75.00

☐ **M43 helmet.** *As above but without decals.* . . . . | 50.00 | 55.00

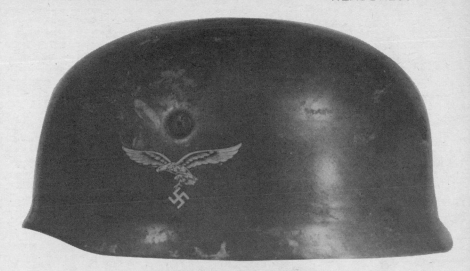

Nazi Paratrooper helmet.

Luftschutz helmet, "Gladiator" pattern.

	Price Range	
☐ **M35 helmet.** *For Africa Corps (DAK), tan, light brown or "sand" color paint, not distinguished by any insignia.*	87.00	95.00
☐ **M35 helmet.** *As above but with painted Africa Corps (DAK) insignia of palm tree and cross.*	145.00	160.00
☐ **M35 helmet.** *For Allgemeine-SS. Black with SS runes on silver shield on right side and red shield with white disk with black swastika on left side.*	475.00	525.00

Nazi M35 Army helmet.

Model 35 helmet for dreaded Allegemeine-SS.

	Price Range	
☐ **Waffen-SS M35 helmet.** *As above but gray/green.*	455.00	500.00
☐ **Waffen-SS M43 helmet.** *As above but with single decal.*	250.00	275.00
☐ **Luftwaffe M35 helmet.** *Blue or gray/blue with Luft-waffe and National decals.*	145.00	160.00
☐ **Luftwaffe M43 helmet.** *As above but with single decal.*	100.00	110.00
☐ **Navy M35 helmet.** *Gray/green with single Navy decal.*	140.00	150.00

M35 Nazi helmet with silver Navy device on the left side.

	Price Range	
☐ **Reichs Labor Service helmet.** *M35 pattern with RAD decal of swastika on spade blade.*	300.00	330.00
☐ **Police M35 helmet.** *Gray/green with police and red, white and black swastika decals.*	130.00	150.00
☐ **Red Cross helmet.** *Luftschutz "gladiator" pattern helmet with single red cross decal (white shield with black stylized Nazi eagle with white swastika on breast and a red cross below) on the left side. Helmet is blue.*	185.00	200.00
☐ **Red Cross helmet.** *Shell painted white overall, large red cross painted across the top of the M35 helmet. The figure "3" is painted on the front of the helmet.*	132.00	145.00
☐ **Transitional helmet.** *1916 and 1918 pattern but with improved lining. Gray/green or blue in color with Nazi insignia.*	100.00	110.00
☐ **World War I Pattern helmet.** *Gray/green, double-dip, with both Army and National decals.*	340.00	375.00
☐ **World War I Pattern helmet.** *For the Allgemeine-SS. Black helmet with both SS and National decals.*	430.00	475.00

Price Range

☐ **As above** *but for Police, with tilted swastika decal and National decal.* 385.00   475.00

☐ **As above** *but for Luftschutz. Blue with Luftschutz decal on front.* 140.00   150.00

Note: During the final years and months of World War I, with a Nazi victory becoming more and more remote, supplies in increasingly short supply, increasing difficulties in organization and even in troop movements, many regulations could not be met. Among other things, there came a time when it became virtually impossible to regulate the pattern of helmets used as well as the decals used to identify units. Captured enemy helmets were pressed into service in a variety of colors and a variety of decals. Naturally all this confusion and lack of regulations has provided an opportunity for dishonest dealers and collectors to improvise a variety of helmets which they pass off as "rare" examples. Again, the collector must be sure of the honesty of the people with whom he deals.

Nazi Rural Police
Motorcycle Crash helmet.

☐ **Rural Police Motorcycle Crash helmet.** *Brown leather hard leather padded skull with heavy brown leather reinforcing ring about outside bottom of skull. Brown leather visor and curtain protecting neck and sides of face. Small Nazi police insignia in silver on front above protective ring. Interesting collector's piece* ..   275.00   350.00

☐ **National Socialist Motor Corps (NSKK) Motorcycle Crash helmet.** *Similar to the above but of black leather. The visor points downward at a greater angle. There is also a black leather covered protective crest on the top and back of the helmet. A large NSKK device in silver and enamel is on the front of the headdress* 200.00   275.00

GERMANY (Federal Republic of Germany)

National Socialist Motor Corps (NSKK) Motorcycle Crash helmet.

Federal Republic of Germany Border Guards helmet.

	Price Range	

☐ **Army helmet.** *Similar to Border Guards helmet but with even greater improved liner, particularly with regard to method of suspension.* 37.00   40.00

☐ **Army helmet.** *Shell similar to that of current American helmet, but with smooth rolled edge. Less flare out at bottom of shell. Liner is suspended from weld on inside top of shell, gray/green color.* 37.00   40.00

☐ **Border Guards helmet.** *Nazi M35 pattern helmet with much improved liner, gray/green. There are no decals on West German helmets.* 37.00   40.00

GERMANY (German Democratic Republic)

☐ **East German helmet.** *Described in text above. Well rounded top to shell, with marked outward flare on all sides. Helmet is lower in back than in front. Inside of shell lined with cork. Well designed suspension, gray/green in color. Some helmets have a small shield in the national colors, black, red and gold, on the left side.* 205.00   225.00

GREAT BRITAIN

☐ **Mark II helmet.** *Similar to standard World War I pattern (which was known as the Mark I helmet). Used during World War II, improved liner and suspension, most often found in rough khaki finish but may be found in black smooth finish.* 15.00   16.50

☐ **Mark III helmet.** *So-called "turtle shell" pattern. Fairly high skull with more pronounced outward flare in front than in back. Small brim with edging, improved liner and suspension, olive drab or khaki.* ... 21.00   23.00

☐ **Paratrooper helmet.** *Very similar in pattern and outline to the Nazi paratrooper helmet but with different liner and suspension. Usually found in olive drab or khaki finish. May also be found in white with identifying devices stenciled or painted on the front.* 50.00   55.00

☐ **Standard World War I Pattern helmet.** *Shallow skull with edged, fairly wide brim. Poor protection to front sides and back of head, looks like an inverted basin, khaki color with rough nonreflecting finish* 15.00   16.50

GREECE

☐ **World War I helmet.** *French M15 Adrian pattern helmet. Dark blue finish, large embossed insignia on front consisting of a Greek cross within a shield with Royal Crown above.* 140.00   150.00

ITALY

☐ **Adrian M15 French Pattern helmet.** *Painted an olive/gray, stenciled in black on the front may be a regimental number under a Royal Crown.* 33.00   35.00

☐ **As above** *but without any distinguishing device on front.* 18.50   20.00

Price Range

☐ **As above** *but with an identifying device on the front consisting of the Cross of Savoy. Used by Savoyan Cavalry Regiment 3.* 65.00   71.00

☐ **As above** *but with blue in finish (shade of blue may vary). On the right side a socket for a plume, on the front the bright metal insignia of the famed Bersaglierie.* 132.00   145.00

☐ **Bersaglierie helmet.** *As above but gray/green and instead of the metal insignia there is stenciled in black the organization badge.* 87.00   95.00

☐ **Cavalry helmet.** *As above but with bright metal front plate consisting of a hunting horn with pierced unit number in the ring of the horn, and with a Royal Crown above.* 100.00   110.00

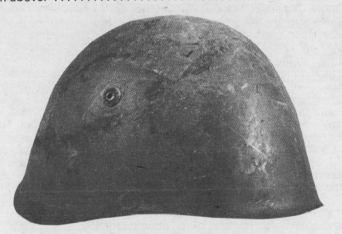

Italian Model 34 helmet.

☐ **Model 34 helmet.** *Worn by all the armed forces during World War II. Fairly deep, well rounded shell with very narrow brim about the bottom. Two ventilation holes, fairly deep dip of helmet over the ears, brim higher in front than in rear. This helmet may appear in several colors. Army helmets are some shade of gray/green, usually dark. A wide variety of stenciled emblems may appear on the front of the helmet. These identify the branch or arm of service and sometimes a unit number. Navy helmets may have a stenciled anchor.*

☐ **As above** *without stenciled identification device.* ...   15.00   16.50

☐ **As above** *with stenciled identification device.* 37.00   40.00

☐ **Model 42 Paratrooper helmet.** *Deep shell with well rounded dome. Sides flare out slightly toward the*

	Price Range	

bottom of the shell. There is no brim. May appear in gray/green or khaki. Heavy liner, well suspended giving considerable protection to the head. **100.00 110.00**

☐ **Siege helmet.** *An odd ball design produced in extremely limited quantities. Undoubtedly the most ugly helmet of modern times. It appears in three versions. All are very heavy, all have a shallow dish dome with almost straight sides. Composed of four parts riveted together, heavy lining, well padded.* **145.00 160.00**

JAPAN

Shortly after World War I Japanese military authorities began the development of a steel combat helmet. Experiments finally developed an interesting design which was standardized. This helmet has a deep shell with well rounded dome. The sides flare out very slightly into a semibrim. Inasmuch as the Japanese military venerated the ancient samurai (warriors), it follows that at least to a minor degree the pattern should resemble that of the ancient fighting men. Also, although the liner is modern, in lieu of a conventional chin strap there was a cloth band arrangement which tied under the chin in the manner in which the ancient helmets were secured. These helmets are usually found painted in some shade of khaki. Helmets may be found without any unit identifying device on the front. Others may be found with an iron, brass or nickel device. Stenciled and painted devices are also found. Army helmets may have a small five-pointed star in front. Navy and Marine helmets may have an anchor or a chrysanthemum superimposed upon an anchor in front. The great majority of Japanese helmets were destroyed following World War II. It has only been recently that a small supply of these helmets has been discovered and they command high prices, even for the stripped shells.

☐ **Helmet shell.** *Original paint, no liner, no insignia.* . . . **28.00 30.00**
☐ **Helmet shell.** *Original paint, no liner, insignia intact.*. **45.00 50.00**
☐ **Helmet with original liner.** *Original paint, no insignia.* **65.00 70.00**
☐ **Helmet with original liner.** *Original paint, insignia intact.* **145.00 160.00**
☐ **Helmet with replaced liner.** *Original paint, no insignia.* **41.00 45.00**
☐ **Helmet with replaced liner.** *Original paint, insignia intact.* **87.00 95.00**
☐ **Paratrooper helmet.** *World War II issue. More conical in profile than the Army helmet. No brim, khaki paint, heavy liner. In lieu of the chin strap typical in paratrooper helmets of other nations, a wide leather section covers the sides and back of the head in the manner of a conventional leather aviator's helmet. Small five-pointed star insignia on front.* **300.00 330.00**

POLAND

☐ **M36 helmet.** *Fairly deep shell with well rounded dome, sides flare out slightly toward the bottom, short visor in front, none in back, no identifying*

Price Range

insignia, painted khaki with an extremely rough (sand) finish. 75.00   85.00

☐ **Polish Forces in France, World War I helmet.** *French M15 Adrian model helmet, painted dark blue. Front plate consisting of a light infantry horn with the Polish Eagle within the ring of the horn.* 200.00   220.00

☐ **Post World War I helmet.** *French M15 Adrian model helmet, painted khaki, no identifying device on front. Liner is a Polish design.* 60.00   65.00

☐ **Post World War I helmet.** *As above but painted blue and with a front plate consisting of the Polish Eagle.*   140.00   150.00

PORTUGAL

British World War I Pattern helmet. *With shallow shell. Skull is deeply ribbed with ribs radiating from the top center of the skull, slightly deeper crown in some examples, painted khaki or olive drab. Helmet has poor ballistic characteristics. Some of these helmets were used during the Spanish Civil War and may have painted devices on the front. Rarely found with the liner intact.*

☐   **As above,** *but without liner.* 15.00   16.50
☐   **As above,** *but with liner.* 37.00   40.00

RUMANIA

☐ **World War I Issue helmet.** *French M15 Adrian model, painted blue/gray. Front plate consisting of an oval upon which appears highly decorative initials "F," "F," back to back, with a small "I" in between (signifying Ferdinand 1st), with Royal Crown above.* 150.00   165.00

RUSSIA (Imperial)

☐ **French M15 Adrian Pattern helmet.** *Various shades of khaki, with metal front plate consisting of the crowned double-headed Imperial Russian Eagle.* 150.00   165.00

RUSSIA (Soviet Union, Union of Soviet Socialist Republics)

☐ **M24 helmet.** *Overall profile similar to that of the French M15 Adrian helmet. Has knob-like ventilator on top in lieu of crest. Different liner, gray/green color.* 150.00   165.00

☐ **M36 helmet.** *Deep, well rounded shell. Fairly broad brim to front and sides, flaring outward with dip over the ear area. Very slight brim in back, green, may be found with painted five-pointed red star on front. All models have a short low crest covering a ventilating slot, improved liner.* 75.00   80.00

☐ **M39 helmet.** *Similar to the M24 but of one-piece construction instead of four-piece construction.* 140.00   150.00

☐ **M40 helmet.** *Deep well rounded skull somewhat similar to U.S. World War II pattern. Very narrow brim, somewhat wider at front and sides than at the back, painted various shades of green.* 75.00   80.00

SPAIN Price Range

Model 21. *This model is sometimes referred to in official Spanish documents as the helmet "with wings" due to the wide flaring brim at sides and back. Well rounded dome with slightly flaring sides toward the bottom. Usually some shade of khaki. Helmet may or may not have very small metal piece attached to the front into which the prong on the back of a crest may be inserted. This crest consists of a crowned Spanish Eagle, in brass, with a red enameled cross on the breast.*

☐ **Helmet.** *As above, with or without small metal piece on front.* 30.00 35.00
☐ **Helmet.** *As above, but with eagle crest.* 37.00 40.00
☐ **M26.** *This model is sometimes referred to in official Spanish Army documents as the helmet "without wings" due to the absence of the wide flaring brim at the sides and back. Otherwise similar to the above.* 30.00 35.00
☐ **Helmet.** *With eagle crest.* 37.00 40.00
Type "Z" helmet. *Similar in profile to the Nazi M35 helmet. Usually some shade of gray/green. The liner is inferior to that of the M35, may or may not have device for holding crest.*
☐ **As above,** *but with or without device for holding crest.* 30.00 35.00
☐ **As above,** *but with eagle crest.* 37.00 40.00

SWEDEN

Swedish Steel
helmet,
model 1921.

☐ **Model 1921.** *Fairly deep skull with medium brim. This brim flares out slightly from sides to back. Painted gray/brown. All have metal shield on front bearing the three crowns of the Royal Arms. Some may also*

Swedish Variant Steel helmet, model 1921. The brim is much broader than that on the standard model 1921.

	Price Range	
have, on each side, a blue shield bearing the crowns in yellow.	35.00	40.00
☐ **Model 1921 Variant.** *As above but with broader brim.*	40.00	45.00
☐ **Model 1937.** *Fairly deep skull with almost straight sides. Extremely narrow brim, may have a variety of liner suspensions, painted gray. On each side of the helmet appears a blue shield with three yellow crowns.*	37.00	40.00

UNITED STATES

☐ **Air Crew Helmet,** *World War II. Very similar to standard World War II helmet but with cut-outs over the ears which are covered by hinged semicupped ear pieces with provision for radio headset.*	25.00	30.00
☐ **Experimental model 2.** *This is the so-called "deep salade" model. It was patterned after the medieval salade. Fairly deep skull flaring out sharply in front to form a visor. The flare was not so sharp on the sides and back. Helmet came down low over the eyes and dipped sharply to provide protection for the sides and back of the head. Rough khaki finish, only a few thousand made.*	275.00	300.00
☐ **Experimental model 8.** *Deep shell with well rounded dome. Medium flare to sides and back. Sides of skull dipped sharply to protect sides and back of head. Has metal visor with eye slots which may be pulled down to cover the entire face to below the chin. Provided limited vision, was clumsy to wear, rough khaki finish, less than 2,000 made.*	320.00	350.00

U.S. Air Crew helmet.

	Price Range	

☐ **"Liberty Bell" model.** *This was another experimental model. This helmet is something of an absurdity. Fairly deep skull flaring sharply out in the front and only slightly to the rear. Medium brim, khaki color. This helmet is not well balanced and is too heavy. Only a few thousand were ever made. Troops testing it gave it an extremely low morale aspect, suggesting that it looked like a Chinese fisherman's hat.* 320.00   350.00

☐ **Navy "Talker" or Antiaircraft Gun Crew helmet.** *Extremely large shell with well rounded dome and slight flare to front, sides and back. Skull had pronounced dip to cover ears and back of head. Helmet large enough to permit comfortable wearing of communication earphones. Extremely heavy padding, painted blue.* 20.00   22.00

☐ **World War I helmet.** *Shallow, basin-like skull with wide brim, rough "sand" khaki color. Either British or American manufacture.* 15.00   16.50

☐ **Model 30.** *As above but with improved liner and suspension.* 10.00   11.00

☐ **World War II helmet.** *The standard helmet of the war and after, including Korea and Vietnam. Deep, well rounded skull with nearly straight sides, small brim (visor) in front and narrow brim to sides and back, fits snugly over a plastic liner of the same shape. This liner is fitted with the suspension. Olive drab color. Helmet is rather well designed.* 20.00   22.00

U.S. Navy "Talker" helmet, World War II.

U.S. World War II helmet.

YUGOSLAVIA   Price Range

☐ **French (Adrian) helmet M15 model.** *Khaki with an identifying device on the front consisting of a crowned double-headed eagle with the state arms.* . .   100.00   110.00

☐ **Helmet of the Socialist Federative Republic of Yugoslavia.** *Similar in profile to the present helmet of the Federal Republic of Germany (West Germany). The side dip and rear visor are not quite so pronounced, however.* 100.00   110.00

☐ **Army helmet model 20.** *Austrian 1918 pattern German helmet taken as war booty, painted gray/green, front plate as French M15 model.* 100.00   110.00

SUN HELMETS

Sun helmets or tropical helmets as they are sometimes known comprise a facet of militaria collecting which is beginning to attract the attention of increasing numbers of collectors. For the most part these helmets are comparatively reasonable in price and the variety is great enough to provide continual interest. Unfortunately, not too much is presently known about these artifacts but as military historians continue to unearth new information, the number of collectors is certain to increase. This will mean, of course, that prices will rise. The collector with a limited purse and the beginning collector could do worse than to start collecting sun helmets.

As is the case with Imperial German headdress, there is an interesting number of German items available. These are of considerable variety. Then, of course, the sun helmet worn by the Nazi Afrika Korps is of interest and is constantly increasing in value. Perhaps the greatest variety of this type of headdress, however, is that to be found in the Italian Army. In fact, the headdress of the Italian Army is a largely unexplored field. It will not be at all surprising if in the not too distant future this area will develop into a major collecting field. The expert in Italian armed forces artifacts is Mr. Rudolfo A. D'Angello of Farmington, Connecticut, who has thoroughly researched the field and who is presently preparing a book on Italian headdress. Italian sun helmets are of a great variety for there was considerable difference in details for the helmets of the Bersaglier, Alpini, Carabiniere, Black Shirts, Army, Navy and Air Force.

The British Army has had sun helmets for many years. These vary in pattern from the high dome model with rear visor longer than the front of the late 1800's to modern patterns which are lower in the skull and have wider brim or visors. These may be either white or khaki. They may or may not have any decoration. Some of the earlier examples have a spike, chin chain and may have an elaborate front plate. Later types may be plain or may have a regimental distinguishing device on one side. Most often these helmets have a pugree or wide band of twisted cloth just above the brim or visors. The famous Royal Marines have a white helmet with a fairly high crown and with an extremely long rear visor. This is worn at times with a gilt ball top and gilt chin chain. At other times it is worn with a simple white ventilator top and leather chin strap. The Royal Marines emblem in large size appears on the front.

The United States armed forces have flirted with the sun helmet from time to time. A need for comfortable hot weather headdress had been apparent for many years but it was not until around the 1870's that much was done about it. At first there apparently was some thought of a helmet very similar to that used in the British Army but after some discussion it was decided that it was too heavy. In 1881 a sun helmet was prescribed for the U.S. Army for hot weather wear. At first this cloth covered cork helmet was issued only in white but later it was also issued in khaki for service wear. This helmet was somewhat smaller and considerably lighter than the British version. The high well rounded skull had a fairly wide brim almost straight down on the sides and with a slightly outward flaring front visor and a somewhat longer rear.

For dress wear a gilt/brass spike and chin chain was authorized for the white helmet. On each side of the white helmet was a gilt/brass button bearing the distinctive device of the arm or service of the wearer. Apparently no front plate was officially authorized for the helmet but there is some evidence that the eagle front plate of the model 1881 helmet was worn at times. On the breast of the eagle there sometimes appeared the device of the arm or service, such as crossed rifles for infantry, crossed cannon for artillery, a castle for the engineers, flaming grenade for ordnance, etc. As might be expected a number of militia units, not satisfied with the more dignified ornamentation of the Regular Army, went in for a far more fancy helmet. These militia specimens might be covered with the more costly felt and elaborate gilt and colored enamel front plates. U.S. Navy officers in the late 1800's and early 1900's at times wore a white helmet similar to that worn by Army officers. This helmet was unadorned except for a gilt Navy button on each side.

During the late 1800's and very early 1900's, U.S. Marines also wore a white helmet for dress. This was adorned by a gilt/brass spike and chin chain and with Marine buttons on the side. At first the front plate consisted of a fairly large U.S. Shield upon which was superimposed a Marine Corps emblem. Later a large Marine Corps emblem alone was worn on the front. A white helmet without spike, chin chain and emblem was authorized for undress wear. This helmet too was similar to that worn by the Army.

Interestingly enough there was a return to the use of the sun helmet in the U.S. forces during the early part of World War II. This was a pressed fiber helmet with cloth cover. It had a medium high skull and a fairly wide brim. These were cheaply made and sold for only a few dollars each. Navy helmets came in white and khaki and were worn by commissioned officers, chief petty officers and certain other designated enlisted personnel. On the front was worn the cap device usually worn by the wearer. The Army and the Marines wore a khaki helmet with the cap device appropriate to the wearer. For a short time Marine officers wore a small square of cordovan leather behind the emblem.

During World War II, Japanese forces at times wore a white or khaki cloth covered cork helmet. The shape of this helmet suggests an oversize Japanese steel combat helmet. These helmets are found with and without a five-point star on the lower front of the helmet.

AMERICAN

☐ **Army Other Ranks helmet,** *c. late 1800's. White or khaki cloth covered cork with fairly high skull and cloth covered domed metal ventilator on the top. Cloth band about the base of the skull. White helmets may or may not have brass side buttons*

U.S. Army Enlisted Man's White Undress Sun helmet, c. late 1800's.

	Price Range	

embossed with the device of the arm or service and with a brass hook at the top rear. This helmet in khaki for service wear and in white for undress. **35.00**   **40.00**

☐ **Above Pattern helmet** in white with brass spike and brass chin chain as worn for dress. **60.00**   **66.00**

☐ **Navy Officer's sun helmet,** c. 1900's. White cloth covered cork, plain helmet without ornamentation. . .   **35.00**   **40.00**

☐ **Marine Officer's Dress helmet,** white cloth covered with gilt spike, chin chain and side buttons and with the Marine Corps emblem superimposed upon the field of the United States. **165.00**   **180.00**

☐ **Marine Officer's White dress helmet,** as above but with front plate consisting of a large Marine Corps emblem. **165.00**   **180.00**

☐ **Enlisted Marine's white helmet,** with either of the two above front plates. **100.00**   **110.00**

☐ **Officer's Fiber sun helmets,** period of World War II, white or khaki for the Navy and khaki for the Army and Marine Corps, complete with Officer's cap insignia. **25.00**   **27.00**

☐ **Enlisted Men's Fiber helmets,** as above but with appropriate enlisted cap insignia on front. **15.00**   **16.00**

BELGIAN

☐ **Officer's sun helmet,** c. 1914. Of the Public Forces of the Belgium Congo. Khaki covered cork helmet, simi-

Price Range

lar in pattern to the British Army sun helmet of that period, ventilator top, khaki pugree. The front plate is the Belgium lion within laurel branches all under the Royal Crown. This device is in gold. Junior noncommissioned officers and other ranks of the Public Forces were native Congolese. All commissioned officers and senior noncommissioned officers were seconded from the Belgium Regular Army. 140.00   150.00

Senior Noncommissioned Officer's sun helmet of the Public Forces of the Belgium Congo.

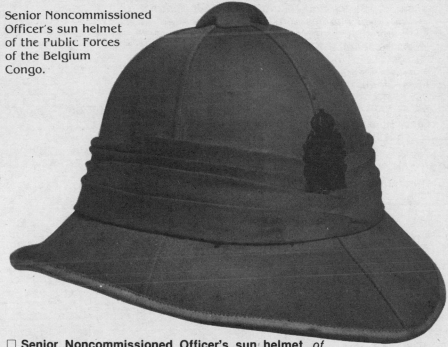

☐ **Senior Noncommissioned Officer's sun helmet,** *of the Public Forces of the Belgium Congo. Similar to the above but with dark bronze front plate.* 120.00   125.00

BRITISH

☐ **Other Ranks sun helmet.** *Khaki covered cork with khaki pugree. This helmet is regimentally identified by a large scarlet patch over the pugree on each side of the helmet bearing the legend "E. LANCASHIRE" in an inverted arc. Brim forms a sharp short visor in front, the sides are straight and the rear visor is medium long.* 150.00   165.00

☐ **Officer's sun helmet,** *c. 1898. As above, but with the gilt and enameled badge of the 21st Company Imperial Yeomanry on the side.* 185.00   200.00

☐ **Other Ranks sun helmet,** *c. 1905. Civil Service Volunteers. Gray cloth covered helmet of conven-*

Price Range

tional pattern with edges bound in black leather. Narrow band of gray cloth about the bottom of the skull in lieu of a pugree. Front plate consisting of a white metal Maltese cross upon which appears a circle bearing the name of the regiment. In the center of the circle appears the three feathers and coronet of the Prince of Wales. Above the cross is a royal crown. 140.00   150.00

☐ **Officer's Royal Marines helmet.** White cloth covered cork helmet of Royal Marines pattern with long rear visor, gilt ball top and gilt chin chain, gilt front plate of the Royal Marines consisting of a heraldic star surmounted by a royal crown. Immediately below the crown appears a ribbon bearing the battle honor "GIBRALTAR." In the center of the star within a laurel wreath appears a circular band upon which is the Royal Marines motto "PER MARE PER TERRAM." In the center of the circle appears the world showing the eastern hemisphere with anchor below. 185.00   200.00

☐ **Other Ranks Royal Marines helmet.** As above but of less costly materials and with brass chin chain, ball top and front plate. 100.00   205.00

GERMAN

☐ **Other Ranks sun helmet,** c. early 1900's. Pattern worn in Asia and East Africa. Dark khaki cloth covered cork helmet with cloth covered domed metal ventilator top. Front plate consists of the Imperial German eagle in gray metal. This eagle differs considerably from the Prussian heraldic eagle. 160.00   175.00

☐ **Other Ranks helmet.** Imperial German Navy detachments in Asia. A white cloth covered cork helmet with cloth covered domed metal ventilator top. White cloth narrow band about the bottom of the skull. The front plate of brass is in the form of the Imperial German eagle superimposed upon a large fouled anchor with the Imperial Crown above. 295.00   325.00

☐ **Officer's Tropical helmet,** c. early 1900's. Light khaki color cloth covered cork helmet with tall gilt spike and cross base, chin scales and trim to visors, gilt Imperial German front plate, large red, white and black rondell under right end of chin scales. 400.00   450.00

☐ **Other Ranks Tropical helmet,** c. early 1900's. Tan cloth covered cork helmet with cloth covered domed metal ventilator. White band (indicating infantry) at base of skull. Red, white and black rondell on right side of helmet. Long tan spine cloth attached to band and hangs down to protect the back of the neck from the sun. Brass Imperial German eagle front plate. . . . 320.00   350.00

☐ **Other Ranks sun helmet,** c. 1914. For duty in Mesopotamia. White or khaki cloth covered helmet similar in pattern to the leather helmet of the era.

German Other Ranks
sun helmet, c. early 1900's.

Imperial German Officer's
Tropical helmet, c. early 1900's.
In this specimen the tall gilt
spike is missing.

Price Range

Conventional round gray metal spike base on top (no spike was worn). Long spine cloth attached to a brown leather spike which encircles the base of the skull. The simple front plate consists merely of a small gray metal cartouche bearing the embossed number of the wearer's regiment. 275.00   300.00

☐ **Other Ranks Tropical helmet,** c. 1915. Khaki cloth covered cork helmet with skull similar to that of the leather helmet with more pronounced front visor and long rear visor. Gray metal spike top on circular base. In lieu of a front plate, the regimental number in red wool appears in large size on the front. This helmet is sometimes found with a gray metal Prussian heraldic eagle. 410.00   450.00

☐ **Officer's sun helmet,** c. early 1900's. Schutztruppen, East Africa. White or khaki cloth covered cork helmet with cloth covered domed ventilator on top, twisted red, white and black cord about the base of the skull, small red, white and black cockard on the lower front of the helmet. 230.00   250.00

☐ **Officer's sun helmet,** c. early 1900's. Medical Officers, East Africa. As above but with twisted gilt braid about the base of the skull. 230.00   250.00

☐ **Other Ranks sun helmets,** Schutztruppen, East Africa. Similar to the above but without the twisted cord about the base of the skull. 160.00   175.00

☐ **General Officer's helmet,** East Asia Occupation Forces. Gray cloth cover over either cork or leather similar to that worn by the home forces, gilt fittings and trim with gilt Imperial Eagle with enameled center, gilt spike. 820.00   900.00

☐ **General Officer's sun helmet,** c. early 1900's. East Asia Occupation Forces. Khaki cloth covered cork helmet of tropical pattern with gilt fittings and gilt Imperial Eagle with enameled device on breast, gold cord over a white band about the base of the skull. . .   730.00   800.00

☐ **General Staff Officer's helmets,** East Asia Occupation Forces. As above but with silver spike, fittings, and front plate. 730.00   800.00

☐ **Officer's helmets,** East Asia Occupation Forces. Generally the same as above except spike, fittings and front plate of brass. No enamel device on the breast of the eagle. This was of brass also. 410.00   450.00

☐ **Other Ranks helmets,** East Asia Occupation Forces, Regiments 1, 2 and 3. Same as those for officers but of lesser quality. 300.00   330.00

ITALIAN

☐ **Field Grade Officer's sun helmet,** c. 1934. Italian Africa Corps. White matted cloth covered cork helmet of tropical pattern with wire mesh ventilators on each side. White cloth covered dome shape metal

Italian Field Grade Officer's sun helmet, Italian Africa Corps.

Price Range

ventilator on top, white cloth pugree. Brass front plate is the badge of the Royal Colonial Infantry consisting of a large light infantry horn superimposed upon crossed rifles with bayonets with Royal Crown above, all resting upon a large red, silver and green cockade of cloth. 205.00   225.00

Italian Other Ranks sun helmet, Italian African Police.

Price Range

☐ **Other Ranks sun helmet,** *Italian African Police. Dark brown cloth covered helmet (cork) of tropical pattern, wire mesh ventilators on sides, brown cloth covered dome shape ventilator on top, brown leather chin strap. Front plate consists of a large bronze eagle of the organization with an enameled Savoy cross within an oval on the breast. Above the eagle's head is a Royal Crown. This badge is superimposed upon a large red, silver and green cockade of cloth.* 115.00   125.00

☐ **Other Ranks sun helmet,** *c. 1925. Italian Africa Corps. Khaki cloth covered cork helmet of tropical pattern, brown leather chin strap, metal mesh ventilator on sides, cloth covered dome shape metal ventilator on top. Large brass front plate of the cross of Savoy on a shield under a royal crown, all superimposed upon a large red, white and green cloth cockade.* 115.00   125.00

☐ **Other Ranks sun helmet,** *Chausseurs. As above but with front plate consisting of crossed lances with lance flags behind a semidome shape center device with Royal Crown above, all superimposed upon a large red, white and green cloth cockade.* 115.00   125.00

☐ **Other Ranks sun helmet,** *Carabinieri. As above except for the front plate which consists of a flaming grenade upon a large red, white and green rosette.* .. 115.00   125.00

☐ **Other Ranks sun helmet,** *Postal and Telegraph Troops. As above but with a large front plate consisting of a postal horn with device within the circle of the horn with eagle and Royal Crown above and interwoven cord design below, all upon a large red, white and green cloth cockade.* 115.00   125.00

☐ **Other Ranks sun helmet,** *1st Artillery Regiment, period of World War II. Khaki cloth covered cork helmet of tropical pattern with cloth covered domed metal ventilator on top, metal mesh ventilators on each side, cloth band about base of skull, knotted cord decoration about top of front visor. Brass front plate consisting of crossed cannons with semi-domed disk below bearing the number "1" in black enamel. Stylized wings appear behind the cannons. Above the cannons is a vertical fasces, all superimposed upon a small red, silver and green rosette. This is a Fascist helmet. The front plates on these Fascist helmets are not as large or as ornate as those of the Kingdom.* 93.00   100.00

JAPANESE

☐ **Other Ranks sun helmet,** *c. World War II. White or khaki cloth covered cork helmet of somewhat heavy design. Helmet is similar in pattern to the Japanese steel combat helmet. May or may not have a five-pointed star device at the bottom front on the narrow cloth band which surrounds the base of the skull.* 205.00   225.00

NAZI

One of the most popular sun helmets among many collectors is that of the Nazi army in Africa and other hot climates. The first sun or tropical helmet was issued to troops fighting in Africa. This was a cloth covered cork helmet of rather conventional pattern with domed cloth covered metal ventilator on top. The edges of the helmet are bound in leather. The helmets issued at first were covered with a canvas-like cloth in either olive/green or khaki. A later issue was covered with brown or olive/green wool. Some experts affirm that the wool cloth covered helmets were most used in Crete and elsewhere. On the right side of the helmet was a small metal shield painted in red, white and black. On the left side was a similar shield bearing a dull silver Wehrmacht eagle on a painted black background. The helmet was provided with a brown leather chin strap. Captured British and Dutch sun helmets were also used. These were fitted with the two metal shields noted above. The price for the original Nazi issued sun helmets is the same for all varieties. Captured helmets may command a slightly higher price because they were in less quantity.

Early model Nazi sun (tropical helmet) with tan (khaki) cover.

	Price Range	
☐ **Nazi sun helmet,** *original issue.*	78.00	85.00
☐ **Captured British or Dutch sun helmet,** *with Nazi shields.*	100.00	120.00

MACHINE GUNS

One of the more interesting areas of military collecting is machine guns and related automatic weapons. IT MAY BE STATED HERE AND NOW THAT UNDER CERTAIN REGULATIONS THE COLLECTING OF MACHINE GUNS IS ENTIRELY LEGAL. This particular area of collecting is growing rapidly. In fact prices are no doubt increasing more rapidly in this area than in any other. Generally speaking this area includes two interests, the collecting of fully operating weapons and the collecting of inactivated guns, commonly known as "dewats."

Machine guns have a most interesting history. The idea of a fully automatic weapon intrigued arms designers and tinkerers virtually since the invention of gun powder. A host of ideas was tried over the years. Even the great Leonardo da Vinci tried his hand. Probably the first attempts, as was da Vinci's, were the so-called multi-barrel "organ" guns with a number of gun barrels fastened in a row to a rigid framework, this giving it a fancied resemblance to the musical instrument. These weapons were fitted with various ignition devices which detonated the charge(s) one at a time or in a very rapid series with the effect that it appeared that they were being fired simultaneously. Also sometimes known as "Quick-Firers," these guns appeared in various forms up until the American Civil War. They were used with but very limited success by both the Union and the Confederacy. Even the best of these guns was highly inaccurate, clumsy to move about and required far too much time to reload.

Various other ideas were experimented with but it was not until just prior to the Civil War that any important breakthrough was made with the introduction of the Gatling gun. The brain child of a Yankee physician, one Dr. Richard Gatling, this weapon consisted basically of a bundle of rifled gun barrels revolving lengthwise around a central axis. Cranked by hand these revolved in such a manner that as each barrel came to the top it was loaded with a cartridge from a magazine. As the rotation continued the breech closed and the cartridge was fired, following which it was ejected, the barrel started upward and the cycle was repeated. Although the Gatling was a much advanced weapon for its day and could attain a rate of fire of around 1000 rounds per minute it found but little favor with the U.S. Armed Forces. On the other hand it was used with great success by the British. Gatling guns are highly prized by collectors and are perhaps the most costly of all weapons in this field.

Other so-called machine guns of this period, and but a few out of many, include the Lowell Battery Gun, the Palmcrantz-Nordenfeldt multi-barrel gun and the Gardner. Rarely if ever do these appear on the collectors' market.

The first true machine gun in every sense of the definition was Sir Hiram Maxim's gun. Maxim was an American genius and gun designer who, like Hotchkiss and others, was unable to interest the U.S. Government and gun manufactures in their inventions. Hiram Maxim went to England where he was knighted for his work. His invention was a **fully** automatic, recoil operated, belt fed weapon. Early models could be set to fire continuously until the entire ammunition supply had been exhausted. Such continuous firing made it difficult to keep the gun on target and quickly heated the water-cooled barrel. It was found to be more practical to arrange the weapon to be fired in short bursts. Shortly after it made its appearance in 1884 it was quickly adopted by Great Britain, Germany, Russia, Spain, Switzerland,

Turkey, Portugal and a host of other nations. In Germany it eventually became known as the Spandau after the name of the arsenal, near Berlin, where it was manufactured. In England it would become known as the Vickers, being made by the Vickers people.

Again the U.S. Government took its time about using a most successful gun. The Maxim was available for use in the Spanish-American War but our military wasn't convinced of the use of machine guns and even the Gatling gun, of which there were some on hand, was not used to any extent. It was not until around World War I that this country ever got around to using the Vickers (Maxim). Maxims are extremely popular with collectors today.

Insofar as machine guns are concerned the U.S. Armed Forces have relied mainly upon the gas-powered, air-cooled weapons developed by John Moses Browning, an American gun designer of rare ability. Some earlier models were water-cooled but all are gas operated. These have appeared in several calibers and designed for differed specific uses. The famous BAR or Browning automatic rifle is one of these variations. All are collector interest.

Other American machine guns of interest to collectors include the Benet-Mercie light machine gun, the Marlin and the Lewis air-cooled machine gun, both the ground version and the aircraft model. Lewis guns made in England and Belgium are equally popular. French machine guns of collector value include the heavy air-cooled weapon and the ugly, inefficient Chauchat machine rifle. Nazi automatic weapons are of course always of great interest and consequently prices of these items are high.

The following guide includes both operating guns and non-operating weapons and are so designated. Machine gun collectors are well aware of the various legal requirements concerning the collecting and possession of these items. Beginning collectors should be positive that they are fully conversant with all requirements. **All these weapons must be registered.** A working or live machine gun is subject to a $200.00 Federal tax payable by the purchaser. This amount is in addition to the selling price of the gun. State and local regulations concerning the possession of both live and dewat weapons vary from state and from local jurisdiction to state and local jurisdiction. Federal tax and registration forms may be obtained from your local or regional office of the Bureau of Alcohol, Tobacco and Firearms Control, U.S. Treasury Department, Internal Revenue Service. This source can also furnish you with a valuable reference booklet entitled "Published Ordinances — FIREARMS. State Laws Relavent to Title 18, U.S. Code, Chapter 44. Publication P-5300.5 (6-78). Representatives of this office can also supply you with any information you may need. State and local authorities can furnish you with necessary information and such forms as may be required.

The following guide gives the lowest prices prevailing at the present time for weapons in good to excellent condition. Prices are constantly increasing. Specimens in better than excellent condition and those with rare serial numbers and markings will always bring considerably more. Most legitimate dealers will render a machine gun inoperative to meet Federal requirements far from $25.00 to $40.00 additional to the selling price.

AUSTRIA

☐ **Schwarzlose machine gun,** *model 1912, 8-mm. Heavy, water-cooled. Complete with long flash hider and tripod mount. Used by Austria in both World Wars I*

Price Range

and II. An interesting gun not often offered but as yet
has not attracted considerable interest. In operating
order. 1450.00   1600.00

BELGIUM

☐ **Lewis machine gun.** *Air-cooled, gas-operated, with
bipod mount. Manufactured by Armes Automatique,
Liege, Belgium. Dated 1913. The barrel cooled by
longitudinal fins enclosed in a cylindrical sleeve, giving it a characteristic appearance. Belgium manufac-
tured Lewis guns are very rare. Operating condition.*   5500.00   6100.00

DENMARK

☐ **Madsen submachine gun,** *model 1950, 9-mm. Most
successful of the Madsen designs, sold widely
throughout the world, gas-operated. Made by Dansk
Industrie Syndikat and so marked. Interesting gun
made by a company no longer in business. Operating
condition.* 1700.00   2100.00

FRANCE

☐ **Chauchat light machine gun or machine rifle,** *8-mm.
Lebel cartridge. Used by both the French and American armies in World War I in spite of the fact that it
was inefficient and troublesome. In operating condi-
tion.* 775.00   850.00

☐ **Hotchkiss heavy machine gun,** *model 1917, 8-mm.
Air-cooled, (Lebel), gas-operated, on tripod mount.
Operating condition.* 2620.00   2900.00

☐ **MAS-38 submachine gun,** *7.65-mm. Sound design but
rather odd looking due to fact that the axis of the barrel and the body and stock are slightly divergent.
Limited production before France occupied by Ger-
man Army. Operating condition.* 1000.00   1100.00

GERMANY (Imperial)

☐ **Maxim heavy machine gun,** *model 1908, 7.92-mm.
This offering on the famous "sled" mount. This is a
rare World War I weapon, much sought after, water-
cooled. Complete with flash hider and in operating
condition.* 3925.00   4350.00

☐ **Maxim heavy machine gun,** *model 1908. Water-
cooled. This specimen is on a tripod mount instead
of the sled mount used by the German Army. It was
produced in great quantities and sold all over the
world. This offering has the Arms of Columbia on the
receiver. In operating condition.* 3430.00   3800.00

☐ **Maxim light machine gun,** *model 08/15, 7.92-mm.
Water-cooled. A modified model 1908 machine gun*

Price Range

*with butt stock, pistol grip and trigger, and short
bipod mount. Although called a light machine gun
during its combat service it required at least two men
to transport it and get it into action. In operating con-
dition. Prized as a World War I exhibit.* 1900.00   2100.00
☐ **Maxim aircraft machine gun,** *(SPANDAU), 7.92-mm.
Air-cooled with perforated cooling jacket and spade
grip. In operating condition, rarely offered.* 2150.00   2600.00

GERMANY (Nazi)

Schmeisser MP-38 machine pistol.

☐ **Schmeiser machine pistol,** *model MP-38, 9-mm. This
and the MP-40 machine pistol were actually designed
by the staff of Erfurter Masccinenwerke B. Giepel
GmbH, commonly known as Erma and were named
Schmeisers for a Schmeiser who managed one of the
Erma plants. Weapon much used by troops of the
Third Reich. Operating condition.* 1900.00   2100.00
☐ **Schmeiser machine pistol,** *model MP-40, 9-mm. Like
above model has folding metal stock, both were
much used paratrooper weapons. Operating condi-
tion.* 1630.00   1800.00
☐ **Schmeiser machine pistol,** *model MP-40, 9-mm. As
above but completely deactivated to meet Federal
requirements.* 1000.00   1100.00
☐ **Bergman machine pistol,** *model MP18/1. 9-mm. Rifle
type butt stock, air-cooled perforated sleeve around
barrel, an early developed machine pistol. Operating
condition.* 910.00   1000.00
☐ **Bergman machine pistol,** *model MP18/1. As above
but rendered completely unoperable in accordance
with Federal law. Makes a most interesting display
piece.* 640.00   700.00
☐ **Mauser general purpose machine gun,** *model MG34,
7.92-mm. Belt fed. A precision built weapon with
folding bipod mount. In operating condition.* 2350.00   2600.00
☐ **Mauser general purpose machine gun,** *model MG34,
7.92-mm. As above but equipped with optic sights
and mounted on special tripod field mount. This*

Price Range

mount was provided with a device which permitted the weapon to fire in a fixed arc without the gunner exposing himself. This gun required a three man crew. Complete and in operating condition. A rare find for the Nazi collector. 3340.00   3700.00

☐ **Mauser general purpose machine gun,** model MG42, 7.92-mm. Much improved version of the above weapon. Probably the best all round machine gun ever developed. It has been widely copied, is still the standard machine gun of the West German Army. With folding bipod and in operating condition. 1540.00   1700.00

☐ **Mauser general purpose machine gun,** model MG42, 7.72-mm. As above, but equipped with the special tripod field mount. 2440.00   2700.00

GREAT BRITAIN

☐ **Bren light machine gun,** .303-mm. A most excellent weapon in its class, rugged, accurate and easy to maintain. Is a modification of a Czech ZB VZ/26 light machine gun manufactured in Brno. The name derives from Brno and Enfield, site of the Royal Small Arms Factory. Still in service in many armies throughout the world. This offering with bipod and in full operating condition. 4520.00   4800.00

British Lanchester submachine gun.

☐ **Lanchester submachine gun,** 9-mm. Design based on the German machine pistol 1928. Rather heavy and was expensive to manufacture, however, is rugged, dependable, accurate weapon. Magazine projects from left side, perforated air-cooling sleeve around barrel, rifle type shoulder stock, fitted with bayonet lug, adopted by the Royal Navy during World War II. This specimen offered complete and in operating order but without the bayonet. 820.00   900.00

☐ **Lewis light machine gun,** .303-mm. World War I classic, made by BSA (British Small Arms). Air-cooled, gas-operated, drum magazine holding 47 rounds, rifle type shoulder stock. Barrel surrounded by series of longitudinal cooling fins enclosed within a cylindrical metal shield, giving it a characteristic profile. Complete with drum magazine and in full operating condition. 1540.00   1700.00

Price Range

☐ **Lewis light machine gun,** *.303-mm. Aircraft version. Shoulder stock replaced with spade grip, no cooling fins nor metal jacket, 96 round drum magazine. A much sought after collector item. Fully operating condition.* 1810.00   2000.00

☐ **Sten Mark I submachine gun,** *9-mm. A much simplified Lanchester design combined with some features of the German MP-40. Crude in appearance but light in weight, compact and rugged. Made by both Enfield and BSA in great quantities as were all models. Metal frame shoulder stock, folding forehand grip, conical flash hider.* 1090.00   1200.00

☐ **Sten Mark II submachine gun,** *9-mm. Improved modification of the above gun. Frame stock replaced with metal tube with flat shoulder plate, no flash hider, simpler construction, much used by French resistance forces, approximately two million made. In operating condition.* 1090.00   1200.00

☐ **Sten Mark III submachine gun,** *9-mm. Yet more simpler construction that the Mark II, rather the same in appearance. Some users affirm that it was the best of all Sten guns. Not produced in great quantity. Fully operating condition.* 1270.00   1400.00

☐ **Sten Mark V submachine gun,** *9-mm. Same basic mechanism as the previous Stens. Wood shoulder stock with fore and rear pistol grips, accommodated the spike bayonet. Used until the 1960's by the British Army. Fully operating condition.* 1360.00   1500.00

ISRAEL

Israel UZI submachine gun.

☐ **Uzi submachine gun,** *9-mm. Design based to some extent on the Czech model 26, easily manufactured, rugged and reliable. Appears with either wood rifle type stock or folding metal stock, thirty-two round box magazine, standard submachine gun of the Israeli Army. Is a very popular weapon and has been exported in quantity to a number of nations including*

Price Range

the Netherlands, Iran, Thailand, Venezuela and West Germany. It has also been made under license in Belgium by the famed Fabrique National. This specimen is offered with box magazine and folding metal stock. Fully operable, rarely available. 5010.00   5621.00

ITALY

☐ **Fiat-Revelli machine gun,** 6.5-mm. Heavy water-cooled. Standard heavy machine gun of the Italian Army during World War I. On tripod mount. Not many offered but not much sought after by collectors. In full operating condition. 1000.00   1100.00

JAPAN

☐ **Aircraft machine gun,** 7.7-mm. A direct copy of the stripped down aircraft version of the famous British Lewis gun. Japanese markings. Operating condition.   2080.00   2300.00
☐ **Light machine gun,** 7.7-mm. A direct copy of the British made Lewis ground machine gun. Japanese markings. Operating condition. 1000.00   1100.00
☐ **M-96 light machine gun,** 6.5-mm. Design based upon the Czech ZB26. These had been captured in quantity in China. A good weapon with magazine and carrying handle on top and with wood rifle type butt stock. Gun is very well made. With bipod. Fully operational.   1720.00   1900.00
☐ **M-96 light machine gun,** 6.5-mm. As above but rendered fully inoperable in accordance with Federal law. 753.00   825.00
☐ **Aircraft machine gun,** 12.7-mm. For fixed wing mounting, from a Zero fighter and so documented. This weapon is an exact copy of the U.S. Browning .50 aircraft gun. This specimen is in near mint condition but has been completely deactivated in accordance with the law. Extremely rare. 2800.00   3100.00
☐ **Taisho 3 heavy machine gun,** 6.5-mm. Air-cooled. This is a big, heavy ugly brute mounted on a tripod, weighing all of 62 pounds. Uses 30 round strip magazine, one of which comes with this offering. Is a direct copy of the Hotchkiss heavy air-cooled machine gun. There is no mistaking the agressive appearance of this weapon. Not often offered for sale. Has flash hider. In full operating condition. 3700.00   4100.00

RUSSIA

☐ **AK-47 Assault Rifle,** 7.62-mm. Designed by Mikhail Kalashnikova and named the Automat Kalashnikova. Standard weapon of the Soviet armed forces. Incorporated very sound design, is well made, rugged and accurate. Has also become standard for the Warsaw

Pact countries and was used by the Viet Cong. In excellent operating condition with magazine 2125.00   2350.00

☐ **Detgyarev DP light machine gun,** *7.62-mm. Interesting air-cooled weapon with drum or pan magazine holding forty-seven rounds. Excellent combat proven weapon which was simple to manufacture. Not phased out of the Soviet forces. Fitted with bipod. This specimen is operable.* 2350.00   2600.00

☐ **Detgyarev RPD light machine gun,** *(Ruchnoi Pulemet Detgyarev), 7.62-mm. Belt fed from drum magazine holding one hundred rounds attached under the gun. Another excellent weapon. Used by the Viet Cong and in the Middle East. With bipod and in fully operable condition.* 2620.00   2900.00

☐ **Sudarev PPS-43 submachine gun,** *7.62-mm. Folding metal stock and with muzzle brake, thirty round detachable box magazine. Not too extensively used by the Russians. Phased out in 1946, some use thereafter by Chinese troops. Full operating condition. An interesting weapon.* 1540.00   1700.00

☐ **Sudarev PPS-43 submachine gun,** *7.65-mm. As above but completely inoperative in accordance with law.*   1045.00   1150.00

☐ **Shpagin PPsh-41 submachine gun,** *(Pistolet Pulyemot Shpagin), 7.62-mm. With seventy-one round drum magazine or thirty-five round vertical box magazine. Wood rifle type butt stock. Not a particularly handsome weapon but thoroughly rugged and trouble free. Rough war emergency appearance but proved operable under all field conditions. Over five million made. Phased out of Russian service around 1950. This offering is complete with both drum and box magazines. Fully operable.* 1495.00   1650.00

UNITED STATES

☐ **M-3 submachine gun,** *(so-called "grease gun"), .45 cal. A rather crude gun but very effective and cheap and easy to manufacture. Retracting wire stock. Thirty round vertical box magazine under gun. Not used in U.S. Armed Forces after the early 1950's but used extensively elsewhere. This offering fully operable and has magazine.* 865.00   952.00

☐ **Browning Automatic Rifle,** *(the famous BAR), model 1918A2, .30 cal. Extremely well made, rugged and accurate. Has a folding bipod, flash hider and carrying handle. Colt made. (The BAR was made by several arms manufacturers in this country and was made abroad under license.). Estimated to have been in use for over fifty years, now obsolete. This specimen is a true collector's item and is in full operating condition complete with box magazine holding twenty rounds.* 3520.00   3900.00

Price Range

☐ **Browning machine gun,** *(COLT), model 1895, .30 cal.
Gas-operated, air-cooled. Popularly known as the
"potato digger" since a system of levers operating
under the gun prevented it from being lowered close
to the ground. Used by the U.S. Navy and Marine
Corps and a few foreign armies but not by the U.S.
Army. Pedstal mounted for shipboard use, on tripod
by ship landing parties and the Marines and on a
chart for the Marines, belt fed. This specimen is fully
operable, and is tripod mounted. Historically this is a
most interesting item, rare.* 3800.00   4200.00

☐ **Browning heavy machine gun,** *model 1917A1, .30 cal.
Water-cooled, belt fed, tripod mounted. This gun and
improved versions was used to a limited extent in
World War I, throughout World War II and in Korea.
Another historically important weapon. In fully
operating order.* 3800.00   4200.00

☐ **Browning M-2 aircraft machine gun,** *.30 cal. Flexible
mounting, air-cooled, spade grip, manual cocking.
Used from introduction to 1940 by U.S. Army Air
Corps, and subsequent Air Force. Fully operable.* . . .   3880.00   4300.00

☐ **Browning M-2 aircraft machine gun,** *.30 cal. For fixed
mounting, has no spade grip nor manual cocking
arrangement. This specimen is also fully operable.*   3430.00   3800.00

☐ **Browning heavy machine gun,** *.50 cal. Water-cooled,
scaled up version of the Browning .30-mm water-
cooled machine gun listed above. Used throughout
World War II, is big and is rugged and is an excellent
display piece. Spade grips, tripod mounted. Fully
operable.* 4880.00   5400.00

☐ **Browning light machine gun,** *model M1919A4, .30 cal.
Tripod mounted, air-cooled, belt fed, pistol grip, two
hundred-fifty round fabric belt. Fully operable.* 3700.00   4100.00

☐ **Browning M2 heavy machine gun,** *.50 cal. Air-cooled,
on tripod mount, double spade grips. Fully operable.*   4970.00   5500.00

☐ **Lewis light machine gun,** *.30 cal. Air-cooled, made by
Savage. (See description under Belgian and British
made Lewis machine guns.) U.S. made Lewis guns
are not as common as those made in Belgium and
England. This is a U.S. Army specimen, complete
with drum magazine and bipod. Fully operable.* 3610.00   4000.00

☐ **Johnson light machine gun,** *model 1941, .39 cal.
Detachable twenty round box magazine, rifle type
wood shoulder stock, pistol grip. Used to a limited
extent by the U.S. Marines and by the Royal Netherlands Marines, as well as by some special U.S. Army
units. An interesting collector's piece. This offering
is fully operable, complete with magazine and bipod.*   865.00   950.00

☐ **Marlin fixed aircraft gun,** *.30 cal. Modified Browning
model 1895 machine gun, to permit use as a fixed air-*

Price Range

craft machine gun. Two hundred fifty round belt fed.
In full operating order. 1810.00   2000.00

☐ **Reising M-55 submachine gun,** .45 cal. Folding wire
stock, staggered twelve or twenty round detachable
box magazine. Made by Harrington and Richardson,
adopted by the U.S. Marines but unpopular because
of the complex mechanism made it prone to jam. Not
used after World War II. Fully operable. 910.00   1000.00

United States Thompson (Colt made), model 1928.

☐ **Thompson ACP submachine gun,** (Colt made), model
1928, .45 cal. U.S. Navy marked. First rejected by
military people the Thompson was made popular in
the 1920's by G-Men and gangsters and the weapon
became known as the "Tommy Gun." Eventually
accepted by the British and the French armies it was
later adopted by U.S. Armed Forces. This weapon
was made in several versions, both military and commercial, and these appear on the market from time to
time. In addition to being made by Colt, later versions
were made by Savage and Auto-Ordnance. The offering here is a U.S. Navy model and is fitted with a
Cutts compensator. It has the usual rifle type wood
shoulder stock and rear pistol grip. It has a twenty
round box magazine and a forearm pistol grip.
Included in this offering is a horizontal wood
forestock and a fifty round drum magazine. All complete and in operating order. This is an extraordinary
desireable and historic collector's piece. 3790.00   4200.00

MACHINE GUN REPRODUCTIONS

Well made replica weapons manufactured from aluminum with a finish
simulating parkerization. All are full size and have moveable cocking
handles. Top covers lift to permit amnunition belts to be inserted. Guns are
not mounted but are designed to accommodate original tripods or other
mounts. Mounts must be supplied by the buyer.

Browning Cal. 30, 1917A1.

Browning Cal. 30. 1919A4.

Browning Cal. 50, heavy barrel, M2.

		Price Range	
☐ **Browning,** *30 cal., model 1917AI*		400.00	440.00
☐ **Browning,** *30 cal., model 1919A4*		300.00	330.00
☐ **Browning,** *40 cal., heavy barrel, model M2*		425.00	468.00
☐ **Browning,** *50 cal., aircraft configuration*		425.00	468.00

MILITARY MINIATURES

The collecting of miniature military figures is of rapidly growing interest. Old toy soldiers of cardboard, tin, lead and other materials are selling for excellent prices. Some of these are flat. Others are in three dimension. Many are but crude and clumsy representations. Toy soldiers of all kinds are now being resurrected from dusty out of the way places and are selling for excellent prices. Quite an industry has grown up about the various areas of specialization, ranging from minutely accurate figures in museum dioramas to run of the mill ill proportioned soldiers put together from kits. Without meaning to down grade toy soldiers and similar figures it is submitted that they are not true militaria. This guide concerns only those items which are large enough and well enough executed to be technically correct in all details. These offerings are true works of art and may be treasured as such apart from their military aspect.

PORCELAIN FIGURES

	Price Range	
☐ **Porcelain figure of Frederich The Great,** *on horseback, in dress uniform, accurate color and detail. A beautifully executed figure in every respect, a Hohe figure. Approximately 8½ inches high.*	925.00	1025.00
☐ **Porcelain standing figure of an Officer of Brunswick Hussars.** *Regiment No. 17, in parade uniform of 1900. All correct color and detail, a Hohe figure. Approximately 9 inches tall.*	475.00	525.00
☐ **Porcelain figure of an Officer of The Guarde du Corps.** *As above, but in gala uniform of 1800. Approximately 8½ inches high.*	475.00	525.00
☐ **Porcelain figure of an Officer of Brunswick Hussars.** *As above, but in parade uniform of 1815. Approximately 9 inches high.*	520.00	575.00
☐ **Porcelain figure of an Officer of Chevaux-Legers de la Maison.** *As above, but in uniform of 1812. Approximately 13 inches high.*	520.00	575.00
☐ **Porcelain figure of an Officer of First Regiment of Cuirassiers.** *As above, but in uniform of 1814. Approximately 13 inches high.*	520.00	575.00
☐ **Porcelain figure of a Trumpeter of the Grenadier zu Pfred.** *In uniform of 1814. Approximately 12 inches high.*	475.00	575.00
☐ **Porcelain figure of Other Ranks of Guard Grenadiers No. 1,** *on porcelain gilt decorated base with gilt initial "N" (Napoleon) on the front. All correct in color and detail, Hohe. Approximately 12 inches high.*	385.00	425.00
☐ **Porcelain figure of a Dragoon.** *As above. 12 inches high.*	385.00	425.00
☐ **Porcelain figure of a Jager zu Pfred.** *As above. Approximately 12 inches high.*	385.00	425.00
☐ **Porcelain figure of a Hussar.** *As above. Approximately 12 inches high.*	385.00	425.00
☐ **Porcelain figure of a Pipe Major of the Irish Guards.** *Limited edition, all correct in color and detail, by Michael Sutty. A true collector's item as are all Sutty figures. 13 inches high.*	1400.00	1550.00
☐ **Porcelain figure of an Officer of Skinner's Horse.** *As above. 12 inches high.*	475.00	525.00
☐ **Porcelain figure of an Officer of Probyn's Horse.** *As above. 11½ inches high.*	498.00	550.00

	Price Range	
☐ **Porcelain figure of a Base Drummer, 1st Dragoon Guards.** *As above. 12 inches high.*	430.00	475.00
☐ **Porcelain figure of a French Horn player, band of the 16th Lancers.** *As above. 12½ inches high.*	408.00	450.00
☐ **Porcelain figure of a French Horn player, band of the 17th Lancers.** *As above. 12½ inches high.*	408.00	450.00
☐ **Porcelain figure of a Cornet player, Horse Guards band.** *As above. 13 inches high.*	408.00	450.00
☐ **Porcelain figure of an Officer of the Welsh Guards.** *As above. 13 inches high.*	408.00	450.00
☐ **Porcelain figure of an Officer of the Scot's Guards.** *As above. 13 inches high.*	408.00	450.00
☐ **Porcelain figures** *by Eugene Lelepvre and Lucien Rousselot. These are extremely well detailed and colored figures but unlike the above they have leather equipage and metal weapons, which add much realism. All are scarce and unique works of military art. Each figure is in a limited edition. All are 9 inches high.*		
☐ **Trompette des Gendarmes,** *uniform of 1725.*	475.00	525.00
☐ **Mameluke,** *uniform of 1815.*	475.00	525.00
☐ **Cuirassier, 11th Cuirassier Regiment,** *uniform of 1810.*	475.00	525.00
☐ **Officer, the Bercheny Hussars,** *uniform of 1730.*	475.00	525.00
☐ **Officer, Gendarmes de la Garde,** *uniform of 1750.* ...	475.00	525.00
☐ **Carabinier,** *uniform of 1812.*	475.00	525.00

JAPANESE FIGURES

Japanese miniature military figures are quite unlike those of any other nation. In each instance they are the work of an artist who has a most intimate knowledge of the arms and armor of the ancient samurai. First the artist made a miniature human figure complete in all detail. He then painstakingly made the weapons to exact scale and fabricated each element of the armor in like fashion. The three miniatures listed here are excellent examples. Each is outstandingly beautiful in its own right. In addition to being a true work of art, each offering permits a detailed study of how the Japanese feudal warrior of noble rank was armed and clothed.

☐ **Figure of a Shogan,** *c. very early 1800's . Armed with a yari or pole arm and with the badge of a samurai, the two sword daisho. Armor is complete in every detail and the helmet is exquisite, is museum quality. Approximately 24 inches high.*	1000.00	1100.00
☐ **Figure of a Kneeling Samurai.** *Beautifully executed, approximately 15 inches high. Armor complete in every detail, armed with the two sword daisho. Interestingly enough this figure in lieu of the conventional helmet is wearing a large flat metal helmet similar to a jingasa. Armor is marked in several places with a family mon. In the right hand of the figure is held a*		

Price Range

saihai, a short rod or shaft with a wisk of tough paper strips attached. This was a sign of rank and was used to give commands. Very beautiful and unusual figure. 730.00   800.00

☐ **Figure of a Japanese Archer,** *c. mid 1800's. Although perhaps not generally known the bow and arrow was the principal weapon of the samurai for many years. Great importance was given to archery training and the bow and arrow was a terrible offensive weapon in the hands of a trained archer. This figure is fully outfitted in archer's armor and carries a typical Japanese bow in his right hand. Complete in every detail. Made by an accomplished artist. This offering is approximately 17 inches high and is displayed in an extremely well made glass case. Excellent collectible. . . . .*   820.00   900.00

HEADDRESS

☐ **Miniature Headdress.** *Officer's dress helmet, French Colonial troops, gilt chin scales, silver and gilt front plate, gilt visor trim, feathered crest. Beautifully detailed. 13 inches high. . . . .*   295.00   325.00

☐ **Miniature headdress.** *c. 1900. Officer's gala helmet of the Garde du Corps. Finely detailed, silver. 10 inches high. . . . .*   475.00   525.00

☐ **Miniature headdress.** *Officer's busby, Emperor Nicholas II of Russia's Hussars (1st Westphalian) Regiment No. 8. This is a most beautiful and impressive example of the jeweler's art, rendered in the highest grade of silver. The details are of the finest, including chin scales, front plate, field badge, busby bag and busby cords. The texture of the fur of the original is reproduced in the metal. 7 inches high. . . .*   3950.00   4400.00

☐ **Miniature headdress.** *c. 1900. Other Ranks Grenadier cap of the 1st Battalion, 1st Guard Regiment of Foot. Well executed in gilt and silver color metal, mounted on small wood base, is rather small. 3½ inches in overall height. . . . .*   93.00   100.00

☐ **Miniature headdress.** *c. 1910. Officer's field cap. In porcelain, white top with red piping, colored Reich and Prussian badges, red cap band, black visor. In the top of the cap are Prussian Arms and flags, interesting. 3 inches high. . . . .*   138.00   150.00

MILITARY MISCELLANY

The foregoing sections of this guide have dealt largely with the items most often sought by military collectors. The following listing includes those artifacts not so commonly collected and in some instances not so readily available. Nonetheless, they are an essential part of the total militaria picture.

Drums have always been popular with military organizations. We know that they were used by military units in ancient Egypt, Assyria and Persia, among others. From the time the drum was first devised it has been used to spur men on to battle, signal messages and movements, and set the cadence for marching. Drums are prized by collectors for a number of reasons including association with a famous regiment or organization and for the very beautiful regimental device or badge which many of them bear. The British Army drums are particularly handsome in this respect. For parade the kettle drums of mounted bands were draped with drum banners of fine cloth with embroidered regimental devices and trim. These banners are much in favor with some collectors.

Paintings and prints of uniforms, battles and portraits of military leaders are the specialties of some collectors. Ofttimes the paintings and color prints of uniforms are the sole clue we have as to the uniforms worn long ago. Paintings and drawings by famous leaders interest some collectors as do their personal possessions. Hitler's original paintings, his letters, jewelry and personal papers are good collectibles as are those of other Nazi leaders. There is a lesser interest in letters, paybooks and other personal items of the men in the ranks. Busts of military leaders are also favorites of some as are small statues with good uniform details.

Regimental badges and belt plates are collected by some, those of the various British regiments being particularly desirable.

A most colorful collectible is the sabretache. The word stems from two German words, **sabre** (sword) and **tasche** (pouch). The origin is said to be with the old Hungarian hussars who wore such tight breeches that they could not accommodate pockets. Therefore, they devised a pouch to wear hanging from the sword belt. Before long they were being worn by hussars and light dragoons of many armies. These items are usually elaborately decorated with bullion and with finely embroidered regimental badges or the royal cypher all worked on fine quality silk or velvet. The sabretache had been phased out of practically all armies by the early 1900's.

Another interesting item is the shoulder belt and pouch. This probably originated with the large leather pouch in which the Seventeenth Century grenadiers carried their grenades. Later smaller pouches were used to carry the paper cartridges in use at the time to protect them from the weather. Mounted officers used them to carry their pistol ammunition. When the need for these no longer existed, the pouch became a highly decorated item of full dress for officers.

The military horse cloth or shabraque is collected by some. This originated as the cloth used under the saddle. Officers of many armies adopted them as yet another dress piece of equipment. These are of extremely fine cloth with bullion trim and beautifully embroidered regimental badges and royal cyphers in the corners.

BATTLE AXES

Price Range

☐ **Executioner's axe,** *c. early 1600's. German. This dreaded axe has an extremely sharp edged cleaver-like blade with a long socket through which a thick sturdy shaft passes. Bright steel with armorer's mark, is rather frightful looking.* 250.00   275.00

Price Range

☐ **Indian All Steel battle axe.** *Shaft terminates in sharp point. The rather narrow blade terminates in a reinforced sharp point for armor piercing.* 295.00   325.00

☐ **Indian axe.** *All steel, long shaft, head has a square hammer on one side, a sharp crescent blue on the other. Blade is decorated with chiselled Arabic script.* 100.00   110.00

☐ **Indian axe.** *Medium length wood shaft with decorative designs, rectangular steel head with sharp edge.* 290.00   320.00

☐ **North African Native battle axe.** *Sturdy polished black wood shaft. Very sharp half disk blade attached to the shaft by a short steel projection which sets the blade slightly out from the shaft. Of crude native workmanship but nonetheless a wicked weapon, of better quality than most native axes.* 120.00   130.00

☐ **Persian battle axe.** *Unusually large double bladed weapon with deep crescent blades, sturdy steel shaft terminating in square sided spike, blades engraved with mounted warriors in combat. This is a fairly rare example.* 1450.00   1600.00

☐ **Persian battle axe.** *Interesting example with three prong blade attached to a wood shaft with steel pointed end, shaft is wound with brass wire.* 109.00   120.00

☐ **Persian battle axe,** *c. early 1700's. Medium length sturdy wood shaft, axe head is square on one end, slightly curved blade. This is a rather common example.* 215.00   235.00

☐ **Pole axe,** *c. early 16th Century. Double-headed with slightly curved sharp blades, long pole, axe head attached to pole by very long steel straps, probably German.* 700.00   775.00

☐ **Russian Pole axe,** *c. early 16th Century. Very long crescent shape blade with "eye" at rear to accommodate the long shaft. The blade extends far enough in front of the shaft so that it could be used for thrusting. A most unusual weapon much used by peasants.* 565.00   625.00

☐ **Saxon Miner's Guild axe,** *c. 1600's. Although not a battle axe, this axe is very often of interest to military collectors. Over 250 years old, it is patterned on the ancient Saxon fighting axe. Unique straight edge blade with square blade extension attaching to a strong wood shaft inlaid with bone carved with mining scenes. This axe was a sign of authority in the guild, very handsome.* 1850.00   2050.00

BELT BUCKLES

GERMANY (Imperial)

☐ **Officer's belt and buckle.** *Belt of good quality brocade in subdued black, silver and red, gray steel*

	Price Range	

buckle with crowned "W" cypher and "II" under a crown, surrounded by a wreath of oak and laurel leaves. **75.00** **80.00**

☐ **Officer's buckle.** *As above but with subdued brown finish.* **46.00** **50.00**

☐ **Other Ranks buckle.** *Brass with silver color rondel with raised edges to form a wide border. In a half arc at the top is "GOTT MIT UNS." In a half arc about the bottom is a wreath. A Prussian crown is in the center. All in high relief.* **30.00** **33.00**

☐ **Other Ranks buckle.** *Gray metal with above rondel stamped, war time issue.* **21.00** **23.00**

☐ **Other Ranks buckle.** *Brass with applied silver color medal Prussian rondel. This buckle is pronounced rectangular in shape and has belt loops on the outside. It is variously known as a telegrapher's or a machine gunner's buckle but the exact determination has yet to be made. A rarity among Imperial Other Ranks buckles.* **185.00** **200.00**

☐ **Other Ranks buckle.** *Brass with applied silver color medal Wurttemberg rondel with raised roped edges enclosing the motto "FURCHTOLS UND TREW" (Faithful and True). In the center the Wurttemberg Arms.* **25.00** **27.00**

☐ **Other Ranks buckle.** *Of dulled blue/gray finish. Rondel in center of buckle has raised edges forming a border with which appears the motto "PROVIDENT-IAE MEMOR" (In Memory of Fortune). Within the center the Saxon Crown.* **41.00** **45.00**

GERMANY (Third Reich)

☐ **Army Officer's buckle.** *Same pattern as Army Other Ranks but buckle of silver.* **41.00** **45.00**

☐ **Army Other Ranks buckle.** *Similar to that of Imperial Army except that the crown is replaced by the Third Reich eagle. The motto "GOT MIT UNS" remained the same.* **23.00** **25.00**

Left: Nazi Belt Buckle Pistol.
Right: Front plate of buckle open and turned down. The block, holding four .22 caliber barrels, is swinging out.

Price Range

☐ **Nazi Belt Buckle Pistol.** *This is undoubtedly one of the most unusual items ever offered to militaria collectors. It is extremely rare, only a* **very** *limited number ever having been made. It was issued as a defense weapon to certainly highly placed Nazi Party officials. Four short .22 caliber barrels are concealed behind a large brass belt buckle attached to a heavy black leather belt. When a release is tripped the buckle swings down on a hinge and the barrels swing out. Each barrel is fired by slight pressure on a trigger. After use the barrels may be reloaded and folded back and the buckle returned to the closed position. On the front of buckle appears the Nazi Party insigne of an eagle grasping a wreath within which is a swastika. This device has been officially identified by the U.S. Government as a curio or relic and is legal to own. Extremely rare.* 17300.00   19200.00

☐ **Red Cross Other Ranks buckle.** *Early pattern. Polished buckle with applied rondel with wreath of laurel leaves in half arc about the border, Geneva cross within.* 20.00   22.00

☐ **Red Cross Other Ranks buckle.** *Pebbled aluminum body with stamped wreath within which is a stylized eagle with folded wings, with swastika on breast holding a Geneva cross.* 41.00   45.00

☐ **Water Protection Police Other Ranks buckle.** *Pebbled aluminum body with stamped gilt rondel attached by prongs. In half arc about top the motto "GOTT MIT UNS," about the bottom a wreath of oak and laurel leaves, in the center a swastika.* 41.00   45.00

BUGLES AND HORNS

☐ **Bugle,** *c. World War I. Brass, complete with mouthpiece. On upper side of bell appears a raised heraldic Prussian Eagle. Some dents to bell but in very good condition.* 70.00   87.00

☐ **Bugle,** *c. World War II. Aluminum, complete with mouthpiece. On upper side of bell appears the insigne of the NSKK, the National Socialist Motor Corps, a Nazi eagle grasping a wreath encircling a swastika with a scroll bearing "N.S.K.K." over the eagle's head. Some dents to bell but good condition.* 65.00   70.00

☐ **Cavalry bugle,** *British Royal Horse Guards, c. late 1800's. Brass mounted copper instrument complete with mouthpiece. Bugle engraved with crowned cypher "VR" and with script initials of the regiment, "RHG," together with the regimental battle honors "WATERLOO/PENINSULA." Attached to the bugle is a very beautiful red silk bugle banner with gold fringe edges. Banner is embroidered in gold bullion thread*

Price Range

with the crowned "VR." The regimental initials and
battle honors also appear in gold bullion thread.
Complete with silk cords and tassels. This is an
important offering of a famous and historical British
cavalry regiment. Excellent condition. 360.00   400.00

☐ **Imperial Bavarian Postal horn.** Brass horn in the traditional postal/huntsman pattern. Is finely engraved with
maker's name and has raised device of the Bavarian
Postal Service. Complete with mouthpiece. Horn
wrapped in cords of the Bavarian national colors,
blue and white, with blue and white tassels. Most
interesting and impressive. 99.00   110.00

BUSTS AND FIGURES

☐ **Bronze Portrait bust of Rudolf Hess.** Very well done,
without base but has lug for mounting. 725.00   805.00

☐ **Bronze Portrait Head of Herman Goering.** Hollow
casting without base but has lug for mounting, well
executed, life size. 995.00   1105.00

☐ **Bronze Portrait Head of Josef Gobbels.** Hollow
casting unmounted but has lug for mounting, life size,
excellent likeness. 995.00   1105.00

☐ **Bronze Portrait Head of Adolph Hitler.** Mounted on
marble base, approximately half life size, good
likeness. 575.00   635.00

☐ **Bronze Portrait Head of Adolph Hitler.** Life size heavy
casting on marble base, blackened finish, much finer
than the above. 700.00   775.00

☐ **Bronze Portrait Head of General von Hindenburg.**
Bronze casting on beautiful marble base, life size,
executed while von Hindenburg was president of the
German Reich, a most attractive bronze. 700.00   775.00

☐ **Bust of Prince Otto von Bismarck,** c. 1894. German
statesman and first chancellor of the German
Empire, beautifully executed bronze bust of Bismarck in civilian clothes wearing a broad brim flat
crown hat, marble base. 475.00   525.00

☐ **Full-length Bronze figure.** Marching German infantryman, c. 1914. Rifle held over left shoulder, excellent action and detail to all parts of uniform. Figure is
singing and wears a sprig of laurel on the left side
of his spiked helmet as was common at that time for
troops leaving for the front. Full 26 inches high,
excellent and unusual. 2905.00   3225.00

☐ **Full-length Heroic Bronze figure.** An American World
War I officer in act of advancing. Wearing helmet with
strap under chin, shirt open at throat, sleeves rolled
back above elbows, semipegged breeches and field
boots, pistol belt and holster at waist. The right arm
is extended with the hand holding a Colt .45-mm

Price Range

automatic pistol. The left hand, held to the rear, holds a trench knife, excellent detail throughout, cast bronze, 25 inches. 1105.00 1225.00

☐ **Full-length Marching Bronze figure.** *A German Jager in field uniform. Jager carries rifle over left shoulder, well done, approximately 12 inches high.* 675.00 735.00

☐ **Full-length Standing Bronze figure.** *Kaiser Wilhelm 1st in a German general's parade uniform. Exceptionally fine detail showing Kaiser's features and decorations. Figure stands with left hand on hip and right resting on a plan on a tree stump. Approximately 12 inches high.* 1105.00 1225.00

☐ **Full-length Standing Bronze figure.** *An underofficer of the 103rd Infantry Regiment (4th Saxon Infantry) in field uniform with left hand on hip and the right hand holding the regimental colors. Excellent detail, about 12 inches high.* 430.00 475.00

☐ **Full-length Standing Ceramic figure.** *General Field Marshal von Moltke, one of the heroes of the Franco-Prussian War. Long blue general's frock coat of the period with blue trousers. Officer's visor cap with Prussian rosette on front. Order of the Iron Cross at neck. Well done and in beautiful color, about 11 inches high.* 140.00 150.00

CARTRIDGE BOXES

☐ **Imperial German Officer's Dress cartridge box.** *A Garde du Corps regiment. Highly polished black leather box with the Star of the Order of the Black Eagle in frosted silver and enamel. Attractive.* 300.00 330.00

☐ **Imperial German Officer's Dress cartridge box.** *26th Dragoon Regiment (Kings Dragoons - 2nd Wurttemberg). Highly polished black leather box with the silver and enameled Star of the Order of the Wurttemberg Crown on the flap. Excellent.* 300.00 330.00

☐ **Imperial German Officer's Dress cartridge box.** *Highly polished black leather with flap trimmed in silver and with a crowned "L" (Ludwig IV) within a wreath, all in silver, in the center of the flap.* 340.00 375.00

☐ **Imperial German Officer's Dress cartridge box.** *Saxon artillery regiments. Polished black leather box with silver flap trimmed in a very fancy gilt border. There is a crowned shield of the Saxon Arms superimposed upon a trophy of flags, all in gilt, on the center of the flap. Very impressive.* 475.00 600.00

☐ **Imperial German Other Ranks Field Service cartridge box,** *(Infantry Regiment No. 42) c. World War I. Thick pebble finished brown leather with belt loops and closure straps. Divided into metal compartments for cartridge clips. Inside top of box stamped in German "J.R. 42."* 20.00 30.00

Price Range

☐ **Prussian Other Ranks Grenadier cartridge box,** *c. 1780's. Large polished black leather box and flap. In the center of the flap is a stamped yellow metal disk with wide border with crown at the top. In the center of the disk is the cypher "FR" (Frederick Rex). On each corner of the flap is a large flaming grenade. The stamping of these decorations, particularly the grenades, lacks finesse. Finish is dulled consistent with age.* 325.00   360.00

☐ **Prussian Other Ranks Artillery cartridge box,** *c. 1700's. Polished black leather box and flap. In the center of the flap is a stamped brass flaming grenade with flames issuing from the top and from each side. In the center of the grenade is the cypher "FWR" (Frederick William Rex). The stamping is in good detail, much better than that in the Other Ranks cartridge box listed above.* 270.00   300.00

☐ **Regiment No. 42** *(Prince Moritz of Anhalt-Dessau's Infantry-5th Pomeranian). Box shows wear but is sound and complete and is an interesting memento of World War I, having been used by a soldier in an old Prussian infantry regiment.* 45.00   50.00

☐ **Third Reich (Nazi) Police Dress cartridge box.** *Highly polished black leather box and flap. In the center of the flap is the large Nazi insignia of stylized eagle with widespread wings grasping a swastika within a wreath, all superimposed across a larger wreath, all in silver color metal. This is a most interesting and seldom seen bit of Nazi memorabilia.* 300.00   330.00

☐ **U.S. Infantryman's cartridge pouch or box.** *Large size of thick black leather with a large "US" within an oval cartouche stamped in the leather in the center of the flap. Tin liners, complete with belt loops and straps and buckles, authentic. In unused condition, dingy from storage.* 125.00   135.00

☐ *In used condition, showing some scuffing and wear.* 70.00   75.00

COLLAR PATCHES AND SHOULDER STRAPS

THIRD REICH

☐ **General Officer's Set of collar patches and shoulder straps.** *Gold wire embroidered general's insignia on red background for collar patches. Gold and silver woven shoulder straps on red background with gilt shoulder strap buttons, excellent.* 175.00   195.00

☐ **General Officer's Single collar patch,** *as above.* 60.00   66.00

☐ **General Officer's shoulder straps.** *Matching pair of patches with insignia in gilt bullion on red background. Two white metal pips on each strap indicating rank of lieutenant general, excellent.* 91.00   100.00

Price Range

☐ **NSDAP (Nazi Political Party) collar patches.** *Red patch with burgundy piping. At top in gold wire embroidery, the Nazi eagle grasping a wreath enclosing a swastika. Under this two oak leaves forming a "V" with two acorns, also in gold wire embroidery. In excellent condition.* 181.00   200.00

☐ **NSDAP (Nazi Political Party) Administrative Officer's collar patch.** *Red background with burgundy piping. In center a metal Nazi eagle, wreath and swastika. Under this a row of oak leaves, all in silver color metal. Left and right patches, excellent.* 82.00   90.00

☐ **Panzer Officer's collar patch.** *Left patch only. Black patch piped in pink. In the center a metal matte gray skull and crossbones with the Roman numeral "XI" beneath in silver embroidery, excellent.* 82.00   90.00

☐ **Panzer Pioneer Officer's collar patch.** *Right patch only consisting of black background upon which appears a silver skull and crossbones. Patch has black/white piping, excellent.* 78.00   80.00

☐ **SA Brigade Leather collar patches.** *A pair. Dark blue patch with silver wire trim to edges. In the center two silver wire oak leaves with acorns and a pip, excellent.* 163.00   180.00

☐ **SS Officer's collar patches.** *A pair. Left is black with silver color wire border, right has the same border with silver color wire SS runes in the center, excellent.* 69.00   75.00

CROSSBOWS

The crossbow was the terror weapon from the time it was introduced some time in the early 1100's until it was rendered obsolete by firearms in the 1500's. Basically, the weapon consists of a heavy bow mounted across a stock at a right angle. A groove runs lengthwise on top of the stock. The short bolt or quarrel is propelled along this groove by the tension of the bow string. Near the rear of the stock is a simple trigger tripping arrangement for releasing the bowstring. It was very effective against the armor of the day and was twice outlawed for use against Christians by reigning Popes. Earlier examples are difficult to come by but later specimens are desirable collector items.

☐ **Crossbow,** *c. late 1500's. German, steel bow, ivory quarrel guide, bowstring appears to be original but is much worn and frayed.* 2350.00   2600.00

☐ **Crossbow,** *c. early 1500's. German, steel bow, no bowstring, well grained wood, ivory mounted, double triggers. An exceptionally well-made high quality weapon.* 2980.00   3300.00

☐ **Crossbow,** *c. early 1500's. German, a rather heavy specimen with steel bow, remains of original bowstring much frayed, heavy wood stock with some*

	Price Range	

carving, ivory mounts, shows age but condition is consistent with age............................... **3250.00** **3600.00**

☐ **Crossbow,** c. 1700's. A late model crossbow with musket-like rear stock and brass mounts, steel bow, bowstring intact, good condition.................. **1180.00** **1300.00**

☐ **Crossbow Arrows or Quarrels.** A set of 10 arrows or quarrels with several different shaped steel heads, wood shafts fletched with leather. Several with sharp pointed heads for use against light armor and several with blunt prongs for use against heavy armor. Quarrels and particularly as many as a set of 10 are seldom offered.................................. **1270.00** **1400.00**

DESK ORNAMENTS

☐ **Desk ornament.** Fixed to a polished black marble base is the bronze replica of a 42-cm howitzer projectile of World War I, complete with rotating bands. On the top of the nose or fuse is a finely detailed Iron Cross. On the top of the body of the projectile is a large finely detailed Imperial German Eagle with the wings extending down over each side. A bronze plaque appears on one side of the top of the base with an inscription which translated from the German reads "The Busy Bertha," this being the name given the big cannon. 4 x 6 x 2 inches. A most interesting memento of World War I. **100.00** **110.00**

☐ **Fascist desk ornament.** Well detailed cast brass Fascist fascine, party symbol of cylindrical bundle of rods with a Roman ax. Mounted on polished round black marble base. Very good. Approximately eight inches high.. **69.00** **75.00**

☐ **Fascist Desk Top Pencil/Pen holder.** Hollow fascine symbol for holding pencils and pens. Of silver color metal with gilt Roman ax. On polished black rounded base. Eleven inches high. Good condition. **64.00** **70.00**

☐ **Imperial German desk ornament,** c. World War I. Large 7 x 7 inch Iron Cross cast in bronze with black background and with raised bright brass edges, crowned royal cypher "FW," oak leaves, and the date "1813," the date of the institution of the Iron Cross order. Mounted on square good quality marble base. Overall height of 10 inches. An excellent article once belonging to a high ranking army official. **302.00** **330.00**

☐ **Iron Cross desk ornament.** Large fully detailed black and silver Iron Cross of the Imperial Era. Cast bronze mounted on a marble base, cross displays crowned "FW" on upper arm, oak leaves in the center and the date "1813" on the bottom arm, nearly 10 inches high. **200.00** **240.00**

Price Range

☐ **Metal desk ornament.** *In the form of a grenadier cap of the 1st Foot Guards (Erstes-Garde-Regiment zu Fuss). Heavy well detailed officer type, mounted on wood base, approximately 3 inches high.* 64.00   70.00

☐ **Nazi Party desk ornament.** *Of gilted bronze mounted on a well polished marble base. Well detailed Nazi Party emblem of eagle standing on wreath encircling a swastika. Overall height of 10 inches.* 168.00   185.00

☐ **Third Reich Panzer Officer's desk ornament.** *Extremely finely detailed cast bronze replica of a Panzerkampfwagen I, Ausf A (tank) of the 1935-1940 period. Has revolving turret. Mounted on a polished marble base. Over all dimensions approximately 6 x 4 x 4 inches. An exceptionally detailed piece.* 136.00   150.00

DRUMS

☐ **Austrian Military drum,** *c. early 1800's. Large drum very colorfully painted with the Austrian double-headed eagle with crown and crowned heraldic shield on breast bearing the initials "FI" of the sovereign Francis 1st. This is an old drum of considerable historic interest. Although not entirely complete, it is in very good condition consistent with its age.* 1180.00   1300.00

☐ **Malta Regiment drum.** *Identified as to the 1st Battalion of that regiment, blue drum with the regimental badge in full color, drum is of the present century and in excellent condition.* 455.00   500.00

☐ **Royal Air Force drum.** *Handsomely painted in full colors with the Royal Arms and the badge of the Royal Air Force, in excellent condition and very beautiful...*   475.00   525.00

☐ **Union Army drum,** *of the Civil War period. The drum is painted a dark blue with a large American Eagle and American Flag, all in full color. Both drum heads intact. Drum is in very good condition consistent with age and the colors are bright considering that the drum is over 100 years old. Unit or organization to which this drum belonged has not been identified but the drum is authentic.* 975.00   1075.00

ENTRENCHING TOOLS

☐ **British Army entrenching tool,** *World War II. Forged steel pick-mattock-shovel blade with center "eye" to accommodate a metal reinforced stout oak handle. Handle has accommodation for the spike bayonet. Complete with spike bayonet and metal scabbard all enclosed in khaki color canvas webbing carrier, very good condition.* 25.00   27.00

☐ **German (Third Reich) Combat Shovel.** *Steel shovel head with stout wood handle, complete with heavy*

German (Third Reich) Combat Shovel.

	Price Range	
leather carrying case, in very good condition and serviceable....................................	40.00	45.00
☐ **U.S. Entrenching Shovel.** *Sharp pointed steel shovel head with saw-teeth along one side, has folding steel handle, complete with olive drab canvas carrier with belt attachments, new condition.*	37.00	40.00

FIELD EQUIPMENT

Price Range

THIRD REICH

☐ **SS Gasoline Can** *(Jerry Can). With stamped SS runes.*	100.00	110.00
☐ **Wehrmacht Ammunition Can.** *Held 250 rounds of ammunition for the MG-34 and the MG-42 machine guns, with handles. If in good, nonrusted condition.*	15.00	16.50
☐ **Wehrmacht Binoculars.** *Standard issue, in useable condition.*	82.00	90.00
☐ **Wehrmacht Blanket.** *Standard issue.*	46.00	50.00
☐ **Wehrmacht Bugle.** *Brass issue item.*	59.00	65.00

Wehrmacht Canteen with Cup.

☐ **Wehrmacht Canteen with Cup.** *Wool covered canteen with inverted cup fitted to top, with attachment......*	37.00	40.00
☐ **Wehrmacht Grenade Bag.** *White canvas............*	100.00	110.00
☐ **Wehrmacht Hand Grenade.** *So-called "potato masher" type, inert.*	125.00	135.00
☐ **Wehrmacht K-98 Rifle Cleaning Kit.** *Complete set of cleaning rod, metal oiler tube, beaded metal pull through chain with stiff bristle brush, all in metal waterproof container.............................*	35.00	38.00
☐ **Wehrmacht Mess Kit.** *Three section.*	25.00	27.00
☐ **Wehrmacht Pioneer (Engineer) Haversack.** *Four compartments with "D" rings.*	60.00	65.00
☐ **Wehrmacht Training Sights.** *For the K-98 Mauser Rifle. These are available in several different types...*	6.70	7.75

Wehrmacht Mess Kit,
three sections, World War II.

JAPANESE ARROWHEADS

Like so many Japanese weapons, Japanese arrowheads are not only
unique in design but they are also minor works of art in themselves. Some of
the better quality combat examples and those used for parades and other
ceremonial purposes were made by celebrated artists and were signed by
them. The great variety of arrowheads and their uniqueness make them
highly desirable collectibles. The rear of the arrowhead was attached to a
long thin sharply pointed prong which fitted into the arrow shaft. There are
an interesting variety of designs depending upon the purpose for which
intended. The so-called **whistling** arrow had a fairly large hollow shaft of
wood or metal, pierced with openings in the top and sides. In flight, the air
rushing through these openings produced a loud whistling sound. Such
arrowheads were used for signaling. The **yasagiha,** or willow leaf pattern, had
straight sides and was sharply pointed. The **torgari** was somewhat similar
but was wider and was sometimes heart shaped. This type was often pierced
with various designs or was inscribed. The **karimata,** rope cutter, are in the
form of a "Y" with very sharp inner edges. These were used to cut ropes and
armor fastenings. The **watakusi,** flesh tearers, are cruel barbed arrowheads.
Some of these have barbs which retract as the arrowhead enters the flesh.
When an attempt is made to extract them the barbs open out inflicting a terri-

ble wound. The following are the types most often found. The very ornate ceremonial arrowheads signed by a famous master may sell for over $1,000.00.

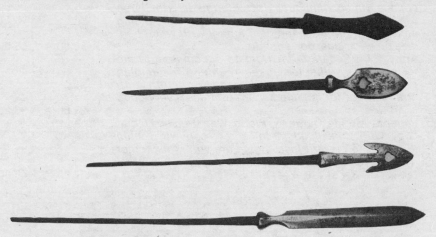

Top: Togari type. Second: Togari type with pierced design. Third: Watakusi type. Bottom: Yasagiha type.

	Price Range	
☐ **Arrowhead,** *c. 1500's. Pronounced spade shape. Signed "Hikohisa."*	123.00	135.00
☐ **Karimato arrowhead,** *c. 1400's. Signed but worn to extent that signature cannot be read. Otherwise very good.*	121.00	155.00
☐ **Togari arrowhead,** *c. 1500's. Decorated with cut out heart. Unsigned.*	105.00	115.00
☐ **Togari arrowhead,** *c. 1500's. Pierced design of a heart and a "boar's eye." Unsigned.*	123.00	135.00
☐ **Togari arrowhead,** *c. 1500's. Pierced design of four ovals about a circle. Signed "Toshimasa."*	132.00	145.00
☐ **Togari arrowhead,** *c. 1500's. Signed "Hikohisa."*	123.00	135.00
☐ **Togari arrowhead,** *c. 1500's. Signed "Rikiju."*	123.00	135.00
☐ **Togari arrowhead,** *c. 1500's. Signed "Yashitado."*	123.00	135.00
☐ **Watakusi arrowhead,** *c. 1600's. Signed "Gatsukane."*	123.00	135.00
☐ **Watakuse arrowhead,** *c. 1600's. Unsigned.*	96.00	105.00
☐ **Whistling arrowhead,** *c. 1500's. Semi-cylindrical horn head pierced on top and sides. Whistling arrows are not as common as the others. The horn head is a little unusual.*	163.00	180.00
☐ **Whistling arrowhead,** *c. 1500's. Wood turnip shape head pierced on top and sides. Unusual.*	150.00	165.00
☐ **Yanagiba arrowhead,** *c. 1500's. Signed "Masonob."*	123.00	135.00
☐ **Yanagiba arrowhead,** *c. 1500's. Unsigned.*	78.00	85.00
☐ **Yanagiha arrowhead,** *c. 1300's. Signed "Nobunaga." An older and classic example.*	154.00	170.00
☐ **Yanagiha arrowhead,** *c. 1700's. Unsigned.*	78.00	85.00

JAPANESE MISCELLANY

Price Range

☐ **Aerial Camera,** *World War II. All metal with black crackle finish, film area is rectangular with large wide view lens at front in cylindrical housing. Folding aerial sight on top, hand held model with wood handles on each side, good condition.* **50.00**   **55.00**

☐ **Army Tabi.** *Separated at front to accommodate big toe apart from other toes, used by snipers in climbing trees, olive drab color. Well made of cloth with arrangement for holding secure to ankles, very good condition, seldom seen.* **28.00**   **30.00**

☐ **Imperial Marine Canteen,** *World War II issue. Metal body with cork lined metal screw cap with chain attached to prevent loss. Complete with khaki color cloth cover upon which appears Japanese characters, shoulder strap, excellent.* **37.00**   **40.00**

Miniature O-No or Battle Ax.

☐ **Miniature O-No or Battle Ax.** *The O-No was the wicked battle ax carried by the military monks or yamabushi of ancient Japan. This beautiful miniature is slightly over 11 inches long, of gilt metal with enameled ax head with Japanese inscription. It comes in a fitted sandle wood case with closely fitted cover. This ax was given in limited numbers to those making a contribution to the Japanese war effort. A Japanese legend appears on the cover of the*

	Price Range	

presentation case. This is a most interesting artifact which is not often seen. **65.00** **70.00**

☐ **Naval Binoculars.** *Large size powerful binoculars with eye pieces set at angle, mounted on metal yoke and pin for mounting in fixture aboard ship, extremely free traverse and elevation, complete with fitted wood case. This is a unique and rare offering, excellent.* **225.00** **245.00**

GAS MASKS

☐ **French gas mask,** *World War I. Extremely early so-called bag type which fit over the head. Crude model which was chemically saturated to absorb gas, not very effective, complete with open top bag with shoulder strap, fair to good condition as are all specimens available, relic only.* **25.00** **27.00**

☐ **French gas mask,** *c. 1934, with steel helmet. So-called marine artillery type. Respirator hose leads from top of mask up, over and back of helmet to canister attached to back of helmet. This type allowed freer movement that the previous types. Not serviceable, relic only, fairly rare.* **170.00** **190.00**

☐ **French gas mask,** *World War II. Interesting model which allowed the canister to be attached directly to the bottom front of the mask or allowed the canister to be connected to the mask through a long hose. No carrying bag, relic only.* **18.50** **25.00**

☐ **German gas mask,** *World War I. Imperial German Army gas mask with large canister attached to the bottom front of the mask. Complete with carrying can and shoulder strap, relic only but in fair to good condition, as are most available.* **37.00** **40.00**

☐ **German gas mask,** *World War I, as above but without the carrying can.* **28.00** **30.00**

☐ **German gas mask,** *Third Reich, World War II issue. Army or Luftwaffe, complete with mask, filter, canister and carrying can with all straps, relic only, very good condition.* **46.00** **50.00**

☐ **German gas mask,** *as above but in excellent condition.* **55.00** **60.00**

☐ **German gas mask,** *Third Reich, World War II issue. The so-called "Volksgasmaske" or people's gas mask for issue to civilians. Large eye pieces and large attached canister, complete in original box of issue with instruction sheet in German, near mint condition but relic only.* **37.00** **40.00**

☐ **Japanese gas mask,** *World War II issue. Semi-rigid face mask with all head straps and large attached canister, without carrying bag, relic only.* **37.00** **40.00**

German Gas Mask and Carrying Can, Third Reich. World War II issue.

	Price Range	
☐ **U.S. gas mask,** *World War I. Complete including mask, hose, canister and bag, good condition but relic only.*	25.00	27.00
☐ **U.S. gas mask,** *present issue. All self-contained, complete with bag, serviceable.*	46.00	50.00

MODELS

☐ **French 155-mm Cannon model,** *c. World War I. Long barrel with split trail and treaded wheels. Although this model is made of wood, it is very detailed and authentic. Trail opens and barrel traverses and elevates, very good.*	145.00	160.00
☐ **Imperial German Bronze model of a Krupp Field Howitzer,** *World War I. Short howitzer type barrel mounted on field carriage with short trail and heavy treaded wheels. A howitzer shell rests at the rear of the trail on a cradle. Extremely well-made and authentic detail, mounted on a black marble base. Apparently made by Krupp as a presentation piece. Excellent and rare.*	300.00	330.00

Price Range

☐ **Mortar model.** *Model of a British mortar of the late 1600's or early 1700's. Exceptionally well made and detailed. Bronze reinforced mortar barrel mounted in bronze open frame on oak wood sled type mount. Barrel is engraved with finely detailed coat of arms superimposed upon trophy of battle flags. Also has original owner's crest as well as proof marks of foundry. Excellent condition and extremely rare.* 1900.00 2200.00

☐ **Naval Cannon model,** *c. mid-1700's. Most unusual model made entirely from marble. Well turned stepped barrel mounted on stepped marble naval type gun carriage with marble wheels. High polish has brought out the exceptional beautiful grain of the marble.* 154.00 170.00

☐ **Naval Cannon model.** *Fairly large size four ringed vented brass barrel mounted on stepped wood naval gun carriage with wood wheels. Brass elevating screw, very authentic detail, model of a mid-1700's cannon but made about 100 years ago.* 145.00 160.00

☐ **Siege Mortar model.** *Period of American Revolution. A fine antique model in brass with reinforcing rings. Mounted on original mahogany bed with exceptionally well-detailed brass features, including trunnion covers. Barrel activated by brass elevating screw as in full size weapon. All in all an excellent model.* 850.00 940.00

☐ **U.S. Cannon model,** *c. Civil War period. Large model of a Napoleon on field carriage with ammunition chest on wheeled carriage. Extremely well-executed both as to craftsmanship and authentic detail. Brass cannon barrel is bored and vented. It is mounted on a detailed brass field carriage with iron wheels. Brass elevating screw, wood ammunition chest with hinged lid mounted on brass field carriage with iron wheels. All gunner's tools with proper attachments. This is a museum piece.* 455.00 500.00

PAPER MEMORABILIA

☐ **Collection of Photographs of Nazi Officials,** *Army and Air Force officers. Each photograph is black and white and is very clear as to detail. Each is carefully mounted on a card bearing in some instances the personal autograph of the person and in other instances a short personal message as well as the autograph. There are at least one hundred photos in the collection, including Hitler, Rommel, Bomberg, Goering, Hesse, Von Rundstead, Milch, and others. This is a rare find for the personal photo and autograph collector.* 3000.00 3300.00

Price Range

☐ **Group of Imperial German Military Documents.** *Consisting of an officer's appointment as second lieutenant; patent of his promotion to first lieutenant, patent for his promotion to captain and finally a patent for his promotion to major in the army of Mecklenburg-Schwerin, signed by the reigning duke, Frederick-Franz. All are in excellent condition.* 123.00   135.00

☐ **Group of Imperial German Military Documents.** *Consisting of the individual's initial order to report to cadet school; a patent appointing him to the grade of Portepee Fhanrich; his certificate from the Prussian War Academy; his promotion to second lieutenant; promotion to first lieutenant; promotion to captain and promotion to major. The last two documents bear the personal signature of Kaiser Wilhelm II. All in excellent condition and interesting.* 145.00   160.00

☐ **Group of German Nurse's Documents.** *An interesting collection of three diplomas certifying her professional training, her workbook showing places of employment with official Nazi stamps, Nazi national insurance card, security card and official identification book containing her photo and personal details. Interesting collection of a person living in a dictatorship.* 100.00   110.00

☐ **Honorary Citizenship Document.** *Cities and towns of the Reich vied with one another in conferring honors on Hitler. One of the most common of these was making him an honorary citizen. Such is the present offering, which is typical. Hand lettered and illuminated in color on parchment.* 250.00   375.00

☐ **Imperial German Iron Cross Award Certificate.** *Dated and named to man in the 21st Infantry Regiment (Von Borcke's Infantry - 4th Pomeranian). For the Second Class Iron Cross.* 40.00   45.00

☐ **Large Framed Photograph of General Field Marshall Von Hindenberg.** *Black and white matte print shows Hindenberg in full uniform of his rank but without the helmet. He is wearing all of his many decorations. Print is mounted with a wide mat, all within an excellent quality glassed wood frame. Of particular interest and importance is Hindenberg's authentic autograph read - "Strength is needed in peace and war," followed by his signature.* 145.00   160.00

☐ **Letter from Eva Braun,** *Hitler's mistress, to a woman friend. Handwritten on her personal gray/blue stationery with the monogram "EB" in the upper left-hand corner, with envelope.* 1375.00   1525.00

☐ **Letter From Prison From Herman Goering,** *to his wife Frau Goering. Brief personal letter about self and wishing her well. Written on official prison camp stationery. Signed "Herman."* 1375.00   1525.00

Price Range

☐ **Nazi Iron Cross Award Certificate.** *Dated and named to a man in 209th Grenadiers. Signed by the Commanding General of the 58th Infantry Division.* 25.00   27.00

☐ **Nazi Navy Chaplain's Cross and Award Document.** *Contrary to what some have believed, there were chaplains in the Nazi armed forces. This unusual offering consists of the chaplain's symbol as a clergyman, a silver Latin pattern cross suspended from a long neck chain. The Honor Award is on excellent quality heavy paper and bears an embossed Nazi eagle stamp. It has a facsimile Hitler signature and the actual signature of Gross-Admiral Raeder. In original folder with gilt eagle on cover.* 975.00   1075.00

☐ **Nazi Party (NSDAP) Membership Book.** *Book is completely `illed in with details concerning the individual and contains his identification photo. With the book is a Membership Honor Pin with gold wreath encircling a black enameled swastika. Book and pin all bear the same party number. These are not too rare but they are extremely popular with collectors and thus cause the price to rise.* 348.00   385.00

☐ **Nazi Party (NSDAP) Membership Book.** *Similar to the above but without the honor pin. This reduces the collectibility considerably.* 78.00   85.00

☐ **Photo and Autograph of Mussolini.** *Large and sharp studio posed matte finish photo with his characteristic scowl. Bust view in Black Shirt uniform without cap. Authentic autograph with dedication to a comrade. Not framed. Approximately twelve by eighteen inches including mat. Fair to good.* 145.00   160.00

☐ **Promotion Order Concerning a Luftwaffe Officer.** *Paper authorizes the promotion of the officer from Generalleutnant (Lieutenant General) to General der Flieger (General of Flyers). The order is embossed with the official seal of the Nazi Records and Orders Commission. It is signed personally by both Hitler and Goering.* 805.00   900.00

☐ **Special Presentation Copy of Hitler's Book "Mein Kampf."** *This is an extraordinary offering. Massive especially printed and bound copy in red leather with silver decoration to covers and spine. Extra fine quality paper and printing. Cover bears above the Nazi eagle with "ADOLPH HITLER" and "MEIN KAMPF" below. The lower half of the cover has a swastika within a square border containing Nordic runes. The cover itself is outlined with a border containing similar runes. The spine is decorated with a swastika and runes. The back cover contains a border of runes in the upper half the arms of the Teleschow family. The lower half of the cover contains a nude mounted warrior brandishing on his left*

Price Range

arm a circular shield upon which appears an ancient form of the swastika. As noted, all this decoration is in silver. The book contains an inscription indicating its presentation to Otto Telschow, a high Nazi official on February 27, 1938. .... 1900.00   2200.00

PORTRAITS

☐ **Bust portrait.** Adolph Hitler standing with arms folded and uncovered, wearing plain uniform. Apparently is an excellent likeness. In gold leaf frame, portrait in oil............................... 835.00   925.00

☐ **Bust portrait.** Adolph Hitler, facing to his right instead of to his left as in the above portrait. Again, is uncovered but wears military overcoat with upturned collar over plain uniform. Again, apparently an excellent likeness. In deep gold leaf frame. 950.00   1050.00

☐ **Bust Portrait in Oil.** Kaiser Wilhelm II of Imperial Germany. He is uncovered but wears the black front and back plates of the gala (parade) uniform of his favorite regiment, the famed Garde du Corps. Portrait shows several neck orders, uniform is white with gold bullion trim, in gold leaf frame............... 1450.00   1600.00

☐ **Full Length portrait,** c. early 1800's. Czar Alexander 1st of Russia wearing a general's uniform. Excellent details of uniform, including cocked hat (held in left hand at side), and decorations, a well-executed portrait. 1270.00   1500.00

☐ **Bust portrait in Oil.** c. early 1800's. A captain in the 5th Bavarian Infantry Regiment. Good detail showing the officer in full regimentals, matted and framed, very good condition............................ 250.00   300.00

☐ **Pastel portrait.** Handsome young lieutenant (bust portrait) in dress uniform of the Kings' Uhlans (1st Hanoverian) No. 13. Again excellent uniform detail, in gold frame. 295.00   325.00

☐ **Portrait in Oil.** King Albert of Saxony (1871-1902) in the full uniform of a General Field Marshal. An extremely well executed portrait showing details of uniform and decorations, as well as an excellent likeness of the king, mounted in extra quality gold frame. 1400.00   1550.00

A few original paintings and drawings by Adolph Hitler are offered from time to time. Apparently only a very few are in private hands, the great majority being in the possession of museums. When offered for sale, the price usually varies between $5,000.00 and $6,000.00. The buyer is advised to secure authentication from an art expert.

RESERVIST'S FLASKS

☐ **Imperial Army reservist's flask.** Although not nearly as much in demand as regimental steins, these

Price Range

flasks which like the steins are mementos of the reservist's active service are good collectibles. The flasks listed here are typical. This particular offering belonged to a reservist of the 151st Infantry Regiment (2nd Ermland Infantry). On the front is a representation of the white regimental shoulder strap with number. The reverse has flags, mottoes and a soldier picture. Flask is of glass enclosed in aluminum and is circular in outline. Long neck with aluminum cap with figures of man and girl riding a goat. Complete with red, white and black shoulder cord. In very good condition. 123.00   135.00

☐ **Imperial Army reservist's flask.** *Similar overall shape to the above but glass flask is enclosed in nickel metal. This one belonged to a reservist of the 15th Infantry Regiment, Prince Frederick of the Netherland's Infantry - 2nd Westphalian. The elaborate front has embosed trophies and relief work. The back has a small compartment which snaps open to contain matches. Long nickel covered neck with cover with man, girl and goat figures, as above. Complete with red, white and black shoulder cord with two dependent tassels.* 136.00   150.00

☐ **Imperial German Navy reservist's flask.** *Navy flasks are few and far between and command a higher price. This offering is of hand painted porcelain within a gilt brass frame. Front is decorated with a scene of deck rating and a petty officer, one on each side of a wreath enclosing the reservist's name. Above are navy flags and a small painting of a battleship. Also has the name of the owner's ship, "SMS WITTLESBACH," and the dates "1904 1907." Rear of flask has scene of seaman leaving for service. Screw on gilt brass cap with Imperial German eagle finial. Red, white and black carrying cord.* 213.00   235.00

☐ **Imperial German reservist's flask.** *14th Hussar Regiment, Landgrave Frederick II of Hesse-Homburg's Hussars, 2nd Hessian. China flask in nickel metal case. Front decorated with a figure of a mounted hussar charging with lance. Bears dates 1905-1908, name of the barracks, Cassel, and regimental identification. Rear bears social scene of hussars and lady friends. Nickeled screw off cap is decorated with an Imperial German eagle finial. Has shoulder cord in the regimental colors of green and white. Excellent and seldom seen.* 145.00   160.00

☐ **Imperial German reservist's flask.** *138th Infantry Regiment, 3rd Lower Alsace Infantry, stationed at Stralsburg. This flask is most unique in that it is bottle shape instead of circular and is enclosed in red leather instead of metal. Pewter screw top cover to*

Price Range

flask opening. Front decorated in color with royal portraits, regimental number, the date "1888" and other designs. Complete with red, white and black shoulder cord. 78.00   85.00

☐ **Third Reich reservist's flask.** *Glass flask enclosed in aluminum. Front of flask has colored design of army motorcycle rider ascending a grade, back of flask has Nazi soldier standing at attention. Red, white and black shoulder cord. The Third Reich flasks are rather plain compared to those of the Imperial German Army. Plain aluminum covered neck and cap.* . . . 51.00   55.00

☐ **Third Reich Artillery reservist's flask.** *Aluminum covered glass flask with front showing Nazi soldier at attention in front of a field piece. Back of flask has view of horse artillery on the march. Aluminum covered neck with plain cap. Red, white and black shoulder cord.* 51.00   55.00

SABRETACHES

☐ **Austrian Officer of Hussars sabretache,** *c. 1830. Red velvet with elaborate gold and silver bullion trim consisting of very fancy borders and with a crowned cypher "F1" (Franz 1st) in the center. Old but in very good condition for its age, very colorful and Austrian examples are not often offered.* 1015.00   1025.00

☐ **British Officer's sabretache.** *The Lancashire Hussars, Victorian Period. Crimson velvet with double row of gilt bullion lace about edges, crowned reverse cypher "VR" in center with crown above, Tudor Rose in center of cypher, all in gilt bullion.* 700.00   775.00

☐ **British Officer's sabretache.** *The Royal Scots Greys. Black leather sabretache bearing the regimental badge.* 208.00   230.00

☐ **British Officer's sabretache.** *The 20th Hussars. Crimson background with two bands of gold lace about the edges. Crowned cypher "VR" in gold bullion appears in center under which appears "20" over an initial "H" within a circle. Under this appears a wreath with a ribbon bearing the honor "PENINSULA" on one side and "SUAKIN 1885" on the other, all embroidered in gold thread, very handsome.* 545.00   600.00

☐ **Officer's sabretache.** *8th Hussar Regiment (Emperor Nicholas II of Russia's Hussars - 1st Wesphalian). Dark blue with wide silver bullion and silver cord trim to edges. Large crowned cypher "FWR" in silver bullion in the center, Imperial German.* 500.00   550.00

Left: British Army Officer's Dress shoulder belt and pouch and a dress pouch. Right: Examples of British Army Officer's sabretaches.

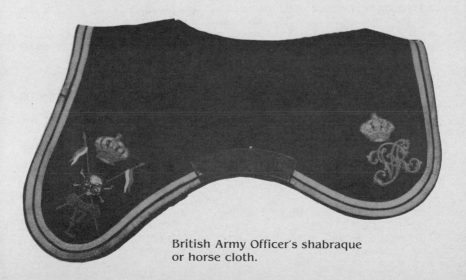

British Army Officer's shabraque
or horse cloth.

SHABRAQUES

Price Range

☐ **British Officer's shabraque.** *The 23rd Light Dragoons. Black cloth with wide band of silver bullion about the edges. In each corner appears the crowned cypher "GR" with "EGYPT" and "23 L.D." below.* 700.00   800.00

☐ **Imperial German shabraque.** *For an officer of the Prussian Guard Field Artillery. Blue cloth with red and black and silver thread edges. In each corner appears the Star of the Order of the Black Eagle in silver bullion thread.* 300.00   330.00

☐ **Imperial German shabraque.** *For an officer of Prussian Guard Grenadiers. Blue cloth with a broad outer edge trim of wide bullion lace and a narrow inner strip. In each forward corner a silver embroidered Star of the Order of the Black Eagle and in each rear corner a large gilt metal flaming grenade.* 300.00   330.00

SHIELDS

Authentic shields are items of growing interest to collectors. For a time they were often sought after for their decorative value but more and more they are being appreciated for their purely military connotation.

☐ **East African shield.** *A very unique shield of native craftsmanship fashioned from a huge turtle shell, long handle projects well above and below shield, most interesting.* 300.00   330.00

☐ **Ethiopian shield.** *Very old shield of heavy hard leather covered with purple velvet and delicate brass overlaid designs, has handle in back, authentic.* 205.00   225.00

☐ **Indian shield.** *Medium size circular steel shield with padded back. Unusual arrangement of six bosses near the edge of shield with larger center boss with sharp spike. Shield is richly etched with geometric designs.* 136.00   150.00

☐ **Indo-Persian shield.** *Large circular steel shield with four wide spread bosses, entire shield covered with engraved Oriental figures. This is a common type shield, often available.* 127.00   140.00

☐ **Persian shield.** *Circular steel shield with brass rim, four wide spread bosses. Shield is richly etched in gold with figures of ancient Persian kings and priests, large size and of extra quality.* 578.00   640.00

☐ **Persian shield.** *Circular brass shield of medium size, padded in back, four bosses, richly decorated in inlaid black, red and blue enameled designs.* 199.00   310.00

☐ **Persian shield.** *Large circular steel shield, padded back, four bosses, beautifully etched in gold with Oriental figures and animals.* 235.00   260.00

☐ **Scots shield** (target), *c. early 1700's. Fairly large circular stout wood shield covered with thick black*

Price Range

leather. Single central boss, row of brass studs around outer edge, circle of brass studs about central boss, eight ray star outlines in brass studs decorate shield, a less ornate example of this type. . .   430.00   475.00

☐ **Scots shield** *(target), c. early 1700's. Fairly large flat circular wood shield covered with brown leather, double row of brass studs about outer edge, no central boss, simple cross made of single rows of studs extending from circle made of two rings of brass studs in center. In the four sections of the shield formed by the cross are rosettes formed in brass studs, one circle or rosette to each quarter. This example is rather well worn but is complete and intact except for some missing studs. Good example.*   510.00   565.00

☐ **Turkish shield.** *Ancient shield of white bronze, circular with four semispherical bosses about center, beautiful gold and red floral design etched over all of shield, handle in back, lined. . . . .*   200.00   220.00

SHOULDER BELT PLATES

☐ **British Officer's shoulder belt plate.** *Royal Welsh Fusiliers. Rectangular gilt on copper plate with the three plumes and cornet of the Prince of Wales within the Garter, all in silver in the center. . . . .*   190.00   210.00

☐ **British Officer's shoulder belt plate.** *The Donegal Militia. Silver on copper rectangular polished plate with the traditional Irish Harp under the Victorian Crown, under the harp is a scroll bearing the word "DONEGAL." . . . .*   215.00   235.00

☐ **British Officer's shoulder belt plate.** *The 9th Foot (The East Norfolk Regiment). Gilt on copper rectangular polished plate bearing the regimental badge of a seated Britannia with British shield on left. Figure holds a spear with British Lion behind, under the figure a scroll bearing the title "IX REGT," a fairly rare plate. . . . .*   215.00   235.00

☐ **British Officer's shoulder belt plate.** *The Prince of Wales Volunteers. Oval silver on copper plate with plain edges, in the center the Prince of Wales plumes and coronet with motto, under this a shield bearing the initial "V" in a capital script letter. . . . .*   100.00   110.00

☐ **British Officer's shoulder belt plate.** *The Royal Marine Light Infantry. Polished gilt on copper rectangular plate with the Royal Crown with crowned lion above in the center. Above a scroll bearing the battle honor "GIBRALTAR," beneath a scroll bearing the motto "PER MARE PER TERRAM." . . . .*   132.00   145.00

☐ **British Officer's shoulder belt plate.** *The 20th Regiment. Large rectangular gilt on copperplate, raised edges and matte finish, in center of plate is laurel*

Price Range

wreath with crown above and with the Roman numerals "XX" within. 127.00   140.00

☐ **Pewter Cross belt plate,** c. early 1700's. Unknown European origin, oval in shape, high relief edge to plate, large crown over unrecognized arms, all in high relief, believed to be from a small independent state or duchy, very good condition. 215.00   235.00

☐ **U.S. Army Cross belt plate,** c. pre-Civil War. Circular brass plate with raised edge, in the center is an American Eagle grasping war arrows and laurel leaves, lead filled back, interesting bit of military Americana. 78.00   85.00

SHOULDER BELTS AND POUCHES

☐ **Austrian Cavalry Officer's shoulder belt and pouch or box,** c. late 1800's. Black leather belt with silver fittings, silver color metal box with gilt crowned double-headed Imperial Austrian Eagle, excellent specimen.   340.00   375.00

☐ **British Cavalry Officer's shoulder belt and pouch.** Leather belt covered with gold bullion trim in intricate pattern, gilt metal fittings, black velvet pouch flap with wide silver lace trim. A large Georgian crown of bullion thread is in the center of the flap. . . .   545.00   600.00

☐ **British Officer's shoulder belt and pouch,** c. early 1900's. The belt of leather trimmed with the gilt regimental lace of The Royal Scots Greys. Gilt belt mounts embossed with thistle design, silver flap to pouch bearing the Regimental (French) Eagle badge, heavily engraved border. 565.00   625.00

☐ **French Other Ranks shoulder belt and pouch.** For a musician of the Third Empire, black highly polished leather shoulder belt with brass trim including a lyre badge, polished leather pouch with brass edge to flap. Brass centerpiece to flap consisting of a trophy of military band instruments topped by a large lyre, interesting example of an Other Ranks shoulder belt and pouch. 140.00   150.00

☐ **Imperial German shoulder belt pouch.** Polished black leather with gilt "FWR" cypher, excellent but pouch alone. 145.00   160.00

☐ **Italian Officer's Dress shoulder belt and pouch.** Black leather belt with gilt trim including the cypher of King Victor Emanuel. Black leather highly polished pouch with silver metal trim, Silver Eagle of Savoy in center, very interesting. 200.00   220.00

☐ **Mecklenburg Officer's shoulder pouch and belt.** 1st Mecklenburg Dragoons (17th Imperial Dragoons), c. late 1800's. Leather shoulder belt with yellow, red and blue trim, with white metal fittings. White metal pouch with yellow metal heraldic star upon which

Price Range

appears the Arms of Mecklenburg in silver. Silver
pickers on chains attached to lion mask boss. These
were used in early days to clean the touch holes of
pistols, rare. 705.00   775.00

SHOULDER STRAPS

☐ **Antiaircraft Searchlight Battalion.** *Red strap with
winged bomb, the initial "S" (Scheinwerfer) and the
numeral "233" all in yellow.* 28.00   30.00

☐ **Imperial German shoulder straps.** *Single strap only,
for the field gray uniform.* . . . .

☐ **3rd Guard Regiment** *(Queen Elizabeth's Guard
Grenadiers). Gray cloth strap with yellow piping and
crowned "E" in red.* 15.00   16.00

☐ **5th Flieger.** *Gray shoulder strap with a winged propellor over the numeral "5" in red, not too common.*   25.00   27.00

☐ **6th Train Battalion.** *Gray shoulder strap piped in blue
with the numeral "6" in red.* 10.00   11.00

☐ **77th Infantry Regiment** *(2nd Hanoverian Infantry).
Gray strap with white piping and the numeral "77."* . .   7.30   8.00

☐ **92nd Infantry Regiment** *(Brunswick Infantry). Gray
strap with white piping and crowned "W" in red.* 17.50   19.00

☐ **106th Infantry Regiment** *(King George's Infantry - 7th
Saxon). Gray strap with Saxon cypher and crown in
red.* 14.50   16.00

☐ **115th Infantry Regiment** *(1st Grand Ducal Hession
Infantry - Lifeguard). Gray shoulder strap with
crowned cypher "EL" in red.* 25.00   27.00

☐ **123rd Infantry Regiment** *(King Charles' Grenadiers-
5th Wurttemberg). Gray strap with crown over Wurt-
temberg cypher in red.* 25.00   27.00

☐ **162nd Infantry Regiment** *(Lubeck Infantry - 3rd
Hanseatic). This is a pre-World War I white strap with
the number "162" in red.* 6.40   7.00

☐ **125th Infantry Regiment** *(Emperor Frederick, King of
Prussia's Infantry - 7th Wurttemberg). Gray strap with
"FR" cypher and crown in red, separately affixed.* . . .   21.00   23.00

TABLE SILVER

☐ **Small Butter Knife.** *Extra high quality silver, bearing
the Goering arms engraved on handle, from the per-
sonal table service of Herman Goering.* 190.00   210.00

☐ **Large Butter Knife.** *As above.* 235.00   260.00

☐ **Dinner Knife.** *From above table service of Herman
Goering, with the Goering arms engraved on the
handle.* 235.00   260.00

☐ **Dinner Fork.** *From same set as above, Goering arms.*   235.00   260.00

☐ **Soup Spoon.** *From one of Hitler's table services,
highest quality silver with Nazi eagle over "AH"
engraved on handle.* 280.00   310.00

Price Range

☐ **Dinner Fork.** *From one of Hitler's table services, high quality silver with raised design of Nazi eagle and initials "AH."* 190.00   210.00

☐ **Luncheon Fork.** *From above service.* 190.00   210.00

☐ **Formal Dinner Napkin.** *High quality cloth in floral design with embroidered Nazi eagle, swastika and initials "AH."* 127.00   140.00

WALL AND TABLE ITEMS

☐ **Fascist Party Headquarters Plaque.** *Sixteen inches long and seven inches high. Gray/green color iron. At each end is a fascine. The rectangular plaque between with raised edges has large raised gold color initials "PFR," for the party name of Fascist Republican Party. Weathered.* 41.00   45.00

☐ **Fascist Wall Devices.** *Flat back carved wood pair of party symbols with blades of iron axes turned toward each other. Twenty-one inches tall, with hanging hooks. Believed to be from the office of a high ranking party official. Very good condition.* 73.00   80.00

☐ **Kaiser Plaque.** *Of bronze, approximately eleven by six inches. Has raised relief edge and high relief of side view of Wilhem II's head and part of shoulders, dressed in the uniform of the Garde du Corps, his favorite regiment. His features and the details of the eagle crest helmet are excellent. Under his royal signature appears "I KNOW OF NO POLITICAL PAR-TIES - ONLY OF GERMANY," in German text. Has sturdy hook on reverse for hanging.* 91.00   100.00

☐ **Imperial German Army Presentation Trophy.** *On top of a tall gilt cylindrical column stands a Garde Eagle with outstretched wings. On the front center of the column is a silver and enameled Star of the Garde du Corps. Mounted on a finely turned, well finished and polished round wood base. Very good condition. Ten inches high overall.* 318.00   350.00

☐ **Military Table Lamp.** *This unique offering consists of a lamp made from the complete metal helmet of an Austrian dragoon officer, c. 1910. The black enameled helmet is complete in every way with gilt trim about the visors, gilt double headed Austrian eagle front plate, ornate gilt chin scales and very high comb with highly embossed lion fighting a serpent on each side. The helmet rests on a highly polished wood base. A metal tube enclosing the electrical cord extends up from the base through a hole pierced through the top of the helmet. Two lamp sockets are attached to the top of the tube and are covered with a large black shade. This is a beautiful lamp but would no doubt make a helmet collector cry to see a rare helmet treated in this way.* 550.00   610.00

WEHRMACT FIELD CLOTHING

Price Range

☐ **Afrika Korps (Africa Corps) Boots.** *Laced canvas and leather. Here again specific sizes are now difficult to obtain. Add $25.00 for wanted size if available. In very good condition.* 260.00   285.00

☐ **Camouflaged Face Mask.** *Cloth hood with eye and nose holes, worn under the helmet, very good condition, rare.* 155.00   170.00

☐ **Camouflaged Jacket.** *Completely reversible, camouflaged on one side and white on the other, very good condition, steadily becoming rare.* 470.00   520.00

☐ **Camouflaged Smock.** *Pullover with laced front, splinter pattern.* 515.00   570.00

☐ **Camouflaged Trousers.** *Completely reversible, as jacket, rare.* 225.00   245.00

☐ **Camouflaged Tunic.** *M-42 type, with four pockets, very good.* 290.00   320.00

☐ **Camouflaged Zeltbahn or Waterproof Shelter Triangle.** *This item could well be listed under field equipment as well as clothing. Strapped to individual field equipment when not in use. Basically part of a shelter tent, it was designed to be used also as a rain cape.* 35.00   38.00

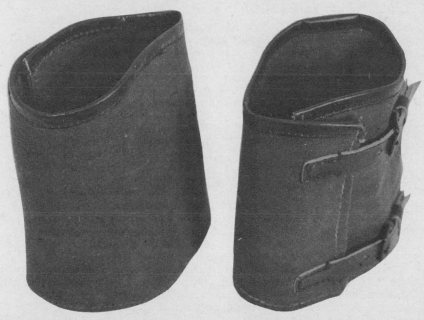

Wehrmacht Canvas Leggings.

	Price Range	

☐ **Leggings.** *Leather or canvas, short height, used with combat shoes in lieu of jackboots.* **12.00** **13.00**

☐ **Motorcyclist's Waterproof Coat.** *A cleverly designed long loose fitting rubberized garment, large pockets. This coat was designed with buttons placed so that the bottom of the coat on each side could easily be fastened about the wearer's legs for more comfort and freedom of movement when astride the motorcycle. A most unique item of clothing rapidly becoming scarce, very good condition.* **127.00** **140.00**

☐ **Panzer (Tank) Black Jacket.** *Short black double-breasted jacket designed especially for tank crews, difficult to find, in very good condition.* **475.00** **525.00**

☐ **Panzer (Tank) Black Trousers.** *Full length, gathered in at the bottom to fit the black leather lanced ankle boots, very good condition.* **100.00** **110.00**

☐ **Panzer Jacket** *(Tank Destroyer and Self-Propelled Assault Gun Units). As above jacket but of field gray material.* **410.00** **450.00**

☐ **Shoes.** *Black and ankle high, regular issue, in very good condition, difficult to obtain exact sizes. If available, add $15.00.* **69.00** **75.00**

SPECIALITY SLEEVE BADGES

☐ **Wehrmacht Other Ranks Trade and speciality sleeve badges.** *All on the left sleeve and are of yellow insignia on a dark green circular or oval background except as noted.*

☐ *Artillery Gun Layer. Vertical shell with flames projecting from top, within a wreath on oval background.* **11.00** **12.00**

☐ **Farrier Instructor.** *Horseshoe with star pip within the shoe on circular background.* **11.00** **12.00**

☐ **Medical Personnel.** *Snake on staff on circular background.* **11.00** **12.00**

☐ **Noncommissioned Officer,** *clothing stores. Gothic "Zg" on circular background.* **11.00** **12.00**

☐ **Noncommissioned Officer,** *supply administration. Gothic "G" on circular background.* **11.00** **12.00**

☐ **Noncommissioned Officer,** *ordnance technician. Gothic "F" on circular background.* **11.00** **12.00**

☐ **Noncommissioned Officer,** *saddler. Gothic "T" on circular background.* **11.00** **12.00**

☐ **Noncommissioned Officer,** *ordnance. Crossed rifles on circular background.* **11.00** **12.00**

☐ **Qualified Farrier.** *Horseshoe on circular background.* **11.00** **12.00**

☐ **Qualified Helmsman,** *engineer assault craft. Vertical anchor upon which is superimposed a small ship's wheel, all in silver on an oval background.* **13.00** **15.00**

☐ **Smoke Projector Operator.** *Vertical mortar shell in white within a white wreath, oval background.* **11.00** **12.00**

☐ **Veterinary Personnel.** *Snake on circular background.* **11.00** **12.00**

PROFICIENCY BADGES

Price Range

☐ **Wehrmacht proficiency badges.** *Worn by both Offi-cers and Other Ranks. All worn on upper right arm.*

☐ *Bergfuher badge. This proficiency badge was of metal and was worn on the left breast. Small metal pin back badge with silver edelweiss with gilt center within a white enameled oval bearing the following title, in Gothic, "HEERSBERGFUHRER." Worn by mountain troops qualified by at least one year of service as a mountain guide.* 60.00   65.00

☐ **Gebirgsjager badge.** *For qualified mountain troops personnel. On a dark green oval appears an edel-weiss flower with pale green stem and leaves, white petals and yellow stamen. This appears within a twisted mountaineering rope of gray with white piton. Design in machine woven high quality silk.* . . . 33.00   35.00

☐ **Jager badge.** *Worn by members of jager divisions and battalions. Dark green oval background with border of pale green rope. In the center of the oval three green oak leaves and an acorn on a brown twig, all in high quality embroidery.* 37.00   40.00

Military Field Police Eagle Army badge. *Appeared on the upper left sleeve of the uniform. Field gray oval cloth background upon which appears a wreath of oak leaves and the police eagle with wings spread beyond the oval. The eagle grasps a circular wreath of oak leaves within which is a swastika. For Officers the design was worked out in silver wire, for Other Ranks the eagle and the wreaths are worked out in orange thread while the swastika is worked out in black thread. Fairly rare, in very good condition.*

☐   **Officer's** 46.00   50.00

☐   **Other Ranks.** 28.00   30.00

☐ **Ski-Jager badge.** *Similar to the above described Jager badge but with the addition of crossed skis in copper/brown. This is by far the rarer of the three badges, for qualified ski riflemen.* 51.00   55.00

☐ **SS Musician's Breast badge.** *Black enameled alumi-num with roped aluminum border and aluminum lyre in center.* 30.00   32.50

MILITARY VEHICLES

Military vehicles have always had an especial fascination for almost every-one. Their very appearance suggests ruggedness and adventure, a chance as it were to escape from the ordinary. Unfortunately for those of modest means military vehicles are fast becoming a part of the antique automobile price complex. Not too many years ago a jeep could be bought for a few dollars as junk. Not so today for it would take in the neighborhood of $10,000 to buy one. The original Jeep was designed as a light military utility vehicle to a design submitted by Willis Overland to the U.S. Army. The first production models were designated Ma's. After the completion of some 16,000 of these the design was improved, including the adoption of a larger fuel tank. Following this the Ford Motor Company was given a contract to manufacture to Willys' design what was known as the Truck, Command and Reconnaissance, ¼ ton, Ford Model GPW. The Jeep soon became universally used among all of the Allied armies and in addition to being used as a utility and command vehicle was armed and used as a combat vehicle. Following World War II the Jeep was modernized in design and was designated the Car Utility M38.

The following prices are those currently prevailing for completely restored or refurbished vehicles in running order.

Left side view,
¾ ton Dodge Command Car.

	Price	Range
☐ **Jeep,** *Willys MB. World War II model.*	7400.00	8200.00
☐ **Jeep,** *Ford GPW. World War II model.*	7400.00	8200.00
☐ **Jeep,** *Model M38. 1951 or 1952 model.*	5600.00	6200.00
☐ **Jeep,** *Model M38-Al. 1952-1954.*	5080.00	5400.00
☐ **Jeep,** *Model M422-Al. 1960-1962.*	6500.00	7200.00
☐ **Jeep,** *Model M151-Al. 1963-1970.*	3890.00	4300.00
☐ **Jeep,** *Model M151-A2. 1970-1974.*	5780.00	6400.00
☐ **Armored Car,** *M-20.*	8400.00	9300.00
☐ **Mule,** *M274.*	2350.00	2600.00
☐ **Command Car,** *Dodge ½ ton.*	8400.00	9400.00
☐ **Command Car,** *Dodge ¾ ton.*	6050.00	6700.00

TANKS

The market on tanks still is difficult to estimate. Prices vary greatly. There is not any great quantity available at the present time. In several instances the price has been arrived at by just how much the buyer was willing to pay. At one time several years ago the small French Renault 2-man light tank and its American version could be had without engine for as little as $100.00. Today the collector may expect to pay several thousands of dollars for the same tanks. The very few Sherman tanks sell for around $3600.00. In view of the extremely fluid state of the market no attempt is made here to assign values.

NAZI BAYONETS, DAGGERS AND SWORDS

By far one of the most popular areas of militaria at the present time is that of edged weapons of the Third Reich. Consequently, there has been a constant increase in prices. This in turn has resulted in what almost amounts to a mass production of so-called "parts daggers" and reproductions. As noted elsewhere in this guide, there are marked differences of opinion as to the acceptance of "parts daggers" and reproductions. One opinion is that there is absolutely no place for them. Another opinion is that they are acceptable as they may be readily identified for what they are.

"Parts daggers" are those made up of genuine parts found in factory storage following World War II, plus new parts struck from original dies. In a few instances, daggers may be found which have been assembled entirely from original parts found after the war. These are usually referred to as "original parts daggers." Reproduction daggers are just that. They are weapons made up of reproduced parts. **Any artifact immediately becomes a FAKE when it is represented as being something other than what it really is.** There are far too many crooks operating in the collectors' field, particularly Third Reich items. Be certain of the honesty of the individual or organization with whom you are dealing. Insist upon proof!

As to the background of these weapons, it may be of some interest to know that the use by modern military organizations is something of an anachronism, a throw back, as it were, to those unsettled times when every person of quality armed himself with dagger or sword or both. Gradually the dagger went into discard. The saber was used for cavalry units and the sword retained for officers and senior noncommissioned officers. Civilians of high degree no longer found it necessary as a weapon or a status symbol. Then the time came when even the sword became merely a symbolic trapping in the military service, used only for ceremonial purposes. Even that died out for most part following World War I, although it has somewhat recently been resurrected for ceremonial purposes in most armed forces.

This was not so in Germany, however, particularly the Germany of Kaiser Wilhelm II and Hitler. In this period every effort was made to add to the respect for authority, both civil and military; from postmen and firemen to the highest government official; from other ranks to field marshals. Human nature being what it is, one of the surest and quickest ways to engender this respect is to clothe authority, both civil and military, both those of low and high degree, in some sort of colorful uniform and give them some symbol of authority, be it a swagger stick, baton, dagger or sword. Hitler, as past master of mob psychology, if ever there was one, knew this full well. With the able assistance of knowledgeable aides, he developed a plurality of uniforms, medals, decorations, accouterments, and fanciful trappings that put Kaiser Wilhelm's activity in the same field to shame.

The Teutonic mind, it seems, has always been attuned to edged weapons. Indeed it appears that they have often made a fetish of such weapons. To a somewhat lesser degree the same has been true of other ethnic groups in central and southern Europe, including the Austrians, Hungarians, Czechs, and Italians. Hitler was, of course, quick to recognize the psychological and propaganda value of edged weapons. In this he was aided and abetted by the cutlery makers of the famed Ruhr Valley. With an abundance of materials at hand, the forebearers of these people had for centuries been blade makers for the military, supplemented by the making of the world's finest cutlery. Military psychology, plus the desire of the weaponsmiths to increase their business, led to a close colaboration with the Nazi authorities to provide for a wide range of edged weapons of many different designs. Army, air force and naval forces, as well as para-military units and civilian organizations, even at lower levels, all had to have their own distinctive edged weapon. Certain variations were permitted in the design of presentation weapons, particularly those to be given to high ranking officials. Movement was always afoot to improve, change or modify existing designs.

In the following list, only those weapons usually available to collectors are noted. It is not deemed worthwhile to list those exotic weapons where only one, two or three specimens are known to exist. Such specimens far exceed the purchasing power of collectors except for the most affluent and for museums.

Fortunately for the collector and historian, there are a number of excellent books available on Nazi edged weapons. These are listed in the Reference section of this guide.

It is important to again note that the prices of all militaria are constantly going higher and higher. The following is a guide to value current at the time this is being written. All prices are for items in excellent condition. A price list of "parts daggers" and reproductions follows this price list.

BAYONETS

	Price Range	
☐ Army Dress bayonet, *short model.*	41.00	45.00
☐ Army Dress bayonet, *long model.*	41.00	45.00
☐ Army Dress bayonet, *with stag grips.*	60.00	65.00
☐ Army Engineer Troops bayonet, *dress.*	115.00	125.00
☐ Fireman's Dress bayonet, *short model.*	60.00	65.00
☐ Fireman's Dress bayonet, *long model.*	60.00	65.00
☐ Fireman's Sawtooth bayonet, *short model.*	125.00	135.00
☐ Fireman's Sawtooth bayonet, *long model.*	125.00	135.00

Mauser Service bayonet, complete with scabbard.

Police Dress bayonet with clamshell langet.

	Price	Range
☐ **Mauser Service bayonet.**	23.00	25.00
☐ **Police Dress bayonet,** *short model.*	275.00	300.00
☐ **Police Dress bayonet,** *with clamshell langet.*	325.00	360.00
☐ **Police Slotted Service bayonet,** *long.*	170.00	185.00
☐ **Police Unslotted Service bayonet,** *long model.*	154.00	170.00

DAGGERS

DEUTSCHE REICHSBAHN (German National Railway System)
☐ **Leader's dagger.** 655.00   725.00

☐ **Leader's dagger for Railway Water Protection Police.**
This unit had responsibility for railway activities in connection with harbors, canals and inland waterways. 865.00   950.00

DEUTSCHER LUFTSPORT-VERBAND or DLV (German Air Sports Formation)
☐ **Flyer's dagger.** *Of some interest is the fact that this is the longest of all standard Third Reich daggers. It was also the pattern for the First Model Luftwaffe dagger.* 1720.00   1900.00

☐ **Flyer's dagger.** 320.00   350.00

DEUTSCHER SCHUTZEN-VERBAND (German Rifle Association)
☐ **Worn by all members when in uniform.** 365.00   400.00

DEUTSCHES ROTES KREUZ or DKR (German Red Cross)
☐ **Hewer for Subordinate Ranks.** *Broad blade with saw-tooth back, square point, designed to do double duty as an identification symbol and as a tool for removing splints, etc.* 154.00   170.00

☐ **Leader's dagger** *(not a hewer).* 320.00   350.00

DIPLOMATEN UND STAATSBEAMTE (Diplomats and Career Officials)
☐ **Dagger for Members of the Foreign Ministry.** *The Foreign Office occupied a most important place in the governments of Germany from the First through the Third Reich. The daggers worn by personnel in these agencies are rare.* 1000.00   1100.00

☐ **Government Official's dagger.** 910.00   1000.00

HEER (Army)
☐ **Officers' dagger,** *with engraved blade.* 275.00   300.00

☐ **Officers' dagger,** *with plain blade.* 132.00   145.00

Nazi Army Officer's dagger with plain blade.

Price Range

HITLER JUGEND or HJ (Hitler Youth)
☐ **Youth Knife.** *Bayonet type hilt with medium width pointed knife blade. This item is very often faked.* ...   73.00   80.00

KREIGSMARINE DAGGER (Navy)
☐ **First model.** *This is the model 1919 Navy dagger with flame shaped pommel. For officers, noncommissioned officers and naval cadets.* 200.00   220.00
☐ **Second Model.** *Pommel in the form of the Nazi eagle with folded wings, for wear as above.* 295.00   325.00

LUFTWAFFE DAGGER (Air Force)

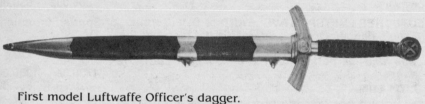

First model Luftwaffe Officer's dagger.

Luftwaffe Officer's dagger, second model.

☐ **First model.** *For officers, officer candidates and non-commissioned officers.* 265.00   290.00
☐ **Second model.** *For officers and officer candidates who had successfully completed prescribed examinations.* 160.00   175.00
☐ **Second model,** *with engraved blade.* 275.00   300.00

NATIONALPOLITISCHE ERZIEHUNGSANSTALT or NPEA (National Political Educational Institute)
☐ **Leader's dagger.** 1550.00   1700.00
☐ **Student dagger.** 325.00   360.00

Price Range

NATIONALSOZIALISTISCHES FLIEGERKORPS or NSFK (National Socialist Flying Corps)
☐ **Model 1937,** *similar to DLV Flyer's knife but with NSFK insignia.* 295.00   325.00

NATIONALSOZIALISTISCHES KRAFFAHRKORPS or NSKK (National Socialist Motor Corps)
☐ **Service model** *for wear by all ranks, prior to 1936.* 160.00   175.00
☐ **Service model** *for all ranks, adopted 1936.* 434.00   480.00

POLIZEI UND FEUERWEHR (Police and Fire Departments)
☐ **Dress Ax.** *Ornamented head with black wood handle. This is a dress version of the practical hand ax required to be carried by all firemen on duty, not carried by fire officials.* 385.00   425.00
☐ **Official's dagger.** *One of the longest blades of all Third Reich daggers.* 305.00   335.00

POSTSCHUTZ (Postal Protection Service)
☐ **Leader's dagger.** 950.00   1050.00

REICHSARBEITSDIENST or RAD (Reichs Labor Service)
☐ **Leader's Pattern Hewer.** *Plastic grips in lieu of the staghorn grips of the former pattern, generally better quality overall.* 325.00   360.00

Reichs Labor Service (RAD) hewer.

☐ **Standard Pattern Hewer,** *worn by all ranks from 1934 to 1937 when a Leader's pattern was introduced, not a dagger but a heavy broad blade knife.* 215.00   235.00

REICHSBUND DEUTSCHE JAGERSCHAFT (German National Hunting Association)
☐ **Knife,** *authorized for wear by all members of the organization. The pattern of the knife worn by all this conservation association was a holdover from that used for many years prior to the Third Reich.* 210.00   345.00

REICHSFORSTDIENST (National Forestry Service)
☐ **Assistant Forester's cutlass.** 310.00   445.00
☐ **Senior Forester's cutlass.** 450.00   495.00

REICHSLUFTSCHUTZBUND or RLB (German Air Protection Federation)
☐ **Leader's dagger,** *first model.* 573.00   635.00
☐ **Subordinate's dagger,** *first model.* 397.00   440.00

	Price Range	
☐ **Leader's dagger,** *second model.*	475.00	525.00
☐ **Subordinate's dagger,** *second model.*	310.00	465.00

SCHUTZSTAFFEL or SS (Elite Guard)
☐ **Service dagger** *for all ranks of the SS.*	273.00	300.00

STURMABTEILUNG or SA DAGGER (Storm Troops)
☐ **Standard model,** *for wear by all ranks. Design follows that of a 16th Century Swiss dagger.*	138.00	150.00
☐ **Rohm Honor dagger.** *As above but bears etched dedication from SA Chief of Staff Ernst Rohm which reads "In Herzlicher Freundschaff Ernst Rohm," or "In Cordial Comradeship, Ernst Rohm."*	560.00	620.00
☐ **As above** *but with inscription ground off. After Rohm's fall from authority and consequent assassination, it was ordered that the inscription be ground off the blade or the dagger destroyed.*	222.00	245.00

TECHNISCHE NORTHILFE or TENO (Technical Emergency Corps)
☐ **Leader's dagger.**	1023.00	1125.00
☐ **Subordinate's Hewer.** *Could be used as a hacking knife in the event of an emergency.*	475.00	525.00

ZOLLDIENST (Customs Service)
This was actually an extension of the dreaded Gestapo and was concerned with border control.

☐ **Land Customs dagger.**	430.00	475.00
☐ **Water Customs dagger.**	1293.00	1425.00

REPRODUCTION DAGGERS (Replica)
☐ **Heer** *(Army)*	90.95	99.95
☐ **Hitler Jugend or HJ** *(Hitler Youth) knife.*	23.50	25.00
☐ **Luftwaffe** *(Air Force).*	90.95	99.95

Hitler Youth Knife replica.

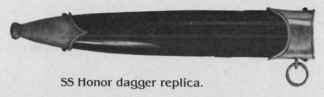

SS Honor dagger replica.

	Price Range	
☐ **Schutzstaffel or SS** *(Elite Guard) honor dagger (Leaders)*	100.00	110.00
☐ **Schutzstaffel or SS** *(Elite Guard) standard service dagger.*	78.00	84.95
☐ **Strumabteilung or SA** *(Storm Troops)*	78.00	84.95

SWORDS

BERGBAU (Miner's Organization)

☐ **Official's sword.**	254.00	280.00

DIPLOMATISCHER DIENST (Diplomatic Service)

☐ **Official's sword.**	2900.00	3200.00

Nazi Army Officer's sword, with plain blade.

HEER (Army)

☐ **Officer's.**	146.00	160.00
☐ **Officer's,** *with engraved blade.*	250.00	275.00
☐ **Officer's,** *with damascus blade.*	588.00	675.00
☐ **Officer's,** *with lionhead pommel.*	180.00	195.00
☐ **Officer's,** *lionhead pommel with engraved blade.*	295.00	325.00
☐ **Officer's saber,** *with nickel finish.*	100.00	110.00
☐ **Officer's saber,** *with brass finish.*	125.00	135.00

KREIGSMARINE (Navy)

☐ **Officer's.**	283.00	315.00

LUFTWAFFE (Air Force)

	Price	Range
☐ **Officer's,** *plain blade*	200.00	220.00
☐ **Officer's,** *engraved blade.*	290.00	320.00

POLIZEI UND FEUERWEHR (Police and Fire Departments)

☐ **Fire department official,** *with leather scabbard*	455.00	500.00
☐ **Police noncommissioned officer.**	150.00	165.00
☐ **Police officer.**	187.00	195.00

SCHUTZSTAFFEL or SS (Elite Guard)

☐ **Noncommissioned Officer.**	254.00	280.00
☐ **Officer Candidate,** *senior pattern.*	270.00	295.00
☐ **Officer Candidate,** *subordinate pattern.*	245.00	270.00
☐ **Officer's sword.**	235.00	370.00

ZOLLDIENST (Customs Service)

☐ **Customs sword** *(land)*	300.00	340.00

ADDENDUM

Upon very rare occasions, an extraordinary Nazi edge weapon will appear for sale on the collectors' market. As was mentioned in the introduction, Goering's wedding sword was put up for auction with a reserve (starting) bid of $60,000.00. The two following examples are rather rare items which at infrequent times may appear for sale. Of course, the value of these one of a kind artifacts increases very rapidly.

Rare Nazi Prototype Dagger (one of a kind.)

☐ **Rare Prototype Dagger.** *This one of a kind weapon by the famous Eickhorn shops is cased and represents the very top in Nazi daggers. Truly a work of art as well as a weapon. Scabbard and fittings are of nickel. Grips are wire wound white plastic. Four well defined swastikas within circles decorate the pommel. Nazi party emblem of eagle and swastika within a wreath on each side of the weapon form the crossguard. Finest quality blade bears the Eickhorn mark. The scabbard is beautifully decorated with a leaf and berry motif with approximately each third of the scabbard further decorated with crossed bands. A dagger of this quality is rarely offered. Consistent with its quality it is fully authenticated.* 23000.00

☐ **Presentation sword,** *given by Heinrich Himmler to his good friend Frederick Weber. High quality damascus blade. Fittings on sword and scabbard are extremely*

Himmler Presentation sword.

Price Range

*high quality silver. Inscription on the blade reads in
translation, "To my Beloved Friend, Frederick Weber.
Presented by H. Himmler, January 30, 1942. Reichs-
fuhrer of the SS." The other side of the blade bears
the legend "My Honor is called Loyalty." Blade elabo-
rately decorated with swastikas and SS runes.* **8400.00**   **9300.00**

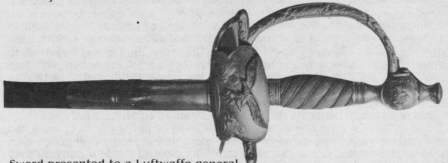

Sword presented to a Luftwaffe general.

☐ **Sword Presented to a Luftwaffe General.** *This specimen was made by the famous Eickhorn firm of swordsmiths. The scabbard had gilt fittings. The light
orange color grip is wound with gilt wire. Pommel
and guard also of gilt. On the folding guard is a silver
Luftwaffe eagle. Blade has blued panels, dedication
from Goering on the blade.* **6600.00**   **7300.00**

ORDERS, DECORATIONS AND MEDALS

The origin of the custom of awarding orders, decorations and medals is
lost far back in antiquity. Ancient China is credited by some military
historians for beginning the giving of awards for valor and service. Others
ascribe it to Old Testament times noting that the famous Jewish historian
Josephus in his monumental work "Antiquities of the Jews" relates that the
Persian conqueror Alexander gave a gold button to Jonathan the high priest
as a reward for leading the Jews in victory over Alexander's Syrian enemies.
We know from historical evidence that both ancient Greece and Rome
recognized outstanding acts of valor by awarding special gifts such as silver

spearheads. This began a custom of giving special weapons for awards which was followed on down through the years by all armies including the United States. This was particularly true in this country during the Revolutionary War, the Mexican War and the Civil War when numbers of special presentation swords were awarded to certain officers.

Before going on to review orders decorations and medals as we know them today, it is necessary that we define just what we are discussing. Generally speaking orders are usually reserved for members of royalty, nobility or to individuals for extremely distinguished civil or military achievement. Those awarded orders became members of an elite group with special privileges. Decorations are **individual** awards for specific acts of gallantry, valor or exceptional meritorious service. On the other hand, medals are given in quantity to many individuals for participation in battles or war. However, at least one decoration, the U.S. Medal of Honor, while strictly a decoration has the word "medal" in its title.

Individual decorations as we know them today most probably began with a special award struck for Sir John Kendal, Prior of the English Knights of St. John for his heroic services in relieving the Island of Rhodes, this in 1480. In succeeding years, there is record that individual awards or decorations were given to certain high-ranking officers. The first campaign medal was given to selected individuals only and not to all who took part in the action. This was the "Ark in the Flood" medal awarded in the name of Elizabeth I in 1558 to commemorate the defeat of the Spanish Armada. The front or obverse of this medal bears the likeness of Elizabeth. The reverse bears the design of an ark-like naval vessel, hence its name. It was awarded to officers only.

The custom of awarding a campaign medal to **all** participants, officers and enlisted men alike originated with the Honorable East India Company which was a government and a law unto itself, employing its own army. Among these medals for service were the Deccan Medal (1778-1784), the Mysore Medal (1791-1792) and the Scringapotam Medal (1799).

The first British Government campaign medal was the Waterloo Medal for all participants in 1816 in that most important and memorable battle to curb the ambitions of Napoleon. So began the custom in the British Service.

The founding fathers of the United States took a dim view of decorations and medals, believing that they were too militaristic and were only a holdover of royal customs. Nonetheless, a few individual swords were made in addition to the usual swords of honor. In commemoration of the evacuation of Boston by the British in 1776, Congress awarded a gold medal to General George Washington. Three years later an award was presented to John Paul Jones for his victory over **H. M. S. Serapis.** These were large plaque-like awards meant for display and not for personal wear.

Washington himself was keenly aware of the value of decorations and medals in creating and maintaining morale and using his authority as Commander-in-Chief, he authorized the Purple Heart. His general order establishing the award is dated August 7, 1782 and reads in part as follows:

"The General, ever desirous to cherish a virtuous ambition in his soldiers, as well as to foster and encourage every species of Military merit, directs that whenever any singularly meritorious action is performed, the author of it shall be permitted to wear on his facings, over his left breast, the figure of a heart in purple cloth, or silk, edged with narrow lace or binding. Not only instances of unusual gallantry, but also of extraordinary fidelity and essential service in any way shall meet with a due reward . . .

The road to glory in a patriot army and a free country is thus opened to all. This order is also to retrospect to the earliest days of the war and to be considered as a permanent one."

Interestingly enough, only three Purple Hearts were awarded under Washington's order. These were received by three sergeants. The Purple Heart did not survive the Revolutionary War. However, it was revived in a different form on Washington's birthday in 1932, by an order of the President of the United States. The medal or rather decoration is given for wounds resulting from enemy action and which require the attention of a medical officer. It is a purple enameled heart within a border of light bronze. The obverse bears the profile of Washington with his coat of arms above. The reverse has a bronze heart with the legend "For Military Merit."

The highest ranking decoration which this country gives is, of course, the Medal of Honor, authorized on December 21, 1861. Originally created for the Navy only, it was authorized for the Army six months later. At first the Medal of Honor could be awarded only to enlisted men. In 1863 the Army authorized its award to officers also. It was not until 1904 that Navy and Marine officers became eligible for it.

The design of the Medal of Honor has been modified through the years. At the present time, there are some differences in the design of the five-pointed star and the central medallion. The Army star is suspended from an American Eagle and bar bearing the word "VALOR." The Navy version has the star suspended from a plain anchor. With the separate establishment of the air arm independent of the Army and designated the Air Force, the award of the Medal of Honor was extended to the new combat arm. More recently, a new design has been instated for the Air Force. A five-pointed star of different design is suspended from a vertical aircraft with thunderbolts all about. This is suspended from a bar bearing the word "VALOR." The neck ribbon of the three awards is a blue ribbon with a flat turnover bearing 13 white stars. The decoration is suspended from this.

A decoration known as the Navy Medal of Honor 1917-1918 was awarded sparingly for valorous service during World War I. This decoration consisted basically of a plain gold cross with a plain anchor on each arm. Between the arms of the cross is a wreath encircling an octagon medallion bearing the Arms of the United States and the legend "UNITED STATES NAVY 1917-1918." The cross is suspended from a blue ribbon upon which are 13 white stars, the ribbon attached to a bar bearing the word "VALOR." The bar was pinned to the neck ribbon. This decoration is very rare.

Our country did not get around to awarding campaign medals until 1898 when the Dewey Medal was authorized. This medal was given to all naval personnel taking part in the battle of Manila Bay during the Spanish-American War. In this action the rapid and accurate gunfire of the American warships under Dewey's command destroyed the Spanish fleet.

For many years it has been the custom of the great majority of nations to award decorations to high officials and ranking military officers of friendly countries. It was not until July 20, 1942 that the United States had a decoration which could be awarded to foreigners. At that time the Legion of Merit was created by Congress. All other American decorations are restricted to our own citizens alone. Our Government now acknowledged that we did need to recognize officials of other countries, particularly in view of close association of our allies in World War II.

The Legion of Merit was created in four degrees for award to foreigners. These degrees are chief commander, commander, officer, and legionnaire. This decoration is awarded to members of our own armed forces without regard to degree, the ribbon and medal of the legionnaire degree being given. The Legion of Merit is awarded to "Personnel of the armed forces of the United States and the Philippines: and personnel of the armed forces of friendly foreign nations who, since September 8, 1939, shall have distinguished themselves by exceptionally meritorious conduct in the performance of outstanding services to the United States."

The basic part of the Legion of Merit is a five-pointed heraldic star. This star has a blue enameled center with 13 white stars surrounded by clouds outlined in gilt. The edges of the white enameled cross are outlined in red enamel and gilt. Crossed war arrows, point outward, appear between the arms of the cross. The star is backed by a green enameled laurel wreath with details in gilt. The chief commander degree is in the form of a three-inch plaque worn on the left breast in the manner of the high decorations awarded in other countries. The commander degree is worn hanging from a neck ribbon. The degrees of officer and legionnaire are worn suspended from a ribbon worn on the right breast. The ribbon for each degree is purple edged in white. This decoration is awarded to members of our own armed forces without regard to degree and the ribbon and medal of the legionnaire degree are worn.

The following price guide does not pretend to list all decorations and medals, only those usually available from dealers and auction houses. The extremely rare items which are not regularly available to collectors are not listed.

In connection with the collecting of decorations and medals given by the United States, it should be noted that Federal law prohibits the sale of such awards but does permit them to be offered on a trade basis. In buying such items, it is required that an article or articles of trade, such as stamps, etc., be exchanged. The nature and value of the trade items can easily be worked out with the dealer.

AUSTRIA

	Price Range	
☐ **Order of Maria Theresa.** *Badge. Order founded in 1757. The second highest order of the Austrian Empire. White enameled slightly modified maltese cross with gold edge. In the center a white enameled ribbon bearing the motto "FORTITUDNI." (Bravery) in gold letters. Red enameled center with horizontal white enameled stripe. Reverse bears a green enameled ribbon bearing the cypher "M.T.F.," (Marie Theresa and her husband Franz.)*	600.00	675.00
☐ **40th Year Anniversary of Coronation of Francis Joseph I.**	28.00	30.00
☐ **Francis Joseph Order.** *With crown.*	40.00	45.00
☐ **1914-1918 Medal.** *With swords.*	20.00	25.00
☐ **Order of Merit,** *First Class. Sash, badge and bow, complete.*	235.00	260.00

Price Range

☐ **Order of the Four Roman Emperors,** *Grand Officer, Second Class. Including breast star, neck badge, neck ribbon, cased.* 440.00 500.00
☐ **Red Cross Medal of Merit.** *For women.* 35.00 38.00
☐ **Signum Laudis,** *Emperor Karl of Austria. With crossed swords.* 18.50 23.50
☐ **60 Year Jubilee Cross of Francis Joseph I.** 18.50 23.50

BELGIUM

☐ **Croix de Guerre.** *With palm.* 40.00 45.00
☐ **Order of Leopold.** *Commander's neck badge, crown suspension, full neck ribbon.* 220.00 250.00
☐ **Order of Leopold II.** *Gold medal of the order, cased.* 39.00 45.00
☐ **World War I Victory Medal.** 20.00 22.00

CANADA

☐ **Air Efficiency Award,** *1944, George VI.* 100.00 125.00
☐ **Defence Medal,** *1945.* 16.00 24.00
☐ **Efficiency Decoration,** *E.II.R. (Elizabeth II).* 75.00 90.00
☐ **Efficiency Decoration,** *G.R.V. (George V).* 40.00 50.00
☐ **Efficiency Decoration,** *G.R.VI (George VI).* 30.00 45.00
☐ **Efficiency Medal,** *Elizabeth II.* 75.00 85.00
☐ **Efficiency Medal,** *George V.* 45.00 55.00
☐ **Efficiency Medal,** *George VI.* 40.00 50.00
☐ **Forces Decoration,** *Elizabeth II.* 50.00 65.00
☐ **Forces Decoration,** *George VI.* 95.00 120.00
☐ **General Service Medal,** *1866, bust of Queen Victoria on circular bronze medallion, Fenian Raids.* 150.00 175.00
☐ **General Service Medal,** *1866-70, Fenian Raids.* 225.00 275.00
☐ **General Service Medal,** *1870, Red River.* 900.00 1100.00
☐ **Korean War Medal,** *1951.* 35.00 45.00
☐ **Medal of Bravery,** *instituted 1972, circular medallion with maple leaf.* 125.00 150.00
☐ **Memorial Cross,** *Elizabeth II.* 35.00 40.00
☐ **Memorial Cross,** *1919, George V.* 15.00 20.00
☐ **Memorial Cross,** *George VI.* 20.00 25.00
☐ **Memorial Plaque,** *1919.* 15.00 20.00
☐ **Mercantile Marine War Medal,** *1919.* 20.00 25.00
Note: In American terminology, "mercantile marine" is "merchant marine."
☐ **Meritorious Service Medal,** *Edward VII, "CANADA" on reverse.* 150.00 175.00
☐ **Meritorious Service Medal,** *GeorgeV, "CANADA" on reverse.* 150.00 175.00
Note: The above medals are identical to corresponding British issues, but for the word "CANADA" on the reverse sides.
☐ **Military Cross,** *Korea.* 100.00 125.00
☐ **Military Cross,** *World War I, cross-within-cross with crowns at each terminal.* 75.00 90.00
☐ **Military Cross,** *World War II.* 75.00 90.00
☐ **Military General Service Medal,** *Chateauguay.* 1200.00 1300.00

	Price Range	
☐ Military General Service Medal, *Chrystler's Farm.* . . .	1300.00	1500.00
☐ Military General Service Medal, *Ft. Detroit.*	1300.00	1500.00
☐ Military General Service Medal, *with multiple clasps.*	2150.00	2300.00
☐ Northwest Canada Medal, *1885.*	500.00	550.00
☐ Order of Canada Medal of Service. *"Service" on one side, maple leaf on reverse.*	175.00	200.00
☐ Order of The Companions of Honour, *oval medallion surmounted by crown.*	RARE	
☐ Royal Canadian Air Force Long Service and Good Conduct Medal, *Elizabeth II.*	85.00	95.00
☐ Royal Canadian Air Force Long Service and Good Conduct Medal, *George VI.*	85.00	95.00
☐ Royal Canadian Cadet Award for Bravery, *1948.*	RARE	
☐ Royal Canadian Humane Association Medal, *gold.* . . .	150.00	175.00
☐ Royal Canadian Humane Association Medal, *silver.* . .	85.00	120.00
☐ Royal Canadian Humane Association Medal, *bronze.*	50.00	75.00
☐ Royal Canadian Navy Long Service and Good Conduct Medal, *Elizabeth II.*	65.00	85.00
☐ Royal Canadian Navy Long Service and Good Conduct Medal, *George V.*	85.00	110.00
☐ Royal Canadian Navy Long Service and Good Conduct Medal, *George V, crowned.*	85.00	110.00
☐ Royal Canadian Navy Long Service and Good Conduct Medal, *George VI.*	85.00	110.00
☐ Royal Canadian Navy Reserve Long Service and Good Conduct Medal, *George VI.*	85.00	110.00
☐ Royal Canadian Navy Reserve Officers' Decoration, *1938.*	65.00	80.00
☐ Royal Canadian Navy Volunteer Officers' Decoration, *1938.*	85.00	110.00
☐ Royal Canadian Navy Volunteer Reserve Long Service and Good Conduct Medal, *George VI.*	85.00	110.00
☐ Star of Courage, *instituted 1972, maple leaves at corners of star.*	225.00	275.00
☐ Volunteer Service Medal, *plain medal.*	18.00	22.00
☐ Volunteer Service Medal, *maple leaf.*	21.00	30.00

CZECHOSLOVAKIA

☐ 1918-1919 Commemorative Medal.	20.00	23.00
☐ Order of Jan Ziska.	240.00	275.00
☐ Order of the Red Banner of Labor.	285.00	320.00
☐ Order of the Slovak Uprising, *1st Class.*	50.00	55.00
☐ Order of the Slovak Uprising, *2nd Class.*	41.00	45.00
☐ 20th Anniversary of the Slovak Uprising.	25.00	30.00
☐ World War I Cross.	21.00	18.50
☐ World War II Cross.	30.00	35.00

FRANCE

☐ Colonial Service Medal.	50.00	55.00
☐ Croix de Guerre.	26.00	30.00

	Price Range	
☐ **Korean Campaign Medal.**	35.00	40.00
☐ **Order of Maritime Merit,** *Commander Degree. Neck badge with ribbon.*	145.00	160.00
☐ **World War I Cross.**	21.00	25.00
☐ **World War I Victory Medal.**	21.00	25.00

GERMAN (Third Reich)

☐ **Armed Services Long Service Awards,** *cornflower blue suspension ribbon.*	30.50	35.00
☐ **Commemorative Medal** *of March 13, 1938 (Anschluss with Austria).*	32.50	37.50
☐ **Commemorative Medal** *of October 1, 1938 (Sudentenlan)*	31.00	35.00
☐ **Decoration for Bravery and Merit** *of the Eastern People (Lithuanians, Lativans and Estonians serving with the Nazi armies.)*		
☐ **1st Class,** *gold, with swords, pin back for breast wear.*	75.00	85.00
☐ **1st Class,** *silver, with swords, pin back for breast wear.*	50.00	55.00
☐ **1st Class,** *gold, cased.*	95.00	105.00
☐ **1st Class,** *silver, cased.*	75.00	95.00
☐ **2nd Class,** *gold, suspension ribbon, green with red stripes, with swords.*	30.00	35.00
☐ **2nd Class,** *silver, suspension ribbon, green with white stripes, with swords.*	25.00	30.00
☐ **2nd Class,** *bronze, green suspension ribbon, with swords.*	21.00	25.00
☐ **18 Year Service Medal,** *silver Maltese cross.*	55.00	60.00
☐ **40 Year Service Medal,** *same as 25 Year Service Medal with addition of a gold oak leaf arrangement in the form of a "V" on the lower part of the suspension ribbon just above the medal ring*	120.00	130.00
☐ **Four Year Service Medal,** *finished in old silver, round medal.*	25.00	30.00
☐ **Hindenburg Cross** *for service in 1914-1918.*	16.00	20.00
☐ **Iron Cross,** *1st Class.*	55.00	65.00
☐ **Iron Cross,** *1st Class, cased.*	65.00	85.00
☐ **Iron Cross,** *2nd Class.*	21.00	25.00
☐ **Knights Cross of the Iron Cross.**	975.00	1175.00
☐ **Mussert Cross.** *With swords. This is a Dutch Nazi award awarded by and named for the head of the Dutch Nazi Party. It was never recognized by Hitler but still is sought after by many Third Reich medal collectors, cased.*	65.00	80.00
☐ **2nd Class Clasp to 1st Class Iron Cross.**	30.00	35.00
☐ **Spanish Cross,** *in gold with swords.*	475.00	550.00
☐ **Spanish Cross,** *in silver with swords.*	400.00	450.00
☐ **Spanish Cross,** *in bronze with swords.*	325.00	360.00
☐ **Spanish Cross,** *in bronze without swords.*	310.00	350.00
☐ **12 Year Service Medal,** *matte gilt finish, round medal.*	30.00	35.00

	Price Range	
☐ **25 Year Service Medal,** *gold Maltese cross.*	71.00	80.00
☐ **War Merit Cross,** *1st Class. With swords, breast badge, cased.*	55.00	60.00
☐ **War Merit Cross,** *1st Class. With swords, breast badge, not cased.*	45.00	50.00
☐ **War Merit Cross,** *1st Class. Without swords, breast badge, cased.*	41.00	45.00
☐ **War Merit Cross,** *1st Class. Without swords, breast badge, not cased.*	31.00	35.00
☐ **War Merit Cross,** *2nd Class. With swords, ribbon suspension.*	22.50	25.00
☐ **War Merit Cross,** *2nd Class. Without swords, ribbon suspension.*		
☐ **War Order of the German Cross.** *This was not a cross in the general use of the word. It was a breast star consisting of a swastika within a wreath mounted on a heraldic star with pin back. It may be so-named because the swastika is a form of cross.*		
☐ In silver.	285.00	310.00
☐ In gold.	295.00	325.00

GERMANY (Imperial)

☐ **Baden Leopold Medal.** *(for service in the Franco-Prussian War) With 1870-1871 bar.*	67.00	75.00
☐ **Baden World War I Honor Medal.** *Medal inscribed "For Baden's Honor," dated 1914-1918.*	25.00	30.00
☐ **Bavarian 1870 Cross for Volunteer Nurses.**	175.00	190.00
☐ **Bavarian Order of Military Merit,** *4th Class. With swords.*	121.00	135.00
☐ **Bavarian 10 Year Service Medal.**	10.00	11.00
☐ **Brunswick Order of Henry the Lion,** *3rd Class.*	375.00	425.00
☐ **Grand Cross to the Iron Cross,** *1914.*	1000.00	1035.00
☐ **Hesse Order of Philip the Good,** *4th Class.*	175.00	190.00
☐ **Iron Cross,** *1st Class, 1870.*	385.00	435.00
☐ **Iron Cross,** *1st Class, World War I, pin back.*	50.00	55.00
☐ **Iron Cross,** *2nd Class, World War I, with ribbon.*	25.00	30.00
☐ **Iron Cross,** *2nd Class, 1870 (Franco Prussian War). With 25 year oak leaf.*	100.00	110.00
☐ **Order of the Black Eagle.** *The highest order awarded by Prussia. Founded 1701. Persons awarded this order were appointed to hereditary nobility. Dark blue enameled eight-point maltese cross with gold edge. A black enameled Prussian eagle, outlined in gold, appears between each arm of the cross. A gold disk with narrow raised edge appears in the center. Upon the disk appears the cypher "FR," (Frederick Rex). Cross was worn on an orange moire neck ribbon. Very handsome. This is the* **badge.**	2800.00	3100.00
☐ **Star** *of the above order is a silver eight point heraldic star. In the center is a large orange enameled disk*		

Price Range

upon which appears a black enameled and gold Prussian eagle. Around this is a white enameled band with gold edges bearing the gold motto "SUUM CUIQUE," (To each his own). Versions of this star appeared on the front plates of elite Prussian Guard units and elsewhere. It is prized by collectors. ...... | 2800.00 | 3100.00

☐ **Order Pour Le Merite (MILITARY).** *The third highest Prussian order. Originated in 1667 as the Order de la Generosite. Fell into disuse. Revived in 1740 in present name and awarded to both civilian and military personnel. After 1810 awarded solely for bravery in combat. The* **badge** *in its early version is a blue enameled maltese cross with gold edges. A gold Prussian eagle appears between the arms of the cross. On the upper arm of the cross appears in gold a crowned "F," (Frederick). On the left arm appears "Pour," while on the right arm appears "le Me." On the lower arm appears "rite." In the center of the cross is a rimed gold medallion bearing the profile of Fredrick the Great. This early version is rather rare. It was worn on a black neck ribbon with a wide silver stripe near each edge.* .... | 3500.00 | 4000.00

☐ **Same as above,** *except second version has no medallion in the center of the cross. Not as rare as the above.* .... | 2500.00 | 3000.00

☐ **Star** *of this order consists of a four-point heraldic star in gold with an enameled band in the center with a gold edge on each side. About the top half appears "POUR LE MERITE" in gold. On the bottom of the band appears a sprig of gold leaves. The profile of Frederick the Great appears in the center. It is reported that only five of these were ever awarded. Consequently they are so rarely offered for sale that it is impossible to establish a price.*

☐ **Order of the Red Eagle.** *The fourth in order of importance of the Prussian orders. Originally founded in Brandenburg-Bayre as the Order de la Sincerite in 1705. In 1734 became the Order of the Red Eagle. When that state was taken over by Prussia the order was reorganized in 1810. Listed below are the classes which have recently been offered for sale. Others appear infrequently from time to time.*

☐ **Badge for Grand Cross.** *This is the highest class of the order. White enameled maltese cross with gold edges. A Prussian eagle in red enamel and gold appears between each arm of the cross. In the center appears a medium width blue enameled circle edged in gold. About the top of the circle, in gold, appears "SINCERE ET CONSTANTER" (Integrity and Perseverance). Upon the gold center is the eagle of Branden-*

Price Range

burg in red enamel with crown above. A beautiful artifact. 1700.00 1900.00

☐ **Badge for Other Classes.** *Similar to the above but consisting of a maltese cross in white enamel with the red enameled Brandenburg eagle in the center. The following have been offered for sale recently:*

☐   **First Class.** 1200.00 1400.00

☐   **Second Class.** 1150.00 1250.00

NOTE: *All of the above classes come with a white neck ribbon with an orange stripe near each edge.*

☐ **Star of the Grand Cross.** *Gold eight point heraldic star with medium width blue enameled circle edged with gold. About the upper part in gold the motto "SINCERE ET CONSTANTER." A laurel sprig in gold at the bottom. An interesting piece. Not too difficult to find.* 1700.00 2000.00

☐ **Star for Other Classes.** *As above, but with silver star in lieu of gold.* 1600.00 1900.00

☐ **Prussian Order of the Royal Crown,** *4th Class.* 72.00 75.00

☐ **Saxon Order of Ernestine,** *Commander Degree. Richly enameled cross, suspended from Ducal Crown, complete with neck ribbon.* 725.00 800.00

☐ **Saxon Order of Ernestine,** *4th Class. Complete with ribbon.* 172.00 200.00

☐ **Saxon Order of the White Falcon.** *With crown and swords, complete with ribbon.* 200.00 225.00

☐ **Saxon Order of Albert,** *2nd Class. Without swords, neck order with ribbon.* 415.00 470.00

☐ **Saxon Order of Albert,** *3rd Class. With crown, swords and wreath, ribbon.* 175.00 195.00

☐ **Saxon Order of Albert,** *4th Class. With swords, ribbon.* 125.00 140.00

☐ **Wilhelm I Commemoration Medal.** 15.00 20.00

☐ **Wurttemberg Medal for Veterans,** *wars of 1793-1815.* 72.00 80.00

☐ **Wurttemberg Silver Medal for Bravery,** *World War I. This offering was for the medal together with the award certificate.* 77.00 85.00

GREAT BRITAIN

☐ **Africa Star,** *1943, plain medal.* 7.50 10.00

☐ **Africa Star,** *Eighth Army.* 10.00 15.00

☐ **African Star.** 13.50 15.00

☐ **Air Crew Europe Star,** *Atlantic.* 20.25 25.00

☐ **Air Crew Europe Star,** *France and Germany.* 20.25 25.00

☐ **Air Crew Europe Star,** *plain medal.* 15.00 20.00

☐ **Air Force Cross,** *after World War II.* 900.00 1000.00

☐ **Air Force Cross,** *World War I.* 1300.00 1600.00

☐ **Air Force Cross,** *World War II.* 1100.00 1250.00

☐ **Air Force Medal,** *Korea.* 200.00 250.00

☐ **Air Force Medal,** *World War I.* 300.00 400.00

	Price Range	
☐ **Air Force Medal,** *World War II.*	250.00	300.00
☐ **Albert Medal,** *heroic actions on land or sea, oval bronze medallion surmounted by crown, classified according to monarch who made presentation:*		
☐ Edward VI.	1500.00	1700.00
☐ Elizabeth II.	1400.00	1500.00
☐ George V.	1400.00	1500.00
☐ George VI.	1400.00	1500.00
☐ Victoria	1500.00	1700.00
☐ **Allied Victory Medal,** *Air.*	15.00	20.00
☐ **Allied Victory Medal,** *awarded to all members of combat battalions in World War I, C.E.F.*	15.00	20.00
☐ **Allied Victory Medal,** *Naval.*	15.00	20.00
☐ **Anglo-Boer War Medal.**	59.00	65.00
☐ **Arctic Medal,** *1857.*	200.00	250.00
☐ **Army Gold Medal (large size),** *instituted 1806, last awarded in 1814. Extremely rare.*	RARE	
☐ **Army Gold Medal (small size),** *Chateauguay.*	RARE	
☐ **Army Gold Medal (small size),** *Chrystler's Farm.*	RARE	
☐ **Army Gold Medal (small size),** *instituted 1806, last awarded in 1814, Ft. Detroit.*	3300.00	3500.00
☐ **Army Long Service and Good Conduct Medal,** *portrait of Edward VII on obverse.*	150.00	200.00
☐ **Army of India,** *one bar "AVA."*	405.00	450.00
☐ **Atlantic Star.**	12.75	14.00
☐ **Atlantic Star,** *Air Crew.*	15.00	20.00
☐ **Atlantic Star,** *France and Germany.*	15.00	20.00
☐ **Atlantic Star,** *plain medal.*	15.00	20.00
☐ **British Victory Medal,** *World War I.*	23.00	25.00
☐ **British War Medal,** *C.E.F.*	10.00	12.00
☐ **British War Medal,** *Naval.*	15.00	20.00
☐ **British War Medal,** *Royal Air Force.*	15.00	20.00
☐ **Burma Star.**	13.50	15.00
☐ **Canada General Service,** *one bar "FENIAN RAID, 1866."*	117.00	130.00
☐ **China Medal,** *1857.*	135.00	150.00
☐ **Colonial Auxiliary Forces Long Service Medal,** *Edward VII.*	100.00	125.00
☐ **Colonial Auxiliary Forces Long Service Medal,** *George V.*	50.00	65.00
☐ **Colonial Auxiliary Forces Long Service Medal,** *Victoria.*	75.00	85.00
☐ **Colonial Auxiliary Forces Officers Decoration,** *E.R.I. VII (Edward VII).*	115.00	130.00
☐ **Colonial Auxiliary Forces Officers Decoration,** *G.R.V. (George V).*	65.00	75.00
☐ **Colonial Auxiliary Forces Officers Decoration,** *V.R.I. (Victoria).*	85.00	100.00
☐ **Conspicuous Gallantry Medal,** *World War II*	2400.00	2600.00
☐ **Crimea Medal,** *one bar "SEBASTOPOL."*	77.00	85.00
☐ **Distinguished Conduct Medal,** *Korea.*	650.00	675.00

	Price Range	
☐ **Distinguished Conduct Medal**, *marked CANADA in upper field, otherwise identical to British version, Boer War (Africa).*	550.00	575.00
☐ **Distinguished Conduct Medal**, *World War I.*	175.00	200.00
☐ **Distinguished Conduct Medal**, *World War II.*	400.00	425.00
☐ **Distinguished Flying Cross.**	385.00	425.00
☐ **Distinguished Flying Cross**, *Korea.*	550.00	575.00
☐ **Distinguished Flying Cross**, *World War I, cross with eagle wings on horizontal bars.*	350.00	375.00
☐ **Distinguished Flying Cross**, *World War II.*	200.00	225.00
☐ **Distinguished Flying Medal**, *World War I, inscribed "For Courage."*	RARE	
☐ **Distinguished Flying Medal**, *World War II.*	350.00	375.00
☐ **Distinguished Service Cross**, *Korea.*	500.00	550.00
☐ **Distinguished Service Cross**, *World War II.*	225.00	250.00
☐ **Distinguished Service Medal**, *Korea.*	RARE	
☐ **Distinguished Service Medal**, *World War II.*	200.00	225.00
☐ **Distinguished Service Order**, *Boer War (Africa).*	325.00	350.00
☐ **Distinguished Service Order**, *crown within cluster, set against cross, Soudan.*	1200.00	1400.00
☐ **Distinguished Service Order**, *George V, cased.*	563.00	625.00
☐ **Distinguished Service Order**, *George VI, 2nd Type, cased.*	563.00	625.00
☐ **Distinguished Service Order**, *Royal Air Force, World War II.*	375.00	400.00
☐ **Distinguished Service Order**, *World War I.*	325.00	350.00
☐ **Distinguished Service Order**, *World War II.*	325.00	350.00
☐ **Edward Medal**, *awarded to civilians for heroic acts, Edward VII.*	550.00	575.00
☐ **Edward Medal**, *George V.*	550.00	575.00
☐ **France and Germany Star**, *Atlantic.*	15.00	20.00
☐ **France and Germany Star**, *for service in France or Germany in World War II, plain medal.*	10.00	12.00
☐ **George Cross**, *World War II, St. George slating the dragon.*	3500.00	4000.00
☐ **George Medal**, *Elizabeth II.*	375.00	425.00
☐ **George Medal**, *St. George slaying dragon, large hanging loop, George VI.*	375.00	425.00
☐ **Imperial Service Medal**, *Edward VII.*	20.00	25.00
☐ **Imperial Service Medal**, *George V (crown).*	20.00	25.00
☐ **Imperial Service Medal**, *George V (star).*	20.00	25.00
☐ **Indian Mutiny Medal**, *one bar "LUCKNOW."*	405.00	450.00
☐ **Indian Order of Merit.**	54.00	60.00
☐ **Indian Service Medal**, *1901-02.*	32.00	35.00
☐ **Indian Service Medal**, *1937-39.*	45.00	50.00
☐ **Italy Star.**	9.00	10.00
☐ **Italy Star**, *for service in Italy during World War II.*	14.00	18.00
☐ **King's and Queen's Commendation for Brave Conduct**, *World War II.*	30.00	35.00
☐ **King's and Queen's Commendation for Valuable Service in the Air**, *World War II.*	30.00	35.00

	Price Range	
☐ **King's Medal for the Champion Shot,** *1923.*	475.00	500.00
☐ **King's South Africa Medal,** *1901-02, presented to soldiers in the Boer War.*	375.00	400.00
☐ **Military Cross,** *Korea.*	100.00	125.00
☐ **Military Cross,** *World War I, cross-within-cross with crowns at each terminal.*	75.00	90.00
☐ **Military Cross,** *World War II.*	75.00	90.00
☐ **Military Medal,** *Korea.*	550.00	625.00
☐ **Military Medal,** *World War I, inscribed "For Bravery in the Field" within cluster, surmounted by initials GR.*	85.00	95.00
☐ **Military Medal,** *World War II.*	250.00	275.00
☐ **Most Ancient and Most Noble Order of the Thistle.** *Originally founded 809, revived 1687. Star of the order. A silver St. Andrew's cross superimposed upon a four-pointed heraldic star. In the center a green enameled circle bearing the motto "NEMO ME IMPUNE LACESSIT," (Nobody attacks me with impunity) in gold. Yellow enamel center with a typical green Scots thistle. This is the second highest British order and is very rare.*	4000.00	4500.00
☐ **Most Distinguished Order of St. Michael and St. George,** *C.M.G.*	250.00	300.00
☐ **Most Distinguished Order of St. Michael and St. George.** *Established 1818. Seventh ranking British order. Badge consists of seven double-pointed arms forming a cross in white enamel with gold edge. Above is a gold crown. In the center a blue enameled circle bearing the motto, in gold, "AUSPICIUM MELIORIS AEVI," (Omen of a better time). In the center of the circle in colored enamel an image of the Archangel St. Michael slaying Satan. The reverse is the same except that the center bears an image of St. George slaying the dragon.*	900.00	1100.00
☐ **Star,** *consists of a seven ray heraldic star in silver with seven gold rays between. Superimposed upon this star is a red enameled cross with gold edge. Superimposed upon the cross is a blue enameled circle with gold edge bearing in gold the motto of the order. Within the circle the image of St. Michael and Satan.*	1000.00	1200.00
☐ **Most Distinguished Order of St. Michael and St. George,** *G.C.M.G.*	850.00	900.00
☐ **Most Distinguished Order of St. Michael and St. George,** *K.C.M.G.*	300.00	350.00
☐ **Most Excellent Order of the British Empire,** *C.B.E.*	175.00	120.00
☐ **Most Excellent Order of the British Empire,** *instituted 1917, G.B.E..*	925.00	975.00
☐ **Most Excellent Order of the British Empire,** *K.B.E.*	450.00	500.00
☐ **Most Excellent Order of the British Empire,** *O.B.E.*	75.00	100.00
☐ **Most Honourable Order of the Bath,** *C.B.*	200.00	250.00
☐ **Most Honourable Order of the Bath,** *G.C.B.*	600.00	650.00

	Price Range	
☐ **Most Honourable Order of the Bath,** *K.C.B.*	300.00	350.00
☐ **Most Noble Order of the Garter.** *Star of the order. A silver eight-point heraldic star. In the center a blue enameled garter bearing in gilt the inscription "HONI SOIT QUI MAL PENSE," (Shame to him who thinks evil). The highest British order. Founded in 1348, it is one of the most honored orders in the world. The Star.*	2500.00	2900.00
☐ **Natal Medal,** *1906.*	95.00	105.00
☐ **Star,** *1914-15.*	20.50	22.50
☐ **Star,** *1914-15, named.*	13.50	15.00
☐ **Naval Gold Medal,** *instituted 1794, last awarded in 1815. Extremely rare.*	RARE	
☐ **Navy General Service Medal,** *Britannia on horse. Extremely rare.*	RARE	
☐ **Nineteen Fourteen (1914) Star,** *crossed swords with ribbon and crown, 1917.*	150.00	175.00
☐ **Nineteen Thirty Nine-1945 Star,** *Battle of Britain.*	RARE	
☐ **Nineteen Thirty Nine-1945 Star,** *plain medal.*	6.00	9.00
☐ **Nineteen Thirty Nine-1945 War Medal,** *inscribed.*	20.00	25.00
☐ **Nineteen Thirty Nine-1945 War Medal,** *1946, uninscribed.*	10.00	15.00
☐ **North West Canada Medal,** *1855, one bar "SASKAT-CHEWAN."*	340.00	375.00
☐ **Order of British India,** *1st Class.*	225.00	250.00
☐ **Order of British India,** *2nd Class.*	270.00	300.00
☐ **Order of Merit,** *crossed swords, "For Merit".*	RARE	
☐ **Order of St. John of Jerusalem,** *Commander.*	75.00	90.00
☐ **Order of St. John of Jerusalem,** *Knight or Dame of Grace.*	150.00	175.00
☐ **Order of St. John of Jerusalem,** *Knight or Dame of Justice.*	150.00	175.00
☐ **Order of St. John of Jerusalem,** *Officer.*	50.00	75.00
☐ **Order of St. John of Jerusalem,** *Serving Brother (Serving Sister).*	50.00	75.00
☐ **Order of the British Empire,** *Commander Grade, cross with crown suspended from neck ribbon, cased.*	263.00	290.00
☐ **Order of the Indian Empire,** *Companion Grade.*	340.00	375.00
☐ **Pacific Star.**	14.50	16.00
☐ **Pacific Star,** *Burma.*	10.00	12.00
☐ **Pacific Star,** *1945, plain medal.*	10.00	12.00
☐ **Permanent Forces of the Empire Long Service and Good Conduct Medal,** *1910.*	85.00	100.00
☐ **Pontifical Zouaves Volunteer Medal,** *portrait of Pope, "ROMA" on bar, 1892.*	125.00	150.00
☐ **Punjab Medal,** *1849.*	180.00	200.00
☐ **Queen's Medal for the Champion Shot of the Air Force,** *1953.*	400.00	450.00
☐ **Queen's South Africa Medal,** *1899-1900, presented to soldiers in the Boer War.*	1400.00	1600.00

	Price Range	
☐ **Same as above,** *but without dates.*	225.00	250.00
☐ **Royal Red Cross,** *1900, awarded only to women, Boer War.*	RARE	
☐ **Royal Red Cross,** *Korea.*	RARE	
☐ **Royal Red Cross,** *World War I.*	90.00	115.00
☐ **Royal Red Cross,** *World War II.*	125.00	150.00
☐ **Royal Victorian Order,** *C.V.O.*	250.00	325.00
☐ **Royal Victorian Order,** *medallion on cross, G.C.V.O.*..	900.00	1000.00
☐ **Royal Victorian Order,** *K.C.V.O.*	650.00	725.00
☐ **Royal Victorian Order Star,** *eight point heraldic star with the cross of the order superimposed upon it.* ...	900.00	1000.00
☐ **Soudan Medal,** *also called Sudan Medal, 1884-85, profile of Queen Victoria facing left.*	775.00	825.00
☐ **South Africa Medal,** *1877-79, one bar "1879."*	167.00	185.00
☐ **Trafalgar Medal,** *1805.*	144.00	160.00
☐ **Victoria Cross,** *1900, Boer War (Africa).*	7500.00	7750.00
☐ **Victoria Cross,** *1866, Fenian Raid.*	RARE	
☐ **Victoria Cross,** *lion rampant, "For Valour," Crimean War.*	RARE	
☐ **Victoria Cross,** *World War I.*	4850.00	5000.00
☐ **Victoria Cross,** *World War II.*	4850.00	5000.00
☐ **Waterloo Medal,** *1815.*	405.00	450.00

IRAN

☐ **Military Honor Cross,** *1st Class, cased.*	63.00	70.00
☐ **Military Merit Award,** *1st Class, cased.*	45.00	50.00
☐ **Military Merit Award,** *2nd Class, cased.*	36.00	40.00

IRAQ

☐ **Order of El Rafidain,** *breast badge, cased.*	126.00	140.00

ITALY

☐ **Combat Cross,** *World War I. Bronze cross suspended from ribbon, with Italian Star in center.*	25.00	30.00
☐ **Ethiopian Service Medal,** *World War II.*	25.00	30.00
☐ **Neck badge on neck ribbon.** *Breast star in addition.*	475.00	525.00
☐ **1915-1918 War Medal.**	20.00	25.00
☐ **Order of the Crown,** *Grand Officer Degree. Neck badge on ribbon, plus breast star, all in fitted case.*	400.00	450.00
☐ **Order of the Crown,** *Knight's Degree.*	35.00	40.00
☐ **Order of the Italian Republic,** *Grand Cross sash and badge.*	300.00	350.00
☐ **Order of Italian Solidarity,** *2nd Class.*	120.00	135.00
☐ **Order of St. Maurice and St. Lazarus,** *Grand Officer, 2nd Class.*		
☐ **Spanish Civil War Medal.** *Awarded to Italians serving in the Spanish Civil War, 1936-1939.*	55.00	60.00

JAPAN

	Price Range	
☐ China Incident Medal.	50.00	55.00
☐ 1894-1895 War Medal.	80.00	85.00
☐ 1904-1905 War Medal.	50.00	55.00
☐ Order of the Golden Kite, *6th Class.*	145.00	160.00
☐ Order of the Golden Kite, *7th Class.*	120.00	135.00
☐ Order of Queen Tamara. *Breast star.*	238.00	265.00
☐ Order of the Rising Sun, *4th Class. In lacquered box.*	150.00	165.00
☐ Order of the Rising Sun, *7th Class. In lacquered box.*	65.00	71.00
☐ Order of the Rising Sun, *8th Class. In lacquered box.*	45.00	50.00
☐ Order of the Sacred Treasure. *Neck badge on cravat.*	400.00	450.00
☐ Order of the Sacred Treasure, *7th Class. Medal suspended from breasts ribbon.*	50.00	55.00

KOREA

☐ Korean War Medal.	30.00	35.00
☐ Order of Military Merit. *Wharang Type 1.*	130.00	145.00
☐ Order of Military Merit. *Wharang Type 2.*	50.00	56.00
☐ Order of Military Merit. *Wharang Type 3.*	49.00	55.00
☐ Vietnam Campaign Medal.	31.00	35.00

NATIONALIST CHINA

☐ Hai Chi Chiang Chang *(Naval Distinction Medal).*	31.00	35.00
☐ Hai Hsun Chiang Chang *(Naval Merit Medal).*	31.00	35.00
☐ Hai Kuang Chiang Chang *(Naval Brilliance Medal).*	31.00	35.00
☐ Hai Kung Chiang Chang *(Naval Achievement Medal).*	31.00	35.00

NETHERLANDS

☐ House Order of Orange. *Neck badge on cravat.*	250.00	290.00
☐ House Order of Orange. *Officer's breast star.*	210.00	250.00
☐ Order of Orange Nassau. *Knight's breast badge.*	175.00	200.00

PORTUGAL

☐ Order of Christ. *Commander's Degree, neck badge on cravat.*	160.00	180.00
☐ Order of Military Merit. *Grand Officer's Degree, breast star.*	150.00	170.00
☐ Order of St. Benedict. *Crown and cross suspended from cravat.*	215.00	250.00
☐ Order of Villa Vicosa. *Grand Officer's Degree, neck badge on cravat with breast star.*	200.00	225.00
☐ Royal House Order of Merit. *Neck badge with crown suspended from cravat.*	215.00	350.00

ROMANIA (Kingdom)

☐ Order of the Star. *Grand Commander's Degree, neck badge with cravat, breast star, cased.*	500.00	560.00

RUSSIA (Imperial)

Price Range

☐ **Imperial Order of Saint Andrew First Called.** *This was the highest order of Imperial Russia. It is extremely beautiful and very rare. Named for the patron saint of Imperial Russia, Saint Andrew, the first of the disciples. Founded by Peter the Great in 1698. Very rarely awarded. Recipients granted great priviledges. The collar consists of seventeen enameled gold sections joined by gold links. These sections alternately consisted of a black double headed Imperial eagle with red center showing Saint George and the dragon; red disk with blue Saint Andrew's cross and the letters "S.A.P.R.," (Saint Andrew Protector of Russia) and a gold and blue trophy of banners and arms upon which is superimposed a blue disk with gold edge with the cypher of Peter the Great in the center. A gold and red crown is at the top of the disk. Although this collar is occasionally offered for sale, it is so infrequent that no price may be given here.*

☐ **Badge,** *consists of the double head Imperial Russian eagle in gold and blue enamel. Superimposed upon the breast of the eagle is the figure of Saint Andrew crucified on his characteristic "X" shape cross. The end of each arm of the cross bears an initial, together reading "S.A.P.R.," (Saint Andrew Protector of Russia). On the reverse of the cross is a ribbon inscribed in Russian "FOR FAITH AND LOYALTY." ...* 12000.00 14000.00

☐ **Star,** *consists of an eight point heraldic silver star. In the center is a wide blue enameled circle edged in gold. Around the upper three fourths of this circle in Russian appears the motto "FOR FAITH AND LOYALTY," in gold. A small decorative device of gold laurel leaves appears at the bottom. Upon the gold center of the star is the Imperial eagle upon which is superimposed a Saint Andrew's cross.* 4750.00 5500.00

☐ **Boxer Rebellion Medal.** 115.00 125.00

☐ **Campaign Medal,** *1857-1859. Silver, suspension ribbon.* 115.00 125.00

☐ **Campaign Medal,** *1859-1864. Silver, suspension ribbon.* 115.00 125.00

☐ **Crimean Medal,** *1854-1855. Silver, suspension ribbon.* 115.00 125.00

☐ **Russo-Japanese Campaign Medal.** 115.00 125.00

☐ **St. George Cross,** *1st Class, bronze.* 150.00 165.00

☐ **St. George Cross,** *3rd Class, silver.* 150.00 165.00

☐ **St. George Medal,** *2nd Class, bronze.* 115.00 130.00

☐ **St. George Medal,** *3rd Class, silver.* 115.00 130.00

☐ **Turkish Campaign Medal,** *1873. Silver, suspension ribbon.* 115.00 130.00

RUSSIA (Soviet)

Price Range

☐ **30th Anniversary of the Soviet Army and Navy.** 35.00   40.00
☐ **Victory over Japan Medal** *(World War II).* 41.00   45.00

SERBIA

☐ **Order of the White Eagle.** *Neck badge with swords with cravat.* 425.00   455.00

SPAIN

☐ **Medal for San Sebastian.** *1836. This medal was awarded to a British Royal Artillery detachment for their support of the Spanish troops at San Sebastian against the French of Napoleon. Silver medal with English Lion on obverse surrounded by the Collar of the Order of the Golden Fleece, all surrounded by the legend "ESPANA AGRADECIA" ("Spain is Grateful.") On the reverse is a cross pattee with the date "1836" in the center, interesting and rare.* 125.00   130.00
☐ **Naval Order of Merit.** *Breast star.* 80.00   90.00
☐ **Order of Alphonso X, the Wise.** *Commander Degree, cross in enamel suspended from cravat.* 95.00   120.00
☐ **Order of Military Merit.** *Breast star.* 41.00   45.00
☐ **Royal Order of St. Hermengildo.** *Set consisting of sash with badge and breast star.* 430.00   550.00
☐ **Royal Order of St. Hermengildo.** *Breast star of the Grand Cross.* 300.00   350.00

THAILAND

☐ **Order of the Crown,** *Knight's Degree.* 30.00   35.00
☐ **Order of the Crown,** *3rd Class. Breast star.* 115.00   130.00
☐ **Order of the White Elephant.** *Silver medal to the order.* 25.00   30.00

TURKEY

☐ **Order of the Medjidjie.** *Commander's Degree. Neck badge with cravat.* 200.00   225.00

UNITED NATIONS

☐ **Korea Medal.** *Bar marked "KOREA" for U.S. troops.*   12.00   15.00
☐ **Korea Medal.** *Bar marked "KOREA" for British troops.* 20.00   25.00
☐ **Korea Medal.** *Bar marked in Korean language, for Korean troops.* 21.00   25.00
☐ **Korea Medal.** *Bar marked in Thai language, for Thai troops.* 21.00   25.00

UNITED STATES

☐ **Air Force Commendation Medal.** 20.00   25.00

Army Distinguished Service Cross.

Bronze Star.

Distinguished Flying Cross.

Legion of Merit, Legionnaire Degree.

	Price Range	
☐ Airman's Medal.	20.00	25.00
☐ American Campaign Medal.	15.00	20.00
☐ American Defense Service Medal.	15.00	20.00
☐ Armed Forces Reserve Medal.	11.00	15.00
☐ Army Commendation Medal.	11.00	15.00
☐ Army Distinguished Service Cross.	100.00	125.00
☐ Army Distinguished Service Medal.	100.00	125.00
☐ Army Mexican Border Medal.	35.00	40.00
☐ Army Occupation of Germany Medal.	21.00	25.00
☐ Army Soldiers Medal.	31.00	35.00
☐ Asiatic-Pacific Area Campaign Medal.	16.00	20.00
☐ Bronze Star.	11.00	15.00
☐ Coast Guard Good Conduct Medal.	26.00	30.00
☐ Dewey Medal *(Navy)*.	65.00	70.00
☐ European-African-Middle Eastern Campaign Medal.	16.00	20.00
☐ Join Services Commendation Medal.	30.00	35.00
☐ Korean Service Medal.	12.00	15.00
☐ Legion of Merit, *Commander Degree, complete with neck ribbon and lapel pin.*	180.00	200.00
☐ Legion of Merit, *Legionnaire Degree.*	31.00	35.00
☐ Marine Corps Expeditionary Medal.	21.00	26.00
☐ Marine Corps Good Conduct Medal.	25.00	30.00
☐ Marine Corps Reserve Medal.	16.00	21.00
☐ Marine Corps Yangtze Service Medal.	36.00	40.00
☐ Medal for Humane Action *(Berlin Air Lift).*	21.00	25.00
☐ Medal of Honor *(Air Force), cased, recent issue.*	550.00	625.00

Medal of Honor, Navy.

Medal of Honor, Navy.

Navy Medal of Honor, 1917-1918.

Navy Cross.

Purple Heart.

	Price Range	
☐ **Medal of Honor** *(Army), cased, recent issue.*	425.00	475.00
☐ **Medal of Honor** *(Navy), cased, recent issue.*	550.00	610.00
☐ **Medal of Honor** *(Navy). This rare specimen is an earlier version of this decoration, being awarded for personal valor during the Spanish-American War. Very few Medals of Honor were awarded during this war. In sale this specimen was accompanied by the award certificate and personal memorabilia of the individual to whom the award was made.*	7300.00	8100.00
☐ **National Defense Service Medal.**	15.00	20.00
☐ **Navy and Marine Corps Medal.**	55.00	60.00
☐ **Navy Antarctic Service Medal.**	21.00	25.00
☐ **Navy Commendation Medal.**	11.00	15.00
☐ **Navy Cross.**	100.00	125.00
☐ **Navy Expeditionary Medal.**	25.00	30.00
☐ **Navy Good Conduct Medal.**	25.00	30.00
☐ **Navy Reserve Medal.**	16.00	20.00
☐ **Purple Heart,** *with ribbon bar.*	25.00	30.00
☐ **Sampson Medal** *(Navy).*	65.00	75.00
☐ **Silver Star.**	50.00	55.00
☐ **Vietnam Service Medal.**	11.00	15.00
☐ **World War I Victory Medal.** *(Battle and sector clasps increase value).*	21.00	25.00
☐ **World War II Victory Medal.**	16.00	20.00

VIETNAM

	Price Range	
☐ Armed Forces Distinguished Service Order, *1st Class.*	35.00	40.00
☐ Armed Forces Distinguished Service Order, *2nd Class.*	35.00	40.00
☐ Armed Forces Honor Medal, *1st Class.*	16.00	20.00
☐ Armed Forces Honor Medal, *2nd Class.*	16.00	20.00
☐ Gallantry Cross, *with palm.*	16.00	20.00
☐ Gallantry Cross, *with bronze star.*	16.00	20.00
☐ National Order of Vietnam, *2nd Class. Star of the order.*	275.00	300.00
☐ Navy Distinguished Service Order, *1st Class.*	36.00	40.00
☐ Navy Distinguished Service Order, *2nd Class.*	36.00	40.00

POSTERS

Recruiting posters present a most interesting field for militaria collectors. The variety is wide yet allows for considerable specialization. Most posters are colorful and represent considerable artistic skill. Indeed, in World War I and II, several famous artists contributed their talents to these recruiting devices. Although older posters usually lack little or any art work, they are most sought after for their historical association. Consequently, these posters command a rather respectable price.

Of course, poster collecting is by no means restricted to those used for recruiting or for other war related activities such as bond drives and such. Posters of various kinds are collected for a whole host of interests. Among other things, posters may be collected solely on their artistic merit, as examples of trends in advertising and so on.

It may possibly come as a surprise to some to know that the idea of the poster itself is ancient. In fact we know that the ancient Egyptian, Greeks and Romans used posters for the purpose of making announcements. Written handbills were circulated in medieval times. With the advent of printing, the production of posters in great quantity was made possible. Early posters usually contained only text material although as the art developed, woodcuts began to be used. Continued improvements in printing and the development of improved methods of reproducing art work, including lithography, opened new and wider vistas.

With the improved methods of reproduction, poster illustrations began to engage the attention of many famous artists. Cheret, Beardsley, Maxfield Parrish, Charles Dana Gibson and the celebrated Toulouse-Lautrec, to name but a few, were poster artists at one time or another. Posters of Toulouse-Lautrec were so popular that soon after they had been posted, they were taken down by collectors before the paste had time to dry. Reproductions of these posters, as well as those of other famous artists, sell readily.

In spite of the use of radio and television advertising, the poster is still a most effective mode of salesmanship and mass communication. Excellent examples of the use of posters are reflected in those for travel, cigarettes and automobiles. These are most colorful and they are but a few among many.

Military recruiting posters, in keeping with the best advertising principles, make use of a whole catalog of appeals. In time of war or international unrest, the appeal is usually patriotic. An appeal to tradition is also frequently used. In older and less sophisticated times, travel and adventure were widely used themes. These are sometimes still used although they are not as attractive as they were when travel was much more limited. The appeal of adventure is always of some appeal to younger recruits. In times past, travel and adventure were particularly appealing to people in the mid-west and a large proportion of Navy and Marine recruits were from that area. In times of economic depression, steady pay and retirement benefits are especially appealing. In these present times education, self-improvement, sports and recreation are perhaps better selling points.

An early Royal Marines recruiting poster, c. 1775, informs the young man that he not only will be able to make an allotment for dependents but he will have ample personal spending money. He is also offered travel and adventure and is told that "The Single Young Man on his Return to Port, finds himself on Shore with his Girl and His Glass, that might be envied by a Nobleman." He was then advised "Take Courage then, seize the Fortune that awaits you, repair to the Royal Marines Rendevous, where in a Flowing Bowl of Punch, in Three Times Three, you shall drink Long live the King, and Success to his Royal Marines." (The use of capitalization on this poster is unique.)

American Marine recruiting posters of this same era make an outright appeal to patriotism, as well as adventure and pay. The lure of prize money from the sale of captured enemy vessels is stressed. Posters of the War of 1812 era stress the same inducements.

Regardless of what some writers affirm, the Mexican War was not too popular to the majority of citizens. Appeals to fill the ranks were directed to enlistments in local and state militia units, a fact reflected by the few surviving recruiting posters of that period. These posters for the most part are devoid of art work except for woodcuts of an American Eagle with a shield on its breast or similar illustrations.

The Civil War produced a profusion of posters in great variety. These range from those utilizing only text material, with an abundance of capital letters, red ink, "scare head" sentences and similar attention getting devices to those making an elaborate, if not artistic, use of woodcut illustrations. Not too often of good workmanship and at times being created by local talent, they treat principally with military scenes or patriotic emblems. Some of these illustrations are merely black and white while others display some color. The majority of the posters of this era are for militia units or privately raised local outfits. Regular Army posters are few and far between and usually are more expensive to buy. Few Navy posters of this era exist. One interesting item of that time is a bombastic broadside headed "THE CONSCRIPT BILL! HOW TO AVOID IT." U.S. NAVY! The obvious appeal was for men to enlist in the service of their choice rather than to be conscripted into the Army. Promotion and pay were stressed as was the prospect of prize money.

Recruiting posters of the late 1800's and early 1900's are few and far between. A Marine poster of 1886, poorly illustrated with a cut of an early steam warship and a Marine in dress uniform on either side, stresses pay and promotion. It was noted that Marine sergeants might have independent command of guard units. In reality, sergeants were few and far between. Unfortunately, the posters of all the armed forces like civilian advertising efforts sometimes stretch the truth. A Marine poster of the early 1900's stresses an opportunity to see the world while an earlier one bears the picture of Admiral George Dewey, of Spanish-American War fame, who said "No finer military organization than the Marine Corps exists in the world." Army posters of the early 1900's are often headed simply "MEN WANTED FOR THE ARMY" with information as to where to enlist. They picture in full color, men in dress blue uniforms or in well-pressed khaki duty uniforms. This particular series of posters had different scenes for the major arms of the service, cavalry, infantry, artillery, etc.

By the time of our entry into World War I, poster art in general had made great progress and advertising in general gave every promise of the great selling force it would later attain. The majority of the recruiting posters of this era are most artistic and much sought after. Among the many well-known artists to volunteer their talent were Howard Chandler Cristy, James Montgomery Flagg and Hamilton Fisher. One of Howard Chandler Cristy's most famous posters shows a beautiful young girl in a sailor's uniform saying: "I WISH I WERE **A MAN**, I'D JOIN THE NAVY, NAVY RESERVE OR COAST GUARD."

James Montgomery Flagg, another famous artist of the day, painted a poster showing a stern face Uncle Sam pointing his finger at the viewer and saying: "I WANT **YOU** FOR THE U.S. ARMY. ENLIST NOW." This poster apparently is a take off from a British Army poster of the period which shows Lord Kitchener doing the pointing. In any event the same idea was also used by the Navy and the Marine Corps. In the Navy version a shapely young lass in a chief petty officer's uniform says, "I WANT YOU FOR THE NAVY." The Marine Corps version shows a handsome and rugged Marine sergeant in dress blue uniform pointing his finger at the viewer and saying, "THE U.S. MARINES WANT YOU."

Some Army posters of World War I sought enlistment of specialists, engineers, truck drivers, mechanics and other skilled people. Others made an appeal for the then new aviation and tank services. These particular posters are worth more on the collectors' market. Generally speaking, the Navy and Marine posters of this era stressed tradition and the Marines were constantly reminding folks that they are the first to fight. The propaganda value of picturing the enemy in as bad a light as possible was frequently used by all the armed forces. At times this bordered on the absurd. One Army poster of this type pictures a menacing ape wearing a German spiked helmet standing on land marked "AMERICA." In his left arm he clutches a seminude fair maiden. In his left hand he holds a heavy club with the word "KULTUR" on it. In the background appears a ruined European city. The text reads "DESTROY THIS MAD BRUTE." "ENLIST U.S. ARMY."

During World War I the Army was "one up" on the other services by introducing a special poster. This depicts three figures, a typical jovial Santa Claus, Uncle Sam in Army uniform and an Army private, walking arm in arm. This poster bears the message, "MERRY CHRISTMAS. PEACE. YOUR GIFT TO THE NATION." This marked the advent of a series of special Christmas theme posters which have been issued from time to time at irregular intervals by each of the armed forces. These vary in execution. Some emphasize the joy of Christmas in the service. Others are of a definite religious theme, showing service people in chapel or in an attitude of reverent contemplation. Others may show service people in a typical Christmas scene with Christmas tree and other decorations. These posters were made in limited numbers and are often more expensive than others.

Between World Wars I and II, the posters of all the services for the most part again used the old themes of travel and adventure, together with some tradition. Aviation came in for special attention and the Navy made a special effort to secure recruits for its submarine and lighter-than-air activities.

World War II posters are usually well executed and colorful. Those seeking volunteers for the women's service are particularly attractive. Again many posters highlighted action, patriotism and tradition.

Since World War II and particularly following our involvement in Korea and Vietnam and the end of the draft, all of the services have had difficulty in meeting recruiting quotas, with the possible exception of the Air Force. A whole multitude of appeals have been made, including the old ones of pride, tradition, travel, adventure, pay and a host of others, as well as the newer appeals of education including both academics and the learning of a skilled trade. Apparently these appeals have not been too successful.

In general, posters of the periods prior to the Civil War are few and far between. Even so there appears to be not too great a demand for them and they are not quite as expensive as one might believe. On the other hand, Civil War posters, although in greater quantity, are perhaps in greater demand than those of any other era. There is some sort of fascination about the Civil War both in this country and abroad, particularly in England. American Civil War societies are not at all uncommon in other countries. Although prices for posters of this period are often far from modest, apparently there have been few attempts to date to produce bogus examples.

World War I posters are rapidly gaining in popularity with a resulting increase in prices. Those for specified services such as tanks, air and engineers are in good demand as are posters by noted artists.

Posters of the period between World Wars are thus far rather reasonably priced but prices are certain to increase. Posters of World War II and after are in fair supply and are also still reasonably priced. Posters of the present day have little value but here again they are certain to increase in value in the future. Collectors with the space to spare might do well to start collecting these.

Some militaria collectors expand their poster collections to include posters of war-related organizations and activities of World Wars I and II, including the Red Cross, the YMCA, war savings bond drives, Civilian Defense, and others. These posters are generally priced in about the same range as the military recruiting posters.

FRANCE

Price Range

☐ **Seven Years War Army poster.** *Seeking cavalry recruits. Poster headed "PREMIER REGIMENT" "DE CALVERIE DE FRANCE." In center of poster is a woodcut of a booted and spurred cavalryman on a rearing horse. Text appeals to price and patriotism, sets out requirements for acceptance, an extremely rare offering very seldom offered in this country.* **950.00   1050.00**

☐ **Seven Years War Army poster.** *Seeking both infantry and cavalry recruits. Across the top of the poster in large letters appears "RECRUES"/"DESTINEES POU LES REGIMENTS"/"DE L'ARMEE D'ALLEMAGNE." In center of poster are two woodcuts, one on the left of an infantryman with musket and the other of a cavalryman on rearing horse.* **950.00   1050.00**

Price Range

☐ **World War II War Bond poster.** *Upper two-thirds of poster is a photo of the open turret of a French tank with tank commander looking forward out of turret hatch, another tank follows. Overhead is a flight of bombing planes, all weapons of early World War II vintage. Lower third of the poster bears the message "SOUSCRIVEZ" (in red letters) and "AUX"/"BONS d'ARMEMENT" (in black).* 59.00   65.00

GERMANY (Third Reich)

☐ **Propaganda poster.** *Against a background of Nazi flags and bursting shells, the half figure of a German infantryman in heroic pose faces the viewer. At the bottom of the poster in large red letters is "DER SIEG WIRD"/"UNSER SEIN!" Full color with greens, blacks and reds predominating.* 50.00   65.00

☐ **Propaganda poster.** *Three-quarter length photo of Hitler against a red and brown background with the legend "Ein Volk, ein Reich, ein Fuhrer" in white across the bottom.* 50.00   65.00

GREAT BRITAIN

☐ **Royal Marines Recruiting poster,** *c. 1805. A rare and interesting poster seeking recruits in the fight against Napoleon. Headed by the Royal Arms of George III, with "G" on one side and "R" on the other. The text is headed "ALL DASHING HIGH-SPIRITED/ YOUNG HEROES WHO WISH TO OBTAIN GLORY IN SERVICE OF THEIR COUNTRY NOW HAVE THE FINEST OPPORTUNITY BY ENTERING THAT ENTER-PRISING CORPS" "THE ROYAL MARINES." The text then goes on to offer good food and quarters plus the inducement of prize money. Obligated service is given as seven years. At the bottom of the poster is admonition "ENGLAND FOREVER" "GOD SAVE THE KING."* 1000.00   1100.00

☐ **World War I War Bond poster.** *Painting of heavy field artillery piece, bags of pounds sterling appear among the shells, well executed in red, white, black and gray.* 73.00   80.00

☐ **World War I Army Recruiting poster.** *This is the famous full color poster showing Lord Kitchener pointing his finger at the observer and saying "YOUR COUNTRY NEEDS YOU." The appeal is direct and requires little explanation. Painted by the British artist Alfred Leete it was one of the most effective recruiting poster of modern times and was copied in subsequent U.S. Army, Navy and Marine Corps posters.* 200.00   220.00

Price Range

☐ **World War II poster.** *Headed "THE BRITISH COM-MONWEALTH OF NATIONS" in yellow upon black. Center of poster is occupied by fighting men in the uniforms of the several Commonwealth armies against a blue background with the Union Jack waving at the right. The word "TOGETHER" appears in large yellow type on black at the bottom of the poster.* **59.00**   **65.00**

☐ **World War II Propaganda poster.** *Against a large photograph of a bombed out village occupying the upper half of the poster, a full length photo of Hitler with right fist extended and with a frown on his face occupies the entire left of the poster. Across the bottom is a quotation from one of Hitler's speeches "ONE IS EITHER A GERMAN OR A CHRISTIAN . . . YOU CANNOT BE BOTH." "- ADOLPH HITLER, 1933."*   **59.00**   **65.00**

SECURITY POSTERS

Certainly some of the most graphic, colorful and hard hitting posters of World War II were those concerning security measures, including careless talk. Some of the best art work is revealed in these. Listed below are a few examples.

☐ **American security poster,** *World War II. Against a background of various shades of red and crimson is a white cross planted in the ground. On one arm hangs an ammunition belt and on the other hangs a steel helmet. Across the top in white "a careless word," across the bottom ". . . another cross." Uncomplicated but very effective.* **64.00**   **70.00**

☐ **American security poster,** *World War II. Full color. This is a tear jerking sentimental job. A tearful young puppy rests its head on the collar of a sailor's blouse which has been thrown over the back of an easy chair. On the wall in the background hangs a service flag with a gold star on it, across the bottom of the poster is ". . . because somebody talked!" If you like sentimentality, this poster is for you.* **50.00**   **55.00**

☐ **American security poster,** *World War II. This is probably by far one of the best executed and effective security posters of the period, art work and detail are excellent. Against a blue sky a dead American paratrooper sags in his parachute harness as his feet touch the ground, in the sky in the background are aircraft and descending paratroopers and on the ground the fire and smoke of battle, across the top in two lines "CARELESS TALK"/". . . got there first." Excellent.* **100.00**   **110.00**

☐ **British security poster,** *World War II. In the background the shadowy face of a soldier is speaking. From his lips a gradually widening spiral emerges to*

Price Range

end near the bottom of the poster in a blood red projectile piercing three British soldiers who fling up their hands in pain and death. Across the top of the poster in red, white and yellow letters appears the admonition "YOUR TALK MAY KILL YOUR COMRADES." Most effective. **91.00**   **100.00**

☐ **German security poster,** *World War II. This poster in white, gray, yellow, black and brown uses shock effect to drive its important message home. Set against a gloomy night sky, a British twin engine bomber emerges from the clouds to begin its bombing run, astride the fuselage is the figure of death as a skeleton with right arms raised to throw a bomb at a lighted doorway and window in a building far below. A figure stands in the doorway casting a long shadow across a street, thus making an excellent target. The admonition to strictly observe black out discipline in the painting is further emphasized in the text, "Der Feind sieht Dein Licht!" "Verdunkeln!" Not altogether a pleasant picture but most graphic.* **100.00**   **110.00**

HOLIDAY POSTERS

As was mentioned in the introduction to this section on posters, the various Armed Forces from time to time have issued special Christmas and holiday posters. These take a variety of forms and themes. Some use paintings for the art work while others use color photographs. Some poster collectors make a specialty of collecting these. Since they are issued irregularly and in limited numbers, they are not too easy to find and usually command a better price than most modern posters. The few following examples, except the first one, are rather typical.

☐ **Army Christmas poster,** *World War I. This is the oldest of this type of poster and is something of a classic, it is difficult to find. Full color poster showing a typical jovial Santa Claus, Uncle Sam in Army uniform and an Army private all smiling, walking arm in arm. The poster reads "MERRY CHRISTMAS" "PEACE" "YOUR GIFT TO YOUR NATION." Interesting and rare.* **140.00**   **150.00**

☐ **Marine Corps Christmas poster.** *Color photo of the upper half of an uncovered Marine corporal in dress blues holding a sprig of holly and a lighted candle in his hands as he lifts his eyes upward, in the background is a large stained glass window, across the bottom is "UNITED STATES MARINES."* **18.50**   **20.00**

☐ **Marine Corps Christmas poster.** *The centerpiece of this poster is a painting showing a Marine enlisted man's white cap with a lighted candle in a holder with a sprig of holly to the right, in the upper right hand corner are the words "ALWAYS"/"FAITHFUL," at the*

Thanksgiving, Navy.

Christmas, Marine, post W. W. II.

British Army, World War I.

Army, Civil War.

Price Range

bottom "U.S. MARINE CORPS." Full color, one of the best of all Marine Christmas posters. Full of dignity, beauty, reverence and meaning. 78.00   85.00

☐ **Marine Corps Christmas poster.** In full color a photo shows a Marine corporal bugler sounding a call, on his right is a Marine private first class at attention holding an American flag with his right hand, on the corporals left is another Marine private first class, also at attention, holding Marine Corps colors in his left hand, all wear dress blues with white caps. In the background is a large decorated Christmas tree, at the top of the poster on a wide holiday ribbon in two lines appears "SEASON'S"/"GREETINGS," across the bottom is "U.S. MARINES." 18.50   20.00

☐ **Navy Christmas poster.** Combination photo and painting, a sailor in blue blouse and white cap bows his head in meditation as a ray of light from above shines on him, in the background are the bridge and part of the flight deck of an aircraft carrier. 28.00   30.00

☐ **Navy holiday poster.** A rather humorous poster filled with happiness and the meaning of the holiday season. A Navy cook puts the final touches on a big cooked turkey, in back of him a sailor looks over each shoulder, all have happy grins, in the lower right corner is one word "NAVY." Very good poster. 37.00   40.00

PATRIOTIC POSTERS

☐ **"Togetherness" poster,** World War I. Full color. A handsome, husky central figure of a workingman holding a hammer walks arm in arm with a sailor on his right and a soldier on his right, all three have a confident smile. The artist for this one is again James Montgomery Flagg. Apparently he didn't do his research on the sailor figure too well for he is wearing a uniform more appropriate to the Spanish-American War than World War I. In the shadow background is a shipyard and a completed transporter, across the bottom of the poster is "TOGETHER WE WILL WIN" and "UNITED STATES SHIPPING BOARD-EMERGENCY FLEET CORPORATION." 151.00   165.00

☐ **Liberty Loan poster,** World War I. Full color. A bandaged and battle weary but broadly smiling American soldier in steel helmet, with his bayoneted rifle held carelessly over his right shoulder, holds a collection of captured German helmets. In the background is a battle scene, to the left of the soldier appears the text "AND THEY THOUGHT WE COULDN'T FIGHT," across the bottom reads "VICTORY LIBERTY LOAN."   32.00   35.00

☐ **Liberty Loan poster,** World War I. Full color poster with large figure of workingman in worn working

Price Range

clothes with sleeves rolled back reaching into his left pocket, in the upper right corner the text reads "SURE! We'll Finish the Job," under the figure appears "VICTORY LIBERTY LOAN." 59.00   65.00

☐ **War Savings Stamp poster,** World War I. Full color poster showing large American eagle with down swept wings in protective posture over small airplane nestlings which are leaving the nest, at the top of the poster is "KEEP HIM FREE," across the bottom is information about War Savings Stamps. As anyone who was a child during this period will remember, in addition to adults, a great appeal was made to public school pupils to save these stamps toward eventual buying of a bond. Imaginative, colorful, well-executed poster by Charles Livingston Bull. 128.00   140.00

☐ **War Bond poster,** World War I. American soldier wearing steel helmet grasps his rifle in his left hand and a grenade in his right, standing on the parapet of a German trench filled with enemy troops. The text reads "Lend the way they fight. Buy Bonds to your UTMOST." War bond posters with a similar theme were used by many nations during both World Wars, by E. M. Ashe. Interesting. 92.00   100.00

☐ **War Bond poster,** World War I. Full color poster showing a large U.S. Mark VIII tank looming over a trench filled with frightened German soldiers, across the top appears "Crush the Prussian," at the bottom appears "BUY A BOND," "3rd Libert Loan." 59.00   65.00

☐ **American patriotic poster,** World War II. This excellent and most effective poster has no text or does it need any for the outstanding painting by the famous artist McCelland Barclay tells the story of the Japanese attack on Pearl Harbor most tellingly. A young American sailor lays sprawled in death across an American flag, his left hand clutches folds of the flag, from the back of his white uniform a Samurai sword protrudes, back of the hilt of the sword is a Japanese flag. An unusual poster with excellent art work. 151.00   165.00

☐ **Civil Defense poster,** World War II. A gray and white American eagle soars in flight toward its prey against a background of red and blue streaks, across the top in white and red appears "AMERICA"/"CALLING" in two lines, under the eagle and to the left appears "Take your place in"/"Civilian Defense" in two lines. The Civil Defense logo of the red letters "CD" within a white triangle upon a blue disk appears in the lower right corner. This is a very effective poster for an important defense activity, not many Civil Defense posters are offered. 41.00   45.00

Price Range

☐ **Food Conservation poster,** *World War II. Impressive poster in red, white, black and blue. Against a blue sky are a red, a white and a blue cargo parachute with a wood case of food attached, across the painting appears "Where our men are fighting"/"Our FOOD is fighting." All this in white except for the word "FOOD" which is in black. Across the bottom of the poster in red appears "BUY WISELY-COOK CARE-FULLY-STORE CAREFULLY-USE LEFTOVERS." Attractive and colorful.* 64.00   70.00

☐ **Navy Day poster,** *World War II. Painting in full color of a flight of Avenger torpedo bombers closing in for a run on a Japanese aircraft carrier, good color and detail. Across the bottom of the painting appears "SPEARHEAD OF VICTORY," under painting appears in two lines "NAVY DAY"/"OCTOBER 21." Well-executed poster by the artist John Falter.* 73.00   80.00

☐ **War Bond poster,** *World War II. Bridge and foredeck of American submarine in this full color poster, one seaman scans the horizon with binoculars while above him another works the shutters of a signal lamp sending the message "FIRE AWAY!" Across the bottom appears "BUY EXTRA BONDS." Interesting.* 69.00   75.00

☐ **War Bond poster,** *World War II. Full color painting of a mother, father and three small children standing at the peak of a hill seen against the rays of the morning sun, off to their left is a white stone cross with a wreath about it, above them in the background in black, gray and blue is President Roosevelt as he appeared just before his death. Under his image are the words from one of his speeches, "In the strength of great hope we must shoulder our common load," under this are the words "BUY VICTORY BONDS." Interesting and impressive, good use of color.* 59.00   65.00

☐ **War Bond poster,** *World War II. "Speed the Day" appears across the top of this sentimental appeal to war bond buyers. Full color art work of a joyous homecoming celebration with a young soldier in uniform with campaign ribbons waves his rifle aloft, a German helmet hangs from his neck. He is astride the shoulders of an admirer, other admirers and a band are around him, colored strings of paper and showers of confetti fill the background. Across the bottom appears "with WAR BONDS." Not noteworthy.* 28.00   30.00

☐ **War Bond poster,** *World War II. This is probably one of the best and most dramatic bond posters of the World War II era. The full color painting shows a tired and grim face soldier carrying five wooden crosses over his left shoulder and a spade in his right hand as*

Army, Civil War.

Army, Civil War.

Army, World War I.

Army Air Service, World War I.

Price Range

*he plods across a graveyard of wooden crosses. The
simple but effective text reads "War Bonds — ARE
CHEAPER THAN WOODEN CROSSES." Excellent art
work and detail.* 59.00   65.00

RECRUITING POSTERS

☐ **Army Civil War Cavalry recruiting poster.** *Large
poster appealing for men with some riding experience. Abundance of text promising the best horses,
equipment, arms, clothing, rations, pay and a bounty.
Pay table lists all ranks from private at $14.00 a
month to sergeant major at $23.00 a month. The inter-
esting feature of this poster is the fine woodcut
showing a mounted officer in the foreground and a
color bearer, soldiers and tents in the background.
Oddly enough, although this is a Civil War poster, the
woodcut shows uniforms of the Mexican War era.
Colorful and interesting.* 290.00   320.00

☐ **Army Civil War recruiting poster.** *Unlike many posters
of this era, this one has a minimum of verbage but is
very effective. Across the top appears "VOLUN-
TEERS WANTED!" in the center appears a large
American eagle with outstretched wings, grasping
laurel leaves and war arrows, in its beak it holds a ribbon with "1776" on one end and "1861" on the other,
below appears the scare line "AN ATTACK ON
WASHINGTON ANTICIPATED!!" with "THE COUN-
TRY TO THE RESCUE!" below this. A poster of this
type is highly valued.* 232.00   255.00

☐ **Army Civil War recruiting poster.** *Another Regular
Army recruiting poster. In large letters appears in six
lines "WANTED!!" / "FOR THE" / "U.S. ARMY." /
"ABLE-BODIED UNMARRIED MEN!" / "FOR 3
YEARS!" / "TWO DOLLARS PAID FOR BRINGING A
RECRUIT!" Under this in much smaller typeface
appears "Apply at," this is followed by a wide blank
space for an address to be inserted, at the very bottom appears "FIFTEENTH INFANTRY, RECRUITING
OFFICER." No art work but the title "U.S. ARMY" is
dressed up with the top half of each letter being a
field with stars while the bottom half of each letter
has wavy stripes. Interesting Regular Army example.*   100.00   110.00

☐ **Army Civil War recruiting poster.** *For Company F of
the Wadsworth Guards. Exceptionally well-executed
woodcut of an American eagle standing on a shield,
in its beak it holds a ribbon bearing the words "THE
UNION NOW AND FOREVER." This is a far better
than average example of a locally produced poster
appealing for 15 men with the usual inducements of
pay, bounty, fame, etc. offered. This particular unit*

Price Range

became part of the famous 104th New York Regiment which served with considerable honor in many major battles of the Civil War. In addition to the art work, this historical association makes this poster desirable. . . .   290.00   320.00

☐ **Army Civil War recruiting poster.** *The attention lines on this item read, in four lines "RECRUITS" / "WANTED" / "BY THE" / "TOWN OF AMESBURY," a bounty of $550.00 is offered. This is an interesting call to fill the ranks of a strickly local unit. No art work. . . . .*   200.00   220.00

☐ **Army Civil War recruiting poster.** *This particular poster dates from the very beginning of the war. It has a large woodcut showing the typical picture of an American eagle standing on a U.S. shield, the ribbon held in its beak reads "THE UNION AND CONSTITUTION FOREVER." Seeks men from Clinton County, New York, to enroll in Harris' Light Cavalry, has usual patriotic appeal. Historically important poster by virtue of fact that this light cavalry outfit became the famed 2nd New York Cavalry Regiment which served with distinction throughout the war. . . .*   295.00   325.00

☐ **Army Civil War recruiting poster.** *This specimen has no art work and consists of 17 lines of scare head type. Enlistments sought for the Philadelphia City Guard to serve 100 days, $50.00 bounty money promised. An extremely plain poster. . . . .*   78.00   85.00

☐ **Army Corps Women's recruiting poster,** *World War II. A most attractive poster. Women's Army Corps private looks upward to text across the top of poster reading "MINE EYES HAVE SEEN THE GLORY." In the background in dark colors is a scene of American soldiers in combat. Across the bottom of the poster is "WOMEN'S ARMY CORPS." The woman model is beautiful and the entire poster is in very good taste. Women's World War II recruiting posters increasing in value. . . . .*   51.00   55.00

☐ **Army Mexican War recruiting poster.** *For one year volunteers. Poster headed "VOLUNTEERS!" in large letters under which is large woodcut of an American eagle with a shield on its breast. In its beak it holds a ribbon bearing the motto "E PLURIBUS UNUM," in its talons the eagle grasps laurel leaves and war arrows, there are 19 stars about the eagle's head. The text of the poster appears for the men of New Hampshire to demonstrate their unerring marksmanship and to ". . . illustrate . . . the fierce, determined, and undaunted bravery that has always characterized her sons." Volunteers are promised the handsome sum of $10.00 a month with $30.00 advance money, in addition, it is stated that Congress "will grant a*

Price Range

handsome bounty in money and ONE HUNDRED
AND SIXTY ACRES OF LAND." Mexican War posters
are seldom seen...................................... **295.00** **325.00**

☐ **Army recruiting poster.** *A fierce looking widespread
winged American eagle grasping laurel leaves and
war arrows stands on a U.S. shield, holding in its
beak a ribbon which carries the message "NO COM-
PROMISE WITH TRAITORS, NO ARGUMENT BUT IN
THE CANNON'S MOUTH." Calls for enlistment in
"COL. OWEN'S REGIMENT ATTACHED TO BAKER'
BRIGADE," pay and rations promised from day of
enrollment. Minimum of text but interesting
woodcut.* **230.00** **250.00**

☐ **Army recruiting poster,** *c. early 1900's. Full color
poster showing cavalrymen watering their mounts.
They wear the khaki field uniform of the era. Across
the top of the poster above the art work appears "The
Horse Is Man's Noblest Companion." Under the picture in three lines appears "JOIN THE" / "CAVALRY" /
"and have a courageous friend." There is space for
the recruiting office address. Colorful and attractive.* **55.00** **60.00**

☐ **Army recruiting poster,** *c. early 1900's. Headed "Men
Wanted for the Army" with space for recruiting office
address at the bottom. Full color painting showing a
five-man gun crew servicing a 3 inch field artillery
piece. In the background an officer uses binoculars,
a soldier records a message and another waves a
semaphore flag. In the foreground an officer and
sergeant talk to a corporal using a field telephone, all
wear khaki uniforms. Art work well done...........* **55.00** **60.00**

☐ **Army recruiting poster,** *c. early 1900's. Shows a
mounted infantry bugler with an infantry sergeant to
the front standing at ease with a rifle, both are in
dress blue uniform. Colorful......................* **55.00** **60.00**

☐ **Army recruiting poster,** *c. early 1900's. The art work
on this poster is well done in full color and shows two
soldiers in fatigue uniforms manning a coast artillery
gun in a fortress scene. Other figures are in khaki
uniform except for a corporal with rifle in dress
blues, space for recruiting office address. ....* **55.00** **60.00**

☐ **Army recruiting poster.** *For the Fourth Delaware
Regiment. Minimum of text material but well laid out.
Promises $100.00 bounty payment plus $13.00 to
$22.00 a month, with a month's pay in advance.
Rations and uniforms to be furnished immediately
upon enlistment. Poster of a type often seen for
recruiting for local units. ....* **118.00** **130.00**

☐ **Army recruiting poster.** *For the "VOSBURGH
CHASSEURS" of the 53rd Regiment of New York
State Volunteers. Has a very good woodcut of a fully*

Army, World War I.

Coast Guard, post World War I.

Marine Corps, c. early 1900's.

Marine Corps, post Civil War.

Price Range

bearded Army officer in full regimentals. It states
that 45 men are wanted to complete Company A. Pay
and bounty are highlighted. Of interest is the state-
ment that "Relief tickets given to families requiring
aid." Attractive................................. 185.00 200.00

☐ **Army recruiting poster,** *post World War I. Post war
appeal for enlistment in a specialized service. Full
color painting of an officer in field uniform, campaign hat and boots standing on top of a signal cart,
views the horizon with binoculars. On the ground a
corporal with headset on is working the controls of a
portable wireless set. Another corporal is writing in a
notebook. The text reads "IF YOU ARE AN ELEC-
TRICIAN MECHANIC OR A TELEGRAPH OPERATOR
YOU BELONG IN THE U.S. ARMY SIGNAL CORPS IF
YOU ARE NOT WE WILL TRAIN YOU. GET IN NOW"
Note the absence of punctuation. A lot of color but
not important.* 18.50 20.00

☐ **Army recruiting poster,** *post World War I. This full col-
or poster was issued a few years after the First World
War. The full length figure of a soldier in combat
uniform of that war stands with Old Glory in his left
hand and a bayonetted rifle in his right. A laurel
wreath hangs down from the muzzle of the rifle. The
soldier wears a steel helmet, web cartridge belt,
spiral leggings and a canteen in its web cover. This is
an older looking soldier whose expression is very
serious. He appears to be standing on a raised bit of
grassy ground and about him are beautiful adoring
women and handsome admiring men. Across the top
of the poster appears "OUR REGULAR ARMY DIVI-
SIONS." Across the bottom is "Honored and
Respected by All." "Enlist for the Infantry — or in
one of the other twelve branches." Information on
the nearest recruiting office appears below. This is
an extremely well done, heroic poster as one might
expect from the artist who was James Montgomery
Flagg. Excellent.* 185.00 200.00

☐ **Army recruiting poster.** *This is a far more interesting
poster than that listed above. This poster is for the
12th Massachusetts Battery. There is a minimum of
text but there is a fine woodcut of an artillery battery
galloping into action.* 187.00 205.00

☐ **Army recruiting poster.** *This is another poster
published by the town of Amesbury, but to which the
town of Salisbury also joined in the appeal for
recruits. Appeal for 80 men is for vacancies in the
field for infantry, cavalry or artillery. Veterans are
offered a bounty of $727.00 while new recruits are
offered the sum of $627.00, payable in installments.*

Price Range

Upon enlistment the men are offered a month's pay of $13.00, the first bounty installment of $62.00, plus a state bounty of $325.00, payable in cash or check. A serious note is added that in event the man is killed, his heirs will receive any unpaid bounty. Interesting but not rare. 118.00   130.00

☐ **Army recruiting poster,** World War I. An Army sentry stands on a hill overlooking the Rhine River in Germany. He wears his trench helmet and holds his Springfield rifle, bayonet attached, at right shoulder arms. At his feet is a battered German steel helmet. Across the river is a castle with the American flag flying over it. Across the bottom of the poster are the words "Die Wacht am Rhein" and the translation below "(The Watch on the Rhine)." In full color. Interesting. 37.00   40.00

☐ **Army recruiting poster,** World War I. "COLUMBIA CALLS" heads this one. A beautiful classical figure of Columbia stands atop the world holding Old Glory in her right hand and a sword in her left. To the lower left appears "ENLIST NOW FOR U.S. ARMY" with address of the nearest recruiting office. To the lower right of the poster appears a poem entitled "Columbia Calls." A bright and colorful poster. Pure appeal to patriotism. 46.00   50.00

☐ **Army recruiting poster,** World War I. Full color poster showing Uncle Sam with his hat and coat at his feet striding forward as he rolls up his sleeves. American eagle and stars in background, text reads "DEFEND YOUR COUNTRY ENLIST NOW." 18.50   20.00

☐ **Army recruiting poster,** World War I. Full color specialized poster. This one is for the Air Service. In the foreground is an American eagle, brown with white head and tail getting the best of a face to face aerial battle with a black Imperial German eagle. In the far background are several war planes. The main text reads "JOIN THE ARMY AIR SERVICE BE AN AMERICAN EAGLE!" Instructions advise the individual to consult his local draft board or write the Army for an illustrated booklet. A much better than average poster. 64.00   70.00

☐ **Army recruiting poster,** World War I. Full color specialized poster appealing for a particular trade. A sergeant wearing a campaign hat and laced canvas leggings with his high collar O.D. uniform stands at attention holding a large American flag in his right hand. In the background is the large castle insignia of the Corps of Engineers. In varying typeface the text reads "JOIN THE ENGINEERS AND MAKE AMERICAN HISTORY FIRST REPLACEMENT REGI-

Price Range

MENT OF ENGINEERS NOW ENLISTING MEN BE-
TWEEN 18 TO 21 AND 31 TO 41 APPLY TO COM-
MANDING OFFICER WASHINGTON BARRACKS,
D.C." 49.00   53.00

☐ **Army recruiting poster,** *World War I. Full color. A grim
looking Uncle Sam holds out a rifle in his left hand
and with his right points to the words "DON'T WAIT."
In the background is a large American flag beneath
which soldiers are marching. Uncomplicated but
most effective.* 51.00   55.00

☐ **Army recruiting poster,** *World War I. This example is
probably the most unattractive poster ever produced.
The hate propaganda borders upon the absurd. Full
color art work shows a menacing ape wearing a German officer's spiked helmet ambling across a stretch
of shoreline marked "AMERICA." In his left arm the
ape holds a seminude maiden. In his right hand he
holds a heavy club marked "KULTUR." In the background appears a ruined European city. Across the
top of the poster appears "DESTROY THIS MAD
BRUTE." At the bottom appears "ENLIST U.S.
ARMY." Poor taste, poor art work.* 10.00   11.00

☐ **Army recruiting poster,** *World War II. American
soldiers in full combat uniforms and equipment
march at "Eyes Right" before a group of rugged Colonial soldiers. In the upper left hand corner is "1778"
and in the upper right hand corner is "1943." This
poster doesn't need much text. The message is clear.
It has hard hitting patriotic and historical appeal.
Excellent full color art work. Appealing.* 46.00   50.00

☐ **Army recruiting poster,** *World War II. Across the top
are the words "WEST POINT OF THE AIR" / "FLYING
CADETS." At the bottom is "U.S. ARMY AIR CORPS."
Smaller type gives information where and how to
apply. Center two-thirds of poster occupied by
scenes of bombers, pursuit planes, training planes
and installations. In color.* 37.50   40.00

☐ **Coast Guard recruiting poster,** *post World War II. A
smiling Coast Guardsman in blue blouse and white
cap looks directly at the viewer. In the background a
Coast Guard cutter with a Coast Guard flying boat
above, all upon a shield. At the bottom in three lines
appears "SERVE" / "in the Armed Forces with the" /
"U.S. COAST GUARD."* 10.75   11.50

☐ **Coast Guard recruiting poster,** *post World War II.
Smiling Coast Guardsman in white uniforms holds
binoculars. In the background is the world globe. In
three lines across the bottom appears "a good look"/
"at your future" / "U.S. COAST GUARD."* 10.75   11.50

☐ **Marine Corps recruiting poster,** *between World Wars
I and II. A handsome young Marine in khaki uniform,*

Marine Corps, post Span.-Amer. W.

Marine Corps, post World War II.

Marine Corps, post World War I.

Marine Corps, World War I.

Price Range

web equipment and rifle hanging from its sling over his left shoulder, gestures with his right hand. The text is to the point. "FOLLOW ME" "ON LAND" "AT SEA AND IN THE AIR" "U.S. MARINES." Steel helmet has the Marine emblem on the front, handsome poster but not much sought after.................... 18.50   20.00

☐ **Marine Corps recruiting poster,** between World Wars I and II. Full color of the stern deck of a heavy cruiser with Marine bugler sounding a call while standing near a crane used to lift seaplanes aboard. Much deck gear about. Text reads "U.S. MARINES." "SOLDIERS WHO GO TO SEA." As above, interesting but not important. Excellent detail and color. 18.50   20.00

☐ **Marine Corps recruiting poster,** c. early 1900's. Headed "MEN WANTED." Small drawing of Marine shore landing party in a tropical scene ashore with battleships offshore. Marines wear khaki uniforms with campaign hats. Two Marines have a very early model Browning aircooled machine gun. Indicates service both ashore and afloat "from the Spanish Main to the Orient" as well as "At Home and Abroad, From China to the West Indies." Not a real attractive poster, lacks professionalism. 20.00   22.00

☐ **Marine Corps recruiting poster,** c. early 1900's. Same text and photos as above, changed art work in center of poster. This one has painting of Marine sergeant in dress blues with his Springfield rifle at "port arms." Another Marine in dress blues is blowing a bugle. Between them is a pedestal with the Marine Corps emblem on it. Not too attractive, lacks professional touch....................................... 42.00   45.00

☐ **Marine Corps recruiting poster,** c. early 1900's. The above art work is smaller size surrounded with photos of Marine activities afloat and ashore. Text simply states "U.S. MARINES" / "SOLDIERS OF THE SEA," with address of recruiting station. Not as attractive as the above. 42.00   45.00

☐ **Marine Corps recruiting poster,** c. early 1900's. This is an excellent poster in full color with art work by a professional artist. Shows a Marine private in dress blue coat, white trousers and white cap cover standing behind a desk in an office/laboratory setting. An extremely handsome type, the Marine holds what appears to be a large text book. Before him on the desk are several articles, including a telephone, blueprints, slide rule, measuring beaker, a sextant and a world globe. Outside a large window is an industrial scene. The only text is to the point "U.S. MARINES." "The service with a Future." A really handsome poster. 46.00   50.00

Price Range

☐ **Marine Corps recruiting poster,** c. early 1900's. This is perhaps the poorest poster issued by the Marines. Poorly executed painting of Marine sergeant in dress blues holding a rifle quite unlike that ever seen in service. Also has a painting of a battleship somewhat similar to the U.S.S. Oregon. At the bottom of the poster is a drawing of a barracks. Brief text reads "MEN WANTED" / "FOR THE" / "U.S. MARINES" / "AN" / "OPPORTUNITY" / "TO SEE" / "THE WORLD"/ "DUTY ON SHORE, AT SEA AND IN" / "OUR ISLAND POSSESSIONS." This followed by address of recruiting station. 18.50   20.00

☐ **Marine Corps recruiting poster,** c. early 1900's. This too is a beautiful poster in full color. It shows a Marine sergeant in dress blues with his Springfield rifle at "right shoulder arms" patrolling a wharf or dock to which a battleship with wire cage masts is moored. In the far background is a Marine barracks with other buildings behind. This is one of the most famous of Marine posters. The Marine is known as "Walking John" and he turns up regularly in a continually updated uniform and modernized background. Otherwise the poster is always the same. The text is simple but effective. "U.S. MARINES." "ACTIVE SERVICE ON LAND AND SEA." At the bottom of the poster is a space for the address of the recruiting office. 55.00   60.00

☐ **Marine Corps recruiting poster,** c. early 1900's. Well-executed painting of two Marines in foreground and battleships with wire cage masts of the period in the background. Marines wear khaki uniforms Montana peak, broad brim campaign hats and laced canvas leggings. One Marine is prone with binoculars. The other stands behind with legs apart signalling with large semaphore flag. The sole text is "U.S. MARINES." Excellent art work. 55.00   60.00

☐ **Marine Corps recruiting poster,** pre-World War II. Full color poster by the well-known Marine artist Colonel Don Dickson. A self-confident and rugged Marine stands with legs apart holding his rifle with both hands. Dressed in khaki uniform with sleeves rolled back. Stands against a background of a large Marine emblem superimposed upon a listing of all the battles the Marines had fought in to that time, beginning with Bladensburg and ending with Tientsin. Across the top is "SERVICE IN THE FOUR CORNERS OF THE GLOBE." Across the bottom is "WE ARE PROUD TO CLAIM THE TITLE OF UNITED STATES MARINE." Typical appeal to pride of corps. 18.50   20.00

☐ **Marine Corps recruiting poster,** pre-World War II. Shows "Walking John" in an updated Marine ser-

Price Range

geants dress blue uniform walking post against an
updated background of a battleship and harbor
scene. The appeal reads "U.S. MARINES" "Active
Service" "Land Sea Air." Good attention to detail,
interesting as all "Walking John" posters are. 23.00 25.00

☐ **Marine Corps recruiting poster,** *post Civil War.* Poster
headed "U.S. MARINE CORPS" / "RECRUITING
SERVICE" in two lines with three woodcuts between
the lines. These are rather crude. In the middle is a
paddlewheel warship with a Marine with musket in
the uniform of the period standing on either side.
Poster seeks men for the Corps for a four year enlistment, notes that Marine sergeants frequently have
independent command of guard units on certain war
vessels, shows pay scale for all ranks from private to
First or Orderly Sergeant of a company. It is related
that one ration a day and an abundant supply of the
best clothing is allowed. Few Marine recruiting post-
ers of this era exist. 290.00 320.00

☐ **Marine Corps recruiting poster,** *post Spanish-American War era.* Poster reads "HE DID HIS DUTY" above
drawing of Admiral George Dewey of Spanish-American War fame. To his left is his quotation "No finer
military organization than the Marine Corps exists in
the World." Under this, in four lines, appears the following "WILL YOU?"/"JOIN FOR ACTIVE SERVICE"/
"LAND AND SEA" / "U.S. MARINES." The last two
lines of text gives the address of the recruiting office. 155.00 170.00

☐ **Marine Corps recruiting poster,** *post World War I.* A
Marine sergeant in more modern dress blues and
with the addition of campaign ribbons and a sharp-
shooter's medal on his left breast points at the
viewer from in front of an entire American flag bear-
ing 48 white stars in the blue field. 73.00 80.00

☐ **Marine Corps recruiting poster,** *post World War II.*
Marine in full combat gear crouches with an automatic rifle. One of another series of posters lifting up
military virtues. Across the top "READY" and across
the bottom "U.S. MARINES." 10.00 11.00

☐ **Marine Corps recruiting poster,** *post World War II.*
The head of a handsome smiling Marine wearing a
white dress cap looks at the viewer. Across the top
"HONOR" and across the bottom in two lines "THE
UNITED STATES MARINE CORPS" / "BUILDS MEN."
This is one of a series of several posters highlighting
a particular virtue. 10.00 11.00

☐ **Marine Corps recruiting poster,** *World War I.* Across
the top appears "E-E-E-YAH-YIP" / "GO OVER WITH"/
"U.S. MARINES." Bottom advises the reader to apply
to his postmaster for information. Fair art work of a

Marine Corps, World War I.

Marine Corps, World War I.

Women's Marine Reserve, W. W. II.

Women's Marine Reserve, W. W. II.

Price Range

Marine in trench helmet and his rifle with bayonet held at high port arms, shouting the above.......... 19.00   21.00

☐ **Marine Corps recruiting poster,** *World War I.* Although there are nine lines of text, the most effective lines are "FIRST TO FIGHT" and "For Fighting — Join the Marines!" Art work shows Marine with Springfield rifle and bayonet landing on a tropical shore with several Marines in the background and a battleship in the background. The Marines shown are much too neat to have ever been in combat. Not too impressive. 18.50   20.00

☐ **Marine Corps recruiting poster,** *World War I.* Another poster with art work by James Montgomery Flagg. Marines in steel helmets wading ashore with rifles held high. Offshore are transports. Text limited to "THE MARINES HAVE LANDED!" Directions to the nearest recruiting station at bottom of poster. Excellent art work as would be expected from this artist. 155.00   170.00

☐ **Marine Corps recruiting poster,** *World War I.* Full color but of rather ordinary art work. A large Marine Corps emblem occupies the top half of this poster. At the upper left is the head of a Marine wearing a campaign hat. At the right is a Marine wearing a steel trench helmet. Both articles of headgear are poorly done. The text reads "THIS DEVICE ON THE HAT OR HELMET MEANS U.S. MARINES FIRST TO FIGHT. An ordinary poster. 18.50   20.00

☐ **Marine Corps recruiting poster,** *World War I.* Full color painting of a Marine officer with Colt automatic pistol in his right hand, in khaki field uniform with a full length American flag in the background. Text reads "FIRST IN THE FIGHT - ALWAYS FAITHFUL -BE A U.S. MARINE." A most effective poster with excellent art work as one might expect for it is by James Montgomery Flagg. 127.00   140.00

☐ **Marine Corps recruiting poster,** *World War I.* Minimum text reading "U.S. MARINES FIRST TO FIGHT FOR DEMOCRACY." Space for recruiting office address. Full color painting of a Marine antiaircraft shipboard gun crew manning their weapon, with a wire cage battleship mast in the background. Apparently they are firing at a Zeppelin which flies overhead. Off to the right is a destroyer. Of all things, the Marines are in action in dress blue uniform. Art work is also very inaccurate in the details of the ship's deck. Not too good. 23.00   25.00

☐ **Marine Corps recruiting poster,** *World War I.* "SPIRIT of 1917" is the attention line on this poster. Below this is a painting of a Marine color guard in a tropical setting with the usual background. On one side is a

Price Range

drawing of a Marine in khaki uniform with campaign hat advancing with his rifle at port arms. On the other side is a Marine in dress blue uniform standing by the breech of a naval deck gun. The remaining text advises the reader to "JOIN THE UNITED STATES MARINES AND BE FIRST IN DEFENSE ON LAND OR SEA" with the address of the recruiting office. Apparently the art work for this one was borrowed from a pre-war poster. **12.00   13.00**

☐ **Marine Corps recruiting poster,** World War I. The artist glamorized this full color poster. Marines in khaki uniforms including campaign hats and canvas leggings follow an officer into some action to which he is pointing. Although it wasn't being done at this time, the artist shows the American flag and the regimental colors being carried into combat. Two Marines are handling Lewis air-cooled machine guns as though they were as light as a rifle. In the right background, war weary peasants amid their shelled homes wave in greeting to the Marines. Offshore are two battleships. All together the picture is far too fanciful and bears little relation to reality. Text reads "U.S. MARINES FIRST TO FIGHT IN FRANCE FOR FREEDOM ENLIST WITH THE 'SOLDERS OF THE SEA!'". **15.00   16.50**

☐ **Marine Corps recruiting poster,** World War I. The art work on this one is by another famous painter, James Montgomery Flagg. A rather handsome civilian with his face set in determination is taking off his coat. At his feet are his hat and a copy of a newspaper with the headlines "HUNS KILL WOMEN AND CHILDREN!" At the top of the poster appears "TELL THAT TO THE MARINES!" The hate motif of the enemy is apparent here. Not as popular as other posters by this artist. **100.00   110.00**

☐ **Marine Corps recruiting poster,** World War I. This example too has indifferent art work probably due to the artist's lack of information on his subject. A Marine in khaki shirt and breeches stands in the bow of a ship's boat holding what is probably meant to be a Lewis air-cooled machine gun. Marines are at the oars. All are wearing the field hat of Spanish-American War vintage. The ship's boat is too small to have stayed afloat with all the Marines it is carrying. Battleship with cage mast in the background. **10.00   11.00**

☐ **Marine Corps recruiting poster,** World War I. This is a funny one. A vicious bulldog with horns emerging from his head wears a steel helmet with the Marine emblem on the front. He is chasing a rather sorry looking dachshund wearing a German officer's spiked helmet. An Iron Cross is tied to the

Price Range

dachshund's tail. *Above this scene appear the words* "TEUFEL HUNDEN GERMAN NICKNAME FOR U.S. MARINES," *below the scene appears* "DEVIL DOG RECRUITING STATION 24 EAST 23rd STREET." *In color. Interesting but not important.* 25.00   27.00

☐ **Marine Corps recruiting poster,** *World War I. This one is beautiful! Occupying most of the full color poster is a beautiful girl in three-quarter length wearing a Marine sergeant's dress blue coat and cap. About her waist is a cartridge belt with shoulder straps in webbing and a bayonet in scabbard. Her right hand rests on the cartridge belt and the left grasps the hilt of the bayonet. In the background are Marines in steel helmets, fixed bayonets on their rifles and colors flying going into combat. The text reads* "IF YOU WANT TO FIGHT JOIN THE MARINES." *This poster is a real work of art. The original was painted by the famous artist Howard Chandler Christy. A real collector's item.* 300.00   330.00

☐ **Marine Corps recruiting poster,** *World War II. A much revised version of* "Walking John." *Here he strides off to the left in full battle gear holding his rifle with bayonet fixed in his right hand and beckons with his left. To the upper right are the words* "LET'S GO!" *At the bottom are the words* "U.S. MARINES." *Much action with good detail.* 32.00   35.00

☐ **Marine Corps recruiting poster,** *World War II. This one shows Marine tanks moving forward through the jungle on Cape Gloucester. Dramatic.* 37.00   40.00

☐ **Marine Corps recruiting poster,** *World War II. Full color fanciful painting of Marines in combat in the jungle. The painting is excellent but has an error in that it shows the American flag and the Regimental color being carried in combat. This just wasn't done. The words* "LET'S GO GET 'EM!" *heads the poster with* "U.S. MARINES" *at the bottom.* 37.00   40.00

☐ **Marine Corps recruiting poster,** *World War II. Painting of a Marine in combat gear advancing through the jungle with his M-1 rifle and fixed bayonet ready for an encounter with the Japanese. The smoke of battle drifts across the scene. Above appears* "LET 'EM HAVE IT." *At the bottom appears* "U.S. MARINES" *with directions to the nearest recruiting station.* 32.00   35.00

☐ **Marine Corps recruiting poster,** *World War II. This poster is but one of a series, each of which carries a painting depicting a scene of one of the Marines' great battles in the South Pacific. All have a brief description of the battle under the painting, the shoulder patch of the units involved and the words* "ENLIST NOW" / "U.S. MARINE CORPS." *The paint-*

Navy, World War I.

Navy, post World War II.

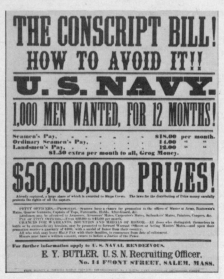

Navy, Civil War.

Navy, World War I.

	Price Range	

ings are by Marine combat artists and they are excellent. This particular poster shows a scene from Guadalcanal with a file of Marines in combat gear struggling forward through the jungle. Interesting and attractive. **37.00**   **40.00**

☐ **Marine Corps Women's Reserve recruiting poster,** World War II. A very beautiful full color poster with a woman Marine officer's head and shoulders occupying most of the space. She is in green uniform with a background of Marines in combat. Under the painting are the words in three lines "BE A MARINE . . ." / "Free a Marine to fight" / "U.S. MARINE CORPS WOMEN'S RESERVE. A most attractive and dignified poster. **32.00**   **35.00**

☐ **Marine Corps Women's Reserve recruiting poster,** World War II. This is probably one of the most beautiful posters of the World War II era. An extremely beautiful woman Marine sergeant in green uniform stands before engine cowling and three-blade propellor of a Marine Corps fighter plane. In the upper right background, a fighter plane zooms by. The woman Marine has a look of dedication and reverence. Across the bottom of the painting are 10 small white stars under a narrow red, white and blue ribbon above which are the words "So Proudly We Serve." Under the painting in two lines appears "U.S. MARINE CORPS" / "Women's Reserve." The painting is extremely well-executed and colors and details are excellent. This is one of the best. **46.00**   **50.00**

☐ **Navy Civil War recruiting poster.** Across the top of this poster in large letters appears, in two lines, "THE CONSCRIPT BILL" "HOW TO AVOID IT!" The poster relates that 1,000 men are needed for 12 months and cites seamen's and landsmen's pay. It is also noted that each sailor receives "grog money." The poster notes to that date $50,000,000.00 prize money had been awarded. According to this poster, promotion was relatively easy. **200.00**   **220.00**

☐ **Navy recruiting poster,** post World War II. Full color poster of three books on left side leaning against four books on the right side to form an arc in which is an aircraft carrier "bows-on." On the backs of the books are the following "SHOP" "HISTORY" "GEOGRAPHY" "MATHEMATICS" "PHYSICS" "ENGLISH" and "SPANISH." Across the top of the poster "stay in school," across the bottom in two lines "your diploma puts everybody ahead" "NAVY." **10.00**   **10.75**

☐ **Navy recruiting poster,** post World War II. This one is an appeal for aviation cadets. The full color painting shows a Navy jet F11F-1 taking off in full flight. In the

Price Range

background are rocket launching cranes with a manned space rocket taking off. To the upper right is the globe as it might appear from outer space. This poster is beautifully done and the details are technically correct. Across the bottom appears "CHOOSE NAVCAD. AOC NAVY." 18.50 20.00

☐ **Navy recruiting poster,** World War I. A rugged handsome seaman with a Colt automatic pistol on a belt on his right hip firmly plants the American flag ashore. In the background a two stack battleship with wire cage mast. Across the bottom of the poster the text reads "ENLIST IN THE NAVY U.S. NAVY RECRUITING STATION" followed by the address. An exceptionally well-done poster with excellent art work, artist was J. Daugherty. Details good. 135.00 145.00

☐ **Navy recruiting poster,** World War I. Exceptionally well-executed full color poster showing a surfacing German U-Boat surrendering to an American destroyer which cuts across the submarine's bow. In the background is a large transport flying the American flag. Excellent detail. This poster by L. A. Shafer is the only World War I poster to show an action at sea. Beautiful and unique. 131.00 145.00

☐ **Navy recruiting poster,** World War I. Full color, top three-fourths of poster has painting of large American eagle with wings partially folded. On its breast is a U.S. shield. Before it appears five sailors wearing white hats. By L. N. Britton. 78.00 85.00

☐ **Navy recruiting poster,** World War I. This specimen is a real tear jerker! Across the top appears in large letters "U.S. NAVY" Three-fourths of the poster is taken up with a painting by the famous artist Charles Dana Gibson (who created the strikingly beautiful Gibson Girl) and which is sentimental to the point of tears. It shows a widow in the center shaking hands with a bareheaded Uncle Sam who stands to her right. To her left stands a very handsome young man with his hat in his hand. The text under the painting reads "Here he is, Sir." "We need him and you too!" The usual recruiting station information appears below. The name of the artist carries this one on. 125.00 150.00

☐ **Navy recruiting poster,** World War I. Yet another poster by James Montgomery Flagg. Dramatic full color painting of a sailor in white uniform grasping the shoulder of a civilian while he gestures toward a beautiful Columbia who holds an American flag and a sword in the background. The civilian is reading a newspaper. The text at the top of the poster reads "THE NAVY NEEDS YOU! DON'T READ HISTORY-MAKE IT!" In the background a battle fleet is dimly seen. Effect and appealing work by a famous artist.. 145.00 160.00

Price Range

☐ **Navy recruiting poster,** *World War II. Here is another beauty. Two handsome seamen in blues are placing a depth charge in its launching gun. The text in three lines reads "Sub Spotted-" / "LET 'EM HAVE IT!" / "LEND A HAND - Enlist in your Navy Today." Excellent color and detail, by the well-known artist McClelland Barclay. Great action.* **59.00   65.00**

☐ **Regular Army recruiting poster.** *This particular poster is somewhat unique in that it is for the Regular Army and is for a particular regiment. In four lines across the top appears "SONS OF" / "NEW-ENGLAND!" / "AROUSE" / "YOUR COUNTRY CALLS YOU!" It goes on to relate that 200 able-bodied men who are unmarried are needed for the 11th Regular Army Infantry. Enlistment is for 3 years. The same bounty of money or land is promised as for volunteers in the militia units. $2.00 is a sum promised to anyone who brings an accepted recruit to the recruiting officer. There is no art work but the unique nature of the poster makes it of added value.* **232.00   255.00**

In view of their uniqueness and price, the following three posters are listed separately. As noted in the foregoing text on the background and history of recruiting posters these three, for the Army, Navy and Marine Corps, all make use of the "I WANT YOU" attention line. As was also noted, all three of these posters apparently are a take off of a famous British Army poster of the period which shows Field Marshal Lord Kitchener pointing and saying "I WANT YOU." They are not likely to be found at militaria dealers or gun shows. It is more probable that they will, when offered, be offered by top flight antique dealers, print and book shops catering to affluent collectors and art galleries frequented by individuals seeking outstanding example of art work by famous artists.

☐ **Army recruiting poster,** *World War I. This is the most sought after of this particular group of posters. It shows a frowning half length Uncle Sam, with hat, pointing his finger at the viewer. In two lines in large letters appears "I WANT YOU" / "FOR THE U.S. ARMY." This is followed by the address of the nearest recruiting station. A most forceful poster with outstanding art work by James Montgomery Flagg.* **610.00   680.00**

☐ **Marine Corps recruiting poster,** *World War I. This is the third and last of this particular series. A very handsome Marine sergeant in dress blues of the period is stepping out from a wide red vertical red bar and before a similar white bar and another red bar. These apparently are the red and white stripes of a very large American flag. He is pointing with his right hand at the viewer. Across the top is "THE U.S. MARINES" and across the bottom is "WANT YOU." This is followed by the recruiting office address. This full color poster is excellently executed and the uniform details are extremely accurate.* **155.00   170.00**

Price Range

☐ **Navy recruiting poster,** *World War I. The next most sought after of this particular series. A very beautiful young woman in a chief petty officer's coat stands with both hands in the pockets. The left sleeve bears a chief's chevrons and two hash marks and is worn over an open throat shirt. A chief's cap is worn at a very jaunty angle. At the upper right of the poster appears "I WANT YOU!" Across the bottom appears "For THE NAVY." Poster executed in full color. The young lady looks like a fashion model. She is painted as only Howard Chandler Christy could paint a beautiful woman. An extremely beautiful poster by a famous artist.* 430.00   480.00

The above selection of posters represents but a few of the hundreds upon hundreds which have been issued throughout the years and which are still being issued. The selection, however, is a typical cross section and gives an excellent indication as to price trends, a trend which is ever upward. It should be noted that in all of his many years dealing in militaria, the author has never seen as wide a variation in military items as there is in posters. Some dealers refuse to handle them because of the wide variation in price. Collectors interested in posters merely as a military collectible will not give large amounts for items. However, historians and art lovers will give an extremely high price for a poster because of its historical or artistic merit. Posters by famous or well-known artists will always bring a premium price.

POWDER FLASKS

Closely associated with powder horns are powder flasks. Like powder horns they were in use for many years following the introduction of firearms. These flasks appear in a great variety of forms and may be made of various metals, leather, and even of horn. They were used world wide. In complete condition they have a spout device to measure the amount of powder released. Since they appear in so many forms and are to be found in some quantity they do not require a great investment. Military flasks generally command a higher price than others.

☐ **Brass flask.** *Deeply embossed shell design on each side, adjustable charger, carrying rings. Still another standard design by the American Flask and Cap Co.* .   91.00   100.00
☐ **Brass flask.** *Deeply embossed with hanging game design on one side only, four carrying rings, adjustable charger. This is another specimen from James Dixon and Sons.* 87.00   95.00
☐ **Brass flask.** *Heavy fluted design all around, adjustable charger, carrying rings. Another standard design from the American Flask and Cap Co.* 78.00   85.00
☐ **Brass flask** *with deeply embossed design of hanging game on each side, adjustable charger, carrying ring. Marked to the American Flask and Cap Co. This old*

Price Range

company was a long time manufacturer of flasks and this offering is one of the popular designs offered by them. **64.00   70.00**

Note: Of some considerable interest is the fact that the original catalogs of American Flask and Cap Co. are very scarce and when available sell for $350.00 or more.

☐ **Brass powder flask** *with embossed feather design about rear. The adjustable telescope measure is intact.* **78.00   85.00**

☐ **Brass powder flask** *with embossed shell design on both sides. The adjustable telescope measure is intact.* **51.00   55.00**

☐ **Brown Leather Covered Brass flask.** *Adjustable charger, complete with carrying rings. This specimen by Frary, Benham & Co.* **73.00   80.00**

☐ **Copper flask.** *Heavily embossed oval cartouche enclosing a classic type hunting horn superimposed upon hunting rifles with hunting hounds, rest of flask fluted, brass charger, two side rings.* **177.00   195.00**

☐ **Copper flask** *of interesting cone form, measuring spout, small carrying ring on each side. Interesting but not rare.* **60.00   65.00**

☐ **Copper flask** *with brass adjustable charger, carrying rings. Flask bears applied oval embossed with the figure of a hunter shooting over his dog. From the famed firm of James Dixon & Sons.* **82.00   90.00**

☐ **Copper powder flask** *embossed with basket work and leaf design, adjustable measure.* **114.00   125.00**

☐ **Copper powder flask** *embossed with tiny stars and disks. Telescope measure is intact. Most attractive.* . **100.00   110.00**

☐ **Copper powder flask** *in the form of an old powder horn. Two suspension rings on top, has plug in lieu of measure. Interesting.* **78.00   85.00**

☐ **Heavy copper flask** *in the form of a gun stock. Elaborately embossed in floral and checkered designs, telescope measure. Its gun stock form makes this a unique offering.* **146.00   160.00**

☐ **Leather Covered Brass flask.** *Plain, large size, four carrying rings, adjustable charger. By James Dixon & Sons.* **37.00   41.00**

☐ **Leather Covered Brass powder flask** *by James Dixon & Sons. Telescope measure is intact.* **82.00   90.00**

☐ **Military flask,** *brass. Obverse deeply embossed with a flaming grenade with smaller grenades and flames encircling the lower half of the larger grenade. Reverse side deeply embossed with the letters "R.G." under a crown, and the date "1728" is engraved under this. Edges of flask elaborately engraved in floral design, engraved brass cover to spout is used as powder measure, carrying loops on*

	Price Range	

each side of flask. Condition consistent with age but sound, military flasks are rare. European. A unique offering. **1360.00 1500.00**

☐ **Military flask.** c. 1827. Large brass flask embossed with light infantry horn or bugle and "PUBLIC PROPERTY" in two lines. Telescope measuring spout. Interesting American Army issue flask. **168.00 185.00**

☐ **Military flask,** heavy copper of the so-called "PEACE" type. Heavily embossed with trophy of crossed flags, cannon and other gear, in the center is an oval design of stars enclosing clasped hands, top bears markings of "Batt'y-Springfield-1857" plug government inspector's marks. Much of original lacquer worn away, otherwise in excellent condition **254.00 280.00**

☐ **Wicker Covered Brass powder flask.** The telescope measure is intact. Wicker covered flasks not too often found. **82.00 90.00**

☐ **Zink powder flask** with brass end, embossed fighting birds on each side. Telescope measure intact. **50.00 55.00**

JAPANESE POWDER FLASKS

Because of their shape, highly lacquered finish and their decoration, Japanese powder flasks **(Hayago),** like so many other Japanese arms, armour and accouterments are beautiful works of art. They attract in many cases an entirely different segment of collectors and therefore are listed separately here. Traditionally these flasks are usually made of leather, wood or papermache. They vary greatly in size and shape. They have for the most part an outlet tube closed by a cap of wood, bone or ivory which has a measuring tube attached.

☐ **Cylindrical Form,** c. 1700's. Ivory mounts. **86.00 95.00**

☐ **Cylindrical Form With One Flat Side.** Beautiful heavily lacquered (brown) wood flask, flat top and bottom, complete with spout, cap and measuring tube. Around top third of flask is a brass band with brass belt hook on flat side of flask, no mon. Interesting and of a form not usually seen. **145.00 160.00**

☐ **Flat Circular Design,** c.1700's. Wood covered with black leather, highly lacquered and decorated with gold family mon, wood cap and measuring tube. **87.00 95.00**

☐ **Flat Circular Design,** c.1700's. Wood with covering of overlapping sections of rawhide, wood cap and measuring tube, has never been lacquered. Obviously used by a commoner, has aged well and is in excellent condition. **100.00 110.00**

☐ **Flat Circular Form,** c. 1700's. Leather with lacquer finish in black, large gold family mon on one side, ivory and measure. Excellent. **136.00 150.00**

☐ **Gourd Shape,** c. 1700's Wood heavily lacquered in black, spout, cap and measuring tube of horn. Not too often found in gourd shape. **91.00 100.00**

Price Range

☐ **Flat Circular Design,** c. 1700's. Decorated with family mon, in gold, wood cap and measuring tube, carrying rings with decorative silk sling.................... 91.00   100.00

☐ **Long Cylindrical Form,** c. 1700's. Lacqured shell decorated with a dragon in raised red lacquer, ivory cap and measure. Very unusual.................. 127.00   140.00

☐ **Rounded Bottlelike Form.** c. 1600's. Wood covered with fine deerskin, cap, spout and measuring tube of ivory, spout is carved in floral designs, all complete. Aged but all intact. Excellent example of nobleman's flask. 259.00   285.00

☐ **Semi-cylindrical Form,** c. 1700's. Wood cap and measure, flask covered with brown lacquer with large family mon, large size, has belt or sash hook at rear. Unusual and beautiful.......................... 127.00   150.00

☐ **Tortise Shell Form,** c. 1700's. Both sides richly lacquered and finished to resemble the shell. Usually cap and measuring tube of wood................. 100.00   110.00

POWDER HORNS

The powder horn, made from the horn of ruminant animals is of ancient origin and was universally used. The large end was sealed and the small end closed by means of a plug. It provided a cheap and convenient method of carrying gun powder. Hung from a cord or strap about the neck it was always conveniently at hand. Interestingly enough the most sought after and the most expensive powder horns are those America examples of the 1700's. Many of these were individually carved and decorated by their one time owners and are one of a kind examples of primitive colonial art. Some have elaborately carved maps, hunting or battle scenes or rural scenes. Many are dated and bear the owners name. Values vary as is only to be expected for individual works of art. Powder horns less elaborately carved and not historically associated are priced in the $800.00 range. Elaborately carved, historically associated examples are now priced in the neighborhood of $2500.00. Plain examples may be had for $125.00. As is usually always the case with rare items, some dishonest characters are making fakes. The collector should be sure of the reliability of the dealer or individual from whom he buys.

RARE AND UNUSUAL

From time to time, rare or unusual "one of a kind" military items will be offered for sale. They are offered infrequently and so have not been listed in the previous sections. Many of these are of museum quality and are rather costly. Also there are some very unique items which are of great interest to collectors and are seldom available. Nonetheless, they are offered at fairly modest prices. It is believed that the following price guide will be of interest to those in search of unique artifacts.

ARTIFACTS   Price Range

☐ **Adolph Hitler's Pocket Watch.** *This authenticated silver cased watch has a plain white face with black Arabic hour numerals and gold hour and second hands. Hitler was wearing this pocket watch when he was wounded by shell fragments, one of which pierced the watch, breaking the glass and destroying the minute hand. Shell fragment hole at 11:00 o'clock. Watch came with authenticating document. This item was offered at auction several years ago at a reserve bid of:* . . . .   2500.00   —

☐ **Herman Goering's Wedding Sword.** *Present to Goering by Luftwaffe officers on the occasion of his marriage to Emmy Sonnemann, a famed German actress. Only the finest design and craftsmanship entered into the fabrication of this unique gift. Made by the ancient and world famous firm of Carl Eickhorn in Solingen, Germany. Elaborate in all details. Upon one side of the blade appears the inscription "10 APRIL 1935 DIE REICHSLUFTWAFFE IHREM OBERFEFEHL-SHABER" (The National Air Force, to its Commander-in Chief, April 10, 1935). The other side bears the inscription "GETREU DEM FUHRER FUR VOLK UND REICH" (Loyal to the Fuhrer, for the People and Nation). Sword offered in handsome glass and wood display case, a most unusual and historic offering. Items such as this are usually in the possession of national museums. This item was offered at auction at a reserve bid of:* . . . .   61000.00   —

☐ **Herman Goering's Yacht.** *Named "Carin II" in honor of his first wife who died of illness, this beautiful motor yacht was presented to Goering by the German automobile industry upon the occasion of his second marriage. As may be expected, it is of the finest materials throughout with regard for both safety and comfort. Tastefully decorated and appointed throughout. White hull bears the Goering arms in color on the bow. The reserve bid was* **over:** . .   800000.00   —

☐ **Japanese Aerial Camera,** *c. World War II. Strikingly similar in overall appearance to a World War I vintage Lewis air-cooled machine gun. Uses 35mm film, black enamel finish with iron and brass fittings, wood grips to pistol stock, aerial machine gun type sight, has numerous markings in Japanese, unusual item.* 200.00   220.00

☐ **Marshal's Baton.** *General Hans model on March 31, 1944 was appointed a field marshal in the Army of the Third Reich in recognition of his command ability. At that time he was presented with this field marshal's baton. It is of cane completely covered with highest quality red velvet. The entire surface of*

Price Range

*the baton is ornamented with gold Third Reich eagles
grasping a swastika alternating with black enamel
and silver Iron Crosses. Ornate pommels are of gold.
On top of one appears the Third Reich eagle and
swastika, on the other appears the Iron Cross. Here
again is a most important historic museum quality
offering. The reserve bid was* **over:** .... **30000.00**   —
*NOTE: It is well to realize that in some instances where very expensive and
extremely one of a kind artifacts are offered for sale, the final price at the
request of the buyer is not made public. The reserve prices noted are the
lowest bid which would be considered.*

GIFT BOX

☐ **Royal gift box,** *c. 1914. Heavy brass box with deeply
stamped lid with the profile of British Princess Mary
in high relief within a circle enclosed within a laurel
wreath. At the top within a cartouche the words
"IMPERIUM BRITANNICUM" and below in another
cartouche the words "CHRISTMAS 1914." Within a
wide border decorated with military and naval scenes
appears the names of the Allies, France, Russia,
Belgium, Japan, Serbia, and Montenegro. Contained
tobacco and cigarettes or candy and was given to all
members of the British armed forces and widows of
prisoners of war and those killed in action. An
interesting military curio of World War I.* **73.00**   **80.00**

☐ **Royal gift box,** *c. 1900. Given in the name of Queen
Victoria to troops in South Africa during the Boer
War. Gold color tin box with red lid. In the center a
large medallion of the head of the Queen, on the right
in large white letters "SOUTH AFRICA" above the
date "1900" in gold. On the left the royal cypher with
the "V" in blue and the "R" in white and the "I" in
gold, all under a gold crown. Along the bottom of the
lid within a blue and white border in a facsimile of the
Queen's handwriting the message "I wish you a
Happy New Year. Victoria R.I." The box was packed
with good quality chocolate bars.* **64.00**   **70.00**

HEADDRESS

☐ **British Army Officer's Shako.** *Of the Waterloo or
Belig pattern. A raised front piece extends above the
body of the shako which is of black felt. The head-
band is of black silk as is the trim to the front. Black
silk rosette and gilt button at top left of shako but no
plume is present, black leather visor, gilt cord drapes
down across the front to form a "V," gilt bullion
tassels hang from the right side. In addition to the
high quality of this piece, the special shako plate
sets it apart and adds considerably to the value. The*

Price Range

large silver cartouche has a raised border and is topped by a Royal Crown. Below this appears a gilt ribbon bearing the battle honor "MINDEN." At left center of the plate is the cypher "GR" (Georgius Rex). At the right center are the Prince of Wales plumes and coronet. At bottom center is a sphinx with the word "EGYPT" below, all in gilt. This identifies the shako as having belonged to an officer of The 23rd Regiment (Royal Welsh Fusiliers). Extremely difficult to find. 4640.00   5100.00

☐ **British Trench Helmet with Face Protector,** c. World War I. This was still another experimental effort to reduce face wounds. Permanently attached to the front of the conventional British "tin hat" is a light brass frame holding a piece of chain mail. The frame could be raised up out of the way when it was not desired to use the protection. Actual use in the trenches proved it to be too cumbersome and reduced the vision too much to be practicable. 550.00   610.00

☐ **French Experimental Trench Helmet with Face Visor.** This helmet with visor was tried by both the U.S. and the French but was not acceptable. Hinged light steel visor pierced with numerous vision slits, visor may be pushed up when not in use, very few were ever made and are rarely offered for sale. 802.00   885.00

☐ **French Shako,** c. 1st Empire. Black felt shako with flat black leather top with a leather band extending around the top of the shako. Black leather visor with white metal edge. White metal chin scales attached to each side by large white metal bosses bearing a stamped lyre device. Front plate consists of large silver crowned eagle standing on a cartouche, the top of which bears an embossed trophy of arms. In the center of the cartouche is the numeral "100." Behind the eagle's head is a red, white and blue cloth cockade with a red plume extending from the top. Shako shows lack of proper care, felt is badly worn and shako slightly out of form. Nonetheless it is a rare example, rather difficult to locate. Bell crowned.   1325.00   1450.00

☐ **Hannover Infantry Officer's Shako,** c. 1866. Medium high black felt cylindrical body with slightly sunken black leather top and wide band of black leather about the bottom. Wide band of gold lace about the top, gold trim to back of black leather visor which has a wide gold lace band about the front, gilt wreath front plate with crown above, within the wreath a white metal horse (the white horse of Hannover). Under the wreath a ribbon bearing the inscription "18. Juni Waterloo 1815." White metal and gilt thick circular field badge. Not often seen. 1640.00   1800.00

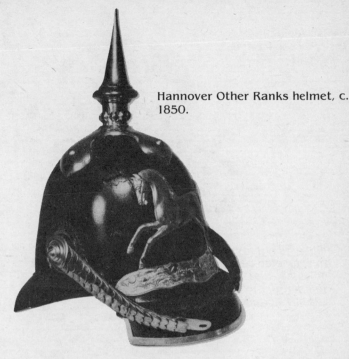

Hannover Other Ranks helmet, c. 1850.

Price Range

☐ **Hannover Other Ranks Helmet,** *c. 1850. High domed black leather skull with brass trimmed front visor and untrimmed back visor. Tall graceful brass spike, base with cross form mounting, brass retaining studs, brass chin scales with red and white rosette on right side. Front plate is a large prancing horse in white metal with white metal representation of ground below. Details are good but do not show the finesse of later stampings. This particular specimen has a small repaired slash on the right front. However, helmet is in very good condition and is a very difficult to locate example.* **800.00   875.00**

☐ **Italian Alpine Infantry Officer's Service Hat.** *1939 pattern. Rank of 1st Lieutenant (tenente). Fine quality gray felt hat with round crown and fairly wide brim turned up in back. Brim is bound in cloth about the edges, wide gray cloth band about bottom of crown, subdued embroidered insignia of eagle with widespread wings, jager horns and crossed rifles. Within the ring of the horns is the figure "6" identifying the wearer as an officer in the 6th Alpine Regiment. On the left side of the hat band is a decorative domed feather holder bearing the Cross of Savoy. The*

Italian Alpine Infantry
Officer's Service hat,
1939 pattern.

Price Range

*feather is cut in the pattern peculiar to this regiment.
An enameled badge affixed to the left side of the hat
indicates that the wearer was a member of the
National Ski Instructor's School. Seldom offered for
sale but almost certain to increase in value.* 180.00   175.00

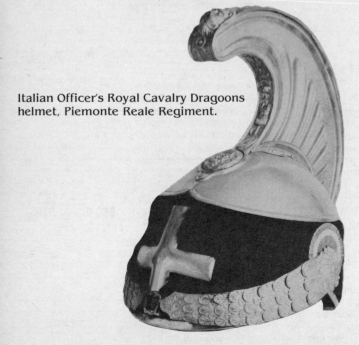

Italian Officer's Royal Cavalry Dragoons
helmet, Piemonte Reale Regiment.

Price Range

☐ **Italian Officer's Royal Cavalry Dragoons Helmet,** *Piemonte Reale Regiment. The basic pattern of this interesting and handsome helmet originated in 1814. This particular specimen is of the type worn for parade until 1939. The skull is of silver covered almost three-fourths of the way up with fine quality sealskin with a silver border at the top. Atop the skull is a highly arched classical Roman type crest decorated with volutes. At the top front is a lion head mask. Down the front is a raised design of Roman arms and armor. At the base of the crest is a brass medallion bearing the monogram of King Victor Emmanul III. This indicated that this specimen was worn from 1901 to 1939. In front is a large Cross of Savoy in silver, ornate chin scales are of brass, under the left chin scale boss is a cockade in red, white and green. To the author's knowledge, this type helmet has been offered for sale not more than four times. . .*   1100.00   1210.00

Italian Parade helmet,
Musketters of the Duce
(Moschettieri del Duce).

☐ **Italian Parade Helmet,** *Musketeers of the Duce (Moschettieri del Duce). The musketeers were Mussolini's personal bodyguards. It was an extremely elite organization with a limited number of members. The skull of this helmet is patterned on the Italian World War II helmet. It has a soft calfkskin and white silk lining. The helmet is entirely black. On the front appears a solid silver skull and crossbones (teschio) attached with two steel prongs. It is impossible to place a value on this item. Only one example is known in this country. It is in the hands of a private collector. This helmet and* **the helmet of the Royal Guard of Tuscany, which was found in an attic**

Price Range

in Connecticut, are listed against the possibility that other examples may be found and their value known.

Italian Royal Guards
(Guardie Regie) helmet,
model of 1920.

☐ **Italian Royal Guards Helmet,** *(Guardie Regie), model of 1920. This parade helmet is of aluminum and is closely patterned after the French Army Adrian trench helmet of World War I. Very large front plate consisting of an eagle grasping the Shield of Savoy which is encircled in a wreath of oak and laurel leaves. This helmet is rarely seen in this country and the front plate is unique and difficult to find. At the present time the interest among American collectors in helmets of this type has not been as great as elsewhere. However, as more become known about them and as helmets from Germany and Russia become harder and harder to find, these helmets will begin a rapid rise in price.* 200.00   220.00

☐ **Nazi Navy Administrative Official's Sun Helmet.** *White canvas covered sun helmet. Large stylized Nazi eagle grasping a wreath, all in silver, with a black swastika in the center of the wreath. White leather chin strap and binding to edge of helmet. Not often offered for sale* 250.00   300.00

☐ **Papal Guard Helmet,** *c. late 1800's. Similar in pattern to the helmet of the Italian Royal Cavalry Dragoons. Well-rounded skull and visors of white metal, lower three-fourths of skull covered with black fur,*

Navy Administrative
Official sun helmet.

Price Range

classical gilt Roman pattern crest decorated with volutes, gilt chin scales, front plate consists of large heraldic star bearing the arms of Pius XI, leather and silk lining to helmet, unusual and hard to find. 575.00   635.00

☐ **Papal State Helmet,** *c. 1905. German spiked helmet (pickelhauben) pattern, polished black leather skull and visors, gilt edge to front visor. Leather backed gilt chin chain with gilt metal cockade with silver ring under the chin chain boss. Large front plate of a heraldric star superimposed upon the Papal Arms. In the center of the star a semidomed circle or disk bearing "PIO" over the Roman numeral "X." Very graceful tall gilt spike with circular base held in place by four star headed screws. This is a most handsome helmet and although hard to find is almost necessary to complete a spiked helmet collection.* 800.00   875.00

☐ **Papal State Helmet.** *c. mid-1800's. Fairly tall conical polished black leather skull with front and rear visors. Similar to the Prussian helmet of the period. Small plain spike with cross type base, attached by four studs. The front plate is large and consists of the papal cypher within a circle surrounded by a floral wreath. Above is the papal crown with crossed keys. Large lion mask attachment on each side of skull for attachment of chin strap. No strap present. All trimmings in brass. And other ranks helmet and old.* 400.00   500.00

Papal State helmet.

Price Range

☐ **Prussian Mirletron or Flugelmutze,** *c. 1842, 5th Land-wehr Hussar Regiment. Black leather body with silver metal "5" on front, on the right side a large Landwehr cross, silver chin scales. At the top right a black and white cloth field badge, black leather top. A long white "wing" lined with black wraps around the top of the headpiece and hangs down on the right side. Rarely if ever seen for sale in this country.* 1550.00   1700.00

Prussian Officer's
Field cap, c. 1843.

Price Range

☐ **Prussian Officer's Field Cap,** *c. 1843. This might be classified by some as a mirletron inasmuch as it appears to be a shorter version of the above. Black felt cylindrical body tapering only slightly in toward the top. Black leather top with a black leather band encircling the cap a third of the way down. Turned up half round felt flap with black leather edge simulates turned back visor. Chin scales are silver. Appearing on the front of the cap is the number "10" in silver while on the side appears the Landwehr Cross also in silver. This is an interesting variation inasmuch as the cross usually appears on the front of the head-dress. On the right above the cross is an officer's field badge of oval form of silver wire with a black velvet center. Silver cap lines terminating in acorns drape from the left top of the cap. Cap is in very good condition for its age, with some fading to felt and tar-nished metal parts and cap lines. Rarely offered for sale. . . . .*   1590.00   1750.00

☐ **Rumanian Officer's Helmet,** *c. 1930's. Polished green leather skull with front and rear visors bound silver color metal. Rear visor is semi-lobster tail pattern. Crest with silver color metal trim and with finely detailed eagle with widespread wings as front piece to crest. Silver color metal chin scales. Front plate consists of intertwined initials "C" (King Carol) with crown above, all in silver color metal. Silver/red/blue metal cockard under chin scale boss on right side. Only three offered for sale in this country. . . . .*   685.00   750.00

☐ **Rumanian Other Ranks Helmet,** *c. late 1800's. Guard Infantry Regiment. Black leather well-rounded skull with front and rear visors trimmed in white metal, white metal spike with cross type base. Spike is very short and has a ball finial. White metal chin scales, white metal front plate consisting of intertwined initials "C" (King Carol) with crown above. Seen at auction twice in this country and a few times abroad, interesting. . . . .*   595.00   650.00

☐ **Russian Other Ranks Dragoon Helmet,** *c. 1910. Polished black leather skull and front and rear visors, front visor edged in brass, brass chin scales, bushy white hair crest extending from side to side of skull. White/orange/black/orange/black cockard under chin scale boss. This helmet was worn by 2nd, 4th, 6th, 8th, 9th, 10th, 12th and 14th Dragoon Regiments. . . . .*   1550.00   1700.00

☐ **Splinter Face Mask,** *c. World War I. Blinding has always been a fear in battle. During World War I many special attempts were made to protect the face and particularly the eyes. Some devices were available from commercial sources and the various governments experimented with protective devices.*

None were successful. This present offering was designed to protect against flying shell splinters. It consists of a ballistic steel mask with good quality russet leather on the outside and suede leather pads on the inside. The eye openings are protected by narrow steel bars. Attached to the bottom of the mask is a chain mail piece designed to cover the lower face, British origin. **154.00   170.00**

Tuscany, Helmet of the Royal Guard, c. 1824 to 1859.

☐ **Tuscany, Helmet of the Royal Guard,** *c. 1824 to 1859. Black leather skull with brass trim to front and rear visors. Skull of modified German design, showing some similarity also to spiked helmets of Russia, Austria and Great Britain of the period. Tall spike with ball finial and cross type base extending well down the sides of the helmet, all in brass. Brass spline down the back, a strip of brass joins the base on each side with the bottom trim, red, white and green rosette on left side. Large front plate of brass consists of the ducal crown over a very ornate cartouche which bears the inscription "LEOPOLDO II" (Leopold II, Duke of Tuscany). Ornate brass chin scales attached at each side with brass bosses, maker's name on interior of helmet. This is one of the*

Price Range

rarest of the rare helmets known today. Only one example is known to exist and it belongs to a collector and historian in the United States. It is impossible to presently set a price on such a specimen. . . . .

☐ **U.S. Enlisted Man's Shako,** *c. early 1800's. Black leather bell crowned shako with large deep visor. Yellow worsted lock chain cord attached to each side of the crown hangs down across the front. The front plate is very small and consists of a brass eagle with widespread wings grasping laurel leaves and arrows. On the eagle's breast is a U.S. shield pierced with the number "3." At the top front of the shako is a black leather rosette in the center of which is a small brass button bearing an American eagle with a U.S. shield on its breast upon which appears the letter "A" indicating artillery. In this specimen the leather is badly flaked and pebbled, and the brass chin scales are absent as is the pompon at the top front. This is true of the majority of surviving U.S. shakos of this era. Interestingly enough, not many examples of early U.S. headdress are available although occasionally one is found in some out-of-the-way place. European headdresses of the era are much more abundant and in better condition. However, these few American examples have great historic value and command a high price for collectors especially interested in military Americana. Although in fair to poor condition, this specimen is much sought after.* . **7500.00   8300.00**   ✦

GERMAN (Imperial)

The following offerings are all Imperial German colonial items of headgear. They are all rather rare and are steadily increasing in price. Imperial German helmet and shako collectors are grasping these as soon as they appear. Very few are available, even in Germany.

☐ **Armorer's Tropical Helmet, Cammeroons and Togo.** *Khaki cloth covered cork helmet, black helmet, band with red edge, Imperial German cockade on left side of helmet band, very scarce.* **770.00   850.00**

☐ **Askari Police Troop Other Ranks Shako.** *Visorless cylindrical shako tapering slightly outward at the top. Of khaki cloth over a formed cardboard body, Imperial German eagle front plate, khaki spine cloth attached at rear. Because of their extremely light construction, not many of these have survived.* **1040.00   1150.00**

☐ **East Asian Train Battalion Tropical Helmet.** *Cork covered with brown cloth. This is a rather unusual looking helmet to say the least. The body is similar to that of the conventional jager shako with flat top. In lieu of the usual visors, there is a downward sloping brim extending all around. This is slightly longer in*

Price Range

back than in front. Brass Imperial German eagle front
plate, two metal ventilation eyelets at the top on
each side, Imperial German cockade. These helmets
have not survived very well over the years. This pres-
ent example in fair condition. 860.00   950.00

☐ **East Asian Infantry Regiment Officer's Helmet.** As
other ranks helmet but of much better quality with
gilt fittings, including chin scales. 1180.00   1300.00

☐ **East Asian Infantry Regiment Other Ranks Helmet.**
Conventional style spiked helmet of field gray felt
over cork with leather visors. Imperial German cockade under leather chin strap, brass spike on round
base, brass Imperial German eagle front plate. 975.00   1075.00

☐ **East Asian Jager Battalion Other Ranks Shako.**
Leather shako with field gray cloth covering to body,
leather visors and crown. Imperial German cockade
under leather chin strap, brass Imperial German front
plate, red/white/black field badge at top front. 1000.00   1100.00

☐ **South West Africa Officer's Hat.** Broad brim gray felt
hat turned up on the right side and held in place
against the crown with a red/white/black Imperial
cockade. Hat brim bound in cornflower blue cloth,
wide cornflower blue cloth hat band. 455.00   500.00

IMPERIAL RUSSIAN MILITARY BADGES

Among all of the orders, decorations and medals of the world, the military
badges of Imperial Russia are no doubt the most rare, interesting and unique
of all. For these reasons they are included in this section. Although perhaps
550 or so different examples of these badges were issued, today they are in
extremely limited supply and it is quite possible that no *complete* collection
exists. For quite some time the province of relatively few collectors, these
articles are now attracting a wider range of interest. As is always the case
when artifacts are in limited supply copies have been produced and the collector must be very careful in acquiring these items.

Officers' badges are of silver and/or gold and many are decorated with fine
enamel work. Those of other ranks are of silver and gold color metal and have
no enamel work.

At this time we are listing just a very few of the more interesting examples.
In our next edition of this guide we plan to go into considerable more detail.
For those desiring the definitive word on these badges we strongly recom-
mend *Badges of Imperial Russia* by Serge Andolenko and Robert Werlich.
This study includes not only military badges but civil and religious also.

Imperial Guard Cossask Regiment of His Majesty.
One of the simplest designs but one of the most
beautiful. A raspberry red maltese cross trimmed in
gold, superimposed upon a four point heraldic star.

☐   Officer's. 750.00   850.00
☐   Other Ranks. 250.00   280.00

Price Range

Moscow Regiment of the Imperial Guard. *Traditional St. Andrew's cross executed in blue enamel with gold edges. In the upper left hand arm appears the initial "S." In the upper right arm appears the initial "A." In the lower left hand arm appears the initial "P." In the lower right arm appears the initial "R." These initials refer to the motto "St. Andrew Protector of Russia." Upon the center of the cross is a mounted St. George in gold slaying a dragon in green gold. The horse is silver.*

☐   Officer's. 900.00   1000.00

☐   Other Ranks. 300.00   325.00

Nicholas Imperial Military Academy. *One of the many military schools. This institution was for the training of officers for the general staff. It is of silver with a wreath of oak and laurel leaves surrounding the double head Imperial eagle, with crown above.*

☐   Officer's. 200.00   300.00

Officer's Aeronautical School. *All silver. A circular floral wreath with crossed swords superimposed upon it. Superimposed upon the swords is a crowned Imperial shield with wings extending from each side.*

☐   Officer's. 700.00   850.00

Officer's Artillery Class, Navy Department. *All silver. An anchor chain forming a circle upon which is superimposed a upright anchor and crossed naval cannons.*

☐   Officer's. 600.00   700.00

Officer's Artillery School. *Wreath of oak and laurel leaves upon which is superimposed the Imperial eagle, with crown above, all in silver. Crossed gold cannons below the eagle.*

☐   Officer's. 700.00   850.00

Officer's Class Naval Aviation, Navy Department. *All silver. Upright winged anchor superimposed upon a circle of anchor chain.*

☐   Officer's. 700.00   850.00

Officer's Mine Laying Class, Navy Department. *All silver. Anchor encircled with an anchor chain. A crossed torpedo and early naval mine are superimposed upon the anchor.*

☐   Officer's. 600.00   700.00

Officer's Submarine Class, Navy Department. *All silver. Anchor chain encircling a stockless anchor which is fouled in its own cable. Superimposed upon the anchor and cable is an early type submarine. This is a rare item, as are all the naval badges.*

☐   Officer's. 700.00   800.00

Preobrazhensky Regiment of the Imperial Guard. *Another badge incorporating a St. Andrew's cross. Cross in blue enamel with gold edges. Superimposed upon this cross is a smaller gold cross bearing the figure of St. Andrew. Within the side and bottom*

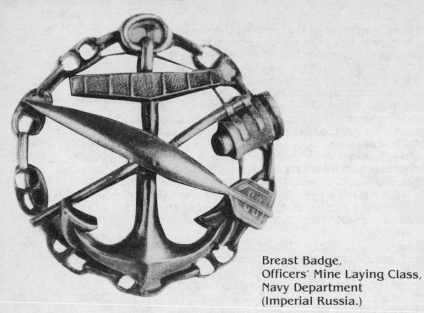

Breast Badge,
Officers' Mine Laying Class,
Navy Department
(Imperial Russia.)

	Price Range	

angles of the cross appear gold double head Imperial
eagles. In the top angle appears a crown.

☐ **Officer's.**	900.00	1000.00
☐ **Other Ranks.**	300.00	325.00

TRENCH ART

So-called because it was made by World War I soldiers of all nations during
the short intervals of time when they had been pulled out of the front lines for
rest. The men cleverly used whatever materials were at hand, including empty
cartridge cases, shell cases, bits of brass and copper. Some are minor works
of art.

☐ **Crucifix.** *Cross made by soldering a cartridge clip to an upright made of Mauser rifle bullets. Brass body of Christ soldered to cross with with the rondel from an other ranks belt buckle forming a halo.*	20.00	25.00
☐ **Decorated Shell Case.** *.75-mm French shell case heavily decorated with incised designs of French flags, trophies of arms and floral wreaths.*	15.00	20.00
☐ **Decorated Shell Case.** *.77-mm Imperial German Artillery shell case highly polished and decorated with incised design of floral wreaths, a large iron cross and a trench helmet. Artistic.*	15.00	20.00
☐ **Shell Case Trophy Cup.** *American, .75-mm shell case to which sturdy but graceful handles have been attached to form a loving or trophy cup. Highly polished.*	15.00	20.00

Trench Art Crucifix.

WEAPONS

Price Range

☐ **British Nordenfelt Rapid Fire Gun.** *Lever operated mechanism fires four barrels in sequence. Traversing and elevating mechanism, gravity feed clips missing, mounted on original base, in very good condition but requires some work to be in firing condition, maker marked brass name plate. Historically important as one of the early successful rapid fire guns to be actually used, many used by the Spanish in the Spanish-American War, seldom offered for sale.* 3675.00   4050.00

☐ **Confederate Cannon.** *An outstanding specimen of the famed smoothbore Confederate "Iron Napoleon." A 12-pounder howitzer barrel with casabel, touch hole has been sealed, threaded holes for holding fuse striker. Right trunnion is marked "--RA & Co.", identifying the owner of the famed Tredegar Iron Works, Richmond, Virginia. At muzzle appears the number "1432." This is a genuine Confederate field piece tube and is very, very seldom ever available to the public.* 6050.00   6700.00

☐ **Confederate Rocket Launcher.** *Rockets, an important weapon used in modern warfare, are of ancient origin and have been used off and on during the centuries. This interesting weapon represents an attempt by the Confederacy to overcome Union superiority in weapons. Open iron circular frame work in lieu of tube or barrel, supported by folding iron rod legs. Large slightly curved metal device*

Price Range

about half way back on frame work is arranged to provide elevation. On brass arm and on wide band encircling the frame work appears in deep stamping "C.S.A./Charleston, S.C./1862/No.5". It has been reported that this weapon was used against the forts in Charleston harbor. This is a historic piece and seldom offered for sale. 3350.00   3700.00

F. P. .45 caliber "Libertador" pistol.

☐ **F.P. .45 caliber "Liberator" pistol.** *A small, cheap, single shot disposeable weapon stamped from sheet tubing. Barrel is a smooth bore steel tube. Furnished in great quantities by the United States to resistance groups of friendly countries during World War II. Maximum effective range is 25 yards or less. Extremely simple in design and manufacture. Interesting.* 75.00   100.00

☐ **Five Barrel Percussion Pistol,** *c. mid-1800's. One of a kind specimen. Very well constructed and machined, probably American, very large brass frame with walnut grips, brass trigger guard. Five steel barrels arranged in a splayed or so-called "duck foot" pattern, curved brass bar locks behind each barrel holding the cartridges. Large hammer has five firing pins which detonate all five charges at the same time, large heavy weapon, unusual.* 1490.00   1650.00

☐ **Full Size Civil War 12 Pound James Rifle.** *Muzzle loading bronze 67 inch barrel mounted on field carriage with large wood iron tired wheels. All original as is the trail, original iron furniture and mounts, rifle is complete with matching limber on similar wheeled*

Price Range

carriage. On one trunnion appears in five lines "AMES CO/FOUNDERS/CHICOPEE/MASS/186I." On the other trunnion appears the date "1861." On each end of the large iron bound ammunition chest on the limber is a large brass plate bearing the information "G&D Cook & Co., New Haven-Carriage Makers-1861." Chest has copper covering and is compartmentalized. On the inside of the chest lid appears the information "Shot-Spherical Case-Canister." All original with just one spot of restoration, very rarely offered and particularly in this fine condition. 14000.00 15500.00

☐ **German Wheel Lock Military Pistol.** Excellent example of this early type firearm, long smoothbore muzzle loading barrel, walnut wood stock with crudely shaped butt extending almost straight back from gun, mechanism intact but requires some cleaning and adjustment. 1450.00 1600.00

☐ **Indian Twin Barrel Rapid Fire Gun.** Mounted on short trail steel field carriage with iron tired wooden wheels, brass elevating and traversing wheels and mechanism. Manually operated by hand crank at right rear which activates mechanism turning large drum or turret type 120 round magazine atop the barrels feeding alternately into the breech mechanism. Has the extremely low serial number "3." Cyrillic markings including information that weapon was manufactured by authority of Royal Nepalese Government. Gun is similar to the American Gardner hand operated machine gun. An extremely rare and unique weapon and only the second ever offered for public sale. 7850.00 8700.00

☐ **Mauser HSc Automatic Pistol.** Marked "NSDAP/SA Gruppe Alpenland" in two lines, identifying the weapon as belonging to the Bavarian Strum Abteilung (Storm Section) of the National Socialist German Labor Party (NSDAP). Special because of its marking. 1180.00 1300.00

☐ **Mid-Eastern Flintlock Musket.** The artistic decoration and workmanship on this artifact would indicate that it was made for royalty or a high ranking noble, entirely Oriental in character. Very long damascus steel smoothbore barrel, flintlock parts decorated with floral designs inlaid in gold, breech and muzzle inlaid with gold. Barrel secured to stock by silver bands, stock and butt stock completely covered with gilted silver decorated with coral stones. In excellent condition, one of a kind and of museum quality...... 3620.00 4000.00

☐ **Walther PPK Automatic Pistol.** This is a special engraved presentation weapon for a highly placed Nazi official. Lavishly engraved and with reddish

Mauser HSC Automatic Pistol.
marked "NSDAP / SA GRUPPE ALPENLAND."

Walther PPK Automatic Pistol.
A special engraved presentation piece
for a highly placed Nazi official.

	Price Range	
brown plastic grips bearing the Nazi Party eagle, wreath and swastika emblem, a choice specimen....	3350.00	3700.00

SPONTOONS

This weapon was also known as an espontoon. It was a development of the European boar spear. Whereas the halberd was most often a weapon and badge of office for sergeants, the spontoon was usually reserved to officers. The exact time of its introduction is not known. However, it appears that it was not used to any extent after the late 1700's. During the period of its use it was part of the weaponry of all armies. Essentially the spontoon consists of a spear head of varying design with a crossbar at the base, the whole being attached to a shaft usually by means of a socket in the base of the spear head. Spontoons used for ceremonial purposes and as a badge of rank, like the halberd, were highly ornamented as opposed to those used for combat. American colonial collectors are especially interested in American made spontoons of the Revolutionary war era. These are in short supply and sell for considerably more than British or European spontoons of the same period.

BRITISH

☐ **Officer's spontoon,** *c. mid-1700's. Broad trowel shape spear point with median ridge. A pierced roughly circular rear to spear point. Obverse side of blade deeply etched with Royal Arms and motto and flags, also bears legend "LE MAINTENDRAL," (I will maintain), reverse engraved with family coat of arms. Spear head attached to original oak shaft with both socket and side straps. Has crossbar. An excellent example, all beautifully done.* .... | 430.00 | 475.00

☐ **Officer's spontoon,** *c. mid-1700's. Long fairly narrow spear head with median ridge, bottom of head has crescent form with sharpened projecting sides, no crossbar, spear head attached to original stout oak shaft by means of both socket and side straps. Normal aging.* .... | 200.00 | 220.00

☐ **Officer's spontoon,** *c. mid-1700's. Well shaped trowel like spear point changing to roughly circular design at rear, median ridge to spear head, all without decoration of any kind, cross bar, attached to heavy wood shaft by means of socket and side straps. Normal aging, no rust. Good example.* .... | 282.00 | 310.00

FRANCE

☐ **Officer's spontoon,** *c. mid-1700's. Medium length leaf type spear blade terminating in sharp point, high median ridge, long socket and side straps, crossbar, a type used by French officers serving in America during Revolutionary War. Is a real weapon, historically interesting.* .... | 435.00 | 480.00

GERMANY

☐ **Officer's spontoon,** *Duchy of Brunswick, c. mid-1700's. Broad spear point with median ridge with roughly oval rear. The blade itself is beautifully and deeply engraved with the cypher "AW," the cypher of the then reigning duke August Wilhelm, with the ducal crown above and a scroll below bearing his motto. Below this is the rearing figure of the "Horse of Hannover" showing the relation to that house, on the rear appears a trophy of arms and flags, crossbar and socket to the rear of this. It was never fitted with side straps, the shaft is missing. The condition of this offering is excellent with no pitting. This is another historically important piece. . . . .*   **700.00**   **775.00**

☐ **Officer's spontoon, Prussia,** *c. late 1700's. Broad spear point with median ridge with elaborately pierced circular rear to spear blade. Spear blade deeply engraved with large crowned cypher "FR" (Frederich Rex), under this is an engraved scroll bearing the words "GARNISON STETTIN." This spontoon is unique in that the head is attached to a long heavy screw by which it was attached to the shaft, the shaft is not present. Some pitting consistent with age, rare. . . . .*   **750.00**   **830.00**

RUSSIA

☐ **Officer's spontoon,** *c. last half 1700's. Broad spear head with rounded point, median ridge, spear head deeply engraved with crowned double-headed Imperial Russian eagle with the double cypher "P" (Czar Paul) in a cartouche on the breast. At the bottom of the eagle device is an open work scroll under which appears the initials "GKW," cross bar to rear of spear head which attaches to stout wood shaft by socket and straps, some pitting to metal, wood shaft intact. Seldom offered. . . . .*   **950.00**   **1050.00**

☐ **Officer's spontoon,** *c. last half 1700's. Fairly broad sharply pointed trowel shape blade with circular rear portion, median ridge to spear head which is elaborately engraved with the double cypher "P" (Czar Paul) under the Imperial Crown, within a wreath. Under this is a cartouche bearing the legend which in translation denotes that this spontoon was for an officer in the Imperial Russian Schleswig-Holstein Infantry Regiment. Crossbar and socket attachment to stout wood shaft, all complete, extremely minor pitting to metal, wood shaft intact. A well preserved weapon which belonged to a historical Imperial Russian Regiment. Not often offered. . . . .*   **1130.00**   **1250.00**

UNITED STATES

Price Range

☐ **Officer's spontoon,** c. mid-1700's. Plain long thin spear head with squared edges at rear, median ridge to spear head, attached to shaft by long socket, the shaft is missing, is completely unadorned and shows age. It appears that both edges of the spear head were sharpened and that it was intended as a practical combat weapon. No crossbar. **790.00   875.00**

☐ **Officer's spontoon,** c. mid-1700's. Large ornate pierced spear head with pierced crescents on each side at rear, attached to a flat top cap-like socket which is fastened to the original pine shaft with a nail on each side, no crossbar, pitting is slight and consistent with age. A rare example. **1950.00   2150.00**

☐ **Officer's spontoon,** c. mid-1700's. Long narrow sharply pointed spear head with median ridge, plain without any ornamentation, edges sharpened, attaches to original shaft with socket and to straps, crossbar. In bright excellent condition, not usually found in such fine condition. **1475.00   1675.00**

STEINS

Steins of all kinds have always enjoyed popularity among collectors. As might be expected, prices vary greatly. Some American advertising steins sell for around $30.00, while steins of the famous German firm of Mettlach demand prices in the neighborhood of $4000.00. Interest in military, or more properly regimental, steins is of comparatively recent importance. Some were on the market following World War I but the greatest interest developed following World War II. Often long treasured family keepsakes, many were sold during the years of desperate economic and morale depression following the end of the war. As is the case in any area of collecting, as more information on steins became available, interest developed rapidly with a resulting escalation in prices.

Although steins, as drinking vessels, have been around for many, many years, it apparently was not until the mid-1800's that regimental steins began to be at all popular. By the end of that century and up until World War I, they had become a valued souvenir of the drafted man's time in service. Upon completion of their active duty (two years for foot troops and three years for mounted), the men were assigned to a reserve. These drafted men or reservists were the only ones in Imperial Germany to purchase steins as mementos of their service days. Regulars did not buy them.

German regimental steins are beautiful artifacts. There is a variety of lid types. Some are flat or semidomed. These bear a decorative design in relief, sometimes an idealized scene of the town in which the unit was stationed. Perhaps the most interesting lids are those with a finial. There is also a variety of these. Perhaps the most common are those found on the steins of infantry units. The finial may be in the form of a single soldier or in the form of a pair of soldiers. The single soldier may be standing at attention, at ease, or even kneeling, with his rifle. Or he may be holding a miniature stein aloft in a silent toast. In the case of two figures, they may be shaking hands or may be in other poses. A few had a fusilier cap, a spiked helmet or a jager shako as a finial. Machine gun units had a miniature of a Maxium machine gun. Field artillery regiments had a field gun as a finial. In some instances the gun would be manned. Horse artillery units would have a mounted artilleryman complete with artillery helmet. Some artillery steins have a finial in the form of a nose fuse and the stein itself may resemble a shell case. Uhlan, dragoon, cuirassier and other mounted units most often had a mounted figure in the uniform of their service. A few steins may have a finial in the form of a well-detailed crown. Railroad units may have a locomotive, while pioneer units may have an anchor and a spade worked into the design. Aviation organizations might have an eagle finial. Naval units generally had a sailor type finial.

Regimental steins are enhanced by colored transfers appearing about the sides. These may show the garrison town, soldiers, sailors, scenes of maneuvers, warships, flags, coats of arms, pictures of royalty and others, in some sort of logical combination. A great many steins will have the unit roster on the back. If the roster is large, part will appear on each side of the handle. The owner's name and rank and the designation of the unit to which he was assigned will appear at the top and bottom of the front of the stein. The exact arrangement may vary. In addition to all this, the stein may have additional colored decorative treatment.

The thumblift attached to the edge of the lid to assist in raising it is also a distinguishing feature of these steins. These are of several varieties. Some are in the form of the coat of arms or the national emblem of the kingdom or state to which the regiment belonged. Others may be in the form of a heraldic eagle, lion or other form.

An interesting feature of the steins is the lithopane appearing on the bottom. The bottom is transparent and when it is held up to the light the design may be plainly seen. These designs most often show a scene of a soldier and his girl or the ruler of the country to which the regiment belongs.

As might be expected, the Nazis did not discourage the use of steins as a morale builder, although the custom was not as widespread as it was in the Imperial Army. Nazi steins were manufactured in several patterns. Although they are not as widely collected as those of Imperial Germany, they are of considerable interest to collectors of Nazi gear and prices are raising steadily. Generally speaking, these Nazi steins are not as colorful or as artistic as those of the old German Army and they were bought by or were gifts to active duty personnel.

It certainly comes as no surprise to know that as popular as stein collecting is, great numbers of reproductions have flooded the market. Here again the inexperienced collector should trade only with reputable persons or seek the advice of an expert. Major John L. Harrell, a retired Army officer, has written a book, "Regimental Steins," which is acknowledged as the "bible" of stein collecting. Major Harrell is probably the outstanding authority on regimental steins in this country. In addition to being a complete illustrated study of the subject, including the detection of reproductions, his book gives a most complete background on the history, tradition and organization of the Imperial German Army and Navy. This book is listed in the reference section of this guide.

The following guide lists but a few of the scores of regimental steins which may be available. However, it is believed that the list is inclusive enough to give an accurate insight into prevailing prices. It is to be remembered that, as is the case with most militaria, prices are steadily increasing. Imperial German regimental steins are listed first, followed by Frei Korps steins, and finally those of the Third Reich.

Price Range

☐ **Bavarian Body Guard Infantry Regimental stein,** *(Bayern Infantrie-Leib-Regiment). This specimen belonged to a member of the 11th Company stationed in Munich 1908-10 and is so named and marked. The Munich town hall occupies the center panel with an early Zeppelin overhead. On one side is the 1909 King's Prize and on the other is the regimental epaulet. The particular unique feature of this stein is the finial which consists of a royal crown placed upon two crossed swords on a pillow. This work is all finely detailed. Thumb lift is a Bavarian lion supporting a crowned Bavarian shield.* **227.00   250.00**

2nd Bavaria Foot Artillery Regimental stein.

Price Range

☐ **2nd Bavarian Foot Artillery Regimental stein.** *In the center panel under a scene of foot artillery in the field is a picture of the garrison town of Metz. Directly under this is the regimental shoulder strap with the numeral "2." To the left of this is the portrait of Wilhelm II and to the right is that of Prince Regent Luitpold. Full-length soldier figure to the left, cone shaped lid with finial of a heavy howitzer and two gun crewmen, dated 1909-11, named.* 300.00 330.00

7th Bavarian Infantry Regimental stein (Prince Leopold's Infantry).

☐ **7th Bavarian Infantry Regimental stein** *(Prince Leopold's Infantry). Front panel has view of Bayreuth where the regiment was garrisoned. There is an early Zeppelin overhead. Below is the regimental shoulder strap with "7" upon it. Transfers to each side, that on*

Price Range

the right of Prince Leopold. On the left side is a sentry and on the right soldiers going into action, finial has a soldier standing beside a Bavarian lion. 227.00   250.00

8th Bavarian Infantry Regimental stein (Grand Duke Frederick of Baden's Infantry).

☐ **8th Bavarian Infantry Regimental stein** *(Grand Duke Frederick of Baden's Infantry). In the center panel is a view of the garrison town of Metz. Under this is the portrait of Grand Duke Friedrich II, with the portrait of Wilhelm II on the left and the portrait of Prince Regent Luitpold on the right. Behind these are crossed rifles and military gear. The regimental shoulder strap with "8" upon it appears to the left. Also to the left is the full-length figure of a soldier, to the right is a training scene. This stein has a prism lid, named. . . . .*   238.00   270.00

Price Range

☐ **19th Bavarian Infantry Regimental stein** *(King Eman-uel III of Italy's Infantry). This example belonged to a member of the 5th Company at the garrison town of Erlanger and is so named and designated. The front panel shows the town of Erlanger, the regimental shoulder strap and coats of arms. To one side are soldiers departing on maneuvers and on the other soldiers on the firing line, two column company roster on the rear. The finial is unusual in being a cut glass prism under which is the picture of a soldier and his girl approaching a sentry house. Dated 1902-04, thumb lift is a Bavarian lion supporting a crowned Bavarian shield.* 227.00   250.00

21st Dragoon Regimental stein
(2nd Baden Dragoons).

Price Range

☐ **21st Dragoon Regimental stein** *(2nd Baden Dragoons). Named and marked to the garrison town of Bruchsal. Center panel shows mounted dragoon at the gallop with white plumed helmet and lance with red and yellow penon. Under this is a trophy of arms topped by a Baden dragoon helmet. This stein is unique in that it belonged to a one year volunteer and is dated 1907-08.* 350.00   385.00

22nd Field Artillery Regimental stein (2nd Westphalian).

☐ **22nd Field Artillery Regimental stein,** *(2nd West-phalian). This interesting stein has a scene of field guns being taken into action. The scene is complete with the mounted drivers and the crews on the car-riages. Scenes of gun crew drill decorate the side*

Price Range

panels. The lower center panel has a black Prussian eagle on the left and a flaming bomb with regimental number on the right. The finial on the high domed lid is a model of a field gun. The thumb lift is in the form of St. Barbara, patron saint of artillerymen. Named and dated 1907-09. . . . . 300.00 330.00

☐ **115th Infantry Regimental stein** *(1st Grand Ducal Hessian Liebgarde). Dated Darmstadt 1902-04. Front shows Hessian ducal crown with trophy, regimental red shoulder strap with gold crowned "L." Sides show soldiers in bivouac and in combat, thumb lift is crowned Hessian lion and shield, named and has double roster on back, domed lid with sitting soldier finial.* 227.00 250.00

☐ **118th Infantry Regimental stein** *(Prince Charles' Infantry - 4th Grand Ducal Hessian). Dated Worms 1899-1901. Front has the ducal crown and gold regimental shoulder board with "118" and trophy shield, sides show soldiers firing from a standing position and in a bivouac. Domed lid with sitting soldier finial, thumb lift is the usual crowned Hessian lion with shield, named* 227.00 250.00

☐ **119th Infantry Regimental stein** *(Queen Olga's Grenadiers - 1st Wurttemberg). Named and is dated Stuttgart 1902-04, bears the cypher of Olga, Queen of Wurttemberg and trophy shield. The finial is in the form of a standing soldier. Thumb lift in the form of the Arms of Wurttemberg.* 200.00 220.00

☐ **127th Infantry Regimental stein** *(9th Wurttemberg Infantry). Named and dated to the garrison town of Ulm 1903-05. Central panel has the regimental shoulder strap bearing the number "127" over which is the Wurttemberg Crown. To each side and behind the shoulder strap is a trophy of rifles, flags, drum, back pack, spiked helmet and other military gear. The domed lid has a finial of the "departing comrade" or "discharged soldier" type consisting of a soldier with rifle and spiked helmet shaking hands with another soldier who holds his field cap in the air.* . . . 218.00 240.00

☐ **SMS Posen stein.** *This stein belonged to a member of the crew of the Imperial German battleship Posen. This example is typical of the tall graceful naval steins with cone like lid. In the center panel are two sailors with an anchor and nautical gear between them. Centered within a life saving ring on the base is a scene of a sailor on shore leave with a girl. Behind this are crossed flags and leaves. Behind one of the sailors in the center panel is the Imperial German war flag. The finial consists of a standing sailor holding the Imperial German Flag. This is a beautiful, unique and most desirable stein.* 750.00 825.00

127 Infantry Regimental stein
(9th Wurttemberg Infantry).

Price Range

☐ **German Frei Korps (Free Corps) stein.** *Frei Korps steins lack the grace and beauty of the Imperial German Regimental Steins. For the most part they are of stoneware and resemble a mug more than anything else. This particular specimen on the front bears in color the Bavarian shield. About the shield is a green wreath tied in red, in a semicircle above the wreath in German is the identity of the Frei Korps unit, the 19th Bavarian Mortar Company. Under the shield in German is the occasion, Christmas 1924.* 80.00   88.00

☐ **Frei Korps Christmas stein.** *21st Signal Battalion. Same stoneware mug shape as above, on front has green wreath with blue and white ribbon. Within the*

SMS Posen stein.
Naval steins such as this example
are fairly rare.

	Price Range	
wreath is a lion head within a circle upon a black diamond, marked Christmas 1919....................	100.00	110.00

☐ **Third Reich Presentation stein.** *To a Luftwaffe lieutenant upon the occasion of his leaving the 36th Luftwaffe Squadron. Stoneware body. On front a red, white and black flag with Iron Cross in center is crossed with the Nazi war flag. Above the flags is the Nazi emblem of eagle, wreath and swastika. An inscription under this reveals that the stein was presented by the officers of the squadron, has pewter lid, names.* ....

181.00   200.00

☐ **Transport Service stein.** *Plain straight sided stein, is of porcelain instead of usual stoneware, front has picture of manned half track pulling a 25-pounder field piece. Above this is "In remembrance of my*

Price Range

service time" in German. Lid has engraved Wermacht eagle and swastika on shield similar to the transfer worn on the steel helmet, plain thumb lift. It is rather interesting to note that this stein lacks the grace and beauty of the Imperial German Regimental steins and it probably would not excite the Imperial German collector at all. Yet the demand for Third Reich militaria by some collectors raises the price of these Nazi steins to the level of the earlier steins. 230.00   250.00

TINNIES

One of the newest fields of militaria collecting is that of propaganda badges of the wartime period. Once the area of a few collectors, it is now fast growing in popularity and is of particular interest to beginning collectors. The items are interesting and are still relatively reasonable. An extensive collection may be assembled for a modest financial outlay. The value of these badges is constantly increasing and provides an interesting investment for the individual of limited means.

The term "tinnie" stems from the very inexpensive stamped tin propaganda badges produced in vast quantities. Now the term has been expanded to include all types of Nazi propaganda badges regardless of composition, whether metal, cloth, paper, plastic or other materials.

Propaganda badges have been and are used all over the world. At election time they are especially popular in this country and there are quite a few collectors who specialize in presidential campaign badges. In the Austrian and Hungarian armies during World War I they became extremely popular, usually indicating that the wearer had donated money to some hospital or charity established for the armed forces. Following World War I, these propaganda badges became very popular in Germany and remained so until well into World War II. Although not worn by the regular military, they were worn by para-military groups and by various Nazi civilian organizations. These badges most often reflected the purpose or ideals of the sponsoring group. Veterans' organizations frequently had a World War I steel trench helmet design. The swastika and various party emblems were also much used.

The entire range of "tinnies" has never been completely cataloged. However, Mr. Ron Manion, an outstanding specialist in militaria has recently published the first volume of a projected series which will cover the subject thoroughly. This well-illustrated and descriptive book is listed in the literature section of this guide. The following listing is far from complete but is a good index as to prices prevailing in the field.

☐ **Austrian World War I,** *rectangular in shape, bearing profile of Emperor Franz Joseph of Austria.* 10.00   11.00
Note: The above is typical of the most common forms of these badges and the price is typical. Rarer types commemorating aviation and naval units will average $25.00.

THIRD REICH BADGES (Nazi)   Price Range

☐ **1933 Commemorative Fifth National Party Day badge.** *Nazi eagle with wreath enclosing swastika with view of Nuremberg under the eagle. Under all is the inscription "NSDAP REICHSPARTEITAG NURNBERG 1933." This is a bronze badge.* 30.00   33.00

☐ **1933 First National Socialist Flying Week,** *Furth-Pfingsten. Bronze badge with stamped design of monoplane superimposed upon a swastika, stylized view of town appears below. About the rim of the oval shape badge appears the legend "ERSTE NS FURTH i/B. PFINGSTEN 1933."* 21.00   23.00

☐ **1934 National Party Day badge.** *Silver color metal in the form of a disk. Occupying the entire center is the stamped figure of a man in what appears to be half armor. There is no helmet on his head. In his mailed right hand he holds an upright stylized short sword. A large shield over the left arm bears a swastika within a circle. About the left side of the badge appears "REICHSPARTEITAG." Across the upper right fourth of the badge appears the date "1934."* 5.50   6.00

☐ **1937 May Day Commemorative.** *A small child standing on the wings of a Nazi eagle with a swastika within a wreath below. The legend "1 MAI 1937" appears across the center of the aluminum badge.* .. 6.40   7.00

☐ **1938 May Day Commemorative.** *A boy and a young girl are shown dancing about a traditional May pole, representing the pleasure of work and its rewards. Below the dancing figures appears the stylized Nazi eagle, swastika and wreath. The legend "1 MAI 1938" appears near the bottom of the badge. This is the next to the last of the May Day commemorative badges, the final one being issued in 1939. The first day of May celebrated the dignity and accomplishments of labor. It was made much of as a holiday.* 6.40   7.00

☐ **1939 NSFK.** *National Sports Competition for Glider Airplane Models held at Wasserkuppe May 26 to 29, 1939. Oval silver color badge with stamped design of nude youth with arms extended to each side holding wings which extend slightly beyond the oval. A large swastika is superimposed across the bottom third of the figure of the youth. In an arc above the head appear the initials "N.S.F.K." Across the lower third of the badge appear the words "NSFK. REICHSWETTBEWERB FUR SEGELFLUGMODELLE WASSERKUPPE. 26. - 29. 5. 39. NS. FLIEGERKORPS."* 25.00   27.00

☐ **German Police Day badge.** *Aluminum, given to those donating for winter help relief in 1934. Six-sided badge with stamped design of a traditional police shako in profile with heraldic rays behind. Above the* shako appear the words "TAG DER DEUTSCHEN POLIZEI." Below the shako appear the words "WINTERHILFWERK. 1934." 11.80 13.00

☐ **Hitler Youth Organization District Meeting badge,** held May 28, 1933 and also commemorating the death of Nazi youth named Schlageter killed at Dusseldorf, the place of the meeting. Stamped rectangular brass badge. On top of badge is a stylized Nazi eagle. Across upper half of the badge appears a large swastika upon which is superimposed a Latin cross which extends from top to bottom of the badge. The legend, in German, reads "HJ GEBEITS JURGENTASGDUSSELDORF 28. 5. 1933 SCHLAGETER." It is most unusual for a Nazi badge to display the Christian cross although the cross in this instance probably symbolizes the death of the youth and not the religious faith................................... 20.88 22.00

☐ **Volkswagen Factory Ground Breaking badge,** May 1938. Gray plastic badge with good detail to design. Across the lower half of a sprocket wheel (gear) enclosing a swastika, a first model Volkswagen is superimposed. Below the car appears, in German, the legend "GRUNDSTEINLEGUNG DES VOLKSWAGENWERKES MAI 1938." 25.00 27.00

☐ **National Association of Former Front Soldiers of World War I 13th Convention badge.** Silver color badge with highly detailed stamped design of a stylized German eagle. On the breast of the eagle appears a well-defined trench helmet with the initials and numeral "13. R.F.S.I." Across the upper edge of the wings appears "BERLIN." 15.50 17.00

☐ **Steel Helmet Association badge.** Identifies veterans of World War I. Silver color metal badge with deeply stamped Iron Cross and the words "Der Stahlhelm," badge in the shape of a World War I trench helmet, words in German script.......................... 20.00 22.00

☐ **Early Nazi Propaganda badge,** promoting sea travel. Cast aluminum badge with detailed design. Oval badge with flying eagle and swastika within a wreath at the top. Occupying the entire center of the badge is a three-mast full rigged ship under full sail. The crown and flukes of an anchor appear at the very bottom of the badge. About the edge in raised letters appears "SEEFAHRT IST NOT. TAG DER DEUTSCHEN SEEARHT. 25.-26. 5. 1935 ("Sea Travel is Necessary, German Sea Travel Day. May 25-26, 1935.") 5.50 6.00

☐ **Gau (Province) Essen Badge.** Gilt upright stylized short sword with swastika on hilt with crossed hammers crossed behind the blade. The head of one hammer bears the date "1925," the other date "1935."

Left: Nurnberg Party Day badge, 1929. Center: Badge of the Steel Helmet Association. Right: (Province) Essen badge. These badges are not to scale.

	Price Range	
The hammers characterize the industrial nature of Essen.	25.00	27.00
☐ **Nurnberg Party Day badge,** *1929. Stamped gray metal with well defined design. The top of the badge has a relief of a part of ols Nurnberg. Immediately under this appears the word "NURNBERG." In the center of the shield shape badge is a World War I trench helmet with a swastika within a wreath on the front. A German eagle with folded wings is perched on top of the helmet. To the left appears the date "1914." To the right appears "1919 N.S.D.A.P." Under the helmet appears "PARTEI TAG 1929" in three lines.*	34.00	37.00
☐ **Third National Party Day badge,** *1927. This is one of the very early Nazi badges and is much sought after by collectors. Although thousands were made, not many have survived. This badge consists of a cloth*		

Price Range

red, white and black rosette upon which is superimposed a small silver color eagle with extended wings grasping a swastika within a circular wreath 38.00   42.00

UNIFORMS

As has already been noted, it is probable that the uniforms of the Papal Guard and the uniforms of the Yeomen of the Guard of Tudor times in England were the first uniforms as we know them today. These, however, were uniforms for only extremely small units and it was not until the reign of Louis XIV of France that an entire army was put in uniform. At that time the French war minister had regulations drawn up not only describing the uniforms to be worn but also the manner of wearing them.

Soon the idea of uniform clothing had been adopted by practically all armies. It was discovered early on that the uniform is one of the greatest aids to that most important military attribute, **esprit de corps.** And among other things, it does create a sense of manliness and makes the fighting man proud of his profession. It sets him apart from the less adventurous civilian. Of greater importance perhaps is the fact that the uniform assists materially in establishing and maintaining discipline. Men dressed in the same uniform can be more readily expected to think and act alike. The uniform also makes for smartness and cleanliness, both important aspects of discipline.

It may be of some interest to note that the Confederate army of the American Civil War was the first large scale unit to benefit from the protective color of the uniform. The continual dwindling state of the finances of the Confederate government, as well as the difficulty in securing uniform cloth from abroad because of the Union Navy blockade eventually led to desperate measures. Except in the few instances when they wore captured Yankee uniforms, the troops were clothed in a cheap homespun cloth which was most often of a so-called "butter-nut brown." This coloration blended in nicely with the background.

The adoption of khaki was also a matter of necessity, howbeit not one of finances. At the time of the Indian Mutiny many British troops in India were uniformed in white, an excellent color for hot weather wear but it made an excellent target. High casualties were being suffered because the natives could easily spot the British against the background. Some inventive souls among the British found that by dyeing their uniforms a mud or dust color they were far less conspicuous. They accomplished this by using coffee, curry powder, mulberry juice or mud. The word **khaki** is a Hindu word which loosely translated means dust color.

Another interesting note on uniforms is the fact that a nation enjoying great military success will often have its uniforms copied by other nations. During the Italian War (against Italy), the French army enjoyed great victories at Magenta and Solferino. Soon thereafter many armies, including those of Great Britain and the United States, adopted French style uniforms. Then when the French were soundly defeated by the Germans in the Franco-Prussian War, many major powers adopted German type uniforms for their armies, including even the **pickelhaube** or spiked helmet. For some years around the end of the 1800's and the early 1900's, United States Army, Marine and Navy Band personnel sported the spiked helmet.

Following World War I many armies adopted the roll collar blouse, smartly pegged breeches and riding and field boots of the British Army. Also adopted was the Sam Brown belt. This belt was devised by General Sir Samuel Brown, V.C., who had lost an arm in battle and designed the waist belt with supporting shoulder belt as an aid in carrying his sword and revolver. In addition to being a practical item, it also gives a smart appearance to the uniform.

The leaders of the Third Reich were quick to recognize the moral value of uniforms and Nazi uniforms are considered by many to be the smartest of all those worn during World War II. In designing the new uniforms, considerable attention was paid to retaining the most colorful and desirable characteristics of the old Imperial Army uniforms. There has always been great respect for tradition in the German service throughout the years, a fact which has paid large dividends in morale.

Of all militaria, uniforms are among the most colorful items. Unfortunately, uniforms are difficult to display unless the collector has an abundance of space, a luxury which not too many collectors can boast. Single items such as a coat or jacket are interesting but lack a certain completeness. Nonetheless, there has been a demand developing for them in recent years. Some collectors will concentrate upon completing a single uniform of a well-known regiment or a uniform of a particular war. These collectors usually insist upon having every authentic item of apparel from underwear, socks and shoes to shirt, tie and headdress. This is difficult to accomplish but is not impossible if the collector is interested in the American Civil War and more recent periods. Earlier periods are represented by bits and pieces and these are very expensive. Missing items must be reproduced, a difficult process when patterns and authentic materials are not available. With regard to price of earlier items an American Loyalist officer's coat, c. 1776, recently sold for $15,000.00!

Reproductions of earlier uniforms are available. An increasing number of collectors have banded together in units named for famous old military organizations. For the most part they devote much time to study and research and their reproductions are fairly true to the originals.

It is still possible to secure parts of World War II uniforms at military surplus goods stores but the supply is rapidly being exhausted. Militaria dealers and auction houses are undoubtedly the best source of older uniforms. Shops handling costumes for theater productions sometimes have desirable articles for sale. As is true in so many areas of military collecting, uniforms of Imperial Germany and the Third Reich are probably the most sought after at the present time. The collector must be careful for there is a super abundance of bogus uniforms being offered as authentic items.

GERMANY (Imperial)

	Price Range	
☐ **Army Tunic,** c. 1917. Extremely plain field gray tunic made without shoulder straps, fly front with concealed buttons, two upper and two lower pockets with flaps closed by buttons. All buttons bear a crown design, tunic is devoid of any decoration.	137.00	150.00
☐ **Artillery Officer's Dress Tunic.** Tunic only. This is a high quality garment, made of ribbed gray material, has a black velvet stand-up collar, black velvet Brandenburg cuffs, round brass buttons down front, about		

Price Range

cuffs and on shoulder straps, red piping around collar, down front of tunic and about cuffs, subdued gray officer type bullion shoulder straps with red underlay and fitted with gilt crossed cannons, lieutenant......   230.00   250.00

☐ **Bavarian Body Guard Infantry Regiment Tunic** *(Bayern Infantrie-Leib-Regiment), c. 1915. This rather drab field gray tunic reflects the characteristics of war time expediency and is in stark contrast to the colorful tunics of the pre-war Imperial German Army tunics. Red piping down the front which is closed by seven buttons bearing the Bavarian heraldic lion, French style cuffs, lower pockets on each side of tunic closed by buttons similar to those down the front, gray shoulder straps with similar buttons at collar end. Printed red Bavarian crown on shoulder straps, white collar litzen (lace) has printed red flashes. The printed crowns and flashes are a far cry from the embroidered work on earlier tunics. Plain but desirable. ....*   200.00   220.00

☐ **82nd Infantry Regiment Tunic** *(2nd Hessian Infantry). Tunic only. Dark blue tunic, red collar with noncommissioned officer gold color lace around the top and down the front. Red Brandenburg cuffs with gold color lace. Red shoulder straps with gilt "82." ......*   160.00   175.00

☐ **5th Hussars Noncommissioned Officer's Attila** *(Prince Blucher's Hussars - Pomeranian). Red attila (jacket) with most elaborate white cord trimming across the front, white cord design knots on sleeves, white cord down the shoulder seam with tombac button at collar end. Noncommissioned officer's lace about collar and around the cuffs, noncommissioned officer's disks on collar, musician's "swallow's" nests on shoulders, beautiful and unusual.............................*   137.00   150.00

☐ **58th Field Artillery Regiment Other Ranks Tunic** *(Minden Field Artillery). Tunic only. Blue with black Swedish cuffs, collar, front of tunic, bottom and cuffs piped in red, black stand-up collar, tombac buttons on front and cuffs, blue shoulder straps bear flaming bomb and "58" in red.....................*   160.00   175.00

☐ **1st Bavarian Infantry Regiment Musician Tunic** *(King's Infantry). Tunic only. Blue tunic with tombac buttons down front, on cuffs and shoulder straps, red stand-up collar and Brandenburg cuffs, top and front of collar and cuffs trimmed with gold color lace. Underoffiizier (noncommissioned officer) disk on each side of collar, rank of feldwebel. Gold lace and red "swallow's" nest on each shoulder, red shoulder straps with crowned cypher in gold, an extremely colorful tunic. ....*   175.00   190.00

☐ **Marine Infantry Officer's Mess jacket.** *Dark blue with high collar trimmed with gold bullion, elaborate*

58th Field Artillery Regiment
(Minden Field Artillery) tunic.
Imperial German Army.

Price Range

Brandenburg type cuffs in white trimmed with silver bullion, buttonholes trimmed in white. Eight tombac buttons down the front and three on each cuff, Navy officer type shoulder straps with gold crown and one pip, indicating the rank of lieutenant. Imperial German Marine Officer's uniforms are not often offered for sale. 304.00   335.00

☐ **92nd Infantry Regiment Tunic** *(Brunswick Infantry). Tunic only. Blue tunic with red stand-up collar and Brandenburg cuffs, red piping down front of tunic, tombac buttons down front, on cuffs and shoulder straps, white shoulder straps upon which appears*

1st Bavarian Infantry Regiment
(King's Infantry) musician's tunic.
Imperial German Army.

	Price Range	
crowned "W," corporal's pattern disk on each side of collar.	160.00	175.00
☐ **13th Field Artillery Regiment Other Ranks Tunic** *(King Charles' Field Artillery-1st Wurttemberg). Tunic only. Dark blue tunic with black stand-up collar, Swedish cuffs, tombac buttons, red shoulder straps with gold cyphers.*	160.00	175.00
☐ **13th Infantry Regiment Tunic** *(Herwath von Bittenfeld's Infantry - 1st Westphalian). Blue tunic with red standup collar, red shoulder straps and red Brandenburg type cuffs. Tombac buttons down the front, on the cuffs and at the end of the shoulder straps, red piping down the front and around bottom of tunic, gold color "13" on shoulder straps.*	160.00	175.00

92nd Infantry Regiment
(Brunswick Infantry) tunic.
Imperial Germany Army.

Price Range

☐ **32nd Field Artillery Regiment Tunic.** *(3rd Saxon Field Artillery). Dark green tunic with tombac buttons down front, on cuffs and at end of shoulder straps, red cuffs and stand-up collar, dark green shoulder straps, piped in red, bearing crowned regimental cypher and crossed cannons in red. Colorful tunic...*   160.00   175.00

☐ **Wurttemberg General Officer's Tunic.** *Excellent quality gray cloth, French cuffs, piped down the front and about the cuffs in red, gold buttons bear the Wurttemberg crown. Four pockets on front of tunic, closed with gold buttons with crown design, general officer pattern bullion shoulder knots and collar decoration, not often offered for sale.* 590.00   650.00

GERMANY (Third Reich)

Third Reich Afrika Kors
(Africa Corps)
Leiutenant General's tunic.

Price Range

☐ **Afrika Korps Lieutenant General's Tunic.** *(Africa Corps). Tunic is of a brown color corduroy cloth with French cuffs, two upper and two lower pockets closed with pebbled gilt buttons, eight gilt pebbled buttons down front of tunic, gold Nazi eagle, wreath and swastika on green cloth backing on right breast. Dark green collar with gold bullion general officer on red patch on each side of collar, gold bullion shoulder knots with lieutenant general's rank pip all on red background.* 610.00   675.00

☐ **Luftwaffe Other Ranks Tunic.** *On the upper left arm the chevrons of an obergefreiter, lower left sleeve has embroidered specialty badge consisting of a*

Luftwaffe Other Ranks Tunic.

Price Range

four-blade propellor between wings, embroidered breast eagle, white piping on shoulder straps, correct collar patches with three wings, correct buttons. This particular offering had the Second Class Iron Cross Ribbon in the top button hole. 410.00   450.00

☐ **Luftwaffe Other Ranks Tunic,** of Oberfeldwebel (Senior Sergeant). Flight collar patches with four gulls and silver braid, shoulder straps piped in yellow with two pips, embroidered breast eagle, four pocket tunic with correct buttons. 160.00   175.00

☐ **SS Evening Dress uniform,** Rank of Unterstrum-fuhrer. This was the most unusual offering of both jacket and trousers instead of only the jacket. Regulation shell jacket with silver on black formal

Price Range

shoulder straps. Jacket has piped French cuffs, left upper sleeve band bearing disk and swastika, right upper arm has the winkel (chevron and star) indicating an ex-Waffen member, right collar patch bears a skull indicating membership (service) in the famed Death Head Unit, left collar patch has correct three rank pips, all correct buttons, complete with SS officer aigulettes. Rare. 3700.00 4100.00

☐ **Waffen General Officer's Tunic.** *At rare intervals an authentic general officer's tunic will be offered for sale or auction and will be in the various general officer ranks. A general officer's tunic in excellent condition, no mothing, no excessive wear and with proper buttons, collar, sleeve and shoulder decoration, insignia and trim and with correct aigulettes will average* 1450.00 1600.00

☐ **Trousers** *for the above general officer's tunic with proper red stripes on outside seams.* 300.00 330.00

☐ **"Riding" breeches,** *as above with stripes.* 300.00 330.00

☐ **Colonel's Tunic.** *With proper piping, decoration and insignia.* 300.00 330.00

☐ **Major and Lower Rank Officer's Tunic.** *All complete.* . 205.00 225.00

☐ **Trousers or "riding" breeches.** *For above officers.* . 64.00 70.00

☐ **Overcoat,** *Officer's, model 36.* 91.00 100.00

☐ **Overcoat,** *Officer's, model 43.* 82.00 90.00

☐ **Overcoat,** *Other Ranks, late war issue.* 73.00 80.00

☐ **Waffen SS Other Ranks Tunic.** *On left arm above elbow the chevrons (winkel) of a noncommissioned officer of the grade of obergefreiter, above this a bevo SS sleeve eagle, on the cuff the title "Reinhard Heydrich," correct shoulder straps, collar and buttons, SS runes on right collar.* 400.00 440.00

GREAT BRITAIN

☐ **Loyalist Officer's Coat.** *As anyone familiar with American history knows, many colonists elected to remain loyal to the Mother Country and joined military units to fight with the British troops. This offering belonged to an officer of one of these units. It is of stout green cloth with red turned back velvet cuffs. Gold lace decoration around buttonholes and across front of coat, gold lace trim on sides of coat and on cuffs. Nearly all of the buttons are still on the coat. These are gilt finish of the so-called "coin" type and bear the initials "RP" (Royal Provincials) under a Royal Crown in relief. The yellow silk lining due to age is somewhat tattered. This is an extremely rare offering. It would be difficult to estimate the historic value of this coat.* 13700.00 15200.00

Price Range

☐ **Officer's Coatee,** c. 1812. This attractive artifact is made of scarlet cloth with blue facings. Five pairs of buttons down the front bearing a crossed baton and sword within a wreath, gilt lace and button decoration on lower sleeves and on tails of coatee, bullion aigulettes. 520.00   575.00

☐ **Officer's Full Dress Uniform,** The Black Watch or The Royal Highland Regiment. This outfit has an officer's feather bonnet complete with the red hackle and the Sphinx badge. The doublet is of fine quality scarlet cloth. The dark blue collar and cuffs has bullion lace trim. White piping to doublet, correct buttons, epaulettes of bullion cord, full dress belt with regimental crest on buckle, silver collar badges, shoulder belt with regimental badge, proper pattern kilt and plaid, silver plaid brooch, full dress sporran with bullion tassels. An extremely colorful outfit not very often encountered. 1000.00   1100.00

PAPAL GUARD

☐ **Tunic and Helmet of the Guardia Nobile.** This is a unique offering which is seldom seen. Black tunic of good cloth with plastron front, two rows of eight buttons each down the front and three on each lower sleeve. The buttons are domed and bear the Papal Arms with "Guardia Nobile." Gilt scaled epaulettes with gilt fringe, collar and cuff are of blue cloth decorated bullion lace, bullion faced sword belt with slings as well as bullion faced shoulder belt with brass pouch which bears a trophy of arms. The classical Roman type helmet is of white metal and has a very high gilt metal crest. The bottom three-quarters of the helmet is covered with black fur. Front of helmet bears a large heraldic star upon which is superimposed the Papal Arms. Gilt chin scales and bosses, helmet lined with silk. 500.00   550.00

UNITED STATES

☐ **Army Air Force Officer's Blouse.** Well tailored of good quality cloth with proper gilt U.S. buttons and cuff braid. Officer's U.S. and winged propellor collar insignia. Pilot's silver wings. 50.00   55.00

☐ **Army Enlisted Man's Field Jack,** World War II. So-called "Eisenhower" jacket of stout OD material. Two pleated pockets. Concealed button front. Embroidered 1st Division patch on left shoulder 18.50   20.00

☐ **Army Enlisted Man's Issue Blouse.** World War I 89th Division patch on upper left sleeve. Bronze U.S. enlisted device on right collar and Signal Corps device on left side. Single overseas chevron 46.00   50.00

U.S. Army
Officer's Light Weight OD tunic.
World War I.

	Price Range	
☐ **Army Enlisted Man's Tailor-Made OD blouse,** *World War I period. On top left sleeve is well-embroidered U.S. Army of Occupation patch. Four bullion overseas chevrons on lower left sleeve, high collar with U.S. rondell or disk on right side and Infantry Headquaters rondell on other, extremely well made.*	50.00	55.00
☐ **Army Officer's High Quality Melton OD Overcoat,** *World War I. Black first lieutenant trefoil braid on lower sleeves, double-breasted with five bone buttons on each side, slash pockets.*	37.00	40.00
☐ **Army Officer's Lightweight OD Tunic,** *World War I. U.S. buttons, U.S. and Signal Corps officer type insignia on each side of stand-up collar, division patch on upper left shoulder.*	41.00	45.00

U.S. Marine Corps
Enlisted Man's coat,
World War II.

Price Range

☐ **Marine Corps Enlisted Man's Coat,** *World War II period. Green coat with four bronze Marine Corps buttons down the front and on each of four pockets. Marine Second Division patch on upper left shoulder. Corporal's stripes and one enlistment stripe on each sleeve. Red "Ruptured Duck" discharge device on green backing on right breast.* 19.75   21.50

☐ **Marine Sergeant OD Wool Blouse,** *World War I period. Four pockets closed with bronze Marine Corps buttons as are pockets. Blouse has high collar with rare collar ornaments consisting of disk bearing Marine Corps emblem. Sergeant's chevrons, all authentic.* 77.00   85.00

WEAPONS

In this section, pistols, revolvers, muskets, rifles, daggers and swords are discussed and listed. Oriental edged weapons, because of their uniqueness, are discussed and listed apart from the others. Brochardt, Luger, Mauser, Walther and the Colt .45 caliber automatics are discussed elsewhere in this volume and so are not discussed here.

Small arms using powder as a propellant originated with the "hand gonne" developed around the middle of the 1300's. These crude, awkward, heavy, inaccurate and undependable pieces were but a small size edition of the large cannons of the very early 1300's. Several versions of these early "hand gonnes" appeared. One had a muzzle loading barrel attached with thongs and iron bands to a long stave which was held between one arm and the body. Another was smaller and was fitted with a short stock which could have permitted it to have been used as a hand carried weapon. Not very much is known about the exact nature of these earliest small arms and very few specimens have survived. In any event it must have required a very brave man to use one.

The earliest method of igniting the propellant powder was simply to touch off some very fine grain priming powder in the touch hole of the gun. At first this apparently was done with the use of a flaming brand. Improvements soon followed. A coil of loosely woven hemp cord, soaked in saltpeter and allowed to dry, burned very slowly when lighted. Known as "slow match" or more often just as "match," it was used to touch off the charge. These coils of "match" could be carried easily by the soldier. Although this was an improvement, it was still far too slow and awkward. A step forward was made when some ingenious fellow thought up the idea of attaching a piece of the "match" to a pivoted holder which could be tripped forward to the touch hole. This was then refined by placing the touch hole on the side of the rear of the barrel, instead of on the top, and placing a small pan beside it to hold the priming powder. This improved method of igniting the powder charge was called a matchlock.

The next development was the wheel lock, c. 1500's. Basically, this was a mechanism involving a spring actuated serrated wheel. A hinged arm holding a piece of iron pyrites was tripped forward and as the trigger was pulled the wheel revolved against the pyrite, resulting in a small shower of sparks which fell into the priming powder. The spring mechanism was wound by means of a key or spanner. This weapon was rather expensive to manufacture and operate and it never received widespread use in the military service except for some elite cavalry units. Its major use was restricted to wealthy men and was used largely as a sporting gun. Gunsmiths and artists were employed to produce lavishly decorated weapons of great price. These guns are much sought after by advanced firearms collectors with an ample purse.

The snaphaunce was the next development, followed by the flintlock. The origin of the snaphaunce, also of the 1500's, is open to question. The mechanism consists of a spring operated "cock" with screw closed jaws which firmly held a piece of selected, shaped flint. The primer pan, which lay in the path of the forward and downward stroke of the "cock" as covered by a frizzen of steel which, when struck by the flint, produced sparks. As this occurred the frizzed moved up to allow the sparks to ignite the powder in the pan beside the touch hole. The relative cheapness of the snaphaunce and its ease of operation made it far more acceptable to military authorities. The flintlock was but a logical refinement of the snaphaunce. It also made use of a flint held in the jaws of the "cock." The improvement lay in the fact that the frizzed, pan and pan cover were built **within** the lock plate. Equally of importance was the development of the prepared cartridge holding both the ball and the powder charge. This cartridge eliminated the necessity of measuring out the charge from a container and forcing it down the gun barrel after which the ball and its patch was rammed home.

The development of the percussion system of ignition opened the modern era of firearms. Several forms of this were tried, the most successful employing a small copper cap containing a pressure sensitive mixture. This cap was placed over a nipple with a tiny opening or tube within it leading to the powder charge within the gun. The falling hammer, activated by a trigger, struck the cap a sharp blow detonating the mixture within the cap which resulted in a flash which traveled down the nipple into powder charge within the rear of the gun barrel. Not very long after this important development, man's inventive mind improved upon the idea, placing the projectile and powder within a metal shell case or cartridge with the detonating charge incorporated within the rear rim (rim fire cartridge) or located at the center rear of the cartridge case (center fire cartridge). The development of the center fire cartridge made possible rapid fire weapons. It may be noted here that the foregoing is a rather simplified description of a highly technical subject.

Along with improving ignition systems, rifling was developed, from whence stems the name rifle. This consists of a series of twisting (turning) lands or grooves within the gun barrel. The projectile or bullet is very slightly larger than the interior circumference produced by the lands. The tremendous pressure entered upon the bullet by the detonating charge forces it to accept the lands thus giving it a rapidly revolving motion along its axis. This revolving or spinning action gives the bullet accuracy in its flight and insures greater distance. All of the above applies to both hand guns and shoulder weapons.

For a complete coverage of weapons, see Stone's *A Glossary of the Construction and Decoration and Use of Arms and Armor in all Countries and in all Times.* This is listed elsewhere in this volume. It is a scholarly, accurate, monumental work and should be in the library of every militaria collector. It is most reasonably priced and may be had from the book dealers listed in this guide.

EDGED WEAPONS

Edged weapons are among the earliest known to man. The place of their origin is unknown as is the exact date of their introduction. However, daggers shaped from reindeer antlers and daggers made of flint indicate a history at least 5000 years old. Copper weapons appeared about 4000 years ago, followed by bronze during the following century. In Europe iron daggers were undoubtedly used as early as 1000 BC.

DAGGERS

Contrary to the belief of some, the dagger is not a short version of the sword. It originated as a short stabbing weapon, was developed independently of the sword and at times was used to support or supplement the longer blade weapon. By medieval times the dagger had been developed into a weapon used to pierce the joints of a fallen foe's armor. In some instances, it was attached to the user's sword belt by a chain or heavy cord to prevent its loss. At other times it was chained directly to the side of the breastplate. Other types with longer and wider blades were used for personal protection and for hand to hand combat. Through the years many types and patterns of daggers were developed, including the **poniard,** which was usually fitted with a narrow, sharply pointed end; the **langue de boeuf,** a dagger with a broad ox tongue-like blade; the Scot's **dirk,** with a fairly long blade of medium width (which developed into the naval **dirk** used by midshipmen and junior officers in the navies of many countries); the **main gauche,** a fairly heavy weapon especially designed to parry a sword thrust and at times had a toothed edge to one side of the blade and quillons formed to catch and break the opponent's sword; the **stiletto,** with a long narrow finely pointed blade, and others.

Arabian Dagger or Jambiya.

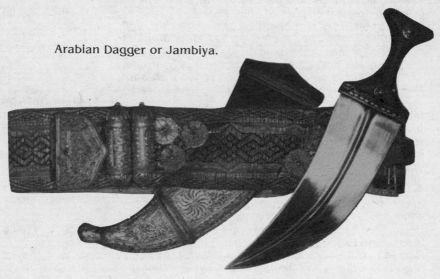

Asia   **Price Range**
- ☐ **Arabian dagger or jambiya.** *This specimen is from Zanzibar. Short very broad double edge curved blade with a ridge down the center, short grips with plain pommel, silver mounted, silver scabbard decorated with intricate designs, elaborate silver braid belt with silver ornaments. This is a wicked dagger which would almost always inflict a fatal wound. Common to all Arabic countries but may vary somewhat from the general pattern according to country.* 590.00   650.00
- ☐ **Imperial Russian Naval Officer's dirk.** *Diamond cross section blade etched with the double-headed Imperial Russian Eagle and the crowned cypher of Nicholas II. Plain brass reversed cross guard with disk finials, squared ivory grips with plain brass ferrules, polished*

Price Range

black leather scabbard with plain brass mounts, interesting 230.00 250.00

☐ **Imperial Turkish Naval Officer's dirk.** *Long straight blade bearing etched designs of fouled anchor, sailing ships and a turban, reversed gilt quillons with central design of fouled anchor, ivory grips, pommel in the shape of a turban, in gilt. Gilted metal shield with gilt mountings.* 122.00 135.00

☐ **Indian katar.** *Blade is strengthened by a central ridge on each side and is thickened at the point to provide extra strength. Hilt lavishly decorated with damasked gold scrolls and other designs, as are the hand grips, complete with pierced steel sheath.* 215.00 230.00

☐ **Indian katar.** *This is a beautiful and extremely high quality example. The highly polished steel blade is designed for armor piercing by being thickened at the point. The brass hilt and grips are highly ornate. The scabbard is covered with green velvet with both the tip and the throat in gold metal highly decorated in repose design.* 975.00 1075.00

☐ **Indian katar or thrusting knife.** *Reputed to be the oldest of all indian knives. This weapon is characterized by two parallel metal bars joined by one or more crosspieces. These metal crosspieces form the hand grip. The blade is usually broad and double-edged. This is a wicked weapon and was often used to pierce armor. Prices vary considerably according to decoration. This particular specimen is from the 1600's and is rather plain. The blade is reinforced and is attached to plain steel hand grips and side pieces* 100.00 110.00

☐ **Indonesian Executioner's kris.** *This specimen is from Sumatra. The long straight double edge blade has a ridge down the center on each side. The point of the blade near the hilt is notched. The decorative ivory grip is set in a decorated brass cup. The highly polished wood sheath is decorated with numerous silver bands. The executioner stood behind the condemned criminal and thrust the kris perpendicularly above the collar bone and downward quickly until it pierced the heart. This type of kris is not as common as the others.* 230.00 250.00

☐ **Indonesian kris.** *This specimen is from Bali. In its various forms, this weapon appears throughout entire Indonesia and at least 40 variations are known. In all variations, however, the blade widens out on one side to a sharp point only at the hilt. This point serves as a guard and may be notched to catch an enemy's blade. Blades will vary from straight to waved on both sides from hilt to point or they may be half straight and half waved. The blades are beautifully forged and may be well-decorated. Scabbards*

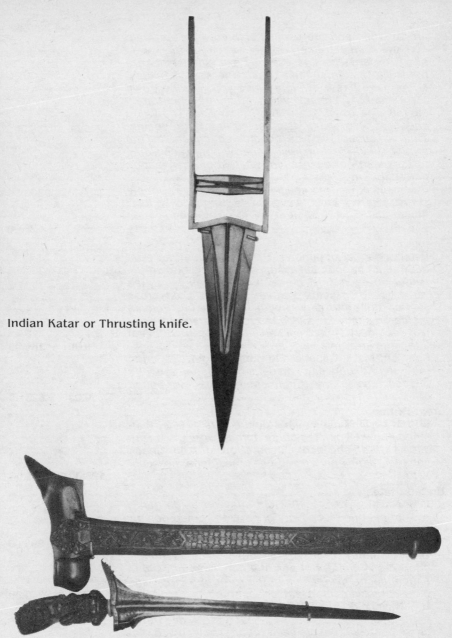

Indian Katar or Thrusting knife.

Indonesian Kris. This specimen is from Bali.

Price Range

are of wood and are usually elaborately decorated. The kris is an extremely deadly weapon in the hands of an expert. The kris used by executioners has a blade much longer than usual. The specimen described here has a straight blade with a ridge down the center. The black wood grips are elaborately carved. The point at the top is notched. The wood sheath is also elaborately carved in a floral design. This specimen may be considered typical of the straight blade pattern kris. Values will vary according to the wealth of decoration lavished on the weapon and scabbard. 125.00   135.00

☐ **Indonesia Kris.** *This specimen is from Java. Double edge watered steel wavy blade the ivory hilt is elaborated carved, point at the top is notched, wood sheath* 45.00   125.00

Europe

☐ **Persian dagger or jambiya.** *Blade about half as wide as Arabian dagger, curved and with a ridge down the center on each side, blade near hilt well-decorated with etched intricate Persian designs. Oval cross section bone hilt carved with the standing Persian prince on each side and with typical Persian decorative designs, flat pommel carved with scene of a lion attacking an antelope.* 140.00   165.00

☐ **Spanish Main Gauche Fighting dagger.** *Tapering fairly long double edge blade, long cross guard with pierced finials, large single shell guard, wire bound grips, ball shape pommel.* 750.00   825.00

Great Britain

☐ **British Navy Midshipman's dirk,** *c. late 1700's. Flattened and well pointed blade, turned ivory grips with gilt oak leaf and acorn decoration, gilt lion mask pommel, highly embossed gilt crosspiece, no scabbard.* 125.00   135.00

United States

☐ **U.S. Naval dirk,** *c. 1810. Gold inlay on blade, fancy cylindrical one piece ivory grips with turned design, ornate cross guard with acorn finials. Straight double edge blade.* 360.00   395.00

☐ **U.S. Naval dirk,** *c. 1812. Well-blued blade, extremely short cross guard, flat pommel cap, ivory grips with simple decorative design in the form of a circle and cross, brass mounted leather scabbard.* 220.00   240.00

☐ **U.S. Naval dirk,** *c. 1820. Gilt finish brass hilt with well defined lion head pommel. Elaborately decorated cross guard with eagle head finials. Well-curved, flat single edge, well-blued blade decorated with etched designs of laurel leaves and trophies. Complete with*

Price Range

*elaborately decorated brass sheath with designs of
laurel leaves and trophies. This is a beautiful and
unusual specimen.* 560.00   620.00

SWORDS

The earliest swords were rather broad with a straightedge or of a leaf pattern. Some military historians believe that the leaf pattern blade is the oldest for there is evidence of it being used during the Bronze Age. Its use continued on through the years and it was a favorite of the classical Greek warriors. One of the most famous swords of later classical times was the **gladius** of the Roman legionnaires. This was a wicked weapon for close combat by any definition. It had a blade which was straight, about two feet long and two inches wide, with a point and an edge on each side. Gradually sword blades became longer. Considerable thought was given as to whether the blade should be single or double-edged, tapered, straight or curved. The saber, a weapon designed primarily for slashing, became important, particularly for mounted troops. Most often with a single edge, curved blade, it soon became the symbol of cavalry. Increasing attention was given to the quality of the steel in the blades and the overall balance of the weapon.

By the early 1500's, the well-proportioned cut and thrust sword had been developed. The hilt and hand guard were given much attention with many patterns, some quite elaborate, being developed. These varied from the basket hilt of the Italian **schiavone** and the Scots broadsword, both with heavy basket hilts, to the simple "D" type hilt. Crossbars, some turned down or up, and other modifications were introduced. Another interesting sword was the **rapier,** with a long two-edged pointed blade. A most deadly weapon in the hands of an expert, it was the favorite of duelists. With the development of modern firearms, the sword became of minor usefulness and today is used mainly as a ceremonial adjunct.

Asia

☐ **Imperial Russian Naval Officer's sword,** *c. mid-1800's.
Slightly curved plain blade, flattened triple bar guard of
gilt brass, flat guard and langets, turned down quillon is
pierced for a sword knot, which is not present. Gilt
brass back strap decorated with Russian script, twisted
gilt copper wire bound black leather grips, black leather
scabbard with gilt brass mounts.* 275.00   300.00

☐ **Imperial Russian Other Ranks Dragoon saber.**
*Slightly curved plain blade, stamped with Russian
spirial markings, the date "1902" and the double-
headed Imperial Russian stamp. Plain brass knuckle
guard with turned down finial pierced for a saber
knot, which is present. Typical Russian spral wood
grip. Guard stamped with regimental markings and
the date "1902." Leather covered wood scabbard
with brass mounts and slots for the socket bayonet.
It was the intention of this arrangement that the
bayonet would always be available. If the bayonet is
present with the saber, the price may be increased by
at least $30.00.* 215.00   235.00

Price Range

☐ **Indian khanda.** *This is the oldest pattern of Indian sword. This specimen is typical. Long, straight double edge cut and thrust blade. The blade widens toward the outer end and has a blunt point. The blade is etched in intricate designs. The large hilt and knuckle guard of steel is inlaid with Sanskrit inscriptions. The large flat disk pommel is unique in that it has a large spike attached to it. This may be used as a grip for the left hand in making a two-handed stroke. It also acts as a guard for the rear of the sword arm. It may also be used as a hand rest when the weapon is sheathed. The inside of the guard and knuckle bow are padded. The scabbard is covered with black velvet.* 310.00 340.00

☐ **Indian tulwar.** *This is an example of an extremely high quality tulwar. Curved single edge blade, hilt, including grips, short quillons, large disk pommel and ring on top of pommel all highly decorated with floral design in green and blue, as are the langets. High quality leather scabbard with throat repeating the design of the hilt, much gold inlay work on metal parts.* 1000.00 1100.00

☐ **Indian tulwar.** *This unusual specimen is an executioner's sword. It has an extremely wide blade for a tulwar. The blade is single edge and is elaborately decorated with gold damasked designs of birds, animals, birds, nobles and scroll work. Chased steel hilt with short quillons and long langets, large disk pommel, chased steel scabbard, desirable item.* 222.00 245.00

☐ **Indian tulwar.** *This weapon is native to India and covers a broad range of sabers. The blades are curved and the hilts usually have short heavy quillons and disk pommels. They may be found with and without knuckle guards. Although the pattern of these weapons is generally the same, the size and ornamentation varies greatly. It is the most common sword in India and is found in great quantity. Values vary greatly according to quality but none are truly expensive. This specimen is typical. Long slightly curved plain blade, all steel hilt with knuckle guard and disk pommel, no scabbard* 73.00 80.00

Europe

☐ **Imperial German Artillery Officer's sword.** *Slightly curved blade, gilt brass guard with reverse "P" knuckle guard, crossed cannons, an amorial shield and a flaming grenade decorate the langets. Heavily decorated back strap, lion head pommel, black enameled metal scabbard, not rare but interesting.* .. 172.00 190.00

☐ **Imperial German Colonial Officer's sword,** *1889 Pattern. This rare specimen is that of an officer serving with colonial troops. Infantry officer's sword with*

long straight plain blade. Gilt hilt, including the
knuckle bow, twisted gilt wire bound fishskin grips
bearing in gilt the crowned Royal cypher "WR" of
Kaiser Wilhelm. The folding counter guard bears the
pierced design of the Imperial German Eagle and not
the Prussian heraldic eagle. This was so because the
German colonial troops were drawn from all the
various German kingdoms, dukedoms and other
states and not from Prussia alone. Complete with
metal scabbard. These colonial officer's swords are
not common. 172.00   190.00

☐ **Imperial German Naval Officer's sword.** Slightly
curved blade, elaborately etched with a crowned
fouled anchor, the Imperial Eagle and other decorations, gilt half basket hilt with crowned fouled anchor
on the turned down counter guard. Embossed back
strap and knuckle guard, lion head pommel with one
red and one green glass eye, twisted gilt wire binding
to ivory grip, black leather scabbard with gilt mounts.   250.00   275.00

☐ **Imperial Italian Air Force Officer's sword.** Long
straight blade of flattened oval cross section. The
blade is elaborately etched with the Imperial Royal
Arms, together with aviation trophies, wings and
floral designs. Cast bronze guard with a design of
overlapping eagle feathers, as is the full back strap,
eagle head pommel, grooved grip of composition,
leather scabbard with bronze mounts. 175.00   190.00

☐ **Indian Army Officer's saber,** c. 1800's. Classic
Mameluke hilt with ivory grips secured by gilt rivets,
pommel pierced for sword knot, gilt back strap
decorated with a design of oak leaves, gilt cross
guard with ears and decorated with scrolls and floral
design, slightly curved blade decorated with etched
floral designs, complete with velvet covered wood
scabbard with three richly decorated gilt mounts, a
beautiful and interesting example. 225.00   245.00

☐ **Italian Venetian schiavona,** c. 1600's. Long straight
wide double edge blade inlaid with a running wolf
and cross and orb marks. The steel full basket hilt
has a thumb ring and curved quillon, silver wire
bound grips and eared silver pommel. This is an
excellent example of the type of weapon after which
the famous Scots backsword was patterned. 1630.00   1800.00

☐ **Prussian Cavalry Officer's sword.** Long straight edge
blade decorated scene of cavalry combat, trophies
and floral designs together with the legend "2
WestfHusaren Reg. No. 11." White metal hilt with
"D" pattern knuckle bow, ribbed composition grip,
large folding counter guard pierced with design of
the Prussian heraldic eagle. Sword is pattern of 1889,
black enameled scabbard. The regiment named is

	Price Range	

the 2nd Westphalian Hussars, No. 11. Weapons marked to particular regiments or organizations are particularly interesting. **140.00 155.00**

☐ **Prussian Infantry Officer's sword,** 1889 pattern. Long straight blade lavishly etched, gilt brass guard, pommel and knuckle guard, twisted gilt wire bound fishskin grips, bearing the Imperial cypher "WRII." Medium size gilt brass folding counter guard with pierced design of Prussian heraldic eagle, black enameled metal scabbard. **127.00 140.00**

Great Britain

☐ **British Army Artillery Officer's dirk,** c. late 1700's. Straight single edged blade lavishly etched with trophies and scrolls, diced ivory grip with stepped pommel, gilt copper cross guard with cannon ball finials, small oval langets engraved with cannon and other military trophies, an excellent example of the hard to find Army officer's dirk, no scabbard. **181.00 200.00**

☐ **British General Officer's saber,** 1831 pattern. Mameluke hilt with ivory grips with two gilt rosettes, hilt pierced for saber knot, richly decorated gilt cross guard, slightly curved blade, complete with brass scabbard with gilt mounts. **400.00 440.00**

☐ **British Light Company Officer's saber,** model 1803. Slightly curved blade beautifully etched, gilt twisted wire bound fishskin grips, richly decorated gilt back strap, lion head pommel, knuckle bow has design of a light infantry bugle horn over "GR." **250.00 275.00**

☐ **British Naval cutlass,** c. early 1800's. Broad slightly curved blade, one piece cast iron cylindrical grips and "D" shape knuckle bow. **180.00 195.00**

☐ **British Naval cutlass,** c. late 1700's. Iron "Figure Eight" knuckle guard, plain cylindrical iron grips, straight single edge blade. This type used by both British and American navies in American Revolution. **150.00 165.00**

☐ **British Naval cutlass,** c. late 1800's. Broad, single edge, slightly curved blade, plain black painted steel guard, plain cylindrical wood grips. **200.00 220.00**

☐ **British Naval Cutlass,** 1900 pattern. Single edge blade, steel hand guard black leather grips with diced design, complete with black leather scabbard with steel mounts, brass frog button. **200.00 220.00**

☐ **British Naval Officer's Dress saber,** 1805. Well curved single edge blade heavily etched with crowned "GR", floral designs and military trophies, gilt copper hilt with langets decorated with engraved fouled anchors. Gilt copper stirrup pattern knuckle bow decorated with laurel leaves, lion head pommel of gilt copper, decorated back strap, black ebony grips bound with

Price Range

twisted gilt wire, polished black leather scabbard
with gilt copper mounts, a rare and interesting saber.   905.00   1000.00

☐ **British Naval Officer's saber,** *1803 pattern.* Plain
slightly curved blade, all copper mounts, pierced
guard and knuckle bow incorporating a crowned
"GR," lion head pommel, ribbed ivory grips with full
back strap, complete with polished black leather
scabbard with copper fittings and with the feathered
device of the Prince of Wales.   145.00   160.00

☐ **British Naval Officer's sword,** *model 1827.* Blued
blade richly etched with design of scrolls together
with crowned "GR" and fouled anchor, gilt copper
hilt. Guard has decoration of crowned fouled anchor,
folding counter guard, lion head pommel, sharkskin
grips with twisted gilt wire. 430.00   475.00

☐ **British Naval Officer's sword,** *c. period of George VI.*
Blade etched with crown, fouled anchor, the Royal
Cypher and a floral design, gilt copper guard with
small folding counter guard, twisted gilt wire bound
fishskin grips, lion head pommel, gilt copper mounts
to the black scabbard, an excellent example. 230.00   250.00

☐ **British Naval Officer's sword,** *c. post 1902.* Straight,
single edge blade elaborately etched with the Royal
Arms, fouled anchor and floral pattern, gilt copper
guard, back strap and lion head pommel, twisted
wire bound sharkskin grips, brass mounted black
leather scabbard. 125.00   135.00

☐ **British Royal Naval Reserve Officer's sword,** *c. Victorian period.* The blade is slightly curved and is
lavishly decorated with etched crown, the initials
"RNR" the Royal Arms, a fouled anchor and floral
designs. Gilt copper half basket guard bearing a
crowned fouled anchor, sharkskin grips with twisted
gilt wire, lion head pommel. 250.00   275.00

☐ **Scottish Basket Hilt Backsword,** *c. 1600's.* Long
single edge blade well marked with cutler's marks,
massive basket hilt of scrolls, bars and panels,
bulbous pommel. This is the characteristic Scots
basket hilt backsword used by Scots troops. Often in
this country it is erroneously referred to as a
claymore. The claymore is a large two-handed sword
Scot's weapon of the 15th and 16th centuries. It has a
long straight blade with straight grip and small pommel. The straight quillons slant slightly toward the
blade. It was known as the **claid-heamh-mor** or
claidhmhichean-mhora. The basket hilt Scots sword
is a back- or broad-sword patterned after the Venetian schiavona. This is a good specimen of the
backsword. 820.00   900.00

Price Range

☐ **Scottish Field Officer's sword,** *c. period of Edward VII. Blade etched with the Royal Crown, Royal Cypher, thistles and other floral designs, half basket guard decorated with floral designs, twisted wire bound fishskin grips, leather covered scabbard with plated mounts, cup pommel.* 175.00   190.00

☐ **Scottish Military dirk set.** *Royal Scots Fusiliers, 21st Regiment, c. Victorian period. Single edge pointed blade with scallop back edge, corded black wood hilt with German silver mounts, pommel is engraved with a thistle and with the identifying "XXI." In its German silver mounted sheath, complete with knife and fork.*   440.00   485.00

United States

☐ **American Revolutionary War hanger.** *Collectors know the "hanger" as a short, single edge sword designed for slashing. It was part of the equipment of the infantry soldier of the early to mid-1700's. This specimen is an example of the colonial blacksmith's art. The turned and polished wood grip narrows slightly at the bottom. The knuckle bow is simply a piece of round iron bar pounded flat at each end. The top attaches to the cap pommel and the lower end is turned down on one side to provide a small shell guard. The single edge blade reveals its local workmanship, no scabbard.* 545.00   600.00

☐ **American Revolutionary War hanger.** *This American made weapon is considerably more sophisticated than the above. Brass wire wound leather covered wire grips, heavy knuckle bow and pommel cap in one piece, lower bow end with flat turned down finial, slightly curved well-made single edge blade, no scabbard.* 475.00   525.00

☐ **Army Cavalry sword,** *model 1913. Patterned after the British Army Model 1905 Cavalry Trooper's sword. So-called Patton saber, having been recommended for adoption by then Colonel George S. Patton. Heavy steel half basket guard reinforced longitudinally by ribs, steel grips incised with a diamond pattern, plain pommel, long tapering straight blade marked on the obverse of the ricasso with "U.S." and the serial number of the sword. Additional markings show its manufacture at the Springfield Armory and the date of manufacture. The steel scabbard is covered with khaki webbing and the throat and tip are blackened. On each side of the throat is a ring to permit the scabbard to be easily attached to the saddle. This weapon was intended for use only when mounted and was not designed for personal wear. This weapon was also issued to members of the Mounted Detachment of the U.S. Marines in the Legation*

U.S. Army Cavalry Sword,
model 1913.

Price Range

guard at Peiping, China, the so-called "horse
Marines."......................................   127.00   140.00

☐ **Army Foot Artillery sword,** *model 1833. During the
middle 1800's the U.S. Army issued this type of short
bladed sword, of the so-called Roman pattern. Brass
scaled grip cast in one piece with a short cross guard
with plain disk finials. Blade marked with the
American Eagle and "N.P. AMES SPRINGFIELD." An
American Eagle appears on the pommel. Hilt
attached to the tang of the blade by three iron*

Price Range

traverse rivets. Similar swords with a variety of hilts were used in England and Europe. The value of these as a weapon is questionable. 154.00 170.00

☐ **Army Officer's sword,** *model 1850. Based on French army model, half basket hilt in gilt with gilt wire wrapped leather covered grips. Phrygian helmet pattern pommel, blade single edge and slightly curved, polished black leather scabbard with gilt/brass fittings. These may be found with several slight variations.* 200.00 220.00

☐ **Army Officer's sword,** *model 1902. Generally similar to the above except that the grips are notched on the inside for the fingers. Full back strap, simple rounded semicap pommel with small caspan top, "D" shape knuckle guard divides into three parts as it becomes the guard. Turned down tear shape finial, nickled scabbard. This is the last model Army sword authorized. Examples will appear in several qualities. Some will have elaborately etched blades and may be named. These will cost more. Blade slightly curved, good quality specimen.* 131.00 165.00

☐ **Army Officer's sword,** *model 1902. Recently made copy manufactured in Spain, blade etched with American Eagle and "US."* 80.00 88.00

☐ **Cavalry saber,** *American Revolutionary War. Another example of an American-made weapon of the period but of rougher workmanship than the above. All iron hilt, leather grips wrapped with iron wire, guard cut from sheet iron with pierced slots on each side of grips. This is part of the narrow knuckle bow which joins a flat cup pommel, slightly curved heavy blade, no scabbard.* 475.00 525.00

☐ **Cavalry saber,** *American Revolutionary War. Large size all brass hilt and two branch knuckle guard, large semioval quillon, large ball pommel, black leather covered grips with brass ferrules at each end, long and fairly wide single edge blade. This is an excellent example of an American made weapon of the period, no scabbard.* 770.00 850.00

☐ **Cavalry saber,** *c. 1776. Long hilt with divided type guard, roughly carved one piece wood grips, iron hand guard and pommel, long single edge blade, metal parts of iron, all roughly forged by some local blacksmith, much patina to all parts, an excellent example of a colonial-made weapon, no scabbard, rare.* 520.00 575.00

☐ **Confederate Foot Artillery sword.** *These may vary somewhat in pattern, some may have almost Bowie knife-like blades, and vary in plan. The average:* 230.00 250.00

☐ **"Grenadier sword."** *European sword made for issue and use in the infant United States, all brass hilt with heavily ribbed grips, fairly long curved single edge blade. Obverse is heavily engraved with lightning bolts and the legend "Grenadier of Virginia" in three lines. Obverse bears the motto "Victory or Death" in three lines. Back of blade stamped with the name of the maker "Klingenthal" together with proof marks. This is a very rare specimen and is considered of great importance to a collector of early American swords.* 2900.00 3200.00

☐ **Heavy Cavalry saber,** *model 1840. Brass semibasket guard joining the Phrygian helmet pattern pommel, slightly curved blade, metal scabbard.* 170.00 185.00

☐ **Light Horse Cavalry saber,** *c. late 1700's. All brass hilt with large lion head pommel, ribbed brass grips, divided "D" type hand guard, broad single edge blade, unmarked, no scabbard.* 750.00 830.00

☐ **Marine Officer's sword,** *regulations of 1859. This is the same pattern as adopted for U.S. Army officers in 1850. Pattern based on a French army model, gilt half basket hilt, pommel in the form of a Phrygian helmet, gilt wire wrapped black leather grips, polished black leather scabbard with gilt mounts, slightly curved blade etched with "UNITED STATES MARINE CORPS."* 320.00 350.00

☐ **Marine Officer's sword,** *regulations of 1875. This is the Mameluke hilt sword worn by Marine officers since that time except for the period of World War II. Earlier specimens will have ivory grips, modern specimens will have plastic, grips secured by two gilt embossed stars, set on a gilt disk flush with grips. The blade is slightly curved and rounded on the back, the words "UNITED STATES MARINES" with a floral design appear on each side of the blade. Some blades bear an etched American flag and Eagle, Anchor and Globe, many bear the name of the owner. Scabbard of nickel-plated iron with gilt bands and tip, bearing a design of laurel leaves. Pommel pierced for sword knot, one piece gilt cross quillon with ears and langets, quillon finials are in the form of an acorn. The readoption of the Mameluke hilt sword prescribed by the 1875 regulations is not, as many suppose, based upon the tradition of that pattern hilt worn by Marine officers according to the 1825 regulations which were said to commemorate the War with the Barbary Pirates. The fact is that the 1875 model sword is similar to that being worn by British generals and field marshals and was so noted by the uniform board which recommended its adoption. These swords will vary in value, the older ones of course being of greater worth.*

	Price Range	

Above sword, c. late 1800's. Ivory grips, scabbard named to the owner. 385.00 425.00

Above sword, World War I period. Ivory grips, named, scabbard. 300.00 330.00

☐ **Above sword,** post World War II. Scabbard, unnamed. 200.00 220.00

☐ **Musician sword,** model 1840. French Army pattern, straight single edge blade, cast brass hilt with "D" knuckle guard, grips ribbed, globular pommel, quillon ends in a slightly flared finial, fairly narrow width blade, may appear with either a black japanned metal scabbard or a polished black leather scabbard. This pattern sword was also worn by U.S. Marine Musicians 145.00 160.00

☐ **Above sword,** but marked "USMC." 175.00 190.00

☐ **Naval Officer's sword,** c. 1810. Knuckle guard in the form of a gilted sea serpent, pommel in the form of a large eagle head holding the upper end of the bow in its beak, gilt wire wrapped leather covered grips. A large finely detailed eagle with wide-spread wings forms the langet on each side, curved blade stamped on each side with an anchor, leather covered scabbard with gilted brass mounts. 655.00 725.00

☐ **Naval Officer's sword,** c. 1820-40. Straight single edge blade, extremely ornate knuckle guard attached at upper end to a plumed helmet shape pommel, mother-of-pearl grips. Fairly large counter guard bears a well-defined American Eagle with outspread wings clasping a fouled anchor. One third of blade nearest guard well-decorated with etched designs, well-decorated metal scabbard. It may be noted here that up until the U.S. Navy Regulations of 1841, the exact pattern of the officer's sword was not prescribed. Consequently they varied greatly, depending upon the officer's fancy and the size of his purse. This present specimen is an excellent item for a collector 475.00 525.00

☐ **Naval Officer's sword,** model 1841. This is the model prescribed for the first time in regulations. Apparently these regulations were not too strictly enforced for although they generally followed the regulation pattern, there were many variations. There are some variations in the design of the eagle pommel, the designs on the langets and the carving decorating the grips. Generally, there is not too great a difference in the price of these swords. The specimen described here has a single edge slightly curved blade with well-defined eagle pommel. The blued blade is etched with a design of acorns and oak leaves, together with an anchor near the guard, *reverse of the blade bears an etched "U.S. NAVY" and the name of the owner, knuckle bow is in the form of a reversed "P" and is decorated with a floral design, ivory grips are carved in an overlapping feather-like design, back strap has a molded design of feathers, there is an acorn at each end of the quillon and there are two counter guards. The obverse is decorated with a design of oak leaves and acorns, reverse guard is plain, scabbard is of highly polished leather with a gilt middle band decorated with an anchor, tip and throat are decorated with a floral design.* 430.00   475.00

U.S. Naval Officer's Sword, model 1852.

☐ **Naval Officer's sword,** *model 1852. The Navy Uniform Regulations of 1852 prescribed a sword which, with some slight modifications, is still worn today (except for the period of World War II). This weapon has a slightly curved cut and thrust blade. The obverse of the blade is decorated with an etched design of floral pattern together with stars, a fouled anchor and other items of a nautical motif. The reverse side is decorated in a similar manner and in most instances will bear "U.S.N." and may have the owner's name. Fishskin bound with twisted gilt wire binds the wood grips, upper end of the gilt "D" knuckle bow is in the form of a dolphin head and joins a Phrygian helmet pattern pommel which is decorated with 13 stars. The knuckle bow branches off and joins the widened quillon to form a counter guard decorated with a pierced "USN" surrounded with oak leaves and acorns, end of the quillon is also decorated with a dolphin head. The scabbard is of highly polished black leather and the gilt throat, middle band and tip are decorated with nautical designs. Since this pattern sword has been in use for so many years, they appear frequently on the collector's market. Those of the Civil War and the earlier period usually have a broader blade, heavier hilt and lighter pebbled fishskin covering on the grips. Prices may vary by reason of the elaborateness of the decoration, quality of materials in the weapon and similar characteristics. Some collectors prefer swords having the former owner's name.*

☐   **Above sword,** *Civil War vintage, inscribed with the name of the former owner, with scabbard* 500.00   550.00

		Price Range	

Above pattern sword, *World War I era, scabbard. . .* — 295.00 — 325.00

Above pattern sword, *post World War II, U.S. made, scabbard.* . . . . — 185.00 — 200.00

Above pattern sword, *post World War II, German made, scabbard.* . . . . — 185.00 — 200.00

Above pattern sword, *post World War II, Spanish import, scabbard.* . . . . — 100.00 — 110.00

☐ **Navy cutlass,** *(Confederate copy), model 1841. Similar to the above but with flat sides to pommel, obverse side of pommel bears "CSN," reverse bears an anchor.* . . . . — 385.00 — 425.00

☐ **Navy cutlass.** *Dated 1808, black japanned slightly concave guard formed of sheet iron, straight single edge blade, marked "N.STARR" on obverse of blade near guard, one piece cylindrical wood grip with iron ferrules at each end. This is a specimen of one of the Nathan Starr contract weapons and is historically important.* . . . . — 385.00 — 425.00

☐ **Navy cutlass,** *model 1841. The hilt of this cutlass differs in pattern from that of other cutlasses. It resembles the scaled hilt of the model 1833 Army Artillery sword. All brass hilt with simulated scales, American Eagle and U.S. Shield appear in relief on each side of pommel, straight wide double-edge blade. On the obverse of the blade appears "N.P. Ames" and Springfield." In three lines on the reverse side of the blade appears "USN"/"1843"/"RC."* . . . . . — 415.00 — 455.00

U.S. Navy Cutlass, model 1860.

☐ **Navy cutlass,** *model 1860. Slightly curved fairly wide blade, brass cup guard, brass pommel of Phrygian helmet pattern, brass wire wound leather cover grips. Ames made, Navy marks.* . . . . — 235.00 — 260.00

☐ **Navy cutlass,** *model 1917. As strange as it may seem, as late as World War I and the era of big battleships and heavy cruisers, there were cutlasses in the arms racks of some fighting ships. The Navy had designed a new model cutlass but was unable to find any manufacturer who would make it, consequently, a very limited number were made by the Navy, and few have reached the collector's market. Large sheet iron half basket guard, wood grips with incised diamond design, painted black, fairly short, slightly curved blade with clipped point and stamped "U.S.N." near* the hilt, all metal parts well-blued. Not a very handsome weapon. **125.00**

☐ **Navy cutlass,** *variant model 1917. Very similar to the above, but the guard has large cut out sections and plain black painted grips. Shortly after World War II large numbers of these were available on the surplus market. There are no markings on these weapons and no authentically documented record exists of their use. Several unsupported accounts have appeared, one to the effect that these weapons were purchased by the U.S. Government for the use of natives in the South Pacific and Asia. These cutlasses appear from time to time at auctions and gun shows but there is no great demand for them at this time. Interesting weapon but not important.* **64.00   70.00**

☐   **As above,** *but grips are of lightly stained wood. Simple in construction but could be very effective weapons, appear with the markings of several European concerns, purely a curio. Some collectors affirm that these were made for use in Indonesia. From time to time they are offered to collectors.* .   **35.00   38.00**

U.S. Navy "Figure 8" Cutlass, c. 1810.

	Price Range	

y "Figure 8" cutlass, c. 1810. *Slightly curved ₁gle edge blade, cylindrical iron grip, the quillon ₁rminates in a simple roll, outside of guard stamped ·US," left side of blade near guard also stamped "US." This is a well-weathered specimen as are nearly all cutlasses of the period. This is a crude copy of the standard Royal Navy cutlass of the period.* . . . . **205.00 | 225.00**

☐ **Non-commissioned Officer's sword,** *model 1840. Similar to musician sword but with longer blade and with kidney shape counter guard on each side of the blade.* . . . . **150.00 | 165.00**

☐ **As above,** *but marked "USMC."* . . . . **185.00 | 200.00**

☐ **Nonregulation 1860 Pattern cutlass.** *This is a specimen of the so-called "Officer's Cutlass" of the Civil War Period. The question is whether it was made for officers who wanted a more rugged combat weapon than the officer's sword or was made for chief petty officers who could afford a fancy yet rugged weapon. In any event, these are beautiful weapons which may be found with slightly different variations in the guard. It appears that these may have been made only on special order. This specimen has a gilted half basket guard with a swirl pattern with the large letters "U" "S" "N" cut out, has the Phrygian helmet pattern gilted pommel of the model 1860 cutlass but it is decorated with a floral motif instead of being plain, grips are wound with gilt wire instead of brass. Made by Ames and so marked. Not many of these weapons were made and they command a good price.* . . . . **1090.00 | 1200.00**

☐ **As above,** *but instead of the swirl pattern guard, above and below the cut out "USN" letters is an engraved floral design, gilt finish to guard, pommel and wire wrapping of grips.* . . . . **1090.00 | 1200.00**

☐ **As above,** *with engraved floral designs but the letters "USN" are also engraved instead of being pierced.* . . . . **590.00 | 650.00**

☐ **Revolutionary War Period cutlass.** *Broad curved single edge blade, shell pattern guard, narrow iron hand guard, bone grips. This is not a graceful weapon but it is a rare example* . . . . **860.00 | 950.00**

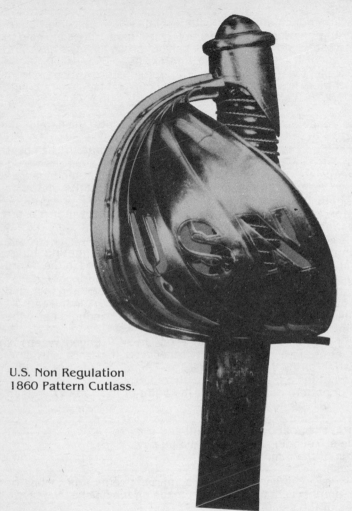

U.S. Non Regulation
1860 Pattern Cutlass.

ORIENTAL EDGED WEAPONS

DAGGERS

Oriental daggers are, for the most part, distinctly different from those of the Western World. Among a great variety of such weapons is the **kris** which has a fairly long and often wavy edge, much wider at the hilt than at the point. It can inflict a deep and nasty wound which is difficult to heal. The grip and hilt are at times quite unique in design. The Hindu **khuttar** with a flat medium length triangular blade and an unusual "H" shape hilt is an interesting but deadly dagger. A variation of this wickedly efficient killer has a spring which when activated expands an apparently single triangular blade into three. The

..rkha **kurkri** is a murderous weapon with a relatively short curved blade ..ich is considerably heavier toward the point. The Gurkha troops are said to ..eep this blade so sharp and keen that they can cut off an enemy's head and ..ne doesn't know about it until he tries to turn his head. The heavier point makes this an excellent weapon to throw. The Burmese **dhaw** may be from six inches to 24 or more inches long. The slightly curved blade has a single edge and is pointed. The **korambi** is a Sumatran dagger with a wicked sickle-type blade.

Japanese edge weapons are of an almost indefinite variety. The **hamidashi** was a dagger with a guard scarcely larger than the grip. Like all Japanese weapons, it was of the finest materials and artistically decorated. The **kozuk** was a small knife-like dagger carried in the scabbard of the Samurai's sword. The blade was single edge and pointed. As was the case with all Japanese weapons, these were made by master armorers or bladesmiths and were highly prized. From their early youth the Samurai were trained in the difficult art of throwing the **kozuk** and it was found useful for throwing into the eyeholes of the iron face mask. The hilts not infrequently were highly executed examples of the metalsmiths art. Although not a weapon, the **kogai** was an interesting adjunct to the noble Japanese warrior's fighting equipment. This skewer pattern implement was also carried at times in the sword scabbard, most usually in the scabbard of the short sword or dagger. It was of steel with an artistically decorated hilt. At times this decoration included the **mon** (identifying mark or symbol) of the owner. It was stuck in the earhole of the severed enemy's head, then was used as a sort of handle to carry the head to the commanding officer for credit.

In the following portion of the price guide on Oriental Edged Weapons some Japanese terms have been used. It is believed that this will allow quicker identification of the various blades. The English words represent a general translation of the Japanese written characters.

BOSHI. Shape or pattern developed near the point of the Japanese blade by the tempering of the blade.

FUCHI. Mouth of the hilt.

FUCHI-KASHIRA. Collar above hand guard and pommel.

HABAKI. Ferule surrounding blade near the guard.

HAMON. Pattern of the temper line.

KASHIRA. Pommel.

KATANA. The long sword carried by the samurai. Twenty four inches or longer in length. Together with the wakizashi made up the **daisho,** one of the identifying badges of the samurai.

KOTO. Old.

KOZUKA. Small knife carried in a pocket in the scabbard of a Japanese sword. Often used as a throwing knife.

KYUGUNTO. Officer's sword, c. 1880-1937.

MENUKI. Ornamentation on the sides of the hilt.

MON. Family crest, approximation of the European and British coat of arms.

MUMEI. Unsigned blade.

NAKAGO. Tang of a Japanese blade. Many bear the signature or other identifying mark of the sword maker.

O-SURIAGE. Shortened tang. May be shortened in later years to cut away the maker's signature.

SAME. Especially selected sharkskin covering the hilts and scabbar
swords and other weapons.

SAYA. Scabbard for a Japanese blade. Often made of wood or of w
lined metal. Frequently lacquered and have mounting corresponding to tho
of the hilt.

SHINGUNTO. Japanese sword of the World War II era.

SHIRASAYA. Literally "white scabbard." Finely finished plain wood hilt
and scabbard for the storage and preservation of extremely fine and costly
blades. Sometimes the scabbard may bear the name of the maker and other
information.

TACHI. Court Sword.

TANTO. Dagger, under twelve inches in length.

TSUBA. Guard of a Japanese sword.

TSUKA. Hilt.

TSUKA-ITO. Silk cord or braid wrapped around the hilt. Wrapping appears
in various patterns.

WAKIZASHI. Shorter of the two swords carried by the samurai. Generally
about eighteen inches long.

YAKIBA. Pattern on Japanese blade formed by temper line harder and
softer steels of blade.

Japanese Dagger or Tanto.

	Price Range	
☐ **Japanese dagger or tanto.** *This beautiful specimen has a short slightly curved blade of good quality, ivory hilt (grips) are artistically carved with figures of armed samurai and floral designs, ivory sheath is also beautifully carved with samurai and battle scenes.*	540.00	600.00
☐ **Japanese dagger or tanto.** *Well-defined temper line pattern, tsuba or hand guard has a deeply incised pattern of waves, inlaid with gold spray, tape bound tsuba or grips with shakudo menuki, complete with green and black striped saya or sheth shakudo kodzuka as waves.*	520.00	575.00
☐ **Japanese tanto.** *Bright clean blade is marked "Kunikane" on the tang, iron tsuba, gold color tsuka-ito over white sharkskin hilt, silver habaki, red lacquered saya with kozuka.*	495.00	550.00
☐ **Japanese tanto.** *Interesting reasonably priced offering. Good quality clean blade with straight temper line, blade is unsigned, interesting ribbed black lacquered hilt with brass insert, brass kogai or skewer fits into saya which is red lacquered.*	270.00	300.00

Price Range

...panese tanto. *This is an extremely fine example. ...he collar above the hand guard, the pommel and the guard are of silver and are en suite, koto blade has two holes in tang, one of which is filled with silver, tang is signed "Tsunahiro," a swordsmith active in the Sagami Providence in the 16th century, blade is in high polish and shows a wide undulating temper line, the boshi has a long turn back, complete with scabbard with silver tip.* 3060.00 3400.00

☐ **Japanese tanto.** *Very good quality koto blade with tang marked "Tsunahiro," a Sixteenth century sword-smith of considerable fame. Has wide and undulating motare temper line, tsuba, fuchi and kashira are of silver and are ensuite, has a kosuka with a silver hilt ensuite with the mounts of the larger weapon, black lacquered saya. This is a much better than usual offering and is in excellent condition.* 2970.00 3300.00

SWORDS

Oriental swords are quite interesting in pattern and are often highly decorated, not infrequently with gold. The **pata** is a weapon with a long straight blade with an "H" type grip enclosed by an armored gauntlet, thus giving full protection to the hand. This weapon is sometimes referred to as a gauntlet sword in western literature. The **parang latok** has a long heavy single edge chopper blade much larger at the point than at the hilt, making it into something like a butcher's cleaver. The **yat** had a long graceful incurving blade. Originally used in Turkey, it soon found favor in North Africa. A weapon of Persian origin which was used in Turkey and India was the **sham-skie.** This was a beautiful weapon with a gracefully curved blade which was particularly effective in the draw-cut. The English word **scimeter** is used to designate this weapon. The **tulwar** was the classical saber type weapon of India. It was fitted with a disk pommel. The guard varied considerably in design, and in some instances, was not even present except for a crossbar type. Guards were usually in the form of an elaborate "D."

Imperial Chinese

These swords are not in great demand except for a few specialist collectors.

☐ **Short sword.** *Plain double-edged fairly wide blade, brass cross guard with devil mask ornamentation and brass pommel, polished plain black wood grips, black lacquered wood scabbard with brass mounts, the throat pierced in Chinese designs.* 250.00 275.00

☐ **Short sword.** *Straight double-edge plain blade, brass guard and pommel, fluted black wood grips, unusual scabbard is covered with tortoise shell and has brass mounts.* 160.00 175.00

☐ **Sword.** *Plain slightly curved single edge blade, plain flat disk brass guard, brass ball shape pommel, black leather grips, black rayskin covered scabbard, brass mounts.* 180.00 200.00

Price Range

☐ **Sword.** *Slightly curved single edge blade lightly decorated with gilt, oval gilt guard pierced with dragon design, squared gilt pommel, grips bound with blue tape, vellum covered scabbard with gilt mounts, scabbard has metal covered square end.* 405.00   450.00

Japanese

The Japanese sword is like no other sword in the world! The single edge blade had three exactly similar curves; the face line, the edge and the back. The blade was very slightly curved. The **katana** was the longer of the two swords usually carried by the samurai. Together the set was one of the symbols of his rank. The shorter of the two swords was known as the **wakizashi.** Together, ensuite, the **katama** and the **wakizashi** made up the **daisho.** Generally speaking, the **katama** was the combat weapon while the **wakizashi** was reserved for use as a secondary weapon and for performing ritualistic suicide or **harakiri.**

It is rather well agreed that no other sword steel, even that of fabled Toledo, equaled that of the Japanese feudal blades. They are fabricated by folding over and over and over again and again alternate layers of soft and wrought iron. By constant hammering, the layers are welded together. This produces a blade with an extremely hard cutting edge (very keen but hard to nick) with the rest of the blade soft and tough, when it has been properly tempered in water. Each master swordsmith had his own highly secret method of tempering the blade and producing the wavy pattern on the blade. The ability of the blade to retain its sharpness is nothing short of uncanny to the western mind. It was not difficult at all to lop off the head of a human or cleave the body to the waist. At times condemned criminals were used to test the keenness of the blade. There are records of blades cutting through the barrel of a machine gun.

Such swords were extremely costly and were passed on from generation to generation. During World War II some sons of ancient noble families carried the same blade which their forebearers had hundreds of years before. In ancient times it was not at all uncommon for a samurai to mortgage all that he owned to purchase a fine blade. It is impossible for the Occidental mind to conceive the reverence with which these blades were held. Just before and during World War II, the Japanese Government arsenals produced samurai pattern swords for officers and noncommissioned officers of senior grade who did not have or could not afford one of the old blades. It doesn't require much knowledge to detect these. The genuine swords of old Japan do, however, require an expert to properly identify them; to determine just when they were made and just who made them. Age alone is not the determining factor. Age is important but of more importance is the reputation of the smith who made the sword. Above all, don't expect any bargains in samurai swords; there just aren't any. Before investing in one of these blades, unless the collector is a master himself, the purchaser should seek the advice of a recognized expert and do business only with a reliable dealer. Names and addresses of qualified experts in identification may be had from weapons curators of the larger museums, from the Japanese Embassy, Washington, D.C., or the Japanese Consul in the larger cities.

Japanese sword furniture also ranks very high in collectibles. **Tsuba** or hand guards are especially sought after. These may take a variety of forms out many are elliptical or square. The better of these were executed by the ancient masters and are works of art in themselves. These guards were easily changed and the samurai might well possess several. There is an almost infinite variety and it is not uncommon for an advanced collector to have several hundred in his collection. Prices usually begin at around $75.00 and range upwards. The **tsuba** are decorated with pierced, embossed, etched and engraved designs. They range in design all the way from the simple to the very complex. It may be a simple geometric design or an elaborate one expressing a philosophy of life. The great variety makes them most interesting.

Another interesting item of dagger and sword furniture which is highly regarded is the **menuki**. These are beautiful ornamental designs appearing on each side of the hilt. They too are in a great variety of designs, including demons, dragons and other mythical creatures, storks and other birds and animals, samurai in combat, and others. Many are of gold.

	Price Range	
☐ **Army Officer's sword**, *World War II. Signed Showa Era blade with a well-defined temper line, typical military scabbard*..............................	340.00	375.00
☐ **Jin-Tachi.** *Very long two-handed sword, not often encountered. Usually carried by an attendant or was slung over the back of the samurai. Blade is slightly over 45 inches long and is unsigned, iron tsuba, black tsuka-ito over white sharkskin hilt, black lacquered saya with rattan trim. This is a most unusual offering, old.*	1800.00	1990.00
☐ **Jitte.** *Medium length steel rod with blunt end and with round ball like pommel. A hook juts out from the rod where it meets the hilt. Primarily used as a defense against the sword but could also be used as an offensive weapon against the eyes or abdomen. Said to have originated in ancient times as a police weapon, later adopted by the samurai. An interesting and historic addition to any Japanese weapons collection.*	78.00	80.00
☐ **Katana.** *Another example in shirasaya mounts. Blade is of very good quality with billowing temper line, O-suriage but the inscription "Hizen no Kuni Ju Omi Daijo" remains. Swordsmith cannot be identified but this is a very old blade.*	1900.00	2100.00
☐ **Katana.** *Blade of the Showa Era is marked "Kunitsugu," old iron tsuba or guard, handle is covered with blue tape laced over white rayskin handle, the collar above the tsuba and the pommel are of iron and are en suite, lacquered scabbard.*	340.00	375.00
☐ **Katana.** *Blue tsuka-ito over white sharkskin hilt, fuchi and kashira are of iron and are ensuite, very old iron tsuba, blade is of the Showa Era and is signed "Knuitsugu," blade is dull, black lacquered saya. In fair condition only.*	253.00	300.00

Price Range

☐ **Katana.** *Dark blue tsuka-ito over white sharkskin hilt, brass fuchi-kashira and kashira are ensuite, brass tsuba, bright blade with nearly straight temper line, black lacquered saya, tang marked "Hyuga Kaneori." An interesting and most reasonable selection for the beginning collector.* **295.00   325.00**

☐ **Katana.** *Excellent blade of the Showa Era type, temper line is narrow and straight, tsuba is of iron and has four lobes, bears the design of a cricket in the grass, tan/brown tsuka-ito over white sharkskin, menuki are in the form of the mon of the Tokugawa family, brown lacquered saya. All in excellent condition. A good collector's piece.* **680.00   750.00**

☐ **Katana.** *Extremely old blade in shirasaya mounts, slightly billowing temper line, Japanese lettering on each side of blade, marked "Hakushu Gatsujo," a famous swordsmith of the 900's.* **3440.00   3800.00**

☐ **Katana.** *Green tsuka-ito over white sharkskin hilt, iron tsuba and kashira, good blade marked "Noshu Seki Ju Kane-haru Saku." Blade thought to be from around the middle of the fifteenth century, black lacquered saya has received considerable rough treatment in the past and needs restoration by an expert, lowering the value of the offering.* **295.00   325.00**

☐ **Katana in storage mounts.** *The storage mounts are called "shirasaya" in Japanese which means "white scabbard." It refers to the plain wood handle and scabbard in which fine blades were stored when not in use. The handle and scabbard are perfectly plain but are beautifully finished and fitted together. This example has a very fine clean blade with a bellowing temper line, tang is lettered "Hizen No Kuni Omi Daito," the name of the maker is not known because that portion of the tang has been cut off. This specimen has been attributed to Fujiwara Tadahiro and is dated around 1648.* **2125.00   2400.00**

☐ **Ken or Temple sword.** *This represents the oldest pattern sword used in Japan. The historical examples found in burial sites are single edge; the later examples are double-edged and may widen close to the point. This fairly typical example has a straight double-edged blade, bearing no signature. The handle is of solid brass, has built in menuke or ornamentation and an elephant design pommel, wood scabbard is brass mounted with brass elephant head at end, handle and the brass throat of the scabbard bear Tokagowa mons.* **723.00   800.00**

☐ **Naval Officer's sword,** *World War II. Clean blade with a straight temper line, gold color lacing over sharkskin handle, brass mounts, handle pierced for*

Japanese Court Sword or Tachi.

Japanese Naval Officer's Sword, World War II.

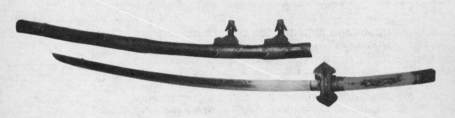

Japanese Katana in storage mounts.

	Price Range	
sword knot, rayskin covered scabbard with brass mounts, single ring suspension. This is a much better than average officer's sword of World War II.	385.00	425.00
☐ **Noncommissioned Officer's sword,** *World War II. Swords of this type were arsenal made in considerable quantity and are usually readily available on the collector's market. This specimen is typical with factory-made blade, tsuba and metal handle, handle made to simulate tape binding, metal scabbard.*	118.00	130.00
☐ **Officer's saber,** *c. World War II. Ornate looking but of inferior quality, may have been intended solely for*		

Price Range

parade wear. Saber and scabbard of general European pattern, bright factory made blade, gilt/brass
wire wrapped white rayskin grips, "D" shape knuckle
guard, pommel and counter guard, highly polished
black leather scabbard with two carrying rings,
gilt/brass mounts. Interesting but not important. 73.00   80.00

☐ **Officer's Sword.** Russo-Japanese War period. Bright
blade with irregular temper line, tang is marked
"Noshu Seki Ju Kanemichi Tsuburu," blade of traditional pattern, brass wire wrapped white sharkskin
hilt with brass pommel and "D" shape knuckle guard.
Nickeled steel scabbard with one carrying ring, hilt
bears the silver mon of the Katabami family. 353.00   400.00

☐ **Other Rank's Cavalry sword.** Russo-Japanese War
era. Newly made samurai pattern blade but rest of
weapon has Occidental appearance. Checkered
wood grips with steel pommel and "D" shape
knuckle guard, steel scabbard with one carrying ring.   100.00   110.00

☐ **Police Officer's sword,** c. 1930's. Long narrow clean
blade, black wire wound hilt with brass pommel, "D"
shape knuckle guard and counter guard, nickeled
steel scabbard. 100.00   110.00

☐ **Police Officer's sword,** c. 1930's. Generally the same
as the above but with tortoise shell grips. 100.00   110.00

☐ **Tachi.** The blade is old and well forged, has a clear
temper line and grain, has been shortened. There are
three holes in the tang and the tang cut off across a
fourth, white rayskin grips with brass mounts and
dragon ornament, adventurine covered scabbard
with decorated brass mounts including two sling
rings for holding the scabbard from the belt instead
of being thrust through the belt as is the case with
the katana. This is an excellent example of this rare
type. 3530.00   3900.00

☐ **Wakizashi.** A rather good offering for a beginning collector. The blade is old and unmarked, needs some
polishing, brass tsuba, tsuka-ito of black silk braid
over white sharkskin black lacquered saya, pocket
for kozuka but it is missing. 277.00   305.00

☐ **Wakizaski.** A rather unique offering. Black silk tsuka-
ito over black sharkskin hilt, hilt is longer than usual,
tang of blade is signed "Kaneyasu," blade appears to
be old, saya is black lacquered. 295.00   325.00

☐ **Wakizashi.** Blade with billowing temper line, square
tsuba pierced with hearts in each corner, the white
rayskin handle is wrapped with brown tape, collar
above the tsuba and the pommel are en suite, black
lacquered scabbard with the Kosuka or small knife in
place. 400.00   440.00

☐ **Wakizashi.** Clean polished blade is unsigned but has
been identified as being a Koto blade from Bitchu

	Price Range	

Province and is old. The yakiba is straight on one side of blade and irregular on the other, gold color tsuka-ito over white sharkskin hilt, silver fuchi and kashira, rather beautiful black lacquered saya with Mother of Pearl specks and with silver mounts, pocket for kosuke but this blade is missing. Weapon in very good condition. 600.00   665.00

□ **Wakizaski,** c. mid-1600's. Early Shinto period. Unsigned blade with clouded tempering, blue tsuka over white sharkskin hilt, black lacquered saya. Good example and inexpensive 363.00   400.00

□ **Wakizashi,** c. early 14th century. Good Koto blade with tang marked "Rai Kuniyasu," blade has straight narrow temper line, blade in shirasaya mounts. Good specimen. 2900.00   3200.00

□ **Wakizashi,** c. mid-1800's. Good temper line to blade, straight grain, good iron tsuba, interesting octopus menuki, fuchi-kashira matches, interesting kozuka decorated with trees and birds, black lacquered saya, unsigned blade. 770.00   850.00

□ **Wakizashi in shira saya.** Straight temper line and good grain, two holes in tang, maker marked to Rai Kuniyasu. Good specimen. 1900.00   2100.00

□ **Wakizashi.** Kashira is brass, fuchi-kashira and tsuba are ensuite, blue tsuka-ito over white sharkskin, blue lacquered saya, unsigned blade cannot be positively dated but has every evidence of being old, therefore, price is low. 303.00   335.00

□ **Wakizashi.** Somewhat unique in that it has black leather wrapping about the white sharkskin covered hilt instead of silk, iron tsuba with gold, silver and copper design, blade is unsigned but has all the characteristics of a Muramasa blade of the 14th century, black lacquered scabbard complete with kosuka. All in excellent condition, extremely collectible. 2900.00   3200.00

□ **Wakizashi.** Tang of the clean blade is marked "Norimitsu," blade may date to the 1300's, old iron tsuba, the white rayskin handle is laced with gold tape, kosuka missing. 2440.00   2700.00

□ **Wakizashi.** This offering is a better than average collector's piece. Koto blade is in excellent condition, good temper line, blade signed by the old and respected sword maker "Masamune," black tsuka-ito over white sharkskin hilt, good iron tsuba with silver design, saya is lacquered cinnabar, nicely made kodzuka is in saya pocket. 4475.00   4950.00

□ **Wakizaski.** Unsigned blade with dragon engraved on one side and a Sanscript letter on the other, old tsuba, brass fuchi and kashira are ensuite, black silk tsuka-ito over white sharkskin hilt, blade is dull but can be made bright by careful polishing. 363.00   400.00

☐ **Wakizaski.** *Unsigned blade with straight temper line, appears to be old but cannot be authenticated, suria-saya mounts with Japanese characters on one side of scabbard. This is a good example of the shirasaya mounts for the beginner.* 300.00   330.00

Japanese Tsuba
or Sword Guards.

Price Range

] **Tsuba.** *These vary greatly in design and quality.*
Listed here are some typical examples.

☐ **Tsuba,** *in dragon design.* 82.00   90.00
☐ **Tsuba,** *iron showing village scene with Mt. Fuji in*
background. 120.00   130.00
☐ **Tsuba,** *pierced in a crab design.* 120.00   130.00
☐ **Tsuba,** *with design of water and reeds in the*
foreground and mountains in the background. 77.00   85.00
☐ **Tsuba,** *with the face of a Buddhist priest.* 205.00   225.00

THE JAPANESE SWORD: WEAPON AND WORK OF ART
© Courtesy David E. J. Pepin 1977

The Japanese sword, more commonly known as the Samurai sword, was a superb weapon. Its unique edge-tempering (compared to the full-blade tempering of the famous Toledo and Damascus swords of Europe) allowed a degree of hardness and razor-sharpness impossible to attain in European swords without danger of brittleness and breakage. The fear and respect which the Japanese warrior and his sword inspired among Oriental foes is recorded in many contemporary accounts. But beyond its quality as a weapon, the Japanese sword is important as one of history's finest expressions of the metalworker's art.

The art of swordmaking required high technical knowledge, great patience, persistence and a true religious devotion. The greatest Japanese swordsmiths led a religious form of life, abstaining from all excesses, and accompanying each step of the work with prayer and ritual.

The actual forging of the blade was a complex process. Strips of two different grades of steel, or of iron and steel, were welded together by the smith's hammer. The resulting billet of metal was then folded upon itself and hammered out again to its original length and thickness. This process was repeated many times, until the final blade consisted of many thin, tightly-welded layers of the original metal. When the forging was completed, the swordsmith used file and scraping knife to give final shape and finish to the blade and tang.

As a result of the forging and finishing processes, the untempered portion of the blade of the Japanese sword frequently shows a unique patterning of the metal similar to wood grain.

The most critical of all the swordmaking processes was the tempering of the edge. The smith began by coating the entire blade with a thin layer of a clay, sand and powdered-charcoal mixture. Then, using a sharp bamboo stick, he inscribed a line a short distance back from the edge. The character of this line — straight, wavy, or irregular — determined the distinctive pattern of the tempered portion of the blade. Variations in shape of the tempering line are among the fine points of classification used by Japanese sword experts.

Material between the scribed line and the edge was removed and the rest of the coating allowed to dry. Then, the swordsmith heated the entire edge over his pine charcoal fire until the proper temperature (judged by the color of the heated metal) was reached. Finally, the glowing blade was plunged into a tank of warm water.

There are four basic types of Japanese swords; two of them short (under 24 inches) and two of them long (over 24 inches) in blade length. The Samurai warrior always carried a pair of sheathed swords — one long and one short — with the types carried depending upon the occasion.

When clad in armor or in formal court dress, the Samurai wore a long sword called the TACHI, slung edge-downward from his girdle or sash. The matching short sword, usually less than 12 inches in length, was a TANTO. It was worn thrust through the girdle and secured by a cord, and like the TACHI, the TANTO was worn edge-downward.

In ordinary dress, the Samurai's long sword was the KATANA. This sword, often nearly three feet in length, was thrust through the girdle, edge-upward. The KATANA was normally considered the fighting sword. Its companion was the WAKIZASHI a sword of between 12 and 24 inches in blade length. It too, was thrust edge-upward through the girdle.

Many Japanese swords were decorated with engraving or inlay work on the blade, although the major decorative work was usually reserved for the TSUBA, or guard; the FUCHI, a collar encircling the hilt at the guard end; and the KISHIRA or pommel-cap. These were often embellished with high-relief carving, engraving, etching, piercing, inlay work, incrustation with precious metals, or a combination of these techniques. The scabbard (SAYA) was usually finished with lacquer, and had decorated metal fittings.

Finishing of the sword hilt (TSUKA) begins with a covering of the white pebbled skin of a ray fish. Then, flat silk braid is wrapped over the hilt in a pattern which leaves a row of lozenge-shaped openings on either side, exposing the white ray skin.

Identification of swords requires removal of the TSUKA, which may be accomplished by carefully forcing out the single tapered wooden peg (MEKUGI) which fastens it to the tang. The TSUKA may then be slid off the tank, revealing the maker's signature and other identifying marks incised in the metal. The signature often consists of the maker's name, his titles, and place at which the sword was made. The date of manufacture, when shown, is usually found on the other side of the tang. Certain patterns of file marks on the tang are also distinctive, aiding the expert in determining the authenticity and dating of the sword.

Monetary value of the Japanese sword obviously depends upon many factors, such as; age, condition, maker and historical associations, but we can all appreciate the value of any of these swords as magnificent examples of the artistic ability and dedication of the Japanese swordsmith.

TYPES OF SWORDS AND DAGGERS

ARMY OFFICERS KATANA
The Saya (scabbard) is usually painted olive drab in color. This type is also found with a leather covered wood Saya. Do not confuse with the all metal handled N.C.O. type. *50% chance for an old blade.*

NAVAL OFFICER'S MODEL
The Navy sword is actually a copy of an old Tachi. It can be easily identified by its SA-ME (occasionally simulated) covered Saya and two hangers. The location of Mons (crests) are the same as the Army sword. This type is also found with a leather covered wood Saya. *40% chance for an old blade.*

MARINE OFFICER'S TYPE
The main distinguishing points of this type are its Helmet design caps (Kashira Kojiri) Its Saya is normally composed of brown laquer over wood. *20% chance for an old blade.*

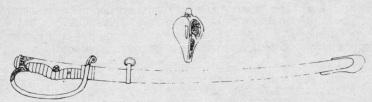

ARMY OFFICER'S SWORD (RUSSO-JAPANESE WAR)
This sword comes in both Army and Navy models. The Tsukas (Handles) are basically the same. There are also two sizes — Large (Katana blade), approximate handle length 10″, Small (Wakizashi blade), approximate handle size 6″. Both have visable Mekugi's (retaining pegs). Do NOT confuse it with Parade or Police sabers (smaller handles, no Mekugi, dull blade). Swords in this type mounting carry old blades most of the time, and should never be passed over without a close examination. *95% chance for an old blade.*

SAMURAI SWORD TERMINOLOGY

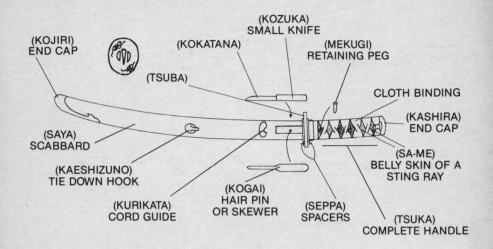

(KOJIRI) END CAP

(KOKATANA)

(KOZUKA) SMALL KNIFE

(MEKUGI) RETAINING PEG

(TSUBA)

CLOTH BINDING

(KASHIRA) END CAP

(SAYA) SCABBARD

(SA-ME) BELLY SKIN OF A STING RAY

(KAESHIZUNO) TIE DOWN HOOK

(KOGAI) HAIR PIN OR SKEWER

(TSUKA) COMPLETE HANDLE

(KURIKATA) CORD GUIDE

(SEPPA) SPACERS

SHINOJI-ZUKURI (STANDARD BLADE STYLE)

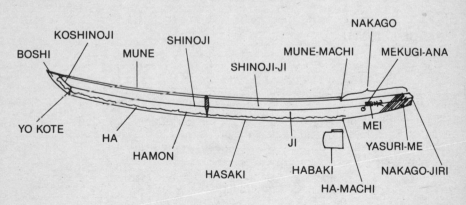

BOSHI

KOSHINOJI

MUNE

SHINOJI

SHINOJI-JI

MUNE-MACHI

NAKAGO

MEKUGI-ANA

YO KOTE

HA

HAMON

HASAKI

JI

HABAKI

HA-MACHI

MEI

YASURI-ME

NAKAGO-JIRI

BLADE VARIATIONS

HIRA-ZUKURI

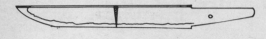

(Flat sides) This is the most sought after style for Wakizashi and Tanto.

UNOKUBI-ZUKURI

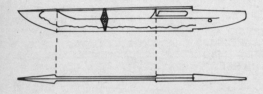

Unokubi-Zukuri style also very desirable.

KEN STYLE

As a rule these are cut down Yari (If not a cut Yari, they are very good).

BLADE LENGTH

Blade length is of the utmost importance in evaluating Japanese sword blades. Therefore, one must know the proper way to measure this. Place yard stick as shown above. Always measure in a straight line. (Do not measure curve.)

Tanto	=	0″ to 12″	Value Medium
Wakizashi	=	12″ to 24″	Value Low
Tachi or Katana	=	24″ to 27¾″	Value Medium High
Tachi or Katana	=	27¾″ to 32″	Value High
Tachi or Katana	=	32″ and up	Value Medium High

It should be remembered that 75% of all blades found to be between 25½″ and 26¼″ are of the military type. Swords of this length should be checked very carefully for Showa Stamps. It should be noted that 29″ to 30½″ is the most desirable length.

HAMON (HEAT-TREATING) VARIATIONS ON BLADES

If difficulty is encountered in seeing the Hamon, it is recommended that the blade be aimed at an incandescent light bulb while looking either just in front of or just behind the reflection of the bulb on the blade and one should be able to distinguish the Hamon with little difficulty even on a blade in reasonably poor polish.

The NIE-NIOI line must be intact for the entire length of the blade, (and should almost appear to be florescent). A gap in this line is known as NIE-NIOI GIRI and is considered one of the most serious flaws, other than in the Manufacture, it can also be caused by excessive heat (i.e. fire or a buffing wheel).

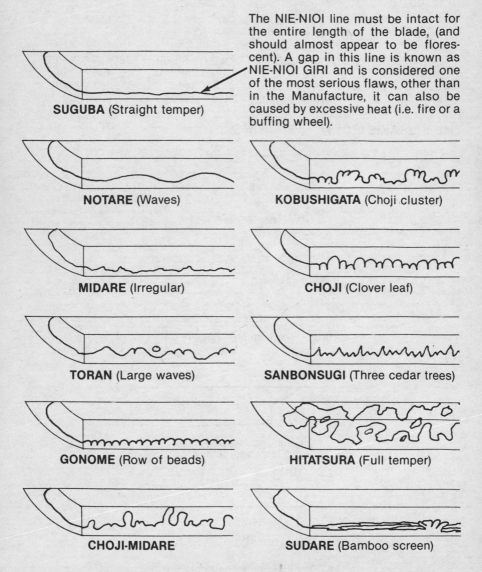

SUGUBA (Straight temper)

NOTARE (Waves)

KOBUSHIGATA (Choji cluster)

MIDARE (Irregular)

CHOJI (Clover leaf)

TORAN (Large waves)

SANBONSUGI (Three cedar trees)

GONOME (Row of beads)

HITATSURA (Full temper)

CHOJI-MIDARE

SUDARE (Bamboo screen)

THE HABAKI (COLLAR OF SLEEVE)

The Habaki (collar of sleeve around the blade) can also serve as an important tip-off in spotting good blades. The type drawn here are usually reserved for use on better blades. It should be noted that any of the above may have a family mon (crest) or other ornate designs.

VARNISHED COPPER

TWO PIECE

GOLD OR SILVER FOIL WRAPPED (with or without design)

SOLID COPPER With Falling Rain Design)

THE KISSAKIS (POINT VARIATIONS)

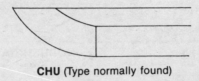

CHU (Type normally found)

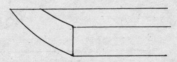

IKUBI (Short, stubby boar's neck)

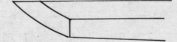

KO (Small, normally found on old Tachi and Katana

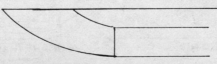

O-KISSAKI (Large, very desirable type)

THE HADA (BLADE GRAIN STRUCTURE) VARIATIONS

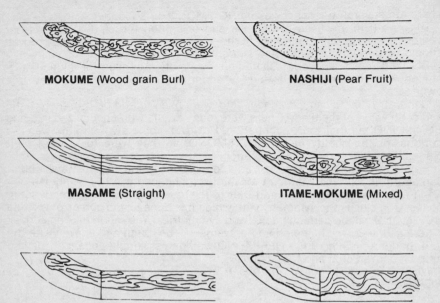

MOKUME (Wood grain Burl)

NASHIJI (Pear Fruit)

MASAME (Straight)

ITAME-MOKUME (Mixed)

ITAME (Wood grain)

AYASUGI (Normally Gassan School)

THE MUNE (BACK STYLE VARIATIONS)

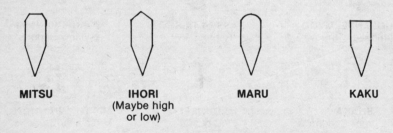

MITSU

IHORI
(Maybe high
or low)

MARU

KAKU

BLADE LAMINATION VARIATIONS (HANDMADE SWORDS)

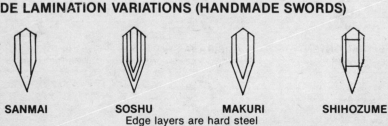

SANMAI

SOSHU
Edge layers are hard steel
Inner layers are softer.

MAKURI

SHIHOZUME

ORIMONO (BLADE ENGRAVINGS)

here are several reasons for using HORIMONO on a blade.

Grooves (HI), are used to balance and or lighten the blade. That was of course of the utmost importance to the experienced swordsman. The grooves should be perfectly smooth, and straight with no uneveness in the valleys.

BONJI (Budist Sandscript Characters), were often applied for religious significance or to bring good fortune, wisdom and bravery, etc. to the swords owner.

Decorative engravings, draggons, etc. were used to add both to the artistic and cash value of the blade. There were many artists who specialized in doing HORIMONO, as their only occupation. However, some swordsmiths were as famous for the quality of their HORIMONO, as they were for that of their blades. This is a very rare combination.

Sometimes horimono has used as a form of deception, to hide flaws and or damage. It is extremely difficult for the inexperienced eye to distinguish bettypween excellent HORIMONO, and that of low quality, done for deceptive purposes. One clue is the symmetry with which it is done ie; the curves of the fine HORIMONO will be perfectly done, and symmetrical, (no rough uneven edges). Where as the curves in the poor engravings will be rough and uneven with the tool marks remaining. Fine HERIMONO was painstakingly polished to eliminate all uneven cuts and tool marks.

Note: It is best to consult an expert when learning to judge the quality of HORIMONO.

SANSCRIPT CHARACTERS — BONJI

KOSANSEI MYOO
"Imbued with love"

BASSRA TAISHO
"Repress evil"

YORU KWANNON
"Willow Buddha"

SHAKA
"The great Buddha"

HAGUNSEI
"Victory star"

MATTO KWANNON
"horse-head Buddha"

BISHAMONTEN
"Bravery"

GUBIRA TAISHO
"A kind palace general"

BUNKYOKUSEI
"Military star"

SHOGUN JIZO BOSATSU
"Supremacy"

DAIJIZAITEN
"Prosperity and freedom"

JUICHIMON KWANNON
"11 face Buddha - see all"

HORIMONO (BLADE ENGRAVINGS)

DURMA

BUDDHA

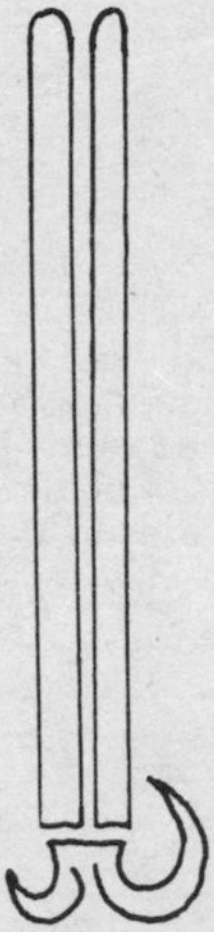

GOMA-BASHI

FUDO

BONJI WITH HORIMONO

GYO KURIKARA

SANKO-TUSKA-KEN

HATAHOKO

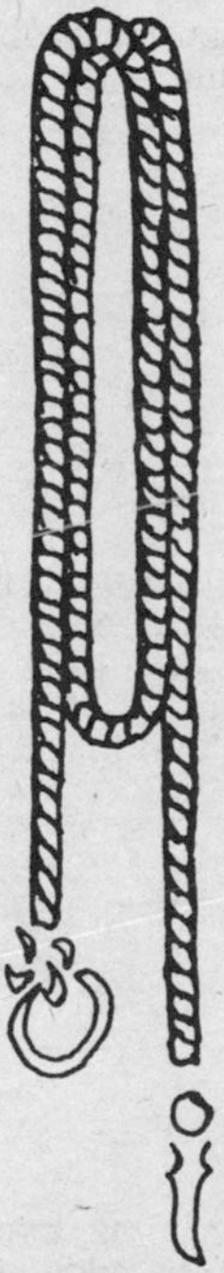

FUDOS ROPE

BUDDHA YARI OR VAJRA FORM

THE NAKAGO (TANG)

UBU, NAKAGO, MU-MEI
(virgin, tang, unsigned)

There is normally a good reason for an UBU NAKAGO being unsigned, 90% of the time the blade either turned out with KIZU or it was a mass production blade. At any rate, use caution in buying an unsigned sword with an UBU NAKAGO.

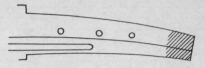

SURIAGE w/HI
(shortened with original groove)

HI should protrude well into the NAKAGO. Note also that YASURI-MEI (file marks), were changed at the time of shortening, and that some of the original YASURI-MEI was left for the purpose of identification.

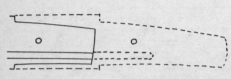

O-SURIAGE
(none of original NAKAGO remaining)

Note that when HI (grooves), are present that they go the entire length of the tang.

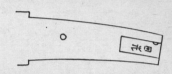

ORIKAESHI-MEI
(folded over signature)

The original NAKAGO has been cut away, with the portion bearing the MEI (signature), left in tact, this portion is then folded into a prepared slot. *Note: An excellent candidate for forgeries.*

MACHI-OKURI

All of the original NAKAGO remains, only the MACHI has been filed forward and a new MEKUGI ANA (hole for the peg), has been added. The signature should be in the proximity of the original hole.

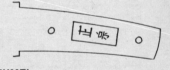

GAKUMEI
(inlayed signature)

This is when the MEI is taken from the cut off portion of the NAKAGO and inlayed in the new NAKAGO. This is one of the most popular methods of faking swords. It is very easy to take a good signature from a broken sword and inlay it in another.

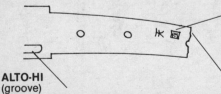

ALTO-HI
(groove)

On this sword you can see that a HI (groove) has been added later, this is often done to hide KIZU, the same is true of blades with ALTO HORIMONO (engravings that were added later.)

It is also common to find a shortened sword with a gold attribution to a popular smith. These attributions have no validity unless signed by a noted expert.

If a SURIAGE is done poorly or crudely it is a sign that the sword was not considered to be a very important one when it was shortened, and therefore is probably not a very good blade.

山城 Yamashiro | 城州 Joshu | 大和 Yamato | 和州 Washu | 河内 Kawachi | 河州 Kashu | 和泉 Izumi | 泉州 Senshu |
攝津 Settsu | 摂州 Sesshu | 伊賀 Iga | 伊州 Ishu | 伊勢 Ise | 勢州 Seishu | 志摩 Shima | 志州 Shishu |
尾張 Owari | 尾州 Bishu | 三河 Mikawa | 三州 Sanshu | 遠江 Totomi | 遠州 Enshu | 駿河 Suruga | 駿州 Sunshu |
甲斐 Kai | 甲州 Koshu | 伊豆 Izu | 豆州 Zushu | 相模 Sagami | 相州 Soshu | 武藏 Musashi | 武州 Bushu |
安房 Awa | 房州 Boshu | 上総 Kazusa | 総州 Soshu | 下総 Shimosa | 総州 Soshu | 常陸 Hitachi | 常州 Joshu |
近江 Omi | 江州 Goshu | 美濃 Mino | 濃州 Noshu | 飛騨 Hida | 飛州 Hishu | 信濃 Shinano | 信州 Shinshu |
上野 Kozuke | 上州 Joshu | 下野 Shimotsuke | 野州 Yashu | 陸奥 Mutsu | 奥州 Oshu | 出羽 Dewa | 羽州 Ushu |
若狭 Wakasa | 若州 Jakushu | 越前 Echizen | 越州 Esshu | 越中 Ecchu | 越州 Esshu | 越後 Echigo | 越州 Esshu |

加賀 Kaga | 加州 Kashu | 能登 Noto | 能州 Noshu | 佐渡 Sado | 佐州 Soshu | 丹波 ... | |
丹後 Tango | 丹州 Tanshu | 但馬 Tajima | 但州 Tanshu | 因幡 Inaba | 因州 Inshu | 伯耆 Hoki | 伯州 Hakushu |
出雲 Izumo | 雲州 Unshu | 石見 Iwami | 石州 Sekishu | 隠岐 Oki | | 土佐 Tosa | |
美作 Mimasaka | 作州 Sakushu | 備前 Bizen | 備州 Bishu | 備中 Bicchu | 備州 Bishu | 備後 Bingo | 備州 Bishu |
安藝 Aki | 藝州 Geishu | 周防 Suo | 防州 Boshu | 長門 Nagato | 長州 Choshu | 筑前 Chikuzen | 筑州 Chikushu |
筑後 Chikugo | 筑州 Chikushu | 豐後 Bungo | 豊州 Hoshu | 豐前 Buzen | 豊州 Hoshu | 肥前 Hizen | 肥州 Hishu |
日向 Hyuga | 日州 Nisshu | 大隅 Osumi | 隅州 Gushu | 薩摩 Satsuma | 薩州 Sasshu | 肥後 Higo | 讃岐 Sanuki |
紀伊 Kii | 紀州 Kishu | 淡路 Awaji | 淡州 Tanshu | 阿波 Awa | 阿州 Ashu | 伊豫 Iyo | 豫州 Yoshu |

1	肥	HI
2	前國	ZEN (NO)
3	國	KUNI
4	住	JU
5	忠	TADA
6	吉	YOSHI
7	作	SAKU

Example 1 — 7 Character MEI

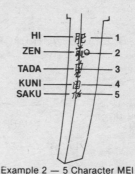

HI	肥	1
ZEN	前	2
TADA	忠	3
KUNI	國	4
SAKU	作	5

Example 2 — 5 Character MEI

In example 1, MEI (signature) charactors 1 & 2 are almost always the Provence name -

3 is usually the Title -

4 is usually JU or living at -

5 & 6 are the makers name -

7 is normally SAKU meaning made this.

You may wish to remember to look for 7 (SAKU) - the two characters that proceed this are usually the makers name. If 7 are not present, the last two are probably the makers name.

In example 2, again 1 & 2 are the Provence name. 3 & 4 are the makers name, and 5 is again SAKU.

JAPANESE SWORD EVALUATION SHEET

NOTE: Rust should never be removed.

UNDESIRABLE BLADE CHARACTERISTICS

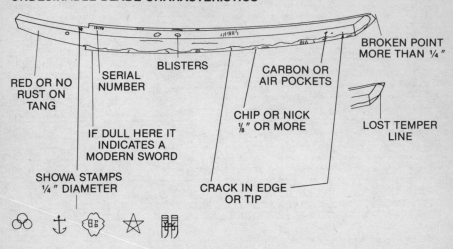

DESIRABLE BLADE CHARACTERISTICS

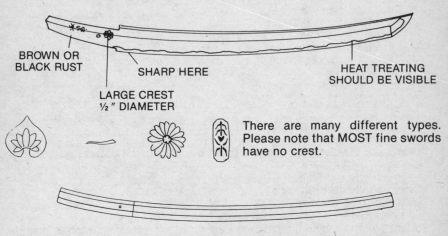

The blade found in a Shira Saya (storage scabbard) should always be checked very closely. Most blades found in this type of mounting are of very good quality, and could be very valuable. The Shira-Saya will resemble a plain white wood cane. Its purpose, however, is to protect a blade prized too highly to be used in battle.

1. Blade length (cutting edge) _____

2. Is the cutting edge sharp where it enters the brass collar? _____
_____

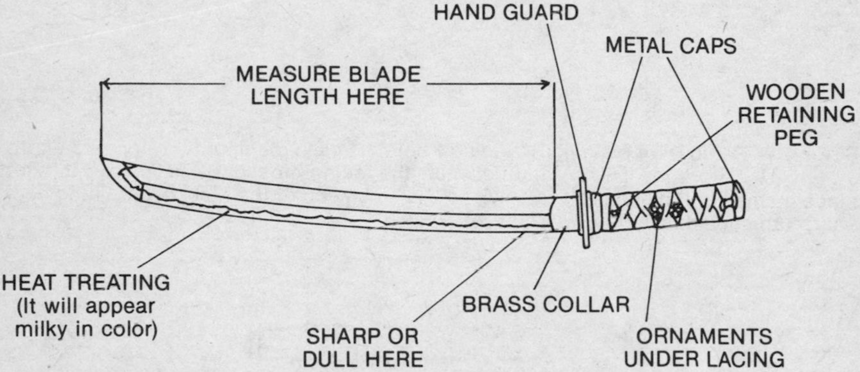

HAND GUARD

METAL CAPS

MEASURE BLADE
LENGTH HERE

WOODEN
RETAINING
PEG

HEAT TREATING
(It will appear
milky in color)

BRASS COLLAR

SHARP OR
DULL HERE

ORNAMENTS
UNDER LACING

3. Are there any chips nicks or cracks on the blade? If so, please measure the depth. What is the type of point and is it damaged?
_____
_____

4. Can heat treating be seen? If so, indicate what type. *(See page 457)*
_____
_____

5. Describe the fittings.
   A. Metal caps at either end of handle _____
_____

   B. Ornaments under lacing _____
_____

   C. Color of lacing _____
_____

   D. Description of handle _____
_____
_____

   E. Indicate scabbard color and the material from which it is made.
_____
_____

6. Indicate the type of Tang *(See page 460)* and the inscription. Follow the steps indicated below to uncover the Tang portion of the blade.

STEP 1 — Removal of Mekugi (Retaining Peg). The Mekugi is normally located approximately 1½" from the TSUBA and between the lacing crossover. To remove it, simply place a small drift punch, (brass only), on the small end of the Mekugi (retaining peg), a sharp tap should dislodge it. (Figure A)

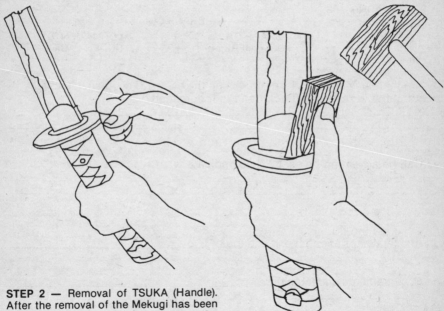

STEP 2 — Removal of TSUKA (Handle). After the removal of the Mekugi has been accomplished, one should grasp the TSUKA (handle) with the left hand, (as illustrated). Holding the sword in an upright (point up), position, with the cutting edge away from the body, strike the left wrist area with the right hand. This should loosen the TSUKA and enable it to be easily removed.

STEP 3 — If step 2 fails, proceed as indicated in Figure C, utilizing a wooden hammer and block, (plastic or Nylon is also accepted), be very careful not to place the drive block on the Tsuba itself, it should rest on the SEPA (spacer). Never use a metal hammer or place the blade in a vice, this will in all probability ruin your sword. (An expensive lesson)

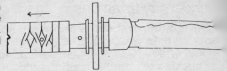

STEP 4 — Now that the TSUKA has been removed, proceed with the removal of the SEPA, TSUBA, and HABAKI, (Figure D). They slide off in the same direction as did the TSUKA.

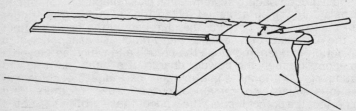

SOFT, STRONG PAPER
(Yellow Tablet Paper is Recommended)

STEP 5 — Place a piece of soft strong paper (yellow tablet paper) over the Tang, rub the paper with a soft lead pencil (do not allow paper to move while making rubbing).

Note: If any difficulty is encountered in using the above method, send a self-addressed envelope to me and I will forward special pressure sensitive paper and instructions to you.

STEP 6 — Please indicate color of rust (red, brown, black). _____

This service is provided free of charge. If you have a sword and would like to have it analyzed, please answer the questions on the previous pages and contact:

DAVID E. J. PEPIN
P. O. Box 354
Grant Park, Illinois 60940

**TELEPHONE: (815) 465-6061 · Illinois Residents
TOLL FREE 1-800-435-5119**

LIFE MEMBER
SOCIETY FOR THE PRESERVATION OF JAPANESE ART SWORDS,
TOKYO, JAPAN

All offerings will be treated in the strictest of confidence and will receive prompt reply. If possible please enclose a photo.

• JAPANESE ARMOUR AND ORIENTAL ART ALSO WANTED •

SKETS AND RIFLES

The ignition systems previously noted applied alike to both hand guns and shoulder held weapons. The earliest arms of this sort were, of course, muzzle-loaders. As was the case with hand guns, arms designers were continually seeking to improve loading procedures, ignition, reliability and accuracy. The ultimate could not be reached until the advent of the metallic cartridge, breechloading and rifling. Captain Patrick Ferguson, of the British Army, was the first to develop a breechloading system which was reliable and practical. This consisted of a screw plug attached to the trigger guard. The trigger guard could be rotated to raise or lower the plug behind the breech. Other systems were the German Dreyse and the French Chassepot which employed a bolt action to open and close the breech and which employed a needle which plunged through the powder charge of a paper cartridge to strike a detonating disk. Although some metallic cartridge breechloaders were made in various countries, it remained for the Mauser brothers, Paul and Wilhelm, to perfect the breechloader. The work of these brothers is noted earlier in this guide. Developed first as a single shot rifle, the system was later fitted with a tubular magazine and later with a box magazine under the chamber. The Mauser became the most copied and most widely used rifle in the world and our own justly famous Springfield model 1903 service rifle was developed from the Mauser.

MUSKETS

Asia   **Price Range**

☐ **Russian Military Flintlock musket,** *c. mid-1700's.*
Cyrillic marks, including that of government arsenal,
full military marks in addition. 860.00   950.00

Europe

☐ **French Army Flintlock musket,** *model 1763, .69 cal.*
Marked to the famous Charleville Arsenal. This pat-
tern musket was also manufactured at the French
Government Arsenals at Maubeuge, Tulle and St.
Etienne, and are so marked. Around 100,000 of these
were furnished to the infant United States by the
French. Regardless of where made, they are all
called "Charlevilles." The first U.S. Government
manufactured musket, the U.S. Flintlock musket,
model 1795, used the Charleville as the pattern.
Those specimens surcharged "U.S." on the rear of
the lockplate indicate that the weapon was owned by
the U.S. Government. Otherwise the musket is of
French Army ownership. 1225.00   1350.00

Great Britain

Brown Bess. This is the familiar name applied to the standard shoulder arm of the British Army for many years. It is of particular interest in this country by reason of the fact that large numbers were captured in the American Revolutionary War and were used by the U.S. Army, Navy and Marine Corps. For a time, indeed, it would seem that the British were the principal suppliers of our best weapons. The term "Brown Bess" apparently was first applied to the British Short Land Musket. The origin of the name is unknown. Some arms historians relate that as issued it had a brightly polished barrel and a highly polished brown stock, this in contrast to the dull black painted stocks of earlier issue muskets. This may account for "Brown." "Bess" may have originated from the German "Busche" or "Buss" for gun. This name could have been easily borrowed from German soldiers then serving in the British Army. It is logical that, with the fighting man's liking to assign a female personality to objects, the soldiers corrupted "Buss" to "Bess" in affection for what to them was an exceptionally good weapon. Brown Bess appeared in several variations, the principal ones which are listed here.

Price Range

☐ **British Army Brown Bess Flintlock musket,** *first model. Rare specimen marked to the "KING'S OWN REG'T." All brass mounts, wrist plate bears regimental musket rack number and unit number, tower marked. This weapon is of special interest inasmuch as the King's Own Regiment (the 4th Foot) served in Boston and at Lexington and Concord. Although in relic condition, musket is historically rare.* 2980.00   3300.00

☐ **British Army Brown Bess Flintlock musket,** *second model. All brass mounts, "Tower" and crowned "GR" marked.* 1000.00   1100.00

☐ **British Army Brown Bess Flintlock musket,** *third model, .78 cal. Brass mounts, on lockplate appears "Tower" with crowned "GR."* 1000.00   1100.00

☐ **British Army Brown Bess Flintlock musket.** *Tower proofed, barrel marked "Kerry M" and bears serial number with inspector's marks, lockplate bears usual Tower and crowned "GR" marks. Stock marked with crowned "GR" and "BO" along with the Broad Arrow. This musket was issued to the County Kerry Militia and is dated 1831.* 500.00   550.00

☐ **British Army Flintlock Cavalry carbine,** *c. early 1700's. Brass mounted, truly a rare specimen. Marked with a crowned "AR" (Queen Anne) with the maker's name "I. Greene." This Queen Anne musket is the immediate forerunner of the famed Brown Bess.* 5600.00   6200.00

☐ **British Army Flintlock Cavalry carbine,** *reign of William IV, .65 cal. Barrel bears crowned "WR" marks and lockplate bears tower mark, with crowned "WR" together with inspector's marks.* 1090.00   1200.00

☐ **British East India Company musket,** *.75 cal. Percussion. All brass mounts, marked with the lion of the East India Company.* 300.00   330.00

☐ **British Naval Brown Bess Flintlock,** *.79 cal. Brass mounts, tower proof, made by Heylin. An interesting specimen with early colonial hex mark on escutcheon, colonial markings and name "W. Young" burned onto the comb, all indicating colonial use.* 1000.00   1100.00

Oriental

☐ **Heavy Japanese Matchlock Wall gun.** *Beautifully made weapon of massive pattern. Barrel inlaid in sil-*

	Price Range	

ver with a dragon design together with the mon of the noble family originally owning the piece, rare. **1900.00 2100.00**

☐ **Heavy Japanese Matchlock Wall gun.** *Flat top barrel with silver inlay design and the mon of the family originally owning the weapon. The barrel also bears, in Japanese, the words "Yamashiro Morifusa Zore." Excellent collector's piece.* **2350.00 2600.00**

☐ **Japanese Matchlock rifle.** *Octagonal barrel inlaid with a dragon design, brass mounted, beautiful polished cherry wood full stock, butt stock decorated with inlaid brass design.* **605.00 675.00**

United States

☐ **Contract Flintlock muskets,** *model 1798. Patterned after the model 1795 Springfield Musket, made by various contractors, quality varies greatly, marked with the maker's name and at times with a U.S. mark, values vary greatly.* **850.00 2050.00**

☐ **Hall Breechloading Flintlock rifle,** *model 1819, .52 cal. Iron mountings. This was the first breechloading arm used by the U.S. Government, the Army and the Navy.* **775.00 1625.00**

☐ **Sharps Box Lock carbine,** *model 1851, .52 cal. Maynard tape primer, breechloading, made for the Army. Sharps and U.S. Government markings.* **1100.00 2600.00**

☐ **Springfield Flintlock musket,** *model 1795, .69 cal. Patterned after the French Army model 1763 flintlock which was furnished to the struggling colonies in some quantity. The first U.S. Government manufactured longarm, several variations exist and collectors specializing in these particular guns often break them down into several subclassifications. Values vary according to year of manufacture.* **1100.00 4600.00**

RIFLES

Asia

☐ **Imperial Russian Army rifle.** *Percussion, brass mounts. This is an interesting specimen which has been converted from a flintlock at the government arsenal. Marked to the Tual Arsenal, dated 1833.* **430.00 475.00**

☐ **Russian Army carbine,** *model 1938, 7.62-mm. Same as model 1938 rifle but carbine type, both rifle and carbine with Russian military markings.* **87.00 95.00**

☐ **Russian Army rifle,** *model 1938, 7.62-mm. Famous Nagant design.* **87.00 95.00**

Europe

☐ **Austrian Mannlicher M1895 rifle,** *11-mm. Straight pull bolt action, one of the first clip loading magazine rifles, the spent clip dropped down through a hole in the magazine after the last round had been fired. Historically important.* **91.00 100.00**

Price Range

☐ **Belgian Mauser FN,** *M50, .30-06 cal. Manufactured in Belgium by famed Fabrique Nationale during the 1950's, M98 action.* **145.00**   **160.00**

☐ **Czechoslovakian Mauser VZ33 Brno,** *M98. Extra high quality Czech made in the famous Brno arsenal, Czech marked.* **96.00**   **105.00**

☐ **French Army Chassepot Bolt Action rifle,** *11-mm. Used self contained paper cartridge with percussion cap in the base, used with considerable effect during Franco-Prussian War, with government and maker marks, interesting historically, not rare.* **200.00**   **220.00**

☐ **French Lebel,** *8-mm. Lebel cartridge, tubular magazine under the barrel. Adopted for the French Army in 1886 and used until early in World War II. Gained considerable fame with the French Foreign Legion and French colonial troops. A historic piece.* **41.00**   **45.00**

☐ **French Army rifle,** *MAS36, 7.5-mm. Belated design to replace the Lebel. Box magazine under the chamber, awkward bolt action with bolt bent sharply forward, squat and ugly looking, bayonet fit in tube under barrel and had to be completely withdrawn and fixed in place, a time consuming operation. This weapon was not much of a success. An interesting example of rifle development and an excellent World War II curio.* **41.00**   **45.00**

☐ **French rifle,** *model '92, 8-mm. Made at the official arsenal at St. Etienne and often referred to as the Model de Ordonnance model '92. Swing out cylinder, right side of weapon swings aside to allow cleaning of weapon. Most interesting collectible.* **32.00**   **35.00**

☐ **German Army Commission rifle.** *Mauser action with Mannlicher clip loading system, usual German marks, clip fed.* **205.00**   **225.00**

☐ **German Army Dreyse Bolt Action rifle,** *model 60. This is the famous so-called "needle gun" which was used so effectively by the Germans in the Franco-Prussian War. Fired a self-contained cartridge with the percussion cap at the front, just behind the bullet. The needle like firing pin penetrated the powder charge to detonate the cap. This was thought to be more effective than if the percussion cap were at the rear. Government proof and inspection marks.*   **520.00**   **575.00**

☐ **German Army Mauser Bolt Action rifle,** *model 1871, 22 l.r. The first of the world famous Mauser rifles. Single shot, one of the very first really successful bolt action rifles using a metallic cartridge, has many government proof and inspection marks, may be*

Price Range

marked to any of several kingdoms, dukedoms and other political divisions of Imperial Germany. Historically interesting, not rare 325.00 355.00

☐ **German Army Mauser,** model 1884. Similar to above but equipped with a tubular magazine under the barrel, bolt actuated cartridge lifter, first of the Mauser magazine rifles, many government proof and inspection marks, may be marked to any of several German states. 275.00 300.00

☐ **German Werder Infantry rifle,** 11.3-mm. Falling block action, adopted by the Bavarian Army in 1869, again the ease and rapidity of action earned it the name of the "Bavarian Lightning Rifle." Used for just a short time. Historically interesting. 42.00 45.00

Mauser Imperial German Army
Bolt Action Rifle, model 1898.
This is the famous Gewehr 98 of World War I.

Mauser Imperial German Army Carbine, model 1898.

☐ **Imperial German Army Mauser Bolt Action rifle,** model 1898. The famous Gewehr 98 of World War I fame, rugged, accurate, dependable. 120.00 130.00

☐ **Imperial German Army Mauser carbine,** model 1898. Short version of the above for cavalry and artillery. .. 120.00 130.00

☐ **Italian Albini-Braendlin Military and Naval rifle,** .60 cal. Single shot rimfire weapon. This most unique breechloader employed a fairly heavy breech block hinged at the forward end to raise manually and fold against the barrel, after the cartridge was seated the block was returned to its closed position, officially adopted by the Italian Navy and by the armies of Belgium, Bavaria and Wurttemberg. Acceptance marks of any of these nations make this an interesting collectible. 137.00 150.00

☐ **Italian Carcano,** model 1891, 6.5-mm. An uninspired design incorporating the Mauser bolt action with the Mannlicher magazine, fed by six-round clip. Imported in great quantities following World War II.......... 28.00 30.00

Price Range

☐ **Italian Vetterli-Vitali.** *Turnbolt action with box maga-zine, bolt action entirely enclosed by the receiver, a modification of the Swiss Vetterli model 1868 rifle, adopted by the Italian Government in 188l. A decora-tor only.* 28.00   30.00

Mauser Nazi Rifle, model 98K.

☐ **Nazi Mauser rifles,** *M98K, 8-mm. All marks, including manufacture, Nazi eagle, proofs, various makers.* 120.00   130.00
☐ **Nazi Mauser rifle,** *SVW M98K. Made during the final months of World War II, made at Oberndorf and used by West Germany.* 145.00   155.00
☐ **Persian Mauser carbine,** *M98, 8-mm. Manufactured in Germany for the Persian Army, Persian crest and markings.* 185.00   200.00
☐ **Spanish Army Mauser rifle,** *model 1893. Bolt action with box magazine fed from rounds stripped from clip as opposed to the Mannlicher system where the clip remained in the magazine until the last round was fired. Magazine contained within the rifle stock instead of protruding below as with the Mannlicher. This rifle was a marked improvement over any then existing, became the basis of Mauser's rifle fame. From this time forward, the Mauser rifle was to become the most widely used bolt action rifle in the world. It went through many modifications but remained basically the same. It was used by nearly all armies of any consequence and, as has been related, the Mauser action was used in the design of the Springfield '03.*
☐ **Spanish Army Mauser rifle,** *model 1893.* 175.00   190.00
☐ **Swiss Army Vetterli Bolt Action rifle,** *10.4-mm. Inter-esting as an early example of the bolt action rifle, has all marks.* 215.00   235.00
☐ **Swiss Schmidt-Rubin Army rifle,** *model 1911, 7.5-mm. Box magazine, excellent example of the straight-pull action, uncommon type, with Swiss government markings.* 110.00   120.00
☐ **Swiss Schmidt-Rubin,** *model 1889, 7.5-mm. The most successful of the straight-pull actions ever devel-oped, box magazine protruding under the rifle holds twelve rounds. Reported to have been extremely accurate but somewhat clumsy to use. Relic only.* 46.00   50.00
☐ **Swiss Schmidt-Rubin,** *model 1931, 7.5-mm. Generally*

Price Range

similar to the above but more compact in design, built to fire a more powerful 7.5-mm cartridge, box magazine holding five rounds located immediately under receiver and does not protrude. 79.00   85.00

☐ **Swiss Vetterli rifle,** model 1868, .41 cal. Rimfire, action similar to that of the Vetterli-Vitali rifle noted above, tubular magazine under the barrel, in service until the early 1890's. Decorator only. 33.00   35.00

Great Britain

☐ **British Army Enfield rifle,** Mark III, .303 Brit Box magazine, characterized by fore stock extending nearly to end of muzzle. The standard of the British Army for many years until World War II. 140.00   150.00

☐ **British Army Enfield rifle,** no. 4, .303 Brit. Government marked, standard of the British Army during World War II. 147.00   160.00

☐ **British Army "Jungle Carbine,"** no. 5, .303 Brit. Box magazine, bolt action as above rifles, government marks. 160.00   175.00

☐ **British Brunswick Army rifle.** Percussion, all brass mounts, has Tower, crowned "VR" and inspector's marks, plus "1865." 500.00   550.00

☐ **British Enfield Percussion rifle,** model 1853, .577 cal. Brass mounts, military marks.   430.00   475.00

☐ **British Enfield Percussion rifle,** model 1853, .577 cal. Section model, full military stock of good walnut, brass furniture except for steel sling swivels, complete with proper sling. 368.00   400.00

☐ **British Enfield Volunteer Percussion rifle,** .577 cal. Birmingham proofed, steel mounts. This is a unique presentation piece. It was given to a member of the First Sussex Rifle Volunteers. Presentation pieces are much sought after. 1020.00   1130.00

☐ **Lee-Enfield rifle,** Mark I. Introduced in 1895. Largely the same as the Magazine rifle, Mark I but with so-called Enfield rifling for use of cordite ammunition, ten round magazine. 160.00   175.00

☐ **Magazine rifle,** Mark I, c. 1890, .303 Brit. Commonly known as the Lee-Medford Rifle, incorporated an eight round box type magazine and a bolt action developed by James Lee, an American arms designer, with a rifled barrel designed by William Metford, an English designer. Powder charge consisted of pressed gunpowder. Interesting historical piece. 160.00   175.00

☐ **British Martini-Henry Army rifle,** .45 cal. Manufactured by Enfield, tubular magazine, lever action, Government marks. 340.00   375.00

☐ **British Snider Army rifle,** .577 cal. Percussion, dated 1885, tower and crowned "VR" marks. This is the

Price Range

famed "Snider" of the Victorian army. Historically interesting. 275.00   300.00

North America (Other than United States)
☐ **Ross Military rifle,** *.303 Brit. Straight pull magazine rifle, clip fed, easily jamed in rough field conditions, incorrect assembly of bolt could result in it being blown back into the firers face, went through a multitude of models in attempt to correct defects, adopted for a short time for the Canadian Militia Units but soon downgraded to a training piece, a few used this way in the United States. A relic only but a rather interesting one.* 51.00   55.00

Oriental
☐ **Japanese Arisaka Standard Service rifle,** *type 38, 6.5-mm. Bolt action, standard Japanese service rifle from 1906 to 1945. Many of these were brought back from Japan and the South Pacific campaigns. A favorite trophy of returning servicemen.* 142.00   155.00
☐ **Japanese Bolt Action Army rifle,** *type 22 (1889), 8-mm. Metallic cartridge.* 100.00   110.00
☐ **Japanese Bolt Action Army rifle,** *type 38 (1905), 6.5-mm. Designed by Colonel Arisaka, has many features of the Mauser turn bolt action.* 100.00   110.00
☐ **Japanese Service rifle,** *type 99 (1939), 7.7-mm. This is a variation of the type 38, not available at beginning of the South Pacific War, but was available in quantity as the war progressed. This weapon is not much sought after except for those specializing in Japanese rifles.* 118.00   130.00
☐ **Japanese rifle,** *11-mm. With French chassepot action, converted from a matchlock, very short butt stock which is inlaid with a fanciful design, interesting but not at all rare.* 250.00   275.00
☐ **Mauser Bolt Action rifle,** *model 1898. Made in Japan for the Royal Siamese Army, bears Tokyo arsenal proof marks plus royal Siamese Crest.* 100.00   110.00

South America
☐ **Mauser Bolt Action carbine,** *model 1891, 7.65-mm.* . .   64.00   70.00
☐ **Mauser Bolt Action rifle,** *model 1891, 7.65-mm. Manufactured for the Argentine Army by Ludwig Loewe.* . .   73.00   80.00

United States
☐ **American Bannerman Bolt Action rifle,** *model 1937, .30-06 cal. During the 1930's, Krag, American Enfield and Springfield '03's were difficult to find. The famous New York City militaria dealer Bannerman & Sons put together a number of rifles for collectors which were made up of surplus parts of the three named rifles. These rifles are now interesting collector items and are becoming rare.* 150.00   165.00

Price Range

☐ **Jenks Breechloading Percussion rifle,** *.54 cal. Unique in that it had a side hammer and was known as a "Mule Ear." Made especially for the U.S. Navy, manufactured by N.P. Ames to the design of William Jenks. Ames, Jenks, Navy markings.* 550.00   1050.00

☐ **Krag Bolt Action rifle,** *model 1892. Designed by two Norwegian Army officers, for whom it was named, all models in the United States. Services in 30-40 Krag center fire, horizontal gate loading (side) magazine, loose rounds fed through open gate and pushed to the left over a spring follower, limited production began for Army in 1894, familiarly known as the Krag although the proper nomenclature is Krag-Jorgensen. Wide range of prices, manufactured in the Springfield Armory.* 775.00   3075.00

☐ **Krag rifle,** *model 1896. Improved version of the above, usual Springfield markings. This model 1896 used by the Army, Navy and Marine Corps whereas the model 1892 was used only by the Army. Fairly common.* 225.00   350.00

☐ **Krag rifle,** *model 1898. Another improved model, similar to the above. Produced in considerable quantity, the majority of which went to the Army also a very few to the Navy and Marine Corps. This is the most common of all U.S. Krag-Jorgensens.* 200.00   325.00

Remington-Keen Magazine Bolt Action Rifle.

☐ **Remington-Keen Magazine Bolt Action rifle,** *.45-.70 cal. This was the first bolt action rifle made by Remington, also made in .40 and .43 caliber, tubular magazine under the barrel, full stocked.*

☐   **Army model.** 650.00   1250.00

☐   **Navy model,** *similar to above but shorter barrel.* . . . 650.00   1250.00

Remington-Lee Bolt Action Magazine Rifle.

☐ **Remington-Lee Bolt Action Magazine rifle,** *.45-.70 cal. Full stocked, made for the Navy, Lee and Navy markings.* 375.00   750.00

☐ **Remington Navy Rolling Block rifle,** *model 1870, .50 cal. Manufactured by Springfield Armory with royalty paid to Remington, marked "USN," "SPRINGFIELD," and the date "1870," plus eagle and anchor marks.* . . 350.00   650.00

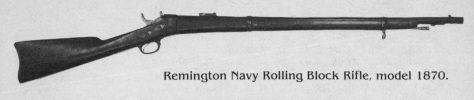

Remington Navy Rolling Block Rifle, model 1870.

Remington Trench Gun, model 1910.

Price Range

☐ **Remington Trench gun,** *model 1910, 12-gauge. Used by U.S. Marines in World War I. This is the model 1910 riot gun, pump action fitted with a bayonet attachment, could be fitted with the model 1917 Enfield bayonet. The Imperial German troops considered this a terror weapon and were greatly afraid of it in close combat. When purchasing this weapon, be sure that it has the bayonet attachment, these were sometimes removed.* 235.00   635.00

☐ **Springfield rifle,** *model 1903. The action of this rifle is based upon the world famous German Mauser Gewehr 98 bolt action, clip fed magazine rifle. The U.S. Government is reported to have paid Mauser $200,000.00 for manufacturing rights. The first of these rifles based on the Mauser action was made in 1900, but they were not very efficient and it was modified in 1903, among other things to use a round nose .30-03 cartridge. It was fitted with a fragil and impractical rod-type bayonet which was housed under the barrel in the manner of a ramrod. The first production model.* 2100.00   3600.00

☐ **Springfield rifle,** *model 1903, .30-03. 1905 modification. This modified model among other things had improved front and rear sights and was fitted with the model 1905 knife-type bayonet designed especially for the new rifle.* 1100.00   2100.00

The famous "Ought Three" Springfield Rifle, model 1903.

Price Range

☐ **Springfield rifle,** *model 1903. Modified to use the pointed .30-06 bullet. This is the version familiarly known as the "Ought Three," the rifle so dear to the hearts of so many marksmen and sharpshooters. It was in production from the time of its introduction in 1906 until around 1936 when it was replaced by the Garand MI, this was longer than any other rifle. Much of its success was due to the reliability of the Mauser action, plus improvements made by American ordnance experts. Many experienced fighting men complained that it was better than the Garand, certainly it was rugged and highly accurate and it was a great favorite with snipers. This rifle was manufactured only in the U.S. Government arsenals at Springfield, Massachusetts, and Rock Island, Illinois, some modifications occur and are listed below.*

☐ **Springfield '03,** *1907-10 manufacture. The first of the series, serial range 269000 to 400000 (approx.)* 300.00   525.00

☐ **Springfield '03,** *1910-17 manufacture. Some slight modifications. As above, manufactured both at Springfield and Rock Island, serial range 400000 to 635000 (approx.)* 250.00   400.00

☐ **Springfield '03,** *1917-21 manufacture. Again some slight modifications. Made both at Springfield and Rock Island, serial range 635000 to 1225000.* 225.00   325.00

☐ **Springfield '03,** *1921-27 manufacture. Some slight improvements over previous versions, again made in both Government arsenals, serial range 1225000 to 12800000 (approx.), many sold as surplus.* 225.00   325.00

☐ **Springfield '03 AI.** *The same old '03 with a full pistol stock, not a new rifle, merely '03 rifles restocked, rather common.* 120.00   245.00

☐ **Springfield '03.** *Modified for the U.S. Air Service, World War I, regular '03 stripped for lightness and fitted with a 25-shot extension magazine, believed made for use of observation balloon crews, about 910 modified. A rare '03.* 1600.00   3100.00

☐ **Springfield '03 Mark I rifle.** *Modified for the Pedersen Device. Upon our entry into World War I, it was found that this country was woefully short of weapons, particularly those of a specialized nature. Among other items, we felt the need for a semiautomatic rifle. As one of the answers to the problems J.D. Pedersen, at the time an arms designer for Remington, devised the so-called Pedersen Device for converting the '03 into a semiautomatic rifle. Officially, it was known as the Automatic Bolt model of 1918 Mark I. Basically, this was a self-contained bolt and return action spring device, it used .30 caliber pistol-type rounds fed from a 40-shot magazine, and was installed in the*

Price Range

'03 action after removing the bolt, however, certain modifications had to be made to accommodate the device. This was done to over 100,000 Springfield '03's, unfortunately, the device was received too late to be of any use in the war, so devices were placed in storage. Although the device was soon outdated by subsequent arms developments, both the modified rifles and the devices were classified SECRET until 1931, then the majority of the devices were destroyed and the rifles were reworked and many were issued to National Guard organizations. The devices themselves are very rare.

☐ **Springfield '03 Mark I rifle.** *Modified for the Pedersen Device. Not altered in any manner.*	275.00	450.00
☐ **Pedersen Device with magazine.**	2800.00	4200.00
☐ **Pedersen Device without magazine.**	2300.00	3600.00
☐ **Metal Carrying Case for the Pedersen Device.**	425.00	775.00
☐ **Spare Magazine Pouch of webbing.**	6.00	11.00

Note: Prior to the advent of the Springfield '03 with its medium length barrel, which in no way affected accuracy, shoulder arms were usually made as a rifle with a long barrel (supposedly to increase accuracy) and the carbine, the same action with a shorter barrel. The shorter barrel permitted easier handling by mounted troops but it was believed by some that accuracy was not as great. The '03 took care of all this. Of course, the concept of the carbine was not given up quickly. Among other things, great quantities were on hand and at times the military mind, particularly in the higher ranks, is reluctant to change.

☐ **U.S. Magazine rifle,** *model 1917. Most often referred to as the "Enfield." As is known this country was woefully short of war material when we entered World War I. In some areas we were fortunate in that a few arms makers were already manufacturing weapons for the Allies. This was the case with the "Enfield." Both Remington and Winchester were making the British Enfield Pattern 14 rifle, together with its bayonet. This weapon used the standard .303 British ammunition. Since enough Springfield '03's were not on hand and could not be produced to arm our rapidly expanding armed forces, it was decided to use the already existing facilities for manufacturing the Enfield, modified to use the American .30 caliber round. This was done and some 466,000 were made by Winchester and some 546,000 by Remington. This rifle was issued to all the armed services but the Marines and Navy used it for training purposes only, the Army used it in combat. All are marked either "REMINGTON" or "WINCHESTER" and "U.S. MODEL 1917."* 125.00   225.00

☐ **Whitney Navy Percussion rifle,** *model 1861, .69 cal. Sometimes known as the Whitney-Plymouth or as the*

Price Range

Plymouth. Designed by Captain, later Admiral, Dahlgren, famous Navy ordnance expert. Designed especially for boarding activities and for arming shore parties. Used by both the Navy and the Marines, an interesting historic piece. Used two types of bayonets, one a Bowie knife pattern, and the other a French sword type. The Bowie type bayonet sells for as much as the rifle. 375.00   850.00

☐ **Winchester Trench gun,** *model 1897. This is the model 1897 riot gun with metal hand guard and bayonet attachment, pump action, external hammer.* 225.00   625.00

☐ **Winchester Trench gun,** *model 1912, 12 gauge. Slide action, metal hand guard, bayonet attachment.* 225.00   625.00

☐ **Enfield bayonet,** *model 1917. For the Winchester trench guns.* 20.00   22.00

PISTOLS (Revolvers and Automatics)

The name "pistol" may have originated from the name of the Italian city of Pistois, where the weapon may have originated, or from **pistole,** an ancient coin whose diameter is said to have been the same as the early hand guns. As used today the term applies to revolvers, automatics and similar hand held guns. As may be expected, the pistol has been experimented with ever since its inception. Attempts have been continually made to increase the rapidity of fire, reliability and accuracy. Early attempts included placing a number of barrels side by side or upon top of each other. The revolving cylinder (containing the cartridges) pistol, known as the revolver, was experimented with for long years. Some of the earliest types had the cylinder revolved by hand for each shot. Then Samuel Colt, using some of the design features developed by Elisha Collier, produced the first successful revolver. Many improvements have been made since, but the credit for making and marketing the first practical weapon of this type must go to Colt. He also was the first to sell the military-the U.S. Army- on its usefulness.

What is popularly called an automatic pistol is actually a semiautomatic. In this regard refer to the section on Lugers in this guide. Although several arms designers of various nationalities may be credited with some form of development of the automatic pistol, it was, of course, Hugo Brochardt who made the first practical weapon of this type. In this country John Moses Browning did pathfinding work in the field and he had considerable influence upon automatic pistol design.

ASIA

☐ **Russian Military pistol,** *model Flintlock. Brass mounted, lockplate bears "Myra 1822," piece is also marked "1834" and "1842." Weapon is of considerable interest in that the escutcheon plate bears the cypher of Czar Alexander 1st.* 565.00   625.00

EUROPE

☐ **Austrian Gasser revolver,** *11-mm. This is a big ugly looking hinged frame, automatic ejecting gun, was a real brute of a weapon which was widely distributed in*

Price Range

*the Balkan countries. Unconfirmed legend is that
every military eligible male in Montenego was required
to own one, this gave rise to its popular name of
Gasser Montengrin. Interesting.* 55.00 60.00

☐ **Austrian Mannlicher Automatic pistol,** *M1901. One of
several Mannlicher pistol designs, delayed blowback
action, chambered for Mannlicher's own specially
designed ammunition. Declared by some to be the
best balanced pistol ever made.* 73.00 80.00

☐ **Austrian Military pistol,** *model Flintlock. Brass
mounted, liege and Austrian Eagle marks. Interesting
although not rare.* 385.00 425.00

☐ **Austrian Montenegrin Gasser Open Frame revolver,**
*11.4-mm. Double action, 6 shot cylinder, bag shape
butt with ivory grips, lanyard ring on butt, weapon
bears the serial number 164495.* 150.00 165.00

☐ **Austrian Rast & Gasser Service revolver,** *8-mm.
Adopted in the late 1800's as the standard service
revolver of the Austro-Hugarian Armies and thousands were made for both the military and the civilian markets, open frame type with six round cylinder
with extractor plate. A big weapon in the old European army tradition.* 46.00 50.00

☐ **Austrian Schwarzlose Automatic Mauser pistol,**
*M1898, 7.63-mm. Although the Schwarzlose heavy
machine gun is well known, the pistol by the same
designer is not, however, the weapon has an interesting history. The few thousand which were made did
not find a ready sale because of the superiority of the
Mauser pistol. The majority were sold to Russian rev-
olutionists but were seized by Russian authorities
while being smuggled into that country, and were
then issued to Russian police. This weapon has a
rotating bolt and employs a locked breech.* 73.00 80.00

☐ **French Army pistol,** *model 1777, .69 cal. Brass
mounted, flintlock, marked to the St. Eteinne Arsenal.* 750.00 830.00
*Note: It is of interest to note that this pistol was supplied in quantity to the
then infant United States. It served as the pattern for the first American
made pistol supplied to the U.S. Navy, the North & Cheney U.S. Flintlock
Pistol, model 1799.*

☐ **French Flintlock pistol,** *Napoleonic era. Brass
mounted, dated 1813 and marked to the Charleville
Arsenal.* 565.00 625.00

☐ **Lefaucheaux Service revolver,** *12-mm. Adopted in
1856 for the French Navy, uses a pin-fire cartridge,
open frame and gate loading. A reliable weapon for
its day, relic only.* 30.00 33.00

☐ **French Military Percussion pistol.** *Lock plate marked
with a crowned "P" over "35," all brass mounts, butt
cap marked with a "T" within a circle over "2115."* ... 320.00 350.00

Price Range

☐ **French Naval Pattern Percussion pistol.** *Barrel marked "Mle 1837," lock plate marked "Mre Rle de Chatelleraut," all brass mounts, breech marked "1839" together with military proof and inspector's marks, butt cap bears "MT" and anchor, belt hook on left side, lanyard ring on butt.* 790.00   875.00

☐ **French Navy Pattern Flintlock pistol,** *officer's model, c. late 1700's. All brass mounted, some engraving.* . .   430.00   475.00

☐ **German Beholla Automatic pistol,** *7.65-mm. Little known, adopted by the Imperial German Army as a substitute standard side arm, fixed-barrel blowback action, a serviceable and rather rugged weapon but of no great merit otherwise. Reported to have been practically difficult to clean in the field.* 25.00   27.00

☐ **German Dreyse Automatic pistol,** *7.65-mm. Seven round magazine in grip, actually designed by Louis Schmeisser, thousands made during World War I and used as a substitute standard pistol by the Imperial Army.* 41.00   45.00

☐ **German Flintlock Battle Ax pistol,** *c. 1750, .56 cal. This is another impractical combination weapon but a good collector's item. Steel belt hook on left side, brass butt cap and action, wood stock encloses a muzzle loading barrel with the muzzle ending at the top of the ax. Action about midway on the stock or handle, spur trigger, no guard, steel ax head with blade with thick spike at rear.* 1270.00   1400.00

☐ **German Jager Automatic pistol,** *7.65-mm. Manufactured during World War I and is unique in that it was constructed of pressed steel parts, a method not used elsewhere until World War I, seven rounds in the handle. Not officially accepted by the Imperial German Army but was privately purchased by officers and other ranks for personal use. An unusual weapon.* 55.00   60.00

☐ **German Reichsrevolver,** *model of 1879, 10.6-mm. This is known as the cavalry model, carried six rounds in revolving cylinder, designed by a commission of the Prussian Army. A so-called officer's model was very similar and was known as the model 1883, its major difference was a longer barrel. Both are gate loaded, single action, solid frame weapons. Used in World War I by the Imperial Army and in World War II by Nazi Volksstrum forces.* 155.00   200.00

☐ **Werder Cavalry pistol,** *11.3-mm. Falling block action, adopted by the Bavarian Army in 1870, ease and rapidity of operation led to its nickname of the "Bavarian Lightning Pistol." Remained in service for but a short time. Interesting curio.* 150.00   200.00

☐ **Italian Beretta,** *model 1915, 7.65-mm. Blowback action, standard pistol of the Italian armed forces*

	Price Range	

during World War I. An excellent which was also used by the military forces of many other nations. . . . **123.00** **135.00**

☐ **Italian Beretta,** *model 1934, 9-mm. Standard with all the Italian armed forces during World War II. Excellent and reliable* **145.00** **160.00**

GREAT BRITAIN

☐ **British "Dragoon" Flintlock pistol,** *c. 1739, .56 cal. Brass mounted, maker marked "Jordan 1739" and crowned "GR." Rare.* **1450.00** **1600.00**

☐ **British "Dragoon" Flintlock pistol.** *Tower proofs, marked "HN," and "H.Nock," brass mounted, Nock was a famous English arms maker.* **1540.00** **1700.00**

☐ **British "Dragoon" Flintlock pistol,** *c. late 1700's, large .75 cal. Brass mounted, tower proof mark and crowned "GR."* **605.00** **670.00**

☐ **British East India Flintlock pistol,** *.67 cal. British proof marks plus British East India Company markings. . . .* **300.00** **330.00**

☐ **British Enfield Mark I revolver,** *.38 cal. "Enfield" is the name popularily applied to arms from the Royal Small Arms Factory, Enfield Lock, Middlesex. After several less than successful efforts by Enfield this was adopted by the British Army as a standard service revolver and continued to be so until the early 1950's, but was first adopted in 1932. A very good weapon.* **70.00** **77.00**

☐ **British Flintlock Coast Guard Pattern pistol,** *.56 cal. Belt hook on left side, lanyard ring on butt. Tower proofed. Crowned "VR" and "Tower 1846" on lock plate.* **430.00** **475.00**

☐ **British Flintlock Military pistol.** *Military proofs plus "Tower" and crowned "WR," also marked "Potts." Interesting specimen.* **405.00** **445.00**

☐ **British New Land Pattern Flintlock pistol.** *Brass mounts, Tower proof marks, plus "Tower" and crowned "GR." Interesting in that trigger guard bears engraved "26," its rack number.* **545.00** **600.00**

☐ **British Sea Service Percussion pistol,** *.56 cal. All brass mounting, belt hook on left side and lanyard ring on butt, Tower proof marks.* **250.00** **275.00**

☐ **British Sea Service Pattern Flintlock pistol,** *.56 cal. Steel belt hook on left side, "Tower" and crowned "GR" marks, brass mounted. It is interesting to note that British arms were captured in some quantity and used by the colonists in the war against the Mother Country.* **550.00** **620.00**

☐ **British Sea Service Pattern Flintlock pistol.** *Similar to the above but with addition of crowned arrow marks.* **635.00** **700.00**

☐ **British Sea Service Pattern Flintlock pistol,** *c. William IV. Similar to above but with crowned "WR" in lieu of crowned "GR."* **1100.00** **1100.00**

Price Range

☐ **British Webley Mark I Royal Navy Automatic,** *.455 Auto. Lanyard rings, magazine release, Webley and Scott markings with date and serial number, dated 1913.* 560.00 620.00

☐ **British Webley Royal Navy Automatic pistol,** *.455 Auto. Webley and Scott markings, dated 1916, marked "N" denoting its acceptance by the Royal Navy and Marines, complete with holster with magazine pouch.* 217.00 240.00

☐ **Scottish Flintlock pistol,** *c. 1735. Usual all steel construction characteristic of such pistols, inlaid kidney shape butt, unique button trigger. Rare.* 1540.00 1700.00

☐ **Scottish Flintlock pistol.** *Both Tower and London proofed. All steel but for rams' horn inlaid butt, marked to "RHR" (The Royal Highland Regiment.) Rare.* 1180.00 1300.00

NORTH AMERICA (Other than United States)

☐ **Mexican Combination Revolver and saber,** *.32 cal. Butt of revolver forms part of hilt and guard, barrel points along the top of the saber blade. Large hand guard engraved with a floral design, the Mexican Eagle and the words "REPUBLICA MEXICANA." Steel scabbard is made to sheath the revolver barrel as well as the saber blade. Most interesting collector's item.* 2775.00 3075.00

UNITED STATES

☐ **Ames Navy Percussion pistol,** *model 1843, .54 cal. Brass mounted, so-called box lock pistol by virtue of the hammer being within the lock plate, allowing the weapon to be thrust through the belt without danger of fouling the hammer. Marked "N. P. AMES" "SPRINGFIELD" "MASS." in three lines, plus "USN" and date together with proof marks, 1842 manufacture.* 1300.00 2300.00

☐ **As above,** *but of 1843, 1844 and 1845 manufacture.* 310.00 660.00

☐ **As above,** *but with U.S. Revenue Service markings instead of U.S. Navy marking ("U.S.R.").* 850.00 1350.00

☐ **Aston & Johnson Percussion pistol,** *model 1842, .54 cal. In connection with percussion pistols it should be noted that many flintlock weapons, both hand-guns and shoulder weapons were converted to the percussion system. The conversion was neither difficult nor expensive and the U.S. Government for reasons of economy favored the conversion. This particular pistol, however, was designed as a percussion weapon, brass mounted, U.S. proof marks, some specimens marked "US" and "H. ASTON" in two lines plus date of manufacture.* 325.00 650.00

☐ **As above,** *but marked "US" "H. ASTON & CO."* . . . 400.00 800.00

☐ **As above,** *but U.S. Navy marked with anchor and naval inspector marks.* 395.00 675.00

Price Range

☐ **Colt Hand Guns.** *The name "Colt" is legendary not only in this country but abroad. A great variety of these guns was made, often in large quantities. It is beyond the scope of this guide to treat with all of these. It is only possible to note which the author deems to be most interesting. The gun collector will want to refer to "Flayderman's Guide to Antique American Firearms" for complete data and prices. This guide is listed in the reference section. It may also be noted at this time that it was the practice of many arms manufacturers to refer to their guns as an "Army" or "Navy" model. This does not necessarily mean that the weapons were ever used by the U.S. services. It did make for good advertising copy. Almost without exception, U.S. Government firearms are well marked to identify them. Of course, some officers and even some enlisted men made private purchases of nonregulation weapons for their own use.*

☐ **Colt Army and Navy revolver,** *new model, all in .38 cal. 6 inch barrel, with Colt and Navy markings.* 170.00   345.00

☐   **As above,** *but with Army markings.* 135.00   285.00

☐ **Colt Army Automatic pistol,** *model 1900. As above but with Army markings.* 425.00   775.00

☐ **Colt Army revolver,** *model 1917, .45 cal. Improved version of the model 1919, much used during World War I and to some extent in World War II. Some officers preferred the revolver over the automatic, claiming it was more reliable and accurate.* 170.00   345.00

☐ **Colt Automatic pistol,** *model 1905, .45 cal. A very limited number of these were made. It was the first Colt automatic pistol in .45 caliber, a caliber much desired by the U.S. Army. Of a total production of slightly over 6000, only around 200 were purchased by the Army. These bear the Colt markings plus government inspector's marks, Lanyard loop on frame.* . . 450.00   875.00

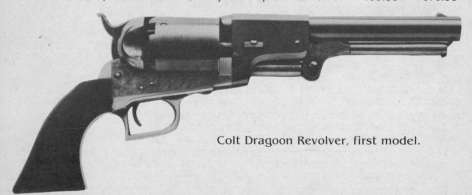

Colt Dragoon Revolver, first model.

Price Range

☐ **Colt Dragoon revolver,** *first model, .44 cal. 6 shot, percussion, marked "ADDRESS SAMI COLT, NEW YORK CITY" and "COLT'S PATENT" in two lines, also has military markings, engraved cylinder.* 1200.00   4200.00

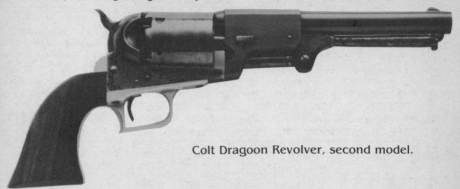

Colt Dragoon Revolver, second model.

☐ **Colt Dragoon revolver,** *second model. Similar to above in most respects but, among other minor differences, the cylinder stop slots are rectangular instead of oval.* 850.00   3550.00

Colt Dragoon Revolver, third model.

☐ **Colt Dragoon revolver,** *third model. Also similar to the above, among minor differences, a rounded trigger guard and rectangular cylinder stop slots, some may be marked "U.S.M.R." or "U.S. DRAGOONS," as is the case with the second model, a few specimens may be marked "C.L. DRAGOONS," and a few specimens may be found with a provision for a shoulder stock. These are of three patterns. The first pattern was provided with two prongs which fit into two slots in the back strap. The second pattern attached by means of a hook which clamped onto the butt and a prong which engaged in a slot in the backstrap. The third pattern and the yoke prolonged on each side to*

Price Range

fit into cutouts in the recoil shield. There was also a
hook which clamped onto the butt. Prices listed here
are for the weapon and the separated stock.

☐	**Weapon alone,** *first and second patterns.*	2600.00	5100.00
☐	**Weapon alone,** *third pattern.*	1600.00	3600.00
☐	**Shoulder stock,** *first and second patterns.*	2600.00	3800.00
☐	**Shoulder stock,** *third pattern.*	1100.00	2850.00

☐ **Colt Hammerless Pocket Automatic pistol,** *model 1903, .32 cal. 8 shot magazine, Colt markings plus "U.S. PROPERTY."* 160.00 410.00

☐ **Colt Marine Corps D.A. revolver,** *model 1905, .38 cal. 6 shot in Colt .38 and Smith & Wesson .38 calibers, Colt and USMC markings. An interesting model but not at all rare.* 300.00 525.00

☐ **Colt Military Automatic pistol,** *model 1902, .38 cal. 8 shot magazine, Browning, Colt and Army markings.* . 425.00 825.00

☐ **Colt Military Automatic pistols,** *model 1911 and model 1911A1. These are discussed and priced in the special section on automatic pistols covering Luger, Mauser, Walther and Colt automatic pistols.* ....

☐ **Colt Navy Automatic pistol,** *model 1900, .38 cal. 7 shot magazine, first Colt production automatic, designed by John Moses Browning, Browning, Colt and Navy markings.* 450.00 850.00

☐ **Colt Navy Double Action revolver,** *model 1889, .38 cal. Swingout cylinder, with Colt and Navy markings.* 225.00 850.00

☐ **Colt U.S. Services revolver,** *model 1909, .45 cal. 5½ inch barrel, lanyard ring on butt, a heavy, reliable, rugged piece.*

☐	**Army model,** *with Colt and Army markings.*	225.00	850.00
☐	**Navy model,** *with Colt and Navy markings.*	275.00	550.00
☐	**Marine Corps model,** *with Colt and USMC markings*	325.00	600.00

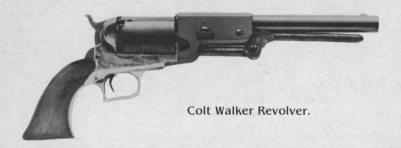

Colt Walker Revolver.

Price Range

☐ **Colt Walker Model revolver,** *.44 cal. 6 shot, percussion type, marked "ADDRESS SAMI COLT NEW YORK CITY" and "US" "1847" in two lines. Government inspection marks, cylinder engraved with Indian vs Ranger fight.* 5200.00   13700.00

☐ **Grant Hammond Military Automatic pistol,** *.45 cal. It is interesting to note the many attempts to secure a U.S. Government contract by submitting a weapon supposably incorporating new ideas. Sometimes these weapons are good but they are not sufficiently superior to justify the time and expense necessary to retool and make other adjustments necessary for production. Such was the case with this particular automatic. It was a .45 caliber* **recoil** *operated weapon of very good characteristics but it was not enough better than the Colt model 1911 to warrant adoption, only a very few test models ever manufactured. This is a fairly rare item.* 3200.00   5200.00

☐ **Harpers Ferry Flintlock pistol,** *model 1805, .54 cal. Brass furniture, first pistol made in a national arsenal. Partially marked with eagle and shield with "US," also marked "HARPERS FERRY," serial number and year of manufacture. Prices vary according to date of manufacture, as well as to condition.*

☐ **1806.**	4225.00	8450.00
☐ **1807.**	2300.00	3300.00
☐ **Model 1808.**	2600.00	3600.00

Navy Elgin Cutlass Pistol.

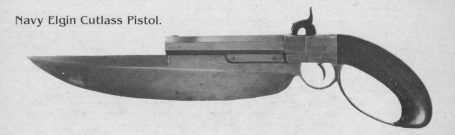

☐ **Navy Elgin Cutlass pistol,** *.54 cal. This is an excellent example of one of the multitude of freak combination weapons produced through the years. Since the introduction of firearms, men have tinkered with the idea of combining them with edged weapons. Firearms have appeared in combination with shields, swords, daggers, spears, halberds and just about every other type of weapon with a blade. They have been universally unsuccessful. In combining the two entirely dissimilar weapons, the better characteristics of each has been sadly modified or even lost.*

Price Range

These weapons proved to be of much greater value to present day collectors than they ever were in the hands of their original users. Several versions of this so-called cutlass pistol appeared, in both military and civilian models. The U.S. Navy version, of which only a very limited number was ever bought by the service, is a percussion pistol in .54 caliber with a cutlass blade 11½ inches long, 2 inches wide, attached to the under side of the barrel. The weapon is 15¾ inches long overall. It was carried in a brass and leather holster. (This holster which is more of a sheath for the blade is worth $750.00 by itself in good condition.) Frame marked "C.B. ALLEN" "SPRING-FIELD" "MASS." in three lines. The serial number appears on various parts. A total of 150 of these pistols was made for the Navy. 4100.00   8200.00

☐ **North Army and Navy Flintlock pistol,** *model 1813, .69 cal. Iron mountings, reputed to be unpopular because of its excessive kick, bears markings of "S. NORTH" over stylized eagle and "U.S." and "MIDLN CON," plus inspector's marks.*

☐   **Army model,** 1800.00   2300.00
☐   **Navy model,** *with steel belt hook on left side.* 2035.00   2535.00
☐ **North & Cheney Flintlock pistol,** *model 1799, .69 cal. Among the very first American made pistols delivered to the infant U.S. Navy, "US" marked with variations of makers names. Very rare, depending upon condition prices vary.* 9600.00   21000.00

North Flintlock Pistol, Transition model 1811.

☐ **North Flintlock pistol,** *Transition model 1811, .69 cal. Brass mounted, marked with eagle above "U. STATES" and "S. NORTH BERLIN CON" in three lines, plus inspector's marks.* 2100.00   4200.00

North Flintlock Pistol, model 1826 (Navy).

Price Range

☐ **North Navy Flintlock pistol,** *model 1826, .54 cal. Iron mounted, brass blade front sight, steel belt hook on left side. A very few specimens will be found with tinned barrels, this was intended to protect the metal from sea spray. Marked with "U.S." over "S. NORTH," plus either "1827" or "1828." Interesting as the last North made Navy pistol.* **1200.00   2400.00**

☐ **North Navy Flintlock pistol,** *model 1808, .64 cal. First pistol made to U.S. Navy specifications, brass mounted, iron hook arrangement on left side to permit it to be hooked onto the belt, no Navy markings, marked "U. STATES" and "S. NORTH BERLIN CON."*   **2200.00   4400.00**

Robert McCormick U.S. Pistol, Contract model 1797-1800.

☐ **Robert McCormick U.S. pistol,** *Contract model 1797-1800, .64 cal. Brass mounted, made for the U.S. Navy, "UNITED STATES" marked, at rear of lockplate, "US" marked on barrel, "KETLAND & CO." appears under the pan, some specimens may have "McCORMICK" appearing on stock.* **5300.00   9400.00**

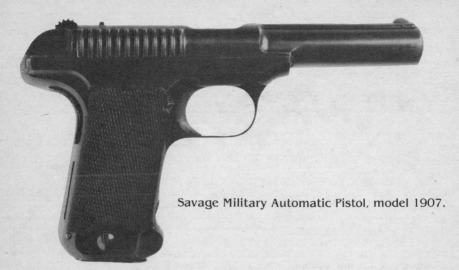

Savage Military Automatic Pistol, model 1907.

Price Range

☐ **Savage Military,** *model 1907, .45 cal. 8 shot magazine, based upon the designs of E.H. Searle, manufactured for the 1907 U.S. Army trials to select an automatic pistol, only about 300 made. This weapon lost out to the Colt .45 caliber automatic, savage markings.*

☐   In original finish. 1050.00   2200.00

☐   If reblued. 550.00   1100.00

☐ **Smith & Wesson Army revolver,** *model 1917, .45 cal. Double action, excellent, rugged service revolver much prized by both officers and enlisted men during World War I. Along with the Colt model 1917 Army revolver was adopted as a wartime expedient when a shortage of automatic pistols developed.* 165.00   340.00

☐ **Smith & Wesson Schofield Single Action Army revolver,** *first model, .45 cal. 6 shot, manufactured in 1875, Smith & Wesson, 7 inch barrel, Smith & Wesson and U.S. markings.* 425.00   900.00

☐ **Smith & Wesson Single Action Army revolver,** *second model. An improved version of the above, Smith & Wesson and Army markings.* 425.00   900.00

☐ **Springfield Flintlock pistol,** *model 1817, .69 cal. Iron mounted with brass blade front sight, "SPRINGFIELD" marked plus date and inspector's marks, together with proof marks. This pistol made up of spare parts of the model 1807 pistol, plus several different locks, thus made, the pistol is referred to as the "first type." A similar pistol, known as the "second type" was constructed from model 1807*

Price Range

pistol parts plus locks from the model 1803 rifle and
newly fabricated locks. Prices between the two types
vary little.. 1100.00 2200.00

Remington Army Revolver, model 1861.

☐ **Remington Army revolver,** *model 1861, .44 cal. 6 shot,
percussion, round cylinder, octagon barrel, Remington and military markings. This weapon was used
much during the American Civil War.* 350.00 625.00

☐ **Remington Army revolver,** *new model, .44 cal. 6 shot,
round cylinder and octagon barrel, a major personal
weapon of the Civil War era, Remington and Army
markings, made in quantity.* 225.00 460.00

☐ **Remington Navy revolver,** *new model, 36 cal. Similar
to the above but somewhat smaller. The Navy ordnance experts decided that a heavier caliber was not
needed in the naval service, Remington and Navy
markings.* 675.00 1575.00

☐ **Remington Navy revolver,** *model 1861, .36 cal. Similar
to the Army model but slightly smaller, Remington
and Navy markings.* 370.00 600.00

☐ **Remington Navy Rolling Block pistol,** *model 1865, .50
cal. Rimfire, spur type trigger, the first of 3 single
shot rolling block model Remington pistols made for
the U.S. Government. Pivoting action breechblock,
usual Remington and U.S. Navy markings.* 500.00 1000.00

☐ **Remington Navy Rolling Block pistol,** *model 1867.
Very similar to the above model but has usual trigger
and trigger guard, Remington and Navy markings....* 350.00 625.00

☐ **Remington Army Rolling Block pistol,** *model 1871.
Very similar to the above pistol but with Army
markings.* 270.00 550.00

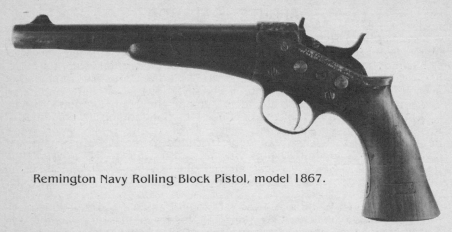

Remington Navy Rolling Block Pistol, model 1867.

JAPANESE PISTOLS

Because of their uniqueness and their specialized interest, these weapons have been listed separately. In many instances, the early Japanese firearms had an extremely short butt or butt stock. This is particularly true of the ancient Japanese shoulder guns and it gives them an odd appearance to Occidental eyes. More recent Japanese firearms follow the general pattern of those of the western world.

Price Range

☐ **Burmese Flintlock Sword pistol,** *c. early 1800's, .46-mm. A beautiful, rare and interesting oddity, flintlock action, brass mounted, highly polished wood stock. The long sharp blade fits nicely into the butt stock, the elongated hilt becoming the barrel of the flintlock musket. Probably not very efficient as a weapon but of value to the collector of weapons oddities.*..................................... 1495.00   1650.00

☐ **Army revolver,** *type 26, dated 1893, 9-mm. Top break, cylinder holds six rounds, apparently a copy of a Smith & Wesson revolver, Japanese marks. Not too well-made, interesting.*............................ 200.00   225.00

☐ **Matchlock pistol,** *c. mid-1800's. This is an interesting and beautiful, yet odd looking, weapon, has external mainspring, brass mounts, weapon full stocked in magnolia wood.* 1000.00   1200.00

☐ **Nambu Automatic pistol,** *model 1904/14, 8-mm. Slotted for a shoulder stock, fairly rare.* 425.00   480.00

☐ **Old Flintlock pistol.** *Brass mounts, Japanese characters on barrel, well-made and old.*................. 1000.00   1200.00

☐ **Percussion Cap pistol,** *.48-mm. Brass mounts, interesting barrel with tulip muzzle.* 850.00   950.00

ABOUT THE AUTHOR

Colonel Robert H. Rankin retired following 32½ years in the United States Marine Corps. He was awarded four campaign and service medals, the Army Commendation Medal and the Navy Legion of Merit. Following his retirement, he served as a consultant to the U.S. Marine Corps Museums and to several arms importers. He is internationally known as a military historian and writer. Born in Ohio, he attended Marshall University and Eastern Kentucky University. He was selected as one of the outstanding 100 graduates of the last hundred years at Eastern Kentucky University. During World War II he authored *Civil Defense Handbook, A Guide to the U.S. Army,* and was co-author of *A Guide to U.S. Army Insignia* and *A Guide to U.S. Navy, Marine Corps and Coast Guard Insignia,* all published by the Whitman Publishing Company. He also served as an editor of books on military subjects for Whitman.

During the post World War II years Colonel Rankin's books included *Uniforms of the Sea Services,* 1962, United States Naval Institute; *Helmets and Headdress of the Imperial German Army,* 1965, N. Flayderman & Co., Inc.; *Uniforms of the Army,* 1967, G. P. Putnam's Sons; *Uniforms of the Marines,* 1970, G. P. Putnam's Sons; *Small Arms of the Sea Services,* 1972, N. Flayderman & Co., and *Military Headdress,* 1976, Arms & Armour Press, London, and Hippocrene Books, New York. He is also co-author of *Immortal Bear* (Story of a Coast Guard Cutter), 1970, G. P. Putnam's Sons.

Colonel Rankin has also published over 200 articles in magazines and journals, including *United States Naval Institute Proceedings, Marine Corps Gazette, Leatherneck, Popular Aviation, Flying, Dare Devil Aces, Flying Aces, Aero Review, Guns, Guns and Ammo, Gun World, Private Pilot, Bow and Arrow, Our Navy, Adventure, The National Guardsman, Air Classics, Hobbies, Shooting Times, Classic Collector, Mechanix Illustrated, Toledo Blade, Louisville Times-Herald, Milwaukee Journal,* and others.

A Fellow of the prestigious Company of Military Historians, he is also a staff book reviewer for *The Retired Officer Magazine,* and is much sought after as a lecturer on military history.

In addition to his Marine Corps commission, Rankin is an Honorary Colonel on the staff of the Governor of Kentucky and an Honorary Admiral on the staff of the Governor of Nebraska.

Colonel Robert H. Rankin
U.S. Marine Corps (Ret.)

DESCRIPTION	DATE PURCHASED	COST	DATE SOLD	PRICE	CONDITION

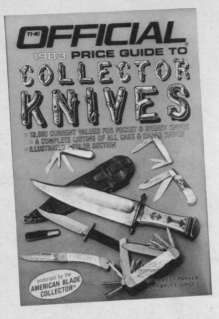

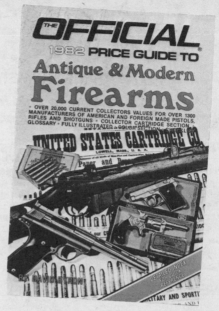

FINALLY...

A practical, easy to read handbook on crisis investing - *for everyone in all income brackets*

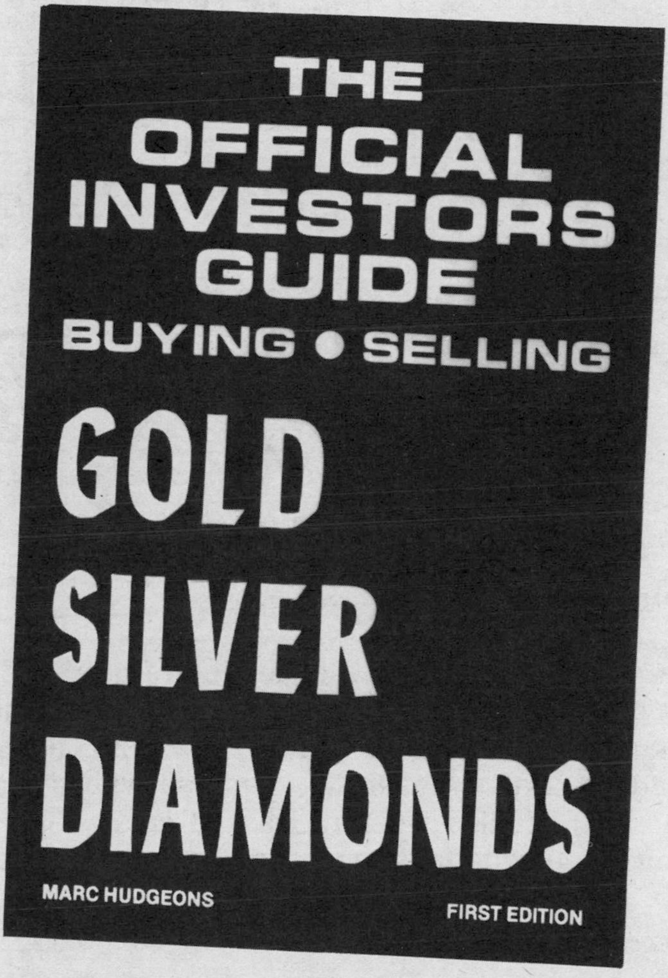

THE OFFICIAL INVESTORS GUIDE

BUYING • SELLING

GOLD

SILVER

DIAMONDS

MARC HUDGEONS

FIRST EDITION

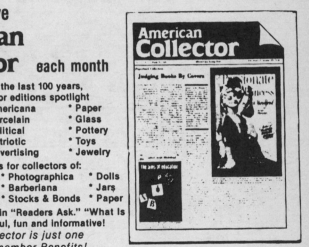

How did your plates do?

Reco's "Little Boy Blue" by John McClelland

UP 214% in 1 Year

Some limited edition plates gained more in the same year, some less, and some not at all ... But Plate Collector readers were able to follow the price changes, step by step, in Plate Price Trends, a copyrighted feature appearing in each issue of the magazine.

PRICE GUIDE SERIES

Antique Wicker

You could be sitting on a **fortune!** Decorators and collectors are driving wicker values to unbelievable highs! This pictorial price guide **positively identifies all types** of Victorian, Turn of the century and Art Deco wicker furniture. **A special illustrated section on wicker repair is included.** *ILLUSTRATED.*

$9.95-1st Edition, 416 pgs., 5⅜″ x 8″, paperback, Order #: 348-1

Bottles Old & New

Over **24,000 current buying and selling prices** of both common and rare collectible bottles . . . ale, soda, bitters, flasks, medicine, perfume, poison, milk and more. **Plus expanded sections on Avon and Jim Beam.** *ILLUSTRATED.*

$9.95-6th Edition, 640 pgs., 5⅜″ x 8″, paperback, Order #: 350-3

Collectible Rock Records

Over **30,000 current prices** of collectible singles, EPs, albums, plus 20,000 memorable song titles recorded by over 1100 artists. **Rare biographies and photos are provided for many well known artists.** *ILLUSTRATED.*

$9.95-3rd Edition, 512 pgs., 5⅜″ x 8″, paperback, Order #: 180-2

Collector Cars

Over **36,000 actual current prices** for 4000 models of antique and classic automobiles — U.S. and foreign. Complete with engine specifications. **Special sections on auto memorabilia values and restoration techniques.** *ILLUSTRATED.*

$9.95-3rd Edition, 544 pgs., 5⅜″ x 8″, paperback, Order #: 181-0

Collector Knives

Over **14,000 buying and selling prices** on U.S. and foreign pocket and sheath knives. **Special sections on bicentennial, commemorative, limited edition, and handmade knives.** By J. Parker & B. Voyles. *ILLUSTRATED.*

$9.95-5th Edition, 640 pgs., 5⅜″ x 8″, paperback, Order #: 324-4

PUBLISHED BY: *THE HOUSE OF COLLECTIBLES, INC.*
1900 PREMIER ROW, ORLANDO, FL 32809   PHONE: (305) 857-9095

MINI PRICE GUIDE SERIES

Pete Rose Baseball Cards

This guide lists **over 44,000 current market values** for baseball cards – Bowman, Burger King, Donruss, Fleer, O-Pee-Chee and Topps. **Includes a full color PETE ROSE limited edition collector card.** *ILLUSTRATED.*
$2.50-2nd Edition, 288 pgs., 4" x 5½", paperback, Order #: 322-8

Comic Books

Young and Old are collecting old comic books for fun **and Profit!** This handy "pocket-sized" price guide lists current market values and detailed descriptions for the most sought-after "collectible" comic books. **Buying, selling and storing tips are provided for the beginning collector.** *ILLUSTRATED.*
$2.50-1st Edition, 240 pgs., 4" x 5½", paperback, Order #: 345-7

O.J. Simpson Football Cards

The world famous O.J. Simpson highlights this comprehensive guide to football card values. **Over 21,000 current collector prices** are listed for: Topps, Bowman, Fleer, Philadelphia and O-Pee-Chee. **Includes a full color O.J. SIMPSON limited edition collector card.** *ILLUSTRATED.*
$2.50-2nd Edition, 256 pgs., 4" x 5½", paperback, Order #: 323-6

Antiques & Flea Markets

Discover the fun and profit of collecting antiques with this handy pocket reference to **over 15,000 types of collectibles.** Avoid counterfeits and learn the secrets to successful buying and selling. *ILLUSTRATED.*
$2.50-1st Edition, 240 pgs., 4" x 5½", paperback, Order #: 308-2

Paperbacks & Magazines

Old discarded paperbacks and magazines could be worth 50-100 times their original cover price. Learn how to identify them. **Thousands** of descriptions and prices show which issues are rare. *ILLUSTRATED.*
$2.50-1st Edition, 240 pgs., 4" x 5½", paperback, Order #: 315-5

Scouting Collectibles

Discover the colorful history behind scouting, relive childhood memories and profit from those old family heirlooms. **Thousands of prices** are listed for all types of Boy and Girl Scout memorabilia. *ILLUSTRATED.*
$2.50-1st Edition, 240 pgs., 4" x 5½", paperback, Order #: 314-7

PUBLISHED BY: *THE HOUSE OF COLLECTIBLES, INC.*
1900 PREMIER ROW, ORLANDO, FL 32809   PHONE: (305) 857-9095

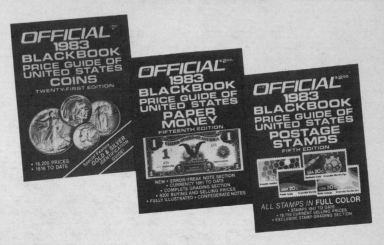